BUSINESS PLUG-INS

TECHNOLOGY PLUG-INS

CORE UNITS

BUSINESS PLUG-INS

TECHNOLOGY PLUG-INS

Business Driven Technology

Paige Baltzan

Daniels College of Business
University of Denver

Amy Phillips

Daniels College of Business
University of Denver

Stephen Haag

Daniels College of Business
University of Denver

Boston   Burr Ridge, IL   Dubuque, IA   New York
San Francisco   St. Louis   Bangkok   Bogotá   Caracas   Kuala Lumpur
Lisbon   London   Madrid   Mexico City   Milan   Montreal   New Delhi
Santiago   Seoul   Singapore   Sydney   Taipei   Toronto

BUSINESS DRIVEN TECHNOLOGY

This book is printed on acid-free paper.

2 3 4 5 6 7 8 9 0 WCK/WCK 0 9 8

ISBN 978-0-07-337674-5
MHID 0-07-337674-4

Publisher: *Paul Ducham*
Developmental editor II: *Trina Hauger*
Marketing director: *Dan Silverburg*
Manager of photo, design & publishing tools: *Mary Conzachi*
Lead production supervisor: *Michael R. McCormick*
Senior designer: *Cara David*
Senior photo research coordinator: *Jeremy Cheshareck*
Senior media project manager: *Greg Bates*
Cover design: *JoAnne Schopler*
Typeface: *10/12 Utopia*
Compositor: *Laserwords Private Limited*
Printer: *Quebecor World Versailles Inc.*

Library of Congress Cataloging-in-Publication Data

Baltzan, Paige.
  Business driven technology / Paige Baltzan, Amy Phillips, Stephen Haag.—3rd ed.
    p. cm.
  Rev. ed. of: Bussiness driven technology / Stephen Haag, Paige Baltzan, Amy Phillips. 2nd ed. c2008.
  Includes index.
  ISBN-13: 978-0-07-337674-5 (alk. paper)
  ISBN-10: 0-07-337674-4 (alk. paper)
  1. Information technology—Management. 2. Management information systems. 3. Information resources management. 4. Industrial management—Technological innovations. I. Phillips Amy (Amy L.). II. Haag, Stephen. III. Haag, Stephen. Business driven technology. IV. Title.
HD30.2.H32 2009
658.4'038—dc22
                                                2008000848

In memory of Allan R. Biggs, my father, my
mentor, and my inspiration.
Paige

To my mother, Jane E. Phillips, with much love
and affection. Without you, I would not be
here.
Amy

For Slim Cummings, James O'Brien, and Steve
Lunce. All truly men among men.
Stephen

TABLE OF CONTENTS

Paige Baltzan

Paige Baltzan teaches in the Department of Information Technology and Electronic Commerce at the Daniels College of Business at the University of Denver. She holds a B.S.B.A specializing in Accounting/MIS from Bowling Green State University and an M.B.A. specializing in MIS from the University of Denver. Paige also teaches online at Strayer University. She is a coauthor of several books including *Business Driven Information Systems, Essentials of Business Driven Information Systems, I-Series,* and a contributor to *Management Information Systems for the Information Age.*

Before joining the Daniels College faculty in 1999, Paige spent several years working for a large telecommunications company and an international consulting firm where she participated in client engagements in the United States as well as South America and Europe. Paige lives in Lakewood, Colorado, with her husband, Tony, and daughters Hannah and Sophie.

Amy Phillips

Amy Phillips teaches in the Department of Information Technology and Electronic Commerce in the Daniels College of Business at the University of Denver. Amy's main teaching and research areas involve Internet and mobile technologies. With her MCT certification, Amy works with developing training material for Microsoft's Web Services platform, .NET. Amy has been teaching for 25 years and has coauthored several textbooks, including *Business Driven Information Systems, Management Information Systems for the Information Age 6e, Internet Explorer 6.0, and PowerPoint 2003.*

Stephen Haag

Stephen Haag is a professor of Information Technology and Electronic Commerce in the Daniels College of Business at the University of Denver. Previously, Stephen has served as Chair of the Department of Information Technology and Electronic Commerce, Director of the Master of Science in Information Technology program, Director of the MBA program, and Associate Dean of Graduate Programs. Stephen holds a BBA and MBA from West Texas State University and a Ph.D. from the University of Texas at Arlington.

Stephen is the author/coauthor of numerous books including *Computing Concepts in Action* (a K-12 textbook), *Interactions: Teaching English as a Second Language* (with his mother and father), *Information Technology: Tomorrow's Advantage Today* (with Peter Keen), *Excelling in Finance, Information Systems Essentials, and Management Information Systems for the Information Age* (now in its 7th edition). He has also written numerous articles appearing in such journals as *Communications of the ACM, Socio-Economic Planning Sciences,* the *International Journal of Systems Science, Managerial and Decision Economics, Applied Economics,* and the *Australian Journal of Management.*

Stephen regularly consults for the federal government with such clients as NASA, Air Force, Environmental Protection Agency, Social Security Administration, Office of Personnel Management, and National Security Agency (NSA). Stephen lives with his family in Highlands Ranch, Colorado.

The overall goal of the Technology Plug-Ins is to provide additional information not covered in the text such as personal productivity using information technology, problem solving using Excel, and decision making using Access. These plug-ins also offer faculty an all-in-one text, avoiding their having to purchase an extra book to support Microsoft Office. These plug-ins offer integration with the core chapters and provide critical knowledge using essential business applications, such as Microsoft Excel, Microsoft Access, and Microsoft Project with hands-on tutorials for comprehension and mastery. Plug-Ins T1 to T12 are located on this textbook's Web site at www.mhhe.com/baltzan.

Plug-In	Description
T1. Personal Productivity Using IT	This plug-in covers a number of things to do to keep a personal computer running effectively and efficiently. The 12 topics covered in this plug-in are: ■ Creating strong passwords. ■ Performing good file management. ■ Implementing effective backup and recovery strategies. ■ Using Zip files. ■ Writing professional e-mails. ■ Stopping spam. ■ Preventing phishing. ■ Detecting spyware. ■ Threads to instant messaging. ■ Increasing PC performance. ■ Using anti-virus software. ■ Installing a personal firewall.
T2. Basic Skills Using Excel 2007	This plug-in introduces the basics of using Microsoft Excel, a spreadsheet program for data analysis, along with a few fancy features. The six topics covered in this plug-in are: ■ Workbooks and worksheets. ■ Working with cells and cell data. ■ Printing worksheets. ■ Formatting worksheets. ■ Formulas. ■ Working with charts and graphics.
T3. Problem Solving Using Excel 2007	This plug-in provides a comprehensive tutorial on how to use a variety of Microsoft Excel functions and features for problem solving. The five areas covered in this plug-in are: ■ Lists ■ Conditional Formatting ■ AutoFilter ■ Subtotals ■ PivotTables
T4. Decision Making Using Excel 2007	This plug-in examines a few of the advanced business analysis tools used in Microsoft Excel that have the capability to identify patterns, trends, and rules, and create "what-if" models. The four topics covered in this plug-in are: ■ IF ■ Goal Seek ■ Solver ■ Scenario Manager
T5. Designing Database Applications	This plug-in provides specific details on how to design relational database applications. One of the most efficient and powerful information management computer-based applications is the relational database. The four topics covered in this plug-in are: ■ Entities and data relationships. ■ Documenting logical data relationships. ■ The relational data model. ■ Normalization.

Plug-in	Description
T6. Basic Skills and Tools Using Access 2007	This plug-in focuses on creating a Microsoft Access database file. One of the most efficient information management computer-based applications is Microsoft Access. Access provides a powerful set of tools for creating and maintaining a relational database. The two topics covered in this plug-in are: ■ Create a new database file. ■ Create and modify tables.
T7. Problem Solving Using Access 2007	This plug-in provides a comprehensive tutorial on how to query a database in Microsoft Access. Queries are essential for problem solving, allowing a user to sort information, summarize data (display totals, averages, counts, and so on), display the results of calculations on data, and choose exactly which fields are shown. The three topics in this plug-in are: ■ Create simple queries using the simple query wizard. ■ Create advanced queries using calculated fields. ■ Format results displayed in calculated fields.
T8. Decision Making Using Access 2007	This plug-in provides a comprehensive tutorial on entering data in a well-designed form and creating functional reports using Microsoft Access. A form is essential to use for data entry and a report is an effective way to present data in a printed format. The two topics in this plug-in are: ■ Creating, modifying, and running forms. ■ Creating, modifying, and running reports.
T9. Designing Web Pages	This plug-in provides a comprehensive assessment into the functional aspects of Web design. Web sites are beginning to look more alike and to employ the same metaphors and conventions. The Web has now become an everyday thing whose design should not make users think. The six topics in this plug-in are: ■ The World Wide Web. ■ Designing for the unknown(s). ■ The process of Web design. ■ HTML basics. ■ Web fonts. ■ Web graphics.
T10. Creating Web Pages Using HTML	This plug-in provides an overview of creating Web pages using the HTML language. HTML is a system of codes that you use to create interactive Web pages. It provides a means to describe the structure of text-based information in a document—by denoting certain text as headings, paragraphs, lists, and so on. The five topics in this plug-in are: ■ An introduction to HTML. ■ HTML tools. ■ Creating, saving, and viewing HTML documents. ■ Apply style tags and attributes. ■ Using fancy formatting. ■ Creating hyperlinks. ■ Displaying graphics.
T11. Creating Web Pages Using Dreamweaver	This plug-in provides a tour of using Dreamweaver to create Web pages. Dreamweaver allows anyone with limited Web page design experience to create, modify, and maintain full-featured, professional-looking pages without having to learn how to code all the functions and features from scratch. The five topics in this plug-in are: ■ Navigation in Dreamweaver. ■ Adding content. ■ Formatting content. ■ Using cascading style sheets. ■ Creating tables.
T12. Creating Gantt Charts with Excel and Microsoft Project	This plug-in offers a quick and efficient way to manage projects. Excel and Microsoft Project are great for managing all phases of a project, creating templates, collaborating on planning processes, tracking project progress, and sharing information with all interested parties. The two topics in this plug-in are: ■ Creating Gantt Charts with Excel. ■ Creating Gantt Charts with Microsoft Project.

Unlike any other MIS text, *Business Driven Technology* discusses various business initiatives first and how technology supports those initiatives second. The premise for this unique approach is that business initiatives should drive technology choices. Every discussion in the text first addresses the business needs and then addresses the technology that supports those needs.

Business Driven Technology offers you the flexibility to customize courses according to your needs and the needs of your students by covering only essential concepts and topics in the five core units, while providing additional in-depth coverage in the business and technology plug-ins.

Business Driven Technology contains 19 chapters (organized into five units), 15 business plug-ins, and 12 technology plug-ins offering you the ultimate flexibility in tailoring content to the exact needs of your MIS or IT course. The unique construction of this text allows you to cover essential concepts and topics in the five core units while providing you with the ability to customize a course and explore certain topics in greater detail with the business and technology plug-ins.

Plug-ins are fully developed modules of text that include student learning outcomes, case studies, business vignettes, and end-of-chapter material such as key terms, individual and group questions and projects, and case study exercises.

We realize that instructors today require the ability to cover a blended mix of topics in their courses. While some instructors like to focus on networks and infrastructure throughout their course, others choose to focus on ethics and security. *Business Driven Technology* was developed to easily adapt to your needs. Each chapter and plug-in is independent so you can:

- Cover any or all of the *chapters* as they suit your purpose.
- Cover any or all of the *business plug-ins* as they suit your purpose.
- Cover any or all of the *technology plug-ins* as they suit your purpose.
- Cover the plug-ins in any order you wish.

Walkthrough

This text is organized around the traditional sequence of topics and concepts in information technology; however, the presentation of this material is nontraditional. That is to say, the text is divided into four major sections: (1) units, (2) chapters, (3) business plug-ins, and (4) technology plug-ins. This represents a substantial departure from existing traditional texts. The goal is to provide both students and faculty with only the most essential concepts and topical coverage in the text, while allowing faculty to customize a course by choosing from among a set of plug-ins that explore topics in more detail. All of the topics that form the core of the discipline are covered, including CRM, SCM, Porter's Five Forces model, value chain analysis, competitive advantage, information security, and ethics.

Business Driven Technology includes four major components:
- 5 Core Units
- 19 Chapters
- 15 Business Plug-Ins
- 12 Technology Plug-Ins

UNITS

1. **Achieving Business Success**
   Chapter 1: Business Driven Technology
   Chapter 2: Identifying Competitive Advantages
   Chapter 3: Strategic Initiatives for Implementing Competitive Advantages
   Chapter 4: Measuring the Success of Strategic Initiatives
   Chapter 5: Organizational Structures That Support Strategic Initiatives

2. **Exploring Business Intelligence**
   Chapter 6: Valuing Organizational Information
   Chapter 7: Storing Organizational Information—Databases
   Chapter 8: Accessing Organizational Information—Data Warehouse

3. **Streamlining Business Operations**
   Chapter 9: Enabling the Organization—Decision Making
   Chapter 10: Extending the Organization—Supply Chain Management
   Chapter 11: Building a Customer-centric Organization—Customer Relationship Management
   Chapter 12: Integrating the Organization from End to End—Enterprise Resource Planning

4. **Building Innovation**
   Chapter 13: Creating Innovative Organizations
   Chapter 14: E-Business
   Chapter 15: Creating Collaborative Partnerships
   Chapter 16: Integrating Wireless Technology in Business

5. **Transforming Organizations**
   Chapter 17: Building Software to Support an Agile Organization
   Chapter 18: Outsourcing in the 21st Century
   Chapter 19: Developing a 21st Century Organization

BUSINESS PLUG-INS

B1	Business Basics	B9	Customer Relationship Management
B2	Business Process	B10	Enterprise Resource Planning
B3	Hardware and Software	B11	E-Business
B4	Enterprise Architectures	B12	Emerging Trends and Technologies
B5	Networks and Telecommunications	B13	Strategic Outsourcing
B6	Information Security	B14	Systems Development
B7	Ethics	B15	Project Management
B8	Supply Chain Management		

TECHNOLOGY PLUG-INS

T1	Personal Productivity Using IT	T8	Decision Making Using Access 2007
T2	Basic Skills Using Excel 2007	T9	Designing Web Pages
T3	Problem Solving Using Excel 2007	T10	Creating Web Pages Using HTML
T4	Decision Making Using Excel 2007	T11	Creating Web Pages Using Dreamweaver
T5	Designing Database Applications	T12	Creating Gantt Charts with Excel
T6	Basic Skills and Tools Using Access 2007		and Microsoft Project
T7	Problem Solving Using Access 2007		

Apply Your Knowledge Projects   Notes
Glossary   Index

Format, Features, and Highlights

Business Driven Technology is state of the art in its discussions, presents concepts in an easy-to-understand format, and allows students to be active participants in learning. The dynamic nature of information technology requires all students, more specifically business students, to be aware of both current and emerging technologies. Students are facing complex subjects and need a clear, concise explanation to be able to understand and use the concepts throughout their careers. By engaging students with numerous case studies, exercises, projects, and questions that enforce concepts, *Business Driven Technology* creates a unique learning experience for both faculty and students.

- **Logical Layout.** Students and faculty will find the text well organized with the topics flowing logically from one unit to the next and from one chapter to the next. The definition of each term is provided before it is covered in the chapter and an extensive glossary is included at the back of the text. Each core unit offers a comprehensive opening case study, introduction, learning outcomes, unit summary, closing case studies, key terms, and making business decision questions. The plug-ins follow the same pedagogical elements with the exception of the exclusion of opening case and closing case studies in the technology plug-ins. Plug-in pointers at the end of the chapters indicate that the discussion at that point may be usefully augmented by specific plug-ins.

- **Thorough Explanations.** Complete coverage is provided for each topic that is introduced. Explanations are written so that students can understand the ideas presented and relate them to other concepts presented in the core units and plug-ins.

- **Solid Theoretical Base.** The text relies on current theory and practice of information systems as they relate to the business environment. Current academic and professional journals cited throughout the text are found in the Notes at the end of the book—a road map for additional, pertinent readings that can be the basis for learning beyond the scope of the unit, chapter, or plug-in.

- **Material to Encourage Discussion.** All units contain a diverse selection of case studies and individual and group problem-solving activities as they relate to the use of information technology in business. Two comprehensive cases at the end of each unit reflect the concepts from the chapters. These cases encourage students to consider what concepts have been presented and then apply those concepts to a situation they might find in an organization. Different people in an organization can view the same facts from different points of view and the cases will force students to consider some of those views.

- **Flexibility in Teaching and Learning.** While most textbooks that are "text only" leave faculty on their own when it comes to choosing cases, *Business Driven Technology* goes much further. Several options are provided to faculty with case selections from a variety of sources including *CIO, Harvard Business Journal, Wired, Forbes, Business 2.0,* and *Time,* to name just a few. Therefore, faculty can use the text alone, the text and a complete selection of cases, or anything in between.

- **Integrative Themes.** Several themes recur throughout the text, which adds integration to the material. Among these themes are value-added techniques and methodologies, ethics and social responsibility, globalization, and gaining a competitive advantage. Such topics are essential to gaining a full understanding of the strategies that a business must recognize, formulate, and in turn implement. In addition to addressing these in the chapter material, many illustrations are provided for their relevance to business practice. These include brief examples in the text as well as more detail presented in the corresponding plug-in(s) (business or technical).

Visual Content Map

Visual Content Map.
Located at the beginning of each unit and serving as a logical outline, the visual content map illustrates the relationship between each unit and its associated plug-ins.

CORE UNITS

Unit 1: Achieving Business Success

Unit 2: Exploring Business Intelligence

Unit 3: Streamlining Business Operations

Unit 4: Building Innovation

Unit 5: Transforming Organizations

BUSINESS PLUG-INS

B1. Business Basics
B2. Business Process
B3. Hardware and Software
B4. Enterprise Architectures
B5. Networks and Telecommunications
B6. Information Security
B7. Ethics
B8. >>Supply Chain Management
B9. >>Customer Relationship Management
B10. >>Enterprise Resource Planning
B11. E-Business
B12. Emerging Trends and Technologies
B13. Strategic Outsourcing
B14. Systems Development
B15. Project Management

TECHNOLOGY PLUG-INS

T1. Personal Productivity Using IT
T2. Basic Skills Using Excel 2007
T3. Problem Solving Using Excel 2007
T4. >>Decision Making Using Excel 2007
T5. Designing Database Applications
T6. Basic Skills and Tools Using Access 2007
T7. Problem Solving Using Access 2007
T8. >>Decision Making Using Access 2007
T9. Designing Web Pages
T10. Creating Web Pages Using HTML
T11. Creating Web Pages Using Dreamweaver
T12. Creating Gantt Charts with Excel and Microsoft Project

Plug-In Pointers

TECHNOLOGY PLUG-IN POINTER

Review the **Technology Plug-In T2 "Basic Skills Using Excel"** for an introduction to Excel including workbooks, worksheets, cells, data, menus, formats, formulas, charts, graphs, and more.

<< BUSINESS PLUG-IN POINTERS

Review the **Business Plug-In B1 "Business Basics"** for an introduction to business fundamentals beginning with the three most common business structures—(1) sole proprietorship, (2) partnership, (3) corporation—and then focusing on the internal operations of a corporation, including accounting, finance, human resources, sales, marketing, operations/production, and management information systems.

Plug-In Pointers. Within the end-of-chapter material, these plug-in pointers provide suggestions of complementary plug-ins that supplement chapter content. For example, Chapter 18 discusses outsourcing collaborative partnerships. For more detail relating to issues surrounding outsourcing, the authors suggest jumping to B13, "Strategic Outsourcing." Plug-in pointers are only suggestions. Feel free to supplement core content with whatever plug-in best fits your teaching needs.

Learning Outcomes and Introduction

Introduction. Located after the Unit Opening Case, the introduction familiarizes students with the overall tone of the chapters. Thematic concepts are also broadly defined.

Learning Outcomes. These outcomes focus on what students should learn and be able to answer upon completion of the chapter or plug-in.

Introduction

Decision making and problem solving in today's electronic world encompass large-scale, opportunity-oriented, strategically focused solutions. The traditional "cookbook" approach to decisions simply will not work in the e-business world. Decision-making and problem-solving abilities are now the most sought-after traits in up-and-coming executives, according to a recent survey of 1,000 executives by Caliper Associates, as reported in *The Wall Street Journal*. To put it mildly, decision makers and problem solvers have limitless career potential.[2]

E-business is the conducting of business on the Internet, not only buying and selling, but also serving customers and collaborating with business partners. (Unit Four discusses e-business in detail.) With the fast growth of information technology and the accelerated use of the Internet, e-business is quickly becoming standard. This unit focuses on technology to help make decisions, solve problems, and find new innovative opportunities. The unit highlights how to bring people together with the best IT processes and tools in complete, flexible solutions that can seize business opportunities (see Figure Unit 3.1). The chapters in Unit 3 are:

- **Chapter Nine**—Enabling the Organization—Decision Making.
- **Chapter Ten**—Extending the Organization—Supply Chain Management.
- **Chapter Eleven**—Building a Customer-centric Organization—Customer Relationship Management.
- **Chapter Twelve**—Integrating the Organization from End to End—Enterprise Resource Planning.

LEARNING OUTCOMES

16.1. Explain how a wireless device helps an organization conduct business anytime, anywhere, anyplace.

16.2. Describe RFID and how it can be used to help make a supply chain more effective.

16.3. List and discuss the key factors inspiring the growth of wireless technologies.

16.4. Describe the business benefits associated with a mobile organization.

Unit Opening Case and Opening Case Study Questions

Unit Opening Case. To enhance student interest, each unit begins with an opening case study that highlights an organization that has been time-tested and value-proven in the business world. This feature serves to fortify concepts with relevant examples of outstanding companies. Discussion of the case is threaded throughout the chapters in each unit.

Opening Case Study Questions. Located at the end of each chapter, pertinent questions connect the Unit Opening Case with important chapter concepts.

UNIT ONE OPENING CASE

Apple—Merging Technology, Business, and Entertainment

Apple Computer Inc., back from near oblivion, is setting the pace in the digital world with innovation and creativity that has been missing from the company for the past 20 years. The introduction of the iPod, a brilliant merger of technology, business, and entertainment, catapulted Apple back into the mainstream.

Capitalizing on New Trends

In 2000, Steve Jobs was fixated on developing video editing software for the Macintosh. But then he realized millions of people were using computers and CD burners to make audio CDs and to download digital songs called MP3s from illegal online services like Napster. Jobs was worried that he was looking in the wrong direction and had missed the MP3 bandwagon.

Jobs moved fast. He began by purchasing SoundStep from Jeff Robbin, a 28-year-old software engineer and former Apple employee. SoundStep was developing software that simplified the importing and compression of MP3 songs. Robbin and a couple of other programmers began writing code from scratch and developed the first version of iTunes for the Mac in less than four months. This powerful and ingenious database could quickly sort tens of thousands of songs in a multitude of ways and find particular tracks in nanoseconds.

OPENING CASE STUDY QUESTIONS

1. Explain how Apple achieved business success through the use of information, information technology, and people.

2. Describe the types of information employees at an Apple store require and compare it to the types of information the executives at Apple's corporate headquarters require. Are there any links between these two types of information?

3. Identify the type of information culture that would have the greatest negative impact on Apple's operations.

Projects and Case Studies

Case Studies. This text is packed with 64 case studies illustrating how a variety of prominent organizations and businesses have successfully implemented many of this text's concepts. All cases promote critical thinking. Company profiles are especially appealing and relevant to your students, helping to stir classroom discussion and interest. For a full list of cases explored in *Business Driven Technology,* turn to the inside back cover.

Apply Your Knowledge Project Overview

Project Number	Project Name	Project Type	Plug-In	Focus Area	Project Level	Skill Set	Page Number
1	Financial Destiny	Excel	T2	Personal Budget	Introductory	Formulas	X
2	Cash Flow	Excel	T2	Cash Flow	Introductory	Formulas	X
3	Technology Budget	Excel	T1, T2	Hardware and Software	Introductory	Formulas	X
4	Tracking Donations	Excel	T2	Employee Relationships	Introductory	Formulas	X
5	Convert Currency	Excel	T2	Global Commerce	Introductory	Formulas	X
6	Cost Comparison	Excel	T2	Total Cost of Ownership	Introductory	Formulas	X
7	Time Management	Excel or Project	T12	Project Management	Introductory	Gantt Charts	X
8	Maximize Profit	Excel	T2, T4	Strategic Analysis	Intermediate	Formulas or Solver	X
9	Security Analysis	Excel	T3	Filtering Data	Intermediate	Conditional Formatting, Autofilter, Subtotal	X
10	Gathering Data	Excel	T3	Data Analysis	Intermediate	Conditional Formatting, PivotTable	X

Chapter One Case: The World Is Flat—Thomas Friedman

In his book, *The World is Flat,* Thomas Friedman describes the unplanned cascade of technological and social shifts that effectively leveled the economic world, and "accidentally made Beijing, Bangalore, and Bethesda next-door neighbors." Chances are good that Bhavya in Bangalore will read your next X-ray, or as Friedman learned firsthand, "Grandma Betty in her bathrobe" will make your JetBlue plane reservation from her Salt Lake City home.

Friedman believes this is Globalization 3.0. "In Globalization 1.0, which began around 1492, the world went from size large to size medium. In Globalization 2.0, the era that introduced us to multinational companies, it went from size medium to size small. And then around 2000 came Globalization 3.0, in which the world went from being small to tiny. There is a difference between being able to make long-distance phone calls cheaper on the Internet and walking around Riyadh with a PDA where you can have all of Google in your pocket. It is a difference in degree that's so enormous it becomes a difference in kind," Friedman states. Figure 1.10 displays Friedman's list of "flatteners."

Friedman says these flatteners converged around the year 2000 and "created a flat world: a global, Web-enabled platform for multiple forms of sharing knowledge and work, irrespective of time, distance, geography, and increasingly, language." At the very moment this platform emerged, three huge economies materialized—those of India, China, and the former Soviet Union—"and 3 billion people who were out of the game, walked onto the playing field." A final convergence may determine the fate of the United States in this chapter of globalization. A "political perfect storm," as Friedman describes it—the dot-com bust, the attacks of 9/11, and the Enron scandal—"distract us completely as a country." Just when we need to face the fact of globalization and the need to compete in a new world, "we're looking totally elsewhere."

Friedman believes that the next great breakthrough in bioscience could come from a 5-year-old who downloads the human genome in Egypt. Bill Gates's view is similar: "Twenty years ago, would you rather have been a B-student in Poughkeepsie or a genius in Shanghai?

FIGURE 1.10

Thomas Friedman's 10 Forces That Flattened the World

1. Fall of the Berlin Wall	The events of November 9, 1989, tilted the worldwide balance of power toward democracies and free markets.
2. Netscape IPO	The August 9, 1995, offering sparked massive investment in fiber-optic cables.
3. Work flow software	The rise of applications from PayPal to VPNs enabled faster, closer coordination among far-flung employees.
4. Open-sourcing	Self-organizing communities, such as Linux, launched a collaborative revolution.
5. Outsourcing	Migrating business functions to India saved money *and* a Third World economy.

Apply Your Knowledge. At the end of this text is a set of 40 projects aimed at reinforcing the business initiatives explored in the text. These projects help to develop the application and problem-solving skills of your students through challenging and creative business-driven scenarios.

Making Decisions

✳ MAKING BUSINESS DECISIONS

1. Improving Information Quality

HangUps Corporation designs and distributes closet organization structures. The company operates five different systems: order entry, sales, inventory management, shipping, and billing. The company has severe information quality issues including missing, inaccurate, redundant, and incomplete information. The company wants to implement a data warehouse containing information from the five different systems to help maintain a single customer view, drive business decisions, and perform multidimensional analysis. Identify how the organization can improve its information quality when it begins designing and building its data warehouse.

2. Information Timeliness

Information timeliness is a major consideration for all organizations. Organizations need to decide the frequency of backups and the frequency of updates to a data warehouse. In a team, describe the timeliness requirements for backups and updates to a data warehouse for

- Weather tracking systems.
- Car dealership inventories.
- Vehicle tire sales forecasts.
- Interest rates.
- Restaurant inventories.
- Grocery store inventories.

3. Entities and Attributes

Martex Inc. is a manufacturer of athletic equipment and its primary lines of business include running, tennis, golf, swimming, basketball, and aerobics equipment. Martex currently supplies four primary vendors including Sam's Sports, Total Effort, The Underline, and Maximum Workout. Martex wants to build a database to help it organize its products. In a group, identify the different types of entity classes and the related attributes that Martex will want to consider when designing the database.

4. Integrating Information

You are currently working for the Public Transportation Department of Chatfield. The department controls all forms of public transportation including buses, subways, and trains. Each department has about 300 employees and maintains its own accounting, inventory, purchasing, and human resource systems. Generating reports across departments is a difficult

End-of-Unit Elements

Searching for Revenue—Google

Google founders Sergey Brin and Larry Page recently made *Forbes* magazine's list of world billionaires. The company is famous for its highly successful search engine.

result. Finally, the search
in a fraction of a second.

* MAKING BUSINESS DECISIONS

1. Improving Information Quality

HangUps Corporation designs and distributes closet organization structures. The company operates five different systems: order entry, sales, inventory management, shipping, and billing. The company has severe information quality issues including missing, inaccurate, redundant, and incomplete information. The company wants to implement a data warehouse containing information from the five different systems to help maintain a single customer view, drive business decisions, and perform multidimensional analysis. Identify how the organization can improv
its data warehouse.

2. Information Timeliness

Information timeliness is a
to decide the frequency of
In a team, describe the time
house for

* KEY TERMS

Analytical information, 75	Data warehouse, 93
Attribute, 81	Entity, 81
Backward integration, 88	Extraction, transformation, and
Business Intelligence	loading (ETL), 93
(BI), 98	Foreign key, 81
Business-critical integrity	Forward integration, 88
constraint, 84	Hierarchical database
Cube, 94	model, 81
Database, 80	Information cleansing or
Database management system	scrubbing, 96
(DBMS), 85	Information granularity, 73
Data-driven Web site, 86	Information integrity, 84
Data mart, 93	Integration, 88
Data mining, 95	Integrity constraint, 84
Data-mining tool, 95	Logical view, 83

Each unit contains complete pedagogical support in the form of:

- **Unit Summary.** Revisiting the unit highlights in summary format.
- **Key Terms.** With page numbers referencing where they are discussed in the text.
- **Two Closing Case Studies.** Reinforcing important concepts with prominent examples from businesses and organizations. Discussion questions follow each case study.
- **Making Business Decisions.** Small scenario-driven projects that help students focus individually on decision making as they relate to the topical elements in the chapters.
- **Apply Your Knowledge.** In-depth projects that help students focus on applying the skills and concepts they have learned throughout the unit.

About the Plug-Ins

The plug-ins are designed to allow faculty to customize their course and cover selected topics in more detail. Students will read core material related to all of the plug-ins in the five units.

As an example, students will learn about various facets of customer relationship management (CRM) most notably in Chapters 11. However, customer relationship management has its own business plug-in. The CRM business plug-in gives both faculty and students the ability to cover CRM in more detail if desired. Likewise, students will receive an introduction to decision making in Unit 3. The Excel technology plug-ins allows coverage of decision-making tools such as PivotTables, Goal Seek, and Scenario Manager.

PLUG-IN

B1 Business Basics

LEARNING OUTCOMES

1. Define the three common business forms.
2. List and describe the seven departments commonly found in most organizations.
3. Describe a transaction and its importance to the accounting department.
4. Identify the four primary financial statements used by most organizations.
5. Define the relationship between sales and marketing, along with a brief discussion of the marketing mix.
6. Define business process reengineering and explain how an organization can use it to transform its business.

Introduction

A sign posted beside a road in Colorado states, "Failing to plan is planning to fail." Playnix Toys posted the sign after successfully completing its 20th year in the toy

Management Focus. By focusing on the business plug-ins, your course will take on a managerial approach to MIS.

Business plug-ins include:

B1	Business Basics
B2	Business Process
B3	Hardware and Software
B4	Enterprise Architectures
B5	Networks and Telecommunications
B6	Information Security
B7	Ethics
B8	Supply Chain Management
B9	Customer Relationship Management
B10	Enterprise Resource Planning
B11	E-Business
B12	Emerging Trends and Technologies
B13	Strategic Outsourcing
B14	Systems Development
B15	Project Management

PLUG-IN

T7 Problem Solving Using Access 2007

LEARNING OUTCOMES

1. Describe the process of using the Query Wizard using Access.
2. Describe the process of using the Design view for creating a query using Access.
3. Describe the process of adding a calculated field to a query using Access.
4. Describe the process of using aggregate functions to calculate totals in queries using Access.
5. Describe how to format results displayed in calculated fields using Access.

Introduction

A *query* is a tool for extracting, combining, and displaying data from one or more tables, according to criteria you specify. For example, in a book inventory database, you could create a query to view a list of all hardcover books with more than 500 pages that you purchased in the past five months. In a query, you can sort information, summarize data (display totals, averages, counts, and so on), display the results of calculations on data, and choose exactly which fields are shown. You can view the results of a query in a tabular format, or you can view the query's data through a form or on a report (which is covered in Plug-In T8, "Decision Making Using Access 2007"). In this plug-in, you will learn how to use the Query Wizard and Query-By-Example (QBE) tool to solve problems using Microsoft Access 2007.

Technical Focus. If hands-on, technical skills are more important, include technical plug-ins in your MIS course.

Technology plug-ins include:

T1	Personal Productivity Using IT
T2	Basic Skills Using Excel 2007
T3	Problem Solving Using Excel 2007
T4	Decision Making Using Excel 2007
T5	Designing Database Applications
T6	Basic Skills and Tools Using Access 2007
T7	Problem Solving Using Access 2007
T8	Decision Making Using Access 2007
T9	Designing Web Pages
T10	Creating Web Pages Using HTML
T11	Creating Web Pages Using Dreamweaver
T12	Creating Gantt Charts with Excel and Microsoft Project

End-of-Plug-In Elements

Each business plug-in contains complete pedagogical support in the form of:

- **Plug-in Summary.** Revisiting the plug-in highlights in summary format.
- **Key Terms.** With page numbers referencing where they are discussed in the text.
- **Two Closing Case Studies.** Reinforcing important concepts with prominent examples from businesses and organizations. Discussion questions follow each case study.
- **Making Business Decisions.** Small scenario-driven projects that help students focus individually on decision making as they relate to the topical elements in the chapters.

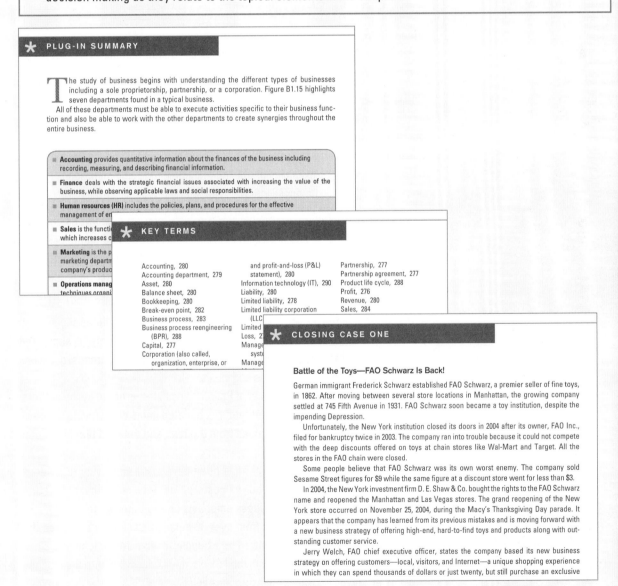

✱ PLUG-IN SUMMARY

The study of business begins with understanding the different types of businesses including a sole proprietorship, partnership, or a corporation. Figure B1.15 highlights seven departments found in a typical business.

All of these departments must be able to execute activities specific to their business function and also be able to work with the other departments to create synergies throughout the entire business.

- **Accounting** provides quantitative information about the finances of the business including recording, measuring, and describing financial information.
- **Finance** deals with the strategic financial issues associated with increasing the value of the business, while observing applicable laws and social responsibilities.
- **Human resources (HR)** includes the policies, plans, and procedures for the effective management of em...
- **Sales** is the functi... which increases c...
- **Marketing** is the p... marketing departm... company's produc...
- **Operations manag...** techniques organi...

✱ KEY TERMS

Accounting, 280
Accounting department, 279
Asset, 280
Balance sheet, 280
Bookkeeping, 280
Break-even point, 282
Business process, 283
Business process reengineering (BPR), 288
Capital, 277
Corporation (also called, organization, enterprise, or

and profit-and-loss (P&L) statement), 280
Information technology (IT), 290
Liability, 280
Limited liability, 278
Limited liability corporation (LLC...
Limited...
Loss, 2...
Manage...
syst...
Manage...

Partnership, 277
Partnership agreement, 277
Product life cycle, 288
Profit, 276
Revenue, 280
Sales, 284

✱ CLOSING CASE ONE

Battle of the Toys—FAO Schwarz Is Back!

German immigrant Frederick Schwarz established FAO Schwarz, a premier seller of fine toys, in 1862. After moving between several store locations in Manhattan, the growing company settled at 745 Fifth Avenue in 1931. FAO Schwarz soon became a toy institution, despite the impending Depression.

Unfortunately, the New York institution closed its doors in 2004 after its owner, FAO Inc., filed for bankruptcy twice in 2003. The company ran into trouble because it could not compete with the deep discounts offered on toys at chain stores like Wal-Mart and Target. All the stores in the FAO chain were closed.

Some people believe that FAO Schwarz was its own worst enemy. The company sold Sesame Street figures for $9 while the same figure at a discount store went for less than $3.

In 2004, the New York investment firm D. E. Shaw & Co. bought the rights to the FAO Schwarz name and reopened the Manhattan and Las Vegas stores. The grand reopening of the New York store occurred on November 25, 2004, during the Macy's Thanksgiving Day parade. It appears that the company has learned from its previous mistakes and is moving forward with a new business strategy of offering high-end, hard-to-find toys and products along with outstanding customer service.

Jerry Welch, FAO chief executive officer, states the company based its new business strategy on offering customers—local, visitors, and Internet—a unique shopping experience in which they can spend thousands of dollars or just twenty, but still purchase an exclusive

Support and Supplemental Material

All of the supplemental material supporting *Business Driven Technology* was developed by the author team to ensure you receive accurate, high-quality, and in-depth content. Included are a complete set of materials that will assist students and faculty in accomplishing course objectives.

For a complete author-narrated overview of the support and supplemental materials of this text, please visit the Online Learning Center.

Online Learning Center (www.mhhe.com/baltzan) The McGraw-Hill Web site for *Business Driven Technology* includes support for students and faculty. All supplements will be available exclusively on the OLC. This will allow the authors to continually update and add to the instructor support materials. The following materials will be available on the OLC:

Video Exercises. Each of the videos that accompany the text is supported by detailed teaching notes on how to turn the videos into classroom exercises where your students can apply the knowledge they are learning after watching the videos.

Online Discussion Questions. This text includes over 30 online discussion questions with narrated overviews for both students and instructors. Post the discussion question and the narrated student overview to your online discussion board. All discussion questions ask students to apply the skills they are learning. Listen to the Instructor narrated overview for examples of grading requirements, common misconceptions, and thought provoking questions you can add in your discussion responses.

Test Bank. This computerized package allows instructors to custom design, save, and generate tests. The test program permits instructors to edit, add, or delete questions from the test banks; analyze test results; and organize a database of tests and students results. In addition to the traditional test bank material, a new test bank will offer Excel and Access questions for testing purposes.

- **Instructor's Manual (IM).** The IM, written by the authors, includes suggestions for designing the course and presenting the material. Each chapter is supported by answers to end-of-chapter questions and problems, and suggestions concerning the discussion topics and cases.
- **PowerPoint Presentations.** A set of PowerPoint slides, created by the authors, accompanies each chapter that features bulleted items that provide a lecture outline, plus key figures and tables from the text, and detailed teaching notes on each slide.
- **Sample Syllabi.** Several syllabi have been developed according to different course lengths—quarters and semesters, as well as different course concentrations such as a business emphasis or a technology focus.
- **Classroom Exercises.** Choose from over 30 detailed classroom exercises that engage and challenge students. For example, if you are teaching systems development, start the class with the "Skyscraper Activity" where the students build a prototype that takes them through each phase of the systems development life cycle. All classroom exercises can be found in the IM.

Supplements:

- Business Driven Teaching Notes
- Online Learning Center
- Instructor's Manual
- PowerPoint Presentations.
- Sample Syllabi
- Classroom Exercises
- Image Library
- Project Files
- Internet Links
- Captivate Files
- Cohesion Case

- **Business Driven Teaching Notes.** The Business Driven Teaching Notes is a comprehensive Excel spreadsheet containing over 150 additional classroom activities, discussion questions, and video clips. You can also turn any of the classroom activities into additional assignments and use the discussion questions for your online courses. You can use the business driven teaching notes to customize your lectures. Each topic in the text is represented by a tab in the workbook. Simply choose the activities you wish to use reorder based on your lecture, and hide any you do not want. Then you can easily print your detailed lecture notes straight from the worksheet.
- **Image Library.** Text figures and tables, as permission allows, are provided in a format by which they can be imported into PowerPoint for class lectures.
- **Project Files.** The authors have provided files for all projects that need further support, such as data files.
- **Internet Links.** Throughout the text are Web site addresses where related material can be obtained from the Web. These sites provide valuable information that, when used with the text, provides a complete, up-to-date coverage of information technology and business.
- **Captivate Files.** A complete set of narrated solution files for all Excel, Access, and Web development projects provide narrated step-by-step detail for each project. These are a great aid to help instructors quickly understand questions and can be posted for students to review, saving instructor time with case reviews.
- **Cohesion Case.** The Broadway Cafe is a running case instructors can use to reinforce core material such as customer relationship management, supply chain management, business intelligence, and decision making. The case has 15 sections that challenge students to develop and expand their grandfather's coffee shop. Students receive hands-on experience in business and learn technology's true value of enabling business. Please note that the Cohesion Case is not a McGraw-Hill product but a Baltzan and Phillips direct product. The case can be found at www.cohesioncase.com.

Media Content

MP3 Content. Harness the power of one of the most popular technology tools students use today—the MP3 player. Our innovative approach allows students to download audio and video presentations right into their MP3 players and take learning materials with them wherever they go. MP3 content icons are placed throughout the text highlighting when we recommend watching the content. The content is also available in Shockwave files so you can watch it on a computer if you choose not to use an MP3 player. This text offers more than 40 MP3 downloads with MP3 IMs to help the instructors turn the MP3s into classroom discussions and exercises.

Video Content. Twenty videos accompany this text and cover topics from entrepreneurship to disaster recovery. Video content icons are placed throughout the text highlighting where we recommend watching the videos. Video IMs are also available so you can turn the videos into engaging classroom activities.

Use our EZ Test Online to help your students prepare to succeed with Apple iPod® iQuiz. Using our EZ Test Online you can make test and quiz content available for a student's Apple iPod®. Students must purchase the iQuiz game application from Apple for 99¢ in order to use the iQuiz content. It works on fifth generation iPods and better. Instructors only need EZ Test Online to produce iQuiz-ready content. Instructors take their existing tests and quizzes and export them to a file that can then be made available to the student to take as a self-quiz on their iPods.

Empowered Instruction

Classroom Performance System
Engage students and assess real-time lecture retention with this simple yet powerful wireless application. You can even deliver tests that instantly grade themselves.

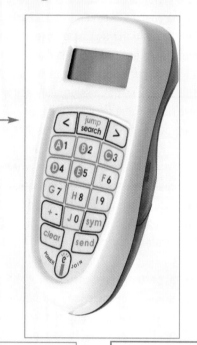

Introduction

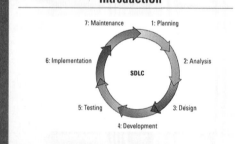

PowerPoint Presentations
Robust, detailed, and designed to keep students engaged. Detailed teaching notes are also included on every slide.

Introduction

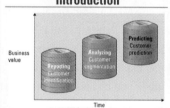

OFFSHORE OUTSOURCING

- Walk the students through the systems development life cycle:
  - *Planning phase*—involves establishing a high-level plan of the intended project and determining project goals
  - *Analysis phase*—involves analyzing end-user business requirements and refining project goals into defined functions and operations of the intended system
  - *Design phase*—involves describing the desired features and operations of the system including screen layouts, business rules, process diagrams, pseudo code, and other documentation
  - *Development phase*—involves taking all of the detailed design documents form the design phase and transforming them into the actual system
  - *Testing phase*—involves bringing all the project pieces together into a special testing environment to test for errors, bugs, and interoperability, in order to verify that the system meets all the business requirements defined in the analysis phase
  - *Implementation phase*—involves placing the system into production so users can begin to perform actual business operations with the system
  - *Maintenance phase*—involves performing changes, corrections, additions, and upgrades to ensure the system continues to meet the business goals

Software Skills & Computer Concepts
MISource provides animated tutorials and simulated practice of the core skills in Microsoft Office 2007 Excel, Access, and PowerPoint.

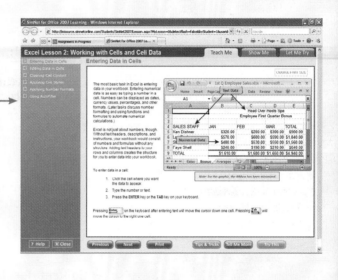

Spend less time reviewing software skills and computer literacy.

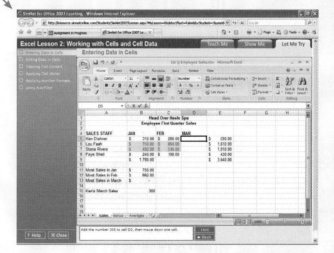

VIDEOS

New videos will be downloadable from the instructor side of the OLC. Selections from our archive of videos from previous years will be delivered upon request.

MBA MIS CASES

Developed by Richard Perle of Loyola Marymount University, these 14 comprehensive cases allow you to add MBA-level analysis to your course. Visit our Web site to review a sample case.

ONLINE LEARNING CENTER

Visit www.mhhe.com/BDT for additional instructor and student resources.

ONLINE COURSES

Content for *Business Driven Technology* is available in WebCT, Blackboard, and PageOut formats to accommodate virtually any online delivery platform.

ACKNOWLEDGMENTS

There are numerous people whom we want to heartily thank for their hard work, enthusiasm, and dedication on the third edition of *Business Driver Technology*.

This text draws from the efforts of a number of people at McGraw-Hill/Irwin. Paul Ducham, our Publisher, thank you for your insight, your intellect, and your continuous support and belief in our abilities—we simply could not have succeeded without you! Trina Hauger, our Development Editor, thank you for always taking the extra time to ask those all-important questions that everyone else seemed to miss. Mary Conzachi, our Manager of Publishing Tools, thank you for making the difficult production process smooth and effortless.

We also thank Brent Gordon (Editorial Director), Sankha Basu (Marketing Manager), Cara David (Designer), Gregory Bates (Media Producer), Rose Range (Supplements Producer), Deborah Sylvester (Production Supervisor), Jen Blankenship (Photo Researcher), and Jeremy Cheshareck (Photo Coordinator), for your support and dedication to the success of this text.

To the faculty at the Daniels College of Business at the University of Denver— Richard Scudder, Don McCubbrey, Paul Bauer, Hans Hultgren, Daivd Paul, Jill Slater, Dan Connolly, and Ked Davisson—thank you. Your feedback, advice, and support is truly valued and greatly appreciated.

Last, but certainly not least, we offer our sincerest gratitude and deepest appreciation to our valuable reviewers whose feedback was instrumental.

Dennis Adams
University of Houston

Kamal Agarwal
Howard University

Syed Imtiaz Ahmad
Eastern Michigan University

Lawrence Andrew
Western Illinois University

Antonio Arreola-Risa
Texas A&M University

Jean-Pierre Auffret
George Mason University

Kristi-Ann L. Berg
Minot State University

Nora M. Braun
Augsburg College

James Cappel
Central Michigan University

Judith P. Carlisle
Dowling College

Gerald J. Carvalho
University of Utah

Casey Cegielski
Auburn University

Elia Chepaltis
Fairfield University

Edward J. Cherian
George Washington University

Beom-Jin Choi
California State University–Sacramento

Joobin Choobineh
Texas A&M University

Phillip D. Coleman
Western Kentucky University

Samuel Coppage
Old Dominion University

Joanna DeFranco-Tommarello
New Jersey Institute of Technology

Roy Dejoie
Purdue University

Robert Denker
Baruch College–CUNY

Charles Downing
Northern Illinois University

Uldarico Rex Dumdum
Marywood University

Richard Egan
New Jersey Institute of Technology

Roland Eichelberger
Baylor University

Michael Eierman
University of Wisconsin–Oshkosh

Juan Esteva
Eastern Michigan University

David Fitoussi
University of California–Irvine

Jerry Fjermestad
New Jersey Institute of Technology

Roger Flynn
University of Pittsburgh

Janet Formichelli
Kent State University

Janos T. Fustos
Metropolitan State College of Denver

Sharyn Hardy Gallagher
University of Massachusetts–Lowell

Michael Gendron
Central Connecticut State University

Edward J. Glantz
Pennsylvania State University

Marvin L. Golland
Polytechnic University, Brooklyn

Robert Gordon
Hofstra University

Diane Graf
Northern Illinois University

Dale D. Gust
Central Michigan University

Don Hardaway
Saint Louis University

Jun He
University of Pittsburgh

Gerald L. Hershey
University of North Carolina, Greensboro

Fred H. Hughes
Faulkner University

Surinder Kahai
SUNY, Binghamton

Rex Karsten
University of Northern Iowa

Joseph Kasten
Dowling College

Yong Jin Kim
Binghamton University

Tracie Kinsley
George Mason University

Elias Kirche
Florida Gulf Coast University

Fred L. Kitchens
Ball State University

Brian J. Klas
Montclair State University

Barbara D. Klein
University of Michigan–Dearborn

Richard Klein
Clemson University

Chang E. Koh
University of North Texas

Gerald Kohers
Sam Houston State University

Rebecca Berens Koop
University of Dayton

Brett J. L. Landry
University of New Orleans

William Lankford
University of West Georgia

Robert Lawton
Western Illinois University

Al Lederer
University of Kentucky

John D. (Skip) Lees
California State University, Chico

Bingguang Li
Albany State University

Shin-Jeng Lin
Le Moyne College

Steve Loy
Eastern Kentucky University

Cindy Joy Marcelis
Temple University

Prosenjit Mazumdar
George Mason University

Dana McCann
Central Michigan University

Charlotte McConn
Pennsylvania State University

Matthew McGowan
Bradley University

Earl McKinney
Bowling Green State University

John Melrose
University of Wisconsin–Eau Claire

Jim Mensching
California State University, Chico

Pam Milstead
Louisiana Tech University

Ellen F. Monk
University of Delaware

Philip F. Musa
The University of Alabama at Birmingham

George Nezlek
Grand Valley State University

Jennifer Nightingale
Duquesne University

Peter Otto
Dowling College

Barry Pasternack
California State University–Fullerton

Gerald Peppers
Howard University

Floyd D. Ploeger
Texas State University–San Marcos

Patricia Quirin
Robert Morris University

T. S. Ragu-Nathan
University of Toledo

Mahesh S. Raisinghani
University of Dallas

Alan Rea
Western Michigan University

Brent Reeves
Abilene Christian University

Paula Ruby
Arkansas State University

Werner Schenk
University of Rochester

Roy Schmidt
Bradley University

David Schroeder
Valparaiso University

Scott Serich
George Washington University

Sherri Shade
Kennesaw State University

Nancy C. Shaw
George Mason University

Betsy Page Sigman
Georgetown University

Marcos P. Sivitanides
Texas State University

Marion S. Smith
Texas Southern University

Ute H. St. Clair
Binghamton University

Robert Szymanski
University of Central Florida

Suzanne Testerman
University of Akron

Amrit Tiwana
Emory University

Yung-Chin Alex Tung
University of Connecticut

Douglas E. Turner
State University of West Georgia

David A. Vance
Mississippi State University

B. Vijayaraman
The University of Akron

Linda Wallace
Virginia Tech

Barbara Warner
University of South Florida

John Wee
University of Mississippi

Rick Weible
Marshall University

Nilmini Wickramsinghe
Cleveland State University

Anita Whitehill
Foothill College

Dennis Williams
California Polytechnic State University

Karen Williams
University of Texas at San Antonio

G. W. K. Willis
Baylor University

Kathleen Wright
Salisbury University

Judy Wynekoop
Florida Gulf Coast University

Ruben Xing
Montclair State University

James E. Yao
Montclair State University

Shu Zou
Temple University

Robert Zwick
Baruch College–CUNY

Business
Driven
Technology

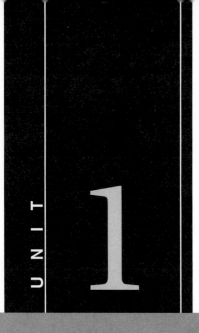

UNIT

1

Achieving Business Success

Apple—Merging Technology, Business, and Entertainment

Apple Computer Inc., back from near oblivion, is setting the pace in the digital world with innovation and creativity that has been missing from the company for the past 20 years. The introduction of the iPod, a brilliant merger of technology, business, and entertainment, catapulted Apple back into the mainstream.

Capitalizing on New Trends

In 2000, Steve Jobs was fixated on developing video editing software for the Macintosh. But then he realized millions of people were using computers and CD burners to make audio CDs and to download digital songs called MP3s from illegal online services like Napster. Jobs was worried that he was looking in the wrong direction and had missed the MP3 bandwagon.

Jobs moved fast. He began by purchasing SoundStep from Jeff Robbin, a 28-year-old software engineer and former Apple employee. SoundStep was developing software that simplified the importing and compression of MP3 songs. Robbin and a couple of other programmers began writing code from scratch and developed the first version of iTunes for the Mac in less than four months. This powerful and ingenious database could quickly sort tens of thousands of songs in a multitude of ways and find particular tracks in nanoseconds.

Jobs next challenged the team to make iTunes portable. He envisioned a Walkman-like player that could hold thousands of songs and be taken anywhere. The idea was to modify iTunes and build a tiny new system for what was basically a miniature computer, along with a user interface that could sort and navigate music files with the same sophistication as iTunes on the Mac. The iPod was born nine months later.

Jobs noticed that one last key element was missing, an online store for buying downloadable songs. Such a store would need an e-business infrastructure that could automatically deliver songs and track billing and payments for conceivably millions of purchases. In the spring of 2003, 18 months after the launch of the iPod, Apple's iTunes Music Store opened for business. The company's goal was to sell 1 million songs in the first six months. It hit this goal in six days.

Capitalizing on the iPod

With millions of iPods in the hands of consumers, other companies are noticing the trend and finding ways to capitalize on the product. John Lin created a prototype of a remote control for the iPod. Lin took his prototype to *Macworld* where he found success. A few months later, Lin's company had Apple's blessing and a commitment for shelf space in its retail stores. "This is how Apple supports the iPod economy," Lin said.

In the iPod-dominated market, hundreds of companies have been inspired to develop more than 500 accessories—everything from rechargers for the car to $1,500 Fendi bags. Eric Tong, vice president at Belkin, a cable and peripheral manufacturer, believes that 75 percent of all iPod owners purchase at least one accessory—meaning that 30 million accessories have been sold. With most of the products priced between $10 and $200, that puts the iPod economy well over $300 million and perhaps as high as $6 billion. Popular iPod accessories include:

- Altec Lansing Technologies—iPod speakers and recharger dock ($150).
- Belkin—TuneCast mobile FM transmitter ($40).
- Etymotic Research—high-end earphones ($150).
- Griffin Technology—iTrip FM transmitter ($35).
- Kate Spade—Geneva faux-croc mini iPod holder ($55).
- Apple—socks set in six colors, green, purple, blue, orange, pink, and gray ($29).
- Apple—digital camera connector ($29).

Capitalizing on the Future

The latest iPod packs music, audiobooks, podcasts, photos, video, contacts, calendars, games, clocks, and locks in a design up to 45 percent slimmer than the original iPod. It also boasts stamina (up to 20 hours of battery life), generous capacity (30GB or 60GB of storage), a great personality (intuitive, customizable menus), and a touch of genius (the Apple Click Wheel). The latest features include:

- **Videos**—Choose from over 2,000 music videos at the iTunes Music Store or purchase ad-free episodes of a favorite ABC or Disney television show and watch them on the go.
- **Podcasts**—The iTunes Podcast Directory features thousands of free podcasts, or radio-style shows, including favorites from such big names as ABC News, Adam Curry, ESPN, KCRW, and WGBH.
- **Audiobooks**—The digital shelves of the iTunes Music Store are stocked with more than 11,000 audiobooks, including such exclusives as the entire Harry Potter series.
- **Photos**—With storage for up to 25,000 photos, iPod users can view photo slide shows—complete with music—on an iPod or on a TV via the optional video cable.

Capitalizing on the iPhone

The Apple iPhone is a revolutionary new mobile phone that allows customers to make a call by simply touching a name or number in an address book, a favorites list, or a call log. It also automatically syncs all contacts from a PC, Mac, or Internet services, and it allows customers to select voice-mail messages in any order—just like e-mail. Customers can easily construct a favorites list for frequently made calls and can quickly merge calls to create conference calls.

The iPhone's most impressive feature is a rich e-mail client. With its advanced Safari browser, one of the most advanced Web browsers to be offered on a portable device, iPhone lets customers see Web pages the way they were designed to be seen, then easily zoom in by simply tapping on the multi-touch display with a finger. Safari also includes built-in Google and Yahoo! search capabilities. The iPhone can multitask, allowing customers to read a Web page while downloading e-mail in the background over wireless networks. Expect the iPhone accessory business to be as powerful and vast as the iPod accessory business. A few of the new iPhone accessories include:

- iPhone Bluetooth headset—$149.
- iPhone doc—$49.
- iPhone stereo headset—$29.
- Apple Doc Connector to USB—$29.

iPod's Impact on the Music Business

In the digital era, the unbundling of CDs through the purchase of individual tracks lets consumers pay far less to get a few of their favorite songs rather than buying an entire album. Many analysts predicted that the iPod's success coupled with the consumer's ability to choose individual song downloads would lead to increased revenues for music businesses. However, the industry is seeing individual downloads cannibalizing album profits and failing to attract new music sales. "I've still never bought a download," said Eneka Iriondo-Coysh, a 21-year-old graphic-design student in London who has owned a 10,000 song-capacity iPod for more than two years. "I do it all from my CDs," mostly hip-hop and soul.

The global music industry has been under siege for years amid declining sales. Record companies suffer from piracy, including billions of dollars in lost revenue due to bootlegged CDs. At the same time, music faces new competition for consumer time and money from video games, DVDs, and mobile phones. At traditional record stores, DVDs and games are taking an increasing amount of shelf space, squeezing out CDs. The music download numbers suggest that the iPod's iconic success is not translating into new music sales the way the evolution from vinyl albums to cassettes and then CDs did. For many users, the portable devices are just another way of stocking and listening to music, not an incentive to buy new music.

iPod Security Leaks

Nike and Apple partnered to create a unique iPod accessory, the Nike iPod SportKit. The Kit consists of two components—a wireless *sensor* that fits into Nike + Air Zoom Moire sneakers and a small white *receiver* that plugs in to an iPod Nano—that communicate using wireless radio protocols. The University of Washington's Department of Science and Engineering recently discovered that customers who use the kit while exercising are subject to an invasion of privacy by becoming a surveillance target. Researchers revealed that security flaws in the new radio-frequency ID-powered device make it easy for tech-savvy stalkers, thieves, and corporations to track every movement an unsuspecting SportKit customer makes. With a simple surveillance tool, a malicious individual could track SportKit owners while they are working out, as well as when they are casually walking around town, a parking lot, or a college campus. With just a few hundred dollars and a little know-how, someone could even plot a SportKit customer's running routes on a Google map without the runner's knowledge. The tracked individuals do not even need to have their iPods with them, just the RFID device.[1]

Introduction

Information is everywhere. Most organizations value information as a strategic asset. Consider Apple and its iPod, iPod accessories, and iTunes Music Store. Apple's success depends heavily on information about its customers, suppliers, markets, and operations for each of these product lines. For example, Apple must be able to predict the number of people who will purchase an iPod to help estimate iPod accessory and iTunes sales within the next year. Estimating too many buyers will lead Apple to produce an excess of inventory; estimating too few buyers will potentially mean lost sales due to lack of product (resulting in even more lost revenues).

Understanding the direct impact information has on an organization's bottom line is crucial to running a successful business. This text focuses on information, business, technology, and the integrated set of activities used to run most organizations. Many of these activities are the hallmarks of business today—supply chain management, customer relationship management, enterprise resource planning, outsourcing, integration, e-business, and others. The five core units of this text cover these important activities in detail. Each unit is divided into chapters that provide individual learning outcomes and case studies. In addition to the five core units, there are technology and business "plug-ins" (see Figure Unit 1.1) that further explore topics presented in the five core units. "Plug-in pointers" provided at the end of each chapter identify the relevant plug-ins.

The chapters in Unit 1 are:

- **Chapter One**—Business Driven Technology.
- **Chapter Two**—Identifying Competitive Advantages.
- **Chapter Three**—Strategic Initiatives for Implementing Competitive Advantages.
- **Chapter Four**—Measuring the Success of Strategic Initiatives.
- **Chapter Five**—Organizational Structures That Support Strategic Initiatives.

Opportunities for Knowledge Workers

FIGURE UNIT 1.1

The Format and Approach of This Text

Business Plug-Ins	CORE UNITS	Technology Plug-Ins
B1. Business Basics	Unit 1: Achieving Business Success	T1. Personal Productivity Using IT
B2. Business Process		T2. Basic Skills Using Excel
B3. Hardware and Software		T3. Problem Solving Using Excel
B4. Enterprise Architectures		T4. Decision Making Using Excel
B5. Networks and Telecommunications	Unit 2: Exploring Business Intelligence	T5. Designing Database Applications
B6. Information Security		T6. Basic Skills Using Access
B7. Ethics		T7. Problem Solving Using Access
B8. Supply Chain Management	Unit 3: Streamlining Business Operations	T8. Decision Making Using Access
B9. Customer Relationship Management		T9. Designing Web Pages
B10. Enterprise Resource Planning	Unit 4: Building Innovation	T10. Creating Web Pages Using HTML
B11. E-Business		T11. Creating Web Pages Using Dreamweaver
B12. Emerging Trends and Technologies	Unit 5: Transforming Organizations	T12. Creating Gantt Charts with Excel and Microsoft Project
B13. Strategic Outsourcing		
B14. Systems Development		
B15. Project Management		

Business Driven Technology

1.1. Compare management information systems (MIS) and information technology (IT).

1.2. Describe the relationships among people, information technology, and information.

1.3. Identify four different departments in a typical business and explain how technology helps them to work together.

1.4. Compare the four different types of organizational information cultures and decide which culture applies to your school.

Information Technology's Role in Business

Students frequently ask, "Why do we need to study information technology?" The answer is simple: Information technology is everywhere in business. Understanding information technology provides great insight to anyone learning about business.

FIGURE 1.1

Technology in *BusinessWeek* and *Fortune*

It is easy to demonstrate information technology's role in business by reviewing a copy of popular business magazines such as *BusinessWeek, Fortune,* or *Fast Company.* Placing a marker (such as a Post-it Note) on each page that contains a technology-related article or advertisement indicates that information technology is everywhere in business (see Figure 1.1). These are *business* magazines, not *technology* magazines, yet they are filled with technology. Students who understand technology have an advantage in business, and gaining a detailed understanding of information technology is important to all students regardless of their area of expertise.

The magazine articles typically discuss such topics as databases, customer relationship management, Web services, supply chain management, security, ethics, business intelligence, and so on. They also focus on companies such as Siebel, Oracle, Microsoft, and IBM. This text explores these topics in detail, along with reviewing the associated business opportunities and challenges.

INFORMATION TECHNOLOGY'S IMPACT ON BUSINESS OPERATIONS

Figure 1.2 highlights the business functions receiving the greatest benefit from information technology, along with the common business goals associated with information technology projects according to *CIO* magazine.[2]

Achieving the results outlined in Figure 1.2, such as reducing costs, improving productivity, and generating growth, is not easy. Implementing a new accounting system or marketing plan is not likely to generate long-term growth or reduce costs across an entire organization. Businesses must undertake enterprisewide initiatives to achieve broad general business goals such as reducing costs. Information technology plays a critical role in deploying such initiatives by facilitating communication and increasing business intelligence. For example instant messaging and WiMax allow people across an organization to communicate in new and innovative ways.[3]

Understanding information technology begins with gaining an understanding of how businesses function and IT's role in creating efficiencies and effectiveness across the organization. Typical businesses operate by functional areas (often called functional silos). Each functional area undertakes a specific core business function (see Figure 1.3).[4]

Functional areas are anything but independent in a business. In fact, functional areas are *interdependent* (see Figure 1.4 on page 11). Sales must rely on information from operations to understand inventory, place orders, calculate transportation costs, and gain insight into product availability based on production schedules. For an organization to succeed, every department or functional area must work together sharing common information and not be a "silo." Information technology can enable departments to more efficiently and effectively perform their business operations.

Any individual anticipating a successful career in business whether it is in accounting, finance, human resources, or operation management must understand the basics of information technology.

FIGURE 1.2

Business Benefits and Information Technology Project Goals

Information Technology Basics

Information technology (IT) is a field concerned with the use of technology in managing and processing information. Today, the term *information technology* has ballooned to encompass many aspects of computing and technology, and the term is more recognizable than ever. The information technology umbrella can be quite large, covering many fields that deal with the use of electronic computers and computer software to convert, store, protect, process, transmit, and retrieve information securely. Information technology can be an important enabler of business success and innovation. This is not to say that IT *equals* business success and innovation or that IT *represents* business success and innovation. Information technology is most useful when it leverages the talents of people. Information technology in and of itself is not useful unless the right people know how to use and manage it effectively.

Management information systems is a business function just as marketing, finance, operations, and human resources are business functions. Formally defined, *management information systems (MIS)* is a general name for the business function and academic discipline covering the application of people, technologies, and procedures—collectively called information systems—to solve business problems.[5]

FIGURE 1.3

Departmental Structure of
a Typical Organization

COMMON DEPARTMENTS IN AN ORGANIZATION

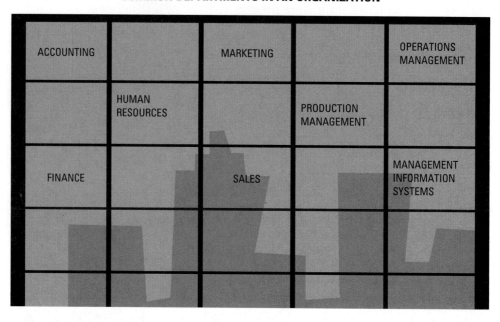

Information
Technology

- **Accounting** provides quantitative information about the finances of the business including recording, measuring, and describing financial information.

- **Finance** deals with the strategic financial issues associated with increasing the value of the business, while observing applicable laws and social responsibilities.

- **Human resources (HR)** includes the policies, plans, and procedures for the effective management of employees (human resources).

- **Sales** is the function of selling a good or service and focuses on increasing customer sales, which increases company revenues.

- **Marketing** is the process associated with promoting the sale of goods or services. The marketing department supports the sales department by creating promotions that help sell the company's products.

- **Operations management** (also called **production management**) includes the methods, tasks, and techniques organizations use to produce goods and services. Transportation (also called logistics) is part of operations management.

- **Management information systems (MIS)** is a general name for the business function and academic discipline covering the application of people, technologies, and procedures—collectively called information systems—to solve business problems.

When beginning to learn about management information systems it is important to understand the following:

- Data, information, and business intelligence.
- IT resources.
- IT cultures.

DATA, INFORMATION, AND BUSINESS INTELLIGENCE

It is important to distinguish between data, information, and business intelligence. *Data* are raw facts that describe the characteristics of an event. Characteristics for a sales event could include the date, item number, item description, quantity ordered, customer name, and shipping details. *Information* is data converted into a meaningful and useful context. Information from sales events could include

FIGURE 1.4

Marketing Working with
Other Organizational
Departments

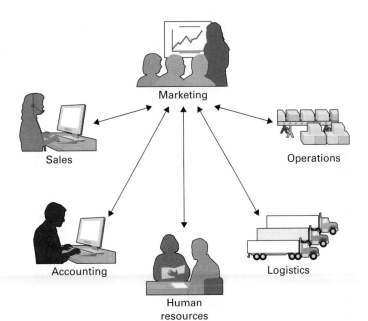

Marketing

Sales

Operations

Accounting

Logistics

Human
resources

Functional organization—Each functional area has its own systems
and communicates with every other functional area (diagram
displays Marketing communicating with all other functional areas
in the organization).

best-selling item, worst-selling item, best customer, and worst customer. **Business intelligence** refers to applications and technologies that are used to gather, provide access to, and analyze data and information to support decision-making efforts. Business intelligence helps companies gain a more comprehensive knowledge of the factors affecting their business, such as metrics on sales, production, and internal operations, which help companies make better business decisions (see Figures 1.5, 1.6, 1.7).

IT RESOURCES

The plans and goals of the IT department must align with the plans and goals of the organization. Information technology can enable an organization to increase efficiency in manufacturing, retain key customers, seek out new sources of supply, and introduce effective financial management.

It is not always easy for managers to make the right choices when using IT to support (and often drive) business initiatives. Most managers understand their business initiatives well, but are often at a loss when it comes to knowing how to use

FIGURE 1.5

Data in an Excel
Spreadsheet

OrderDate	ProductName	Quantity	Unit Price	Total Sales	Unit Cost	Total Cost	Profit	Customer	SalesRep
04-Jan-10	Mozzarella cheese	41	24	984	18	738	246	The Station	Debbie Fernande
04-Jan-10	Romaine lettuce	90	15	1,350	14	1,260	90	The Station	Roberta Cross
05-Jan-10	Red onions	27	12	324	8	216	108	Bert's Bistro	Loraine Schultz
06-Jan-10	Romaine lettuce	67	15	1,005	14	938	67	Smoke House	Roberta Cross
07-Jan-10	Black olives	79	12	948	6	474	474	Flagstaff House	Loraine Schultz
07-Jan-10	Romaine lettuce	46	15	690	14	644	46	Two Bitts	Loraine Schultz
07-Jan-10	Romaine lettuce	52	15	780	14	728	52	Pierce Arrow	Roberta Cross
08-Jan-10	Red onions	39	12	468	8	312	156	Mamm'a Pasta Palace	Loraine Schultz
09-Jan-10	Romaine lettuce	66	15	990	14	924	66	The Dandelion	Loraine Schultz
10-Jan-10	Romaine lettuce	58	15	870	14	812	58	Carmens	Loraine Schultz
10-Jan-10	Pineapple	40	33	1,320	28	1,120	200	The Station	Loraine Schultz

Rows of data in an Excel spreadsheet.

FIGURE 1.6

Data Turned into
Information

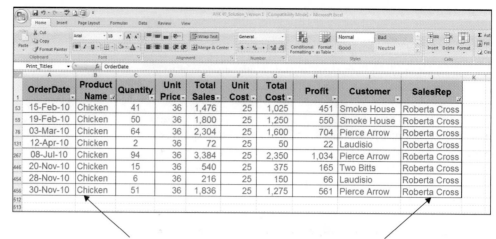

Data features, such as Autofilter, turn data into information.
This view shows all of Roberta Cross's chicken sales.

FIGURE 1.7

Information Turned into
Business Intelligence

Distribution Analysis		
Question	Name	Total
Who is Bob's best customer by total sales?	Pierce Arrow	$ 56,789
Who is Bob's worst customer by total sales	Smoke House	$ 3,456
Who is Bob's best customer by profit?	Laudisio	$ 45,777
Who is Bob's worst customer by profit?	Carmens	$ 4,555
What is Bob's best selling product by total sales?	Chicken	$ 34,234
What is Bob's worst selling product by total sales?	Black olives	$ 567
What is Bob's best selling product by profit?	Peppers	$ 22,444
What is Bob's worst selling product by profit?	Red onions	$ 2,443
Who is Bob's best sales representative by profit?	Loraine Schultz	$ 98,989
Who is Bob's worst sales representative by profit?	Roberta Cross	$ 4,567
What is the best sales representative's best selling product (by total profit)?	Red onions	$ 24,343
Who is the best sales representative's best customer (by total profit)?	Flagstaff House	$ 1,234
What is the best sales representative's worst selling product (by total profit)?	Romaine lettuce	$ 45,678
Who is the best sales representative's worst customer (by total profit)?	Bert's Bistro	$ 5,678

Advanced analytical tools, such as Pivot Tables, uncover business
intelligence in the data. For example, best customer, worst
customer, and best sales representative's best selling product.

and manage IT effectively in support of those initiatives. Managers who understand
what IT is, and what IT can and cannot do, are in the best position for success.

Putting It All Together

In essence,

- *People* use
- *information technology* to work with
- *information* (see Figure 1.8).

Those three key resources—people, information, and information technology
(in that order of priority)—are inextricably linked. If one fails, they all fail. Most
important, if one fails, then chances are the business will fail.

IT CULTURES

An organization's culture plays a large role in determining how successfully it will share information. Culture will influence the way people use information (their information behavior) and will reflect the importance that company leaders attribute to the use of information in achieving success or avoiding failure. Four common information-sharing cultures exist in organizations today: information-functional, information-sharing, information-inquiring, and information-discovery (see Figure 1.9).[6]

An organization's IT culture can directly affect its ability to compete in the global market. If an organization operates with an information-functional culture it will have a great degree of difficulty operating. Getting products to market quickly and creating a view of its end-to-end (or entire) business from sales to billing will be a challenge. If an organization operates with an information-discovery culture it will be able to get products to market quickly and easily see a 360-degree view of its entire organization. Employees will be able to use this view to better understand the market and create new products that offer a competitive advantage.

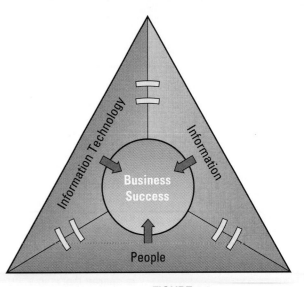

FIGURE 1.8

The Relationship among People, Information, and Information Technology

FIGURE 1.9

Different Information Cultures found in Organizations

Organizational Information Cultures	
Information-Functional Culture	Employees use information as a means of exercising influence or power over others. For example, a manager in sales refuses to share information with marketing. This causes marketing to need the sales manager's input each time a new sales strategy is developed.
Information-Sharing Culture	Employees across departments trust each other to use information (especially about problems and failures) to improve performance.
Information-Inquiring Culture	Employees across departments search for information to better understand the future and align themselves with current trends and new directions.
Information-Discovery Culture	Employees across departments are open to new insights about crises and radical changes and seek ways to create competitive advantages.

OPENING CASE STUDY QUESTIONS

1. Explain how Apple achieved business success through the use of information, information technology, and people.

2. Describe the types of information employees at an Apple store require and compare it to the types of information the executives at Apple's corporate headquarters require. Are there any links between these two types of information?

3. Identify the type of information culture that would have the greatest negative impact on Apple's operations.

In his book, *The World is Flat,* Thomas Friedman describes the unplanned cascade of techno-logical and social shifts that effectively leveled the economic world, and "accidentally made Beijing, Bangalore, and Bethesda next-door neighbors." Chances are good that Bhavya in Bangalore will read your next X-ray, or as Friedman learned firsthand, "Grandma Betty in her bathrobe" will make your JetBlue plane reservation from her Salt Lake City home.

Friedman believes this is Globalization 3.0. "In Globalization 1.0, which began around 1492, the world went from size large to size medium. In Globalization 2.0, the era that introduced us to multinational companies, it went from size medium to size small. And then around 2000 came Globalization 3.0, in which the world went from being small to tiny. There is a difference between being able to make long-distance phone calls cheaper on the Internet and walking around Riyadh with a PDA where you can have all of Google in your pocket. It is a difference in degree that's so enormous it becomes a difference in kind," Friedman states. Figure 1.10 displays Friedman's list of "flatteners."

Friedman says these flatteners converged around the year 2000 and "created a flat world: a global, Web-enabled platform for multiple forms of sharing knowledge and work, irrespective of time, distance, geography, and increasingly, language." At the very moment this platform emerged, three huge economies materialized—those of India, China, and the former Soviet Union—"and 3 billion people who were out of the game, walked onto the playing field." A final convergence may determine the fate of the United States in this chapter of globalization. A "political perfect storm," as Friedman describes it—the dot-com bust, the attacks of 9/11, and the Enron scandal—"distract us completely as a country." Just when we need to face the fact of globalization and the need to compete in a new world, "we're looking totally elsewhere."

Friedman believes that the next great breakthrough in bioscience could come from a 5-year-old who downloads the human genome in Egypt. Bill Gates's view is similar: "Twenty years ago, would you rather have been a B-student in Poughkeepsie or a genius in Shanghai?

FIGURE 1.10

Thomas Friedman's 10 Forces That Flattened the World

1. Fall of the Berlin Wall	The events of November 9, 1989, tilted the worldwide balance of power toward democracies and free markets.
2. Netscape IPO	The August 9, 1995, offering sparked massive investment in fiber-optic cables.
3. Work flow software	The rise of applications from PayPal to VPNs enabled faster, closer coordination among far-flung employees.
4. Open-sourcing	Self-organizing communities, such as Linux, launched a collaborative revolution.
5. Outsourcing	Migrating business functions to India saved money *and* a Third World economy.
6. Offshoring	Contract manufacturing elevated China to economic prominence.
7. Supply-chaining	Robust networks of suppliers, retailers, and customers increased business efficiency.
8. Insourcing	Logistics giants took control of customer supply chains, helping mom-and-pop shops go global.
9. Informing	Power searching allowed everyone to use the Internet as a "personal supply chain of knowledge."
10. Wireless	Wireless technologies pumped up collaboration, making it mobile and personal.

Twenty years ago you'd rather be a B-student in Poughkeepsie. Today, it is not even close. You'd much prefer to be the genius in Shanghai because you can now export your talents anywhere in the world."[7]

Questions

1. Do you agree or disagree with Friedman's assessment that the world is flat? Be sure to justify your answer.
2. What are the potential impacts of a flat world for a student performing a job search?
3. What can students do to prepare themselves for competing in a flat world?
4. Identify a current flattener not mentioned on Friedman's list.

<< BUSINESS PLUG-IN POINTERS

Review the **Business Plug-In B1 "Business Basics"** for an introduction to business fundamentals beginning with the three most common business structures—(1) sole proprietorship, (2) partnership, (3) corporation—and then focusing on the internal operations of a corporation, including accounting, finance, human resources, sales, marketing, operations/ production, and management information systems.

Review the **Business Plug-In B2 "Business Process."** This plug-in dives deeper into the world of business by reviewing business processes, continuous process improvement, business process reengineering, and business process modeling. There are a number of sample business process models diagramming such processes as order entry, online bill payment, e-business processes, and process improvement.

Review the **Business Plug-In B3 "Hardware and Software"** to cover the two basic categories of information technology. Information technology can be composed of the Internet, a personal computer, a cell phone that can access the Web, a personal digital assistant, or presentation software. All of these technologies help to perform specific information processing tasks. This plug-in covers the basics including terminology, business uses, and common characteristics.

Review the **Business Plug-In B4 "Enterprise Architectures,"** which includes the plans for how an organization will build, deploy, use, and share its data, processes, and IT assets. To support the volume and complexity of today's user and application requirements, information technology needs to take a fresh approach to enterprise architectures by constructing smarter, more flexible environments that protect it from system failures and crashes. A solid enterprise architecture can decrease costs, increase standardization, promote reuse of IT assets, and speed development of new systems. The end result is that the right enterprise architecture can make IT cheaper, strategic, and more responsive.

Review the Business Plug-In B5 "Networks and Telecommunications" for a detailed look at telecommunication systems and networks. Businesses around the world are moving to network infrastructure solutions that allow greater choice in how they go to market; the solutions have a global reach. These alternatives include wireless, voice-over Internet protocol (VoIP), and radio-frequency identification (RFID). This plug-in takes a detailed look at key telecommunication, network, and wireless technologies that are integrating businesses around the world.

Review the Technology Plug-In T1 "Personal Productivity Using IT" for a walk-through on how to take advantage of your computer's many features, including data management, antivirus software, zip files, backup solutions, e-mail etiquette, PC performance, and spam control.

2

Identifying Competitive Advantages

2.1. Explain why competitive advantages are typically temporary.

2.2. List and describe each of the five forces in Porter's Five Forces Model.

2.3. Compare Porter's three generic strategies.

2.4. Describe the relationship between business processes and value chains.

Identifying Competitive Advantages

To survive and thrive, an organization must create a competitive advantage. A ***competitive advantage*** is a product or service that an organization's customers place a greater value on than similar offerings from a competitor. Unfortunately, competitive advantages are typically temporary because competitors often seek ways to duplicate the competitive advantage. In turn, organizations must develop a strategy based on a new competitive advantage.

Panera
Bread

When an organization is the first to market with a competitive advantage, it gains a first-mover advantage. The ***first-mover advantage*** occurs when an organization can significantly impact its market share by being first to market with a competitive advantage. FedEx created a first-mover advantage several years ago when it developed its customer self-service software allowing people and organizations to request a package pick-up, print mailing slips, and track packages online. Other parcel delivery services quickly followed with their own versions of the software. Today, customer self-service on the Internet is a standard for doing business in the parcel delivery industry.

As organizations develop their competitive advantages, they must pay close attention to their competition through environmental scanning. ***Environmental scanning*** is the acquisition and analysis of events and trends in the environment external to an organization. Information technology has the opportunity to play an important role in environmental scanning. For example, Frito-Lay, a premier provider of snack foods such as Cracker Jacks and Cheetos, does not just send its representatives into grocery stores to stock shelves—they carry handheld computers and record the product offerings, inventory, and even product locations of competitors. Frito-Lay uses this information to gain business intelligence on everything from how well competing products are selling to the strategic placement of its own products.

Organizations use three common tools to analyze and develop competitive advantages: (1) the Five Forces Model, (2) the three generic strategies, and (3) value chains.

The Five Forces Model—Evaluating Business Segments

Organizations frequently face a decision as to whether to enter a new industry or industry segment. Michael Porter's Five Forces Model is a useful tool to aid in this

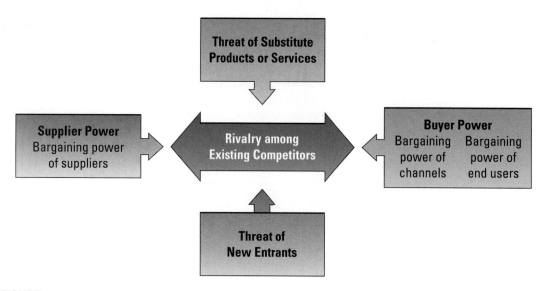

FIGURE 2.1

Porter's Five Forces Model

challenging decision. The **Five Forces Model** helps determine the relative attractiveness of an industry and includes the following five forces (see Figure 2.1):

1. Buyer power.
2. Supplier power.
3. Threat of substitute products or services.
4. Threat of new entrants.
5. Rivalry among existing competitors.

The following introduction to each force provides detailed examples of how information technology can develop a competitive advantage.

Competitive
Advantage

BUYER POWER

Buyer power in the Five Forces Model is high when buyers have many choices of whom to buy from and low when their choices are few. To reduce buyer power (and create a competitive advantage), an organization must make it more attractive for customers to buy from it than from its competition. One of the best IT-based examples is the loyalty programs that many organizations offer. **Loyalty programs** reward customers based on the amount of business they do with a particular organization. The travel industry is famous for its loyalty programs such as frequent-flyer programs for airlines and frequent-stayer programs for hotels.

Keeping track of the activities and accounts of many thousands or millions of customers covered by loyalty programs is not practical without large-scale IT systems. Loyalty programs are a good example of using IT to reduce buyer power. Because of the rewards (e.g., free airline tickets, upgrades, or hotel stays) travelers receive, they are more likely to be loyal to or give most of their business to a single organization.

SUPPLIER POWER

Supplier power in the Five Forces Model is high when buyers have few choices of whom to buy from and low when their choices are many. Supplier power is the converse of buyer power: A supplier organization in a market will want buyer power to be low. A **supply chain** consists of all parties involved, directly or indirectly, in the procurement of a product or raw material. In a typical supply chain, an organization will probably be both a supplier (to customers) and a customer (of other supplier organizations) (see Figure 2.2).

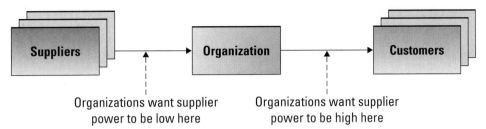

FIGURE 2.2

An Organization within the
Supply Chain

Organizations want supplier
power to be low here

Organizations want supplier
power to be high here

As a buyer, the organization can create a competitive advantage by locating alternative supply sources. IT-enabled business-to-business (B2B) marketplaces can help. A **business-to-business (B2B) marketplace** is an Internet-based service that brings together many buyers and sellers. One important variation of the B2B marketplace is a private exchange. A **private exchange** is a B2B marketplace in which a single buyer posts its needs and then opens the bidding to any supplier who would care to bid. Bidding is typically carried out through a reverse auction. A **reverse auction** is an auction format in which increasingly lower bids are solicited from organizations willing to supply the desired product or service at an increasingly lower price. As the bids get lower and lower, more and more suppliers drop out of the auction. Ultimately, the organization with the lowest bid wins. Internet-based reverse auctions are an excellent example of the way that information technology can reduce supplier power for an organization and create a competitive advantage.

THREAT OF SUBSTITUTE PRODUCTS OR SERVICES

The **threat of substitute products or services** in the Five Forces Model is high when there are many alternatives to a product or service and low when there are few alternatives from which to choose. Ideally, an organization would like to be in a market in which there are few substitutes for the products or services it offers. Of course, that is seldom possible in any market today, but an organization can still create a competitive advantage by using switching costs. **Switching costs** are costs that can make customers reluctant to switch to another product or service.

A switching cost need not have an associated *monetary* cost. Amazon.com offers an example. As customers purchase products at Amazon.com over time, Amazon begins to develop a unique profile of their shopping and purchasing habits. When a customer visits Amazon.com repeatedly, Amazon can begin to offer products tailored to that particular customer based on the customers' profile. If the customer decides to shop elsewhere, there is an associated switching cost because the new site will not have the profile of the customer's past purchases. In this way Amazon.com has reduced the threat of substitute products or services by tailoring customer offerings and creating a "cost" to the consumer to switch to another online retailer.

THREAT OF NEW ENTRANTS

The **threat of new entrants** in the Five Forces Model is high when it is easy for new competitors to enter a market and low when there are significant entry barriers to entering a market. An **entry barrier** is a product or service feature that customers have come to expect from organizations in a particular industry and must be offered by an entering organization to compete and survive. For example, a new bank must offer its customers an array of IT-enabled services, including ATM use, online bill paying, and account monitoring. These are significant barriers to entering the banking market. At one time, the first bank to offer such services gained a valuable first-mover advantage, but only temporarily, as other banking competitors developed their own IT systems.

RIVALRY AMONG EXISTING COMPETITORS

Rivalry among existing competitors in the Five Forces Model is high when competition is fierce in a market and low when competition is more complacent. Although competition is always more intense in some industries than in others, the overall trend is toward increased competition in almost every industry.

The retail grocery industry is intensively competitive. While Kroger, Safeway, and Albertson's in the United States compete in many different ways, essentially they try to beat or match the competition on price. Most of them have loyalty programs that give shoppers special discounts. Customers get lower prices while the store gathers valuable information on buying habits to craft pricing strategies. In the future, expect to see grocery stores using wireless technologies to track customer movement throughout the store and match it to products purchased to determine purchasing sequences. Such a system will be IT-based and a huge competitive advantage to the first store to implement it.

Since margins are quite low in the grocery retail market, grocers build efficiencies into their supply chains, connecting with their suppliers in IT-enabled information partnerships such as the one between Wal-Mart and its suppliers. Communicating with suppliers over telecommunications networks rather than using paper-based systems makes the procurement process faster, cheaper, and more accurate. That equates to lower prices for customers and increased rivalry among existing competitors.

The Three Generic Strategies—Creating a Business Focus

Once the relative attractiveness of an industry is determined and an organization decides to enter that market, it must formulate a strategy for entering the new market. An organization can follow Porter's three generic strategies when entering a new market: (1) broad cost leadership, (2) broad differentiation, or (3) a focused strategy. Broad strategies reach a large market segment, while focused strategies target a niche market. A focused strategy concentrates on either cost leadership or differentiation. Trying to be all things to all people, however, is a recipe for disaster, since it is difficult to project a consistent image to the entire marketplace. Porter suggests that an organization is wise to adopt only one of the three generic strategies. (See Figure 2.3.)

FIGURE 2.3

Porter's Three Generic Strategies

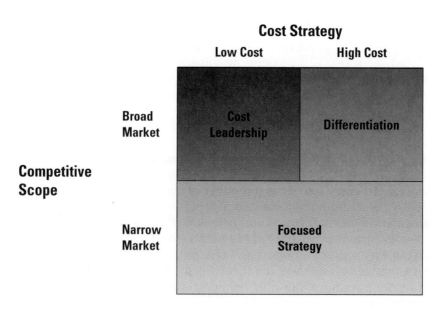

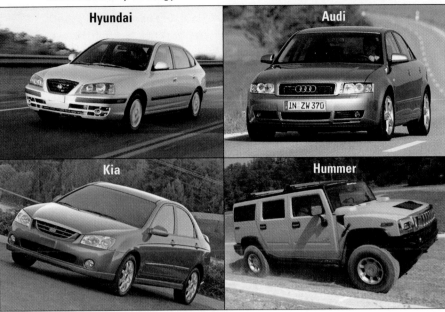

FIGURE 2.4

Three Generic Strategies
in the Auto Industry

To illustrate the use of the three generic strategies, consider Figure 2.4. The matrix shown demonstrates the relationships among strategies (cost leadership versus differentiation) and market segmentation (broad versus focused).

- **Hyundai** is following a broad cost leadership strategy. Hyundai offers low-cost vehicles, in each particular model stratification, that appeal to a large audience.
- **Audi** is pursuing a broad differentiation strategy with its Quattro models available at several price points. Audi's differentiation is safety, and it prices its various Quattro models (higher than Hyundai) to reach a large, stratified audience.
- **Kia** has a more focused cost leadership strategy. Kia mainly offers low-cost vehicles in the lower levels of model stratification.
- **Hummer** offers the most focused differentiation strategy of any in the industry (including Mercedes-Benz).

Value Chain Analysis—Targeting Business Processes

Once an organization enters a new market using one of Porter's three generic strategies, it must understand, accept, and successfully execute its business strategy. Every aspect of the organization contributes to the success (or failure) of the chosen strategy. The business processes of the organization and the value chain they create play an integral role in strategy execution. Figure 2.5 combines Porter's Five Forces and his three generic strategies creating business strategies for each segment.[8]

VALUE CREATION

A *business process* is a standardized set of activities that accomplish a specific task, such as processing a customer's order. To evaluate the effectiveness of its business processes, an organization can use Michael Porter's value chain approach. An organization creates value by performing a series of activities that Porter identified as the value chain. The *value chain* approach views an organization as a series of

Generic Strategies			
Industry Force	Cost Leadership	Differentiation	Focused
Entry Barriers	Ability to cut price in retaliation deters potential entrants.	Customer loyalty can discourage potential entrants.	Focusing develops core competencies that can act as an entry barrier.
Buyer Power	Ability to offer lower price to powerful buyers.	Large buyers have less power to negotiate because of few close alternatives.	Large buyers have less power to negotiate because of few alternatives.
Supplier Power	Better insulated from powerful suppliers.	Better able to pass on supplier price increases to customers.	Suppliers have power because of low volumes, but a differentiation-focused firm is better able to pass on supplier price increases.
Threat of Substitutes	Can use low price to defend against substitutes.	Customers become attached to differentiating attributes, reducing threat of substitutes.	Specialized products and core competency protect against substitutes.
Rivalry	Better able to compete on price.	Brand loyalty to keep customers from rivals.	Rivals cannot meet differentiation-focused customer needs.

FIGURE 2.5

Generic Strategies and
Industry Forces

processes, each of which adds value to the product or service for each customer. To create a competitive advantage, the value chain must enable the organization to provide unique value to its customers. In addition to the firm's own value-creating activities, the firm operates in a value system of vertical activities including those of upstream suppliers and downstream channel members. To achieve a competitive advantage, the firm must perform one or more value-creating activities in a way that creates more overall value than do competitors. Added value is created through lower costs or superior benefits to the consumer (differentiation).

Organizations can add value by offering lower prices or by competing in a distinctive way. Examining the organization as a value chain (actually numerous distinct but inseparable value chains) leads to the identification of the important activities that add value for customers and then finding IT systems that support those activities. Figure 2.6 depicts a value chain. Primary value activities, shown at the bottom of the graph, acquire raw materials and manufacture, deliver, market,

FIGURE 2.6

A Graphical Depiction of a
Value Chain

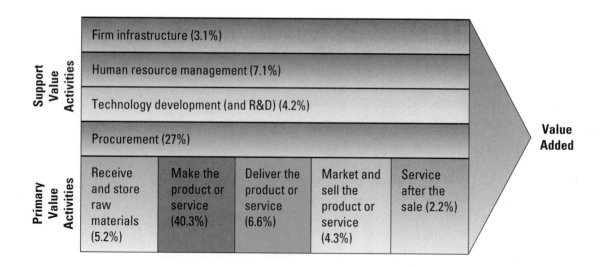

sell, and provide after-sales services. Support value activities, along the top of the graph, such as firm infrastructure, human resource management, technology development, and procurement, support the primary value activities.

The goal here is to survey the customers and ask them the extent to which they believe each activity adds value to the product or service. This generates a quantifiable metric, displayed in percentages in Figure 2.6, for how each activity adds value (or reduces value). The competitive advantage decision then is to (1) target high value-adding activities to further enhance their value, (2) target low value-adding activities to increase their value, or (3) perform some combination of the two.

Organizations should attempt to use information technology to add value to both primary and support value activities. One example of a primary value activity facilitated by IT is the development of a marketing campaign management system that could target marketing campaigns more efficiently, thereby reducing marketing costs. The system would also help the organization better pinpoint target market needs, thereby increasing sales. One example of a support value activity facilitated by IT is the development of a human resources system that could more efficiently reward employees based on performance. The system could also identify employees who are at risk of leaving their jobs, allowing the organization to find additional challenges or opportunities that would help retain these employees and thus reduce turnover costs.

Value chain analysis is a highly useful tool in that it provides hard and fast numbers for evaluating the activities that add value to products and services. An organization can find additional value by analyzing and constructing its value chain in terms of Porters' Five Forces (see Figure 2.7). For example, if an organization wants to decrease its buyers' or customers' power it can construct its value chain activity of "service after the sale" by offering high levels of quality customer service. This will increase the switching costs for its customers, thereby decreasing their power.

Strategy

FIGURE 2.7

The Value Chain and Porter's Five Forces

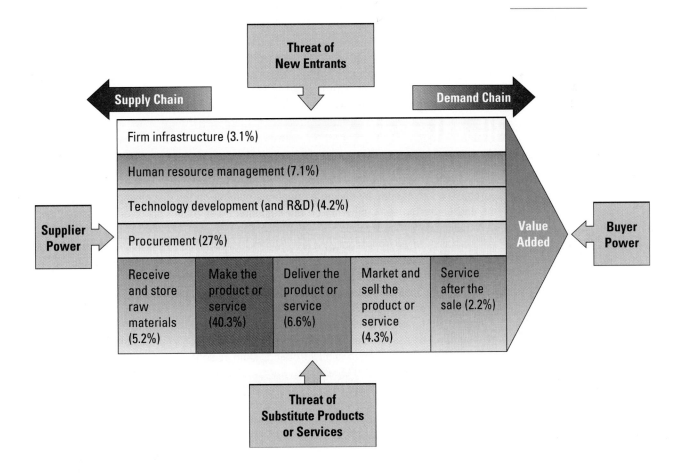

Analyzing and constructing its support value activities can help an organization decrease the threat of new entrants. Analyzing and constructing its primary value activities can help an organization decrease the threat of substitute products or services.

A company can implement its selected strategy by means of programs, budgets, and procedures. Implementation involves organization of the firm's resources and motivation of the employees to achieve objectives. How the company implements its chosen strategy can have a significant impact on its success. In a large company, the personnel implementing the strategy are usually different from those formulating the strategy. For this reason, proper communication of the strategy is critical. Failure can result if the strategy is misunderstood or if lower-level managers resist its implementation because they do not understand the process for selecting the particular strategy.

An organization must continually adapt to its competitive environment, which can cause its business strategy to change. To remain successful, an organization should use Porter's Five Forces, the three generic strategies, and value chain analysis to adopt new business strategies.

OPENING CASE STUDY QUESTIONS

1. How can Apple use environmental scanning to gain business intelligence?

2. Using Porter's Five Forces Model, analyze Apple's buyer power and supplier power.

3. Which of the three generic strategies is Apple following?

4. Which of Porter's Five Forces did Apple address through the introduction of the iPhone?

Chapter Two Case: Say "Charge It" with Your Cell Phone

Wireless operators, credit card companies, and retailers are working on a technology that allows customers to purchase items by using their cell phones. For example, a customer could purchase a can of soda by dialing a telephone number on the dispensing machine and have the charge for the soda show up on the customer's cell phone bill. Working prototypes are currently in use in South Korea, Japan, and Europe.

The ability to charge items to a cell phone has significant business potential because, unlike in the United States, credit cards are not nearly as popular in other countries. In Japan and China, for example, people are much more likely to have a cell phone than a credit card.

Japanese consumers use credit cards for only 5.6 percent of their personal spending compared with 33 percent of U.S. consumer spending.

The payoff for credit card companies and cell phone operators from this technology could be enormous. By associating a credit card with a cell phone, banks and credit card companies hope to persuade consumers to buy products, such as soda, with their cell phones instead of pocket change. Of course, they will reap transaction fees for each transaction. Mobile phone operators see the technology as a way to increase traffic on their networks as well as to position cell phones as an even more useful and, thus, essential device for consumers. Retailers envision easier transactions also leading to more sales.

MasterCard International and Nokia are currently testing a cell phone credit card for the U.S. market. The phones have a special chip programmed with the user's credit card information and a radio-frequency transmitting circuit. Consumers can simply tap their phone on a special device at a checkout counter equipped with a receiving device that costs the retailer about $80. Betsy Foran-Owens, vice president for Product Services at MasterCard International, commented that with this technology, "You don't even have to get off your phone to pay. You can just tap this thing down at the register." She also noted, "If you're not going to carry cash around, what are you going to carry? Your mobile phone."

The only players who might not look favorably on the technology are the traditional telephone companies, who must certainly view the technology as just one more threat to their traditional telephone business.[9]

Questions

1. Do you view this technology as a potential threat to traditional telephone companies? If so, what counterstrategies could traditional telephone companies adopt to prepare for this technology?
2. Using Porter's Five Forces describe the barriers to entry for this new technology.
3. Which of Porter's three generic strategies is this new technology following?
4. Describe the value chain of the business of using cell phones as a payment method.
5. What types of regulatory issues might occur due to this type of technology?
6. How could Apple's iPhone use this technology to gain a competitive advantage?

Strategic Initiatives for Implementing Competitive Advantages

3.1. List and describe the four basic components of supply chain management.

3.2. Explain customer relationship management systems and how they can help organizations understand their customers.

3.3. Summarize the importance of enterprise resource planning systems.

3.4. Identify how an organization can use business process reengineering to improve its business.

Strategic Initiatives

Trek, a leader in bicycle products and accessories, gained more than 30 percent of the worldwide market by streamlining operations through the implementation of several IT systems. According to Jeff Stang, director of IT and operational accounting, the most significant improvement realized from the new systems was the ability to obtain key management information to drive business decisions in line with the company's strategic goals. Other system results included a highly successful Web site developed for the 1,400 Trek dealers where they could enter orders directly, check stock availability, and view accounts receivable and credit summaries. Tonja Green, Trek channel manager for North America, stated, "We wanted to give our dealers an easier and quicker way to enter their orders and get information. Every week the number of Web orders increases by 25 to 30 percent due to the new system."[10]

This chapter introduces high-profile strategic initiatives that an organization can undertake to help it gain competitive advantages and business efficiencies—supply chain management, customer relationship management, business process reengineering, and enterprise resource planning. Each of these strategic initiatives is covered in detail throughout this text. This chapter provides a brief introduction only.

Supply Chain Management

Rocketboom

To understand a supply chain, consider a customer purchasing a Trek bike from a dealer. On one end, the supply chain has the customer placing an order for the bike with the dealer. The dealer purchases the bike from the manufacturer, Trek. Trek purchases raw materials such as packaging material, metal, and accessories from many different suppliers to make the bike. The supply chain for Trek encompasses every activity and party involved in the process of fulfilling the order from the customer for the new bike.

Supply chain management (SCM) involves the management of information flows between and among stages in a supply chain to maximize total supply chain effectiveness and profitability. The four basic components of supply chain management are:

1. **Supply chain strategy**—the strategy for managing all the resources required to meet customer demand for all products and services.

2. **Supply chain partners**—the partners chosen to deliver finished products, raw materials, and services including pricing, delivery, and payment processes along with partner relationship monitoring metrics.

3. **Supply chain operation**—the schedule for production activities including testing, packaging, and preparation for delivery. Measurements for this component include productivity and quality.

4. **Supply chain logistics**—the product delivery processes and elements including orders, warehouses, carriers, defective product returns, and invoicing.

Dozens of steps are required to achieve and carry out each of the above components. SCM software can enable an organization to generate efficiencies within these steps by automating and improving the information flows throughout and among the different supply chain components.

Wal-Mart and Procter & Gamble (P&G) implemented a tremendously successful SCM system. The system linked Wal-Mart's distribution centers directly to P&G's manufacturing centers. Every time a Wal-Mart customer purchases a P&G product, the system sends a message directly to the factory alerting P&G to restock the product. The system also sends an automatic alert to P&G whenever a product is running low at one of Wal-Mart's distribution centers. This real-time information allows P&G to efficiently make and deliver products to Wal-Mart without having to maintain large inventories in its warehouses. The system also generates invoices and receives payments automatically. The SCM system saves time, reduces inventory, and decreases order-processing costs for P&G. P&G passes on these savings to Wal-Mart in the form of discounted prices.[11]

Figure 3.1 diagrams the stages of the SCM system for a customer purchasing a product from Wal-Mart. The diagram demonstrates how the supply chain is dynamic and involves the constant flow of information between the different parties. For example, the customer generates order information by purchasing a product from Wal-Mart. Wal-Mart supplies the order information to its warehouse or distributor. The warehouse or distributor transfers the order information to the manufacturer, who provides pricing and availability information to the store and replenishes the product to the store. Payment funds among the various partners are transferred electronically.[12]

Effective and efficient supply chain management systems can enable an organization to:

- Decrease the power of its buyers.
- Increase its own supplier power.
- Increase switching costs to reduce the threat of substitute products or services.

Supply
Chain

FIGURE 3.1

Supply Chain for a Product
Purchased from Wal-Mart

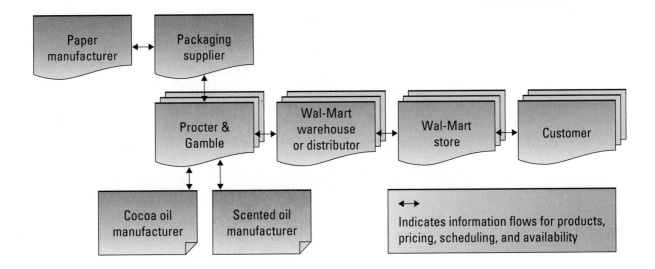

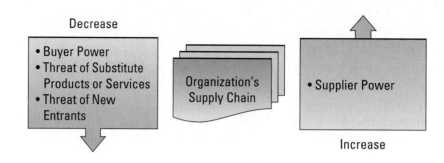

- Create entry barriers thereby reducing the threat of new entrants.
- Increase efficiencies while seeking a competitive advantage through cost leadership (see Figure 3.2).

Customer Relationship Management

Today, most competitors are simply a mouse-click away. This intense marketplace has forced organizations to switch from being sales focused to being customer focused.

Charles Schwab recouped the cost of a multimillion-dollar customer relationship management system in less than two years. The system, developed by Siebel, allows the brokerage firm to trace each interaction with a customer or prospective customer and then provide services (retirement planning, for instance) to each customer's needs and interests. The system gives Schwab a better and more complete view of its customers, which it can use to determine which customers are serious investors and which ones are not. Automated deposits from paychecks, for example, are a sign of a serious investor, while stagnant balances signal a nonserious investor. Once Schwab is able to make this determination, the firm allocates its resources accordingly, saving money by not investing time or resources in subsidizing nonserious investors.[13]

Customer relationship management (CRM) involves managing all aspects of a customer's relationship with an organization to increase customer loyalty and retention and an organization's profitability. CRM allows an organization to gain insights into customers' shopping and buying behaviors in order to develop and implement enterprisewide strategies. Kaiser Permanente undertook a CRM strategy to improve and prolong the lives of diabetics. After compiling CRM information on 84,000 of its diabetic patients among its 2.4 million northern California members, Kaiser determined that only 15 to 20 percent of its diabetic patients were getting their eyes checked routinely. (Diabetes is the leading cause of blindness.) As a result, Kaiser is now enforcing more rigorous eye-screening programs for diabetics and creating support groups for obesity and stress (two more factors that make diabetes even worse). This CRM-based "preventive medicine" approach is saving Kaiser considerable sums of money and saving the eyesight of diabetic patients.[14]

Figure 3.3 provides an overview of a typical CRM system. Customers contact an organization through various means including call centers, Web access, e-mail, faxes, and direct sales. A single customer may access an organization multiple times through many different channels. The CRM system tracks every communication between the customer and the organization and provides access to CRM information within different systems from accounting to order fulfillment. Understanding all customer communications allows the organization to communicate effectively with each customer. It gives the organization a detailed understanding of each customer's products and services record regardless of the customer's preferred communication channel. For example, a customer service representative

FIGURE 3.3

CRM Overview

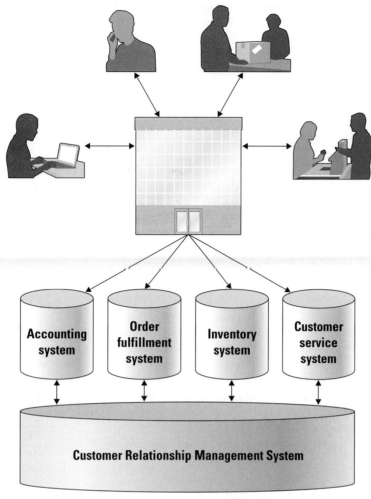

Customer Relationship Management System

←→ Customer information flows
are represented by arrows.

can easily view detailed account information and history through a CRM system when providing information to a customer such as expected delivery dates, complementary product information, and customer payment and billing information.

CRM STRATEGY

Eddie Bauer ships 110 million catalogs a year, maintains two Web sites, and has over 600 retail stores. The company collects information through customer transactions and analyzes the information to determine the best way to market to each individual customer. Eddie Bauer discovered that customers who shop across all three of its distribution channels—catalogs, Web sites, and stores—spend up to five times more than customers who shop through only one channel.

Michael Boyd, director of CRM at Eddie Bauer, stated, "Our experience tells us that CRM is in no way, shape, or form a software application. Fundamentally, it is a business strategy to try to optimize profitability, revenue, and satisfaction at an individual customer level. Everything in an organization, every single process, every single application, is a tool that can be used to serve the CRM goal."[15]

It is important to realize that CRM is not just technology, but also a strategy that an organization must embrace on an enterprise level. Although there are many technical components of CRM, it is actually a process and business goal simply enhanced by technology. Implementing a CRM system can help an organization identify customers and design specific marketing campaigns tailored to each customer, thereby increasing customer spending. A CRM system also allows an organization to treat customers as individuals, gaining important insights into their buying preferences and behaviors and leading to increased sales, greater profitability, and higher rates of customer loyalty.

Business Process Reengineering

A **business process** is a standardized set of activities that accomplish a specific task, such as processing a customer's order. **Business process reengineering (BPR)** is the analysis and redesign of workflow within and between enterprises. The concept of BPR traces its origins to management theories developed as early as the 19th century. The purpose of BPR is to make all business process the best-in-class. Frederick Taylor suggested in the 1880s that managers could discover the best processes for performing work and reengineer the processes to optimize productivity. BPR echoes the classical belief that there is one best way to conduct tasks. In Taylor's time, technology did not allow large companies to design processes in a cross-functional or cross-departmental manner. Specialization was the state-of-the-art method to improve efficiency given the technology of the time.[16]

BPR reached its heyday in the early 1990s when Michael Hammer and James Champy published their best-selling book, *Reengineering the Corporation*. The authors promoted the idea that radical redesign and reorganization of an enterprise (wiping the slate clean) sometimes was necessary to lower costs and increase quality of service and that information technology was the key enabler for that radical change. Hammer and Champy believed that the workflow design in most large corporations was based on invalid assumptions about technology, people, and organizational goals. They suggested seven principles of reengineering to streamline the work process and thereby achieve significant improvement in quality, time management, and cost (see Figure 3.4).[17]

FINDING OPPORTUNITY USING BPR

Companies frequently strive to improve their business processes by performing tasks faster, cheaper, and better. Figure 3.5 displays different ways to travel the same road. A company could improve the way that it travels the road by moving from foot to horse and then from horse to car. However, true BPR would look at taking a different path. A company could forget about traveling on the same old road and use an airplane to get to its final destination. Companies often follow the same indirect path for doing business, not realizing there might be a different, faster, and more direct way of doing business.[18]

Creating value for the customer is the leading factor for instituting BPR, and information technology often plays an important enabling role. Radical and

Business
Process

FIGURE 3.4

Seven Principles of
Business Process
Reengineering

Seven Principles of Business Process Reengineering	
1	Organize around outcomes, not tasks.
2	Identify all the organization's processes and prioritize them in order of redesign urgency.
3	Integrate information processing work into the real work that produces the information.
4	Treat geographically dispersed resources as though they were centralized.
5	Link parallel activities in the workflow instead of just integrating their results.
6	Put the decision point where the work is performed, and build control into the process.
7	Capture information once and at the source.

fundamentally new business processes enabled Progressive Insurance to slash the claims settlement from 31 days to four hours. Typically, car insurance companies follow this standard claims resolution process: The customer gets into an accident, has the car towed, and finds a ride home. The customer then calls the insurance company to begin the claims process, which usually takes over a month (see Figure 3.6).[19]

Progressive Insurance improved service to its customers by offering a mobile claims process. When a customer has a car accident he or she calls in the claim on the spot. The Progressive claims adjustor comes to the accident and performs a mobile claims process, surveying the scene and taking digital photographs. The adjustor then offers the customer on-site payment, towing services, and a ride home (see Figure 3.6).[20]

A true BPR effort does more for a company than simply improve it by performing a process better, faster, and cheaper. Progressive Insurance's BPR effort redefined best practices for its entire industry. Figure 3.7 displays the different types of change an organization can achieve, along with the magnitude of change and the potential business benefit.[21]

FIGURE 3.5

Better, Faster, Cheaper or BPR

PITFALLS OF BPR

One hazard of BPR is that the company becomes so wrapped up in fighting its own demons that it fails to keep up with its competitors in offering new products or services. While American Express tackled a comprehensive reengineering of its credit card business, MasterCard and Visa introduced a new product—the corporate procurement card. American Express lagged a full year behind before offering its customers the same service.[22]

Enterprise Resource Planning

Today's business leaders need significant amounts of information to be readily accessible with real-time views into their businesses so that decisions can be made when they need to be, without the added time of tracking data and generating reports. *Enterprise resource planning (ERP)* integrates all departments and functions throughout an organization into a single IT system (or integrated set of IT systems) so that employees can make decisions by viewing enterprisewide information on all business operations.

Many organizations fail to maintain consistency across business operations. If a single department, such as sales, decides to implement a new system without

FIGURE 3.6

Auto Insurance Claims Processes

Company A: Claims Resolution Process   Progressive Insurance: Claims Resolution Process

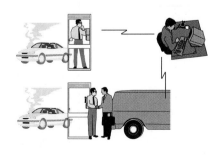

| Resolution Cycle Time: 3–8 weeks | Resolution Cycle Time: 30 min–3 hours |

FIGURE 3.7

The Benefits and
Magnitude of Change

Process Change Spectrum

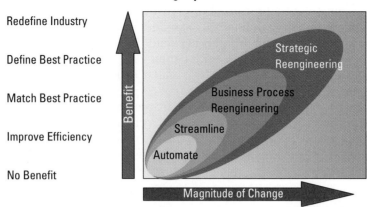

considering the other departments, inconsistencies can occur throughout the company. Not all systems are built to talk to each other and share data, and if sales suddenly implements a new system that marketing and accounting cannot use or is inconsistent in the way it handles information, the company's operations become siloed. Figure 3.8 displays sample data from a sales database, and Figure 3.9 displays samples from an accounting database. Notice the differences in data formats, numbers, and identifiers. Correlating this data would be difficult, and the inconsistencies would cause numerous reporting errors from an enterprisewide perspective.

Los Angeles is a city of 3.5 million, with 44,000 city employees, and a budget of $4 billion. Yet a few years ago each department conducted its own purchasing. That meant 2,000 people in 600 city buildings and 60 warehouses were ordering material. Some 120,000 purchase orders (POs) and 50,000 checks per year went to more than 7,000 vendors. Inefficiency was rampant.

"There was a lack of financial responsibility in the old system, and people could run up unauthorized expenditures," said Bob Jensen, the city's ERP project manager. Each department maintained its own inventories on different systems. Expense-item

FIGURE 3.8

Sales Information Sample

OrderDate	ProductName	Quantity	Unit Price	Unit Cost	Customer ID	SalesRep ID
Monday, January 04, 2010	Mozzarella cheese	41.5	$ 24.15	$ 15.35	AC45	EX-107
Monday, January 04, 2010	Romaine lettuce	90.65	$ 15.06	$ 14.04	AC45	EX-109
Tuesday, January 05, 2010	Red onions	27.15	$ 12.08	$ 10.32	AC67	EX-104
Wednesday, January 06, 2010	Romaine lettuce	67.25	$ 15.16	$ 10.54	AC96	EX-109
Thursday, January 07, 2010	Black olives	79.26	$ 12.18	$ 9.56	AC44	EX-104
Thursday, January 07, 2010	Romaine lettuce	46.52	$ 15.24	$ 11.54	AC32	EX-104
Thursday, January 07, 2010	Romaine lettuce	52.5	$ 15.26	$ 11.12	AC84	EX-109
Friday, January 08, 2010	Red onions	39.5	$ 12.55	$ 9.54	AC103	EX-104
Saturday, January 09, 2010	Romaine lettuce	66.5	$ 15.98	$ 9.56	AC4	EX-104
Sunday, January 10, 2010	Romaine lettuce	58.26	$ 15.87	$ 9.50	AC174	EX-104
Sunday, January 10, 2010	Pineapple	40.15	$ 33.54	$ 22.12	AC45	EX-104
Monday, January 11, 2010	Pineapple	71.56	$ 33.56	$ 22.05	AC4	EX-104
Thursday, January 14, 2010	Romaine lettuce	18.25	$ 15.00	$ 10.25	AC174	EX-104
Thursday, January 14, 2010	Romaine lettuce	28.15	$ 15.26	$ 10.54	AC44	EX-107
Friday, January 15, 2010	Pepperoni	33.5	$ 15.24	$ 10.25	AC96	EX-109
Friday, January 15, 2010	Parmesan cheese	14.26	$ 8.05	$ 4.00	AC96	EX-104
Saturday, January 16, 2010	Parmesan cheese	72.15	$ 8.50	$ 4.00	AC103	EX-109
Monday, January 18, 2010	Parmesan cheese	41.5	$ 24.15	$ 15.35	AC45	EX-107
Monday, January 18, 2010	Romaine lettuce	90.65	$ 15.06	$ 14.04	AC45	EX-109
Wednesday, January 20, 2010	Tomatoes	27.15	$ 12.08	$ 10.32	AC67	EX-104
Thursday, January 21, 2010	Peppers	67.25	$ 15.16	$ 10.54	AC96	EX-109
Thursday, January 21, 2010	Mozzarella cheese	79.26	$ 12.18	$ 9.56	AC44	EX-104
Saturday, January 23, 2010	Black olives	46.52	$ 15.24	$ 11.54	AC32	EX-104
Sunday, January 24, 2010	Mozzarella cheese	52.5	$ 15.26	$ 11.12	AC84	EX-109
Tuesday, January 26, 2010	Romaine lettuce	39.5	$ 12.55	$ 9.54	AC103	EX-104
Wednesday, January 27, 2010	Parmesan cheese	66.5	$ 15.98	$ 9.56	AC4	EX-104
Thursday, January 28, 2010	Peppers	58.26	$ 15.87	$ 9.50	AC174	EX-104
Thursday, January 28, 2010	Mozzarella cheese	40.15	$ 33.54	$ 22.12	AC45	EX-104
Friday, January 29, 2010	Tomatoes	71.56	$ 33.56	$ 22.05	AC4	EX-104
Friday, January 29, 2010	Peppers	18.25	$ 15.00	$ 10.25	AC174	EX-104

FIGURE 3.9

Accounting Information Sample

OrderDate	ProductName	Quantity	Unit Price	Total Sales	Unit Cost	Total Cost	Profit	Customer	SalesRep
04-Jan-10	Mozzarella cheese	41	24	984	18	738	246	The Station	Debbie Fernandez
04-Jan-10	Romaine lettuce	90	15	1,350	14	1,260	90	The Station	Roberta Cross
05-Jan-10	Red onions	27	12	324	8	216	108	Bert's Bistro	Loraine Schultz
06-Jan-10	Romaine lettuce	67	15	1,005	14	938	67	Smoke House	Roberta Cross
07-Jan-10	Black olives	79	12	948	6	474	474	Flagstaff House	Loraine Schultz
07-Jan-10	Romaine lettuce	46	15	690	14	644	46	Two Bitts	Loraine Schultz
07-Jan-10	Romaine lettuce	52	15	780	14	728	52	Pierce Arrow	Roberta Cross
08-Jan-10	Red onions	39	12	468	8	312	156	Mamm'a Pasta Palace	Loraine Schultz
09-Jan-10	Romaine lettuce	66	15	990	14	924	66	The Dandelion	Loraine Schultz
10-Jan-10	Romaine lettuce	58	15	870	14	812	58	Carmens	Loraine Schultz
10-Jan-10	Pineapple	40	33	1,320	28	1,120	200	The Station	Loraine Schultz
11-Jan-10	Pineapple	71	33	2,343	28	1,988	355	The Dandelion	Loraine Schultz
14-Jan-10	Romaine lettuce	18	15	270	14	252	18	Carmens	Loraine Schultz
14-Jan-10	Romaine lettuce	28	15	420	14	392	28	Flagstaff House	Debbie Fernandez
15-Jan-10	Pepperoni	33	53	1,749	35	1,155	594	Smoke House	Roberta Cross
15-Jan-10	Parmesan cheese	14	8	112	4	56	56	Smoke House	Loraine Schultz
16-Jan-10	Parmesan cheese	72	8	576	4	288	288	Mamm'a Pasta Palace	Roberta Cross
18-Jan-10	Parmesan cheese	10	8	80	4	40	40	Mamm'a Pasta Palace	Loraine Schultz
18-Jan-10	Romaine lettuce	42	15	630	14	588	42	Smoke House	Roberta Cross
20-Jan-10	Tomatoes	48	9	432	7	336	96	Two Bitts	Loraine Schultz
21-Jan-10	Peppers	29	21	609	12	348	261	The Dandelion	Roberta Cross
21-Jan-10	Mozzarella cheese	10	24	240	18	180	60	Mamm'a Pasta Palace	Debbie Fernandez
23-Jan-10	Black olives	98	12	1,176	6	588	588	Two Bitts	Roberta Cross
24-Jan-10	Mozzarella cheese	45	24	1,080	18	810	270	Carmens	Loraine Schultz
26-Jan-10	Romaine lettuce	58	15	870	14	812	58	Two Bitts	Loraine Schultz
27-Jan-10	Parmesan cheese	66	8	528	4	264	264	Flagstaff House	Loraine Schultz
28-Jan-10	Peppers	85	21	1,785	12	1,020	765	Pierce Arrow	Loraine Schultz
28-Jan-10	Mozzarella cheese	12	24	288	18	216	72	The Dandelion	Debbie Fernandez
29-Jan-10	Tomatoes	40	9	360	7	280	80	Pierce Arrow	Roberta Cross

mismatches piled up. One department purchased one way, others preferred a different approach. Mainframe-based systems were isolated. The city chose an ERP system as part of a $22 million project to integrate purchasing and financial reporting across the entire city. The project resulted in cutting the check processing staff in half, processing POs faster than ever, reducing the number of workers in warehousing by 40 positions, decreasing inventories from $50 million to $15 million, and providing a single point of contact for each vendor. In addition, $5 million a year has been saved in contract consolidation.[23]

Figure 3.10 shows how an ERP system takes data from across the enterprise, consolidates and correlates the data, and generates enterprisewide organizational reports. Original ERP implementations promised to capture all information onto one true "enterprise" system, with the ability to touch all the business processes within the organization. Unfortunately, ERP solutions have fallen short of these promises, and typical implementations have penetrated only 15 to 20 percent of

Corporate Data

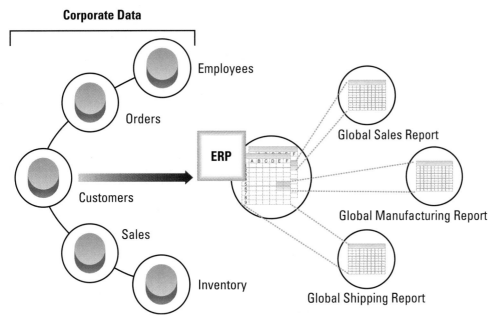

Employees
Orders
Customers
Sales
Inventory

ERP

Global Sales Report

Global Manufacturing Report

Global Shipping Report

FIGURE 3.10

Enterprise Resource Planning System

the organization. The issue ERP intends to solve is that knowledge within a majority of organizations currently resides in silos that are maintained by a select few, without the ability to be shared across the organization, causing inconsistency across business operations.[24]

Chapter Three Case: Consolidating Touchpoints for Saab

Saab Cars USA imports more than 37,000 Saab sedans, convertibles, and wagons annually and distributes the cars to 220 U.S. dealerships. Saab competes in the premium automotive market, and its primary rivals attract customers through aggressive marketing campaigns, reduced prices, and inexpensive financing. Saab decided that the answer to beating its competition was not to spend capital on additional advertising, but to invest in Siebel Automotive, a customer relationship management system.

Until recently, the company communicated with its customers through three primary channels: (1) dealer network, (2) customer assistance center, (3) lead management center. Traditionally, each channel maintained its own customer database, and this splintered approach to managing customer information caused numerous problems for the company. For example, a prospective customer might receive a direct-mail piece from Saab one week, then an e-mail with an unrelated offer from a third-party marketing vendor the next week. The local dealer might not know of either activity, and therefore might deliver an ineffective pitch when the customer visited the showroom that weekend. Al Fontova, direct marketing manager with Saab Cars USA, stated he had over 3 million customer records and 55 files at three different vendors. Analyzing this information in aggregate was complicated, inefficient, and costly.

Saab required a solution that would provide a consolidated customer view from all three touchpoints. In 2002, Saab implemented the Siebel CRM solution, which provides Saab's call center employees with a 360-degree view of each customer, including prior service-related questions and all the marketing communications they have received. Known internally as "TouchPoint," the Siebel application provides Saab's dealers with a powerful Web-based solution for coordinating sales and marketing activities. These tracking capabilities enable Saab to measure the sales results of specific leads, recommend more efficient selling techniques, and target its leads more precisely in the future. Using Siebel Automotive, Saab received the following benefits:

- Direct marketing costs decreased by 5 percent.
- Lead follow-up increased from 38 percent to 50 percent.
- Customer satisfaction increased from 69 percent to 75 percent.
- Saab gained a single view of its customers across multiple channels.[25]

Questions

1. Explain how implementing a CRM system enabled Saab to gain a competitive advantage.
2. Estimate the potential impact to Saab's business if it had not implemented a CRM system.
3. What additional benefits could Saab receive from implementing a supply chain management system?
4. Create a model of Saab's potential supply chain.
5. How is Saab's CRM implementation going to influence its SCM practices?

TECHNOLOGY PLUG-IN POINTER

Review the **Technology Plug-In T2 "Basic Skills Using Excel"** for an introduction to Excel including workbooks, worksheets, cells, data, menus, formats, formulas, charts, graphs, and more.

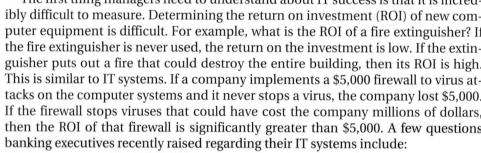
Measuring the Success of Strategic Initiatives

4.1. Compare efficiency IT metrics and effectiveness IT metrics.

4.2. List and describe five common types of efficiency IT metrics.

4.3. List and describe four types of effectiveness IT metrics.

4.4. Explain customer metrics and their importance to an organization.

Online Job
Search
Industry

Measuring Information Technology's Success

IT has become an important part of organizations' strategy, competitive advantage, and profitability. There is management pressure to build systems faster, better, and at minimum cost. The return on investment that an organization can achieve from the money it spends on IT has come under increased scrutiny from senior business executives and directors. Consequently, IT now has to operate like other parts of the organization, being aware of its performance and its contribution to the organization's success and opportunities for improvement. So what is it that managers need to know about measuring the success of information technology?

The first thing managers need to understand about IT success is that it is incredibly difficult to measure. Determining the return on investment (ROI) of new computer equipment is difficult. For example, what is the ROI of a fire extinguisher? If the fire extinguisher is never used, the return on the investment is low. If the extinguisher puts out a fire that could destroy the entire building, then its ROI is high. This is similar to IT systems. If a company implements a $5,000 firewall to virus attacks on the computer systems and it never stops a virus, the company lost $5,000. If the firewall stops viruses that could have cost the company millions of dollars, then the ROI of that firewall is significantly greater than $5,000. A few questions banking executives recently raised regarding their IT systems include:

■ Is the internal IT operation performing satisfactorily?

■ Should I outsource some or all of the IT operations?

■ How is my outsourcer performing?

■ What are the risk factors to consider in an IT project?

■ What questions should be asked to ensure an IT project proposal is realistic?

■ What are the characteristics of a healthy project?

■ Which factors are most critical to monitor to ensure the project remains on track?

Peter Drucker, a famous management guru, once stated that if you cannot measure it, you cannot manage it. Managers need to ask themselves how they are going to manage IT projects if they cannot find a way to measure the projects.[26]

IT professionals know how to install and maintain information systems. Business professionals know how to run a successful business. But how does a company decide if an information system helps make a business successful?

The answer lies in the metrics. Designing metrics requires an expertise that neither IT nor business professionals usually possess. Metrics are about neither technology nor business strategy. The questions that arise in metrics design are almost philosophical: How do you define success? How do you apply quantifiable measures to business processes, especially qualitative ones like customer service? What kind of information best reflects progress, or the lack of it?

Key performance indicators (KPIs) are the measures that are tied to business drivers. Metrics are the detailed measures that feed those KPIs. Performance metrics fall into a nebulous area of business intelligence that is neither technology- nor business-centered, but this area requires input from both IT and business professionals to find success. Cisco Systems implemented a cross-departmental council to create metrics for improving business process operations. The council developed metrics to evaluate the efficiency of Cisco's online order processing and discovered that due to errors, more than 70 percent of online orders required manual input and were unable to be automatically routed to manufacturing. By changing the process and adding new information systems, within six months the company doubled the percentage of orders that went directly to manufacturing.[27]

Effective
Business

Efficiency and Effectiveness

Organizations spend enormous sums of money on IT to compete in today's fast-paced business environment. Some organizations spend up to 50 percent of their total capital expenditures on IT. To justify these expenditures, an organization must measure the payoff of these investments, their impact on business performance, and the overall business value gained.

Efficiency and effectiveness metrics are two primary types of IT metrics. *Efficiency IT metrics* measure the performance of the IT system itself including throughput, speed, and availability. *Effectiveness IT metrics* measure the impact IT has on business processes and activities including customer satisfaction, conversion rates, and sell-through increases. Peter Drucker offers a helpful distinction between efficiency and effectiveness. Drucker states that managers "Do things right" and/or "Do the right things." Doing things right addresses efficiency—getting the most from each resource. Doing the right things addresses effectiveness—setting the right goals and objectives and ensuring they are accomplished.[28]

Effectiveness focuses on how well an organization is achieving its goals and objectives, while efficiency focuses on the extent to which an organization is using its resources in an optimal way. The two—efficiency and effectiveness—are definitely interrelated. However, success in one area does not necessarily imply success in the other.

Benchmarking—Baseline Metrics

Regardless of what is measured, how it is measured, and whether it is for the sake of efficiency or effectiveness, there must be *benchmarks,* or baseline values the system seeks to attain. *Benchmarking* is a process of continuously measuring system results, comparing those results to optimal system performance (benchmark values), and identifying steps and procedures to improve system performance.

Consider e-government worldwide as an illustration of benchmarking efficiency IT metrics and effectiveness IT metrics (see survey results in Figure 4.1). From an

Efficiency	Effectiveness
1. United States (3.11)	1. Canada
2. Australia (2.60)	2. Singapore
3. New Zealand (2.59)	3. United States
4. Singapore (2.58)	4. Denmark
5. Norway (2.55)	5. Australia
6. Canada (2.52)	6. Finland
7. United Kingdom (2.52)	7. Hong Kong
8. Netherlands (2.51)	8. United Kingdom
9. Denmark (2.47)	9. Germany
10. Germany (2.46)	10. Ireland

FIGURE 4.1

Comparing Efficiency IT and Effectiveness IT Metrics for E-Government Initiatives

effectiveness point of view, Canada ranks number one in terms of e-government satisfaction of its citizens. (The United States ranks third.) The survey, sponsored by Accenture, also included such attributes as CRM practices, customer-service vision, approaches to offering e-government services through multiple-service delivery channels, and initiatives for identifying services for individual citizen segments. These are all benchmarks at which Canada's government excels.[23]

In contrast, the *United Nations Division for Public Economics and Public Administration* ranks Canada sixth in terms of efficiency IT metrics. (It ranked the United States first.) This particular ranking based purely on efficiency IT metrics includes benchmarks such as the number of computers per 100 citizens, the number of Internet hosts per 10,000 citizens, the percentage of the citizen population online, and several other factors. Therefore, while Canada lags behind in IT efficiency, it is the premier e-government provider in terms of effectiveness.[29]

Governments hoping to increase their e-government presence would benchmark themselves against these sorts of efficiency and effectiveness metrics. There is a high degree of correlation between e-government efficiency and effectiveness, although it is not absolute.

The Interrelationships of Efficiency and Effectiveness IT Metrics

Efficiency IT metrics focus on the technology itself. Figure 4.2 highlights the most common types of efficiency IT metrics.

While these efficiency metrics are important to monitor, they do not always guarantee effectiveness. Effectiveness IT metrics are determined according to an organization's goals, strategies, and objectives. Here, it becomes important to consider the strategy an organization is using, such as a broad cost leadership strategy (Wal-Mart, for example), as well as specific goals and objectives such as increasing new customers by 10 percent or reducing new-product development cycle times to six months. Broad, general effectiveness metrics are outlined in Figure 4.3.

In the private sector, eBay constantly benchmarks its information technology efficiency and effectiveness. Maintaining constant Web site availability and optimal throughput performance is critical to eBay's success.[30] Jupiter Media Metrix ranked

FIGURE 4.2

Common Types of Efficiency IT Metrics

Efficiency IT Metrics	
Throughput	The amount of information that can travel through a system at any point.
Transaction speed	The amount of time a system takes to perform a transaction.
System availability	The number of hours a system is available for users.
Information accuracy	The extent to which a system generates the correct results when executing the same transaction numerous times.
Web traffic	Includes a host of benchmarks such as the number of page views, the number of unique visitors, and the average time spent viewing a Web page.
Response time	The time it takes to respond to user interactions such as a mouse click.

Effectiveness IT Metrics	
Usability	The ease with which people perform transactions and/or find information. A popular usability metric on the Internet is degrees of freedom, which measures the number of clicks required to find desired information.
Customer satisfaction	Measured by such benchmarks as satisfaction surveys, percentage of existing customers retained, and increases in revenue dollars per customer.
Conversion rates	The number of customers an organization "touches" for the first time and persuades to purchase its products or services. This is a popular metric for evaluating the effectiveness of banner, pop-up, and pop-under ads on the Internet.
Financial	Such as return on investment (the earning power of an organization's assets), cost-benefit analysis (the comparison of projected revenues and costs including development, maintenance, fixed, and variable), and break-even analysis (the point at which constant revenues equal ongoing costs).

FIGURE 4.3

Common Types of Effectiveness IT Metrics

eBay as the Web site with the highest visitor volume (efficiency) for the fourth year in a row, with an 80 percent growth from the previous year. The eBay site averaged 8 million unique visitors during each week of the holiday season that year with daily peaks exceeding 12 million visitors. To ensure constant availability and reliability of its systems, eBay implemented ProactiveNet, a performance measurement and management-tracking tool. The tool allows eBay to monitor its environment against baseline benchmarks, which helps the eBay team keep tight control of its systems. The new system has resulted in improved system availability with a 150 percent increase in productivity as measured by system uptime.[31]

Be sure to consider the issue of security while determining efficiency and effectiveness IT metrics. When an organization offers its customers the ability to purchase products over the Internet it must implement the appropriate security—such as encryption and Secure Sockets Layers (SSLs; denoted by the lock symbol in the lower right corner of a browser window and/or the "s" in https). It is actually inefficient for an organization to implement security measures for Internet-based transactions as compared to processing nonsecure transactions. However, an organization will probably have a difficult time attracting new customers and increasing Web-based revenue if it does not implement the necessary security measures. Purely from an efficiency IT metric point of view, security generates some inefficiency. From an organization's business strategy point of view, however, security should lead to increases in effectiveness metrics.

FIGURE 4.4

The Interrelationships between Efficiency and Effectiveness

Figure 4.4 depicts the interrelationships between efficiency and effectiveness. Ideally, an organization should operate in the upper right-hand corner of the graph, realizing both significant increases in efficiency and effectiveness. However, operating in the upper left-hand corner (minimal effectiveness with increased efficiency) or the lower right-hand corner (significant effectiveness with minimal efficiency) may be in line with an organization's particular strategies. In general, operating in the lower left-hand corner (minimal efficiency and minimal effectiveness) is not ideal for the operation of any organization.

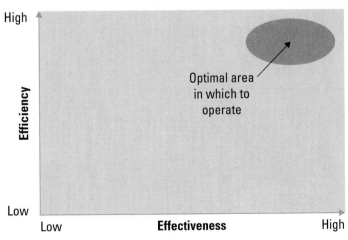

Metrics for Strategic Initiatives

What is a metric? A metric is nothing more than a standard measure to assess performance in a particular area. Metrics are at the heart of a good, customer-focused management system and any program directed at continuous improvement. A focus on customers and performance standards shows up in the form of metrics that assess the ability to meet customers' needs and business objectives.

Business leaders want to monitor key metrics in real-time to actively track the health of their business. Most business professionals are familiar with financial metrics. Different financial ratios are used to evaluate a company's performance. Companies can gain additional insight into their performance by comparing financial ratios against other companies in their industry. A few of the more common financial ratios include:

- Internal rate of return (IRR)—the rate at which the net present value of an investment equals zero.

- Return on investment (ROI)—indicates the earning power of a project and is measured by dividing the benefits of a project by the investment.

- Payback method —number of years to recoup the cost of an initiative based on projected annual net cash flow.

- Break-even analysis—determines the volume of business required to make a profit at the current prices charged for the products or services. For example, if a promotional mailing costs $1,000 and each item generates $50 in revenue, the company must generate 20 sales to break even and cover the cost of the mailing. The break-even point is the point at which revenues equal costs. The point is located by performing a break-even analysis. All sales over the break-even point produce profits; any drop in sales below that point will produce losses (see Figure 4.5).

Most managers are familiar with financial metrics but unfamiliar with information system metrics. The following metrics will help managers measure and manage their strategic initiatives:

- Web site metrics.
- Supply chain management (SCM) metrics.
- Customer relationship management (CRM) metrics.
- Business process reengineering (BPR) metrics.
- Enterprise resource planning (ERP) metrics.

FIGURE 4.5

Break-Even Analysis

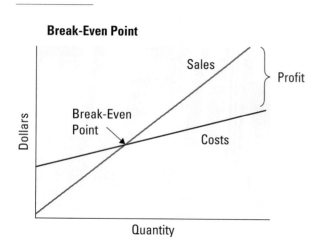

Break-Even Point

WEB SITE METRICS

Most companies measure the traffic on a Web site as the primary determinant of the Web site's success. However, heavy Web site traffic does not necessarily indicate large sales. Many organizations with lots of Web site traffic have minimal sales. A company can use Web traffic analysis or Web analytics to determine the revenue generated, the number of new customers acquired, any reductions in customer service calls, and so on. The Yankee Group reports that 66 percent of companies determine Web site success solely by measuring the amount of traffic. New customer acquisition ranked second on the list at 34 percent, and revenue generation ranked third at 23 percent. Figure 4.6 displays a few metrics managers should be familiar with to help measure Web site success along

FIGURE 4.6

Web Site Metrics

Web Site Metrics
■ **Abandoned registrations:** Number of visitors who start the process of completing a registration page and then abandon the activity.
■ **Abandoned shopping carts:** Number of visitors who create a shopping cart and start shopping and then abandon the activity before paying for the merchandise.
■ **Click-through:** Count of the number of people who visit a site, click on an ad, and are taken to the site of the advertiser.
■ **Conversion rate:** Percentage of potential customers who visit a site and actually buy something.
■ **Cost-per-thousand (CPM):** Sales dollars generated per dollar of advertising. This is commonly used to make the case for spending money to appear on a search engine.
■ **Page exposures:** Average number of page exposures to an individual visitor.
■ **Total hits:** Number of visits to a Web site, many of which may be by the same visitor.
■ **Unique visitors:** Number of unique visitors to a site in a given time. This is commonly used by Nielsen/Net ratings to rank the most popular Web sites.

Metrics

FIGURE 4.7

Supply Chain Management Metrics

Supply Chain Management Metrics
■ **Back order:** An unfilled customer order. A back order is demand (immediate or past due) against an item whose current stock level is insufficient to satisfy demand.
■ **Customer order promised cycle time:** The anticipated or agreed upon cycle time of a purchase order. It is a gap between the purchase order creation date and the requested delivery date.
■ **Customer order actual cycle time:** The average time it takes to actually fill a customer's purchase order. This measure can be viewed on an order or an order line level.
■ **Inventory replenishment cycle time:** Measure of the manufacturing cycle time plus the time included to deploy the product to the appropriate distribution center.
■ **Inventory turns (inventory turnover):** The number of times that a company's inventory cycles or turns over per year. It is one of the most commonly used supply chain metrics.

with an organization's strategic initiatives. A Web-centric metric is a measure of the success of Web and e-business initiatives. Of the hundreds of Web-centric metrics available, some are general to almost any Web or e-business initiative and others are dependent on the particular initiative.[32]

SUPPLY CHAIN MANAGEMENT (SCM) METRICS

Supply chain management metrics can help an organization understand how it's operating over a given time period. Supply chain measurements can cover many areas including procurement, production, distribution, warehousing, inventory, transportation, and customer service. However, a good performance in one part of the supply chain is not sufficient. A supply chain is only as strong as its weakest link. The solution is to measure all key areas of the supply chain. Figure 4.7 displays common supply chain management metrics.[33]

CUSTOMER RELATIONSHIP MANAGEMENT (CRM) METRICS

Wondering what CRM metrics to track and monitor using reporting and real-time performance dashboards? Best practice is no more than seven (plus or minus two) metrics out of the hundreds possible should be used at any given management level. Figure 4.8 displays common CRM metrics tracked by organizations.

FIGURE 4.8

CRM Metrics

Sales Metrics	Service Metrics	Marketing Metrics
■ Number of prospective customers	■ Cases closed same day	■ Number of marketing campaigns
■ Number of new customers	■ Number of cases handled by agent	■ New customer retention rates
■ Number of retained customers	■ Number of service calls	■ Number of responses by marketing campaign
■ Number of open leads	■ Average number of service requests by type	■ Number of purchases by marketing campaign
■ Number of sales calls	■ Average time to resolution	■ Revenue generated by marketing campaign
■ Number of sales calls per lead	■ Average number of service calls per day	■ Cost per interaction by marketing campaign
■ Amount of new revenue	■ Percentage compliance with service-level agreement	■ Number of new customers acquired by marketing campaign
■ Amount of recurring revenue	■ Percentage of service renewals	■ Customer retention rate
■ Number of proposals given	■ Customer satisfaction level	■ Number of new leads by product

BUSINESS PROCESS REENGINEERING (BPR) AND ENTERPRISE RESOURCE PLANNING (ERP) METRICS

Business process reengineering and enterprise resource planning are large, organizationwide initiatives. Measuring these types of strategic initiatives is extremely difficult. One of the best methods is the balanced scorecard. This approach to strategic management was developed in the early 1990s by Drs. Robert Kaplan of the Harvard Business School and David Norton. Addressing some of the weaknesses and vagueness of previous measurement techniques, the balanced scorecard approach provides a clear prescription as to what companies should measure in order to balance the financial perspective.[34]

The *balanced scorecard* is a management system, in addition to a measurement system, that enables organizations to clarify their vision and strategy and translate them into action. It provides feedback around both the internal business processes and external outcomes in order to continuously improve strategic performance and results. When fully deployed, the balanced scorecard transforms strategic planning from an academic exercise into the nerve center of an enterprise. Kaplan and Norton describe the innovation of the balanced scorecard as follows:

> The balanced scorecard retains traditional financial measures. But financial measures tell the story of past events, an adequate story for industrial age companies for which investments in long-term capabilities and customer relationships were not critical for success. These financial measures are inadequate, however, for guiding and evaluating the journey that information age companies must make to create future value through investment in customers, suppliers, employees, processes, technology, and innovation.[35]

The balanced scorecard views the organization from four perspectives, and users should develop metrics, collect data, and analyze their business relative to each of these perspectives:

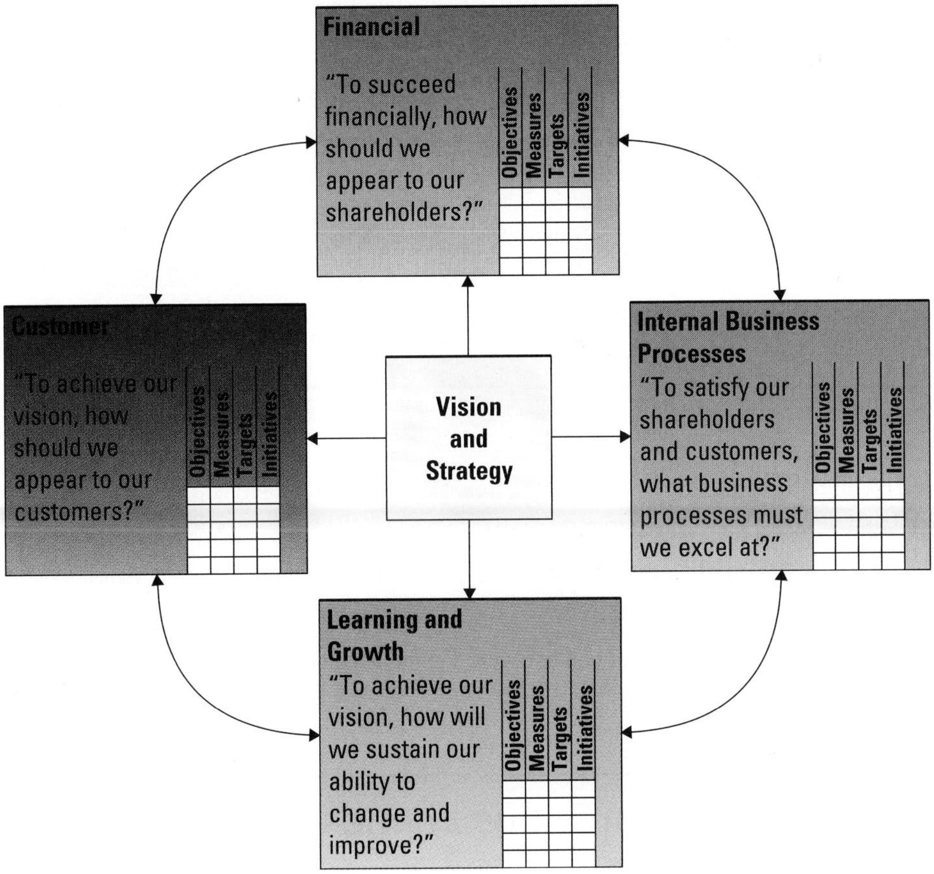

FIGURE 4.9

The Four Primary
Perspectives of the
Balanced Scorecard

- The learning and growth perspective.
- The internal business process perspective.
- The customer perspective.
- The financial perspective (see Figure 4.9).[36]

Recall that companies cannot manage what they cannot measure. Therefore, metrics must be developed based on the priorities of the strategic plan, which provides the key business drivers and criteria for metrics that managers most desire to watch. Processes are then designed to collect information relevant to these metrics and reduce it to numerical form for storage, display, and analysis. Decision makers examine the outcomes of various measured processes and strategies and track the results to guide the company and provide feedback. The value of metrics is in their ability to provide a factual basis for defining:

- Strategic feedback to show the present status of the organization from many perspectives for decision makers.
- Diagnostic feedback into various processes to guide improvements on a continuous basis.
- Trends in performance over time as the metrics are tracked.
- Feedback around the measurement methods themselves and which metrics should be tracked.
- Quantitative inputs to forecasting methods and models for decision support systems.[37]

One warning regarding metrics—do not go crazy. The trick is to find a few key metrics to track that provide significant insight. Remember to tie metrics to other financial and business objectives in the firm. The key is to get good insight without becoming a slave to metrics. The rule of thumb is to develop seven key metrics, plus or minus two.[38]

OPENING CASE STUDY QUESTIONS

1. Formulate a strategy describing how Apple can use efficiency IT metrics to improve its business.

2. Formulate a strategy describing how Apple can use effectiveness IT metrics to improve its business.

3. List three CRM metrics Apple should track, along with the reasons these metrics will add value to Apple's business strategy.

4. List three SCM metrics Apple should track, along with the reasons these metrics will add value to Apple's business strategy.

5. How can Apple use the balanced scorecard to make its business more efficient?

Chapter Four Case: How Do You Value Friendster?

Jonathan Abrams is keeping quiet about how he is going to generate revenue from his Web site, Friendster, which specializes in social networking. Abrams is a 33-year-old Canadian software developer whose experiences include being laid off by Netscape and then moving from one start-up to another. In 2002, Abrams was unemployed, not doing well financially, and certainly not looking to start another business, when he developed the idea for Friendster. He quickly coded a working prototype and watched in amazement as his Web site took off.

The buzz around social networking start-ups has been on the rise. A number of high-end venture capital (VC) firms, including Sequoia and Mayfield, have invested more than $40 million into social networking start-ups such as LinkedIn, Spoke, and Tribe Networks. Friendster received over $13 million in venture capital from Kleiner, Perkins, Caufield, Byers, and Benchmark Capital, which reportedly valued the company at $53 million—a startling figure for a company that had yet to generate even a single dime in revenue.

A year after making its public debut, Friendster was one of the largest social networking Web sites, attracting over 5 million users and receiving more than 50,000 page views per day. The question is how do efficiency metrics, such as Web traffic and page views, turn into cash flow? Everyone is wondering how Friendster is going to begin generating revenue.

The majority of Abrams's competitors make their money by extracting fees from their subscribers. Friendster is going to continue to let its subscribers meet for free but plans to charge them for premium services such as the ability to customize their profile page. The company also has plans to extend beyond social networking to an array of value-added services such as friend-based job referrals and classmate searches. Abrams is also looking into using his high-traffic Web site to tap into the growing Internet advertising market.

Abrams does not appear concerned about generating revenue or about potential competition. He states, "Match.com has been around eight years, has 12 million users, and has spent many millions of dollars on advertising to get them. We're a year old, we've spent zero dollars on advertising, and in a year or less, we'll be bigger than them—it's a given."

The future of Friendster is uncertain. Google offered to buy Friendster for $30 million even though there are signs, both statistical and anecdotal, that Friendster's popularity may have peaked.[39]

Questions

1. How could you use efficiency IT metrics to help place a value on Friendster?

2. How could you use effectiveness IT metrics to help place a value on Friendster?

3. Explain how a venture capital company can value Friendster at $53 million when the company has yet to generate any revenue.

4. Explain why Google would be interested in buying Friendster for $30 million when the company has yet to generate any revenue.

5. Google purchased You Tube for $1.65 billion. Do you think this was a smart investment? Why or why not?

Organizational Structures That Support Strategic Initiatives

5.1. Compare the responsibilities of a chief information officer (CIO), chief technology officer (CTO), chief privacy officer (CPO), chief security officer (CSO), and chief knowledge officer (CKO).

5.2. Explain the gap between IT people and business people and the primary reason this gap exists.

5.3. Define the relationship between security and ethics.

Organizational Structures

Employees across the organization must work closely together to develop strategic initiatives that create competitive advantages. Understanding the basic structure of a typical IT department including titles, roles, and responsibilities will help an organization build a cohesive enterprisewide team.

IT Roles and Responsibilities

Raven Biotechnologies

Information technology is a relatively new functional area, having been around formally in most organizations only for about 40 years. Job titles, roles, and responsibilities often differ dramatically from organization to organization. Nonetheless, clear trends are developing toward elevating some IT positions within an organization to the strategic level.

Most organizations maintain positions such as chief executive officer (CEO), chief financial officer (CFO), and chief operations officer (COO) at the strategic level. Recently there are more IT-related strategic positions such as chief information officer (CIO), chief technology officer (CTO), chief security officer (CSO), chief privacy officer (CPO), and chief knowledge officer (CKO).

J. Greg Hanson is proud to be the first CIO of the U.S. Senate. Contrary to some perceptions, the technology found in the Senate is quite good, according to Hanson. Hanson's responsibilities include creating the Senate's technology vision, leading the IT department, and deploying the IT infrastructure. Hanson must work with everyone from the 137 network administrators to the senators themselves to ensure that everything is operating smoothly. Hanson is excited to be the first CIO of the U.S. Senate and proud of the sense of honor and responsibility that comes with the job.[40]

The ***chief information officer (CIO)*** is responsible for (1) overseeing all uses of information technology and (2) ensuring the strategic alignment of IT with business goals and objectives. The CIO often reports directly to the CEO. (See Figure 5.1 for the average CIO compensation.) CIOs must possess a solid and detailed understanding of every aspect of an organization coupled with tremendous insight into the capability of IT. Broad functions of a CIO include:

1. *Manager*—ensure the delivery of all IT projects, on time and within budget.

2. *Leader*—ensure the strategic vision of IT is in line with the strategic vision of the organization.

3. *Communicator*—advocate and communicate the IT strategy by building and maintaining strong executive relationships.[41]

Although CIO is considered a position within IT, CIOs must be concerned with more than just IT. According to a recent survey (see Figure 5.2), most CIOs ranked "enhancing customer satisfaction" ahead of their concerns for any specific aspect of IT. CIOs with the broad business view that customer satisfaction is more crucial and critical than specific aspects of IT should be applauded.[42]

The *chief technology officer (CTO)* is responsible for ensuring the throughput, speed, accuracy, availability, and reliability of an organization's information technology. CTOs are similar to CIOs, except that CIOs take on the additional responsibility for effectiveness of ensuring that IT is aligned with the organization's strategic initiatives. CTOs have direct responsibility for ensuring the *efficiency* of IT systems throughout the organization. Most CTOs possess well-rounded knowledge of all aspects of IT, including hardware, software, and telecommunications.

The *chief security officer (CSO)* is responsible for ensuring the security of IT systems and developing strategies and IT safeguards against attacks from hackers and viruses. The role of a CSO has been elevated in recent years because of the number of attacks from hackers and viruses. Most CSOs possess detailed knowledge of networks and telecommunications because hackers and viruses usually find their way into IT systems through networked computers.

The *chief privacy officer (CPO)* is responsible for ensuring the ethical and legal use of information within an organization. CPOs are the newest senior executive position in IT. Recently, 150 of the Fortune 500 companies added the CPO position to their list of senior executives. Many CPOs are lawyers by training, enabling them to understand the often complex legal issues surrounding the use of information.[43]

The *chief knowledge officer (CKO)* is responsible for collecting, maintaining, and distributing the organization's knowledge. The CKO designs programs and systems that make it easy for people to reuse knowledge. These systems create repositories of organizational documents, methodologies, tools, and practices, and they establish methods for filtering the information. The CKO must continuously encourage employee contributions to keep the systems up-to-date. The CKO can contribute directly to the organization's bottom line by reducing the learning curve for new employees or employees taking on new roles.

Danny Shaw was the first CKO at Children's Hospital in Boston. His initial task was to unite information from disparate systems to enable analysis of both the efficiency and effectiveness of the hospital's care. Shaw started by building a series of small, integrated information systems that quickly demonstrated value. He then gradually built on those successes, creating a knowledge-enabled organization one layer at a time. Shaw's information systems have enabled administrative and clinical operational analyses.[44]

All the above IT positions and responsibilities are critical to an organization's success. While many organizations may not have a different individual for each of these positions, they must have leaders taking responsibility for all these areas of concern. The individuals responsible for enterprisewide IT and IT-related issues must provide guidance and support to the organization's employees. Figure 5.3 displays the personal skills pivotal for success in an executive IT role.

Industry	Average CIO Compensation
Wholesale/Retail/Distribution	$243,304
Finance	$210,547
Insurance	$197,697
Manufacturing	$190,250
Medical/Dental/Health Care	$171,032
Government	$118,359
Education	$ 93,750

FIGURE 5.1

Average CIO Compensation by Industry

FIGURE 5.2

What Concerns CIOs the Most?

Percentage	CIO's Concerns
94%	Enhancing customer satisfaction
92	Security
89	Technology evaluation
87	Budgeting
83	Staffing
66	ROI analysis
64	Building new applications
45	Outsourcing hosting

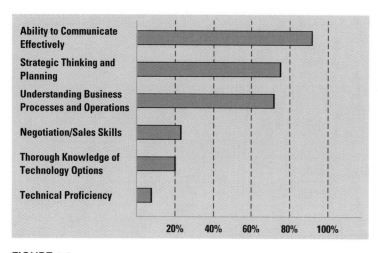

FIGURE 5.3

Skills Pivotal for Success
in Executive IT Roles

The Gap between Business Personnel and IT Personnel

One of the greatest challenges today is effective communication between business personnel and IT personnel. Business personnel possess expertise in functional areas such as marketing, accounting, sales, and so forth. IT personnel have the technological expertise. Unfortunately, a communications gap often exists between the two. Business personnel have their own vocabularies based on their experience and expertise. IT personnel have their own vocabularies consisting of acronyms and technical terms. Effective communication between business and IT personnel should be a two-way street with each side making the effort to better understand the other (including through written and oral communication).

IMPROVING COMMUNICATIONS

Business personnel must seek to increase their understanding of IT. Although they do not need to know every technical detail, it will benefit their careers to understand what they can and cannot accomplish using IT. Business managers and leaders should read business-oriented IT magazines, such as *InformationWeek* and *CIO*, to increase their IT knowledge.

At the same time, an organization must develop strategies for integrating its IT personnel into the various business functions. Too often, IT personnel are left out of strategy meetings because of the belief they do not understand the business so they will not add any value. That is a dangerous position to take. IT personnel must understand the business if the organization is going to determine which technologies can benefit (or hurt) the business. With a little effort to communicate, IT personnel, by providing information on the functionality available in CRM systems, might add tremendous value to a meeting about how to improve customer service. Working together, business and IT personnel have the potential to create customer-service competitive advantages.

It is the responsibility of the CIO to ensure effective communications between business and IT personnel. While the CIO assumes the responsibility on an enterprisewide level, it is also each employee's responsibility to communicate effectively on a personal level.

Organizational Fundamentals—Ethics and Security

Ethics and security are two fundamental building blocks that organizations must base their businesses on. Such events as the Enron and Martha Stewart scandals along with 9/11 have shed new light on the meaning of ethics and security. When the behavior of a few individuals can destroy billion-dollar organizations because of a lapse in ethics or security, the value of highly ethical and highly secure organizations should be evident. Review the Ethics and Security plug-ins to gain a detailed understanding of these topics. Due to the importance of these topics, they will be readdressed throughout this text.

ETHICS

Ian Clarke, the inventor of a file-swapping service called Freenet, decided to leave the United States for the United Kingdom, where copyright laws are more lenient. Wayne Rosso, the inventor of a file-sharing service called Grokster, left the United States for Spain, again saying goodbye to tough U.S. copyright protections. File sharing encourages a legal network of shared thinking that can improve drug research, software development, and flow of information. The United States copyright laws, designed decades before the Internet was invented, make file sharing and many other Internet technologies illegal.[45]

The ethical issues surrounding copyright infringement and intellectual property rights are consuming the e-business world. Advances in technology make it easier and easier for people to copy everything from music to pictures. Technology poses new challenges for our *ethics*—the principles and standards that guide our behavior toward other people. Review Figure 5.4 for an overview of concepts, terms, and ethical issues stemming from advances in technology.

Ethics

In today's electronic world, privacy has become a major ethical issue. *Privacy* is the right to be left alone when you want to be, to have control over your own personal possessions, and to not be observed without your consent. Some of the most problematic decisions organizations face lie in the murky and turbulent waters of privacy. The burden comes from the knowledge that each time employees make a decision regarding issues of privacy, the outcome could sink the company some day.

The Securities and Exchange Commission (SEC) began inquiries into Enron's accounting practices on October 22, 2001. David Duncan, the Arthur Andersen partner in charge of Enron, instructed his team to begin destroying paper and electronic Enron-related records on October 23, 2001. Kimberly Latham, a subordinate to Duncan, sent instructions on October 24, 2001, to her entire team to follow Duncan's orders and even compiled a list of computer files to delete. Arthur Andersen blames Duncan for destroying thousands of Enron-related documents. Duncan blames the Arthur Andersen attorney, Nancy Temple, for sending him a memo instructing him to destroy files. Temple blames Arthur Andersen's document deletion policies.[46]

Privacy

Regardless of who is to blame, the bigger issue is that the destruction of files after a federal investigation has begun is both unethical and illegal. A direct corporate order to destroy information currently under federal investigation poses a dilemma for any professional. Comply, and you participate in potentially criminal activities; refuse, and you might find yourself looking for a new job.[47]

Privacy is one of the biggest ethical issues facing organizations today. Trust between companies, customers, partners, and suppliers is the support structure of the e-business world. One of the main ingredients in trust is privacy. Widespread fear about privacy continues to be one of the biggest barriers to the growth of e-business. People are concerned their privacy will be violated as a consequence of interactions on the Web. Unless an organization can effectively address this issue of privacy, its customers, partners, and suppliers may lose trust in the organization, which hurts its business. Figure 5.5 displays the results from a *CIO* survey as to how privacy issues reduce trust for e-business.[48]

Intellectual property	Intangible creative work that is embodied in physical form.
Copyright	The legal protection afforded an expression of an idea, such as a song, video game, and some types of proprietary documents.
Fair use doctrine	In certain situations, it is legal to use copyrighted material.
Pirated software	The unauthorized use, duplication, distribution, or sale of copyrighted software.
Counterfeit software	Software that is manufactured to look like the real thing and sold as such.

FIGURE 5.4

Issues Affected by Technology Advances

FIGURE 5.5

Primary Reasons Privacy
Issues Reduce Trust for
E-Business

1. Loss of personal privacy is a top concern for Americans in the 21st century.

2. Among Internet users, 37 percent would be "a lot" more inclined to purchase a product on a Web site that had a privacy policy.

3. Privacy/security is the number one factor that would convert Internet researchers into Internet buyers.

SECURITY

State Farm Bank

Smoking is not just bad for a person's health; it seems that it is also bad for company security, according to a new study. With companies banning smoking inside their offices, smokers are forced outside—usually to specific smoking areas in the back of the building. The doors leading out to them are a major security hole, according to a study undertaken by NTA Monitor Ltd., a U.K.-based Internet security tester.

NTA's tester was able to easily get inside a corporate building through a back door that was left open so smokers could easily and quickly get out and then back in, according to the company. Once inside, the tester asked an employee to take him to a meeting room, claiming that the IT department had sent him. Even without a pass, he reportedly gained access unchallenged and was then able to connect his laptop to the company's network.[49]

Organizational information is intellectual capital. Just as organizations protect their assets—keeping their money in an insured bank or providing a safe working environment for employees—they must also protect their intellectual capital. An organization's intellectual capital includes everything from its patents to its transactional and analytical information. With security breaches on the rise and computer hackers everywhere, an organization must put in place strong security measures to survive.

The Health Insurance Portability and Accountability Act (HIPAA) protects the privacy and security of personal health records and has the potential to impact every business in the United States.[50] HIPAA affects all companies that use electronic data interchange (EDI) to communicate personal health records. HIPAA requires health care organizations to develop, implement, and maintain appropriate security measures when sending electronic health information. Most important, these organizations must document and keep current records detailing how they are performing security measures for all transmissions of health information. On April 21, 2005, security rules for HIPAA became enforceable by law.[51]

According to recent Gartner polls, less than 10 percent of all health care organizations have begun to implement the security policies and procedures required by HIPAA. The Health Information Management Society estimates that 70 percent of all health care providers failed to meet the April 2005 deadline for privacy rule compliance. Health care organizations need to start taking HIPAA regulations seriously since noncompliance can result in substantial fines and even imprisonment.[52]

Beyond the health care industry, all businesses must understand the importance of information security, even if it is not enforceable by law. **Information security** is a broad term encompassing the protection of information from accidental or intentional misuse by persons inside or outside an organization. With current advances in technologies and business strategies such as CRM, organizations are able to determine valuable information—such as who are the top 20 percent of their customers who produce 80 percent of their revenues. Most organizations view this type of information as valuable intellectual capital, and they are implementing security measures to prevent the information from walking out the door or falling into the wrong hands.

Security

Adding to the complexity of information security is the fact that organizations must enable employees, customers, and partners to access all sorts of information electronically to be successful. Doing business electronically automatically creates tremendous information security risks for organizations. There are many technical aspects of security, but the biggest information security issue is not technical, but human. Most information security breaches result from people misusing

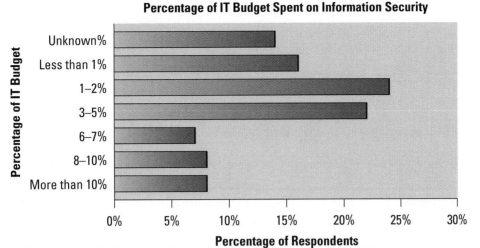

Percentage of IT Budget Spent on Information Security

FIGURE 5.6

Organizational Spending
on Information Security

an organization's information either intentionally or inadvertently. For example, many individuals freely give up their passwords or leave them on sticky notes next to their computers, leaving the door wide open to intruders.

Figure 5.6 displays the typical size of an organization's information security budget relative to the organization's overall IT budget from the CSI/FBI 2004 Computer Crime and Security Survey. Forty-six percent of respondents indicated that their organization spent between 1 and 5 percent of the total IT budget on security. Only 16 percent indicated that their organization spent less than 1 percent of the IT budget on security.[53]

Figure 5.7 displays the spending per employee on computer security broken down by both public and private industries. The highest average computer security investment per employee was found in the transportation industry.[54]

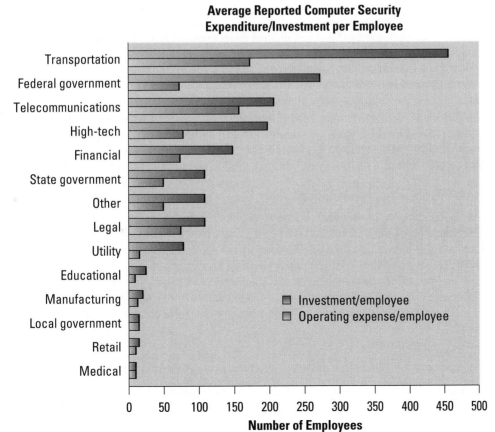

Average Reported Computer Security Expenditure/Investment per Employee

FIGURE 5.7

Computer Security
Expenditures/Investments
by Industry

Security is perhaps the most fundamental and critical of all the technologies/disciplines an organization must have squarely in place to execute its business strategy. Without solid security processes and procedures, none of the other technologies can develop business advantages.

Chapter Five Case: Executive Dilemmas in the Information Age

The vast array of business initiatives from supply chain management, customer relationship management, business process reengineering, and enterprise resource planning makes it clear that information technology has evolved beyond the role of mere infrastructure to the support of business strategy. Today, in more and more industries, IT is a business strategy and is quickly becoming a survival issue.

Board and executive team agendas are increasingly peppered with, or even hijacked by, a growing range of IT issues from compliance to ethics and security. In most companies today, computers are key business tools. They generate, process, and store the majority of critical business information. Executives must understand how IT can affect a business by successfully addressing a wide range of needs—from large electronic discovery projects to the online review of document collections by geographically dispersed teams. A few examples of executive IT issues follow.

Stolen Proprietary Information

A computer company investigated to determine if an executive who accepted a job with a competitor stole proprietary information. The hard drive from the executive's laptop and desktop machine were forensically imaged. The analysis established that the night before the executive left, he downloaded all of the company's process specifications and distributor agreements, which he then zipped and e-mailed to the competitor. Additionally, reconstruction of deleted files located e-mails between the executive and the competitor discussing his intent to provide the proprietary information if he was offered additional options in the new company.

Sexual Harassment

A woman employed by a large defense contractor accused her supervisor of sexual harassment. The woman was fired from her job for poor performance and subsequently sued her ex-boss and the former employer.

A computer company was retained by the plaintiff's attorneys to investigate allegations of the former supervisor's harassing behavior. After making a forensic image backup of the ex-boss's hard drive, the forensic company was able to recover deleted electronic messages that showed the ex-boss had a history of propositioning women under his supervision for "special favors." A situation that might have been mired in a "he said/she said" controversy was quickly resolved; the woman got her job back, and the real culprit was terminated.

Stolen Trade Secrets

The board of directors of a technical research company demoted the company's founder and CEO. The executive, disgruntled because of his demotion, was later terminated. It was subsequently determined that the executive had planned to quit about the same time he was fired and establish a competitive company. Upon his termination, the executive took home two computers; he returned them to the company four days later, along with another company computer that he had previously used at home. Suspicious that critical information had been taken, the company's attorneys sent the computers to a computer forensic company for examination.

After making a forensic image backup of the hard drives, the forensic analysis identified a file directory that had been deleted during the aforementioned four-day period that had the same name as the competing company the executive had established. A specific search of the deleted files in this directory identified the executive's "to do list" file. This file indicated the executive planned to copy the company's database (valued at $100 million) for his personal use. Another item specified the executive was to "learn how to destroy evidence on a computer."

The computer forensic company's examination also proved that the executive had been communicating with other competing companies to establish alliances, in violation of the executive's nondisclosure agreement with the company. It was also shown that numerous key company files were located on removable computer storage media that had not been turned over by the executive to the company.[55]

Questions

1. Explain why understanding technology, especially in the areas of security and ethics, is important for a CEO. How do a CEO's actions affect the organizational culture?

2. Identify why executives in nontechnological industries need to worry about technology and its potential business ramifications.

3. Describe why continuously learning about technology allows an executive to better analyze threats and opportunities.

4. Identify three things that a CTO, CPO, or CSO could do to prevent the above issues.

<< BUSINESS PLUG-IN POINTERS

Review the Business Plug-In B6 "Information Security" for an overview of security issues and features including information security policies and plans, hackers, viruses, public key encryption, digital certificates, digital signatures, firewalls, and authentication, authorization, and detection and response technologies.

Review the Business Plug-In B7 "Ethics" for an overview of privacy laws, ethical computer use policy, Internet use policy, information privacy policy, acceptable use policy, e-mail privacy policy, anti-spam policy, monitoring technologies, and monitoring policies.

U nderstanding and working with technology have become an integral part of life in the 21st century. Most students take courses in various disciplines in their educational careers, such as in marketing, operations management, management, finance, accounting, and information technology, each of which is designed to provide insight into the tasks of each functional area. In the business world, these are all intertwined and inextricably linked.

Information technology can be an important enabler of business success and innovation and is most useful when it leverages the talents of people. Technology in and of itself is not useful unless the right people know how to use and manage it effectively.

Organizations use information technology to capture, process, organize, distribute, and massage information. Information technology enables an organization to:

- Integrate all functional areas and the tasks they perform.
- Gain an enterprisewide view of its operations.
- Efficiently and effectively utilize resources.
- Realize tremendous market and industry growth by gaining insight into the market at large (through environmental scanning) and insight into internal operations.

KEY TERMS

Balanced scorcard, 42
Benchmark, 37
Benchmarking, 37
Business intelligence, 11
Business process, 21, 30
Business process
   reengineering (BPR), 30
Business-to-business (B2B)
   marketplace, 19
Buyer power, 18
Chief information officer
   (CIO), 46
Chief knowledge officer
   (CKO), 47
Chief privacy officer (CPO), 47
Chief security officer
   (CSO), 47
Chief technology officer
   (CTO), 47
Competitive advantage, 17
Copyright, 49
Counterfeit software, 49

Customer relationship
   management (CRM), 28
Data, 10
Effectiveness IT metrics, 37
Efficiency IT metrics, 37
Enterprise resource planning
   (ERP), 31
Entry barrier, 19
Environmental scanning, 17
Ethics, 49
Fair use doctrine, 49
First-mover advantage, 17
Five Forces Model, 18
Information, 10
Information accuracy, 38
Information security, 50
Information technology
   (IT), 9
Intellectual property, 49
Key performance indicator
   (KPI), 37
Loyalty program, 18

Management information
   systems (MIS), 9
Pirated software, 49
Privacy, 49
Private exchange, 19
Response time, 38
Reverse auction, 19
Rivalry among existing
   competitors, 20
Supplier power, 18
Supply chain, 18
Supply chain management
   (SCM), 26
System availability, 38
Switching cost, 19
Threat of new entrants, 19
Threat of substitute products or
   services, 19
Throughput, 38
Transaction speed, 38
Value chain, 21
Web traffic, 38

How Levi's Jeans Got into Wal-Mart

People around the world recognize Levi's as an American icon, the cool jeans worn by movie stars James Dean and Marilyn Monroe. However, the company failed to keep up with the fast-changing tastes of American teenagers. In particular, it missed the trend to baggy jeans that caught hold in the mid-1990s. Sales plummeted from $7.1 billion in 1996 to $4.1 billion in 2003, and Levi Strauss & Co.'s U.S. market share dropped from 18.7 percent in 1997 to 12 percent in 2003, a huge decline in both dollars and market share.

Analyzing and Responding to What Happened

Competition hit Levi Strauss on both the high and low ends. Fashion-conscious buyers were drawn to high-priced brands like Blue Cult, Juicy, and Seven, which had more fashion cachet than Levi's. On the low end, parents were buying Wrangler and Lee jeans for their kids because on average they cost about $10 less than Levi's Red Tab brand. Wrangler and Lee were also the brands they found at discount retailers such as Wal-Mart, Target, and T. J. Maxx. David Bergen, Levi's chief information officer (CIO), described the company as "getting squeezed," and "caught in the jaws of death."

CEO Philip A. Marineau came to Levi Strauss from PepsiCo in 1999, a year after he helped PepsiCo surpass Coca-Cola in sales for the first time. Marineau recruited Bergen in 2000 from Carstation.com. Marineau quickly realized that turning Levi's around would entail manufacturing, marketing, and distributing jeans that customers demanded, particularly customers at the low end where the mass market was located.

Bergen was eager to join Marineau's team because of his background in clothing, retailing, and manufacturing with companies such as The Gap and Esprit de Corps in the 1980s. He knew that Marineau's plan to anticipate customer wants would require up-to-date IT applications such as data warehousing, data mining, and customer relationship management (CRM) systems. He also knew that selling to mass market retailers would require upgrades to Levi's supply chain management (SCM) systems, and he understood that globalization would necessitate standardized enterprise resource planning (ERP) systems. Overall, it was a challenge any ambitious CIO would covet. After all, designing and installing IT systems that drive and achieve key business initiatives is what it is all about.

Joining Wal-Mart

Wal-Mart was a pioneer in supply chain management systems, having learned early on that driving costs out of the supply chain would let the company offer products to customers at the lowest possible prices, while at the same time assuring that products the customers demanded were always on the stores shelves. Becoming one of Wal-Mart's 30,000 suppliers is not easy. Wal-Mart insists that its suppliers do business using up-to-date IT systems to manage the supply chain—not just the supply chain between Wal-Mart and its suppliers, but the supply chains between the suppliers and their suppliers as well. Wal-Mart has strict supply chain management system requirements that its business partners must meet.

Wal-Mart's requirements presented Levi Strauss with a serious hurdle to overcome because its supply chain management systems were in bad shape. Executives did not even have access to key information required to track where Levi products were moving in the supply chain. For example, they did not know how many pairs of jeans were in the factory awaiting shipment, how many were somewhere en route, or how many had just been unloaded at a customer's warehouse. According to Greg Hammann, Levi's U.S. chief customer officer, "Our supply chain could not deliver the services Wal-Mart expected."

Bergen created a cross-functional team of key managers from IT, finance, and sales to transform Levi's systems to meet Wal-Mart's requirements. Their recommendations included network upgrades, modifications to ordering and logistics applications, and data warehouse improvements. Although Bergen realized that about half the changes required to accommodate the state-of-the-art demands of Wal-Mart would be a waste of resources because these systems were being replaced by a new SAP enterprise software system over the next five years, the company could not wait for the SAP installation if it wanted Wal-Mart's business now, so it decided to move forward with the changes.

Levi's successful transformation of its supply chain management system allowed the company to partner with Wal-Mart. The company introduced at Wal-Mart its new signature line, which sells for around $23 and has fewer details in the finish than Levi's other lines; no trademark pocket stitching or red tab, for example. Wal-Mart wants big-name brands to lure more affluent customers into its stores, while still maintaining the low price points all Wal-Mart customers have come to expect. Wal-Mart Senior Vice President Lois Mikita notes that Wal-Mart "continues to tailor its selection to meet the needs of customers from a cross section of income levels and lifestyles." She also states she is impressed with the level of detail Levi's has put into its systems transformation efforts to "make the execution of this new launch 100 percent."

Achieving Business Success Through IT

Bergen's changes were a success and the percentage of products delivered on time quickly rose from 65 percent to 95 percent primarily because of the updated supply chain management system. Levi's total sales were also up in the third and fourth quarters of 2003, for the first time since 1996. In 2003, Levi's appeared on NPD Fashionworld's top 10 list of brands preferred by young women, ending an absence of several years. Marshall Cohen, a senior industry analyst at NPD Groups Fashionworld, a research group that tracks apparel and footwear market trends, noted that Levi's "hadn't been close to that for a while. Teens hadn't gravitated toward Levi's in years. That was incredible. A lot of that has to do with having the right style in the right place at the right time." The improved systems, Cohen noted, also helped the company get the right sizes to the right stores.

Another highly successful IT system implemented by Levi Strauss is a digital dashboard that executives can display on their PC screens. The dashboard lets an executive see the status of a product as it moves from the factory floor to distribution centers to retail stores. For example, the dashboard can display how Levi's 501 jeans are selling at an individual Kohl's store compared to forecasted sales. "When I first got here, I didn't see anything," Hammann says. "Now I can drill down to the product level."

The digital dashboard alerts executives to trends that under the previous systems would have taken weeks to detect. For example, in 2002 Levi Strauss started to ship Dockers Stain Defender pants. Expected sales for the pants were around 2 million pairs. The digital dashboard quickly notified key executives that the trousers were selling around 2.5 million pairs.

This information enabled them to adjust production upward in time to ship more pants, meet the increased demand, and avoid lost sales. The company also uses the systems to control supply during key seasonal sales periods such as back-to-school and Christmas.

"If I look overconfident, I'm not," says Bergen. "I'm very nervous about this change. When we trip, we have to stand up real quick and get back on the horse, as they say." As if to reinforce Bergen's point, Gib Carey, a supply chain analyst at Bain, notes, "The place where companies do fail is when they aren't bringing anything new to Wal-Mart. Wal-Mart is constantly looking at 'How can I get the same product I am selling today at a lower price somewhere else?' "[56]

Questions

1. Explain how Levi Strauss & Co. achieved business success through the use of information, information technology, and people.

2. Using Porter's Five Forces Model, analyze Levi Strauss's buyer power and supplier power. Which of Porter's Five Forces did Levi Strauss address through the implementation of its updated supply chain management system?

3. Which of the three generic strategies is the company following?

4. Evaluate how Levi Strauss can gain business intelligence through the implementation of a customer relationship management system.

5. How can Levi Strauss use efficiency IT metrics and effectiveness IT metrics to improve its business?

6. David Bergen, Levi Strauss CIO, put together a cross-functional team of key managers from IT, finance, and sales to transform the company's systems to meet Wal-Mart's requirements. Analyze the relationships between these three business areas and determine why Bergen chose them to be a part of his cross-functional team.

7. Predict what might happen to Wal-Mart's business if it failed to secure its partner's information and all sales information for all products was accidentally posted to an anonymous Web site.

 UNIT CLOSING CASE TWO

Business 2.0: Bad Business Decisions

Business 2.0 magazine looked at the top 100 bad business decisions of all time including bungled layoffs, customer-service snafus, executive follies, and other madness. Five of the top 10 bad business decisions of all time were made because business personnel did not understand information technology; these five are highlighted below. Perhaps one good reason to pay attention in this course is so that you will not end-up on Business 2.0's bad business decisions![57]

Bad Business Decision 3 of 10: Starbucks

Winner: Dumbest Moment—Marketing

Starbucks directs baristas in the Southeastern United States to e-mail a coupon for a free iced coffee to friends and family members. But e-mail knows no geographic boundaries and, worse, can be printed repeatedly.

After the e-mail spreads to every corner of the country and is reproduced en masse, Starbucks yanks the offer, leading disgruntled customer Kelly Coakley to file a $114 million class-action lawsuit.

Bad Business Decision 4 of 10: Radioshack

Winner: Dumbest Moment—Human Resources

From: RadioShack
To: RadioShack employees
Subject: Your former job
RadioShack fires 400 staffers via e-mail. Affected employees receive a message that reads, "The work force reduction notification is currently in progress. Unfortunately your position is one that has been eliminated."

Bad Business Decision 7 of 10: AOL

Winner: Dumbest Moment—Data Security

In an "attempt to reach out to the academic community with new research tools," AOL releases the search queries of 657,000 users.

Though AOL insists that the information contains no personally identifiable data, *The New York Times* and other news outlets promptly identify a number of specific users, including searcher No. 4417749, soon-to-be-ex-AOL-subscriber Thelma Arnold of Lilburn, Georgia, whose queries include "women's underwear" and "dog that urinates on everything."

The gaffe leads to the resignation of AOL's chief technology officer and a half-billion-dollar class-action lawsuit.

Bad Business Decision 8 of 10: UCLA

Winner: Dumbest Moment—E-Commerce

On the morning of April 3, 2006, Amazon.com sends an e-mail headed "UCLA Wins!" to virtually everyone to whom it has ever sold a sports-related item, attempting to hawk a cap celebrating the Bruins' stirring victory in college basketball's championship game.

Just one problem: The game isn't scheduled to be played until later that night. When it is, UCLA is trounced by Florida, 73–57.

Bad Business Decision 9 of 10: Bank of America

Winner: Dumbest Moment—Outsourcing

After Bank of America announces plans to outsource 100 tech support jobs from the San Francisco Bay Area to India, the American workers are told that they must train their own replacements in order to receive their severance payments.

Here are a few other bad ones that did not make the top 10, but are worth mentioning.

Bad Business Decision: McDonald's

Guess the translator took the phrase "viral marketing" a bit too literally. McDonald's runs a promotional contest in Japan in which it gives away 10,000 Mickey D's-branded MP3 players.

The gadgets come preloaded with 10 songs—and, in some cases, a version of the QQPass family of Trojan horse viruses, which, when uploaded to a PC, seek to capture passwords, user names, and other data and then forward them to hackers.

Bad Business Decision: General Motors

Then again, viral marketing can be messed up in English too. As part of a cross promotion with the NBCTV show *The Apprentice*, GM launches a contest to promote its Chevy Tahoe SUV. At Chevyapprentice.com, viewers are given video and music clips with which to create their own 30-second commercials.

Among the new Tahoe ads that soon proliferate across the Web are ones with taglines like "Yesterday's technology today" and "Global warming isn't a pretty SUV ad—it's a frightening reality."

Bad Business Decision: New York Times Company

We were wondering how Billy the paperboy could afford that gold-plated Huffy. News carriers and retailers in Worcester, Massachusetts, get an unexpected bonus with their usual shipment of the *Telegram & Gazette:* the credit and debit card numbers of 240,000 subscribers to the paper and its sister publication, the *Boston Globe,* both owned by the New York Times Co.

The security breach is the result of a recycling program in which paper from the *Telegram & Gazette*'s business office is reused to wrap bundles of newspapers.

Bad Business Decision: Sony

PC-B-Q. Defects in batteries made by Sony for portable computing cause a handful of note-books to burst into spectacularly photogenic flames.

The end result is the biggest computer-related recall ever, as Dell replaces the batteries in more than 4 million laptops. In short order, Apple (1.8 million), Lenovo/IBM (500,000), and others do the same.[58]

QUESTION

1. Explain why understanding information technology and management information systems can help you achieve business success—or more importantly, help you avoid business disasters—regardless of your major.

MAKING BUSINESS DECISIONS

1. Competitive Analysis

Cheryl O'Connell is the owner of a small, high-end retailer of women's clothing called Excelus. Excelus's business has been successful for many years, largely because of Cheryl's ability to anticipate the needs and wants of her loyal customer base and provide them with personalized service. Cheryl does not see any value in IT and does not want to invest any capital in something that will not directly affect her bottom line. Develop a proposal describing the potential IT-enabled competitive opportunities or threats Cheryl might be missing by not embracing IT. Be sure to include a Porter's Five Forces analysis and discuss which one of the three generic strategies Cheryl should pursue.

2. Using Efficiency and Effectiveness Metrics

You are the CEO of a 500-bed acute care general hospital. Your internal IT department is responsible for running applications that support both administrative functions (e.g., patient accounting) as well as medical applications (e.g., medical records). You need assurance that your IT department is a high quality operation in comparison to similar hospitals. What metrics should you ask your CIO to provide you to give the assurance you seek? Provide the reasoning behind each suggested metric. Also, determine how the interrelationship between efficiency metrics and effectiveness metrics can drive your business's success.

3. Building Business Relationships

Synergistics Inc. is a start-up company that specializes in helping businesses build successful internal relationships. You have recently been promoted to senior manager of the Business and IT Relationship area. Sales for your new department have dwindled over the last two years for a variety of reasons including the burst of the technological stock bubble, recent economic conditions, and a poorly communicated business strategy. Your first task on the job is to prepare a report detailing the following:

- Fundamental reasons for the gap between the IT and business sides.
- Strategies you can take to convince your customers that this is an area that is critical to the success of their business.
- Strategies your customers can follow to ensure that synergies exist between the two sides.

4. Acting Ethically

Assume you are an IT manager and one of your projects is failing. You were against the project from the start; however, the project had powerful sponsorship from all of the top executives. You know that you are doomed and that the project is doomed. The reasons for the failure are numerous including the initial budget was drastically understated, the technology is evolving and not stable, the architecture was never scaled for growth, and your resources do not have the necessary development skills for the new technology. One of your team leads has come to you with a plan to sabotage the project that would put the project out of its misery without assigning any blame to the individuals on the project. Create a document detailing how you would handle this situation.

5. Determining IT Organizational Structures

You are the chief executive officer for a start-up telecommunications company. The company currently has 50 employees and plans to ramp up to 3,000 by the end of the year. Your first task is to determine how you are going to model your organization. You decide to address the IT department's organizational structure first. You need to consider if you want to have a CIO, CPO, CSO, CTO, and CKO, and if so, what their reporting structure will look like and why. You also need to determine the different roles and responsibilities for each executive position. Once you have compiled this information, put together a presentation describing your IT department's organizational structure.

6. Comparing CRM Vendors

As a team, search the Internet for at least one recent and authoritative article that compares or ranks customer relationship management systems. Select two packages from the list and compare their functions and features as described in the article(s) you found as well as on each company's Web site. Find references in the literature where companies that are using each package have reported their experiences, both good and bad. Draw on any other comparisons you can find. Prepare a presentation for delivery in class on the strengths and weaknesses of each package, which one you favor, and why.

7. Applying the Three Generic Strategies

The unit discussed examples of companies that pursue differentiated strategies so that they are not forced into positions where they must compete solely on the basis of price.

Pick an industry and have your team members find and compare two companies, one that is competing on the basis of price and another that has chosen to pursue a differentiated strategy enabled by the creative use of IT. Some industries you may want to consider are clothing retailers, grocery stores, airlines, and personal computers. Prepare a presentation for the class on the ways that IT is being used to help the differentiating company compete against the low-cost provider. Before you begin, spend some class time to make sure each team selects a different industry if at all possible.

8. The Five Forces Model

Your team is working for a small investment company that specializes in technology investments. A new company, Geyser, has just released an operating system that plans to compete with Microsoft's operating systems. Your company has a significant amount of capital invested in Microsoft. Your boss, Jan Savage, has asked you to compile a Porter's Five Forces analysis for Microsoft to ensure that your company's Microsoft investment is not at risk.

* APPLY YOUR KNOWLEDGE

1. Capitalizing on Your Career

Business leaders need to be involved in information technology—any computer-based tool that people use to work with information and support the information and information-processing needs of an organization—for the following (primary) reasons:

- The sheer magnitude of the dollars spent on IT must be managed to ensure business value.
- Research has consistently shown that when business leaders are involved in information technology, it enables a number of business initiatives, such as gaining a competitive advantage, streamlining business processes, and even transforming entire organizations.
- Research has consistently shown that when business leaders are not involved in IT, systems fail, revenue is lost, and even entire companies can fail as a result of poorly managed IT.

One of the biggest challenges facing organizations is, "How do we get general business leaders involved in IT?" Research has shown that involvement is highly correlated with personal experience with IT and IT education, including university classes and IT executive seminars. Once general business leaders understand IT through experience and education, they are more likely to be involved in IT, and more likely to lead their organizations in achieving business success through IT.

Project Focus

1. Search the Internet to find examples of the types of technologies that are currently used in the field or industry that you plan to pursue. For example, if you are planning on a career in accounting or finance, you should become familiar with financial systems such as Oracle Financials. If you are planning a career in logistics or distribution, you should research supply chain management systems. If you are planning a career in marketing, you should research customer relationship management systems, blogs, and e-marketing.
2. IT is described as an enabler/facilitator of competitive advantage, organizational effectiveness, and organizational efficiency. As a competitive tool, IT can differentiate an organization's products, services, and prices from its competitors by improving product quality, shortening product development or delivery time, creating new IT-based products and

services, and improving customer service before, during, and after a transaction. Search the Internet and find several examples of companies in the industry where you plan to work that have achieved a competitive advantage through IT.

3. Create a simple report of your findings; include a brief overview of the type of technologies you found and how organizations are using them to achieve a competitive advantage.

2. Achieving Alignment

Most companies would like to be in the market-leading position of JetBlue, Dell, or Wal-Mart, all of which have used information technology to secure their respective spots in the marketplace. These companies have a relentless goal of keeping the cost of technology down by combining the best of IT and business leadership.

It takes more than a simple handshake between groups to start on the journey toward financial gains; it requires operational discipline and a linkage between business and technology units. Only recently have companies not on the "path for profits" followed the lead of their successful counterparts, requiring more operational discipline from their IT groups as well as more IT participation from their business units. Bridging this gap is one of the greatest breakthroughs a company can make.

Companies that master the art of finely tuned, cost-effective IT management will have a major advantage. Their success will force their competitors to also master the art or fail miserably. This phenomenon has already occurred in the retail and wholesale distribution markets, which have had to react to Wal-Mart's IT mastery, as one example. Other industries will follow. This trend will change not only the face of IT, but also the future of corporate America.

As world markets continue to grow, the potential gains are greater than ever. However, so are the potential losses. The future belongs to those who are perceptive enough to grasp the significance of IT and resourceful enough to synchronize business management and information technology.

Project Focus

1. Use any resource to answer the question, "Why is business-IT alignment so difficult?" Use the following questions to begin your analysis:
   a. How do companies prioritize the demands of various business units as they relate to IT?
   b. What are some of the greatest IT challenges for the coming year?
   c. What drives IT decisions?
   d. Who or what is the moving force behind IT decisions?
   e. What types of efficiency metrics and effectiveness metrics might these companies use to measure the impact of IT?
   f. How can a company use financial metrics to monitor and measure IT investments?
   g. What are some of the issues with using financial metrics to evaluate IT?

3. Market Dissection

To illustrate the use of the three generic strategies, consider Figure AYK.1. The matrix shown demonstrates the relationships among strategies (cost leadership versus differentiation) and market segmentation (broad versus focused).

- Hyundai is following a broad cost leadership strategy. Hyundai offers low-cost vehicles, in each particular model stratification, that appeal to a large audience.

- Audi is pursuing a broad differentiation strategy with its Quattro models available at several price points. Audi's differentiation is safety and it prices its various Quattro models (higher than Hyundai) to reach a large, stratified audience.

Cost Leadership strategy	Differentiation strategy

Broad market

Focused market

FIGURE AYK.1

Porter's Three Generic
Strategies

- Kia has a more focused cost leadership strategy. Kia mainly offers low-cost vehicles in the lower levels of model stratification.
- Hummer offers the most focused differentiation strategy of any in the industry (including Mercedes-Benz).

Project Focus Focus

Create a similar graph displaying each strategy for a product of your choice. The strategy must include an example of the product in each of the following markets: (1) cost leadership, broad market, (2) differentiation, broad market, (3) cost leadership, focused market, and (4) differentiation, focused market. Potential products include:

- Cereal
- Dog food
- Soft drinks
- Computers
- Shampoo
- Snack foods
- Jeans
- Sneakers
- Sandals
- Mountain bikes
- TV shows
- Movies

4. Grading Security

Making The Grade is a nonprofit organization that helps students learn how to achieve better grades in school. The organization has 40 offices in 25 states and more than 2,000 employees. The company wants to build a Web site to offer its services online. Making The Grade's online services will provide parents seven key pieces of advice for communicating with their children to help them achieve academic success. The Web site will offer information on how to maintain open lines of communication, set goals, organize academics, regularly track progress, identify trouble spots, get to know their child's teacher, and celebrate their children's successes.

Project Focus

You and your team work for the director of information security. Your team's assignment is to develop a document discussing the importance of creating information security polices and an information security plan. Be sure to include the following:

- The importance of educating employees on information security.
- A few samples of employee information security policies specifically for Making The Grade.
- Other major areas the information security plan should address.
- Signs the company should look for to determine if the Web site is being hacked.
- The major types of attacks the company should expect to experience.

5. Eyes Everywhere

The movie *Minority Report* chronicled a futuristic world where people are uniquely identifiable by their eyes. A scan of each person's eyes gives or denies them access to rooms, computers, and anything else with restrictions. The movie portrayed a black market in new eyeballs to help people hide from the authorities. (Why did they not just change the database entry instead? That would have been much easier, but a lot less dramatic.)

The idea of using a biological signature is entirely plausible since biometrics is currently being widely used and is expected to gain wider acceptance in the near future because forging documents has become much easier with the advances in computer graphics programs and color printers. The next time you get a new passport, it may incorporate a chip that has your biometric information encoded on it. Office of Special Investigations agents with fake documents found that it was relatively easy to enter the United States from Canada, Mexico, and Jamaica, by land, sea, and air.

The task of policing the borders is daunting. Some 500 million foreigners enter the country every year and go through identity checkpoints. More than 13 million permanent-resident and border-crossing cards have been issued by the U.S. government. Also, citizens of 27 countries do not need visas to enter this country. They are expected to have passports that comply with U.S. specifications that will also be readable at the border.

In the post-9/11 atmosphere of tightened security, unrestricted border crossing is not acceptable. The Department of Homeland Security is charged with securing the nation's borders, and as part of this plan, new entry/exit procedures were instituted at the beginning of 2003. An integrated system, using biometrics, will be used to identify foreign visitors to the United States and reduce the likelihood of terrorists entering the country.

Early in 2003, after 6 million biometric border-crossing cards had been issued, a pilot test conducted at the Canadian border detected more than 250 imposters. The testing started with two biometric identifiers: photographs for facial recognition and fingerprint scans. As people enter and leave the country, their actual fingerprints and facial features are compared to the data on the biometric chip in the passport.[59]

Project Focus

In a group, discuss the following:

1. How do you feel about having your fingerprints, facial features, and perhaps more of your biometric features encoded in documents like your passport? Explain your answer.
2. Would you feel the same way about having biometric information on your driver's license as on your passport? Why or why not?

3. Is it reasonable to have different biometric identification requirements for visitors from different nations? Explain your answer. What would you recommend as criteria for deciding which countries fall into what categories?

4. The checkpoints U.S. citizens pass through upon returning to the country vary greatly in the depth of the checks and the time spent. The simplest involves simply walking past the border guards who may or may not ask you your citizenship. The other end of the spectrum requires that you put up with long waits in airports where you have to line up with hundreds of other passengers while each person is questioned and must produce a passport to be scanned. Would you welcome biometric information on passports if it would speed the process, or do you think that the disadvantages of the reduction in privacy, caused by biometric information, outweigh the advantages of better security and faster border processing? Explain your answer.

6. Setting Boundaries

Even the most ethical people sometimes face difficult choices. Acting ethically means behaving in a principled fashion and treating other people with respect and dignity. It is simple to say, but not so simple to do since some situations are complex or ambiguous. The important role of ethics in our lives has long been recognized. As far back as 44 B.C., Cicero said that ethics are indispensable to anyone who wants to have a good career. Having said that, Cicero, along with some of the greatest minds over the centuries, struggled with what the rules of ethics should be.

Our ethics are rooted in our history, culture, and religion, and our sense of ethics may shift over time. The electronic age brings with it a new dimension in the ethics debate—the amount of personal information that we can collect and store, and the speed with which we can access and process that information.[60]

Project Focus

In a group, discuss how you would react to the following situations:

1. A senior marketing manager informs you that one of her employees is looking for another job and she wants you to give her access to look through her e-mail.
2. A vice president of sales informs you that he has made a deal to provide customer information to a strategic partner, and he wants you to burn all of the customer information onto a DVD.
3. You are asked to monitor your employee's e-mail to discover if he is sexually harassing another employee.
4. You are asked to install a video surveillance system in your office to watch if employees are taking office supplies home with them.
5. You are looking on the shared network drive and discover that your boss's entire hard drive has been copied to the network for everyone to view. What do you do?
6. You have been accidentally copied on an e-mail from the CEO, which details who will be the targets of the next round of layoffs. What would you do?

7. Porter's Five Forces

Porter's Five Forces Model is an easy framework to understand market forces. Break into groups and choose two products from the list below to perform a Porter's Five Forces analysis.

- Laptop computer and desktop computer.
- PDA and laptop computer.
- iPod and Walkman.
- DVD player and VCR player.
- Digital camera and Polaroid camera.

- Cell phone and Blackberry PDA.
- Coca-Cola plastic bottle and Coca-Cola glass bottle.
- GPS device and a road atlas.
- Roller skates and Rollerblades.
- Digital books and printed books.
- Digital paper and paper.

8. Measuring Efficiency and Effectiveness

In a group, create a plan to measure the efficiency and effectiveness of this course and recommendations on how you could improve the course to make it more efficient and more effective. You must determine ways to benchmark current efficiency and effectiveness and ways to continuously monitor and measure against the benchmarks to determine if the course is becoming more or less efficient and effective (class quizzes and exams are the most obvious benchmarks). Be sure your plan addresses the following:

- Design of the classroom.
- Room temperature.
- Lighting and electronic capabilities of the classroom.
- Technology available in the classroom.
- Length of class.
- E-mail and instant messaging.
- Students' attendance.
- Students' preparation.
- Students' arrival time.
- Quizzes and exams (frequency, length, grades).

9. Discovering Reengineering Opportunities

In an effort to increase efficiency, your college has hired you to analyze its current business processes for registering for classes. Analyze the current business processes from paying tuition to registering for classes and determine which steps in the process are:

- Broken
- Redundant
- Antiquated

Be sure to define how you would reengineer the processes for efficiency.

10. Reorganizing an Organization

The AAA Management Company specializes in the management of rental properties and generates over $20 million in revenues each year and has more than 2,000 employees throughout the United States, Canada, and Mexico. The company has just hired a new CEO, David Paul. David is planning to reorganize the company so that it operates more efficiently and effectively. Next is the new organizational structure that he plans to present to the board of directors on Monday. Break into groups and explain the advantages and disadvantages of such a reporting structure. Reorganize the reporting structure in the way that will be most beneficial to the operations of the company, being sure to justify the new structure.

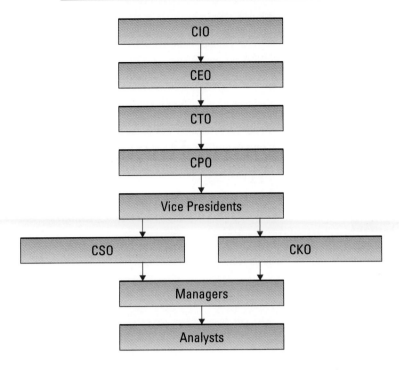

AAA Management's New Organizational Structure

CIO → CEO → CTO → CPO → Vice Presidents

CSO / CKO → Managers → Analysts

11. Contemplating Sharing

Bram Cohen is the creator of one of the most successful peer-to-peer (P2P) programs ever developed, BitTorrent. BitTorrent allows users to quickly upload and download enormous amounts of data, including files that are hundreds or thousands of times bigger than a single MP3. BitTorrent's program is faster and more efficient than traditional P2P networking.

Cohen showed his code to the world at a hacker conference, as a free, open source project aimed at computer users who need a cheap way to swap software online. But the real audience turns out to be TV and movie fanatics. It takes hours to download a ripped episode of *Alias* or *Monk* off Kazaa, but BitTorrent can do it in minutes. As a result, more than 20 million people have downloaded the BitTorrent application. If any one of them misses a favorite TV show, no worries. Surely, someone has posted it as a "torrent." As for movies, if you can find it at Blockbuster, you can probably find it online somewhere—and use BitTorrent to download it. "Give and ye shall receive" became Cohen's motto, which he printed on T-shirts and sold to supporters.[61]

Project Focus

There is much debate surrounding the ethics of peer-to-peer networking. Do you believe BitTorrent is ethical or unethical? Justify your answer.

UNIT 2

Exploring Business Intelligence

It Takes a Village to Write an Encyclopedia

The concept of gathering all the world's knowledge in a single place goes back to the ancient Library of Alexandria, but the modern concept of a general-purpose, widely distributed, printed encyclopedia dates from shortly before the 18th century. The Internet has expanded on the concept with the development of Wikipedia. Founded by Jimmy Wales, Wikipedia is a project to produce a free content encyclopedia that can have thousands of contributors and be edited by anyone, and it now contains millions of articles and pages worldwide. Wikipedia ranks among the top 15 online destinations worldwide.

A wiki is a type of Web site connected to a database that allows users to easily add and edit content and is especially suited for collaborative writing. The name is based on the Hawaiian term *wiki,* meaning quick, fast, or to hasten. In essence, wiki is a simplification of the process of creating Web pages combined with a database that records each individual change, so that at any time, a page can be reverted to any of its previous states. A wiki system may also provide tools that allow users to easily monitor the constantly changing state of the wiki and discuss the issues that emerge in trying to achieve a general consensus about wiki content.

Wikipedia Tightens the Reins

Wikipedia is exploding with information. The site originally allowed unrestricted access so that people could contribute without registering. As with any database management system, governance is a key issue. Without governance, there is no control over how information is published and maintained.

When you research Wikipedia, you find stories about how competing companies are removing and editing each other's entries in Wikipedia to gain market share. The *Washington Post* reported that Capitol Hill is playing "WikiPolitics" by editing representatives' and senators' biographies and speeches. Wikipedia had to temporarily block certain Capitol Hill Web addresses from altering entries.

Wikipedia recently began tightening its rules for submitting entries following the disclosure that it ran a piece falsely implicating a man in the Kennedy assassinations.

John Seigenthaler Sr., who was Robert Kennedy's administrative assistant in the early 1960s, wrote an article revealing that Wikipedia had run a biography claiming Seigenthaler had been suspected in the assassinations of the former attorney general and his brother, President John F. Kennedy. Wikipedia now requires users to register before they can create and edit articles.

Wikipedia has grown into a storehouse of pieces on topics ranging from medieval art to nanotechnology. The volume of content is possible because the site relies on volunteers, including many experts in their fields, to submit entries and edit previously submitted articles. The Web site hopes that the registration requirement will limit the number of stories being created. "What we're hopeful to see is that by slowing that down to 1,500 a day from several thousand, the people who are monitoring this will have more ability to improve the quality," Wales said. "In many cases the types of things we see going on are impulse vandalism."

The Future of Wiki

Can the wisdom of crowds trump the genius of Google? Wales believes that it not only can, but it will. Wales plans to launch a new search engine called Wikiasari, and hopes that it could someday overtake Google as the Web search leader.

Like Wikipedia, Wikiasari will rely on the support of a volunteer community of users. The idea is that Web surfers and programmers will be able to bring their collective intelligence to bear, to fine-tune search results and make the experience more effective for everyone. "If you search in Google, a lot of the results are very, very good and a lot of the results are very, very bad," Wales says. What that shows, Wales says, is that mathematical formulas alone do not produce consistently relevant results. "Human intelligence is still a very important part of the process," he says.

People can contribute to Wikiasari in one of two ways. The first is by enabling ordinary computer users to rerank search results. When a user performs a search on Wikiasari, the engine will return results based on a formula akin to Google's Page-Rank system, which determines relevance by counting the number of times other Web pages link to a specific page, among other things. Unlike Google, however, users will then be able to reorder the results based on which links they find most useful by selecting an edit function. Wikiasari's servers will then store the new results along with the original query. When the same query is made in the future, Wikiasari will return the results in the order saved by most users.

Potential Web users with programming knowledge have a second way to contribute. Wikiasari's technology is based on Apache's open-source Web search software Lucene and Nutch, and Wales plans to unveil all the company's computer code to the outside world. This kind of open-source development is in sharp contrast to the approach of the leading search engines, which do not release their search ranking formulas. Yet Wales contends that his open approach will ultimately prevail, because anyone any place in the world can weigh in with tweaks to Wikiasari's code to help return more relevant results.

A Fly in the Wiki

Wikipedia will fail in four years, crushed under the weight of an automated assault by marketers and others seeking online traffic. So says law professor Eric Goldman, who predicts Wikipedia's downfall. Goldman, a professor at the Santa Clara University School of Law, argues that Wikipedia will see increasingly vigorous efforts to subvert its editorial process, much as Digg.com has seen. As marketers become more determined and turn to automated tools to alter Wikipedia entries to generate online traffic, Goldman predicts Wikipedians will burn out trying to keep entries clean.

"Thus, Wikipedia will enter a death spiral where the rate of junkiness will increase rapidly until the site becomes a wasteland," Goldman writes. "Alternatively, to prevent this death spiral, Wikipedia will change its core open-access architecture, increasing the database's vitality by changing its mission somewhat."

As precedent, Goldman cites the fate of the Open Directory Project, a user-edited Web directory, which he says "is now effectively worthless." "I love Wikipedia," Goldman concludes. "I use it every day. Based on the stats from my Google personalized search, Wikipedia is the Number one site I click on from Google search results. So I'm not rooting for it to fail. But the very architecture of Wikipedia contains the seeds of its own destruction. Without fame or fortune, I don't think Wikipedia's incentive system is sustainable."[1]

Introduction

Information is powerful. Information is useful in telling an organization how its current operations are performing and estimating and strategizing how future operations might perform. New perspectives open up when people have the right information and know how to use it. The ability to understand, digest, analyze, and filter information is a key to success for any professional in any industry. Unit Two demonstrates the value an organization can uncover and create by learning how to manage, access, analyze, and protect organizational information. The chapters in Unit Two are:

- **Chapter Six**—Valuing Organizational Information.
- **Chapter Seven**—Storing Organizational Information—Databases.
- **Chapter Eight**—Accessing Organizational Information—Data Warehouse.

Valuing Organizational Information

6.1. Describe the broad levels, formats, and granularities of information.

6.2. Differentiate between transactional and analytical information.

6.3. List, describe, and provide an example of each of the five characteristics of high quality information.

6.4. Assess the impact of low quality information on an organization and the benefits of high quality information on an organization.

Organizational Information

Google recently reported a 200 percent increase in sales of its new Enterprise Search Appliance tool. Companies use the tool within an enterprise information portal (EIP) to search corporate information for answers to customer questions and to fulfill sales orders. Hundreds of Google's customers are already using the tool—Xerox, Hitachi Data Systems, Nextel Communications, Procter & Gamble, Discovery Communications, Cisco Systems, Boeing. The ability to search, analyze, and comprehend information is vital for any organization's success. The incredible 200 percent growth in sales of Google's Search Appliance tool is a strong indicator that organizations are coveting technologies that help organize and provide access to information.[2]

Information is everywhere in an organization. When addressing a significant business issue, employees must be able to obtain and analyze all the relevant information so they can make the best decision possible. Organizational information comes at different levels and in different formats and "granularities." *Information granularity* refers to the extent of detail within the information (fine and detailed or coarse and abstract). Employees must be able to correlate the different levels, formats, and granularities of information when making decisions. For example, if employees are using a supply chain management system to make decisions, they might find that their suppliers send information in different formats and granularity at different levels. One supplier might send detailed information in a spreadsheet, another supplier might send summary information in a Word document, and still another might send aggregate information from a database. Employees will need to compare these different types of information for what they commonly reveal to make strategic SCM decisions. Figure 6.1 displays types of information found in organizations.

Successfully collecting, compiling, sorting, and finally analyzing information from multiple levels, in varied formats, exhibiting different granularity can provide tremendous insight into how an organization is performing. Taking a hard look at organizational information can yield exciting and unexpected results such as potential new markets, new ways of reaching customers, and even new ways of doing business.

Digital
Domain

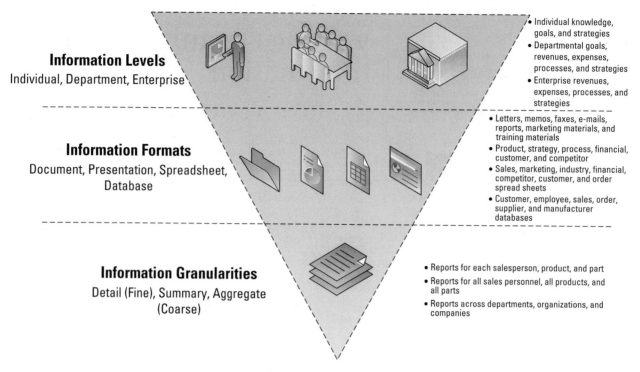

Information Levels
Individual, Department, Enterprise

- Individual knowledge, goals, and strategies
- Departmental goals, revenues, expenses, processes, and strategies
- Enterprise revenues, expenses, processes, and strategies

Information Formats
Document, Presentation, Spreadsheet, Database

- Letters, memos, faxes, e-mails, reports, marketing materials, and training materials
- Product, strategy, process, financial, customer, and competitor
- Sales, marketing, industry, financial, competitor, customer, and order spread sheets
- Customer, employee, sales, order, supplier, and manufacturer databases

Information Granularities
Detail (Fine), Summary, Aggregate (Coarse)

- Reports for each salesperson, product, and part
- Reports for all sales personnel, all products, and all parts
- Reports across departments, organizations, and companies

FIGURE 6.1

Levels, Formats, and Granularities of Organizational Information

Information

Samsung Electronics took a detailed look at over 10,000 reports from its resellers to identify "lost deals" or orders lost to competitors. The analysis yielded the enlightening result that 80 percent of lost sales occurred in a single business unit, the health care industry. Furthermore, Samsung was able to identify that 40 percent of its lost sales in the health care industry were going to one particular competitor. Before performing the analysis, Samsung was heading into its market blind. Armed with this valuable information, Samsung is changing its selling strategy in the health care industry by implementing a new strategy to work more closely with hardware vendors to win back lost sales.[3]

Not all companies are successful at managing information. Staples, the office-supplies superstore, opened its first store in 1986 with state-of-the-art technology. The company experienced rapid growth and soon found itself overwhelmed with the resulting volumes of information. The state-of-the-art technology quickly became obsolete, and the company was unable to obtain any insight into its massive volumes of information. A simple query such as identifying the customers who purchased a computer, but not software or peripherals, took hours. Some queries required several days to complete and by the time the managers received answers to their queries it was too late for action.[4]

After understanding the different levels, formats, and granularities of information, it is important to look at a few additional characteristics that help determine the value of information. These characteristics are type (transactional and analytical), timeliness, and quality.

The Value of Transactional and Analytical Information

Transactional information encompasses all of the information contained within a single business process or unit of work, and its primary purpose is to support the performing of daily operational tasks. Examples of transactional information are withdrawing cash from an ATM, making an airline reservation, or purchasing stocks. Organizations capture and store transactional information in databases, and they use it when performing operational tasks and repetitive decisions such as analyzing daily sales reports and production schedules to determine how much inventory to carry.

Analytical information encompasses all organizational information, and its primary purpose is to support the performing of managerial analysis tasks. Analytical information includes transactional information along with other information such as market and industry information. Examples of analytical information are trends, sales, product statistics, and future growth projections. Analytical information is used when making important ad hoc decisions such as whether the organization should build a new manufacturing plant or hire additional sales personnel. Figure 6.2 displays different types of transactional and analytical information.

The Value of Timely Information

The need for timely information can change for each business decision. Some decisions require weekly or monthly information while other decisions require daily information. Timeliness is an aspect of information that depends on the situation. In some industries, information that is a few days or weeks old can be relevant while in other industries information that is a few minutes old can be almost worthless. Some organizations, such as 911 centers, stock traders, and banks, require consolidated, up-to-the-second information, 24 hours a day, seven days a week. Other organizations, such as insurance and construction companies, require only daily or even weekly information.

Real-time information means immediate, up-to-date information. *Real-time systems* provide real-time information in response to query requests. Many organizations use real-time systems to exploit key corporate transactional information. In a survey of 700 IT executives by Evans Data Corp., 48 percent of respondents said they were already analyzing information in or near real-time, and another 25 percent reported plans to add real-time systems.[5]

The growing demand for real-time information stems from organizations' need to make faster and more effective decisions, keep smaller inventories, operate more efficiently, and track performance more carefully. But timeliness is relative. Organizations need fresh, timely information to make good decisions. Information also needs to be timely in the sense that it meets employees' needs—but no more. If employees can absorb information only on an hourly or daily basis, there is no need to gather real-time information in smaller increments. For example, MBIA Insurance Corp. uses overnight updates to feed its real-time systems. Employees use

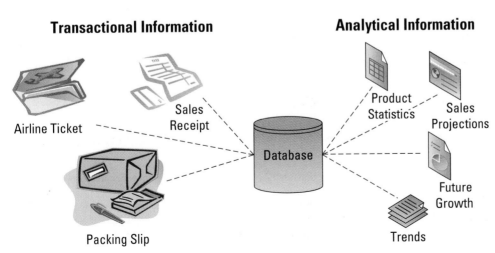

FIGURE 6.2

Transactional versus Analytical Information

this information to make daily risk decisions for mortgages, insurance policies, and other services. The company found that overnight updates were sufficient, as long as users could gain immediate access to the information they needed to make business decisions during the day.[6]

Most people request real-time information without understanding one of the biggest pitfalls associated with real-time information—continual change. Imagine the following scenario: Three managers meet at the end of the day to discuss a business problem. Each manager has gathered information at different times during the day to create a picture of the situation. Each manager's picture may be different because of this time discrepancy. Their views on the business problem may not match since the information they are basing their analysis on is continually changing. This approach may not speed up decision making, and may actually slow it down.

The timeliness of the information required must be evaluated for each business decision. Organizations do not want to find themselves using real-time information to make a bad decision faster.

The Value of Quality Information

Westpac Financial Services (WFS), one of the four major banks in Australia, serves millions of customers from its many core systems, each with its own database. The databases maintain information and provide users with easy access to the stored information. Unfortunately, the company failed to develop information-capturing standards, which led to inconsistent organizational information. For example, one system had a field to capture e-mail addresses while another system did not. Duplicate customer information among the different systems was another major issue, and the company continually found itself sending conflicting or competing messages to customers from different operations of the bank. A customer could also have multiple accounts within the company, one representing a life insurance policy and one representing a credit card. WFS had no way to identify that the two different customer accounts were for the same customer.

WFS had to solve its information quality problems immediately if it was to remain competitive. The company purchased NADIS (Name & Address Data Integrity Software), a software solution that filters customer information, highlighting missing, inaccurate, and redundant information. Customer service ratings are on the rise for WFS now that the company can operate its business with a single and comprehensive view of each one of its customers.[7]

Business decisions are only as good as the quality of the information used to make the decisions. Figure 6.3 reviews five characteristics common to high quality information: accuracy, completeness, consistency, uniqueness, and timeliness. Figure 6.4 highlights several issues with low quality information including:

1. The first issue is *missing* information. The customer's first name is missing. (See #1 in Figure 6.4.)

FIGURE 6.3

Five Common Characteristics of High Quality Information

Accuracy	Are all the values correct? For example, is the name spelled correctly? Is the dollar amount recorded properly?
Completeness	Are any of the values missing? For example, is the address complete including street, city, state, and zip code?
Consistency	Is aggregate or summary information in agreement with detailed information? For example, do all total fields equal the true total of the individual fields?
Uniqueness	Is each transaction, entity, and event represented only once in the information? For example, are there any duplicate customers?
Timeliness	Is the information current with respect to the business requirements? For example, is information updated weekly, daily, or hourly?

Labels around the table:
1. Missing information (no first name)
2. Incomplete information (no street)
5. Inaccurate information (invalid e-mail)

ID	Last Name	First Name	Street	City	State	Zip	Phone	Fax	E-mail
113	Smith		123 S. Main	Denver	CO	80210	(303) 777-1258	(303) 777-5544	ssmith@aol.com
114	Jones	Jeff	12A	Denver	CO	80224	(303) 666-6868	(303) 666-6868	(303) 666-6868
115	Roberts	Jenny	1244 Colfax	Denver	CO	85231	759-5654	853-6584	jr@msn.com
116	Robert	Jenny	1244 Colfax	Denver	CO	85231	759-5654	853-6584	jr@msn.com

3. Probable duplicate information (similar names, same address, phone number)
4. Potential wrong information (are the phone and fax numbers the same or is this an error?)
6. Incomplete information (missing area codes)

FIGURE 6.4

Low Quality Information Example

2. The second issue is *incomplete* information since the street address contains only a number and not a street name.

3. The third issue is a probable *duplication* of information since the only slight difference between the two customers is the spelling of the last name. Similar street addresses and phone numbers make this likely.

4. The fourth issue is potential *wrong* information because the customer's phone and fax numbers are the same. Some customers might have the same number for phone and fax line, but the fact that the customer also has this number in the e-mail address field is suspicious.

5. The fifth issue is definitely an example of *inaccurate* information since a phone number is located in the e-mail address field.

6. The sixth issue is *incomplete* information since there is not a valid area code for the phone and fax numbers.

Recognizing how low quality information issues occur will allow organizations to begin to correct them. The four primary sources of low quality information are:

1. Online customers intentionally enter inaccurate information to protect their privacy.

2. Different systems have different information entry standards and formats.

3. Call center operators enter abbreviated or erroneous information by accident or to save time.

4. Third-party and external information contains inconsistencies, inaccuracies, and errors.[8]

Addressing the above sources of information inaccuracies will significantly improve the quality of organizational information and the value that can be extracted from the information.

UNDERSTANDING THE COSTS OF POOR INFORMATION

Using the wrong information can lead to making the wrong decision. Making the wrong decision can cost time, money, and even reputations. Every business decision is only as good as the information used to make the decision. Bad information can cause serious business ramifications such as:

- Inability to accurately track customers, which directly affects strategic initiatives such as CRM and SCM.
- Difficulty identifying the organization's most valuable customers.

- Inability to identify selling opportunities and wasted revenue from marketing to nonexisting customers and nondeliverable mail.
- Difficulty tracking revenue because of inaccurate invoices.
- Inability to build strong relationships with customers—which increases buyer power.

UNDERSTANDING THE BENEFITS OF GOOD INFORMATION

High quality information can significantly improve the chances of making a good decision and directly increase an organization's bottom line. Lillian Vernon Corp., a catalog company, used Web analytics to discover that men preferred to shop at Lillian Vernon's Web site instead of looking through its paper catalog. Based on this information, the company began placing male products more prominently on its Web site and soon realized a 15 percent growth in sales to men.[9]

Another company discovered that Phoenix, Arizona, is not a good place to sell golf clubs, even with its high number of golf courses. An analysis revealed that typical golfers in Phoenix are either tourists or conventioneers. These golfers usually bring their clubs with them while visiting Phoenix. The analysis further revealed that two of the best places to sell golf clubs in the United States are Rochester, New York, and Detroit, Michigan.[10]

There are numerous examples of companies that have used their high quality information to make solid strategic business decisions. High quality information does not automatically guarantee that every decision made is going to be a good one, since people ultimately make decisions. But such information ensures that the basis of the decisions is accurate. The success of the organization depends on appreciating and leveraging the true value of timely and high quality information.

OPENING CASE STUDY QUESTIONS

1. Determine if an entry in Wikipedia is an example of transactional information or analytical information.

2. Describe the impact to Wikipedia if the information contained in its database is of low quality.

3. Review the five common characteristics of high quality information and rank them in order of importance to Wikipedia.

4. Explain how Wikipedia is resolving the issue of poor information.

Chapter Six Case: Fishing for Quality

The Alaska Department of Fish and Game requires high quality information to manage the state's natural resources, specifically to increase fishing yields, while ensuring the future of many species. Using fish counts, the department makes daily decisions as to which districts will be open or closed to commercial fishing. If the department receives poor information from fish counts, then either too many fish escape or too many are caught. Allowing too many salmon to swim upstream could deprive fishermen of their livelihoods. Allowing too many to be caught before they swim upstream to spawn could diminish fish populations—yielding devastating effects for years to come.

Because of the incredible size of Alaskan fisheries, the Commercial Fisheries Division's decisions have global impact. Its information is relied upon by individual fishermen who want to know the best places to fish, by corporations around the world that need information on which to base business strategies for seafood processing and marketing, by researchers, and by legislators. With so much at stake, the Division of Commercial Fisheries set out to improve the quality of its information by implementing a system that can gather the information from remote parts of the state and analyze it quickly to determine the daily outcomes.

Originally, the department captured information in spreadsheets that were e-mailed from station to station before being entered into the system. There was no central information set to work from, and more often than not, the information was low quality. Decisions were based on inaccurate and, because of delays in posting, untimely information.

With the implementation of an Oracle database, the department significantly improved the quality and timeliness of its information. Each time a commercial fishing boat within Alaska's jurisdiction unloads at a processing plant, the catch is weighed and details of the catch, such as species caught, weight, and quantity, are recorded on a fish ticket. This information is entered into the new system. To gather fish escapement information from remote areas, field workers positioned in towers scan rivers to visibly count fish. This information is radioed in the next morning.

Information from fish processed the previous day is keyed in by 10:00 a.m., and one hour later, the managers and fisheries across the state have all the information they require to make accurate decisions. They then announce on the radio and on their Web site, which receives more than 3,000 hits on an average day, whether or not fishermen can fish that day.

Fisheries are now managed with timely, centralized, and accurate information. Web pages summarize daily catches for certain areas, like Bristol Bay, whose annual sockeye salmon season, which lasts only a few weeks, is closely monitored by fish processors worldwide. With the enormous quantities of fish caught, salmon fisheries worldwide adjust their production levels based on the results of the annual Bristol Bay sockeye salmon season. This is just one reason producing fast, quality information is critical to managing Alaska's natural resources.[11]

Questions

1. Describe the difference between transactional and analytical information and determine which type the Alaska Department of Fish and Game is using to make decisions.

2. Explain the importance of quality information for the Alaska Department of Fish and Game.

3. Review the five common characteristics of high quality information and rank them in order of importance for the Alaska Department of Fish and Game.

4. Do the managers at the Alaska Department of Fish and Game have all the information they require to make an accurate decision? Explain the statement "it is never possible to have all of the information required to make the best decision possible."

CHAPTER 7

Storing Organizational Information—Databases

7.1. Define the fundamental concepts of the relational database model.

7.2. Evaluate the advantages of the relational database model.

7.3. Compare relational integrity constraints and business-critical integrity constraints.

7.4. Describe the benefits of a data-driven Web site.

7.5. Describe the two primary methods for integrating information across multiple databases.

Storing Organizational Information

Organizational information is stored in a database. Applications and programs, such as supply chain management systems, and customer relationship management systems, access the data in the database so the program can consult it to answer queries. The records retrieved in answer to questions become information that can be used to make decisions. The computer program used to manage and query a database is known as a database management system (DBMS). The properties and design of database systems are included in the study of information science.

The central concept of a database is that of a collection of records, or pieces of information. Typically, a given database has a structural description of the type of facts held in that database: This description is known as a schema. The schema describes the objects that are represented in the database and the relationships among them. There are a number of different ways of organizing a schema, that is, of modeling the database structure: These are known as database models (or data models). The most commonly used model today is the relational model, which represents all information in the form of multiple related tables each consisting of rows and columns. This model represents relationships by the use of values common to more than one table. Other models, such as the hierarchical model, and the network model, use a more explicit representation of relationships.

Many professionals consider a collection of data to constitute a database only if it has certain properties; for example, if the data are managed to ensure integrity and quality, if it allows shared access by a community of users, if it has a schema, or if it supports a query language. However, there is no definition of these properties that is universally agreed upon. [12]

Relational Database Fundamentals

There are many different models for organizing information in a database, including the hierarchical database, network database, and the most prevalent—the relational database model. Broadly defined, a **database** maintains information about various types of objects (inventory), events (transactions), people (employees), and places (warehouses). In a ***hierarchical database model,*** information is organized into a tree-like structure that allows repeating information using parent/child relationships in such a way that it cannot have too many relationships. Hierarchical structures were widely used in the first mainframe database management systems. However, owing to their restrictions, hierarchical structures often cannot be used to relate to structures that exist in the real world. The ***network database model*** is a flexible way of representing objects and their relationships. Where the hierarchical model structures data as a tree of records, with each record having one parent record and many children, the network model allows each record to have multiple parent and child records, forming a lattice structure. The ***relational database model*** is a type of database that stores information in the form of logically related two-dimensional tables. This text focuses on the relational database model.

Database

Consider how the Coca-Cola Bottling Company of Egypt (TCCBCE) implemented an inventory-tracking database to improve order accuracy by 27 percent, decrease order response time by 66 percent, and increase sales by 20 percent. With over 7,400 employees, TCCBCE owns and operates 11 bottling plants and 29 sales and distribution centers, making it one of the largest companies in Egypt.

Traditionally, the company sent distribution trucks to each customer's premises to take orders and deliver stock. Many problems were associated with this process including numerous information entry errors, which caused order-fulfillment time to take an average of three days. To remedy the situation, Coca-Cola decided to create presales teams equipped with handheld devices to visit customers and take orders electronically. On returning to the office, the teams synchronized orders with the company's inventory-tracking database to ensure automated processing and rapid dispatch of accurate orders to customers.[13]

ENTITIES AND ATTRIBUTES

Figure 7.1 illustrates the primary concepts of the relational database model—entities, entity classes, attributes, keys, and relationships. An ***entity*** in the relational database model is a person, place, thing, transaction, or event about which information is stored. A table in the relational database model is a collection of similar entities. The tables of interest in Figure 7.1 are *CUSTOMER, ORDER, ORDER LINE, PRODUCT,* and *DISTRIBUTOR.* Notice that each entity class (the collection of similar entities) is stored in a different two-dimensional table. ***Attributes,*** also called fields or columns, are characteristics or properties of an entity class. In Figure 7.1 the attributes for *CUSTOMER* include *Customer ID, Customer Name, Contact Name,* and *Phone.* Attributes for *PRODUCT* include *Product ID, Product Description,* and *Price.* Each specific entity in an entity class (e.g., Dave's Sub Shop in the *CUSTOMER* table) occupies one row in its respective table. The columns in the table contain the attributes.

KEYS AND RELATIONSHIPS

To manage and organize various entity classes within the relational database model, developers must identify primary keys and foreign keys and use them to create logical relationships. A ***primary key*** is a field (or group of fields) that uniquely identifies a given entity in a table. In *CUSTOMER,* the *Customer ID* uniquely identifies each entity (customer) in the table and is the primary key. Primary keys are important because they provide a way of distinguishing each entity in a table.

A ***foreign key*** in the relational database model is a primary key of one table that appears as an attribute in another table and acts to provide a logical relationship between the two tables. Consider Hawkins Shipping, one of the distributors appearing in the *DISTRIBUTOR* table. Its primary key, *Distributor ID,* is DEN8001. Notice that *Distributor ID* also appears as an attribute in the ORDER table. This establishes the fact that Hawkins Shipping (*Distributor ID* DEN8001) was responsible

FIGURE 7.1

Potential Relational
Database for Coca-Cola
Bottling Company of Egypt
(TCCBCE)

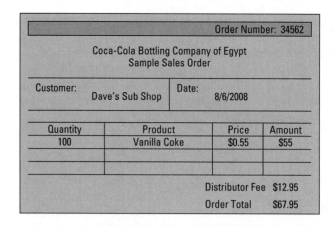

CUSTOMER

Customer ID	Customer Name	Contact Name	Phone
23	Dave's Sub Shop	David Logan	(555)333-4545
43	Pizza Palace	Debbie Fernandez	(555)345-5432
765	T's Fun Zone	Tom Repicci	(555)565-6655

ORDER

Order ID	Order Date	Customer ID	Distributor ID	Distributor Fee	Total Due
34561	7/4/2008	23	DEN8001	$22.00	$145.75
34562	8/6/2008	23	DEN8001	$12.95	$67.95
34563	6/5/2008	765	NY9001	$29.50	$249.50

ORDER LINE

Order ID	Line Item	Product ID	Quantity
34561	1	12345AA	75
34561	2	12346BB	50
34561	3	12347CC	100
34562	1	12349EE	100
34563	1	12345AA	100
34563	2	12346BB	100
34563	3	12347CC	50
34563	4	12348DD	50
34563	5	12349EE	100

DISTRIBUTOR

Distributor ID	Distributor Name
DEN8001	Hawkins Shipping
CHI3001	ABC Trucking
NY9001	Van Distributors

PRODUCT

Product ID	Product Description	Price
12345AA	Coca-Cola	$0.55
12346BB	Diet Coke	$0.55
12347CC	Sprite	$0.55
12348DD	Diet Sprite	$0.55
12349EE	Vanilla Coke	$0.55

for delivering orders 34561 and 34562 to the appropriate customer(s). Therefore, *Distributor ID* in the *ORDER* table creates a logical relationship (who shipped what order) between *ORDER* and *DISTRIBUTOR*.

Relational Database Advantages

From a business perspective, database information offers many advantages, including:

- Increased flexibility.
- Increased scalability and performance.
- Reduced information redundancy.
- Increased information integrity (quality).
- Increased information security.

INCREASED FLEXIBILITY

Databases tend to mirror business structures, and a good database can handle changes quickly and easily, just as any good business needs to be able to handle changes quickly and easily. Equally important, databases provide flexibility in allowing each user to access the information in whatever way best suits his or her needs. The distinction between logical and physical views is important in understanding flexible database user views. The *physical view* of information deals with the physical storage of information on a storage device such as a hard disk. The *logical view* of information focuses on how users logically access information to meet their particular business needs. This separation of logical and physical views is what allows each user to access database information differently. That is, while a database has only one physical view, it can easily support multiple logical views. In the previous database illustration, for example, users could perform a query to determine which distributors delivered shipments to Pizza Palace last week. At the same time, another person could perform some sort of statistical analysis to determine the frequency at which Sprite and Diet Coke appear on the same order. These represent two very different logical views, but both views use the same physical view.

Consider another example—a mail-order business. One user might want a CRM report presented in alphabetical format, in which case last name should appear before first name. Another user, working with a catalog mailing system, would want customer names appearing as first name and then last name. Both are easily achievable, but different logical views of the same physical information.

INCREASED SCALABILITY AND PERFORMANCE

The official Web site of The American Family Immigration History Center, www .ellisisland.org, generated over 2.5 billion hits in its first year of operation. The site offers easy access to immigration information about people who entered America through the Port of New York and Ellis Island between 1892 and 1924. The database contains over 25 million passenger names correlated to 3.5 million images of ships' manifests.[14]

Only a database could "scale" to handle the massive volumes of information and the large numbers of users required for the successful launch of the Ellis Island Web site. *Scalability* refers to how well a system can adapt to increased demands. *Performance* measures how quickly a system performs a certain process or transaction. Some organizations must be able to support hundreds or thousands of online users including employees, partners, customers, and suppliers, who all want to access and share information. Databases today scale to exceptional levels, allowing all types of users and programs to perform information-processing and information-searching tasks.

REDUCED INFORMATION REDUNDANCY

Redundancy is the duplication of information, or storing the same information in multiple places. Redundant information occurs because organizations frequently capture and store the same information in multiple locations. The primary problem with redundant information is that it is often inconsistent, which makes it difficult to determine which values are the most current or most accurate. Not having correct information is confusing and frustrating for employees and disruptive to an organization. One primary goal of a database is to eliminate information redundancy by recording each piece of information in only one place in the database. Eliminating information redundancy saves space, makes performing information updates easier, and improves information quality.

INCREASED INFORMATION INTEGRITY (QUALITY)

Information integrity is a measure of the quality of information. Within a database environment, *integrity constraints* are rules that help ensure the quality of information. Integrity constraints can be defined and built into the database design. The database (more appropriately, the database management system, which is discussed below) ensures that users can never violate these constraints. There are two types of integrity constraints: (1) relational integrity constraints and (2) business-critical integrity constraints.

    Relational integrity constraints are rules that enforce basic and fundamental information-based constraints. For example, an operational integrity constraint would not allow someone to create an order for a nonexistent customer, provide a markup percentage that was negative, or order zero pounds of raw materials from a supplier. *Business-critical integrity constraints* enforce business rules vital to an organization's success and often require more insight and knowledge than relational integrity constraints. Consider a supplier of fresh produce to large grocery chains such as Kroger. The supplier might implement a business-critical integrity constraint stating that no product returns are accepted after 15 days past delivery. That would make sense because of the chance of spoilage of the produce. These types of integrity constraints tend to mirror the very rules by which an organization achieves success.

    The specification and enforcement of integrity constraints produce higher quality information that will provide better support for business decisions. Organizations that establish specific procedures for developing integrity constraints typically see a decline in information error rates and an increase in the use of organizational information.

INCREASED INFORMATION SECURITY

Information is an organizational asset. Like any asset, the organization must protect its information from unauthorized users or misuse. As systems become increasingly complex and more available over the Internet, security becomes an even bigger issue. Databases offer many security features including passwords, access levels, and access controls. Passwords provide authentication of the user who is gaining access to the system. Access levels determine who has access to the different types of information, and access controls determine what type of access they have to the information. For example, customer service representatives might need read-only access to customer order information so they can answer customer order inquiries; they might not have or need the authority to change or delete order information. Managers might require access to employee files, but they should have access only to their own employees' files, not the employee files for the entire company. Various security features of databases can ensure that individuals have only certain types of access to certain types of information.

Databases can increase personal security as well as information security. The Chicago Police Department (CPD) has relied on a crime-fighting system called Citizen and Law Enforcement Analysis and Reporting (CLEAR). CLEAR electronically streamlines the way detectives enter and access critical information to help them solve crimes, analyze crime patterns, and ultimately promote security in a proactive manner. The CPD enters 650,000 new criminal cases and 500,000 new arrests into CLEAR each year.[15]

Database Management Systems

Ford's European plant manufactures more than 5,000 vehicles a day and sells them in over 100 countries worldwide. Every component of every model must conform to complex European standards, including passenger safety standards and pedestrian and environmental protection standards. These standards govern each stage of Ford's manufacturing process from design to final production. The company needs to obtain many thousands of different approvals each year to comply with the standards. Overlooking just one means the company cannot sell the finished vehicle, which brings the production line to a standstill and could potentially cost Ford up to 1 million euros per day. Ford built the Homologation Timing System (HTS), based on a relational database, to help it track and analyze these standards. The reliability and high performance of the HTS have helped Ford substantially reduce its compliance risk.[16]

A database management system is used to access information from a database. A ***database management system (DBMS)*** is software through which users and application programs interact with a database. The user sends requests to the DBMS and the DBMS performs the actual manipulation of the information in the database. There are two primary ways that users can interact with a DBMS: (1) directly and (2) indirectly, as displayed in Figure 7.2. In either case, users access the DBMS and the DBMS accesses the database.

DATA-DRIVEN WEB SITES

The pages on a Web site must change according to what a site visitor is interested in browsing. Consider for example, a company selling sports cars. A database is

FIGURE 7.2

Interacting Directly and Indirectly with a Database through a DBMS

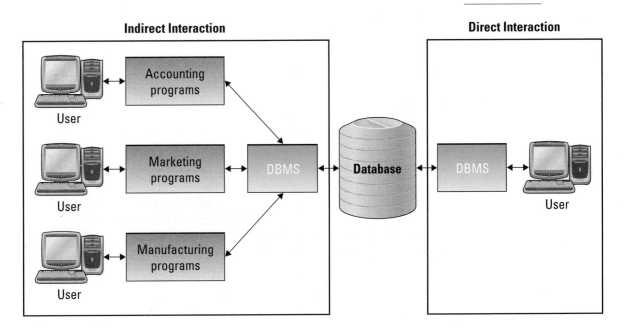

created with information on each of the currently available cars (e.g., make, model, engine details, year, a photograph, etc.). A visitor to the Web site clicks on Porsche, for example, enters the price range he or she is interested in, and hits "Go." The visitor is presented with information on available cars within the price range and an invitation to purchase or request more information from the company. Via a secure administration area on the Web site, the company has the ability to modify, add, or remove cars to the database.[17]

A *data-driven Web site* is an interactive Web site kept constantly updated and relevant to the needs of its customers through the use of a database. Data-driven Web sites are especially useful when the site offers a great deal of information, products, or services. Web site visitors are frequently angered if they are buried under an avalanche of information when searching a Web site. A data-driven Web site invites visitors to select and view what they are interested in by inserting a query. The Web site analyzes the query and then custom builds a Web page in real-time that satisfies the query. Figure 7.3 displays a Wikipedia user querying business intelligence and the database sending back the appropriate Web page that satisfies the user's request.[18]

Data-Driven Web Site Business Advantages

When building a Web site, ask two primary questions to determine if the Web site needs a database:

1. How often will the content change?
2. Who will be making the content changes?

For a general informational Web site with static information, it is best to build a "static" Web site—one that a developer can update on an as-needed basis, perhaps a few times a year. A static Web site is less expensive to produce and typically meets business needs.

For a Web site with continually changing information—press releases, new product information, updated pricing, etc.—it is best to build a data-driven Web site. Figure 7.4 displays the many advantages associated with a data-driven Web site.[19]

FIGURE 7.3

Wikipedia—Data-Driven Web Site

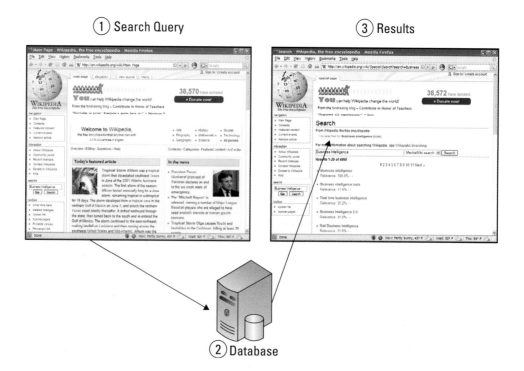

① Search Query   ③ Results

② Database

Data-Driven Web Site Advantages
■ **Development:** Allows the Web site owner to make changes any time—all without having to rely on a developer or knowing HTML programming. A well-structured, data-driven Web site enables updating with little or no training.
■ **Content management:** A static Web site requires a programmer to make updates. This adds an unnecessary layer between the business and its Web content, which can lead to misunderstandings and slow turnarounds for desired changes.
■ **Future expandability:** Having a data-driven Web site enables the site to grow faster than would be possible with a static site. Changing the layout, displays, and functionality of the site (adding more features and sections) is easier with a data-driven solution.
■ **Minimizing human error:** Even the most competent programmer charged with the task of maintaining many pages will overlook things and make mistakes. This will lead to bugs and inconsistencies that can be time consuming and expensive to track down and fix. Unfortunately, users who come across these bugs will likely become irritated and may leave the site. A well-designed, data-driven Web site will have "error trapping" mechanisms to ensure that required information is filled out correctly and that content is entered and displayed in its correct format.
■ **Cutting production and update costs:** A data-driven Web site can be updated and "published" by any competent data-entry or administrative person. In addition to being convenient and more affordable, changes and updates will take a fraction of the time that they would with a static site. While training a competent programmer can take months or even years, training a data-entry person can be done in 30 to 60 minutes.
■ **More efficient:** By their very nature, computers are excellent at keeping volumes of information intact. With a data-driven solution, the system keeps track of the templates, so users do not have to. Global changes to layout, navigation, or site structure would need to be programmed only once, in one place, and the site itself will take care of propagating those changes to the appropriate pages and areas. A data-driven infrastructure will improve the reliability and stability of a Web site, while greatly reducing the chance of "breaking" some part of the site when adding new areas.
■ **Improved stability:** Any programmer who has to update a Web site from "static" templates must be very organized to keep track of all the source files. If a programmer leaves unexpectedly, it could involve re-creating existing work if those source files cannot be found. Plus, if there were any changes to the templates, the new programmer must be careful to use only the latest version. With a data-driven Web site, there is peace of mind, knowing the content is never lost—even if your programmer is.

FIGURE 7.4

Data-Driven Web Site Advantages

Data-Driven Business Intelligence

Companies can gain business intelligence by viewing the data accessed and analyzed from their Web site. Figure 7.5 displays how running queries or using analytical tools, such as a Pivot Table, on the database that is attached to the Web site can offer insight into the business, such as items browsed, frequent requests, items bought together, etc.

Integrating Information among Multiple Databases

Until the 1990s, each department in the United Kingdom's Ministry of Defense (MOD) and Army headquarters had its own systems, each system had its own database, and sharing information among the departments was difficult. Manually inputting the same information multiple times into the different systems was also time consuming and inefficient. In many cases, management could not even compile the information it required to answer questions and make decisions.

The Army solved the problem by integrating its systems, or building connections between its many databases. These integrations allow the Army's multiple systems to automatically communicate by passing information between the databases, eliminating the need for manual information entry into multiple systems because after entering the information once, the integrations send the information immediately to all other databases. The integrations not only enable the different departments to share information, but have also dramatically increased the quality of the

FIGURE 7.5

BI in a Data-Driven Web Site

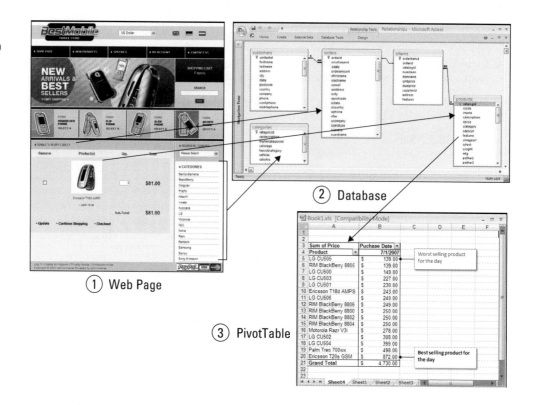

① Web Page

② Database

③ PivotTable

information. The Army can now generate reports detailing its state of readiness and other vital issues, nearly impossible tasks before building the integrations among the separate systems.[20]

An *integration* allows separate systems to communicate directly with each other. Similar to the UK's Army, an organization will probably maintain multiple systems, with each system having its own database. Without integrations, an organization will (1) spend considerable time entering the same information in multiple systems and (2) suffer from the low quality and inconsistency typically embedded in redundant information. While most integrations do not completely eliminate redundant information, they can ensure the consistency of it across multiple systems.

An organization can choose from two integration methods. The first is to create forward and backward integrations that link processes (and their underlying databases) in the value chain. A *forward integration* takes information entered into a given system and sends it automatically to all downstream systems and processes. A *backward integration* takes information entered into a given system and sends it automatically to all upstream systems and processes.

Figure 7.6 demonstrates how this method works across the systems or processes of sales, order entry, order fulfillment, and billing. In the order entry system, for example, an employee can update the information for a customer. That information, via the integrations, would be sent upstream to the sales system and downstream to the order fulfillment and billing systems.

Ideally, an organization wants to build both forward and backward integrations, which provide the flexibility to create, update, and delete information in any of the systems. However, integrations are expensive and difficult to build and maintain and most organizations build only forward integrations (sales through billing in Figure 7.6). Building only forward integrations implies that a change in the initial system (sales) will result in changes occurring in all the other systems. Integration of information is not possible for any changes occurring outside the initial system, which again can result in inconsistent organizational information. To address this issue, organizations can enforce business rules that all systems, other than the initial system, have read-only access to the integrated information. This will require

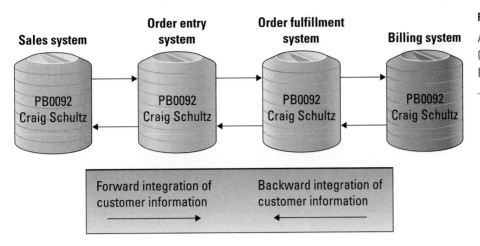

users to change information in the initial system only, which will always trigger the integration and ensure that organizational information does not get out of sync.

The second integration method builds a central repository for a particular type of information. Figure 7.7 provides an example of customer information integrated using this method across four different systems in an organization. Users can create, update, and delete customer information only in the central customer information database. As users perform these tasks on the central customer information database, integrations automatically send the new and/or updated customer information to the other systems. The other systems limit users to read-only access of the customer information stored in them. Again, this method does not eliminate redundancy—but it does ensure consistency of the information among multiple systems.

FIGURE 7.7

Integrating Customer
Information among
Databases

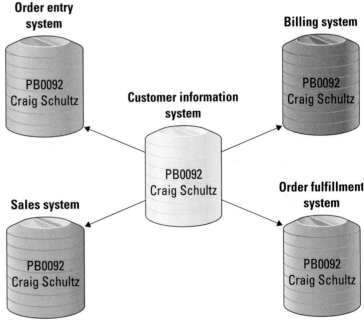

1. Identify the different types of entity classes that might be stored in Wikipedia's database.

2. Explain why database technology is so important to Wikipedia's business model.

3. Explain the difference between logical and physical views and why logical views are important to Wikipedia's customers.

More than 145,000 consumers nationwide were placed at risk by a recent data theft at database giant ChoicePoint. Criminals tricked the company by posing as legitimate businesses to gain access to the various ChoicePoint databases, which contain a treasure trove of consumer data, including names, addresses, Social Security numbers, credit reports, and other information. At least 50 suspicious accounts had been opened in the name of nonexistent debt collectors, insurance agencies, and other companies, according to the company.

Without a doubt, databases are one of the most important IT tools that organizations use today. Databases contain large repositories of detailed data. When a transaction occurs, a sale, for example, a database stores every detail of the transaction including customer name, customer address, credit card number, products purchased, discounts received, and so on.

Organizations must carefully manage their databases. This management function includes properly organizing the information in these repositories in the most efficient way, ensuring that no erroneous information ever enters the databases, and—most important—protecting the information from thieves and hackers.

Information is a valuable commodity, and, sadly, this makes it a target for theft. Organizations store large amounts of customer information including Social Security numbers, credit card numbers, and bank account numbers—just think of the information stored at eBay, Amazon, or the IRS. When someone steals personal information (not necessarily by taking it from the person, but rather stealing it from a company), that person becomes a victim of identity theft. Consider this short list of organizations that have lost information and the huge numbers of customers affected.

- Bank of America: 1.2 million customers.
- CardSystems: 40 million customers.
- Citigroup: 3.9 million customers.
- DSW Shoe Warehouse: 1.4 million customers.
- TJX Companies: 45.6 million customers.
- Wachovia: 676,000 customers.

Adding up the numbers, almost 90 million people had their personal information either stolen or lost through organizations.

Business Accountability in Data Security

Companies may soon face stiff penalties for wayward data security practices. Massachusetts is considering legislation that would require companies to pay for any costs associated with a data breach of their IT systems. This move to protect customer data in Massachusetts comes at a fitting time, as two prominent retailers in the area, TJX Companies and Stop & Shop, wrestle with the aftermath of significant breaches that have exposed some of their customers to fraud.

Much of the expense associated with stopping fraudulent activity, such as canceling or reissuing credit or debit cards, stopping payment, and refunding customers, has been absorbed by the banks issuing credit or debit cards to the victims. The merchant banks that allow businesses such as TJX and Stop & Shop stores to accept credit and debit card transactions are penalized with fines from Visa, MasterCard, and other credit card organizations if the merchants they work with are found to violate the payment card industry's data security standards.

But the businesses who have had customer data stolen have largely suffered only from the costs to offer customers free credit-monitoring services and to repair a tarnished public image. In the case of popular retailers, this tarnish is easily polished away when juicy sales incentives are offered to get customers back.

Massachusetts House Bill 213, sponsored by Rep. Michael Costello, proposes to amend the Commonwealth's general laws to include a section that would require any corporation or other commercial entity whose sensitive customer information is stolen to notify customers about the data breach and also make companies liable to card-issuing banks for the costs those banks incur because of the breach and any subsequent fraudulent activity. This would include making businesses cover the costs to cancel or reissue cards, stop payments or block transactions with respect to any such account, open or reopen an account, and issue any refund or credit made to any customer of the bank as a result of unauthorized transactions.

The Massachusetts legislation is a key step in compelling companies to invest in better data security. Passage of this bill would put Massachusetts ahead of other states in terms of protecting customer data and spreading out the penalties so that both financial institutions and retailers have incentives to improve security. Security vendors are likely to be watching Massachusetts very closely, as the bill also would create an urgent need for companies doing business in that state to invest in ways to improve their ability to protect customer data. If the companies will not do this on their own, then holding them accountable for their customers' financial losses may be just what is needed to stop the next data breach from occurring. [21]

Questions

1. How many organizations have your personal information, including your Social Security number, bank account numbers, and credit card numbers?

2. What information is stored at your college? Is there a chance your information could be hacked and stolen from your college?

3. What can you do to protect yourself from identity theft?

4. Do you agree or disagree with changing laws to hold the company where the data theft occurred accountable? Why or why not?

5. What impact would holding the company liable where the data theft occurred have on large organizations?

6. What impact would holding the company liable where the data theft occurred have on small businesses?

<< TECHNOLOGY PLUG-IN POINTERS

Review **Technology Plug-In T5 "Designing Database Applications"** for an overview of the steps to follow while designing a small database application, including defining entity classes, identifying primary and foreign keys, and completing the first three steps of normalization (up through and including eliminating many-to-many relationships).

Review **Technology Plug-In T6 "Basic Skills Using Access"** for a comprehensive tutorial on how to create tables and define relationships..

Accessing Organizational Information—Data Warehouse

8.1. Describe the roles and purposes of data warehouses and data marts in an organization.

8.2. Compare the multidimensional nature of data warehouses (and data marts) with the two-dimensional nature of databases.

8.3. Identify the importance of ensuring the cleanliness of information throughout an organization.

8.4. Explain the relationship between business intelligence and a data warehouse.

Accessing Organizational Information

Applebee's Neighborhood Grill & Bar posts annual sales in excess of $3.2 billion and is actively using information from its data warehouse to increase sales and cut costs. The company gathers daily information for the previous day's sales into its data warehouse from 1,500 restaurants located in 49 states and seven countries. Understanding regional preferences, such as patrons in Texas preferring steaks more than patrons in New England, allows the company to meet its corporate strategy of being a neighborhood grill appealing to local tastes. The company has found tremendous value in its data warehouse by being able to make business decisions about customers' regional needs. The company also uses data warehouse information to perform the following:

- Base labor budgets on actual number of guests served per hour.
- Develop promotional sale item analysis to help avoid losses from overstocking or understocking inventory.
- Determine theoretical and actual costs of food and the use of ingredients.[22]

History of Data Warehousing

In the 1990s as organizations began to need more timely information about their business, they found that traditional operational information systems were too cumbersome to provide relevant data efficiently and quickly. Operational systems typically include accounting, order entry, customer service, and sales and are not appropriate for business analysis for the following reasons:

- Information from other operational applications is not included.
- Operational systems are not integrated, or not available in one place.
- Operational information is mainly current—does not include the history that is required to make good decisions.
- Operational information frequently has quality issues (errors)—the information needs to be cleansed.

- Without information history, it is difficult to tell how and why things change over time.
- Operational systems are not designed for analysis and decision support.[23]

During the latter half of the 20th century, the numbers and types of databases increased. Many large businesses found themselves with information scattered across multiple platforms and variations of technology, making it almost impossible for any one individual to use information from multiple sources. Completing reporting requests across operational systems could take days or weeks using antiquated reporting tools that were designed to execute the business rather than run the business. From this idea, the data warehouse was born as a place where relevant information could be held for completing strategic reports for management. The key here is the word *strategic* as most executives were less concerned with the day-to-day operations than they were with a more overall look at the model and business functions.

A key idea within data warehousing is to take data from multiple platforms/technologies (as varied as spreadsheets, databases, and word files) and place them in a common location that uses a common querying tool. In this way operational databases could be held on whatever system was most efficient for the operational business, while the reporting/strategic information could be held in a common location using a common language. Data warehouses take this a step further by giving the information itself commonality by defining what each term means and keeping it standard. An example of this would be gender, which can be referred to in many ways (Male, Female, M/F, 1/0), but should be standardized on a data warehouse with one common way of referring to each sex (M/F).[24]

This design makes decision support more readily available without affecting day-to-day operations. One aspect of a data warehouse that should be stressed is that it is *not* a location for *all* of a business's information, but rather a location for information that is interesting, or information that will assist decision makers in making strategic decisions relative to the organization's overall mission.

Data warehousing is about extending the transformation of data into information. Data warehouses offer strategic level, external, integrated, and historical information so businesses can make projections, identify trends, and decide key business issues. The data warehouse collects and stores integrated sets of historical information from multiple operational systems and feeds them to one or more data marts. It may also provide end-user access to support enterprisewide views of information.[25]

Data Warehouse

Data Warehouse Fundamentals

A **data warehouse** is a logical collection of information—gathered from many different operational databases—that supports business analysis activities and decision-making tasks. The primary purpose of a data warehouse is to aggregate information throughout an organization into a single repository in such a way that employees can make decisions and undertake business analysis activities. Therefore, while databases store the details of all transactions (for instance, the sale of a product) and events (hiring a new employee), data warehouses store that same information but in an aggregated form more suited to supporting decision-making tasks. Aggregation, in this instance, can include totals, counts, averages, and the like. Because of this sort of aggregation, data warehouses support only analytical processing.

The data warehouse modeled in Figure 8.1 compiles information from internal databases or transactional/operational databases and external databases through **extraction, transformation, and loading (ETL),** which is a process that extracts information from internal and external databases, transforms the information using a common set of enterprise definitions, and loads the information into a data warehouse. The data warehouse then sends subsets of the information to data marts. A **data mart** contains a subset of data warehouse information. To distinguish between

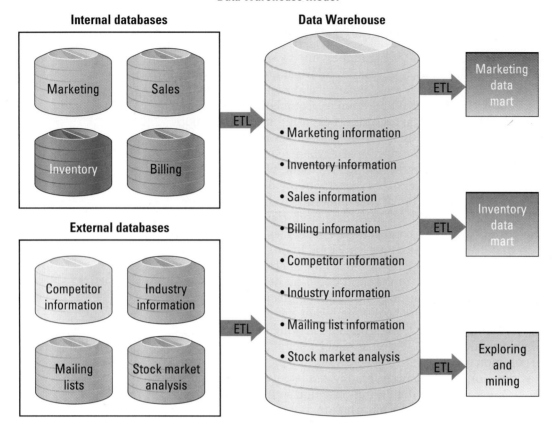

Data Warehouse Model

Internal databases

Marketing

Sales

Inventory

Billing

External databases

Competitor information

Industry information

Mailing lists

Stock market analysis

ETL

Data Warehouse

- Marketing information
- Inventory information
- Sales information
- Billing information
- Competitor information
- Industry information
- Mailing list information
- Stock market analysis

ETL → Marketing data mart

ETL → Inventory data mart

ETL → Exploring and mining

FIGURE 8.1

Model of a Typical Data Warehouse

data warehouses and data marts, think of data warehouses as having a more organizational focus and data marts as having focused information subsets particular to the needs of a given business unit such as finance or production and operations.

Lands' End created an organizationwide data warehouse so all its employees could access organizational information. Lands' End soon found out that there could be "too much of a good thing." Many of its employees would not use the data warehouse because it was simply too big, too complicated, and had too much irrelevant information. Lands' End knew there was valuable information in its data warehouse, and it had to find a way for its employees to easily access the information. Data marts were the perfect solution to the company's information overload problem. Once the employees began using the data marts, they were ecstatic at the wealth of information. Data marts were a huge success for Lands' End.[26]

MULTIDIMENSIONAL ANALYSIS AND DATA MINING

A relational database contains information in a series of two-dimensional tables. In a data warehouse and data mart, information is multidimensional, meaning it contains layers of columns and rows. For this reason, most data warehouses and data marts are *multidimensional databases*. A *dimension* is a particular attribute of information. Each layer in a data warehouse or data mart represents information according to an additional dimension. A ***cube*** is the common term for the representation of multidimensional information. Figure 8.2 displays a cube (cube *a*) that represents store information (the layers), product information (the rows), and promotion information (the columns).

Once a cube of information is created, users can begin to slice and dice the cube to drill down into the information. The second cube (cube *b*) in Figure 8.2 displays a slice representing promotion II information for all products, at all stores. The

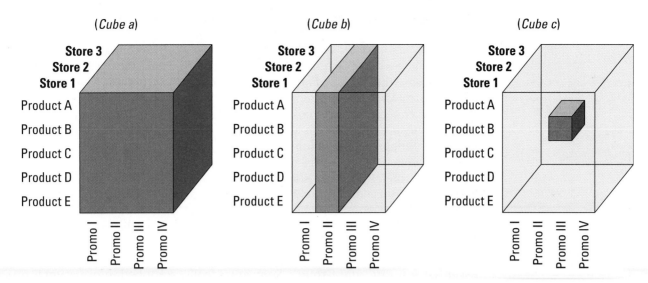

(Cube a)   (Cube b)   (Cube c)

FIGURE 8.2

A Cube of Information
for Performing a
Multidimensional Analysis
on Three Different Stores,
for Five Different Products,
and Four Different
Promotions

third cube (cube *c*) in Figure 8.2 displays only information for promotion III, product B, at store 2. By using multidimensional analysis, users can analyze information in a number of different ways and with any number of different dimensions. For example, users might want to add dimensions of information to a current analysis including product category, region, and even forecasted versus actual weather. The true value of a data warehouse is its ability to provide multidimensional analysis that allows users to gain insights into their information.

Data warehouses and data marts are ideal for off-loading some of the querying against a database. For example, querying a database to obtain an average of sales for product B at store 2 while promotion III is under way might create a considerable processing burden for a database, essentially slowing down the time it takes another person to enter a new sale into the same database. If an organization performs numerous queries against a database (or multiple databases), aggregating that information into a data warehouse could be beneficial.

Data mining is the process of analyzing data to extract information not offered by the raw data alone. For example, Ruf Strategic Solutions helps organizations employ statistical approaches within a large data warehouse to identify customer segments that display common traits. Marketers can then target these segments with specially designed products and promotions.[27]

Data mining can also begin at a summary information level (coarse granularity) and progress through increasing levels of detail (drilling down), or the reverse (drilling up). To perform data mining, users need data-mining tools. **Data-mining tools** use a variety of techniques to find patterns and relationships in large volumes of information and infer rules from them that predict future behavior and guide decision making. Data-mining tools for data warehouses and data marts include query tools, reporting tools, multidimensional analysis tools, statistical tools, and intelligent agents.

Sega of America, one of the largest publishers of video games, uses a data warehouse and statistical tools to distribute its annual advertising budget of more than $50 million. With its data warehouse, product line specialists and marketing strategists "drill" into trends of each retail store chain. Their goal is to find buying trends that help them determine which advertising strategies are working best and how to reallocate advertising resources by media, territory, and time.[28]

INFORMATION CLEANSING OR SCRUBBING

Maintaining quality information in a data warehouse or data mart is extremely important. The Data Warehousing Institute estimates that low quality information costs

U.S. businesses $600 billion annually. That number may seem high, but it is not. If an organization is using a data warehouse or data mart to allocate dollars across advertising strategies (such as in the case of Sega of America), low quality information will definitely have a negative impact on its ability to make the right decision.[29]

To increase the quality of organizational information and thus the effectiveness of decision making, businesses must formulate a strategy to keep information clean. This is the concept of information cleansing or scrubbing. ***Information cleansing or scrubbing*** is a process that weeds out and fixes or discards inconsistent, incorrect, or incomplete information.

Specialized software tools use sophisticated algorithms to parse, standardize, correct, match, and consolidate data warehouse information. This is vitally important because data warehouses often contain information from several different databases, some of which can be external to the organization. In a data warehouse, information cleansing occurs first during the ETL process and second on the information once it is in the data warehouse. Companies can choose information cleansing software from several different vendors including Oracle, SAS, Ascential Software, and Group 1 Software. Ideally, scrubbed information is error free and consistent.

Dr Pepper/Seven Up, Inc., was able to integrate its myriad databases in a data warehouse (and subsequently data marts) in less than two months, giving the company access to consolidated, clean information. Approximately 600 people in the company regularly use the data marts to analyze and track beverage sales across multiple dimensions, including various distribution routes such as bottle/can sales, fountain food-service sales, premier distributor sales, and chain and national accounts. The company is now performing in-depth analysis of up-to-date sales information that is clean and error free.[30]

Looking at customer information highlights why information cleansing is necessary. Customer information exists in several operational systems. In each system all details of this customer information could change from the customer ID to contact information (see Figure 8.3). Determining which contact information is accurate and correct for this customer depends on the business process that is being executed.

Figure 8.4 displays a customer name entered differently in multiple operational systems. Information cleansing allows an organization to fix these types of inconsistencies and cleans the information in the data warehouse. Figure 8.5 displays the typical events that occur during information cleansing.

Achieving perfect information is almost impossible. The more complete and accurate an organization wants its information to be, the more it costs (see Figure 8.6). The trade-off for perfect information lies in accuracy versus completeness. Accurate information means it is correct, while complete information means there are no blanks. A birth date of 2/31/10 is an example of complete but inaccurate information

FIGURE 8.3

Contact Information in Operational Systems

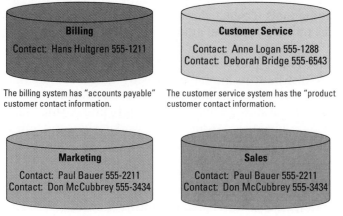

Billing
Contact: Hans Hultgren 555-1211

The billing system has "accounts payable" customer contact information.

Customer Service
Contact: Anne Logan 555-1288
Contact: Deborah Bridge 555-6543

The customer service system has the "product customer contact information.

Marketing
Contact: Paul Bauer 555-2211
Contact: Don McCubbrey 555-3434

Sales
Contact: Paul Bauer 555-2211
Contact: Don McCubbrey 555-3434

The marketing and sales system has "decision maker" customer contact information.

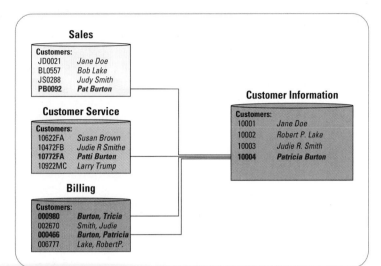

FIGURE 8.4

Standardizing Customer Name from Operational Systems

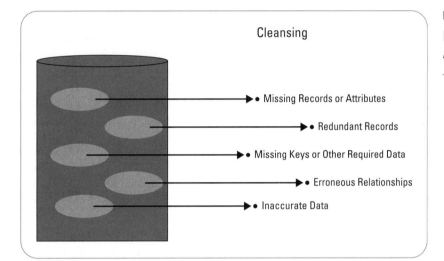

FIGURE 8.5

Information Cleansing Activities

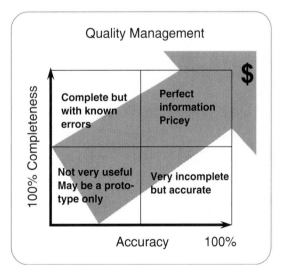

FIGURE 8.6

Accurate and Complete Information

(February 31 does not exist). An address containing Denver, Colorado, without a ZIP code is an example of incomplete information that is accurate. For their information, most organizations determine a percentage high enough to make good decisions at a reasonable cost, such as 85 percent accurate and 65 percent complete.

Business Intelligence

Business intelligence (BI) refers to applications and technologies that are used to gather, provide access to, and analyze data and information to support decision-making efforts. An early reference to business intelligence occurs in Sun Tzu's book titled *The Art of War.* Sun Tzu claims that to succeed in war, one should have full knowledge of one's own strengths and weaknesses and full knowledge of the enemy's strengths and weaknesses. Lack of either one might result in defeat. A certain school of thought draws parallels between the challenges in business and those of war, specifically:

- Collecting information.
- Discerning patterns and meaning in the information.
- Responding to the resultant information.[31]

Business Intelligence

Before the start of the information age in the late 20th century, businesses sometimes collected information from nonautomated sources. Businesses then lacked the computing resources to properly analyze the information and often made commercial decisions based primarily on intuition.

As businesses started automating more and more systems, more and more information became available. However, collection remained a challenge due to a lack of infrastructure for information exchange or to incompatibilities between systems. Reports sometimes took months to generate. Such reports allowed informed long-term strategic decision making. However, short-term tactical decision making continued to rely on intuition.

In modern businesses, increasing standards, automation, and technologies have led to vast amounts of available information. Data warehouse technologies have set up repositories to store this information. Improved ETL has increased the speedy collecting of information. Business intelligence has now become the art of sifting through large amounts of data, extracting information, and turning that information into actionable knowledge.

ENABLING BUSINESS INTELLIGENCE

Competitive organizations accumulate business intelligence to gain sustainable competitive advantage, and they may regard such intelligence as a valuable core competence in some instances. The principal BI enablers are technology, people, and corporate culture.[32]

Technology

Even the smallest company with BI software can do sophisticated analyses today that were unavailable to the largest organizations a generation ago. The largest companies today can create enterprisewide BI systems that compute and monitor metrics on virtually every variable important for managing the company. How is this possible? The answer is technology—the most significant enabler of business intelligence.

People

Understanding the role of people in BI allows organizations to systematically create insight and turn these insights into actions. Organizations can improve their decision making by having the right people making the decisions. This usually means a manager who is in the field and close to the customer rather than an analyst rich in data but poor in experience. In recent years "business intelligence for the masses" has been an important trend, and many organizations have made great strides in providing sophisticated yet simple analytical tools and information to a much larger user population than previously possible.

Culture

A key responsibility of executives is to shape and manage corporate culture. The extent to which the BI attitude flourishes in an organization depends in large part on the organization's culture. Perhaps the most important step an organization can take to encourage BI is to measure the performance of the organization against a set of key indicators. The actions of publishing what the organization thinks are the most important indicators, measuring these indicators, and analyzing the results to guide improvement display a strong commitment to BI throughout the organization.

OPENING CASE STUDY QUESTIONS

1. Determine how Wikipedia could use a data warehouse to improve its business operations.

2. Explain why Wikipedia must cleanse or scrub the information in its data warehouse.

3. Explain how a company could use information from Wikipedia to gain business intelligence.

Chapter Eight Case: Mining the Data Warehouse

According to a Merrill Lynch survey in 2006, business intelligence software and data-mining tools were at the top of CIOs' technology spending list. Following are a few examples of how companies are using data warehousing and data-mining tools to gain valuable business intelligence.

Ben & Jerry's

These days, when we all scream for ice cream, Ben & Jerry's cuts through the din by using integrated query, reporting, and online analytical processing technology from BI software vendor Business Objects. Through an Oracle database and with BI from Business Objects, Ben & Jerry's tracks the ingredients and life of each pint. If a consumer calls in with a complaint, the consumer affairs staff matches the pint with which supplier's milk, eggs, cherries, or whatever did not meet the organization's near-obsession with quality.

The BI tools let Ben & Jerry's officials access, analyze, and act on customer information collected by the sales, finance, purchasing, and quality-assurance departments. The company can determine what milk customers prefer in the making of the ice cream. The technology helped Ben & Jerry's track more than 12,500 consumer contacts in 2005. The information ranged from comments about the ingredients used in ice cream to queries about social causes supported by the company.

California Pizza Kitchen

California Pizza Kitchen (CPK) is a leading casual dining chain in the premium pizza segment with a recognized consumer brand and an established, loyal customer base. Founded in 1985, there are currently more than 130 full-service restaurants in over 26 states, the District of Columbia, and five foreign countries.

Before implementing its BI tool, Cognos, CPK used spreadsheets to plan and track its financial statements and line items. The finance team had difficulty managing the volumes of data, complex calculations, and constant changes to the spreadsheets. It took several weeks of two people working full time to obtain one version of the financial statements and future forecast. In addition, the team was limited by the software's inability to link cells and calculations across multiple spreadsheets, so updating other areas of corporate records became a time-consuming task. With Cognos, quarterly forecasting cycles have been reduced from eight days to two days. The finance team can now spend more time reviewing the results rather than collecting and entering the data.

Noodles & Company

Noodles & Company has more than 70 restaurants throughout Colorado, Illinois, Maryland, Michigan, Minnesota, Texas, Utah, Virginia, and Wisconsin. The company recently purchased Cognos BI tools to help implement reporting standards and communicate real-time operational information to field management throughout the United States.

Before implementing the first phase of the Cognos solution, IT and finance professionals spent days compiling report requests from numerous departments including sales and marketing, human resources, and real estate. Since completing phase one, operational Cognos reports are being accessed on a daily basis through the Noodles & Company Web site. This provides users with a single, 360-degree view of the business and consistent reporting throughout the enterprise.

Noodles & Company users benefit from the flexible query and reporting capabilities, allowing them to see patterns in the data to leverage new business opportunities. Cognos tools can pull information directly from a broad array of relational, operational, and other systems.[33]

Questions

1. Explain how Ben & Jerry's is using business intelligence tools to remain successful and competitive in a saturated market.

2. Identify why information cleansing is critical to California Pizza Kitchen's business intelligence tool's success.

3. Illustrate why 100 percent accurate and complete information is impossible for Noodles & Company to obtain.

4. Describe how each of the companies above is using BI to gain a competitive advantage.

TECHNOLOGY PLUG-IN POINTERS>>

Review **Technology Plug-In T3 "Problem Solving Using Excel"** for a comprehensive tutorial on how to create and sort a list in a workbook, use filters, organize and analyze entries by using subtotals, and create summary information by using pivot tables and pivot charts.

Review **Technology Plug-In T7 "Problem Solving Using Access"** for a comprehensive tutorial on using the query-by-example tool to select data from a table or tables, as well as to sort and filter data.

The five common characteristics of quality information include accuracy, completeness, consistency, uniqueness, and timeliness. The costs to an organization of having low quality information can be enormous and could result in revenue losses and ultimately business failure. Databases maintain information about various types of objects, events, people, and places and help to alleviate many of the problems associated with low quality information such as redundancy, integrity, and security.

A data warehouse is a logical collection of information—gathered from many different operational databases—that supports business analysis activities and decision-making tasks. Data marts contain a subset of data warehouse information. Organizations gain tremendous insight into their business by mining the information contained in data warehouses and data marts.

Understanding the value of information is key to business success. Employees must be able to optimally access and analyze organizational information. The more knowledge employees have concerning how the organization stores, maintains, provides access to, and protects information the better prepared they will be when they need to use that information to make critical business decisions.

KEY TERMS

Analytical information, 75
Attribute, 81
Backward integration, 88
Business Intelligence
    (BI), 98
Business-critical integrity
    constraint, 84
Cube, 94
Database, 80
Database management system
    (DBMS), 85
Data-driven Web site, 86
Data mart, 93
Data mining, 95
Data-mining tool, 95

Data warehouse, 93
Entity, 81
Extraction, transformation, and
    loading (ETL), 93
Foreign key, 81
Forward integration, 88
Hierarchical database
    model, 81
Information cleansing or
    scrubbing, 96
Information granularity, 73
Information integrity, 84
Integration, 88
Integrity constraint, 84
Logical view, 83

Network database
    model, 81
Performance, 83
Physical view, 83
Primary key, 81
Real-time information, 75
Real-time system, 75
Redundancy, 84
Relational database
    model, 81
Relational integrity
    constraint, 84
Scalability, 83
Transactional information, 74

Harrah's—Gambling Big on Technology

The large investment made by Harrah's Entertainment Inc. in its information technology strategy has been tremendously successful. The results of Harrah's investment include:

- 10 percent annual increase in customer visits.
- 33 percent increase in gross market revenue.
- Yearly profits of over $208 million.
- Highest three-year ROI (return on investment) in the industry.
- A network that links over 42,000 gaming machines in 26 casinos across 12 states.
- Rated number six of the 100 best places to work in IT for 2003 by *ComputerWorld* magazine.
- Recipient of 2000 Leadership in Data Warehousing Award from the Data Warehousing Institute (TDWI), the premier association for data warehousing.

The casino industry is highly competitive. Bill Harrah was a man ahead of his time when he opened his first bingo parlor in 1937 with the commitment of getting to know each one of his customers. In 1984, Phil Satre, president and CEO of Harrah's, continued a commitment to customers. In search of its competitive advantage, Harrah's invested in an enterprisewide technology infrastructure to maintain Bill Harrah's original conviction: "Serve your customers well and they will be loyal."

Harrah's Commitment to Customers

Harrah's recently implemented its patented Total Rewards™ program to help build strong relationships with its customers. The program rewards customers for their loyalty by tracking their gaming habits across its 26 properties and currently maintains information on over 19 million customers, information the company uses to analyze, predict, and maximize each customer's value.

One major reason for the company's success is Harrah's implementation of a service-oriented strategy. Total Rewards allows Harrah's to give every customer the appropriate amount of personal attention, whether it's leaving sweets in the hotel room or offering free meals. Total Rewards works by providing each customer with an account and a corresponding card that the player swipes each time he or she plays a casino game. The program collects information on the amount of time the customers gamble, their total winnings and losses, and their betting strategies. Customers earn points based on the amount of time they spend gambling, which they can then exchange for comps such as free dinners, hotel rooms, tickets to shows, and even cash.

Total Rewards helps employees determine which level of service to provide each customer. When a customer makes a reservation at Harrah's, the service representative taking the call can view the customer's detailed information including the customer's loyalty level, games typically played, past winnings and losses, and potential net worth. If the service representative notices that the customer has a Diamond loyalty level, for example, the service representative knows that customer should never have to wait in line and should always receive free upgrades to the most expensive rooms.

"Almost everything we do in marketing and decision making is influenced by technology," says Gary Loveman, Harrah's chief operating officer. "The prevailing wisdom in this business is that the attractiveness of property drives customers. Our approach is different. We stimulate demand by knowing our customers. For example, if one of our customers always vacations at Harrah's in April, they will receive a promotion in February redeemable for a free weekend in April."

Gaining Business Intelligence with a Data Warehouse

Over 90 million customers visit Harrah's each year, and tracking a customer base larger than the population of Australia is a challenge. To tackle it, Harrah's began developing a system called WINet (Winner's Information Network). WINet links all Harrah's properties, allowing the company to collect and share customer information on an enterprisewide basis. WINet collects customer information from all the company transactions, game machines, and hotel management and reservations systems and places the information in a central data warehouse. Information in the data warehouse includes both customer and gaming information recorded in hourly increments. The marketing department uses the data warehouse to analyze customer information for patterns and insights, which allows it to create individualized marketing programs for each customer based on spending habits. Most important, the data warehouse allows the company to make business decisions based on information, not intuition.

Casinos traditionally treat customers as though they belong to a single property, typically the place the customer most frequently visits. Harrah's was the first casino to realize the potential of rewarding customers for visiting more than one property. Today, Harrah's has found that customers who visit more than one of its properties represent the fastest growing revenue segment. In the first two years of the Total Rewards program, the company received a $100 million increase in revenue from customers who gambled at more than one casino.

Harrah's also uses business intelligence to determine gaming machine performance. Using the data warehouse, Harrah's examines the performance and cost structure of each individual gaming machine. The company can quickly identify games that do not deliver optimal operational performance and can make a decision to move or replace the games. The capability to assess the performance of each individual slot machine has provided Harrah's with savings in the tens of millions of dollars. CIO Tim Stanley stated, "As we leverage more data from our data warehouse and increase the use and sophistication of our decision science analytical tools, we expect to have many new ways to improve customer loyalty and satisfaction, drive greater revenues, and decrease our costs as part of our ongoing focus on achieving sustainable profitability and success."

Information Security and Privacy

Some customers have concerns about Harrah's information collection strategy since they want to keep their gambling information private. The good news for these customers is that casinos are actually required to be more mindful of privacy concerns than most companies. For example, casinos cannot send marketing material to any underage persons. To adhere to strict government regulations, casinos must ensure that the correct information security and restrictions are in place. Many other companies actually make a great deal of money by selling customer information. Harrah's will not be joining in this trend since its customer information is one of its primary competitive advantages.

The Future of Harrah's

Harrah's current systems support approximately $140,000 in revenue per hour (that's almost $25 million weekly). In the future, Harrah's hopes to become device-independent by allowing employees to access the company's data warehouse via PDAs, handheld computers, and even cell phones. "Managing relationships with customers is incredibly important to the health of our business," Stanley says. "We will apply whatever technology we can to do that."[26]

Questions

1. Identify the effects poor information might have on Harrah's service-oriented business strategy.

2. Summarize how Harrah's uses database technologies to implement its service-oriented strategy.

3. Harrah's was one of the first casino companies to find value in offering rewards to customers who visit multiple Harrah's locations. Describe the effects on the company if it did not build any integrations among the databases located at each of its casinos.

4. Estimate the potential impact to Harrah's business if there is a security breach in its customer information.

5. Explain the business effects if Harrah's fails to use data-mining tools to gather business intelligence.

6. Identify three different types of data marts Harrah's might want to build to help it analyze its operational performance.

7. Predict what might occur if Harrah's fails to clean or scrub its information before loading it into its data warehouse.

8. How could Harrah's use data mining to increase revenue?

 UNIT CLOSING CASE TWO

Searching for Revenue—Google

Google founders Sergey Brin and Larry Page recently made *Forbes* magazine's list of world billionaires. The company is famous for its highly successful search engine.

How Google Works

Figure Unit 2.1 displays the life of an average Google query. The Web server sends the query to the index servers. The content inside the index server is similar to the index at the back of a book—it tells which pages contain the words that match any particular query term. Then the query travels to the document servers, which actually retrieve the stored documents and generate snippets to describe each search result. Finally, the search engine returns the results to the user. All these activities occur within a fraction of a second.

Google consists of three distinct parts:

1. The Web crawler, known as Googlebot, finds and retrieves Web pages and passes them to the Google indexer. Googlebot functions much like a Web browser. It sends a request for a Web page to a Web server, downloads the entire page, and then hands it off to Google's indexer. Googlebot can request thousands of different Web pages simultaneously.

2. The indexer indexes every word on each page and stores the resulting index of words in a huge database. This index is sorted alphabetically by search term, with each index

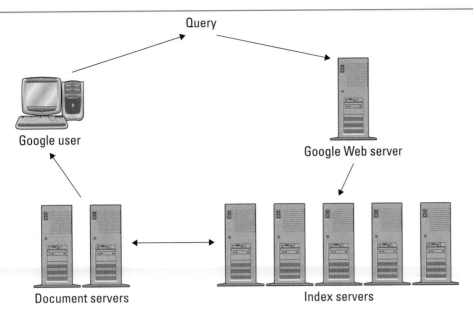

Query

Google user

Google Web server

Document servers

Index servers

entry storing a list of documents in which the term appears and the location within the text where it occurs. Indexing the full text of Web pages allows Google to go beyond simply matching single search terms. Google gives more priority to pages that have search terms near each other and in the same order as the query. Google can also match multi-word phrases and sentences.

3. The query processor compares the search query to the index and recommends the documents that it considers most relevant. Google considers over a hundred factors in determining which documents are most relevant to a query, including the popularity of the page, the position and size of the search terms within the page, and the proximity of the search terms to one another. The query processor has several parts, including the user interface (search box), the "engine" that evaluates queries and matches them to relevant documents, and the results formatter.

Selling Words

Google's primary line of business is its search engine; however, the company does not generate revenue from people using its site to search the Internet. It generates revenue from the marketers and advertisers that are paying to place their ads on the site.

Around 200 million times each day, people from all over the world access Google to perform searches. AdWords, a part of the Google site, allows advertisers to bid on common search terms. The advertisers simply enter in the keywords they want to bid on and the maximum amounts they want to pay per click, per day. Google then determines a price and a search ranking for those keywords based on how much other advertisers are willing to pay for the same terms. Pricing for keywords can range from 5 cents to $3 a click. A general search term like "tropical vacation" costs less than a more specific term like "Hawaiian vacation." Whoever bids the most for a term appears in a sponsored advertisement link either at the top or along the side of the search-results page.

Paid search is the ultimate in targeted advertising because consumers type in exactly what they want. One of the primary advantages of paid search Web programs such as AdWords is that customers do not find it annoying, as is the problem with some forms of Web advertising such as banner ads and pop-up ads. According to the Interactive Advertising Bureau, overall industry revenues from paid search surpassed banner ads in the third quarter of 2003.

"A big percentage of queries we get are commercial in nature," confirms Salar Kamangar, Google's director of product management. "It is a marketplace where the advertisers tell us about themselves by telling us how much each lead is worth. They have an incentive to bid how much they really want to pay, because if they underbid, their competitors will get more traffic."

Kamangar came up with the AdWords concept and oversees that part of the business today. AdWords, which launched in 2005, accounts for the vast majority of Google's annual revenue and the company has over 150,000 advertisers in its paid-search program, up from zero in 2002.

Expanding Google

Google has a secret weapon working for its research and development department—hackers. Hackers actually develop many of the new and unique ways to expand Google. The company elicits hacker ideas through its application program interface (API), a large piece of the Google code. The API enables developers to build applications around the Google search engine. By making the API freely available, Google has inspired a community of programmers that are extending Google's capabilities. "It's working," states Nelson Minar, who runs the API effort. "We get clever hacks, educational uses, and wacky stuff. We love to see people do creative things with our product." A few of the successful user-developed applications include:

- **Banana Slug**—www.bananaslug.com. For customers who hit a dead end with Google search, the site adds a random word to search text that generates surprising results.
- **Cookin' with Google**—www.researchbuzz.org. Enter the ingredients that are in the fridge and the site returns potential recipes for those ingredients.
- **Google Alert**—www.googlealert.com. Google Alert automatically searches the Web for information on a topic and returns the results by e-mail.
- **RateMyProfessors.com**—www.ratemyprofessors.com. The goal of this site was to create a place where students could rank their teachers. However, too many jokesters typing in false professor names such as "Professor Harry Leg" and "Professor Ima Dog" left the information on the site questionable. The developers turned to the Google API to create an automatic verification tool. If Google finds enough mentions in conjunction with a professor or university then it considers the information valid and posts it to the Web site.

Stopping Google

As part of its Google Print Library Project, the company is working to scan all or parts of the book collections of the University of Michigan, Harvard University, Stanford University, the New York Public Library, and Oxford University. It intends to make those texts searchable on Google and to sell advertisements on the Web pages.

The Authors Guild filed a lawsuit against Google, alleging that its scanning and digitizing of library books constitutes a massive copyright infringement. "This is a plain and brazen violation of copyright law," Nick Taylor, president of the New York-based Authors Guild, said in a statement about the lawsuit, which is seeking class-action status. "It's not up to Google or anyone other than the authors, the rightful owners of these copyrights, to decide whether and how their works will be copied."

In response, Google defended the program in a company blog posting. "We regret that this group chose to sue us over a program that will make millions of books more discoverable to the world—especially since any copyright holder can exclude their books from the program," wrote Susan Wojcicki, vice president of product management. "Google respects copyright. The use we make of all the books we scan through the Library Project is fully consistent with both the fair use doctrine under U.S. copyright law and the principles underlying copyright law itself, which allow everything from parodies to excerpts in book reviews."[35]

Questions

1. Determine if Google's search results are examples of transactional or analytical information.
2. Describe the impact on Google's business if the search information it presented to its customers was of low quality.

3. Explain how the Web site RateMyProfessors.com solved its problem of poor information.

4. Identify the different types of entity classes that might be stored in Google's indexing database.

5. Identify how Google might use a data warehouse to improve its business.

6. Explain why Google would need to cleanse the information in its data warehouse.

7. Identify a data mart that Google's marketing and sales department might use to track and analyze its AdWords revenue.

 MAKING BUSINESS DECISIONS

1. Improving Information Quality

HangUps Corporation designs and distributes closet organization structures. The company operates five different systems: order entry, sales, inventory management, shipping, and billing. The company has severe information quality issues including missing, inaccurate, redundant, and incomplete information. The company wants to implement a data warehouse containing information from the five different systems to help maintain a single customer view, drive business decisions, and perform multidimensional analysis. Identify how the organization can improve its information quality when it begins designing and building its data warehouse.

2. Information Timeliness

Information timeliness is a major consideration for all organizations. Organizations need to decide the frequency of backups and the frequency of updates to a data warehouse. In a team, describe the timeliness requirements for backups and updates to a data warehouse for

- Weather tracking systems.
- Car dealership inventories.
- Vehicle tire sales forecasts.
- Interest rates.
- Restaurant inventories.
- Grocery store inventories.

3. Entities and Attributes

Martex Inc. is a manufacturer of athletic equipment and its primary lines of business include running, tennis, golf, swimming, basketball, and aerobics equipment. Martex currently supplies four primary vendors including Sam's Sports, Total Effort, The Underline, and Maximum Workout. Martex wants to build a database to help it organize its products. In a group, identify the different types of entity classes and the related attributes that Martex will want to consider when designing the database.

4. Integrating Information

You are currently working for the Public Transportation Department of Chatfield. The department controls all forms of public transportation including buses, subways, and trains. Each department has about 300 employees and maintains its own accounting, inventory, purchasing, and human resource systems. Generating reports across departments is a difficult task and usually involves gathering and correlating the information from the many different systems. It typically takes about two weeks to generate the quarterly balance sheets and profit and loss statements. Your team has been asked to compile a report recommending what the Public Transportation Department of Chatfield can do to alleviate its information and system issues. Be sure that your report addresses the various reasons departmental reports are presently difficult to obtain as well as how you plan to solve this problem.

5. Explaining Relational Databases

You have been hired by Vision, a start-up recreational equipment company. Your manager, Holly Henningson, is unfamiliar with databases and their associated business value. Holly has asked you to create a report detailing the basics of databases. Holly would also like you to provide a detailed explanation of relational databases along with their associated business advantages.

✱ APPLY YOUR KNOWLEDGE

1. Determining Information Quality Issues

Real People is a magazine geared toward working individuals that provides articles and advice on everything from car maintenance to family planning. *Real People* is currently experiencing problems with its magazine distribution list. Over 30 percent of the magazines mailed are returned because of incorrect address information, and each month it receives numerous calls from angry customers complaining that they have not yet received their magazines. Below is a sample of *Real People*'s customer information. Create a report detailing all of the issues with the information, potential causes of the information issues, and solutions the company can follow to correct the situation.

ID	First Name	Middle Initial	Last Name	Street	City	State	ZIP Code
433	M	J	Jones	13 Denver	Denver	CO	87654
434	Margaret	J	Jones	13 First Ave.	Denver	CO	87654
434	Brian	F	Hoover	Lake Ave.	Columbus	OH	87654
435	Nick	H	Schweitzer	65 Apple Lane	San Francisco	OH	65664
436	Richard	A		567 55th St.	New York	CA	98763
437	Alana	B	Smith	121 Tenny Dr.	Buffalo	NY	142234
438	Trevor	D	Darrian	90 Fresrdestil	Dallas	TX	74532

2. Mining the Data Warehouse

Alana Smith is a senior buyer for a large wholesaler that sells different types of arts and crafts to greeting card stores such as Hallmark. Alana's latest marketing strategy is to send all of her customers a new line of hand-made picture frames from Russia. Alana's data support her decision for the new line. Her analysis predicts that the frames should sell an average of 10 to 15 per store, per day. Alana is excited about the new line and is positive it will be a success.

One month later Alana learns that the frames are selling 50 percent below expectations and averaging between five and eight frames sold daily in each store. Alana decides to access the company's data warehouse to determine why sales are below expectations. Identify several different dimensions of data that Alana will want to analyze to help her decide what is causing the problems with the picture frame sales.

3. Cleansing Information

You are working for BI, a start-up business intelligence consulting company. You have a new client that is interested in hiring BI to clean up its information. To determine how good your work is, the client would like your analysis of the following spreadsheet.

CUST ID	First Name	Last Name	Address	City	State	ZIP	Phone	Last Order Date
233620	Christopher	Lee	12421 W Olympic Blvd	Los Angeles	CA	75080-1100	(972)680-7848	4/18/2002
233621	Bruce	Brandwen	268 W 44th St	New York	PA	10036-3906	(212)471-6077	5/3/2002
233622	Glr	Johnson	4100 E Dry Creek Rd	Littleton	CO	80122-3729	(303)712-5461	5/6/2002
233623	Dave	Owens	466 Commerce Rd	Staunton	VA	24401-4432	(540)851-0362	3/19/2002
233624	John	Coulbourn	124 Action St	Maynard	MA	1754	(978)987-0100	4/24/2002
233629	Dan	Gagliardo	2875 Union Rd	Cheektowaga	NY	14227-1461	(716)558-8191	5/4/2002
23362	Damanceee	Allen	1633 Broadway	New York	NY	10019-6708	(212)708-1576	
233630	Michael	Peretz	235 E 45th St	New York	NY	10017-3305	(212)210-1340	4/30/2002
							(608)238-9690	
233631	Jody	Veeder	440 Science Dr	Madison	WI	53711-1064	X227	3/27/2002
233632	Michael	Kehrer	3015 SSE Loop 323	Tyler	TX	75701	(903)579-3229	4/28/
233633	Erin	Yoon	3500 Carillon Pt	Kirkland	WA	98033-7354	(425)897-7221	3/25/2002
233634	Madeline	Shefferly	4100 E Dry Creek Rd	Littleton	CO	80122-3729	(303)486-3949	3/33/2002
233635	Steven	Conduit	1332 Enterprise Dr	West Chester	PA	19380-5970	(610)692-5900	4/27/2002
233636	Joseph	Kovach	1332 Enterprise Dr	West Chester	PA	19380-5970	(610)692-5900	4/28/2002
233637	Richard	Jordan	1700 N	Philadelphia	PA	19131-4728	(215)581-6770	3/19/2002
233638	Scott	Mikolajczyk	1655 Crofton Blvd	Crofton	MD	21114-1387	(410)729-8155	4/28/2002
233639	Susan	Shragg	1875 Century Park E	Los Angeles	CA	90067-2501	(310)785-0511	4/29/2002
233640	Rob	Ponto	29777 Telegraph Rd	Southfield	MI	48034-1303	(810)204-4724	5/5/2002
233642	Lauren	Butler	1211 Avenue Of The Americas	New York	NY	10036-8701	(212)852-7494	4/22/2002
233643	Christopher	Lee	12421 W Olympic Blvd	Los Angeles	CA	90064-1022	(310)689-2577	3/25/2002
233644	Michelle	Decker	6922 Hollywood Blvd	Hollywood	CA	90028-6117	(323)817-4655	5/8/2002
233647	Natalia	Galeano	1211 Avenue Of The Americas	New York	NY	10036-8701	(646)728-6911	4/23/2002
233648	Bobbie	Orchard	4201 Congress St	Charlotte	NC	28209-4617	(704)557-2444	5/11/2002
233650	Ben	Konfino	1111 Stewart Ave	Bethpage	NY	11714-3533	(516)803-1406	3/19/2002
233651	Lenee	Santana	1050 Techwood Dr NW	Atlanta	GA	30318-KKRR	(404)885-2000	3/22/2002
233652	Lauren	Monks	7700 Wisconsin Ave	Bethesda	MD	20814-3578	(301)771-4772	3/19/2005
233653	Mark	Woolley	10950 Washington Blvd	Culver City	CA	90232-4026	(310)202-2900	4/20/2002
233654	Stan	Matthews	1235 W St NE	Washington	DC	20018-1107	(202)608-2000	3/25/2002

4. Different Dimensions

The focus of data warehousing is to extend the transformation of data into information. Data warehouses offer strategic level, external, integrated, and historical information so businesses can make projections, identify trends, and make key business decisions. The data warehouse collects and stores integrated sets of historical information from multiple operational systems and feeds them to one or more data marts. It may also provide end-user access to support enterprisewide views of information.

Project Focus

You are currently working on a marketing team for a large corporation that sells jewelry around the world. Your boss has asked you to look at the following dimensions of data to determine which ones you want in your data mart for performing sales and market analysis (see Figure AYK.1). As a team, categorize the different dimensions ranking them from 1 to 5, with 1 indicating that the dimension offers the highest value and must be in your data mart and 5 indicating that the dimension offers the lowest value and does not need to be in your data mart.

FIGURE AYK.1

Data Warehouse Data

Dimension	Value (1–5)	Dimension	Value (1–5)
Product number		Season	
Store location		Promotion	
Customer net worth		Payment method	
Number of sales personnel		Commission policy	
Customer eating habits		Manufacturer	
Store hours		Traffic report	
Salesperson ID		Customer language	
Product style		Weather	
Order date		Customer gender	
Product quantity		Local tax information	
Ship date		Local cultural demographics	
Current interest rate		Stock market closing	
Product cost		Customer religious affiliation	
Customer's political affiliation		Reason for purchase	
Local market analysis		Employee dress code policy	
Order time		Customer age	
Customer spending habits		Employee vacation policy	
Product price		Employee benefits	
Exchange rates		Current tariff information	
Product gross margin			

5. Understanding Search

Pretend that you are a search engine. Choose a topic to query. It can be anything such as your favorite book, movie, band, or sports team. Search your topic on Google, pick three or four pages from the results, and print them out. On each printout, find the individual words from your query (such as "Boston Red Sox" or "The Godfather") and use a highlighter to mark each word with color. Do that for each of the documents that you print out. Now tape those documents on a wall, step back a few feet, and review your documents. If you did not know what the rest of a page said and could only judge by the colored words, which document do you think would be most relevant? Is there anything that would make a document look more relevant? Is it better to have the words be in a large heading or to occur several times in a smaller font? Do you prefer it if the words are at the top or the bottom of the page? How often do the words need to appear? Come up with two or three things you would look for to see if a document matched a query well. This exercise mimics search engine processes and should help you understand why a search engine returns certain results over others.

UNIT 3

Streamlining Business Operations

Second Life: Succeeding in Virtual Times

Second Life is a virtual world built and owned by its residents. It opened to the public in 2003, and today is inhabited by millions of residents from around the world. The three main parts to Second Life are:

- **The World:** The world of Second Life is constantly changing and growing. It is filled with hundreds of games, from multi-player role-playing games to puzzles and grid-wide contests. There are also dance clubs, shopping malls, space stations, vampire castles' and movie theaters. To find something to do at any time of the day or night, residents simply open the Search menu and click on Events for a listing of discussions, sports, commercial, entertainment, games, pageants, education, arts and culture, and charity/support groups.

- **The Creations:** Second Life is dedicated to creativity. Everything in Second Life is resident-created, from the strobe lights in the nightclubs to the cars (or spaceships) in driveways. Imagine tinkering with the steering and handling program of a motorcycle while a friend tweaks the shape of the fuel tank and gives it a wicked flame paint job, in-world and in real-time, before taking it for a spin down a newly created road to look for land to buy. Have you ever wondered what it would be like to have a pair of black leather wings? Build them and give it a go.

- **The Marketplace:** The Marketplace currently supports millions of U.S. dollars in monthly transactions. This commerce is handled with the in-world unit of trade, the Linden dollar, which can be converted to U.S. dollars at several thriving online Linden dollar exchanges. Users can make real money in a virtual world because Second Life has a fully integrated economy designed to reward risk, innovation, and craftsmanship. Residents create their own virtual goods and services. Residents retain the intellectual property rights of their creations and can sell them at various in-world venues. Businesses succeed by the ingenuity, artistic ability, entrepreneurial acumen, and good reputation of their owners. Residents who have amassed lots of Linden dollars are matched with residents who want to buy Linden dollars at LindeX (the official Linden dollar exchange) or at other unaffiliated third-party exchanges.

Businesses on Second Life

Second Life is an exciting new venue for collaboration, business ventures, distance learning, new media studies, and marketing. Business possibilities on Second Life are endless; a few examples include:

- Hold a virtual meeting with sales managers located in Europe and Asia.
- Present new sales initiatives and discuss them with the team real-time.
- Build a new world that allows Second Life residents to interact with company products or services and test new designs and concepts before introducing them to the real world.
- Sell products and services in Second Life by creating an event to promote the product: a concert, a class, a famous speaker, a party, a contest. Many companies are excited about the numerous ways they can use Second Life to support their business. A few companies paving the way on Second Life include:

1-800-flowers.com	H&R Block	Sony
Adidas	IBM	Sprint
Amazon	Intel	Student Travel Association
American Apparel	Kraft Food	Starwood Hotels
American Cancer Society	Lacoste	Sundance Channel
BBC Radio 1	Major League Baseball	Toyota
Best Buy Co. Inc.	Mazda	Universal Motown Records
BMW	Mercedes-Benz	Visa
Calvin Klein	Microsoft	Warner bros. Music
Circuit City	MTV	Weather Channel
Cisco	NASA	*Wired* magazine
Coca-Cola	National Basketball Association	Xerox
Coldwell Banker		Yahoo
Comcast	NBC	Yankee Stadium
Crayola	Nissan	
Dell	NPR	

Second Life Success Stories

Virtual Dublin

John Mahon, known as Ham Rambler in Second Life, created the popular city of Dublin. His company, PickSL.net, builds community-based businesses in Second Life. Dublin, as John explains, started with an Irish bar, some great barmen, and plenty of good-spirited conversation. Since then, it has become a destination location in Second Life. "I joined Second Life more than two years ago," John says. "I felt what was missing was a comfortable, easygoing place to meet, talk, and interact. In other words: a good Irish bar. Everyone knows what a good Irish bar is. It needs no marketing. So I built the bar, and it was incredibly successful. I streamed in Irish music. There were lots of friendly people. I didn't start Dublin as a commercial project. It started as a bar where people could gather, hang out, and bring their friends. And then it became clear that people wanted more and that I should build a city around the bar. Build a larger context, in other words. That's where Dublin came from. It's a place people will go," John says.

Infinite Vision Media

The interactive marketing agency Infinite Vision Media specializes in 3D Web spaces. Once part of the original team that created the lovely Dublin region, IVM now uses its deep real-world experience in advertising, branding, architecture, and programming to create immersive experiences for Second Life residents.

Neo-Realms Entertainment

As a game and content developer, Neo-Realms Entertainment has hooked the big one in Second Life. The flagship game, Neo-Realms Fishing, can be played at three different fishing camps in-world. "We created the first fishing camp in 2004," says co-founder and designer Steven McCall (known as Sweegy Manilow in Second Life). Steve and his fellow Neo-Realmers, Thanh Ha and Bryan King, were casting in real-world ponds when they realized the dearth of fishing games online. "We thought, 'All MMPGs really need fishing,' " Steve says, laughing. Although it sounded a little esoteric, it turned out that the threesome had their fingers on the pulse of consumer taste. Their little fishing expedition became a huge hit. Featuring various rod and bait types, their system offers fishing quests, reward points redeemable for prizes, and daily multiplayer tournaments for prizes and money. "It's also just a good place to hang out with your friends and socialize," says Steve.

Crescendo Design

In the real world of Wisconsin, architect Jon Brouchoud and his team at Crescendo Design create custom homes and sell plans for Springboard Homes. Their goal is to make energy-efficient, green design features more affordable. Jon and his team have found Second Life to be a great architectural tool. They use Second Life both within their company and among long-distance clients to create virtual designs and structures.

Global Kids

Global Kids is a nonprofit group working to prepare urban youth to become global citizens and community leaders. With help from Main Grid content creators and consultants like The Magicians and the Electric Sheep Company, Global Kids created a program where students in New York City collaborate with Teen Grid Residents from around the world. The teens had to finish the interactive adventure to participate in a real-world essay contest. Winners of the contest received cash prizes (in U.S. dollars) and were part of an awards ceremony co-broadcast into the Teen Grid and on stage in New York City.

American Apparel

American Apparel opened a store in Second Life on Lerappa Island (Lerappa is apparel spelled backward). Resident Aimee Weber was responsible for the build. What makes this opening so special is that it makes an exclusive offer for Second Life residents. Purchasers at the in-world American Apparel store will get a notecard with a promotional code offering a real life discount at American Apparel's online store.

Sire Records/Regina Spektor

Recently, Sire Records and musician Regina Spektor launched an interactive, virtual listening party for her fourth album, Begin to Hope, inside Second Life. Songs from the album were available at six listening posts in a virtual New York City loft in-world.

Marvin the Robot

When Rivers Run Red was asked to create Marvin the Robot for the film *Hitchhikers Guide to the Galaxy,* Justin Bovington headed for Second Life. Rivers Run Red is an innovative marketing and communication firm located in the United Kingdom, and Justin is Fizik Baskerville, a developer in Second Life where he creates his ideas and makes them real. With Marvin, Justin successfully demonstrated Second Life's viability as a development platform—blurring the line between Second Life and real life.[1]

Introduction

Decision making and problem solving in today's electronic world encompass large-scale, opportunity-oriented, strategically focused solutions. The traditional "cookbook" approach to decisions simply will not work in the e-business world. Decision-making and problem-solving abilities are now the most sought-after traits in up-and-coming executives, according to a recent survey of 1,000 executives by Caliper Associates, as reported in *The Wall Street Journal*. To put it mildly, decision makers and problem solvers have limitless career potential.[2]

E-business is the conducting of business on the Internet, not only buying and selling, but also serving customers and collaborating with business partners. (Unit Four discusses e-business in detail.) With the fast growth of information technology and the accelerated use of the Internet, e-business is quickly becoming standard. This unit focuses on technology to help make decisions, solve problems, and find new innovative opportunities. The unit highlights how to bring people together with the best IT processes and tools in complete, flexible solutions that can seize business opportunities (see Figure Unit 3.1). The chapters in Unit 3 are:

- **Chapter Nine**—Enabling the Organization—Decision Making.
- **Chapter Ten**—Extending the Organization—Supply Chain Management.
- **Chapter Eleven**—Building a Customer-centric Organization—Customer Relationship Management.
- **Chapter Twelve**—Integrating the Organization from End to End—Enterprise Resource Planning.

FIGURE UNIT 3.1

Decision-Enabling, Problem-Solving, and Opportunity-Seizing Systems

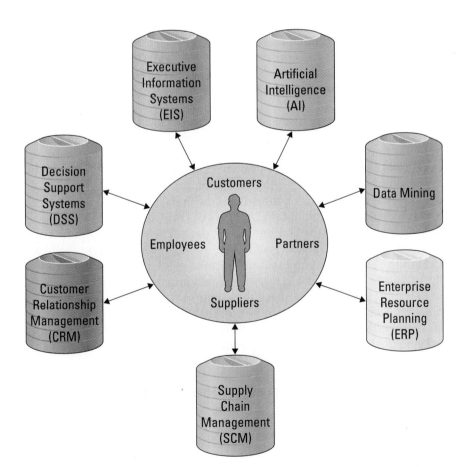

CHAPTER	9	Enabling the Organization—Decision Making

9.1. Define the systems organizations use to make decisions and gain competitive advantages.

9.2. Describe the three quantitative models typically used by decision support systems.

9.3. Describe the relationship between digital dashboards and executive information systems.

9.4. List and describe four types of artificial intelligence systems.

9.5. Describe three types of data-mining analysis capabilities.

Decision Making

Disney
Imagineering

What is the value of information? The answer to this important question varies. Karsten Solheim would say that the value of information is its ability to lower a company's handicap. Solheim, an avid golfer, invented a putter, one with a "ping," that led to a successful golf equipment company and the Ping golf clubs. Ping Inc., a privately held corporation, was the first to offer customizable golf clubs. And Ping thanks information technology for the explosion of its business over the past decade.

Ping prides itself on being a just-in-time manufacturer that depends on a highly flexible information system to make informed production decisions. The system scans Ping's vast amounts of order information and pulls orders that meet certain criteria such as order date, order priority, and customer type. Ping then places the appropriate inventory orders allowing the company to maintain only 5 percent of its inventory in its warehouse. Ping depends on its flexible information systems for both decision support and operational problem solving.[3]

Business is accelerating at a breakneck pace. The more information a business acquires, the more difficult it becomes to make decisions. Hence, the amount of information people must understand to make good decisions is growing exponentially. In the past, people could rely on manual processes to make decisions because they had only limited amounts of information to deal with. Today, with massive volumes of available information it is almost impossible for people to make decisions without the aid of information systems. Figure 9.1 highlights the primary reasons dependence on information systems to make decisions and solve problems is growing and will continue to grow.

A ***model*** is a simplified representation or abstraction of reality. Models can calculate risks, understand uncertainty, change variables, and manipulate time. Decision-making information systems work by building models out of organizational information to lend insight into important business issues and opportunities. Figure 9.2 displays three common types of decision-making information systems used in organizations today. Each system uses different models to assist in decision making, problem solving, and opportunity capturing. These systems include:

Reasons for Growth of Decision-Making Information Systems
1. **People need to analyze large amounts of information**—Improvements in technology itself, innovations in communication, and globalization have resulted in a dramatic increase in the alternatives and dimensions people need to consider when making a decision or appraising an opportunity.
2. **People must make decisions quickly**—Time is of the essence and people simply do not have time to sift through all the information manually.
3. **People must apply sophisticated analysis techniques, such as modeling and forecasting, to make good decisions**—Information systems substantially reduce the time required to perform these sophisticated analysis techniques.
4. **People must protect the corporate asset of organizational information**—Information systems offer the security required to ensure organizational information remains safe.

FIGURE 9.2

IT Systems in an Enterprise

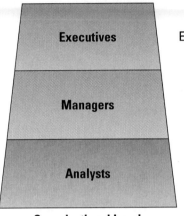

Executives — Executive Information Systems (EIS)

Managers — Decision Support Systems (DSS)

Analysts — Transaction Processing Systems (TPS)

Organizational Levels

- Transaction processing systems.
- Decision Support Systems.
- Executive Imformation Systems.

Transaction Processing Systems

The structure of a typical organization is similar to a pyramid. Organizational activities occur at different levels of the pyramid. People in the organization have unique information needs and thus require various sets of IT tools (see Figure 9.3). At the lower levels of the pyramid, people perform daily tasks such as processing transactions. *Online transaction processing (OLTP)* is the capturing of transaction and event information using technology to (1) process the information according to defined business rules, (2) store the information, and (3) update existing information to reflect the new information. During OLTP, the organization must capture every detail of transactions and events. A *transaction processing system (TPS)* is the basic business system that serves the operational level (analysts) in an organization. The most common example of a TPS is an operational accounting system such as a payroll system or an order-entry system.

Moving up through the organizational pyramid, people (typically managers) deal less with the details ("finer" information) and more with meaningful aggregations of information ("coarser" information) that help them make broader decisions for the organization. (Granularity means fine and detailed or "coarse" and abstract information.) *Online analytical processing (OLAP)* is the manipulation of information to create business intelligence in support of strategic decision making.

FIGURE 9.3

Enterprise View of
Information and
Information Technology

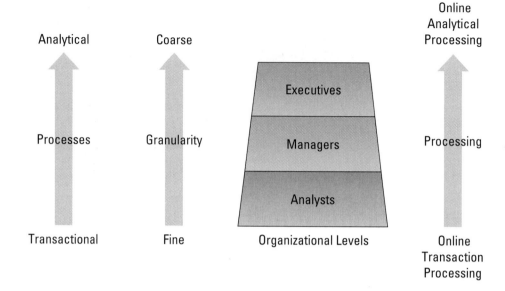

Decision Support Systems

At limousine and transportation company BostonCoach, the most critical process for managers is dispatching a fleet of hundreds of vehicles as efficiently as possible. BostonCoach requires a real-time dispatching system that considers inventory, customer needs, and soft dimensions such as weather and traffic. Researchers at IBM's Thomas J. Watson Research Center built BostonCoach a mathematical algorithm for a custom dispatch system that combines information about weather, traffic conditions, driver locations, and customer pickup requests and tells BostonCoach dispatchers which cars to assign to which customers. The system is so efficient that, after launching it in Atlanta, BostonCoach experienced a 20 percent increase in revenues.[4]

A **decision support system (DSS),** such as BostonCoach's, models information to support managers and business professionals during the decision-making process. Three quantitative models are typically used by DSSs: (1) sensitivity analysis, (2) what-if analysis, and (3) goal-seeking analysis.

1. **Sensitivity analysis** is the study of the impact that changes in one (or more) parts of the model have on other parts of the model. Users change the value of one variable repeatedly and observe the resulting changes in other variables.

2. **What-if analysis** checks the impact of a change in an assumption on the proposed solution. For example, "What will happen to the supply chain if a hurricane in South Carolina reduces holding inventory from 30 percent to 10 percent?" Users repeat this analysis until they understand all the effects of various situations. Figure 9.4 displays an example of what-if analysis using Microsoft Excel. The tool is calculating the net effect of a 20 percent increase in sales on the company's bottom line.

3. **Goal-seeking analysis** finds the inputs necessary to achieve a goal such as a desired level of output. Instead of observing how changes in a variable affect other variables as in what-if analysis, goal-seeking analysis sets a target value (a goal) for a variable and then repeatedly changes other variables until the target value is achieved. For example, "How many customers are required to purchase our new product line to increase gross profits to $5 million?" Figure 9.5 displays a goal-seeking scenario using Microsoft Excel. The model is seeking the monthly mortgage payment needed to pay off the remaining balance in 130 months.

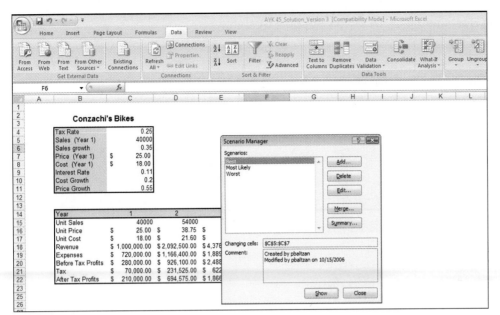

FIGURE 9.4

Example of What-If
Analysis in Microsoft
Excel

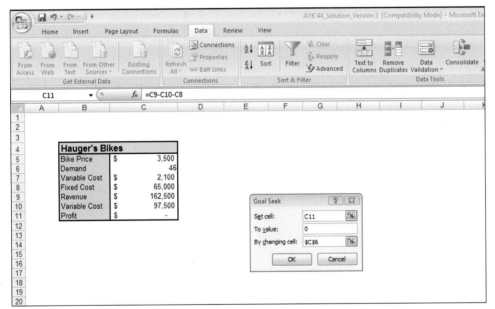

FIGURE 9.5

Example of Goal-Seeking
Analysis in Microsoft
Excel

One national insurance company uses DSSs to analyze the amount of risk the
company is undertaking when it insures drivers who have a history of driving under
the influence of alcohol. The DSS discovered that only 3 percent of married male
homeowners in their forties received more than one DUI. The company decided
to lower rates for customers falling into this category, which increased its revenue
while mitigating its risk.[5]

Figure 9.6 displays how a TPS is used within a DSS. The TPS supplies transaction-
based data to the DSS. The DSS summarizes and aggregates the information from
the many different TPS systems, which assists managers in making informed decisions. Burlington Northern and Santa Fe Railroad (BNSF) regularly tests its railroad
tracks. Each year hundreds of train derailments result from defective tracks. Using
a DSS to schedule train track replacements helped BNSF decrease its rail-caused
derailments by 33 percent.[6]

Transaction Processing Systems   Decision Support Systems

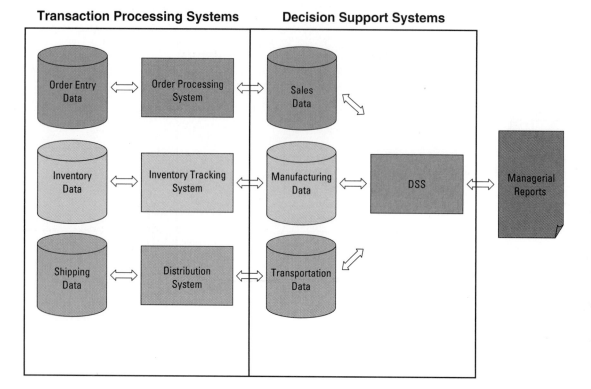

FIGURE 9.6

Interaction Between TPSs
and DSSs

Decisions

Executive Information Systems

An *executive information system (EIS)* is a specialized DSS that supports senior-level executives within the organization. An EIS differs from a DSS because an EIS typically contains data from external sources as well as data from internal sources (see Figure 9.7).

Consolidation, drill-down, and slice-and-dice are a few of the capabilities offered in most EISs.

- *Consolidation* involves the aggregation of information and features simple roll-ups to complex groupings of interrelated information. Many organizations track financial information at a regional level and then consolidate the information at a single global level.

- *Drill-down* enables users to get details, and details of details, of information. Viewing monthly, weekly, daily, or even hourly information represents drill-down capability.

- *Slice-and-dice* is the ability to look at information from different perspectives. One slice of information could display all product sales during a given promotion. Another slice could display a single product's sales for all promotions.[7]

DIGITAL DASHBOARDS

A common feature of an EIS is a digital dashboard. *Digital dashboards* integrate information from multiple components and tailor the information to individual preferences. Digital dashboards commonly use indicators to help executives quickly identify the status of key information or critical success factors. Following is a list of potential features included in a dashboard designed for a senior executive of an oil refinery:

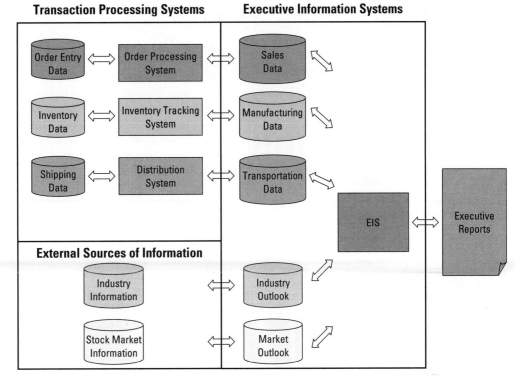

External Sources of Information

FIGURE 9.7

Interaction Between TPSs and EISs

- A hot list of key performance indicators, refreshed every 15 minutes.
- A running line graph of planned versus actual production for the past 24 hours.
- A table showing actual versus forecasted product prices and inventories.
- A list of outstanding alerts and their resolution status.
- A graph of crude-oil stock market prices.
- A scroll of headline news from Petroleum Company news, an industry news service.

Digital dashboards, whether basic or comprehensive, deliver results quickly. As digital dashboards become easier to use, more executives can perform their own analysis without inundating IT personnel with questions and requests for reports. According to an independent study by Nucleus Research, there is a direct correlation between use of digital dashboards and companies' return on investment (ROI). Figure 9.8 and Figure 9.9 display two different digital dashboards from Visual Mining.[8]

EIS systems, such as digital dashboards, allow executives to move beyond reporting to using information to directly impact business performance. Digital dashboards help executives react to information as it becomes available and make decisions, solve problems, and change strategies daily instead of monthly.

Verizon Communications CIO Shaygan Kheradpir tracks 100-plus major IT systems on a single screen called "The Wall of Shaygan." Every 15 seconds, a new set of charts communicating Verizon's performance flashes onto a giant LCD screen in Kheradpir's office. The 44 screen shots cycle continuously, all day long, every day. The dashboard includes more than 300 measures of business performance that fall into one of three categories:

1. **Market pulse**—examples include daily sales numbers, market share, and subscriber turnover.
2. **Customer service**—examples include problems resolved on the first call, call center wait times, and on-time repair calls.
3. **Cost driver**—examples include number of repair trucks in the field, repair jobs completed per day, and call center productivity.

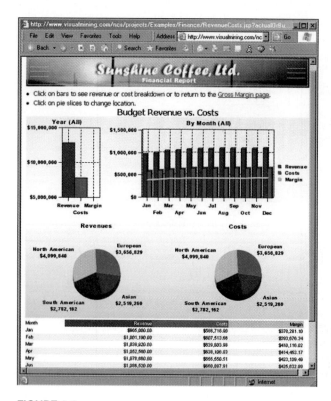

FIGURE 9.8

Visual Mining, NetCharts Corporate Financial Dashboard

Kheradpir has memorized the screens and can tell at a glance when the lines on the charts are not trending as expected. The system informs him of events such as the percentage of customer calls resolved by voice systems, number of repair trucks in the field, and amount of time to resolve an IT system issue. The dashboard works the same way for 400 managers at every level of Verizon. There are two primary types of executive informative system: artificial intelligence and data mining.[9]

Artificial Intelligence (AI)

Executive information systems are starting to take advantage of artificial intelligence to help executives make strategic decisions. RivalWatch, based in Santa Clara, California, offers a strategic business information service using artificial intelligence that enables organizations to track the product offerings, pricing policies, and promotions of online competitors. Clients can determine the competitors they want to watch and the specific information they wish to gather, ranging from products added, removed, or out of stock to price changes, coupons offered, and special shipping terms. Clients can check each competitor, category, and product either daily, weekly, monthly, or quarterly.

"Competing in the Internet arena is a whole different ballgame than doing business in the traditional brick-and-mortar world because you're competing with the whole world rather than the store down the block or a few miles away," said Phil

FIGURE 9.9

Visual Mining, NetCharts Marketing Communications Dashboard

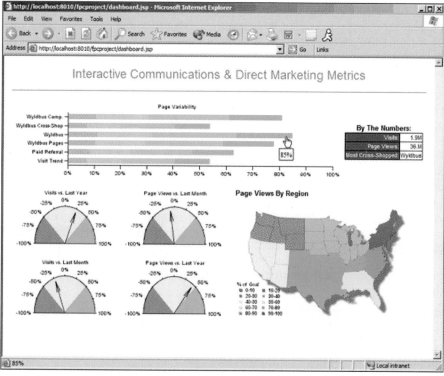

Lumish, vice president of sales and marketing at RivalWatch.com. "With new products and campaigns being introduced at a breakneck pace, e-businesses need new tools to monitor the competitive environment, and our service is designed specifically to meet that need."[10]

Intelligent systems are various commercial applications of artificial intelligence. *Artificial intelligence (AI)* simulates human intelligence such as the ability to reason and learn. AI systems can learn or understand from experience, make sense of ambiguous or contradictory information, and even use reasoning to solve problems and make decisions effectively. AI systems can perform such tasks as boosting productivity in factories by monitoring equipment and signaling when preventive maintenance is required. The ultimate goal of AI is the ability to build a system that can mimic human intelligence. AI systems are beginning to show up everywhere:

- At Manchester Airport in England, the Hefner AI Robot Cleaner alerts passengers to security and nonsmoking rules while it scrubs up to 65,600 square feet of floor per day. Laser scanners and ultrasonic detectors keep it from colliding with passengers.

- Shell Oil's SmartPump keeps drivers in their cars on cold, wet winter days. It can service any automobile built after 1987 that has been fitted with a special gas cap and a windshield-mounted transponder that tells the robot where to insert the pump.

- Matsushita's courier robot navigates hospital hallways, delivering patient files, X-ray films, and medical supplies.

- The FireFighter AI Robot can extinguish flames at chemical plants and nuclear reactors with water, foam, powder, or inert gas. The robot puts distance between the human operator and the fire.[11]

AI systems dramatically increase the speed and consistency of decision making, solve problems with incomplete information, and resolve complicated issues that cannot be solved by conventional computing. There are many categories of AI systems; four of the most familiar are: (1) expert systems, (2) neural networks, (3) genetic algorithms, and (4) intelligent agents.

EXPERT SYSTEMS

Expert systems are computerized advisory programs that imitate the reasoning processes of experts in solving difficult problems. Human expertise is transferred to the expert system and users can access the expert system for specific advice. Most expert systems reflect expertise from many humans and can therefore perform better analysis than any single expert. Typically, the system includes a knowledge base containing various accumulated experience and a set of rules for applying the knowledge base to each particular situation. The best-known expert systems play chess and assist in medical diagnosis. Expert systems are the most commonly used form of AI in the business arena because they fill the gap when human experts are difficult to find, hard to retain, or too expensive.

Examples of AI Systems

NEURAL NETWORKS

A *neural network,* also called an *artificial neural network,* is a category of AI that attempts to emulate the way the human brain works. The types of decisions for which neural networks are most useful are those that involve pattern or image recognition because a neural network can learn from the information it processes. Neural networks analyze large quantities of information to establish patterns and characteristics in situations where the logic or rules are unknown.

The finance industry is a veteran in neural network technology and has been relying on various forms of it for over two decades. The industry uses neural networks to review loan applications and create patterns or profiles of applications that fall into two categories: approved or denied. One neural network has become the standard for detecting credit card fraud. Since 1992, this technology has slashed fraud by 70 percent for U.S. Bancorp. Now, even small credit unions are required to use the software in order to qualify for debit-card insurance from Credit Union National Association. Additional examples of neural networks include:[12]

- Citibank uses neural networks to find opportunities in financial markets. By carefully examining historical stock market data with neural network software, Citibank financial managers learn of interesting coincidences or small anomalies (called market inefficiencies). For example, it could be that whenever IBM stock goes up, so does Unisys stock. Or it might be that a U.S. Treasury note is selling for 1 cent less in Japan than it is in the United States. These snippets of information can make a big difference to Citibank's bottom line in a very competitive financial market.

- In Westminster, California, a community of 87,000 people, police use neural network software to fight crime. With crime reports as input, the system detects and maps local crime patterns. Police say that with this system they can better predict crime trends, improve patrol assignments, and develop better crime prevention programs.

- Fingerhut, the mail-order company based in Minnesota, has 6 million people on its customer list. To determine which customers were and were not likely to order from its catalog, Fingerhut recently switched to neural network software. The company finds that the new software is more effective and expects to generate millions of dollars by fine-tuning its mailing lists.

- Fraud detection widely uses neural networks. Visa, MasterCard, and many other credit card companies use a neural network to spot peculiarities in individual accounts. MasterCard estimates neural networks save it $50 million annually.

- Many insurance companies (Cigna, AIG, Travelers, Liberty Mutual, Hartford) along with state compensation funds and other carriers use neural network software to identify fraud. The system searches for patterns in billing charges, laboratory tests, and frequency of office visits. A claim for which the diagnosis was a sprained ankle but included an electrocardiogram would be flagged for the account manager.

- FleetBoston Financial Corporation uses a neural network to watch transactions with customers. The neural network can detect patterns that may indicate a customer's growing dissatisfaction with the company. The neural network looks for signs like decreases in the number of transactions or in the account balance of one of FleetBoston's high-value customers.

Neural networks' many features include:

- Learning and adjusting to new circumstances on their own.
- Lending themselves to massive parallel processing.
- Functioning without complete or well-structured information.

- Coping with huge volumes of information with many dependent variables.
- Analyzing nonlinear relationships in information (they have been called fancy regression analysis systems).

The biggest problem with neural networks to date has been that the hidden layers are hidden. It is difficult to see how the neural network is learning and how the neurons are interacting. Newer neural networks no longer hide the middle layers. With these systems, users can manually adjust the weights or connections, giving them more flexibility and control.

Fuzzy logic is a mathematical method of handling imprecise or subjective information. The basic approach is to assign values between 0 and 1 to vague or ambiguous information. The higher the value, the closer it is to 1. The value zero is used to represent nonmembership, and the value one is used to represent membership. For example, fuzzy logic is used in washing machines that determine by themselves how much water to use or how long to wash (they continue washing until the water is clean). In accounting and finance, fuzzy logic allows people to analyze information with subjective financial values (like intangibles such as goodwill) that are very important considerations in economic analysis. Fuzzy logic and neural networks are often combined to express complicated and subjective concepts in a form that makes it possible to simplify the problem and apply rules that are executed with a level of certainty.[13]

GENETIC ALGORITHMS

A *genetic algorithm* is an artificial intelligence system that mimics the evolutionary, survival-of-the-fittest process to generate increasingly better solutions to a problem. A genetic algorithm is essentially an optimizing system: It finds the combination of inputs to yield the best outputs.

Genetic algorithms are best suited to decision-making environments in which thousands, or perhaps millions, of solutions are possible. Genetic algorithms can find and evaluate solutions with many more possibilities, faster and more thoroughly than a human. Organizations face decision-making environments for all types of problems that require optimization techniques such as the following:

- Business executives use genetic algorithms to help them decide which combination of projects a firm should invest in, taking complicated tax considerations into account.
- Investment companies use genetic algorithms to help in trading decisions.
- Telecommunication companies use genetic algorithms to determine the optimal configuration of fiber-optic cable in a network that may include as many as 100,000 connection points. The genetic algorithm evaluates millions of cable configurations and selects the one that uses the least amount of cable.[14]

INTELLIGENT AGENTS

An *intelligent agent* is a special-purpose knowledge-based information system that accomplishes specific tasks on behalf of its users. Intelligent agents use their knowledge base to make decisions and accomplish tasks in a way that fulfills the intentions of a user. Intelligent agents usually have a graphical representation such as "Sherlock Holmes" for an information search agent.

Intelligence

One of the simplest examples of an intelligent agent is a shopping bot. A *shopping bot* is software that will search several retailer Web sites and provide a comparison of each retailer's offerings including price and availability. Increasingly, intelligent agents handle the majority of a company's Internet buying and selling and handle such processes as finding products, bargaining over prices, and executing transactions. Intelligent agents also have the capability to handle all supply chain buying and selling.

Another application for intelligent agents is in environmental scanning and competitive intelligence. For instance, an intelligent agent can learn the types of competitor information users want to track, continuously scan the Web for it, and alert users when a significant event occurs.

By 2010, some 4 million AI robots are expected to populate homes and businesses, performing everything from pumping gas to delivering mail. According to a new report by the United Nations and the International Federation of Robotics, more than half the AI robots will be toys and the other half will perform services. Bots will deactivate bombs, clean skyscraper windows, and vacuum homes.[15]

Multi-Agent Systems and Agent-Based Modeling

What do cargo transport systems, book distribution centers, the video game market, a flu epidemic, and an ant colony have in common? They are all complex adaptive systems and thus share some common characteristics. By observing parts of the ecosystem, like ant or bee colonies, artificial intelligence scientists can use hardware and software models that incorporate insect characteristics and behavior to (1) learn how people-based systems behave; (2) predict how they will behave under a given set of circumstances; and (3) improve human systems to make them more efficient and effective. This concept of learning from ecosystems and adapting their characteristics to human and organizational situations is called biomimicry.

In the last few years, AI research has made much progress in modeling complex organizations as a whole with the help of multi-agent systems. In a multi-agent system, groups of intelligent agents have the ability to work independently and to interact with each other. The simulation of a human organization using a multi-agent system is called agent-based modeling. Agent-based modeling is a way of simulating human organizations using multiple intelligent agents, each of which follows a set of simple rules and can adapt to changing conditions.

Agent-based modeling systems are being used to model stock market fluctuations, predict the escape routes that people seek in a burning building, estimate the effects of interest rates on consumers with different types of debt, and anticipate how changes in conditions will affect the supply chain, to name just a few. Examples of companies that have used agent-based modeling to their advantage include:

- Southwest Airlines—to optimize cargo routing.
- Procter & Gamble—to overhaul its handling of what the company calls its "supply network" of 5 billion consumers in 140 countries.
- Air Liquide America—to reduce production and distribution costs of liquefied industrial gases.
- Merck & Co.—to find more efficient ways of distributing anti-AIDS drugs in Africa.
- Ford Motor Co.—to build a model of consumer preferences and find the best balance between production costs and customers' demands.
- Edison Chouest Offshore LLC—to find the best way to deploy its service and supply vessels in the Gulf of Mexico.[16]

Data Mining

Wal-Mart consolidates point-of-sale details from its 3,000 stores and uses AI to transform the information into business intelligence. Data-mining systems sift instantly through the information to uncover patterns and relationships that would elude an army of human researchers. The results enable Wal-Mart to predict sales of every product at each store with uncanny accuracy, translating into huge savings in inventories and maximum payoff from promotional spending. Figure 9.10 displays the average organizational spending on data-mining tools.[17]

Data-mining software typically includes many forms of AI such as neural networks and expert systems. Data-mining tools apply algorithms to information sets to uncover inherent trends and patterns in the information, which analysts use to develop new business strategies. Analysts use the output from data-mining tools to build models that, when exposed to new information sets, perform a variety of data analysis functions. The analysts provide business solutions by putting together the analytical techniques and the business problem at hand, which often reveals important new correlations, patterns, and trends in information. A few of the more common forms of data-mining analysis capabilities include cluster analysis, association detection, and statistical analysis.

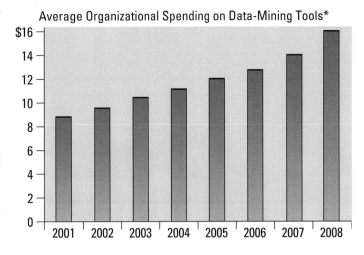

Average Organizational Spending on Data-Mining Tools*

FIGURE 9.10

Data-Mining Tools
Investment Forecast

* In millions of dollars

CLUSTER ANALYSIS

Cluster analysis is a technique used to divide an information set into mutually exclusive groups such that the members of each group are as close together as possible to one another and the different groups are as far apart as possible. Cluster analysis is frequently used to segment customer information for customer relationship management (CRM) systems to help organizations identify customers with similar behavioral traits such as clusters of best customers or onetime customers. Cluster analysis also uses neural networks because of their ability to uncover naturally occurring patterns in information.

Such data-mining tools that "understand" human language are finding unexpected applications in medicine. IBM and the Mayo Clinic unearthed hidden patterns in medical records, discovering that infant leukemia has three distinct clusters, each of which probably benefits from tailored treatments. Caroline A. Kovac, general manager of IBM Life Sciences, expects that mining the records of cancer patients for clustering patterns will turn up clues pointing the way to "tremendous strides in curing cancer."[18]

ASSOCIATION DETECTION

Whirlpool Corporation, a $4.3 billion home and commercial appliance manufacturer, employs hundreds of R&D engineers, data analysts, quality assurance specialists, and customer service personnel who all work together to ensure that each generation of appliances is better than the previous generation. Whirlpool is an example of an organization that is gaining business intelligence with association detection data-mining tools.[19]

Association detection reveals the degree to which variables are related and the nature and frequency of these relationships in the information. Whirlpool's warranty analysis tool, for instance, uses statistical analysis to automatically detect potential issues, provide quick and easy access to reports, and perform multidimensional analysis on all warranty information. This association detection data-mining tool enables Whirlpool managers to take proactive measures to control product defects even before most of its customers are aware of the defect. The tool also allows Whirlpool's personnel to devote more time to value-added tasks such as ensuring high quality on all products rather than waiting for or manually analyzing monthly reports.[20]

Many people refer to association detection algorithms as association rule generators because they create rules to determine the likelihood of events occurring

together at a particular time or following each other in a logical progression. Percentages usually reflect the patterns of these events, for example, "55 percent of the time, events A and B occurred together," or "80 percent of the time that items A and B occurred together, they were followed by item C within three days."

One of the most common forms of association detection analysis is market basket analysis. ***Market basket analysis*** analyzes such items as Web sites and checkout scanner information to detect customers' buying behavior and predict future behavior by identifying affinities among customers' choices of products and services. Market basket analysis is frequently used to develop marketing campaigns for cross-selling products and services (especially in banking, insurance, and finance) and for inventory control, shelf-product placement, and other retail and marketing applications.

STATISTICAL ANALYSIS

Statistical analysis performs such functions as information correlations, distributions, calculations, and variance analysis, just to name a few. Data-mining tools offer knowledge workers a wide range of powerful statistical capabilities so they can quickly build a variety of statistical models, examine the models' assumptions and validity, and compare and contrast the various models to determine the best one for a particular business issue.

Kraft is the producer of instantly recognizable food brands such as Oreo, Ritz, DiGiorno, and Kool-Aid. The company implemented two data-mining applications to assure consistent flavor, color, aroma, texture, and appearance for all of its lines of foods. One application analyzed product consistency and the other analyzed process variation reduction (PVR).

The product consistency tool SENECA (Sensory and Experimental Collection Application) gathers and analyzes information by assigning precise definitions and numerical scales to such qualities as chewy, sweet, crunchy, and creamy. SENECA then builds models, histories, forecasts, and trends based on consumer testing and evaluates potential product improvements and changes.

The PVR tool ensures consistent flavor, color, aroma, texture, and appearance for every Kraft product since even small changes in the baking process can result in huge disparities in taste. Evaluating every manufacturing procedure, from recipe instructions to cookie dough shapes and sizes, the PVR tool has the potential to generate significant cost savings for each product. Using these types of data-mining techniques for quality control and cluster analysis makes sure that the billions of Kraft products that reach consumers annually will continue to taste great with every bite.[21]

Forecasting is a common form of statistical analysis. Formally defined, ***forecasts*** are predictions made on the basis of time-series information. ***Time-series information*** is time-stamped information collected at a particular frequency. Examples of time-series information include Web visits per hour, sales per month, and calls per day. Forecasting data-mining tools allow users to manipulate the time-series information for forecasting activities. When discovering trends and seasonal variations in transactional information, use a time-series forecast to change the transactional information by units of time, such as transforming weekly information into monthly or seasonal information or hourly information into daily information. Companies base production, investment, and staffing decisions on a host of economic and market indicators in this manner. Forecasting models allow organizations to consider all sorts of variables when making decisions.

Nestlé Italiana is part of the multinational giant Nestlé Group and currently dominates Italy's food industry. The company improved sales forecasting by 25 percent with its data-mining forecasting solution that enables the company's managers to make objective decisions based on facts instead of subjective decisions based on intuition.

Determining sales forecasts for seasonal confectionery products is a crucial and challenging task. During Easter, Nestlé Italiana has only four weeks to market, deliver, and sell its seasonal products. The Christmas time frame is a little longer, lasting from six to eight weeks, while other holidays such as Valentine's Day and Mother's Day have shorter time frames of about one week.

The company's data-mining solution gathers, organizes, and analyzes massive volumes of information to produce powerful models that identify trends and predict confectionery sales. The business intelligence created is based on five years of historical information and identifies what is important and what is not important. Nestlé Italiana's sophisticated data-mining tool predicted Mother's Day sales forecasts that were 90 percent accurate. The company has benefited from a 40 percent reduction in inventory and a 50 percent reduction in order changes, all due to its forecasting tool. Determining sales forecasts for seasonal confectionery products is now an area in which Nestlé Italiana excels.[22]

Today, vendors such as Business Objects, Cognos, and SAS offer complete data-mining decision-making solutions. Moving forward, these companies plan to add more predictive analytical capabilities to their products. Their goal is to give companies more "what-if" scenario capabilities based on internal and external information.

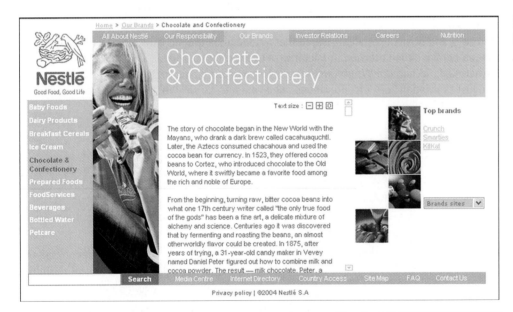

Nestlé—Excelling at Forecasting

OPENING CASE STUDY QUESTIONS

1. How could companies use Second Life for new product or service decision making?

2. How could financial companies use neural networks in Second Life to help their businesses?

3. How could a company such as Nike use decision support systems on Second Life to help its business?

4. How could an apparel company use Second Life to enhance decision making for a new product or service offering?

The DARPA Grand Challenge was designed to leverage American ingenuity to develop autonomous vehicle technologies that can be used by the military. Created in response to a Congressional and U.S. Department of Defense (DoD) mandate with the goal of saving lives on the battlefield, the DARPA Grand Challenge brings together individuals and organizations from industry, the R&D community, government, the armed services, and academia, and includes students, backyard inventors, and automotive enthusiasts.

DARPA Grand Challenge 2004

The DARPA Grand Challenge 2004 field test of autonomous ground vehicles ran from Barstow, California, to Primm, Nevada, and offered a $1 million prize. From the qualifying round at the California Speedway, 15 finalists emerged to attempt the Grand Challenge. However, the prize went unclaimed as no vehicles were able to complete the difficult desert route.

DARPA Grand Challenge 2005

The DARPA Grand Challenge 2005 was held on October 8, 2005, in the Mojave Desert and offered a $2 million prize to the team that completed the course the fastest in under 10 hours. Five teams completed the Grand Challenge course of 132 miles over desert terrain, and Stanley, the Stanford Racing Team's car, garnered the $2 million prize with a winning time of 6 hours, 53 minutes.

The Grand Challenge demonstrated that autonomous ground vehicles can travel long distances across difficult terrain at militarily relevant rates of speed. DARPA Director Dr. Tony Tether said, "When the Wright brothers flew their little plane, they proved it could be done, and just as aviation 'took off' after those achievements, so will the very exciting and promising robotics technologies displayed here today."[23]

Questions

1. Describe how the DoD is using AI to improve its operations and save lives.
2. Explain why the DoD would use an event, such as the DARPA Grand Challenge, to further technological innovation.
3. Describe how autonomous vehicles could be used by organizations around the world to improve business efficiency and effectiveness.
4. The Ansari X is another technological innovation competition focusing on spacecraft. To win the $10 million Ansari X Prize, a private spacecraft had to be the first to carry the weight equivalent of three people to an altitude of 62.14 miles twice within two weeks. SpaceShipOne, a privately built spacecraft, won the $10 million Ansari X Prize on October 4, 2004. Describe the potential business impacts of the Ansari X competition.

TECHNOLOGY PLUG-IN POINTERS >>

Review **Technology Plug-In T4 "Decision Making Using Excel"** for a comprehensive tutorial using decision analysis tools including Scenario Manager, Goal Seek, and Solver.

Review **Technology Plug-In T8 "Decision Making Using Access"** for a comprehensive tutorial on building well-designed forms and creating strategic reports.

Extending the Organization—Supply Chain Management

LEARNING OUTCOMES

10.1. List and describe the components of a typical supply chain.

10.2. Define the relationship between decision making and supply chain management.

10.3. Describe the four changes resulting from advances in IT that are driving supply chains.

10.4. Summarize the best practices for implementing a successful supply chain management system.

Supply Chain Management

Companies that excel in supply chain operations perform better in almost every financial measure of success, according to a report from Boston-based AMR Research Inc. When supply chain excellence improves operations, companies experience a 5 percent higher profit margin, 15 percent less inventory, 17 percent stronger "perfect order" ratings, and 35 percent shorter cycle times than their competitors. "The basis of competition for winning companies in today's economy is supply chain superiority," says Kevin O'Marah, vice president of research at AMR Research. "These companies understand that value chain performance translates to productivity and market-share leadership. They also understand that supply chain leadership means more than just low costs and efficiency; it requires a superior ability to shape and respond to shifts in demand with innovative products and services."[24]

Basics of Supply Chain

The average company spends nearly half of every dollar that it earns on production needs—goods and services it needs from external suppliers to keep producing. A **supply chain** consists of all parties involved, directly or indirectly, in the procurement of a product or raw material. **Supply chain management (SCM)** involves the management of information flows between and among stages in a supply chain to maximize total supply chain effectiveness and profitability.

In the past, companies focused primarily on manufacturing and quality improvements within their four walls; now their efforts extend beyond those walls to influence the entire supply chain including customers, customers' customers, suppliers, and suppliers' suppliers. Today's supply chain is a complex web of suppliers, assemblers, logistic firms, sales/marketing channels, and other business partners linked primarily through information networks and contractual relationships. SCM systems enhance and manage the relationships. The supply chain has three main links (see Figure 10.1):

1. Materials flow from suppliers and their upstream suppliers at all levels.

2. Transformation of materials into semi-finished and finished products, or the organization's own production processes.

3. Distribution of products to customers and their downstream customers at all levels.

Greater Chicago
Food Depository

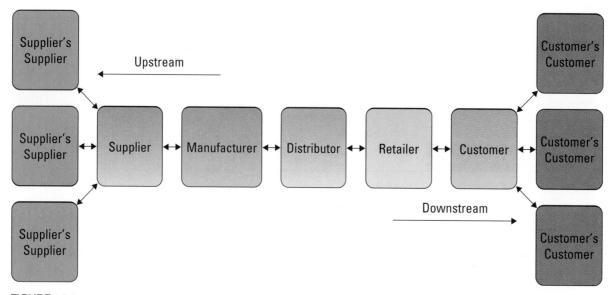

FIGURE 10.1

A Typical Supply Chain

Organizations must embrace technologies that can effectively manage and oversee their supply chains. SCM is becoming increasingly important in creating organizational efficiencies and competitive advantages. Best Buy checks inventory levels at each of its 750 stores in North America as often as every half-hour with its SCM system, taking much of the guesswork out of inventory replenishment. Supply chain management improves ways for companies to find the raw components they need to make a product or service, manufacture that product or service, and deliver it to customers. Figure 10.2 highlights the five basic components for supply chain management.[25]

Technology advances in the five SCM components have significantly improved companies' forecasting and business operations in the last few years. Businesses today have access to modeling and simulation tools, algorithms, and applications that can combine information from multiple sources to build forecasts for days, weeks, and months in advance. Better forecasts for tomorrow result in better preparedness today.

Mattel Inc. spent the past several years investing heavily in software and processes that simplify its supply chain, cut costs, and shorten cycle times. Using supply chain management strategies the company cut weeks out of the time it takes to design, produce, and ship everything from Barbies to Hot Wheels. Mattel installed optimization software that measures, tweaks, and validates the operations of its seven distribution centers, seven manufacturing plants, and other facilities that make up its vast worldwide supply chain. Mattel improved forecasting from monthly to weekly. The company no longer produces more inventory than stores require and delivers inventory upon request. Mattel's supply chain moves quickly to make precise forecasts that help the company meet demand.[26]

Information Technology's Role in the Supply Chain

As companies evolve into extended organizations, the roles of supply chain participants are changing. It is now common for suppliers to be involved in product development and for distributors to act as consultants in brand marketing. The notion of virtually seamless information links within and between organizations is an essential element of integrated supply chains.

Information technology's primary role in SCM is creating the integrations or tight process and information linkages between functions within a firm—such as

FIGURE 10.2

The Five Basic Supply
Chain Management
Components

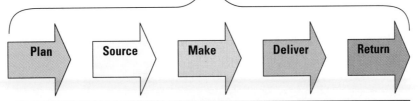

Company

SCM
Advantages

THE FIVE BASIC SUPPLY CHAIN MANAGEMENT COMPONENTS
1. **Plan** – This is the strategic portion of supply chain management. A company must have a plan for managing all the resources that go toward meeting customer demand for products or services. A big piece of planning is developing a set of metrics to monitor the supply chain so that it is efficient, costs less, and delivers high quality and value to customers.
2. **Source** – Companies must carefully choose reliable suppliers that will deliver goods and services required for making products. Companies must also develop a set of pricing, delivery, and payment processes with suppliers and create metrics for monitoring and improving the relationships.
3. **Make** – This is the step where companies manufacture their products or services. This can include scheduling the activities necessary for production, testing, packaging, and preparing for delivery. This is by far the most metric-intensive portion of the supply chain, measuring quality levels, production output, and worker productivity.
4. **Deliver** – This step is commonly referred to as logistics. *Logistics* is the set of processes that plans for and controls the efficient and effective transportation and storage of supplies from suppliers to customers. During this step, companies must be able to receive orders from customers, fulfill the orders via a network of warehouses, pick transportation companies to deliver the products, and implement a billing and invoicing system to facilitate payments.
5. **Return** – This is typically the most problematic step in the supply chain. Companies must create a network for receiving defective and excess products and support customers who have problems with delivered products.

marketing, sales, finance, manufacturing, and distribution—and between firms, which allow the smooth, synchronized flow of both information and product between customers, suppliers, and transportation providers across the supply chain. Information technology integrates planning, decision-making processes, business operating processes, and information sharing for business performance management (see Figure 10.3). Considerable evidence shows that this type of supply chain integration results in superior supply chain capabilities and profits.[27]

FIGURE 10.3

The Integrated Supply
Chain

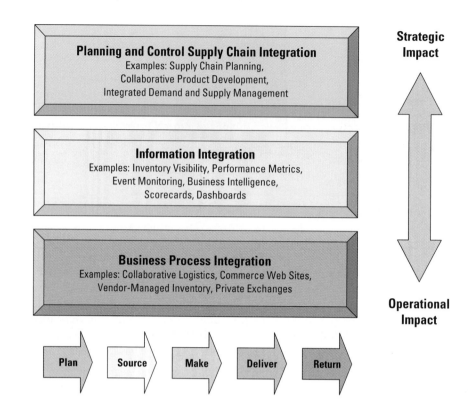

Adaptec, Inc., of California manufactures semiconductors and markets them to the world's leading PC, server, and end-user markets through more than 115 distributors and thousands of value-added resellers worldwide. Adaptec designs and manufactures products at various third-party locations around the world. The company uses supply chain integration software over the Internet to synchronize planning. Adaptec personnel at the company's geographically dispersed locations communicate in real time and exchange designs, test results, and production and shipment information. Internet-based supply chain collaboration software helped the company reduce inventory levels and lead times.[28]

Although people have been talking about the integrated supply chain for a long time, it has only been recently that advances in information technology have made it possible to bring the idea to life and truly integrate the supply chain. Visibility, consumer behavior, competition, and speed are a few of the changes resulting from information technology advances that are driving supply chains (see Figure 10.4).

FIGURE 10.4

Factors Driving Supply
Chain Management

VISIBILITY

Supply chain visibility is the ability to view all areas up and down the supply chain. Changing supply chains requires a comprehensive strategy buoyed by information technology. Organizations can use technology tools that help them integrate upstream and downstream, with both customers and suppliers.

To make a supply chain work most effectively, organizations must create visibility in real time. Organizations must know about customer events triggered downstream, but so must their suppliers and their suppliers' suppliers. Without this information, partners throughout the supply chain, can experience a bullwhip effect, in which disruptions intensify throughout the chain. The *bullwhip effect* occurs when distorted product demand information passes from one entity to the next throughout the supply chain. The misinformation regarding a slight rise in demand for a product could cause different members in the supply chain to stockpile inventory. These changes ripple throughout the supply chain, magnifying the issue and creating excess inventory and costs.[29]

Today, information technology allows additional visibility in the supply chain. Electronic information flows allow managers to view their suppliers' and customers' supply chains. Some organizations have completely changed the dynamics of their industries because of the competitive advantage gained from high visibility in the supply chain. Dell is the obvious example. The company's ability to get product to the customer and the impact of the economics have clearly changed the nature of competition and caused others to emulate this model.[30]

CONSUMER BEHAVIOR

The behavior of customers has changed the way businesses compete. Customers will leave if a company does not continually meet their expectations. They are more demanding because they have information readily available, they know exactly what they want, and they know when and how they want it. **Demand planning software** generates demand forecasts using statistical tools and forecasting techniques. Companies can respond faster and more effectively to consumer demands through supply chain enhancements such as demand planning software. Once an organization understands customer demand and its effect on the supply chain it can begin to estimate the impact that its supply chain will have on its customers and ultimately the organization's performance. The payoff for a successful demand planning strategy can be tremendous. A study by Peter J. Metz, executive directory of the MIT Center for e-business, found that companies have achieved impressive bottom-line results from managing demand in their supply chains, averaging a 50 percent reduction in inventory and a 40 percent increase in timely deliveries.[31]

SCM Future

COMPETITION

Supply chain management software can be broken down into (1) supply chain planning software and (2) supply chain execution software—both increase a company's ability to compete. **Supply chain planning (SCP) software** uses advanced mathematical algorithms to improve the flow and efficiency of the supply chain while reducing inventory. SCP depends entirely on information for its accuracy. An organization cannot expect the SCP output to be accurate unless correct and up-to-date information regarding customer orders, sales information, manufacturing capacity, and delivery capability is entered into the system.

An organization's supply chain encompasses the facilities where raw materials, intermediate products, and finished goods are acquired, transformed, stored, and sold. These facilities are connected by transportation links, where materials and products flow. Ideally, the supply chain consists of multiple organizations that function as efficiently and effectively as a single organization, with full information visibility. **Supply chain execution (SCE) software** automates the different steps and stages of the supply chain. This could be as simple as electronically routing orders from a manufacturer to a supplier. Figure 10.5 details how SCP and SCE software correlate to the supply chain.[32]

General Motors, Ford, and DaimlerChrysler made history when the three automotive giants began working together to create a unified supply chain planning/execution system that all three companies and their suppliers could leverage. The combined automotive giants' purchasing power is tremendous with GM spending $85 billion per year, Ford spending $80 billion per year, and DaimlerChrysler spending $73 billion per year. The ultimate goal is to process automotive production from ordering materials and forecasting demand to making cars directly to consumer specifications through the Web. The automotive giants understand the impact strategic supply chain planning and execution can have on their competition.[33]

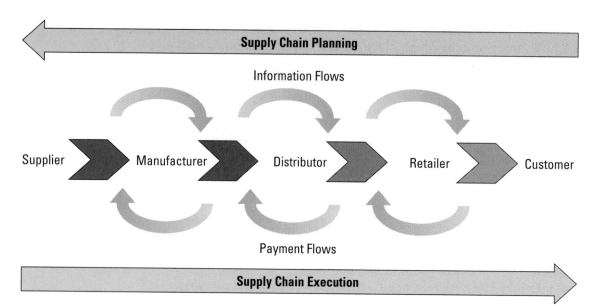

FIGURE 10.5

Supply Chain Planning and Supply Chain Execution Software's Correlation to the Supply Chain

SPEED

During the past decade, competition has focused on speed. New forms of servers, telecommunications, wireless applications, and software are enabling companies to perform activities that were once never thought possible. These systems raise the accuracy, frequency, and speed of communication between suppliers and customers, as well as between internal users. Another aspect of speed is the company's ability to satisfy continually changing customer requirements efficiently, accurately, and quickly. Timely and accurate information is more critical to businesses than ever before. Figure 10.6 displays the three factors fostering this change.[34]

Supply Chain Management Success Factors

To succeed in today's competitive markets, companies must align their supply chains with the demands of the markets they serve. Supply chain performance is now a distinct competitive advantage for companies proficient in the SCM area. Perdue Farms excels at decision making based on its supply chain management system. Perdue Farms moves roughly 1 million turkeys, each within 24 hours of processing, to reach holiday tables across the nation yearly. The task is no longer as complicated as it was before Perdue Farms invested $20 million in SCM technology. SCM makes Perdue more adept at delivering the right number of turkeys, to the right customers, at the right time.[35]

To achieve success such as reducing operating costs, improving asset productivity, and compressing order cycle time, an organization should follow the seven principles of supply chain management outlined in Figure 10.7.

These seven principles run counter to previous built-in functional thinking of how companies organize, operate, and serve customers. Old concepts of supply chains are typified by discrete manufacturing, linear structure, and a focus on buy-sell transactions ("I buy from my suppliers, I sell to my customers"). Because the traditional supply chain is spread out linearly, some suppliers are removed from the end customer. Collaboration adds the value of visibility for these companies. They benefit by knowing

FIGURE 10.6

Three Factors Fostering Speed

Factors Fostering Supply Chain Speed
1. Pleasing customers has become something of a corporate obsession. Serving the customer in the best, most efficient, and most effective manner has become critical, and information about issues such as order status, product availability, delivery schedules, and invoices has become a necessary part of the total customer service experience.
2. Information is crucial to managers' abilities to reduce inventory and human resource requirements to a competitive level.
3. Information flows are essential to strategic planning for and deployment of resources.

Seven Principles of Supply Chain Management
1. Segment customers by service needs, regardless of industry, and then tailor services to those particular segments.
2. Customize the logistics network and focus intensively on the service requirements and on the profitability of the preidentified customer segments.
3. Listen to signals of market demand and plan accordingly. Planning must span the entire chain to detect signals of changing demand.
4. Differentiate products closer to the customer, since companies can no longer afford to hold inventory to compensate for poor demand forecasting.
5. Strategically manage sources of supply, by working with key suppliers to reduce overall costs of owning materials and services.
6. Develop a supply chain information technology strategy that supports different levels of decision making and provides a clear view (visibility) of the flow of products, services, and information.
7. Adopt performance evaluation measures that apply to every link in the supply chain and measure true profitability at every stage.

FIGURE 10.7

Seven Principles of Supply Chain Management

immediately what is being transacted at the customer end of the supply chain (the end customer's activities are visible to them). Instead of waiting days or weeks (or months) for the information to flow upstream through the supply chain, with all the potential pitfalls of erroneous or missing information, suppliers can react in near real-time to fluctuations in end-customer demand.

Dell Inc. offers one of the best examples of an extremely successful SCM system. Dell's highly efficient build-to-order business model enables it to deliver customized computer systems quickly. As part of the company's continual effort to improve its supply chain processes, Dell deploys supply chain tools to provide global views of forecasted product demand and materials requirements, as well as improved factory scheduling and inventory management.[36]

Organizations should study industry best practices to improve their chances of successful implementation of SCM systems. The following are keys to SCM success.

Lill 1154

MAKE THE SALE TO SUPPLIERS

The hardest part of any SCM system is its complexity because a large part of the system extends beyond the company's walls. Not only will the people in the organization need to change the way they work, but also the people from each supplier that is added to the network must change. Be sure suppliers are on board with the benefits that the SCM system will provide.

WEAN EMPLOYEES OFF TRADITIONAL BUSINESS PRACTICES

Operations people typically deal with phone calls, faxes, and orders scrawled on paper and will most likely want to keep it that way. Unfortunately, an organization cannot disconnect the telephones and fax machines just because it is implementing a supply chain management system. If the organization cannot convince people that using the software will be worth their time, they will easily find ways to work around it, which will quickly decrease the chances of success for the SCM system.

ENSURE THE SCM SYSTEM SUPPORTS THE ORGANIZATIONAL GOALS

It is important to select SCM software that gives organizations an advantage in the areas most crucial to their business success. If the organizational goals support highly efficient strategies, be sure the supply chain design has the same goals.

DEPLOY IN INCREMENTAL PHASES AND MEASURE AND COMMUNICATE SUCCESS

Design the deployment of the SCM system in incremental phases. For instance, instead of installing a complete supply chain management system across the company and all suppliers at once, start by getting it working with a few key suppliers, and then move on to the other suppliers. Along the way, make sure each step is adding value through improvements in the supply chain's performance. While a big-picture perspective is vital to SCM success, the incremental approach means the SCM system should be implemented in digestible bites, and also measured for success one step at a time.

BE FUTURE ORIENTED

The supply chain design must anticipate the future state of the business. Because the SCM system likely will last for many more years than originally planned, managers need to explore how flexible the systems will be when (not if) changes are required in the future. The key is to be certain that the software will meet future needs, not only current needs.[37]

SCM Success Stories

Figure 10.8 depicts the top reasons more and more executives are turning to SCM to manage their extended enterprises. Figure 10.9 lists several companies using supply chain management to drive operations.

Apple Computer initially distributed its business operations over 16 legacy applications. Apple quickly realized that it needed a new business model centered around an integrated supply chain to drive performance efficiencies. Apple devised an implementation strategy that focused on specific SCM functions—finance, sales, distribution, and manufacturing—that would most significantly help its business. The company decided to deploy leading-edge functionality with a new business model that provided:

- Build-to-order and configure-to-order manufacturing capabilities.
- Web-enabled configure-to-order order entry and order status for customers buying directly from Apple at Apple.com.
- Real-time credit card authorization.
- Available-to-promise and rules-based allocations.
- Integration to advanced planning systems.

FIGURE 10.8

Top Reasons Executives Use SCM to Manage Extended Enterprises

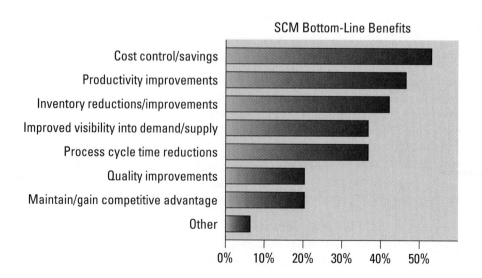

Since its SCM system went live, Apple has experienced substantial benefits in many areas including measurable improvements in its manufacturing processes, a decrease by 60 percent in its build-to-order and configure-to-order cycle times, and the ability to process more than 6,000 orders daily.[38]

Companies Using Supply Chain to Drive Operations	
Dell	Business grows 17 percent per year with a $40 billion revenue base.
Nokia	Supply chain best practices are turning ideas into profitable businesses.
Procter & Gamble	Consumer-driven supply chain is the defining architecture for large consumer companies. Best practices in product innovation and supply chain effectiveness are tops.
IBM	Hardware supply chain product-development processes overhauled to the tune of 70 percent better, faster, and cheaper.
Wal-Mart Stores	Everyday low prices define the customer demand driving Wal-Mart's partner integrated supply chain.
Toyota Motor	Lean is one of the top three best practices associated with benchmarked supply chain excellence.
The Home Depot	Cutting-edge supply chain management improved logistics and innovative services.
Best Buy	SCM has radically thinned inventories and delivered enviable business positions.
Marks & Spencer	A pioneer in the use of radio frequency identification (RFID) in stores, Marks & Spencer manages to grow and stay lean.

FIGURE 10.9

Companies Using Supply Chain Management Technologies to Drive Operations

OPENING CASE STUDY QUESTIONS

1. Would you need supply chain management systems in a virtual world such as Second Life? Why or why not?

2. How could a real company augment its supply chain management system through Second Life?

3. If you were an apparel company, such as Nike or REI, what would your virtual SCM system look like? Create a drawing of this system and be sure to include all upstream and downstream participants.

Chapter Ten Case: BudNet

Every time a six-pack moves off the shelf, Anheuser-Busch's top-secret nationwide data network, BudNet, knows. BudNet is Anheuser-Busch's secret weapon and one of the reasons that Anheuser's share (by volume) of the $74.4 billion U.S. beer market inched up to 50.1 percent from 48.9 percent.

Dereck Gurden, a sales representative for Sierra Beverage, one of about 700 U.S. distributors that work for Anheuser-Busch, manages an 800-square-mile territory in California's

Central Valley. His customers include 7-Eleven, Buy N Save, and dozens of liquor marts and restaurants. When Gurden enters one of his customers' stores he already knows what products are selling, which campaigns are successful, and what needs to be done to help the customer's business.

When entering a store, Gurden checks his handheld PC, which displays vital store information. "First I'll scroll through and check the accounts receivable, make sure everything's current," he says. "Then it'll show me an inventory screen with a four-week history. I can get past sales, package placements—facts and numbers on how much of the sales they did when they had a display in a certain location." Gurden also walks around the store and inputs competitor information into his handheld PC relating to product displays, pricing strategies, and promotions.

How BudNet Works

Information is entered into BudNet nightly from several thousand beer distributors and sales representatives. The information allows Anheuser-Busch managers to constantly adjust production and fine-tune marketing campaigns. The system works as follows:

1. Sales representatives collect new orders and track competitors' marketing efforts on PDAs and laptops.
2. Distributors compile the information and transmit it daily to Anheuser corporate headquarters.
3. Anheuser brand managers analyze the information and make decisions for distributors.
4. Distributors log on to BudNet to get the latest intelligence.
5. Sales representatives rearrange displays and rotate stock based on the recommendations.

Anheuser-Busch uses BudNet's information to constantly change marketing strategies, to design promotions to suit the ethnic makeup of its markets, and as early warning radar that detects where rivals might have an edge. "If Anheuser-Busch loses shelf space in a store in Clarksville, Tennessee, they know it right away," says Joe Thompson, president of Independent Beverage Group, a research and consulting firm. "They're better at this game than anyone, even Coca-Cola."

According to dozens of analysts, beer industry veterans, and distributor executives, Anheuser has made a deadly accurate science out of determining what beer lovers are buying, as well as when, where, and why. The last time you bought a six-pack of Bud Light at the corner store, Anheuser servers most likely recorded what you paid, when that beer was brewed, whether you purchased it warm or chilled, and whether you could have gotten a better deal down the street. BudNet has not just added efficiency into the beer supply chain; it is changing the dynamics of the industry.[39]

Questions

1. Describe how an SCM system can help a distributor such as Anheuser-Busch make its supply chain more effective and efficient.
2. SCM is experiencing explosive growth. Explain why this statement is true using BudNet as an example.
3. Evaluate BudNet's effect on each of the five factors that are driving SCM success.

BUSINESS PLUG-IN POINTER>>

Review **Business Plug-In B8 "Supply Chain Management"** for a detailed look at how an organization can create a supply chain strategy focusing on efficiency and effectiveness through the use of the four primary drivers of supply chain management—facilities, inventory, transportation, and information.

Building a Customer-centric Organization—Customer Relationship Management

11.1. Compare operational and analytical customer relationship management.

11.2. Identify the primary forces driving the explosive growth of customer relationship management.

11.3. Define the relationship between decision making and analytical customer relationship management.

11.4. Summarize the best practices for implementing a successful customer relationship management system.

Customer Relationship Management (CRM)

MTV

After 1-800-Flowers.com achieved operational excellence in the late 1990s, it turned to building customer intimacy to continue to improve profits and business growth. The company turned brand loyalty into brand relationships by using the vast amounts of information it collected to better understand customers' needs and expectations. The floral delivery company adopted SAS Enterprise Miner to analyze the information in its CRM systems. Enterprise Miner sifts through information to reveal trends, explain outcomes, and predict results so that businesses can increase response rates and quickly identify their profitable customers. With the help of Enterprise Miner, 1-800-Flowers.com is continuing to thrive, with 27 percent annual increases in revenue.[40]

CRM is a business philosophy based on the premise that those organizations that understand the needs of individual customers are best positioned to achieve sustainable competitive advantage in the future. Many aspects of CRM are not new to organizations; CRM is simply performing current business better. Placing customers at the forefront of all thinking and decision making requires significant operational and technology changes, however.

A customer strategy starts with understanding who the company's customers are and how the company can meet strategic goals. *The New York Times* understands this and has spent the past decade researching core customers to find similarities among groups of readers in cities outside the New York metropolitan area. Its goal is to understand how to appeal to those groups and make *The New York Times* a national newspaper, expanding its circulation and the "reach" it offers to advertisers. *The New York Times* is growing in a relatively flat publishing market and has achieved a customer retention rate of 94 percent in an industry that averages roughly 60 percent.[41]

As the business world increasingly shifts from product focus to customer focus, most organizations recognize that treating existing customers well is the best source of profitable and sustainable revenue growth. In the age of e-business, however, an organization is challenged more than ever before to truly satisfy its customers. CRM will allow an organization to:

- Provide better customer service.
- Make call centers more efficient.

- Cross-sell products more effectively.
- Help sales staff close deals faster.
- Simplify marketing and sales processes.
- Discover new customers.
- Increase customer revenues.

The National Basketball Association's New York Knicks are becoming better than ever at communicating with their fans. Thanks to a CRM solution, the New York Knicks' management now knows which season-ticket holders like which players, what kind of merchandise they buy, and where they buy it. Management is finally able to send out fully integrated e-mail campaigns that do not overlap with other marketing efforts.[42]

Recency, Frequency, and Monetary Value

An organization can find its most valuable customers by using a formula that industry insiders call RFM—recency, frequency, and monetary value. In other words, an organization must track:

- How recently a customer purchased items (recency).
- How frequently a customer purchases items (frequency).
- How much a customer spends on each purchase (monetary value).

Once a company has gathered this initial customer relationship management (CRM) information, it can compile it to identify patterns and create marketing campaigns, sales promotions, and services to increase business. For example, if Ms. Smith buys only at the height of the season, then the company should send her a special offer during the off-season. If Mr. Jones always buys software but never computers, then the company should offer him free software with the purchase of a new computer.[43]

CRM technologies can help organizations track RFM and answer tough questions such as who are their best customers and which of their products are the most profitable. This chapter details the different operational and analytical CRM technologies an organization can use to strengthen its customer relationships and increase revenues.

The Evolution of CRM

Knowing the customer, especially knowing the profitability of individual customers, is highly lucrative in the financial services industry. Its high transactional nature has always afforded the financial services industry more access to customer information than other industries have, but it has embraced CRM technologies only recently.

Barclays Bank is a leading financial services company operating in more than 70 countries. In the United Kingdom, Barclays has over 10 million personal customers and about 9.3 million credit cards in circulation, and it serves 500,000 small-business customers. Barclays decided to invest in CRM technologies to help gain valuable insights into its business and customers.

With its new CRM system, Barclays' managers are better able to predict the financial behavior of individual customers and assess whether a customer is likely to pay back a loan in full and within the agreed upon time period. This helps Barclays manage its profitability with greater precision because it can charge its customers a more appropriate rate of interest based on the results of the customer's risk assessment. Barclays also uses a sophisticated customer segmentation system to identify groups of profitable customers, both on a corporate and a personal level, which it can then target for new financial products. One of the most valuable pieces of information

CRM
Advantages

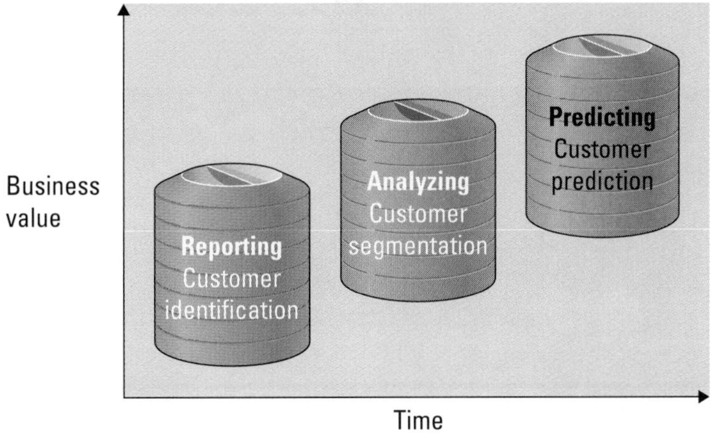

FIGURE 11.1

Evolution of CRM

Barclays discovered was that about 50 percent of its customers are not profitable and that less than 30 percent of its customers provide 90 percent of its profits.[44]

There are three phases in the evolution of CRM: (1) reporting, (2) analyzing, and (3) predicting (see Figure 11.1). CRM reporting technologies help organizations identify their customers across other applications. CRM analysis technologies help organizations segment their customers into categories such as best and worst customers. CRM predicting technologies help organizations make predictions regarding customer behavior such as which customers are at risk of leaving.

Both operational and analytical CRM technologies can assist in customer reporting (identification), customer analysis (segmentation), and customer prediction. Figure 11.2 highlights a few of the important questions an organization can answer using CRM technologies.[45]

The Ugly Side of CRM: Why CRM Matters More Now than Ever Before

Business 2.0 ranked "You—the customer" as number one in the top 50 people who matter most in business. It has long been said that the customer is always right, but for a long time companies never really meant it. Now, companies have no choice as the power of the customer grows exponentially as the Internet grows. You—or rather, the collaborative intelligence of tens of millions of people, the networked

FIGURE 11.2

Reporting, Analyzing, and Predicting Examples

REPORTING "Asking What Happened"	ANALYZING "Asking Why It Happened"	PREDICTING "Asking What Will Happen"
What is the total revenue by customer?	Why did sales not meet forecasts?	What customers are at risk of leaving?
How many units did we manufacture?	Why was production so low?	What products will the customer buy?
Where did we sell the most products?	Why did we not sell as many units as last year?	Who are the best candidates for a mailing?
What were total sales by product?	Who are our customers?	What is the best way to reach the customer?
How many customers did we serve?	Why was customer revenue so high?	What is the lifetime profitability of a customer?
What are our inventory levels?	Why are inventory levels so low?	What transactions might be fradulent?

you—continually create and filter new forms of content, anointing the useful, the relevant, and the amusing and rejecting the rest. You do it on Web sites like Amazon, Flickr, and YouTube, via podcasts and SMS polling, and on millions of self-published blogs. In every case, you have become an integral part of the action as a member of the aggregated, interactive, self-organizing, auto-entertaining audience. But the "You Revolution" goes well beyond user-generated content. Companies as diverse as Delta Air Lines and T-Mobile are turning to you to create their ad slogans. Procter & Gamble and Lego are incorporating your ideas into new products. You constructed open-source software and are its customer and its care-taker. None of this should be a surprise, since it was you—your crazy passions and hobbies and obsessions—that built out the Web in the first place. And somewhere out there, you are building Web 3.0. We do not yet know what that is, but one thing is for sure: It will matter. Figure 11.3 displays a few examples of the power of the people.[46]

Customer Relationship Management's Explosive Growth

Brother International Corporation experienced skyrocketing growth in its sales of multifunction centers, fax machines, printers, and labeling systems in the late 1990s. Along with skyrocketing sales growth came a tremendous increase in cus-tomer service calls. When Brother failed to answer the phone fast enough, prod-uct returns started to increase. The company responded by increasing call center capacity, and the rate of returns began to drop. However, Dennis Upton, CIO of Brother International, observed that all the company was doing was answering the phone. He quickly realized that the company was losing a world of valuable market intelligence (business intelligence) about existing customers from all those tele-phone calls. The company decided to deploy SAP's CRM solution. The 1.8 million calls Brother handled dropped to 1.57 million, which reduced call center staff from 180 agents to 160 agents. Since customer demographic information is now stored and displayed on the agent's screen based on the incoming telephone number, the company has reduced call duration by an average of one minute, saving the com-pany $600,000 per year.[47]

In the context of increasing business competition and mature markets, it is eas-ier than ever for informed and demanding customers to defect since they are just a click away from migrating to an alternative. When customers buy on the Inter-net, they see, and they steer, entire value chains. The Internet is a "looking glass," a two-way mirror, and its field of vision is the entire value chain. While the Internet cannot totally replace the phone and face-to-face communication with customers, it can strengthen these interactions and all customer touch points. Customer Web interactions become conversations, interactive dialogs with shared knowledge, not just business transactions. Web-based customer care can actually become the focal point of customer relationship management and provide breakthrough benefits for both the enterprise and its customers, substantially reducing costs while improving service.

According to an AMR Research survey of more than 500 businesses in 14 key vertical markets, half of all current CRM spending is by manufacturers. Current users are allocating 20 percent of their IT budgets to CRM solutions. Those who

FIGURE 11.4

CRM Business Drivers

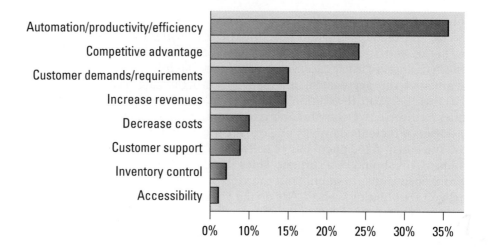

FIGURE 11.5

CRM Spending ($ billions)

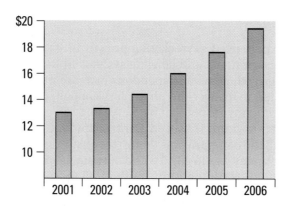

have not invested in CRM may soon come on board: Of the respondents in the study who are not currently using CRM, roughly one-third plan to implement these types of technology solutions within the next year. Figure 11.4 displays the top CRM business drivers, and Figure 11.5 displays the CRM spending over the past few years.[48]

Using Analytical CRM to Enhance Decisions

Joe Guyaux knows the best way to win customers is to improve service. Under his leadership and with the help of Siebel CRM, the PNC retail banking team increased new consumer checking customers by 19 percent in 2003. Over two years, PNC retained 21 percent more of its consumer checking households as well as improved customer satisfaction by 9 percent.[49]

The two primary components of a CRM strategy are operational CRM and analytical CRM. **Operational CRM** supports traditional transactional processing for day-to-day front-office operations or systems that deal directly with the customers. **Analytical CRM** supports back-office operations and strategic analysis and includes all systems that do not deal directly with the customers. The primary difference between operational CRM and analytical CRM is the direct interaction between the organization and its customers. See Figure 11.6 for an overview of operational CRM and analytical CRM.

Patagonia

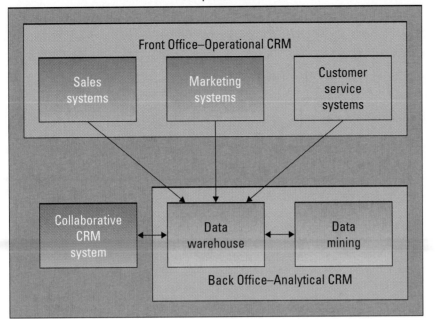

Enterprise CRM

Front Office–Operational CRM

Sales systems

Marketing systems

Customer service systems

Collaborative CRM system

Data warehouse

Data mining

Back Office–Analytical CRM

FIGURE 11.6

Operational CRM and Analytical CRM

Maturing analytical CRM and behavioral modeling technologies are helping numerous organizations move beyond "legacy benefits" like enhanced customer service and retention to systems that can truly improve business profitability. Unlike operational CRM that automates call centers and sales forces with the aim of enhancing customer transactions, analytical CRM solutions are designed to dig deep into a company's historical customer information and expose patterns of behavior on which a company can capitalize. Analytical CRM is primarily used to enhance and support decision making and works by identifying patterns in customer information collected from the various operational CRM systems.

For many organizations, the power of analytical CRM solutions provides tremendous managerial opportunities. Depending on the specific solution, analytical CRM tools can slice-and-dice customer information to create made-to-order views of customer value, spending, product affinities, percentile profiles, and segmentations. Modeling tools can identify opportunities for cross-selling, up-selling, and expanding customer relationships.

Personalization occurs when a Web site can know enough about a person's likes and dislikes that it can fashion offers that are more likely to appeal to that person. Many organizations are now utilizing CRM to create customer rules and templates that marketers can use to personalize customer messages.

The information produced by analytical CRM solutions can help companies make decisions about how to handle customers based on the value of each and every one. Analytical CRM can help make decisions as to which customers are worth investing in, which should be serviced at an average level, and which should not be invested in at all.

CRM Success

Customer Relationship Management Success Factors

CRM solutions make organizational business processes more intelligent. This is achieved by understanding customer behavior and preferences, then realigning product and service offerings and related communications to make sure they are synchronized with customer needs and preferences. If an organization is implementing a CRM system, it should study the industry best practices to help ensure a successful implementation (see Figure 11.7).[50]

FIGURE 11.7

CRM Implementation
Strategies

CRM Implementation Strategies

1. **Clearly Communicate the CRM Strategy**—Boise Office Solutions spent $25 million implementing a successful CRM system. One primary reason for the system's success was that Boise started with a clear business objective for the system: to provide customers with greater economic value. Only after establishing the business objective did Boise Office Solutions invest in CRM technology to help meet the goal. Ensuring that all departments and employees understand exactly what CRM means and how it will add value to the organization is critical. Research by Gartner Dataquest indicates that enterprises that attain success with CRM have interested and committed senior executives who set goals for what CRM should achieve, match CRM strategies with corporate objectives, and tie the measurement process to both goals and strategies.

2. **Define Information Needs and Flows**—People who perform successful CRM implementations have a clear understanding of how information flows in and out of their organization. Chances are information comes into the organization in many different forms over many different touchpoints.

3. **Build an Integrated View of the Customer**—Essential to a CRM strategy is choosing the correct CRM system that can support organizational requirements. The system must have the corresponding functional breadth and depth to support strategic goals. Remember to take into account the system's infrastructure including ease of integration to current systems, discussed in greater detail later in this unit.

4. **Implement in Iterations**—Implement the CRM system in manageable pieces—in other words avoid the "big bang" implementation approach. It is easier to manage, measure, and track the design, building, and deployment of the CRM system when it is delivered in pieces. Most important, this allows the organization to find out early if the implementation is headed for failure and thus either kill the project and save wasted resources or change direction to a more successful path.

5. **Scalability for Organizational Growth**—Make certain that the CRM system meets the organization's future needs as well as its current needs. Estimating future needs is by far one of the hardest parts of any project. Understanding how the organization is going to grow, predicting how technology is going to change, and anticipating how customers are going to evolve are very difficult challenges. Taking the time to answer some tough questions up front will ensure the organization grows into, instead of out of, its CRM system.

CRM is critical to business success. It is the key competitive strategy to stay focused on customer needs and to integrate a customer-centric approach throughout an organization. CRM can acquire enterprisewide knowledge about customers and improve the business processes that deliver value to an organization's customers, suppliers, and employees. Using the analytical capabilities of CRM can help a company anticipate customer needs and proactively serve customers in ways that build relationships, create loyalty, and enhance bottom lines.

OPENING CASE STUDY QUESTIONS

1. Why is it important for any company to use CRM strategies to manage customer information?

2. How are CRM strategies in Second Life different from CRM strategies in the real world?

3. If the virtual world is the first point of contact between a company and its customers, how might that transform the entire shopping experience?

4. How could companies use Second Life to connect with customers that would be difficult or too expensive in the real world?

Chapter Eleven Case: The Ritz-Carlton—Specializing in Customers

Bill Kapner, CEO of financial software provider Bigdough, checked into the Ritz-Carlton in Palm Beach, Florida. Before introducing himself, he was greeted—by name—at the front desk. Then a reception clerk asked, "Will you be having sushi tonight?" The interesting thing about these conversations is that Kapner never mentioned his fondness for Japanese cuisine. "I was wowed," he said.

Ritz-Carlton is the only service company to have won the prestigious Malcolm Baldrige National Quality Award twice—in 1992 and 1999. Companies worldwide strive to be "the Ritz-Carlton" of their industries. In 2000, the company launched the Ritz-Carlton Leadership Center, where anyone can study the brand's cult of customer service for $2,000. The center has addressed topics such as "talent benchmarking" and "empowerment using customer recognition to boost loyalty" for more than 800 companies, including Starbucks, Microsoft, and Coca-Cola. The following six steps can be followed and implemented by any company to become the Ritz-Carlton of its industry:

1. **Make customer service an elite club.** Ritz-Carlton has devised a rigorous interview process to identify the positive team players who, according to in-house statistics, become top performers. Executives believe that the company is effective not only in picking great talent, but also in conveying the message that working at Ritz-Carlton is a privilege.

2. **Once you have the right people, indoctrinate them.** Ritz-Carlton spends about $5,000 to train each new hire. It begins with a two-day introduction to company values (it's all about the service) along with a 21-day course focused on job responsibilities, such as a bellman's 28 steps to greeting a guest: "A warm and sincere greeting. Use the guest's name, if and when possible." Tracy Butler Hamilton, a retired bond trader who has stayed at a Ritz-Carlton in Atlanta several times, recalls that the hotel's bartenders remembered not only her name, but also the name and favorite drink of her brother, who would sometimes visit. "He wasn't even staying at the hotel," Hamilton said.

3. **Treat staffers the way they should treat customers.** The Ritz-Carlton motto—"We are ladies and gentlemen serving ladies and gentlemen"—might sound corny, but it is taken seriously. The company celebrates not just employee birthdays, but also employment anniversaries. Regardless of position, every staff member can spend as much as $2,000 without management approval to resolve a guest's problem. Employees say the exemption lets them make a personal impact on a guest's experience, resulting in higher job satisfaction. The median annual nonmanagement turnover rate at luxury hotels is 44 percent; at Ritz-Carlton, it is only 25 percent.

4. **Offer "memorable" service.** "What others call complaints," said John Timmerman, vice president for quality and productivity, "we call opportunities." A tired euphemism elsewhere, the idea is truly embraced at Ritz-Carlton. In one case, an administrative assistant at Ritz-Carlton Philadelphia overheard a guest lamenting that he had forgotten to pack formal shoes and would have to wear hiking boots to an important meeting; early the next morning, she delivered to the awestruck man a new pair in his size and favorite color. (In a more intimate example, a housekeeper recently traded shoes with a woman who needed a different pair.)

5. **Talk about values and stoke enthusiasm.** Every day at the chain's 57 hotels, all 25,000 Ritz-Carlton employees participate in a 15-minute "lineup" to talk about one of the basics. The ritual makes Ritz-Carlton one of the few large companies that set aside time for a daily discussion of core values.

6. **Eschew technology, except where it improves service.** Other hotels may be experimenting with automated check-in kiosks, but not Ritz-Carlton. "Not in a million years," said Vivian Deuschl, the company's vice president for public relations. "We will not replace human service with machines." But porters and doormen wear headsets, so when they spot your name on luggage tags, they can radio the information to the front desk. In addition, an in-house database called the Customer Loyalty Anticipation Satisfaction System stores guest preferences, such as whether an individual likes Seagram's ginger ale or Canada Dry. The software also alerts front-desk clerks when a guest who has stayed at other Ritz-Carltons has a habit of inquiring about the best sushi in town.[51]

Questions

1. What are the two different types of CRM and how has the Ritz-Carlton used them to become a world-class customer-service business?

2. Determine which of Ritz-Carlton's six steps of customer service is the most important for its business.

3. Rank Ritz-Carlton's six steps of customer service in order of greatest to least importance in a CRM strategy for an online book-selling business such as Amazon.com.

4. Describe three ways Ritz-Carlton can extend its customer reach by performing CRM functions over the Internet.

5. The sixth step states to eschew technology—"We will not replace human service with machines." Do you agree that customer service and satisfaction would decrease at Ritz-Carlton if it used technology such as automatic check-in kiosks? Why or why not? Do you think that Ritz-Carlton might find itself at a competitive disadvantage to hotels that are embracing technology to become more efficient and effective? Why or why not?

<<BUSINESS PLUG-IN POINTER

Review **Business Plug-In B9 "Customer Relationship Management"** for a complete overview of CRM strategies along with a detailed look at the many different technologies that sales, marketing, and customer service departments can use to strengthen customer relationships.

<table>
<tr><td>CHAPTER</td><td>12</td><td>Integrating the Organization from End to End—Enterprise Resource Planning</td></tr>
</table>

CHAPTER *12* Integrating the Organization from End to End—Enterprise Resource Planning

LEARNING OUTCOMES

12.1. Describe the role information plays in enterprise resource planning systems.

12.2. Identify the primary forces driving the explosive growth of enterprise resource planning systems.

12.3. Explain the business value of integrating supply chain management, customer relationship management, and enterprise resource planning systems.

Enterprise Resource Planning (ERP)

Enterprise resource planning systems serve as the organization's backbone in providing fundamental decision-making support. In the past, departments made decisions independent of each other. ERP systems provide a foundation for collaboration between departments, enabling people in different business areas to communicate. ERP systems have been widely adopted in large organizations to store critical knowledge used to make the decisions that drive performance.

To be competitive, organizations must always strive for excellence in every business process enterprisewide, a daunting challenge if the organization has multisite operations worldwide. To obtain operational efficiencies, lower costs, improve supplier and customer relations, and increase revenues and market share, all units of the organization must work together harmoniously toward congruent goals. An ERP system will help an organization achieve this.

Hot Topics

One company that has blazed a trail with ERP is Atlanta-based United Parcel Service of America, Inc. (UPS). UPS has developed a number of Web-based applications that track information such as recipient signatures, addresses, time in transit, and other shipping information. These services run on an SAP foundation that UPS customers can connect to using real-time ERP information obtained from the UPS Web site. Currently, 6.2 million tracking requests pass through the company's Web site each day. By automating the information delivery process, UPS has dramatically reduced the demand on its customer service representatives. Just as important, UPS has improved relationships with its business partners—in effect integrating its business with theirs—by making it easier for consumers to find delivery information without leaving the Web site of the merchant.[52]

The heart of an ERP system is a central database that collects information from and feeds information into all the ERP system's individual application components (called modules), supporting diverse business functions such as accounting, manufacturing, marketing, and human resources. When a user enters or updates information in one module, it is immediately and automatically updated throughout the entire system, as illustrated in Figure 12.1.

ERP automates business processes such as order fulfillment—taking an order from a customer, shipping the purchase, and then billing for it. With an ERP system, when a customer service representative takes an order from a customer, he or she has all the information necessary to complete the order (the customer's credit rating and order history, the company's inventory levels, and the delivery schedule).

FIGURE 12.1

ERP Integration Data Flow

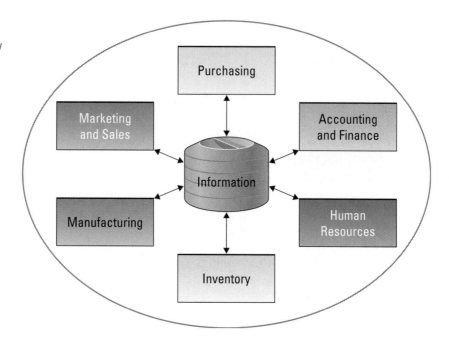

Everyone else in the company sees the same information and has access to the database that holds the customer's new order. When one department finishes with the order, it is automatically routed via the ERP system to the next department. To find out where the order is at any point, a user need only log in to the ERP system and track it down, as illustrated in Figure 12.2. The order process moves like a bolt of lightning through the organization, and customers get their orders faster and with fewer errors than ever before. ERP can apply that same magic to the other major business processes, such as employee benefits or financial reporting.[53]

Bringing the Organization Together

In most organizations, information has traditionally been isolated within specific departments, whether on an individual database, in a file cabinet, or on an employee's PC. ERP enables employees across the organization to share information across a

FIGURE 12.2

ERP Process Flow

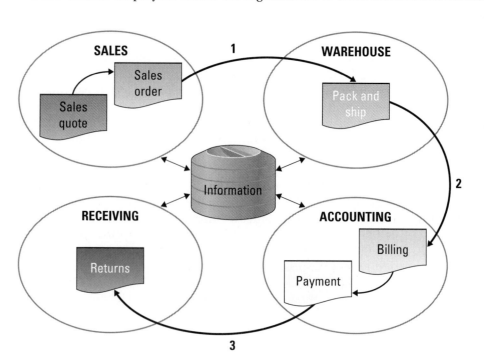

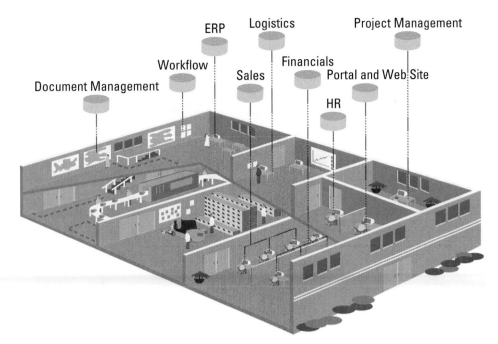

FIGURE 12.3

The Organization before ERP

single, centralized database. With extended portal capabilities, an organization can also involve its suppliers and customers to participate in the workflow process, allowing ERP to penetrate the entire value chain, and help the organization achieve greater operational efficiency (see Figures 12.3 and 12.4).[54]

ERP Success

The Evolution of ERP

Originally, ERP solutions were developed to deliver automation across multiple units of an organization, to help facilitate the manufacturing process and address issues such as raw materials, inventory, order entry, and distribution.

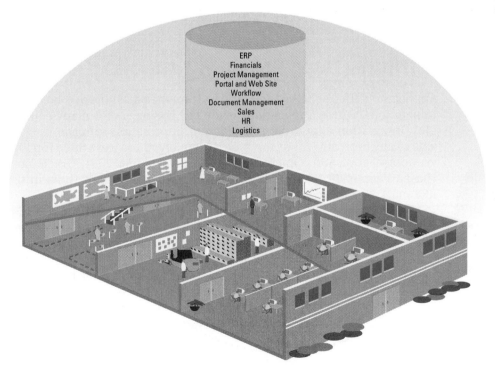

FIGURE 12.4

ERP—Bringing the Organization Together

FIGURE 12.5

The Evolution of ERP

ERP
- Materials Planning
- Order Entry
- Distribution
- General Ledger
- Accounting
- Shop Floor Control

Extended ERP
- Scheduling
- Forecasting
- Capacity Planning
- e-Commerce
- Warehousing
- Logistics

ERP-II
- Project Management
- Knowledge Management
- Workflow Management
- Customer Relationship Management
- Human Resource Management
- Portal Capability
- Integrated Financials

| 1990 | 2000 | Present |

However, ERP was unable to extend to other functional areas of the company such as sales, marketing, and shipping. It could not tie in any CRM capabilities that would allow organizations to capture customer-specific information, nor did it work with Web sites or portals used for customer service or order fulfillment. Call center or quality assurance staff could not tap into the ERP solution, nor could ERP handle document management, such as cataloging contracts and purchase orders.[55]

ERP has grown over the years to become part of the extended enterprise. From its beginning as a tool for materials planning, it has extended to warehousing, distribution, and order entry. With its next evolution, ERP expands to the front office including CRM. Now administrative, sales, marketing, and human resources staff can share a tool that is truly enterprisewide. To compete on a functional level today, companies must adopt an enterprisewide approach to ERP that utilizes the Internet and connects to every facet of the value chain. Figure 12.5 shows how ERP has grown since the 1990s to accommodate the needs of the entire organization.[56]

FIGURE 12.6

SCM Market Overview

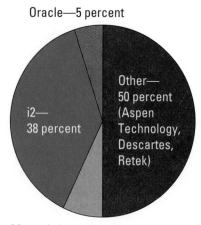

Oracle—5 percent

i2—38 percent

Other—50 percent (Aspen Technology, Descartes, Retek)

Manugistics—7 percent

Integrating SCM, CRM, and ERP

Applications such as SCM, CRM, and ERP are the backbone of e-business. Integration of these applications is the key to success for many companies. Integration allows the unlocking of information to make it available to any user, anywhere, anytime. Originally, there were three top ERP vendors—PeopleSoft, Oracle, and SAP. In December 2004, Oracle purchased PeopleSoft for $10 billion, leaving two main competitors in the ERP market—Oracle and SAP.

Most organizations today have no choice but to piece their SCM, CRM, and ERP applications together since no one vendor can respond to every organizational need; hence, customers purchase applications from multiple vendors. Oracle and SAP both offer CRM and SCM components. However, these modules are not as functional or flexible as the modules offered by industry leaders of SCM and CRM such as Siebel and i2 Technologies, as depicted in Figures 12.6 and 12.7. As a result, organizations face the challenge of integrating their systems. For example, a single organization might choose its CRM components from Siebel, SCM components from i2, and financial components and HR management components from Oracle. Figure 12.8 displays the general audience and purpose for each of these applications that have to be integrated.

From its roots in the California Gold Rush era, San Francisco–based Del Monte Foods has grown to become the nation's largest producer and distributor of premium quality processed fruits, vegetables, and tomato products. With annual sales of over $3 billion, Del Monte is also one of the country's largest producers, distributors, and marketers of private-label food and pet products with a powerful portfolio of brands including Del Monte, StarKist, Nature's Goodness, 9Lives, and Kibbles 'n Bits.

Del Monte's acquisition of StarKist, Nature's Goodness, 9Lives, and Kibbles 'n Bits from the H. J. Heinz Company required an integration between Del Monte's and H. J. Heinz's business processes. Del Monte needed to overhaul its IT infrastructure, migrating from multiple platforms including UNIX and mainframe systems and consolidating applications centrally on a single system. The work required integration of business processes across manufacturing, financial, supply chain, decision support, and transactional reporting areas.

The revamp of Del Monte's architecture stemmed from a strategic decision. Del Monte decided to implement an ERP system to support its entire U.S. operations, with headquarters in San Francisco, operations in Pittsburgh, and distribution centers and manufacturing facilities across the country. The company concluded that the only way it could unite its global operations and open its system to its customers, which are mainly large retailers, was through the use of an ERP system. Among other key factors was the need to embrace an e-business strategy. The challenge facing Del Monte was to select an ERP system to merge multiple systems quickly and cost effectively. If financial and customer service targets were to be achieved, Del Monte needed to integrate new businesses that

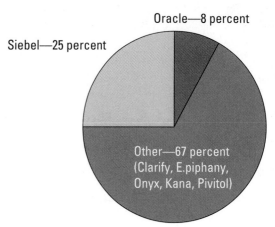

FIGURE 12.7

CRM Market Overview

ERP Solutions

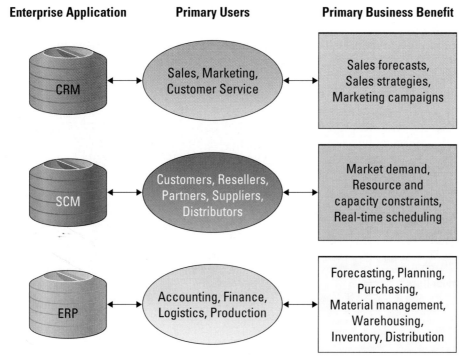

FIGURE 12.8

Primary Users and Business Benefits of Strategic Initiatives more than doubled the size of the company. Since implementing the ERP system, customers and trading partners are now provided with a single, consistent, and integrated view of the company.[57]

Integration Tools

Effectively managing the transformation to an integrated enterprise will be critical to the success of the 21st century organization. The key is the integration of the disparate IT applications. An integrated enterprise infuses support areas, such as finance and human resources, with a strong customer orientation. Integrations are achieved using *middleware*—several different types of software that sit in the middle of and provide connectivity between two or more software applications. Middleware translates information between disparate systems. *Enterprise application integration (EAI) middleware* represents a new approach to middleware by packaging together commonly used functionality, such as providing prebuilt links to popular enterprise applications, which reduces the time necessary to develop solutions that integrate applications from multiple vendors. A few leading vendors of EAI middleware include Active Software, Vitria Technology, and Extricity. Figure 12.9 displays the data points where these applications integrate and illustrates the underlying premise of architecture infrastructure design.

Companies run on interdependent applications, such as SCM, CRM, and ERP. If one application performs poorly, the entire customer value delivery system is affected. For example, no matter how great a company is at CRM, if its SCM system does not work and the customer never receives the finished product, the company will lose that customer. The world-class enterprises of tomorrow must be built on the foundation of world-class applications implemented today.

Coca-Cola's business model is a common one among well-known franchisers. Coca-Cola gets the majority of its $18 billion in annual revenue from franchise fees it earns from bottlers all over the world. Bottlers, along with the franchise, license Coke's secret recipe and many others including recipes for Odwalla, Nestea, Minute Maid, and Sprite. Now Coca-Cola hopes that bottlers will also buy into adopting common business practices using a service-oriented architecture ERP system.

The target platform chosen by Coca-Cola is mySAP enterprise resource planning (ERP) by SAP. If it works, Coca-Cola and its bottlers stand to make and save a lot of money, and SAP will be able to position itself as one of the dominant players in

FIGURE 12.9

Integrations between SCM, CRM, and ERP Applications

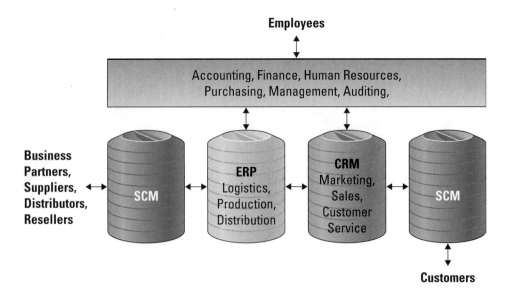

SoA-enabled ERP. Already, Coca-Cola and many of its bottlers use versions of SAP for finance, manufacturing, and a number of administrative functions. But Coca-Cola wants everyone to move to a "services" architecture environment.

Coca-Cola hopes that this services standardization will make its supply chain more efficient and reduce costs. In explaining why a services approach is so vitally important, Jean-Michel Ares, CIO of Coca-Cola, stated, "That will allow bottlers to converge one step at a time, one process area at a time, one module at a time, at a time that's right for the bottler. We can march across the bottling world incrementally."[58]

Enterprise Resource Planning's Explosive Growth

Cisco Systems Inc., a $22 billion producer of computer-network equipment, is using an ERP system to create a consolidated trial balance sheet and a consolidated income statement within a half day of a fiscal quarter's close, compared with two weeks more than five years ago when Cisco was a $4 billion company. What's more, during those years, the time devoted to transaction processing has fallen from 65 percent to 35 percent, and finance group expenses, as a percentage of the total company revenues, have fallen from 2 percent to 1.3 percent. All that has occurred even as Cisco added people to its finance department to keep pace with the company's growth. The ERP system gives Cisco executives a look at revenues, expenses, margins, and profits every day of every month.[59]

Business in the 21st century is complex, fluid, and customer-centric. It requires stringent, yet flexible processes and communications systems that extend globally and respond instantaneously. The processes and systems must be integrated. No part of the enterprise can escape the pressure to deliver measurable results. Here are a few reasons ERP solutions have proven to be such a powerful force:

- ERP is a logical solution to the mess of incompatible applications that had sprung up in most businesses.
- ERP addresses the need for global information sharing and reporting.
- ERP is used to avoid the pain and expense of fixing legacy systems.[60]

To qualify as a true ERP solution, the system not only must integrate various organization processes, but also must be:

- **Flexible**—An ERP system should be flexible in order to respond to the changing needs of an enterprise.
- **Modular and open**—An ERP system has to have an open system architecture, meaning that any module can be interfaced with or detached whenever required without affecting the other modules. The system should support multiple hardware platforms for organizations that have a heterogeneous collection of systems. It must also support third-party add-on components.
- **Comprehensive**—An ERP system should be able to support a variety of organizational functions and must be suitable for a wide range of business organizations.
- **Beyond the company**—An ERP system must not be confined to organizational boundaries but rather support online connectivity to business partners or customers.

ERP as a business concept resounds as a powerful internal information management nirvana: Everyone involved in sourcing, producing, and delivering the company's product works with the same information, which eliminates redundancies, cuts wasted time, and removes misinformation.

1. If you operated a business entirely on Second Life would you require an ERP system? Why or why not?

2. How would an ERP system be used in Second Life to support a global organization?

Chapter Twelve Case: Gearing Up at REI

Recreational Equipment Inc. (REI) boasts annual revenues between $500 million and $1 billion and more than 10,000 employees. According to Forrester Research, REI is an industry leader for its "best practice" multichannel CRM strategy, which allows customers to seamlessly purchase products at the company's 70 retail stores as well as by telephone, through mail order, and on the Internet.

REI's Internet Strategy

To boost in-store sales, REI developed a comprehensive Internet strategy. In June 2003, REI.com launched free in-store pickup for customers who ordered online. The belief was that people who visit stores to collect their online purchases might spend more money upon seeing the colorful displays of clothing, climbing gear, bikes, and camping equipment.

REI's strategy paid off. "One out of every three people who buy something online will spend an additional $90 in the store when they come to pick something up," said Joan Broughton, REI's vice president of multichannel programs. That tendency translated into a healthy 1 percent increase in store sales. Broughton's motto is "a sale is a sale is a sale—whether online, in stores, or through catalogs." The Internet is not an isolated channel with its own operational metrics or exclusive customer group.

As the Web has matured as a retail channel, consumers have turned to online shopping as an additional place to interact with a retailer rather than as a replacement for existing channels such as stores or catalogs. According to Jupiter Research, while its prediction of $117 billion in online sales for 2008 represents only 5 percent of total retail sales, the company estimates that 30 percent of offline sales will be influenced by consumers' online research. Essentially, that means retailers will need to leverage their online properties in ways that are synergistic with and complementary to their offline operations.

REI's CRM Strategy

REI.com was one of the first companies to offer a broad selection of outdoor gear plus expert advice and in-depth information about outdoor products and recreation online. The highly successful Web site currently receives over 2.5 million visitors per day, and online sales represent 15 percent of REI's total sales revenue.

REI realized it could provide a consistent and seamless customer experience whether the customer is shopping via its Web site or at its in-store kiosks by consolidating its four disparate database systems into one customer relationship management system. The system integrates multiple sales channels to manage mail orders, in-store special orders, kiosk operations, and REI Adventures, the company's adventure travel service. This gives the company a complete view of all customers regardless of their shopping preference. In addition to finding items such as backpacks, bicycles, or tents through the system, customers can also research hiking trails, camping guides, and cycling techniques.

The system is providing REI with the confidence it needs to expand customer service, such as the new REI store pickup. REI has also expanded its multichannel philosophy to include services.

In February 2004, the company launched an integrated gift registry that allows people to set up lists for gifts that can be purchased in any retail channel. The registry also allows consumers to post messages to other site visitors, seeking information or specific, hard-to-find products. Customers can create a gift registry in several ways: Visit a store and use a kiosk or scan products with a handheld device, call customer service, or visit REI.com. Once a registry is set up, REI sends e-mail to a designated list of recipients, complete with a link to a personalized registry page. According to Brad Brown, REI's vice president of information services, the registry is a way to expand sales among consumers who do not traditionally shop at REI.

REI's SCM Strategy

REI offers free in-store pickup for online orders as a strategy specifically designed to get people into the stores. To make that strategy as cost-efficient as possible, the company uses the same trucks that restock its stores to fulfill online orders slated for in-store pickup. To do this, REI had to integrate order information from its Web site and replenishment orders from its stores.

Integrating the two types of order information was not complex, Brown said. What was difficult, however, was coordinating fulfillment of both online and replenishment orders because "orders placed on the Web [by customers] are nothing like replenishment orders that stores place," he said. Online orders are picked from the warehouse at the time of the order and then put in a queue until the appropriate truck is loaded, whereas store orders are picked by an automated replenishment system that typically picks orders at one time based on either a weekly or biweekly replenishment schedule.

To make in-store pickup a reality, Brown's group wrote a "promise algorithm" that informs customers of a delivery date when they place an online order. Timing can get tricky when orders are placed the day before a truck is scheduled to depart the warehouse with a store-replenishment delivery. For example, if an online order is placed on a Monday night and a truck is scheduled to depart Tuesday morning, the system promises the customer a pickup date of a week later, as if the order would be placed on the following week's truck. However, REI will shoot for fulfilling the order that night; if it can do it, REI (and, ultimately, the customer) is happy because the order arrives sooner than was promised.

Creating effective business-to-consumer retail Web sites entails more than simply calculating sales figures; it also involves multiple projects and delivering the functionality that users expect while mitigating risk and change.[61]

Questions

1. What business impact could REI gain by using a digital dashboard from its ERP system?
2. How can REI benefit from using artificial intelligence to support its business operations?
3. How does REI's ERP system help employees improve their decision-making capabilities and highlight potential business opportunities?
4. How could an SCM system improve REI's business operations?
5. Provide an illustration of REI's SCM system including all upstream and downstream participants.
6. Determine two pieces of customer information that REI could extrapolate from its ERP system that would help it manage its business more effectively.
7. How can an ERP system help REI gain business intelligence in its operations?
8. What is the business benefit for REI in integrating its CRM, SCM, and ERP systems?

<< BUSINESS PLUG-IN POINTER

Review **Business Plug-In B10 "Enterprise Resource Planning"** for a detailed analysis of different ERP strategies and best practices. The plug-in also focuses on the two basic groups of ERP systems—core and extended.

Today, organizations of various sizes are proving systems that support decision making and opportunity seizing are essential to thriving in the highly competitive electronic world. We are living in an era when information technology is a primary tool, knowledge is a strategic asset, and decision making and problem solving are paramount skills. The tougher, larger, and more demanding a problem or opportunity is, and the faster and more competitive the environment is, the more important decision-making and problem-solving skills become. This unit discussed numerous tools and strategic initiatives that an organization can take advantage of to assist in decision making:

- Supply chain management (SCM)—managing information flows within the supply chain to maximize total supply chain effectiveness and profitability.

- Customer relationship management (CRM)—managing all aspects of customers' relationships with an organization to increase customer loyalty and retention and an organization's profitability.

- Enterprise resource planning (ERP)—integrating all departments and functions throughout an organization into a single IT system (or integrated set of IT systems) so that managers and leaders can make enterprisewide decisions by viewing enterprisewide information on all business operations.

✳ KEY TERMS

Analytical CRM, 148
Artificial intelligence (AI), 125
Association detection, 129
Bullwhip effect, 136
Cluster analysis, 129
Consolidation, 122
Decision support system (DSS), 120
Demand planning software, 137
Digital dashboard, 122
Drill-down, 122
E-business, 117
Enterprise application integration (EAI) middleware, 158
Executive information system (EIS), 122

Expert system, 125
Forecast, 130
Fuzzy logic, 127
Genetic algorithm, 127
Goal-seeking analysis, 120
Intelligent agent, 127
Intelligent system, 125
Logistics, 135
Market basket analysis, 130
Middleware, 158
Model, 118
Neural network or artificial neural network, 126
Online analytical processing (OLAP), 119
Online transaction processing (OLTP), 119

Operational CRM, 148
Personalization, 149
Sensitivity analysis, 120
Shopping bot, 127
Slice-and-dice, 122
Supply chain, 133
Supply chain execution (SCE) software, 137
Supply chain management (SCM), 133
Supply chain planning (SCP) software, 137
Supply chain visibility, 136
Transaction processing system (TPS), 119
Time-series information, 130
What-if analysis, 120

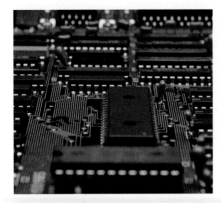  

Dell's Famous Supply Chain

Speed is at the core of everything Dell does. Dell assembles nearly 80,000 computers every 24 hours. The computer manufacturer has done more than any other company when it comes to tweaking its supply chain. More than a decade ago, Dell carried 20 to 25 days of inventory in a sprawling network of warehouses. Today, Dell does not have a single warehouse and carries only two hours of inventory in its factories and a maximum of just 72 hours across its entire operation. Dell's vast, global supply chain is in constant overdrive making the company one of the fastest, most hyperefficient organizations on the planet.

Disaster Occurs

In 2002, a 10-day labor lockout shut down 29 West Coast ports extending from Los Angeles to Seattle, idled 10,000 union dockworkers, and blocked hundreds of cargo ships from unloading raw materials and finished goods. The port closings paralyzed global supply chains and ultimately cost U.S. consumers and businesses billions of dollars.

Analysts expected Dell, with its just-in-time manufacturing model, would be especially hard hit when parts failed to reach its two U.S.-based factories. Without warehouses filled with motherboards and hard drives the world's largest PC maker would simply find itself with nothing to sell within a matter of days. Dell knew all too well that its ultra-lean, high-speed business model left it vulnerable to just such a situation. "When a labor problem or an earthquake or a SARS epidemic breaks out, we've got to react quicker than anyone else," said Dick Hunter, the company's supply chain expert. "There's no other choice. We know these things are going to happen; we must move fast to fix them. We just can't tolerate any kind of delay."

Fortunately, the same culture of speed and flexibility that seems to put Dell at the mercy of disruptions also helps it deal with them. Dell was in constant, round-the-clock communication with its parts makers in Taiwan, China, and Malaysia and its U.S.-based shipping partners. Hunter dispatched a "tiger team" of 10 logistics specialists to Long Beach, California, and other ports; they worked with Dell's carrying and freight-forwarding networks to assemble a contingency plan.

When the tiger team confirmed that the closings were all but certain, Dell moved into high gear. It chartered 18 airplanes (747s) from UPS, Northwest Airlines, and China Airlines. A 747 holds the equivalent of 10 tractor-trailers—enough parts to manufacture 10,000 PCs. The bidding for the planes grew fierce, running as high as $1 million for a one-way flight from Asia to the West Coast. Dell got in the bidding early and kept costs around $500,000 per plane. Dell also worked with its Asia-based suppliers to ensure that its parts were always at the Shanghai and Taipei airports in time for its returning charters to land, reload, refuel, and take off. The company was consistently able to get its planes to the United States and back within 33 hours, which kept its costs down and its supply chain moving.

Meanwhile, Dell had people on the ground in every major harbor. In Asia, the freight specialists saw to it that Dell's parts were the last to be loaded onto each cargo ship so they would be unloaded first when the ship hit the West Coast. The biggest test came when the ports reopened and companies scrambled to sort through the backed-up mess of thousands of containers. Hunter's tiger team had anticipated this logistical nightmare. Even though Dell had PC components in hundreds of containers on 50 ships, it knew the exact moment when each component cycled through the harbor, and it was among the first to unload its parts and speed them to its factories in Austin, Texas, and Nashville, Tennessee. In the end, Dell did the impossible: It survived a 10-day supply chain blackout with roughly 72 hours of inventory without delaying a single customer order.

The aftershocks of the port closings reverberated for weeks. Many companies began to question the wisdom of running so lean in an uncertain world, and demand for warehouse space soared as they piled up buffer inventory to ensure against labor unrest, natural disasters, and terrorist attacks.

Building a "Dell-like" Supply Chain

Dell's ultimate competitive weapon is speed, which gives the technical giant's bottom line a real boost. Figure Unit 3.2 displays a five-point plan for building a fast supply chain—direct from Dell.[62]

Questions

1. Identify a few key metrics a Dell marketing executive might want to monitor on a digital dashboard.
2. Determine how Dell can benefit from using decision support systems and executive information systems in its business.
3. Describe how Dell has influenced visibility, consumer behavior, competition, and speed though the use of IT in its supply chain.
4. Explain the seven principles of SCM in reference to Dell's business model.
5. Identify how Dell can use CRM to improve its business operations.
6. Explain how an ERP system could help Dell gain business intelligence.

FIGURE UNIT 3.2

How to Build a Dell-like Supply Chain

Dell-Like Supply Chain Plan
1. **The supply chain starts with the customer.** By cutting out retailers and selling directly to its customers, Dell is in a far better position to forecast real customer demand.
2. **Replace inventory with information.** To operate with close to zero inventory, Dell communicates constantly with its suppliers. It sends out status updates three times a day from its assembly plants; every week it updates its quarterly demand forecasts. By making communication its highest priority, Dell ensures the lowest possible inventory.
3. **If you cannot measure it, you cannot manage it.** Dell knows what works because it measures everything from days in inventory to the time it takes to build a PC. As Dell slashed those numbers, it got more efficient.
4. **Complexity slows you down.** Dell cut the number of its core PC suppliers from several hundred to about 25. It standardized critical PC components, which streamlined its manufacturing. Dell got faster by making things simpler.
5. **Create a watershed mind-set.** Dell is not content with incremental improvement; it demands massive change. Each year, it wants its Austin-based PC-assembly plant—already very fast—to improve production by 30 percent. "You don't get a big result if you do not challenge people with big goals," Dell CEO Kevin Rollins said.

Revving Up Sales at Harley-Davidson

Harley-Davidson produces 290,000 motorcycles and generates over $4 billion in net revenues yearly. There is a mystique associated with a Harley-Davidson motorcycle. No other motorcycle in the world has the look, feel, and sound of a Harley-Davidson, and many people consider it a two-wheeled piece of art. Demand for Harley-Davidson motorcycles outweighs supply. Some models have up to a two-year wait list. Harley-Davidson has won a number of awards including:

- Rated second in *ComputerWorld*'s Top 100 Best Places to Work in IT in 2003.
- Rated 51st in *Fortune*'s 100 Best Companies to Work For in 2003.
- Rated first in *Fortune*'s 5 Most Admired Companies in the motor vehicles industry.
- Rated first in the Top 10 Sincerest Corporations by the *Harris Interactive Report.*
- Rated second in the Top 10 Overall Corporations by the *Harris Interactive Report.*

Harley-Davidson's Focus on Technology

Harley-Davidson's commitment to technology is paying off: In 2003 it decreased production costs and inventories by $40 million as a direct result of using technology to increase production capacity. The company's technology budget of $50 million is more than 2 percent of its revenue, which is far above the manufacturing industry average. More than 50 percent of this budget is devoted to developing new technology strategies.

Harley-Davidson focuses on implementing e-business strategies to strengthen its market share and increase customer satisfaction. Over 80 projects were in development in 2003, and the majority of the new projects focused on sharing information, gaining business intelligence, and enhancing decision making.

Talon, Harley-Davidson's proprietary dealer management system, is one of its most successful technology initiatives. Talon handles inventory, vehicle registration, warranties, and point-of-sale transactions for all Harley-Davidson dealerships. The system performs numerous time-saving tasks such as checking dealer inventory, automatically generating parts orders, and allowing the company to review and analyze information across its global organization. Talon gives Harley-Davidson managers a 360-degree view into enterprisewide information that supports strategic goal setting and decision making throughout all levels of the organization.

Building Supplier Relationships

Harley-Davidson invests time, energy, and resources into continually improving its company-to-company strategic business initiatives such as supply chain management. The company understands and values the importance of building strong relationships with its suppliers. To develop these important relationships the company deployed Manugistics, an SCM system that allows it to do business with suppliers in a collaborative, Web-based environment. The company plans to use the SCM software to better manage its flow of materials and improve collaboration activities with its key suppliers.

Building Customer Relationships

Each time a customer reaches out to the company, Harley-Davidson has an opportunity to build a trusting relationship with that particular customer. Harley-Davidson realizes that it takes more than just building and selling motorcycles to fulfill the dreams of its customers. For this reason, the company strives to deliver unforgettable experiences along with its top quality products.

Harley-Davidson sells over $500 million worth of parts and accessories to its loyal followers. Ken Ostermann, Harley-Davidson's manager of electronic commerce and communications, decided that the company could increase these sales if it could offer the products online. The dilemma facing Ostermann's online strategy was that selling jackets, saddlebags, and T-shirts directly to consumers would bypass Harley-Davidson's 650 dealers, who depend on the high-margin accessories to fuel their businesses' profits. Ostermann's solution was to build an online store, Harley-Davidson.com, which prompts customers to select a participating Harley-Davidson dealership before placing any online orders. The selected dealership is then responsible for fulfilling the order. This strategy has helped ensure that the dealers remain the focal point of customers' buying experiences.

To guarantee that every customer has a highly satisfying online buying experience, the company asks the dealers to agree to a number of standards including:

- Checking online orders twice daily.
- Shipping online orders within 24 hours.
- Responding to customer inquiries within 24 hours.

The company still monitors online customer metrics such as time taken to process orders, number of returned orders, and number of incorrect orders, ensuring that Harley-Davidson delivers on its message of prompt, excellent service consistently to all its loyal customers. The company receives over 1 million visitors a month to its online store. Customer satisfaction scores for the Web site moved from the extremely satisfied level to the exceptional level in a year.

Another of Harley-Davidson's customer-centric strategies is its Harley's Owners Group (HOG), established in 1983. HOG is the largest factory-sponsored motorcycle club in the world with more than 600,000 members. HOG offers a wide array of events, rides, and benefits to its members. HOG is one of the key drivers helping to build a strong sense of community among Harley-Davidson owners. Harley-Davidson has built a customer following that is extremely loyal, a difficult task to accomplish in any industry.

Harley-Davidson's Corporate Culture

Harley-Davidson employees are the engine behind its outstanding performance and the foundation of the company's overall success. Harley-Davidson believes in a strong sense of corporate ethics and values, and the company's top five core values serve as a framework for the entire corporation:

1. Tell the truth.
2. Be fair.
3. Keep your promises.
4. Respect the individual.
5. Encourage intellectual curiosity.

The company credits its core values as the primary reason it won the two prestigious awards from the *Harris Interactive Report,* one of the most respected consumer reviews for corporate sincerity, ethics, and standards. Sticking to strong ethics and values is and will continue to be a top priority for the company and its employees.

To enhance its enterprise further Harley-Davidson plans to keep taking advantage of new technologies and strategies including a Web-based approach to accessing information and an enterprisewide system to consolidate procurement at its eight U.S. facilities.[63]

Questions

1. Explain how Talon helps Harley-Davidson employees improve their decision-making capabilities.

2. Identify a few key metrics a Harley-Davidson marketing executive might want to monitor on a digital dashboard.

3. How can Harley-Davidson benefit from using decision support systems and executive information systems in its business?

4. How would Harley-Davidson's business be affected if it decided to sell accessories directly to its online customers? Include a brief discussion of the ethics involved with this decision.

5. Evaluate the HOG CRM strategy and recommend an additional benefit Harley-Davidson could provide to its HOG members to increase customer satisfaction.

6. How could Harley-Davidson's SCM system, Manugistics, improve its business operations?

7. Provide a potential illustration of Harley-Davidson's SCM system including all upstream and downstream participants.

8. Explain how an ERP system could help Harley-Davidson gain business intelligence in its operations.

✳ MAKING BUSINESS DECISIONS

1. Implementing an ERP System

Blue Dog Inc. is a leading manufacturer in the high-end sunglasses industry. Blue Dog Inc. reached record revenue levels of over $250 million last year. The company is currently deciding on the possibility of implementing an ERP system to help decrease production costs and increase inventory control. Many of the executives are nervous about making such a large investment in an ERP system due to its low success rates. As a senior manager at Blue Dog Inc. you have been asked to compile a list of the potential benefits and risks associated with implementing an ERP system along with your recommendations for the steps the company can take to ensure a successful implementation.

2. DSS and EIS

Dr. Rosen runs a large dental conglomerate—Teeth Doctors—that staffs over 700 dentists in six states. Dr. Rosen is interested in purchasing a competitor called Dentix that has 150 dentists in three additional states. Before deciding whether to purchase Dentix, Dr. Rosen must consider several issues:

- The cost of purchasing Dentix.
- The location of the Dentix offices.
- The current number of customers per dentist, per office, and per state.
- The merger between the two companies.
- The professional reputation of Dentix.
- Other competitors.

Explain how Dr. Rosen and Teeth Doctors can benefit from the use of information systems to make an accurate business decision in regard to the potential purchase of Dentix.

3. SCM, CRM, and ERP

Jamie Ash is interested in applying for a job at a large software vendor. One of the criteria for the job is a detailed understanding of strategic initiatives such as SCM, CRM, and ERP. Jamie has no knowledge of any of these initiatives and cannot even explain what the acronyms mean. Jamie has come to you for help. She would like you to compile a summary of the three initiatives including an analysis of how the three are similar and how they are different. Jamie would also like to perform some self-training via the Web so be sure to provide her with several additional links to key Web sites that offer detailed overviews on SCM, CRM, and ERP.

4. Customer Relationship Management Strategies

On average, it costs an organization six times more to sell to a new customer than to sell to an existing customer. As the co-owner of a medium-sized luggage distributor, you have recently been notified by your EIS systems that sales for the past three months have decreased by an average of 17 percent. The reasons for the decline in sales are numerous, including a poor economy, people's aversion to travel because of the terrorist attacks, and some negative publicity your company received regarding a defective product line. In a group, explain how implementing a CRM system can help you understand and combat the decline in sales. Be sure to justify why a CRM system is important to your business and its future growth.

5. Finding Information on Decision Support Systems

You are working on the sales team for a small catering company that maintains 75 employees and generates $1 million in revenues per year. The owner, Pam Hetz, wants to understand how she can use decision support systems to help grow her business. Pam has an initial understanding of DSS systems and is interested in learning more about what types are available, how they can be used in a small business, and the cost associated with different DSS systems. In a group, research the Web site www.dssresources.com and compile a presentation that discusses DSS systems in detail. Be sure to answer all Pam's questions on DSS systems in the presentation.

6. Analyzing Dell's Supply Chain Management System

Dell's supply chain strategy is legendary. Essentially, if you want to build a successful SCM system your best bet is to model your SCM system after Dell's. In a team, research Dell's supply chain management strategy on the Web and create a report discussing any new SCM updates and strategies the company is using that were not discussed in this text. Be sure to include a graphical presentation of Dell's current supply chain model.

7. Gaining Business Intelligence from Strategic Initiatives

You are a new employee in the customer service department at Premier One, a large pet food distributor. The company, founded by several veterinarians, has been in business for three years and focuses on providing nutritious pet food at a low cost. The company currently has 90 employees and operates in seven states. Sales over the past three years have tripled and the manual systems currently in place are no longer sufficient to run the business. Your first task is to meet with your new team and create a presentation for the president and chief executive officer describing supply chain management, customer relationship management, and enterprise resource planning systems. The presentation should highlight the main benefits Premier One can receive from these strategic initiatives along with any additional added business value that can be gained from the systems.

1. Great Stories

With the advent of the Internet, when customers have an unpleasant customer experience, the company no longer has to worry about them telling a few friends and family; the company has to worry about them telling everyone. Internet service providers are giving consumers frustrated with how they were treated by a company another means of fighting back. Free or low-cost computer space for Internet Web sites is empowering consumers to tell not only their friends, but also the world about the way they have been treated. A few examples of disgruntled customer stories from the Internet include:

- **Bad Experience with Blue Marble Biking**—Tourist on biking tour is bitten by dog, requires stitches. Company is barred from hotel because of incident, and in turn it bars the tourist from any further tours.
- **Best Buy Receipt Check**—Shopper declines to show register receipt for purchase to door guard at Lakewood Best Buy, which is voluntary. Employees attempt to seize cart, stand in shopper's path, and park a truck behind shopper's car to prevent departure.
- **Enterprise Rent-A-Car Is a Failing Enterprise**—Enterprise Rent-A-Car did not honor reservations, did not have cars ready as stated, rented cars with nearly empty tanks, and charged higher prices to corporate account holders.

Project Focus

The Internet is raising the stakes for customer service. With the ability to create a Web site dedicated to a particular issue, a disgruntled customer can have nearly the same reach as a manufacturer. The Internet is making it more difficult for companies to ignore their customers' complaints. In a group, search the Web for the most outrageous story of a disgruntled customer. A few places to start include:

- **Complain Complain (complaincomplain.net)**—provides professionally written, custom complaint letters to businesses.
- **The Complaint Department (www.thecomplaintdepartment.ca)**—a for-fee consumer complaint resolution and letter writing service.
- **The Complaint Station (www.thecomplaintstation.com)**—provides a central location to complain about issues related to companies' products, services, employment, and get rich quick scams.
- **Complaints.com Consumer Complaints (www.complaints.com)**—database of consumer complaints and consumer advocacy.
- **Baddealings.com (www.baddealings.com)**—forum and database on consumer complaints and scams on products and services.

2. Classic Car Problems

Classic Cars Inc. operates high-end automotive dealerships that offer luxury cars along with luxury service. The company is proud of its extensive inventory, top-of-the-line mechanics, and especially its exceptional service, which even includes a cappuccino bar at each dealership.

The company currently has 40 sales representatives at four locations. Each location maintains its own computer systems, and all sales representatives have their own contact management systems. This splintered approach to operations causes numerous problems including customer communication issues, pricing strategy issues, and inventory control issues. A few examples include:

- A customer shopping at one dealership can go to another dealership and receive a quote for a different price for the same car.
- Sales representatives are frequently stealing each other's customers and commissions.
- Sales representatives frequently send their customers to other dealerships to see specific cars and when the customer arrives, the car is not on the lot.
- Marketing campaigns are not designed to target specific customers; they are typically generic, such as 10 percent off a new car.
- If a sales representative quits, all of his or her customer information is lost.

Project Focus

You are working for Customer One, a small consulting company that specializes in CRM strategies. The owner of Classic Cars Inc., Tom Repicci, has hired you to help him formulate a strategy to put his company back on track. Develop a proposal for Tom detailing how a CRM system can alleviate the company's issues and create new opportunities.

3. Building Visibility

Visionary companies are building extended enterprises to best compete in the new Internet economy. An extended enterprise combines the Internet's power with new business structures and processes to eliminate old corporate boundaries and geographic restrictions. Networked supply chains create seamless paths of communication among partners, suppliers, manufacturers, retailers, and customers. Because of advances in manufacturing and distribution, the cost of developing new products and services is dropping, and time to market is speeding up. This has resulted in increasing customer demands, local and global competition, and increased pressure on the supply chain.

To stay competitive, companies must reinvent themselves so that the supply chain—sourcing and procurement, production scheduling, order fulfillment, inventory management, and customer care—is no longer a cost-based back-office exercise, but rather a flexible operation designed to effectively address today's challenges.

The Internet is proving an effective tool in transforming supply chains across all industries. Suppliers, distributors, manufacturers, and resellers now work together more closely and effectively than ever. Today's technology-driven supply chain enables customers to manage their own buying experiences, increases coordination and connectivity among supply partners, and helps reduce operating costs for every company in the chain.[64]

Project Focus

In the past, assets were a crucial component of success in supply chain management. In today's market, however, a customer-centric orientation is key to retaining competitive advantage. Using the Internet and any other resources available, develop a strategic plan for implementing a networked, flexible supply chain management system for a start-up company of your choice. Research Netflix if you are unfamiliar with how start-up companies are changing the supply chain. Be sure that your supply chain integrates all partners—manufacturers, retailers, suppliers, carriers, and vendors—into a seamless unit and views customer relationship management as a key competitive advantage. There are several points to consider when creating your customer-centric supply chain strategy:

- Taking orders is only one part of serving customer needs.
- Businesses must fulfill the promise they make to customers by delivering products and information upon request—not when it is convenient for the company.
- Time to market is a key competitive advantage. Companies must ensure uninterrupted supply, and information about customer demands and activities is essential to this requirement.

- Cost is an important factor. Companies need to squeeze the costs from internal processes to make the final products less expensive.
- Reducing design-cycle times is critical, as this allows companies to get their products out more quickly to meet customer demand.

4. Netflix Your Business

Netflix reinvented the video rental business using supply chain technology. Netflix, established in 1998, is the largest online DVD rental service, offering flat-rate rental-by-mail to customers in the United States. Headquartered in Los Gatos, California, it has amassed a collection of 80,000 titles and over 6.8 million subscribers. Netflix has over 42 million DVDs and ships 1.6 million a day, on average, costing a reported $300 million a year in postage. On February 25, 2007, Netflix announced the delivery of its billionth DVD.

The company provides a monthly flat-fee service for the rental of DVD movies. A subscriber creates an ordered list, called a rental queue, of DVDs to rent. The DVDs are delivered individually via the United States Postal Service from an array of regional warehouses (44 in 29 states). A subscriber keeps a rented DVD as long as desired but has a limit on the number of DVDs (determined by subscription level) that can be checked out at any one time. To rent a new DVD, the subscriber mails the previous one back to Netflix in a prepaid mailing envelope. Upon receipt of the disc, Netflix ships another disc in the subscriber's rental queue.[65]

Project Focus

Netflix's business is video rental, but it used technology to revamp the supply chain to completely disrupt the entire video rental industry. Reinvent IT is a statewide contest where college students can propose a new business that they will reinvent by revamping the supply chain (such as Netflix has done). You want to enter and win the contest. Reinvent a traditional business, such as the video rental business, using supply chain technologies.

5. Finding Shelf Space at Wal-Mart

Wal-Mart's business strategy of being a low-cost provider by managing its supply chain down to the minutia has paid off greatly. Each week, approximately 100 million customers, or one-third of the U.S. population, visit Wal-Mart's U.S. stores. Wal-Mart is currently the world's largest retailer and the second largest corporation behind ExxonMobil. It was founded by Sam Walton in 1962 and is the largest private employer in the United States and Mexico. Wal-Mart is also the largest grocery retailer in the United States, with an estimated 20 percent of the retail grocery and consumables business, and the largest toy seller in the United States, with an estimated 45 percent of the retail toy business, having surpassed Toys "R" Us in the late 1990s.

Wal-Mart's business model is based on selling a wide variety of general merchandise at "always low prices." The reason Wal-Mart can offer such low prices is due to its innovative use of information technology tools to create its highly sophisticated supply chain. Over the past decade, Wal-Mart has famously invited its major suppliers to jointly develop powerful supply chain partnerships. These are designed to increase product flow efficiency and, consequently, Wal-Mart's profitability.

Many companies have stepped up to the challenge, starting with the well-known Wal-Mart/Procter & Gamble alliance, which incorporated vendor-managed inventory, category management, and other intercompany innovations. Wal-Mart's CFO became a key customer as P&G's objective became maximizing Wal-Mart's internal profitability. Unlike many other retailers, Wal-Mart does not charge a slotting fee to suppliers for their products to appear in the store. Alternatively, Wal-Mart focuses on selling more popular products and often pressures store managers to drop unpopular products in favor of more popular ones, as well as pressuring manufacturers to supply more popular products.[66]

You are the owner of a high-end collectible toy company. You create everything from authentic sports figure replicas to famous musicians and movie characters including Babe Ruth, Hulk Hogan, Mick Jagger, Ozzy Osbourne, Alien, and the Terminator. It would be a huge win for your company if you could get your collectibles into Wal-Mart. Compile a strategic plan highlighting the steps required to approach Wal-Mart as your supply chain partner. Be sure to address the pros and cons of partnering with Wal-Mart, including the cost to revamp your current supply chain to meet Wal-Mart's tough supply chain requirements.

6. Shipping Problems

Entrepreneurship is in Alyssa Stuart's blood. Alyssa has been starting businesses since she was 10 years old, and she finally has the perfect business of custom-made furniture. Customers who visit Alyssa's shop can choose from a number of different fabrics and 50 different styles of couch and chair designs to create their custom-made furniture. Once the customer decides on a fabric pattern and furniture design, the information is sent to China where the furniture is built and shipped to the customer via the West Coast. Alyssa is excited about her business; all of her hard work has finally paid off as she has over 17,000 customers and 875 orders currently in the pipe.

Project Focus

Alyssa's business is booming. Her high quality products and outstanding customer service have created an excellent reputation for her business. But Alyssa's business is at risk of losing everything and she has come to you for help solving her supply chain issues.

Yesterday, a dockworkers union strike began and shut down all of the West Coast shipping docks from San Francisco to Canada. Work will resume only when the union agrees to new labor contracts, which could take months. Alyssa has asked you to summarize the impact of the dock shutdown on her business and create a strategy to keep her business running, which is especially difficult since Alyssa guarantees 30-day delivery on all products or the product is free. What strategies do you recommend for Alyssa's business to continue working while her supply chain is disrupted by the dockworkers' strike?

7. Political Supply Chains

The U.S. government has crafted a deal with the United Arab Emirates (UAE) that would let a UAE-based firm, Dubai Ports World (DPW), run six major U.S. ports. If the approval is unchallenged, Dubai Ports World would run the ports of New York, New Jersey, Baltimore, New Orleans, Miami, and Philadelphia. Currently, London-based Peninsular and Oriental Steam Navigation Co. (P&O), the fourth largest port operator in the world, runs the six ports. But the $6.8 billion sale of P&O to DPW would effectively turn over North American operations to the government-owned company in Dubai. [67]

Project Focus

Some citizens are worried that the federal government may be outsourcing U.S. port operations to a company prone to terrorist infiltration by allowing a firm from the United Arab Emirates to run port operations within the United States. You have been called in on an investigation to determine the potential effects on U.S. businesses' supply chains if these ports were shut down due to terrorist activities. The United Arab Emirates has had people involved in terrorism. In fact, some of its financial institutions laundered the money for the 9/11 terrorists. Create an argument for or against outsourcing these ports to the UAE. Be sure to detail the effect on U.S. businesses' supply chains if these ports are subjected to terrorist acts.

8. JetBlue on YouTube

JetBlue took an unusual and interesting CRM approach by using YouTube to apologize to its customers. JetBlue's founder and CEO, David Neeleman, apologized to customers via YouTube after a very, very bad week for the airline: 1,100 flights canceled due to snow storms and thousands of irate passengers. Neeleman's unpolished, earnest delivery makes this apology worth accepting. But then again, we were not stuck on a tarmac for eight hours. With all of the new advances in technology and the many ways to reach customers, do you think using YouTube is a smart approach? What else could JetBlue do to help gain back its customers' trust?

Project Focus

You are the founder and CEO of GoodDog, a large pet food manufacturing company. Recently, at least 16 pet deaths have been tied to tainted pet food, fortunately not manufactured by your company. A recall of potentially deadly pet food has dog and cat owners studying their animals for even the slightest hint of illness and swamping veterinarians nationwide with calls about symptoms both real and imagined. Create a strategy for using YouTube as a vehicle to communicate with your customers as they fear for their pets' lives. Be sure to highlight the pros and cons of using YouTube as a customer communication vehicle. Are there any other new technologies you could use as a customer communication vehicle that would be more effective than YouTube?

9. Second Life CRM

The virtual world of Second Life could become the first point of contact between companies and customers and could transform the whole customer experience. Since it began hosting the likes of Adidas, Dell, Reuters, and Toyota, Second Life has become technology's equivalent of India or China—everyone needs an office and a strategy involving it to keep their shareholders happy. But beyond opening a shiny new building in the virtual world, what can such companies do with their virtual real estate?

Like many other big brands, PA Consulting has its own offices in Second Life and has learned that simply having an office to answer customer queries is not enough. Real people, albeit behind avatars, must be staffing the offices—in the same way having a Web site is not enough if there is not a call center to back it up when a would-be customer wants to speak to a human being. The consultants believe call centers could one day ask customers to follow up a phone call with them by moving the query into a virtual world.

Unlike many corporate areas in the virtual world, the National Basketball Association incorporates capabilities designed to keep fans coming back, including real-time 3-D diagrams of games as they are being played.[68]

Project Focus

You are the executive director of CRM at StormPeak, an advanced AI company that develops robots. You are in charge of overseeing the first virtual site being built in Second Life. Create a CRM strategy for doing business in a virtual world. Here are a few questions to get you started:

- How will customer relationships be different in a virtual world?
- What is your strategy for managing customer relationships in this new virtual environment?
- How will supporting Second Life customers differ from supporting traditional customers?
- How will supporting Second Life customers differ from supporting Web site customers?
- What customer security issues might you encounter in Second Life?
- What customer ethical issues might you encounter in Second Life?

UNIT 4

Building Innovation

eBay—The Ultimate E-Business

Pierre Omidyar was just 28 when he sat down over a long holiday weekend to write the original computer code for what eventually became an Internet super brand—the auction site eBay. Omidyar viewed auctions as a fair mechanism for Internet commerce where sellers could set their minimum prices, and buyers could then determine an item's market value by bidding up to what they were willing to pay. A novel feedback system could allow buyers and sellers to rate each other, helping minimize fraud by enabling the community to police itself. "I really wanted to give the individual the power to be a producer as well. It was letting the users take responsibility for building the community," Omidyar would later explain.

The site launched on Labor Day, September 4, 1995, under the title of Auction Web, soon to be renamed after the site's domain name—eBay.com (a shortening of Echo Bay, Omidyar's consulting firm). The service was free at first, but started charging to cover Internet service provider costs.

A National Marketplace

Omidyar's auction Web site, eBay.com, took off. It provided something novel that its users craved: an efficient national marketplace with a strong community built on fairness and trust. A photography student looking for a used camera could choose from models across the nation and trust the timely delivery of the product. The owner of a vintage clothing store could sell to collectors nationwide. The community would expose a deceptive or fraudulent user and ban them from the marketplace.

Entrepreneurs in record numbers began setting up shop on eBay. According to a survey conducted for eBay by ACNielsen International Research, more than 1 million people support themselves by selling items on eBay, up from 75,000 in 2002. In addition to these professional eBay sellers, another 1.5 million individuals supplement their income by selling on eBay.

The stock market value of Omidyar's innovative company grew to $2 billion in just three years, and his site's staying power as an economic engine was evident. Jeffrey Skoll, a Stanford MBA, joined the company in 1996 after the site was already profitable. In March 1998, Meg Whitman took over as president and CEO. In September 1998, eBay launched a successful public offering, making both Omidyar and Skoll billionaires—three years after Omidyar created eBay. As of 2005, Omidyar's 214 million eBay shares were worth about $8 billion.

Collaborating with eBay

This e-business is collaborating with marketplace, payment, and communication companies that add value for its customers.

Marketplace—The U.S. Postal Service

People who sell items on eBay all have one thing in common: They need to ship their goods to their customers. To support this growing economic force, eBay and the U.S. Postal Service created an innovative economic and educational opportunity.

The Postal Service's bread and butter—first-class mail—is beset by rising costs and falling use. E-mail and faxes have reduced the amount of mail sent each day, but the Postal Service still bears the cost of delivering to every business and home, six days a week. Package shipping, however, remains a profitable and booming business, as evidenced by the number and earnings of private shippers in the market.

The Postal Service offers free boxes and heavy-duty envelopes for shippers using overnight or priority mail. To make it easier for those in the vanguard of the new, digital economy, the Postal Service will pick up shipments from the sender, and its Web site sells mailing labels with postage included that can be printed out from a home computer. Over 20 million shipping labels with postage were printed via the eBay/Postal Service link in 2005. Customers can also link to the United Parcel Service site, but eBay does not have a formal relationship with Federal Express.

Payment—PayPal

Founded in 1998, PayPal, an eBay company, enables any individual or business with an e-mail address to securely, easily, and quickly send and receive payments online. PayPal's service builds on the existing financial infrastructure of bank accounts and credit cards and utilizes the world's most advanced proprietary fraud prevention systems to create a safe, global, real-time payment solution.

PayPal has quickly become a global leader in online payment solutions with 96 million account members worldwide. Buyers and sellers on eBay, online retailers, online businesses, as well as traditional off-line businesses are transacting with PayPal, available in 55 countries.

Communication—Skype

Skype, a global Internet communications company, allows people everywhere to make free, unlimited, superior quality voice calls via its innovative peer-to-peer software.

Since its launch in August 2003, Skype has been downloaded more than 163 million times in 225 countries and territories. Fifty-four million people are registered to use Skype's free services, with over 3 million simultaneous users on the network at any one time. Skype adds about 150,000 users a day.

In September 2005, eBay acquired Skype for approximately $2.6 billion, anticipating that Skype will streamline and improve communications between buyers and sellers as it is integrated into the eBay marketplace. Buyers will gain an easy way to talk to sellers quickly and get the information they need, and sellers can more easily build relationships. The auction company hopes the acquisition will strengthen its global marketplace and payments platform, while opening several new lines of business and creating significant new opportunities for the company.

Unforeseen Dangers of Collaboration

"Communications is at the heart of e-commerce and community," said Meg Whitman. "By combining the two leading e-commerce franchises, eBay and PayPal, with the leader in Internet voice communications, Skype, we will create an extraordinarily powerful environment for business on the Net."

In October 2005, one month after eBay's acquisition of Skype, a press release discussed two critical flaws in Skype's software, one of which could allow malicious hackers to take control of compromised systems and another that could allow attackers to crash the client software. While fixes for the issues were being addressed, businesses asked their users to refrain from using voice services based on proprietary protocols like Skype while on corporate networks because of network security issues. Perhaps Skype might not be the collaborative tool of choice for eBay.[1]

Introduction

One of the biggest forces changing business is the Internet. Technology companies like Intel and Cisco were among the first to seize the Internet to overhaul their operations. Intel deployed Web-based automation to liberate its 200 salesclerks from tedious order-entry positions. Instead, salesclerks concentrate on customer relationship management functions such as analyzing sales trends and pampering customers. Cisco handles 75 percent of its sales online, and 45 percent of online orders never touch employees' hands. This type of Internet-based ordering has helped Cisco hike productivity by 20 percent over the past few years.[2]

E-business is the conducting of business on the Internet, not only buying and selling, but also serving customers and collaborating with business partners. Organizations realize that putting up simple Web sites for customers, employees, and partners does not create an e-business. E-business Web sites must create a buzz, much as Amazon has done in the book-selling industry. E-business Web sites must be innovative, add value, and provide useful information. In short, the site must build a sense of community and collaboration, eventually becoming the port of entry for business. This unit focuses on the opportunities and advantages found with developing collaborative partnerships in e-business and includes:

- **Chapter Thirteen**—Creating Innovative Organizations.
- **Chapter Fourteen**—E-Business.
- **Chapter Fifteen**—Creating Collaborative Partnerships.
- **Chapter Sixteen**—Integrating Wireless Technology in Business.

13 | Creating Innovative Organizations

13.1. Compare disruptive and sustaining technologies.

13.2. Explain how the Internet caused disruption among businesses.

13.3. Define the relationship between the Internet and the World Wide Web.

13.4. Describe the Internet's impact on information along with how these changes are affecting businesses.

Disruptive Technology

Polaroid, founded in 1937, produced the first instant camera in the late 1940s. The Polaroid camera was one of the most exciting technological advances the photography industry had ever seen. By using a Polaroid camera, customers no longer had to depend on others to develop their pictures. The technology was innovative and the product was high-end. The company eventually went public, becoming one of Wall Street's most prominent enterprises, with its stock trading above $60 in 1997. In 2002, the stock was down to 8 cents and the company declared bankruptcy.[3]

How could a company like Polaroid, which had innovative technology and a captive customer base, go bankrupt? Perhaps company executives failed to use Porter's Five Forces to analyze the threat of substitute products or services. If they had, would they have noticed the two threats, one-hour film processing and digital cameras, that eventually stole Polaroid's market share? Would they have understood that their customers, people who want instant access to their pictures without having a third party involved, would be the first to use one-hour film processing and the first to purchase digital cameras? Could the company have found a way to compete with one-hour film processing and the digital camera to save Polaroid?

Most organizations face the same dilemma as Polaroid—the criteria an organization uses to make business decisions for its present business could possibly create issues for its future business. Essentially, what is best for the current business could ruin it in the long term. Some observers of our business environment have an ominous vision of the future—digital Darwinism. ***Digital Darwinism*** implies that organizations that cannot adapt to the new demands placed on them for surviving in the information age are doomed to extinction.[4]

Spawn.com

DISRUPTIVE VERSUS SUSTAINING TECHNOLOGY

A ***disruptive technology*** is a new way of doing things that initially does not meet the needs of existing customers. Disruptive technologies tend to open new markets and destroy old ones. A ***sustaining technology,*** on the other hand, produces an improved product customers are eager to buy, such as a faster car or larger hard drive. Sustaining technologies tend to provide us with better, faster, and cheaper products in established markets. Incumbent companies most often lead sustaining

FIGURE 13.1

Disruptive and Sustaining
Technologies

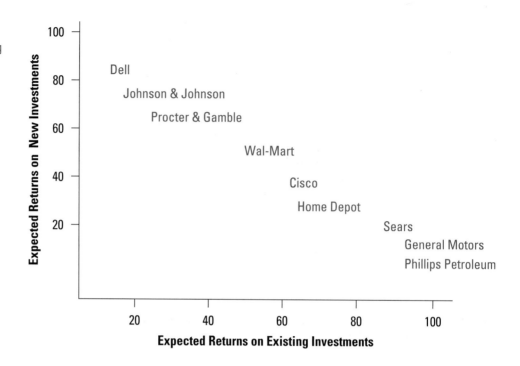

Disruption

technology to market, but virtually never lead in markets opened by disruptive technologies. Figure 13.1 displays companies that are expecting future growth to occur from new investments (disruptive technology) and companies that are expecting future growth to occur from existing investments (sustaining technology).

Disruptive technologies typically cut into the low end of the marketplace and eventually evolve to displace high-end competitors and their reigning technologies. Sony is a perfect example of a company that entered the low end of the marketplace and eventually evolved to displace its high-end competitors. Sony started as a tiny company that built portable, battery-powered transistor radios people could carry around with them. The sound quality of Sony's transistor radios was poor because the transistor amplifiers were of lower quality than traditional vacuum tubes, which produce a better sound. But customers were willing to overlook sound quality for the convenience of portability. With the experience and revenue stream from the portables, Sony improved its technology to produce cheap, low-end transistor amplifiers that were suitable for home use and used those revenues to improve the technology further, which produced better radios.[5]

The *Innovator's Dilemma,* a book by Clayton M. Christensen, discusses how established companies can take advantage of disruptive technologies without hindering existing relationships with customers, partners, and stakeholders. Companies like Xerox, IBM, Sears, and DEC all listened to existing customers, invested aggressively in technology, had their competitive antennae up, and still lost their market-dominant positions. Christensen states that these companies may have placed too much emphasis on satisfying customers' current needs, while neglecting to adopt new disruptive technology that will meet customers' future needs, thus causing the companies to eventually fail. Figure 13.2 highlights several companies that launched new businesses by capitalizing on disruptive technologies.[6]

THE INTERNET—BUSINESS DISRUPTION

When the Internet was in its early days, no one had any idea how massive it would become. Computer companies did not think it would be a big deal; neither did the phone companies or cable companies. Difficult to access and operate, it seemed likely to remain an arcane tool of the Defense Department and academia. However,

Company	Disruptive Technology
Charles Schwab	Online brokerage
Hewlett-Packard	Microprocessor-based computers; ink-jet printers
IBM	Minicomputers; personal computers
Intel	Low-end microprocessors
Intuit	QuickBooks software; TurboTax software; Quicken software
Microsoft	Internet-based computing; operating system software; SQL and Access database software
Oracle	Database software
Quantum	3.5-inch disks
Sony	Transistor-based consumer electronics

FIGURE 13.2

Companies That Capitalized on Disruptive Technology

the Internet grew, and grew, and grew. It began with a handful of users in the mid-1960s and reached 1 billion by 2005 (see Figures 13.3 and 13.4). Estimates predict there will be more than 3 billion Internet users by 2010. Already, villages in Indonesia and India have Internet access before they have electricity.[7]

Evolution of the Internet

During the Cold War in the mid-1960s, the U.S. military decided it needed a bomb-proof communications system, and thus the concept for the Internet was born. The system would link computers throughout the country allowing messages to get though even if a large section of the country was destroyed. In the early days, the only linked computers were at government think tanks and a few universities. The Internet was essentially an emergency military communications system operated by the Department of Defense's Advanced Research Project Agency (ARPA) and called ARPANET. Formally defined, the **Internet** is a global public network of computer networks that pass information from one to another using common

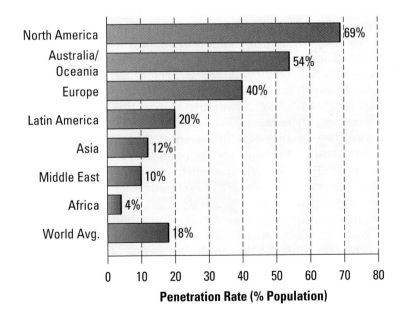

FIGURE 13.3

Internet Penetration by World Region

FIGURE 13.4

World Internet Users

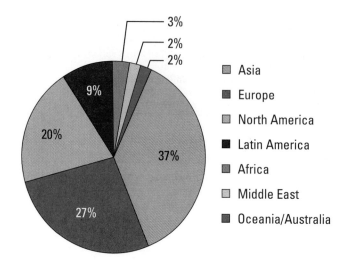

- Asia
- Europe
- North America
- Latin America
- Africa
- Middle East
- Oceania/Australia

computer protocols. ***Protocols*** are the standards that specify the format of data as well as the rules to be followed during transmission.

In time, every university in the United States that had defense-related funding installed ARPANET computers. Gradually, the Internet moved from a military pipeline to a communications tool for scientists. As more scholars came online, system administration transferred from ARPA to the National Science Foundation. Years later, businesses began using the Internet, and the administrative responsibilities were once again transferred. Today, no one party operates the Internet; however, several entities oversee the Internet and set standards including:

- Internet Engineering Task Force (IETF): The protocol engineering and development arm of the Internet.
- Internet Architecture Board (IAB): Responsible for defining the overall architecture of the Internet, providing guidance and broad direction to the IETF.
- Internet Engineering Steering Group (IESG): Responsible for technical management of IETF activities and the Internet standards process.

EVOLUTION OF THE WORLD WIDE WEB

Internet

People often interchange the terms *Internet* and the *World Wide Web*, but these terms are not synonymous. Throughout the 1960s, 1970s, and 1980s, the Internet was primarily used by the Department of Defense to support activities such as e-mail and transferring files. The Internet was restricted to noncommercial activities, and its users included government employees, researchers, university professors, and students. The World Wide Web changed the purpose and use of the Internet.

The ***World Wide Web (WWW)*** is a global hypertext system that uses the Internet as its transport mechanism. ***Hypertext transport protocol (HTTP)*** is the Internet standard that supports the exchange of information on the WWW. By defining universal resource locators (URLs) and how they can be used to retrieve resources anywhere on the Internet, HTTP enables Web authors to embed hyperlinks in Web documents. HTTP defines the process by which a Web client, called a browser, originates a request for information and sends it to a Web server, a program designed to respond to HTTP requests and provide the desired information. In a hypertext system, users navigate by clicking a hyperlink embedded in the current document. The action displays a second document in the same or a separate browser window. The Web has quickly become the ideal medium for publishing information on the Internet and serves as the platform for the electronic economy. Figure 13.5 displays the reasons for the popularity and growth in the WWW.

FIGURE 13.5

Reasons for World Wide
Web Growth

Reasons for Growth of the World Wide Web
■ The microcomputer revolution made it possible for an average person to own a computer.
■ Advancements in networking hardware, software, and media made it possible for business PCs to be inexpensively connected to larger networks.
■ Browser software such as Microsoft's Internet Explorer and Netscape Navigator gave computer users an easy-to-use graphical interface to find, download, and display Web pages.
■ The speed, convenience, and low cost of e-mail have made it an incredibly popular tool for business and personal communications.
■ Basic Web pages are easy to create and extremely flexible.

The WWW remained primarily text-based until 1991 when two events occurred that would forever change the Web and the amount and quality of information available (see Figure 13.6). First, Tim Berners-Lee built the first Web site on August 6, 1991 (http://info.cern.ch/—the site has been archived). The site provided details about the World Wide Web including how to build a browser and set up a Web server. It also housed the world's first Web directory, since Berners-Lee later maintained a list of other Web sites apart from his own.[8]

Second, Marc Andreesen developed a new computer program called the NCSA Mosaic (National Center for Supercomputing Applications at the University of Illinois) and gave it away! The browser made it easier to access the Web sites that had started to appear. Soon Web sites contained more than just text; they also had sound and video files (see Figure 13.7). These pages, written in the hypertext markup language (HTML), have links that allow the user to quickly move from one document to another, even when the documents are stored in different computers. Web browsers read the HTML text and convert it into a Web page.[9]

By eliminating time and distance, the Internet makes it possible to perform business in ways not previously imaginable. The *digital divide* is when those with access to technology have great advantages over those without access to technology. People living in the village of Siroha, India, must bike five miles to find a telephone. For over 700 million rural people living in India, the digital divide was a way of life,

FIGURE 13.6

The Internet's Impact on
Information

Internet's Impact on Information	
Easy to compile	Searching for information on products, prices, customers, suppliers, and partners is faster and easier when using the Internet.
Increased richness	*Information richness* refers to the depth and breadth of information transferred between customers and businesses. Businesses and customers can collect and track more detailed information when using the Internet.
Increased reach	*Information reach* refers to the number of people a business can communicate with, on a global basis. Businesses can share information with numerous customers all over the world.
Improved content	A key element of the Internet is its ability to provide dynamic relevant content. Buyers need good content descriptions to make informed purchases, and sellers use content to properly market and differentiate themselves from the competition. Content and product description establish the common understanding between both parties to the transaction. As a result, the reach and richness of that content directly affects the transaction.

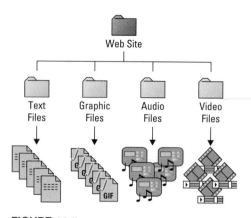

FIGURE 13.7

File Formats Offered over the WWW

until recently. Media Lab Asia sells telephony and e-mail services via a mobile Internet kiosk mounted on a bicycle, which is known as an "info-thelas." The kiosk has an onboard computer equipped with an antenna for Internet service and a specially designed all-day battery. Over 2,000 villages have purchased the kiosk for $1,200, and another 600,000 villages are interested.[10]

WEB 2.0

Web 2.0's vast disruptive impact is just beginning. *Web 2.0* is a set of economic, social, and technology trends that collectively form the basis for the next generation of the Internet—a more mature, distinctive medium characterized by user participation, openness, and network effects. Although the term suggests a new version of the World Wide Web, it does not refer to an update to Web technical specifications; instead, it refers to changes in the ways software developers and end-users use the Web as a platform. According to Tim O'Reilly, "Web 2.0 is the business revolution in the computer industry caused by the move to the Internet as platform, and an attempt to understand the rules for success on that new platform." Figure 13.8 displays the move from Web 1.0 to Web 2.0, and Figure 13.9 displays the timeline of Web 1.0 and Web 2.0.[11]

More than just the latest technology buzzword, Web 2.0 is a transformative force that is propelling companies across all industries toward a new way of doing business. Those who act on the Web 2.0 opportunity stand to gain an early-mover advantage in their markets. What is causing this change? Consider the following raw demographic and technological drivers:

- One billion people around the globe now have access to the Internet.
- Mobile devices outnumber desktop computers by a factor of two.
- Nearly 50 percent of all U.S. Internet access is now via always-on broadband connections.

Combine these drivers with the fundamental laws of social networks and lessons from the Web's first decade, and you get Web 2.0, the next-generation, user-driven, intelligent Web:

- In the first quarter of 2006, MySpace.com signed up 280,000 new users each day and had the second most Internet traffic of any Web site.
- By the second quarter of 2006, 50 million blogs were created—new ones were added at a rate of two per second.
- In 2005, eBay conducted 8 billion API-based Web services transactions.[12]

FIGURE 13.8

The Move from Web 1.0 to Web 2.0

Web 1.0		Web 2.0
Doubleclick	-->	Google Adsense
Ofoto	-->	Flickr
Akamai	-->	Bittorrent
Mp3.Com	-->	Napster
Britannica Online	-->	Wikipedia
Personal Web Sites	-->	Blogging
Evite	-->	Upcoming.Org And EVDB
Domain Name Speculation	-->	Search Engine Optimization
Page Views	-->	Cost Per Click
Screen Scraping	-->	Web Services
Publishing	-->	Participation
Content Management Systems	-->	Wikis
Directories (Taxonomy)	-->	Tagging ("Folksonomy")
Stickiness	-->	Syndication

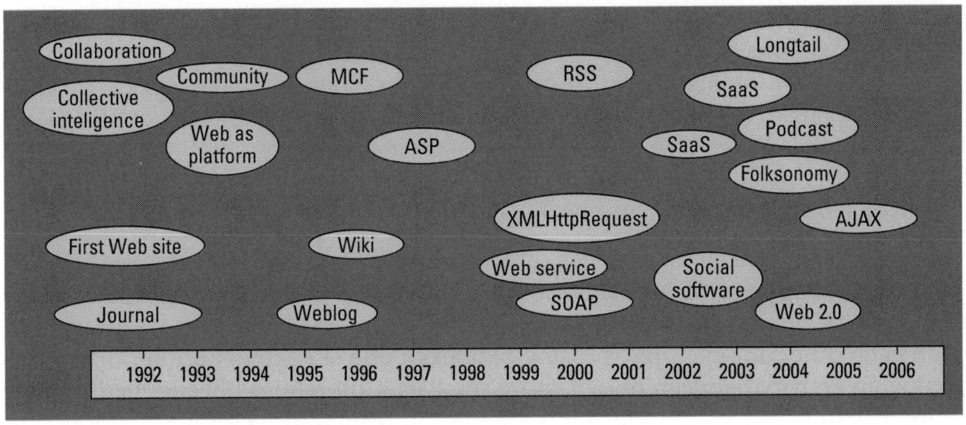

FIGURE 13.9

Timeline of Web 1.0

THE FUTURE—WEB 3.0

Web 3.0 is a term that has been coined with different meanings to describe the evolution of Web usage and interaction among several separate paths. These include transforming the Web into a database, a move toward making content accessible by multiple nonbrowser applications, the leveraging of artificial intelligence technologies, or the semantic Web. The **semantic Web** is an evolving extension of the World Wide Web in which Web content can be expressed not only in natural language, but also in a format that can be read and used by software agents, thus permitting them to find, share, and integrate information more easily. It derives from W3C director Sir Tim Berners-Lee's vision of the Web as a universal medium for data, information, and knowledge exchange. There is considerable debate as to what the term *Web 3.0* means, but many agree it encompasses one or more of the following:

1. Transforming the Web into a database.

2. An evolutionary path to artificial intelligence.

3. The realization of the semantic Web and SOA.

4. Evolution toward 3D.

Transforming the Web into a Database

The first step toward a Web 3.0 is the emergence of the data-driven Web as structured data records are published to the Web in formats that are reusable and able to be queried remotely. Because of the recent growth of standardized query language for searching across distributed databases on the Web, the data-driven Web enables a new level of data integration and application interoperability, making data as openly accessible and linkable as Web pages. The data-driven Web is the first step on the path toward the full semantic Web. In the data-driven Web phase, the focus is on making structured data available using databases. The full semantic Web stage will widen the scope such that both structured data and even what is traditionally thought of as unstructured or semistructured content (such as Web pages, documents, e-mail, etc.) will be widely available in common formats.[13]

An Evolutionary Path to Artificial Intelligence

Web 3.0 has also been used to describe an evolutionary path for the Web that leads to artificial intelligence that can reason about the Web in a quasi-human fashion. Some skeptics regard this as an unobtainable vision. However, companies such as IBM and Google are implementing new technologies that are yielding surprising information, such as predicting hit songs by mining information on college music

Web sites. There is also debate over whether the driving force behind Web 3.0 will be intelligent systems, or whether intelligence will emerge in a more organic fashion, from systems of intelligent people, such as via collaborative filtering services like del.icio.us, Flickr, and Digg that extract meaning and order from the existing Web and how people interact with it.[14]

The Realization of the Semantic Web and SOA

Related to the artificial intelligence direction, Web 3.0 could be the realization of a possible convergence of the semantic Web and service-oriented architecture (SOA). A *service-oriented architecture (SOA)* is a collection of services that communicate with each other, for example, passing data from one service to another or coordinating an activity between one or more services. Companies have longed to integrate existing systems in order to implement information technology support for business processes that cover the entire business value chain. The main drivers for SOA adoption are that it links computational resources and promotes their reuse. Enterprise architects believe that SOA can help businesses respond more quickly and cost-effectively to changing market conditions. This style of architecture can simplify interconnection to—and usage of—existing IT (legacy) assets.[15]

Evolution toward 3D

Another possible path for Web 3.0 is toward the three-dimensional vision championed by the Web3D Consortium. This would involve the Web transforming into a series of 3D spaces, taking the concept realized by Second Life further. This could open up new ways to connect and collaborate using 3D shared spaces.[16]

OPENING CASE STUDY QUESTIONS

1. Do you agree that eBay founder Pierre Omidyar used disruptive technology to change the auction business? Why or why not?

2. Create a Porter's Five Forces analysis highlighting eBay's market position. Be sure to highlight any new technologies that have the potential to disrupt eBay's business.

3. What types of ethical dilemmas will an online business such as eBay face that a traditional company would not face?

4. What types of security issues will an online business such as eBay face that a traditional company would not face?

Chapter Thirteen Case: Failing to Innovate

It is a sad but common tale—a dynamic company comes up with an innovative new product that utilizes cutting-edge technology in an exciting way that generates lots of hype and attention. But for some reason this new product fails to click with the masses and falls into oblivion, only to see other products gain massive success by following in its footsteps.

It's not always a case of right technology at the wrong time. Sometimes these first movers failed to build on their innovation, instead sitting on their initial achievements and letting more nimble competitors refine their idea into something more attractive and functional. And some just made too many mistakes to succeed.

Obtaining the first-mover advantage is critical to any business that wants to compete in the Internet economy. However, gaining a first-mover advantage is typically temporary, and without remaining innovative the company can soon fail. Here is a list of the top 10 first movers that flopped, according to Jim Rapoza of eWeek.

1. **Apple Newton PDA**—When it was launched in the early '90s, the Apple Newton was first lauded but later mocked because of its failings (it even had the honor of being spoofed on *The Simpsons*. But one can draw a straight line from the Newton to current products such as tablet PCs, smart phones, and the new Apple iPhone.

2. **PointCast**—In 1997, one of the hottest products found on the desktop of nearly every IT worker was PointCast, which delivered selected news items directly to the desktop. It quickly launched the "push" craze, which just as quickly imploded spectacularly. But today's RSS and news feeds all owe a debt to PointCast.

3. **Gopher Protocol**—It was so close. Launched just before the Web itself, Gopher quickly became popular in universities and business. Using search technology, it worked very much like a Web site, but it could not compete with the Web itself.

4. **VisiCalc**—Often lauded as the first killer application for the PC, the VisiCalc spreadsheet was a must-have for early PC-enabled businesses but quickly fell behind more polished spreadsheets from Lotus and Microsoft.

5. **Atari**—For those of a certain age, the word *Atari* is synonymous with video games. The pioneer in home gaming consoles failed to innovate in the face of more nimble competitors.

6. **Diamond Rio**—For $200 and with 32MB of RAM (with a SmartMedia slot for memory expansion), the Rio helped launch the MP3 revolution. That is, until white earbuds and a thing called the iPod took over.

7. **Netscape Navigator**—Netscape Navigator was essentially the Web for users in the early to mid-1990s. But Netscape could not withstand the Microsoft onslaught, along with plenty of mistakes the company made itself, and now only lives on as the original basis of the Mozilla browsers.

8. **AltaVista**—Not the first search engine, but the first to use many of the natural language technologies common today and the first to gain real Web popularity, AltaVista failed to keep up with technological changes.

9. **Ricochet Networks**—Nothing created geek lust like sitting next to someone who had a Ricochet card plugged into the laptop. Look, she is in a cab and accessing the Internet at ISDN speeds! But Richochet never expanded to enough cities to be a serious player.

10. **IBM Simon Phone**—The iPhone's $499 price is nothing compared with the $900 price tag the IBM Simon had when it finally became available in 1994. But it pioneered most of the features found in today's smart phones and even beat the iPhone when it came to a buttonless touch-screen interface.[17]

Questions

1. If these companies all had a first-mover advantage, then why did the products fail?
2. For each of the above determine if the technology used was disruptive or sustaining.
3. Choose one of the products above and determine what the company could have done to prevent the product from failing.
4. Can you name another technology product that failed? Why did it fail? What could the company have done differently for it to succeed?

Review **Technology Plug-In T9 "Designing Web Pages"** for an overview of the functional aspects of Web design including the basic steps involved in Web site development.

Review **Technology Plug-In T10 "Creating Web Pages Using HTML"** for an overview of using HTML to create Web pages including how to format text, insert hyperlinks, add graphics, and organize content.

14 E-Business

14.1. Compare e-commerce and e-business.

14.2. Compare the four types of e-business models.

14.3. Describe the benefits and challenges associated with e-business.

14.4. Explain the differences among e-shops, e-malls, and online auctions.

E-Business

Tom Anderson and Chris DeWolf started MySpace, a social networking Web site that offers its members information about the independent music scene around the country representing both Internet culture and teenage culture. Musicians sign up for free MySpace home pages where they can post tour dates, songs, and lyrics. Fans sign up for their own Web pages to link to favorite bands and friends. MySpace is the world's second most popular English-language Web site with over 100 million users.[18]

Night Agency

One of the biggest benefits of the Internet is its ability to allow organizations to perform business with anyone, anywhere, anytime. *E-commerce* is the buying and selling of goods and services over the Internet. E-commerce refers only to online transactions. *E-business,* derived from the term *e-commerce,* is the conducting of business on the Internet, not only buying and selling, but also serving customers and collaborating with business partners. The primary difference between e-commerce and e-business is that e-business also refers to online exchanges of information, for example, a manufacturer allowing its suppliers to monitor production schedules or a financial institution allowing its customers to review their banking, credit card, and mortgage accounts.

In the past few years, e-business seems to have permeated every aspect of daily life. Both individuals and organizations have embraced Internet technologies to enhance productivity, maximize convenience, and improve communications globally. From banking to shopping to entertainment, the Internet has become integral to daily life. Figure 14.1 provides examples of a few of the industries using e-business.

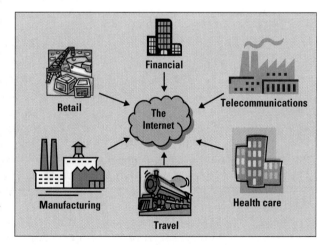

FIGURE 14.1

Overview of Several Industries Using E-Business

E-Business Models

An *e-business model* is an approach to conducting electronic business on the Internet. E-business transactions take place between two major entities—businesses and consumers. All e-business activities happen within the framework of two types

E-Business Term	Definition
Business-to-business (B2B)	Applies to businesses buying from and selling to each other over the Internet.
Business-to-consumer (B2C)	Applies to any business that sells its products or services to consumers over the Internet.
Consumer-to-business (C2B)	Applies to any consumer that sells a product or service to a business over the Internet.
Consumer-to-consumer (C2C)	Applies to sites primarily offering goods and services to assist consumers interacting with each other over the Internet.

	Business	Consumer
Business	B2B	B2C
Consumer	C2B	C2C

FIGURE 14.2

Basic E-Business Models

of business relationships: (1) the exchange of products and services between businesses (business-to-business, or B2B) and (2) the exchange of products and services with consumers (business-to-consumer, or B2C) (see Figure 14.2).

The primary difference between B2B and B2C are the customers; B2B customers are other businesses while B2C markets to consumers. Overall, B2B relations are more complex and have higher security needs; plus B2B is the dominant e-business force, representing 80 percent of all online business. Figure 14.3 illustrates all the e-business models: business-to-business, business-to-consumer, consumer-to-consumer, and consumer-to-business.[19]

EBags is a true e-business success story. It is thriving as the world's leading online provider of bags and accessories for all lifestyles. With 180 brands and over 8,000 products, eBags has sold more than 4 million bags since its launch in March 1999. It carries a complete line of premium and popular brands, including Samsonite, JanSport, The North Face, Liz Claiborne, and Adidas. The company has received several awards for excellence in online retailing including the Circle of Excellence Platinum Award from Bizrate.com, Web Site of the Year from *Catalog Age* magazine, and Email Marketer of the Year from ClickZ.MessageMedia. This success can be attributed to

FIGURE 14.3

E-Business Models

Business-to-Business (B2B)

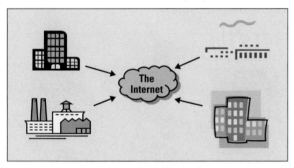

Business-to-Consumer (B2C)

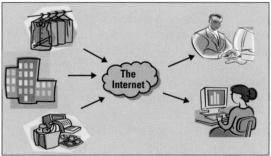

Consumer-to-Business (C2B)

Consumer-to-Consumer (C2C)

eBags' commitment to providing each customer with superior service, 24 hours a day, 365 days a year, including convenient, real-time UPS order tracking. According to Jon Nordmark, CEO of eBags.com, "From a customer perspective, we've spent a great deal of time developing pioneering ways to guide our shoppers to the bags and accessories that enhance their lifestyles through function and fashion."[20]

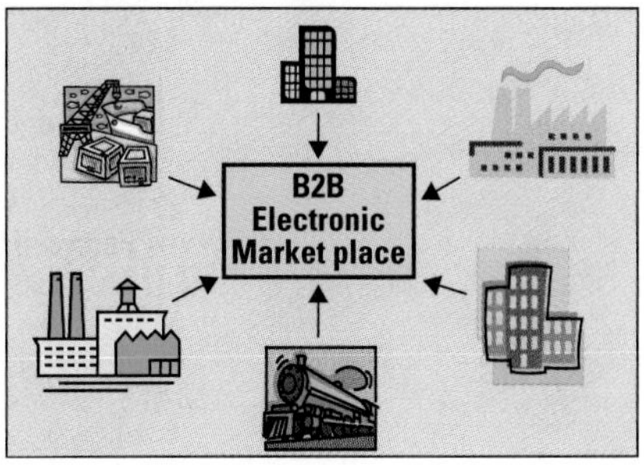

BUSINESS-TO-BUSINESS (B2B)

Business-to-business (B2B) applies to businesses buying from and selling to each other over the Internet. Online access to data, including expected shipping date, delivery date, and shipping status, provided either by the seller or a third-party provider, is widely supported by B2B models. Electronic marketplaces represent a new wave in B2B e-business models. *Electronic marketplaces,* or *e-marketplaces,* are interactive business communities providing a central market space where multiple buyers and sellers can engage in e-business activities (see Figure 14.4). They present structures for conducting commercial exchange, consolidating supply chains, and creating new sales channels. Their primary goal is to increase market efficiency by tightening and automating the relationship between buyers and sellers. Existing e-marketplaces allow access to various mechanisms in which to buy and sell almost anything, from services to direct materials.

BUSINESS-TO-CONSUMER (B2C)

Business-to-consumer (B2C) applies to any business that sells its products or services to consumers over the Internet. Carfax has been in the vehicle history report business for 20 years with an original customer base of used-car dealers. "The Internet was just a new way for us to reach the consumer market," Carfax President Dick Raines said. Carfax spent $20 million on print and TV ads to attract customers to its Web site. Customers can purchase a Carfax report for $14.95 or six days of reports for $19.95. Carfax has now launched a partnership program for small auto dealers' Web sites and a cash-back program offering customers 20 percent of revenues received for their referrals. "We continue to look for more and more ways to add value," Raines said. Common B2C e-business models include e-shops and e-malls.[21]

E-Shop

An *e-shop,* sometimes referred to as an *e-store* or *e-tailer,* is a version of a retail store where customers can shop at any hour of the day without leaving their home or office. These online stores sell and support a variety of products and services. The online businesses channeling their goods and services via the Internet only, such as Amazon.com, are called pure plays. The others are an extension of traditional retail outlets that sell online as well as through a traditional physical store. They are generally known as "bricks and clicks" or "clicks and mortar" organizations, such as the Gap (www.gap.com) and Best Buy (www.bestbuy.com) (see Figure 14.5).

FIGURE 14.4

Business-to-Business E-Marketplace Overview

E-Business

FIGURE 14.5

Types of Businesses

Business Types	
Brick-and-mortar business	A business that operates in a physical store without an Internet presence.
Pure-play (virtual) business	A business that operates on the Internet only without a physical store. Examples include Amazon.com and Expedia.com.
Click-and-mortar business	A business that operates in a physical store and on the Internet. Examples include REI and Barnes and Noble.

FIGURE 14.6

Online Auctions

Online Auctions	
Electronic Auction (e-auction)	Sellers and buyers solicit consecutive bids from each other and prices are determined dynamically.
Forward Auction	An auction that sellers use as a selling channel to many buyers and the highest bid wins.
Reverse Auction	An auction that buyers use to purchase a product or service, selecting the seller with the lowest bid.

E-Mall

An *e-mall* consists of a number of e-shops; it serves as a gateway through which a visitor can access other e-shops. An e-mall may be generalized or specialized depending on the products offered by the e-shops it hosts. Revenues for e-mall operators include membership fees from participating e-shops, advertising, and possibly a fee on each transaction if the e-mall operator also processes payments. E-shops in e-malls benefit from brand reinforcement and increased traffic as visiting one shop on the e-mall often leads to browsing "neighboring" shops. An example of an e-mall is the Arizona e-mall www.1az1.com/shopping.

CONSUMER-TO-BUSINESS (C2B)

Consumer-to-business (C2B) applies to any consumer that sells a product or service to a business over the Internet. One example of this e-business model is Priceline.com where bidders (or customers) set their prices for items such as airline tickets or hotel rooms, and a seller decides whether to supply them. The demand for C2B e-business will increase over the next few years due to customers' desires for greater convenience and lower prices.

CONSUMER-TO-CONSUMER (C2C)

Consumer-to-consumer (C2C) applies to sites primarily offering goods and services to assist consumers interacting with each other over the Internet. The Internet's most successful C2C online auction Web site, eBay, links like-minded buyers and sellers for a small commission. Figure 14.6 displays the different types of online auctions.

C2C online communities, or virtual communities, interact via e-mail groups, Web-based discussion forums, or chat rooms. C2C business models are consumer-driven and opportunities are available to satisfy most consumers' needs, ranging from finding a mortgage to job hunting. They are global swap shops based on customer-centered communication. One C2C community, KazaA, allows users to download MP3 music files, enabling users to exchange files. Figure 14.7 highlights the different types of C2C communities that are thriving on the Internet.

FIGURE 14.7

C2C Communities

C2C Communities
■ **Communities of interest**—People interact with each other on specific topics, such as golfing and stamp collecting.
■ **Communities of relations**—People come together to share certain life experiences, such as cancer patients, senior citizens, and car enthusiasts.
■ **Communities of fantasy**—People participate in imaginary environments, such as fantasy football teams and playing one-on-one with Michael Jordan.

E-Business Benefits and Challenges

According to an NUA Internet Survey, the Internet links more than 1 billion people worldwide. Experts predict that global Internet usage will nearly triple between 2006 and 2010, making e-business a more significant factor in the global economy. As e-business improves, organizations will experience benefits and challenges alike. Figure 14.8 details e-business benefits for an organization.[22]

The Internet is forcing organizations to refocus their information systems from the inside out. A growing number of companies are already using the Internet to streamline their business processes, procure materials, sell products, automate customer service, and create new revenue streams. Although the benefits of e-business systems are enticing, developing, deploying, and managing these systems is not always easy. Unfortunately, e-business is not something a business can just go out and buy. Figure 14.9 details the challenges facing e-business.

A key element of e-marketplaces is their ability to provide not only transaction capabilities but also dynamic, relevant content to trading partners. The original e-business Web sites provided shopping cart capabilities built around product catalogs. As a result of the complex e-marketplace that must support existing business processes and systems, content is becoming even more critical for e-marketplaces. Buyers need good content description to make informed purchases, and sellers use content to properly market and differentiate themselves from the competition. Content and product description establish the common understanding between both parties to the transaction. As a result, the accessibility, usability, accuracy, and richness of that content directly affect the transaction. Figure 14.10 on page 195 displays the different benefits and challenges of various e-marketplace revenue models.

E-Business Success

Mashups

A **Web mashup** is a Web site or Web application that uses content from more than one source to create a completely new service. The term is typically used in the context of music; putting Jay-Z lyrics over a Radiohead song makes something old become new. The Web version of a mashup allows users to mix map data, photos, video, news feeds, blog entries and so on. Content used in mashups is typically sourced from an **application programming interface (API),** which is a set of routines, protocols, and tools for building software applications. A good API makes

E-Business Benefits	
Highly Accessible	Businesses can operate 24 hours a day, 7 days a week, 365 days a year.
Increased Customer Loyalty	Additional channels to contact, respond to, and access customers helps contribute to customer loyalty.
Improved Information Content	In the past, customers had to order catalogs or travel to a physical facility before they could compare price and product attributes. Electronic catalogs and Web pages present customers with updated information in real time about goods, services, and prices.
Increased Convenience	E-business automates and improves many of the activities that make up a buying experience.
Increased Global Reach	Businesses, both small and large, can reach new markets.
Decreased Cost	The cost of conducting business on the Internet is substantially smaller than traditional forms of business communication.

FIGURE 14.8

E-Business Benefits

FIGURE 14.9

E-Business Challenges

E-Business Challenges	
Protecting Consumers	Consumers must be protected against unsolicited goods and communication, illegal or harmful goods, insufficient information about goods or their suppliers, invasion of privacy, and cyberfraud.
Leveraging Existing Systems	Most companies already use information technology to conduct business in non-Internet environments, such as marketing, order management, billing, inventory, distribution, and customer service. The Internet represents an alternative and complementary way to do business, but it is imperative that e-business systems integrate existing systems in a manner that avoids duplicating functionality and maintains usability, performance, and reliability.
Increasing Liability	E-business exposes suppliers to unknown liabilities because Internet commerce law is vaguely defined and differs from country to country. The Internet and its use in e-business have raised many ethical, social, and political issues, such as identity theft and information manipulation.
Providing Security	The Internet provides universal access, but companies must protect their assets against accidental or malicious misuse. System security, however, must not create prohibitive complexity or reduce flexibility. Customer information also needs to be protected from internal and external misuse. Privacy systems should safeguard the personal information critical to building sites that satisfy customer and business needs. A serious deficiency arises from the use of the Internet as a marketing means. Sixty percent of Internet users do not trust the Internet as a payment channel. Making purchases via the Internet is considered unsafe by many. This issue affects both the business and the consumer. However, with encryption and the development of secure Web sites, security is becoming less of a constraint for e-businesses.
Adhering to Taxation Rules	The Internet is not yet subject to the same level of taxation as traditional businesses. While taxation should not discourage consumers from using electronic purchasing channels, it should not favor Internet purchases over store purchases either. Instead, a tax policy should provide a level playing field for traditional retail businesses, mail-order companies, and Internet-based merchants. The Internet marketplace is rapidly expanding, yet it remains mostly free from traditional forms of taxation. In one recent study, uncollected state and local sales taxes from e-business were projected to exceed $60 billion in 2008.

it easier to develop a program by providing all the building blocks. A programmer puts the blocks together. Most operating environments, such as Microsoft Windows, provide an API so that programmers can write applications consistent with the operating environment. Many people experimenting with mashups are using Microsoft, Google, eBay, Amazon, Flickr, and Yahoo APIs, which has led to the creation of mashup editors. ***Mashup editors*** are WSYIWYGs (What You See Is What You Get) for mashups. They provide a visual interface to build a mashup, often allowing the user to drag and drop data points into a Web application.[23]

Whoever thought technology could help sell bananas? Dole Organic now places three-digit farm codes on each banana and creates a mashup using Google Earth and its banana database. Socially and environmentally conscious buyers can plug the numbers into Dole's Web site and look at a bio of the farm where the bananas were raised. The site tells the story of the farm and its surrounding community, lists its organic certifications, posts some photos, and offers a link to satellite images of the farm in Google Earth. Customers can personally monitor the production and

Revenue Models	Advantages	Limitations
Transaction fees	■ Can be directly tied to savings (both process and price savings) ■ Important revenue source when high level of liquidity (transaction volume) is reached	■ If process savings are not completely visible, use of the system is discouraged (incentive to move transactions offline) ■ Transaction fees likely to decrease with time
License fees	■ Creates incentives to do many transactions ■ Customization and back-end integration leads to lock-in of participants	■ Up-front fee is a barrier to entry for participants ■ Price differentiation is complicated
Subscription fees	■ Creates incentives to do transactions ■ Price can be differentiated ■ Possibility to build additional revenue from new user groups	■ Fixed fee is a barrier to entry for participants
Fees for value-added services	■ Service offering can be differentiated ■ Price can be differentiated ■ Possibility to build additional revenue from established and new user groups (third parties)	■ Cumbersome process for customers to continually evaluate new services
Advertising fees	■ Well-targeted advertisements can be perceived as value-added content by trading participants ■ Easy to implement	■ Limited revenue potential ■ Overdone or poorly targeted advertisements can be disturbing elements on the Web site

FIGURE 14.10

The Benefits and Challenges of Various E-Marketplace Revenue Models

treatment of their fruit from the tree to the grocer. The process assures customers that their bananas have been raised to proper organic standards on an environmentally friendly, holistically minded plantation. Other interesting mashups include:

- **1001 Secret Fishing Holes:** Over a thousand fishing spots in national parks, wildlife refuges, lakes, campgrounds, historic trails etc. (Google Maps API).
- **25 Best Companies to Work For:** Map of the 100 best U.S. companies to work for as rated by *Fortune* magazine (Google Maps API).
- **Album Covers:** Uses the Amazon API and an Ajax-style user interface to retrieve CD/DVD covers from the Amazon catalog (Amazon eCommerce API).
- **Gawker:** A handy mashup for keeping up with celebrity sightings in New York City. Readers are encouraged to e-mail as soon as the celeb is spotted (Google Maps API).
- **Gigul8tor:** Provides a data entry page where bands can enter information about upcoming gigs and venues. Gigul8tor displays a list of possible locations depending on the venue engine and enters event information right into Eventful in an interface designed just for bands. It shows how different user interfaces could be built in front of Eventful with mashup techniques.
- **GBlinker:** A Google pin wired to a serial port so it flashes when e-mail arrives.
- **OpenKapow:** Offers a platform for creating Web-based APIs, feeds, and HTML snippets from any Web site, taking mashup possibilities way beyond the more than 300 APIs offered on ProgrammableWeb.
- **The Hype Machine:** Combines blog posts from a set of curated music blogs with Amazon sales data and upcoming events. The Hype Machine tracks songs and discussion posted on the best blogs about music. It integrates with iTunes to take customers right from the Web page to the track they are interested in. If the customer prefers buying through Amazon, The Hype Machine figures out what CD page to display.

- **Zillow:** Sophisticated home valuation tools with 65 million listings and extensive data on comparables (Microsoft Virtual Earth API).
- **ProgrammableWeb:** The favorite community Web site of mashup developers provides comprehensive listings of APIs available on the Web and includes forums where developers can discuss how to best use them.[24]

OPENING CASE STUDY QUESTIONS

1. Identify the type of e-business model eBay is using and explain why it has been so successful.

2. Other major Web sites, like Amazon.com and Yahoo!, have entered the e-marketplace with far less success than eBay. How has eBay maintained its dominant position?

3. What are the three different types of online auctions and which one is eBay using?

Chapter Fourteen Case: eBiz

Amazing things are happening on the Internet, things nobody would believe. Here are two stories that demonstrate how innovation, creativity, and a great idea can turn the Internet into a cash cow.

A Million Dollar Homepage

The Million Dollar Homepage is a Web site conceived by Alex Tew, a 21-year-old student from Cricklade, Wiltshire, England, to help raise money for his university education. Launched on August 26, 2005, the Web site is said to have generated a gross income of $1,037,100 and has a current Google PageRank of 7.

The index page of the site consists of a 1000 by 1000 pixel grid (1 million pixels), on which he sells image-based links for $1 per pixel, in minimum 10 by 10 blocks. A person who buys one or more of these pixel blocks can design a tiny image that will be displayed on the block, decide which URL the block will link to, and write a slogan that appears when the cursor hovers over the link. The aim of the site was to sell all of the pixels in the image, thus generating $1 million of income for the creator, which seems to have been accomplished. On January 1, 2006, the final 1,000 pixels left were put up for auction on eBay. The auction closed on January 11 with the winning bid of $38,100. This brought the final tally to $1,037,100 in gross income. See the Million Dollar Homepage on the next page.[25]

One Red Paper Clip

The Web site One Red Paperclip was created by Kyle MacDonald, a Canadian blogger who bartered his way from a single paper clip to a house in a series of trades spanning almost one year. MacDonald began with one red paper clip on July 14, 2005. By July 5, 2006, a chain of bartering had ultimately led to trading a movie role for a two-story farmhouse in Kipling, Saskatchewan. On July 7, 2006—almost exactly one year after MacDonald began his experiment—the deed to the house was signed. In September, at the housewarming party

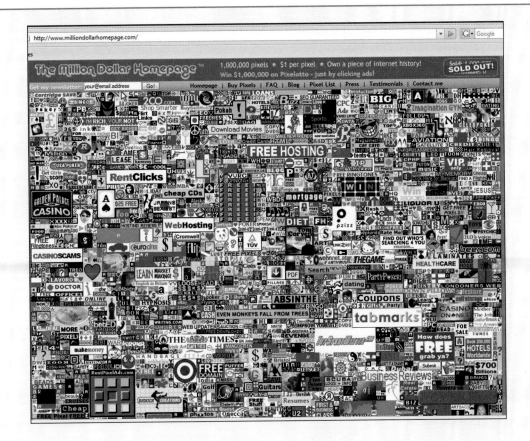

where 12 of the 14 traders were present, he proposed to his girlfriend and she accepted. The wedding ring was made from the original red paper clip he got back from the first woman to have agreed to trade with him.

Following is the timeline, based on the Web site and as summarized by the BBC:

- On July 14, 2005, MacDonald went to Vancouver and traded the paper clip for a fish-shaped pen.
- MacDonald then traded the pen the same day for a hand-sculpted doorknob from Seattle, Washington, which he nicknamed Knob-T.
- On July 25, 2005, MacDonald traveled to Amherst, Massachusetts, with a friend to trade the Knob-T for a Coleman camp stove (with fuel).
- On September 24, 2005, he went to San Clemente, California, and traded the camp stove for a Honda generator, from a U.S. Marine.
- On November 16, 2005, MacDonald made a second (and successful) attempt (after having the generator confiscated by the New York City Fire Department) in Maspeth, Queens, to trade the generator for an "instant party": an empty keg, an IOU for filling the keg with the beer of the holder's choice, and a neon Budweiser sign.
- On December 8, 2005, he traded the "instant party" to Quebec comedian and radio person-ality Michel Barrette for a Ski-doo snowmobile.
- Within a week of that, MacDonald traded the snowmobile for a two-person trip to Yahk, British Columbia, in February 2006.
- On or about January 7, 2006, the second person on the trip to Yahk traded MacDonald a cube van for the privilege.
- On or about February 22, 2006, he traded the cube van for a recording contract with Metal Works in Toronto.

- On or about April 11, 2006, MacDonald traded the recording contract to Jody Gnant for a year's rent in Phoenix, Arizona.
- On or about April 26, 2006, he traded the one year's rent in Phoenix, Arizona, for one afternoon with Alice Cooper.
- On or about May 26, 2006, MacDonald traded the one afternoon with Alice Cooper for a KISS motorized snow globe.
- On or about June 2, 2006, he traded the KISS motorized snow globe to Corbin Bernsen for a role in the film *Donna on Demand*.
- On or about July 5, 2006, MacDonald traded the movie role for a two-story farmhouse in Kipling, Saskatchewan.

Questions

1. How else can you use the Internet to raise money?
2. What types of businesses could benefit from trading on the Internet?
3. Can you think of any other disruptive or non-traditional ways that you could use the Internet?

BUSINESS PLUG-IN POINTER>>

Review **Business Plug-In B11 "E-Business Models"** for an overview of how business functions are using the Internet to reshape the way they conduct business and explore the complex network of suppliers, distributors, and customers who deal with each other via the Internet.

Creating Collaborative Partnerships

Teams, Partnerships, and Alliances

To be successful—and avoid being eliminated by the competition—an organization must constantly undertake new initiatives, address both minor and major problems, and capitalize on significant opportunities. To support these activities, an organization often will create and utilize teams, partnerships, and alliances because the expertise needed is beyond the scope of a single individual or organization. These teams, partnerships, and alliances can be formed internally among a company's employees or externally with other organizations (see Figure 15.1).

Businesses of all sizes and in all markets have witnessed the benefits of leveraging their IT assets to create competitive advantage. Whereas information technology efforts in the past were aimed at increasing operational efficiency, the advent and proliferation of network-based computing (the Internet being the most visible, but not only, example) has enabled organizations to build systems with which all sorts of communities can interact. The ultimate result will allow organizations to do business with customers, business partners, suppliers, governments and regulatory agencies, and any other community relevant to their particular operation or activity.

Solution People

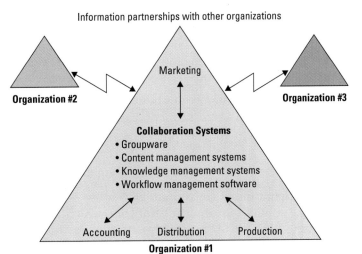

FIGURE 15.1

Teams, Partnerships, and Alliances Within and External to an Organization

Information partnerships with other organizations

Organization #2

Organization #3

Marketing

Collaboration Systems
- Groupware
- Content management systems
- Knowledge management systems
- Workflow management software

Accounting   Distribution   Production

Organization #1

In the same way that organizations use internal teams, they are increasingly forming alliances and partnerships with other organizations. The ***core competency*** of an organization is its key strength, a business function that it does better than any of its competitors. Apple Computer is highly regarded for its strength in product design, while Accenture's core competency is the design and installation of information systems. A ***core competency strategy*** is one in which an organization chooses to focus specifically on what it does best (its core competency) and forms partnerships and alliances with other specialist organizations to handle nonstrategic business processes. Strategic alliances enable businesses to gain competitive advantages through access to a partner's resources, including markets, technologies, and people. Teaming up with another business adds complementary resources and capabilities, enabling participants to grow and expand more quickly and efficiently, especially fast-growing companies that rely heavily on outsourcing many areas of their business to extend their technical and operational resources. In the outsourcing process, they save time and boost productivity by not having to develop their own systems from scratch. They are then free to concentrate on innovation and their core business.

Information technology makes such business partnerships and alliances easier to establish and manage. An ***information partnership*** occurs when two or more organizations cooperate by integrating their IT systems, thereby providing customers with the best of what each can offer. The advent of the Internet has greatly increased the opportunity for IT-enabled business partnerships and alliances. Amazon developed a profitable business segment by providing e-business outsourcing services to other retailers that use Amazon's Web site software. Some well-known retailers partnering with Amazon include Office Depot and Target.[26]

Collaboration Systems

Collaboration

Heineken USA has shortened its inventory cycle time for beer production and distribution from three months to four weeks. By using its collaborative system to forecast demand and expedite shipping, the company has dramatically cut inventory levels and shipping costs while increasing sales.

Over the past few years most business processes have changed on various dimensions (e.g., flexibility, interconnectivity, coordination style, autonomy) because of market conditions and organizational models. Frequently, information is located within physically separated systems as more and more organizations spread their reach globally. This creates a need for a software infrastructure that enables collaboration systems.

A ***collaboration system*** is an IT-based set of tools that supports the work of teams by facilitating the sharing and flow of information. Collaboration solves specific business tasks such as telecommuting, online meetings, deploying applications, and remote project and sales management (see Figure 15.2).

Collaboration systems allow people, teams, and organizations to leverage and build upon the ideas and talents of staff, suppliers, customers, and business partners. It involves unique business challenges that:

- Include complex interactions between people who may be in different locations and desire to work across function and discipline areas.

- Require flexibility in work process and the ability to involve others quickly and easily.

- Call for creating and sharing information rapidly and effortlessly within a team.

Most organizations collaborate with other companies in some capacity. Consider the supplier-customer relationship, which can be thought of in terms of a continuous life cycle of engagement, transaction, fulfillment, and service activities. Rarely do companies excel in all four life cycle areas, either from a business process or from a technology-enabled aspect. Successful organizations identify and invest in their core competencies, and outsource or collaborate for those competencies that are not core to them. Collaboration systems fall into one of two categories:

1. **Unstructured collaboration** (sometimes referred to as **information collaboration**) includes document exchange, shared whiteboards, discussion forums, and e-mail. These functions can improve personal productivity, reducing the time spent searching for information or chasing answers.

2. **Structured collaboration** (or **process collaboration**) involves shared participation in business processes, such as workflow, in which knowledge is hard-coded as rules. This is beneficial in terms of improving automation and the routing of information.

Regardless of location or format—be it unstructured or structured—relevant accurate information must be readily and consistently available to those who need it anytime, anywhere, and on any device. The integration of IT systems enables an organization to provide employees, partners, customers, and suppliers with the ability to access, find, analyze, manage, and collaborate on content. The collaboration can be done across a wide variety of formats, languages, and platforms. Figure 15.3 illustrates many of the typical collaborative functions within most organizations.

Lockheed Martin Aeronautics Company's ability to share complex project information across an extended supply chain in real time was key in its successful bid for a $19 billion Department of Defense (DoD) contract to build 21 supersonic stealth fighters. New government procurement rules require defense contractors to communicate effectively to ensure that deadlines are met, costs are controlled, and projects are managed throughout the life cycle of the contract.[27]

FIGURE 15.2

Collaborative Business Areas

FIGURE 15.3

Typical Collaborative Business Functions

Function	Collaborator(s)	Business Function(s)
Planning and forecasting	Supplier, customer	Real-time information sharing (forecast information and sales information)
Product design	Supplier, customer	Document exchange, computer-aided design (CAD)
Strategic sourcing	Supplier	Negotiation, supplier performance management
Component compatibility testing	Supplier	Component compatibility
Pricing	Supplier, customer	Pricing in supply chain
Marketing	Supplier, customer	Joint/cooperative marketing campaigns, branding
Sales	Customer	Shared leads, presentations, configuration and quotes
Make-to-order	Customer	Requirements, capabilities, contract terms
Order processing	Supplier, customer	Order solution
Fulfillment: Logistics and service	Supplier, customer	Coordination of distribution
International trade logistics	Customer	Document exchange, import/export documents
Payment	Customer	Order receipt, invoicing
Customer service/support	Supplier, customer	Shared/split customer support

In anticipation of the contract, the Fort Worth, Texas, unit of Lockheed Martin Corporation developed a real-time collaboration system that can tie together its partners, suppliers, and DoD customers via the Internet. The platform lets participants collectively work on product design and engineering tasks as well as supply chain and life cycle management issues. Lockheed will host all transactions and own the project information. The platform will let DoD and Lockheed project managers track the daily progress of the project in real time. This is the first major DoD project with such a requirement. The contract, awarded to the Lockheed unit and partners Northrop Grumman Corp. and BAE Systems, is the first installment in what could amount to a $200 billion program for 3,000 jet fighters over 40 years. The strengths of the collaboration process lie with the integration of many systems, namely:[29]

- Knowledge management systems
- Content management systems
- Workflow management systems
- Groupware systems

Knowledge Management Systems

Knowledge management (KM) involves capturing, classifying, evaluating, retrieving, and sharing information assets in a way that provides context for effective decisions and actions. It is best to think of KM in the broadest context. Succinctly put, KM is the process through which organizations generate value from their intellectual and knowledge-based assets. Most often, generating value from such assets involves codifying what employees, partners, and customers know, and sharing that information among employees, departments, and even with other companies to devise best practices. The definition says nothing about technology; while KM is often facilitated by IT, technology by itself is not KM.

Think of a golf caddie as a simplified example of a knowledge worker. Good caddies do more than carry clubs and track down wayward balls. When asked, a good caddie will give advice to golfers, such as, "The wind makes the ninth hole play 15 yards longer." Accurate advice may lead to a bigger tip at the end of the day. The golfer, having derived a benefit from the caddie's advice, may be more likely to play that course again. If a good caddie is willing to share what he knows with other caddies, then they all may eventually earn bigger tips. How would KM work to make this happen? The caddie master may decide to reward caddies for sharing their knowledge by offering them credits for pro shop merchandise. Once the best advice is collected, the course manager would publish the information in notebooks (or make it available on PDAs) and distribute them to all the caddies. The end result of a well-designed KM program is that everyone wins. In this case, caddies get bigger tips and deals on merchandise, golfers play better because they benefit from the collective experience of caddies, and the course owners win because better scores lead to repeat business.[30]

KM IN BUSINESS

KM has assumed greater urgency in American business over the past few years as millions of baby boomers prepare to retire. When they punch out for the last time, the knowledge they gleaned about their jobs, companies, and industries during their long careers will walk out with them—unless companies take measures to retain their insights. In addition, CIOs who have entered into outsourcing agreements must address the thorny issue of transferring the knowledge of their full-time staff members, who are losing their jobs because of an outsourcing deal, to the outsourcer's employees.[31]

Knowledge can be a real competitive advantage for an organization. Information technology can distribute an organization's knowledge base by interconnecting people and digitally gathering their expertise. The primary objective of knowledge management is to be sure that a company's knowledge of facts, sources of information, and solutions are readily available to all employees whenever it is needed.

Such knowledge management requires that organizations go well beyond providing information contained in spreadsheets, databases, and documents. It must include expert information that typically resides in people's heads. A **knowledge management system (KMS)** supports the capturing, organization, and dissemination of knowledge (i.e., know-how) throughout an organization. It is up to the organization to determine what information qualifies as knowledge.

Knowledge
Management

EXPLICIT AND TACIT KNOWLEDGE

Not all information is valuable. Individual companies must determine what information qualifies as intellectual and knowledge-based assets. In general, intellectual and knowledge-based assets fall into one of two categories: explicit or tacit. As a rule, **explicit knowledge** consists of anything that can be documented, archived, and codified, often with the help of IT. Examples of explicit knowledge are assets such as patents, trademarks, business plans, marketing research, and customer lists.

Tacit knowledge is the knowledge contained in people's heads. The challenge inherent in tacit knowledge is figuring out how to recognize, generate, share, and manage knowledge that resides in people's heads. While information technology in the form of e-mail, instant messaging, and related technologies can help facilitate the dissemination of tacit knowledge, identifying it in the first place can be a major obstacle. Shadowing and joint problem solving are two best practices for transferring or re-creating tacit knowledge inside an organization.[32]

Shadowing

With shadowing, less experienced staff observe more experienced staff to learn how the more experienced counterparts approach their work. Dorothy Leonard and Walter Swap, two knowledge management experts, stress the importance of having the protégé discuss his or her observations with the expert to deepen the dialog and crystallize the knowledge transfer.

Joint Problem Solving

Another sound approach is joint problem solving by expert and novice. Because people are often unaware of how they approach problems or do their work and therefore cannot automatically generate step-by-step instructions for doing whatever they do, having a novice and expert work together on a project will bring the expert's approach to light. The difference between shadowing and joint problem solving is that shadowing is more passive. With joint problem solving, the expert and the novice work hand in hand on a task.[33]

Information is of little use unless it is analyzed and made available to the right people, at the right place, and at the right time. To get the most value from intellectual assets, knowledge must be shared. An effective KMS system should help do one or more of the following:

- Foster innovation by encouraging the free flow of ideas.
- Improve customer service by streamlining response time.
- Boost revenues by getting products and services to market faster.

- Enhance employee retention rates by recognizing the value of employees' knowledge.

- Streamline operations and reduce costs by eliminating redundant or unnecessary processes.

A creative approach to knowledge management can result in improved efficiency, higher productivity, and increased revenues in practically any business function. Figure 15.4 indicates the reasons organizations launch KMS.

Software is helping ChevronTexaco Corporation improve how it manages the assets in oil fields by enabling employees in multiple disciplines to easily access and share the information they need to make decisions. ChevronTexaco teams of 10 to 30 people are responsible for managing the assets, such as the drilling equipment, pipelines, and facilities, for a particular oil field. Within each team, earth scientists and various engineers with expertise in production, reservoir, and facilities work together to keep the oil field up and running. Each member of the asset team needs to communicate with other members to make decisions based on the collection and analysis of huge amounts of information from various departments. Individual team members can look at information from the perspective of their own department.

This has helped ChevronTexaco achieve a 30 percent productivity gain, a 50 percent improvement in safety performance, and more than $2 billion in operating cost reductions. Through KMSs, ChevronTexaco has restructured its gasoline retailing business and now drills oil and gas wells faster and cheaper.[34]

Not every organization matches ChevronTexaco's success with KM. Numerous KM projects have failed over the past few years, generating an unwillingness to undertake—or even address—KM issues among many organizations. However, KM is an effective tool if it is tied directly to discrete business needs and opportunities. Beginning with targeted projects that deliver value quickly, companies can achieve the success that has proved elusive with many big-bang approaches. Successful KM projects typically focus on creating value in a specific process area, or even just for a certain type of transaction. Companies should start with one job at a time—preferably the most knowledge-oriented one—and build KM into a job function in a way that

FIGURE 15.4

Key Reasons
Organizations Launch
Knowledge Management
Systems

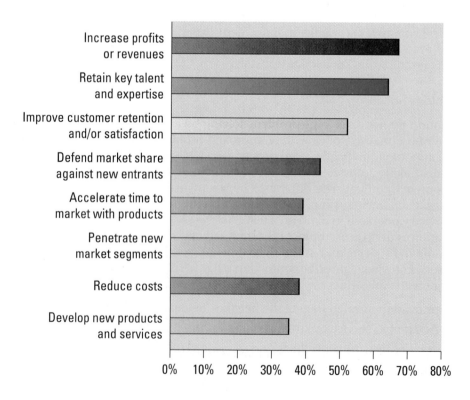

actually helps employees do their work better and faster, then expand to the next most knowledge-intensive job, and so on. Celebrating even small success with KM will help build a base of credibility and support for future KM projects.[35]

KM TECHNOLOGIES

KM is not a purely technology-based concept. Organizations that implement a centralized database system, electronic message board, Web portal, or any other collaborative tool in the hope that they have established a KMS are wasting both their time and money.

Although tools don't make a KMS, such a system does need tools, from standard, off-the-shelf e-mail packages to sophisticated collaboration tools designed specifically to support community building and identity. Generally, KMS tools fall into one or more of the following categories:[36]

- Knowledge repositories (databases).
- Expertise tools.
- E-learning applications.
- Discussion and chat technologies.
- Search and data mining tools.

KM AND SOCIAL NETWORKING

Companies that have been frustrated by traditional KM efforts are increasingly looking for ways to find out how knowledge flows through their organization, and social networking analysis can show them just that. *Social networking analysis (SNA)* is a process of mapping a group's contacts (whether personal or professional) to identify who knows whom and who works with whom. In enterprises, it provides a clear picture of how far-flung employees and divisions work together and can help identify key experts in the organization who possess the knowledge needed to, say, solve a complicated programming problem or launch a new product.

M&M maker Mars used SNA to identify how knowledge flows through its organizations, who holds influence, who gives the best advice, and how employees share information. The Canadian government's central IT unit used SNA to establish which skills it needed to retain and develop, and to determine who, among the 40 percent of the workforce that was due to retire within five years, had the most important knowledge and experience to begin transferring to others.[37]

SNA is not a replacement for traditional KM tools such as knowledge databases or portals, but it can provide companies with a starting point for how best to proceed with KM initiatives. As a component to a larger KM strategy, SNA can help companies identify key leaders and then set up a mechanism, such as communities of practice, so that those leaders can pass on their knowledge to colleagues. To identify experts in their organizations, companies can use software programs that track e-mail and other kinds of electronic communication.[38]

Content Management Systems

A *content management system* provides tools to manage the creation, storage, editing, and publication of information in a collaborative environment. As a Web site grows in size and complexity, the business must establish procedures to ensure that things run smoothly. At a certain point, it makes sense to automate this process and use a content management system to manage this effectively. The content management system marketplace is complex, incorporating document management, digital asset management, and Web content management. Figure 15.5 highlights the three primary types of content management systems. Figure 15.6 lists the major content management system vendors.

Common Types of Content Management Systems	
Document management system (DMS)	DMS—Supports the electronic capturing, storage, distribution, archiving, and accessing of documents. A DMS optimizes the use of documents within an organization independent of any publishing medium (for example, the Web). A DMS provides a document repository with information about other information. The system tracks the editorial history of each document and its relationships with other documents. A variety of search and navigation methods are available to make document retrieval easy. A DMS manages highly structured and regulated content, such as pharmaceutical documentation.
Digital asset management (DAM) system	DAM—Though similar to document management, DAM generally works with binary rather than text files, such as multimedia file types. DAM emphasizes file manipulation and conversion, for example, converting GIF files to JPEG.
Web content management (WCM) system	WCM—Adds an additional layer to document and digital asset management that enables publishing content both to intranets and to public Web sites. In addition to maintaining the content itself, WCM systems often integrate content with online processes like e-business systems.

FIGURE 15.5

Common Types of Content Management Systems

WORKING WIKIS

Wikis are Web-based tools that make it easy for users to add, remove, and change online content. *Business wikis* are collaborative Web pages that allow users to edit documents, share ideas, or monitor the status of a project. Most people are familiar with Wikipedia, one of the largest online collaboration Web sites. Employees also use wikis to collaborate; for example, companies such as Intel, Motorola, IBM, and Sony use them for a host of tasks, from setting internal meeting agendas to posting documents related to new products. Many companies rely on wikis to engage customers in ongoing discussions about products. Wikis for Motorola and T-Mobile handsets serve as continually updated user guides. TV networks including ABC and CBS are creating fan wikis that let viewers interact with each other as they unravel mysteries from such shows as *Lost* and *CSI: Crime Scene Investigation.*[39]

A handful of tech-savvy employees at two very different European companies began dabbling in the use of wikis and witnessed a rapid spread of wikis at both companies—Finnish handset-maker Nokia and London- and Frankfurt-based

FIGURE 15.6

Major Content Management System Vendors

Vendors	Strengths	Weaknesses	Costs
Documentum www.documentum.com	Document and digital asset management	Personalization features not as strong as competitors	Major components start at less than $100,000
FatWire www.fatwire.com	Web content management	May not scale to support thousands of users	SPARK, $25,000; Update Engine, $70,000 and up
InterWoven www.interwoven.com	Collaboration, enterprise content management	Requires significant customization	InterWoven 5 Platform, $50,000; average cost for a new customer, $250,000
Percussion www.percussion.com	Web content management	May not scale to support thousands of users	Rhythmyx Content Manager, about $150,000
Stellent www.stellent.com	Document conversion to Web-ready formats	Engineering for very large implementations with thousands of users	Content and Collaboration Servers, $50,000 to $250,000 each
Vignette www.vignette.com	Personalization	Document management and library services are not as robust as others	V6 Multisite Content Manager, $200,000 and up; V6 Content Suite, $450,000 and up

investment bank Dresdner Kleinwort. Nokia estimates at least 20 percent of its 68,000 employees use wiki pages to update schedules and project status, trade ideas, edit files, and so on. "It's a reversal of the normal way things are done," says Stephen Johnston, senior manager for corporate strategy at Nokia, who helped pioneer the technology. Where Nokia once bought outside software to help foster collaboration, now "some of the most interesting stuff is emerging from within the company itself," says Johnston.

It is a similar tale at Dresdner Kleinwort. A few pioneers in the IT department at its London office sent a program called Socialtext to several groups to see how it might be used to facilitate different IT tasks. The wiki program spread so quickly that Dresdner Kleinwort decided to launch its own corporate wiki. By October 2006, the bank's 5,000 employees had created more than 6,000 individual pages and logged about 100,000 hits on the company's official wiki.

The experience of Nokia and Dresdner Kleinwort offer insight into how to nurture the use of a radically new technology to change the way organizations work. Clearly, not everyone recognizes the value of wikis right way. The initial efforts at Dresdner, for example, confused employees and had to be refined to make the technology easier to use. More important than tweaking the technology was a simple edict from one of the proponents: Do not send e-mails, use the wiki. Gradually, employees embraced the use of the wiki, seeing how it increased collaboration and reduced time-consuming e-mail traffic.[40]

Workflow Management Systems

A **workflow** defines all the steps or business rules, from beginning to end, required for a business process. Therefore, **workflow management systems** facilitate the automation and management of business processes and control the movement of work through the business process. Work activities can be performed in series or in parallel and involve people and automated computer systems. In addition, many workflow management systems allow the opportunity to measure and analyze the execution of the process because workflow systems allow the flow of work between individuals and/or departments to be defined and tracked. Workflow software helps automate a range of business tasks and electronically route the right information to the right people at the right time. Users are notified of pending work, and managers can observe status and route approvals through the system quickly.

There are two primary types of workflow systems: messaging-based and database-based. **Messaging-based workflow systems** send work assignments through an e-mail system. The workflow system automatically tracks the order for the work to be assigned and, each time a step is completed, the system automatically sends the work to the next individual in line. For example, each time a team member completes a piece of the project, the system would automatically send the document to the next team member.

Database-based workflow systems store documents in a central location and automatically ask the team members to access the document when it is their turn to edit the document. Project documentation is stored in a central location and team members are notified by the system when it is their turn to log in and work on their portion of the project.

Either type of workflow system helps to present information in a unified format, improves teamwork by providing automated process support, and allows team members to communicate and collaborate within a unified environment. Figure 15.7 lists some typical features associated with workflow management systems.

New York City was experiencing a record number of claims, ranging from injuries resulting from slips on sidewalks to medical malpractice at city hospitals. The city processes over 30,000 claims and incurs $250 million in claim costs annually.

Workflow Feature	Description
Process definition tool	A graphical or textual tool for defining a business process. Each activity within the process is associated with a person or a computer application. Rules are created to determine how the activities progress across the workflow and which controls are in place to govern each activity.
Simulation, prototyping, and piloting	Some systems allow workflow simulation or create prototype and/or pilot versions of a particular workflow to test systems on a limited basis before going into production.
Task initiation and control	The business process defined above is initiated and the appropriate resources (either human and/or IT related) are scheduled and/or engaged to complete each activity as the process progresses.
Rules-based decision making	Rules are created for each step to determine how workflow-related information is to be processed, routed, tracked, and controlled. As an example, one rule might generate e-mail notifications when a condition has been met. Another rule might implement conditional routing of documents and tasks based on the content of fields.
Document routing	In simple systems, this is accomplished by passing a file or folder from one recipient to another (e.g., an e-mail attachment). In sophisticated systems, document routing is completed by checking the documents in and out of a central repository. Both systems might allow for "redlining" of the documents so that each person in the process can add their own comments without affecting the original document.
Applications to view and manipulate information	Word-processors, spreadsheets, and production systems are used to allow workers to create, update, and view information.
Work list	Current tasks are quickly identified along with such things as a due date, goal date, and priority by using work lists. In some systems, an anticipated workload is displayed as well. These systems analyze where jobs are in the workflow and how long each step should take, and then estimate when various tasks will reach a worker's desk.
Task automation	Computerized tasks are automatically invoked. These might include such things as letter writing, e-mail notices, or execution of production systems. Task automation often requires customization of the basic workflow product.
Event notification	Employees can be notified when certain milestones occur or when workload increases.
Process monitoring	The workflow system can provide an organization with valuable information on current workload, future workload, bottlenecks (current or potential), turn-around time, or missed deadlines.
Tracking and logging of activities	Information about each step can be logged. This might include such things as start and completion times, worker(s) assigned to the task, and key status fields. Later, this information can be used to analyze the process or to provide evidence that certain tasks were in fact completed.

FIGURE 15.7

Workflow Management
System Features

Claims are generally filed with the Comptroller's Office, which investigates them and offers to settle meritorious claims. The New York City Comptroller's Office, with the assistance of its consultants Xerox and Universal Systems Inc., utilized a workflow management system to enhance revenues and decrease operating costs. With the implementation of the Omnibus Automated Image Storage Information System (OAISIS) for processing contracts and claims, New York City will save over $20 million. Numerous city organizations were involved in the workflow management system, including Bureau of Law and Adjustment, Office of Contracts/Administration, Management and Accounting Systems, and Bureau of Information Systems.[41]

In supporting all these organizations, the system performs many functions that were previously labor-intensive and detracted from the quality and efficiency of investigations. The workflow management system screens claims to determine accordance with statutory requirements. Acknowledgment letters are generated automatically, with little or no resource allocation involved in assignment of claims or routing of claims to specific work locations. Status letters are automatically generated by the system for certain claim types, thus allowing the Comptroller's Office to keep claimants informed two months, five months, and one year from the date of their filing. All this is done automatically by the workflow management system.

Workflow management systems allow management to schedule individual systematic claim reviews without disrupting the investigation. Management can also see the entire claim process graphically and determine bottlenecks. Deployment of additional resources to needed areas occurs without a management analysis of a particular process problem.

Groupware Systems

Groupware is software that supports team interaction and dynamics including calendaring, scheduling, and videoconferencing. Organizations can use this technology to communicate, cooperate, coordinate, solve problems, compete, or negotiate. While traditional technologies like the telephone qualify as groupware, the term refers to a specific class of technologies relying on modern computer networks, such as e-mail, newsgroups, videophones, and chat rooms. Groupware systems fall along two primary categories (see Figure 15.8):

1. Users of the groupware are working together at the same time (real-time or synchronous groupware) or different times (asynchronous groupware).

2. Users are working together in the same place (colocated or face-to-face) or in different places (non-colocated or distance).

The groupware concept integrates various systems and functionalities into a common set of services or a single (client) application. In addition, groupware can represent a wide range of systems and methods of integration. Figure 15.9 displays the advantages groupware systems offer an organization over single-user systems.

Lotus Notes is one of the world's leading software solutions for collaboration that combines messaging, groupware, and the Internet. The structure of Notes allows it to track, route, and manage documents. Systems that lend themselves to Notes involve tracking, routing, approval, document management, and organization.[42]

Toyota developed an intranet system to promote information sharing within the company and to raise productivity. Unfortunately, the company's conventional e-mail system became overloaded, generating problems. Users did not receive incoming messages and were not able to send messages. Individual departments had introduced their own e-mail systems, which were not always compatible. Messages to other mail systems, including those outside the company, experienced delays. To deal with these difficulties, Toyota's information systems

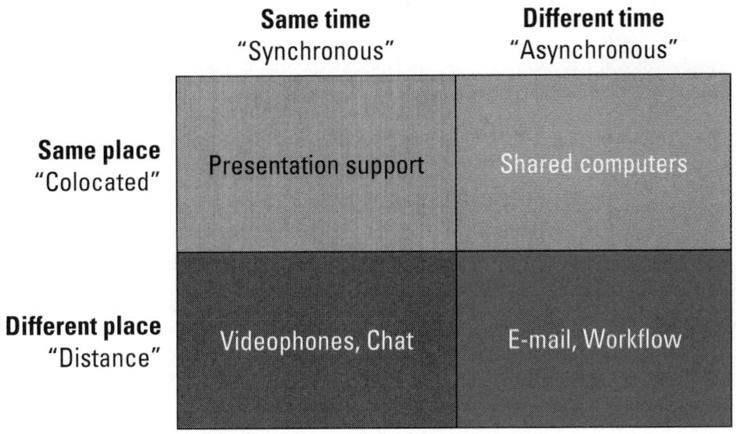

	Same time "Synchronous"	Different time "Asynchronous"
Same place "Colocated"	Presentation support	Shared computers
Different place "Distance"	Videophones, Chat	E-mail, Workflow

FIGURE 15.8

Groupware Systems

FIGURE 15.9

Groupware Advantages

Groupware System Advantages
Facilitating communication (faster, easier, clearer, more persuasive)
Enabling telecommuting
Reducing travel costs
Sharing expertise
Forming groups with common interests where it would not be possible to gather a sufficient number of people face-to-face
Saving time and cost in coordinating group work
Facilitating group problem solving

department reviewed the e-mail system and restructured it so that e-mail, now recognized as an important communication tool, is utilized more effectively in business transactions.[43]

VIDEOCONFERENCING

A **videoconference** is a set of interactive telecommunication technologies that allow two or more locations to interact via two-way video and audio transmissions simultaneously. It has also been called visual collaboration and is a type of groupware. Videoconferencing uses telecommunications of audio and video to bring people at different sites together for a meeting. This can be as simple as a conversation between two people in private offices (point-to-point) or involve several sites (multi-point) with more than one person in large rooms at different sites. Besides the audio and visual transmission of people, videoconferencing can be used to share documents, computer-displayed information, and whiteboards.[44]

Simple analog videoconferences could be established as early as the invention of the television. Such videoconferencing systems consisted of two closed-circuit television systems connected via cable. During the first manned space flights, NASA used two radio frequency (UHF or VHF) links, one in each direction. TV channels routinely use this kind of videoconferencing when reporting from distant locations, for instance. Then mobile links to satellites using special trucks became rather common (see Figure 15.10 for an example of videoconferencing).

FIGURE 15.10

Videoconferencing

Videoconferencing is now being introduced to online networking Web sites to help businesses form profitable relationships quickly and efficiently without leaving their place of work. Several factors support business use of videoconferencing, including:[45]

- Over 60 percent of face-to-face communication is nonverbal. Therefore, an enriched communications tool such as videoconferencing can promote an individual's or a team's identity, context, and emotional situation.

- 56 percent of business professionals waste an estimated 30 minutes a day using inefficient communication methods, costing businesses an estimated $297 billion annually.

- The latest technology is available with reliable and easy-to-use conferencing, fostering collaboration at meetings.

- Enterprises that fail to use modern communications technologies run the very real risk of falling behind their competition.[35]

WEB CONFERENCING

Web conferencing blends audio, video, and document-sharing technologies to create virtual meeting rooms where people "gather" at a password-protected Web site. There, they can chat in conference calls or use real-time text messages. They can mark up a shared document as if it were a blackboard, and even watch live software demos or video clips.

Perhaps the biggest surprise about Web conferencing is its simplicity. Users only need to set up an account and download a few small software files. The best part about a Web conference is that attendees do not have to have the same hardware or software. Every participant can see what is on anyone else's screen, regardless of the application being used (see Figure 15.11 for an example of Web conferencing).[46]

Even with its video features, Web conferencing is not quite like being there—or like being in a sophisticated (and pricey) videoconferencing facility. Still, professionals can accomplish more sitting at their desks than in an airport waiting to make travel connections. A growing number of companies are offering Web conferencing. Leaders in this industry include WebEx, SameTime 2, and Elluminate Live.

FIGURE 15.11

Web Conferencing

INSTANT MESSAGING

E-mail is by far the dominant collaboration application, but real-time collaboration tools like instant messaging are creating a new communication dynamic within organizations. ***Instant messaging*** (sometimes called ***IM*** or ***IMing***) is a type of communications service that enables someone to create a kind of private chat room with another individual in order to communicate in real time over the Internet. In 1992, AOL deployed IM to the consumer market, allowing users to communicate with other IMers through a buddy list. Most of the popular instant messaging programs provide a variety of features, such as:

- Web links: Share links to favorite Web sites.
- Images: Look at an image stored on someone else's computer.
- Sounds: Play sounds.
- Files: Share files by sending them directly to another IMer.
- Talk: Use the Internet instead of a phone to talk.
- Streaming content: Receive real-time or near-real-time stock quotes and news.
- Instant messages: Receive immediate text messages.

Commercial vendors such as AOL and Microsoft offer free instant messaging tools. Real-time collaboration, such as instant messaging, live Web conferencing, and screen or document sharing, creates an environment for decision making. AOL, Microsoft's MSN, and Yahoo! have begun to sell enterprise versions of their instant messaging services that match the capabilities of business-oriented products like IBM's Lotus Sametime. Figure 15.12 demonstrates the IM application presence within IT systems.

IBM Lotus software has released new versions of its real-time collaboration platform, IBM Lotus Instant Messaging and IBM Lotus Web Conferencing, plus its mobile counterpart, IBM Lotus Instant Messaging Everyplace. These built-for-business products let an organization offer presence awareness, secure instant messaging, and Web conferencing. The products give employees instant access to colleagues and company information regardless of time, place, or device.[47]

The bigger issue in collaboration for organizations is cultural. Collaboration brings teams of people together from different regions, departments, and even companies—people who bring different skills, perceptions, and capabilities. A formal collaboration strategy helps create the right environment as well as the right systems for team members.

FIGURE 15.12

Instant Messaging
Application

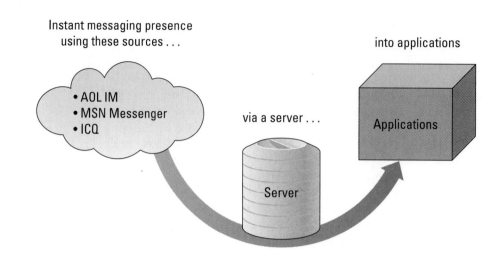

Instant messaging presence using these sources . . .

- AOL IM
- MSN Messenger
- ICQ

via a server . . .

into applications

Server

Applications

OPENING CASE STUDY QUESTIONS

1. Identify which systems eBay could use to collaborate internally.

2. Explain which Internet technologies have facilitated the way in which eBay collaborates with both its customers and business partners.

3. List the four collaboration systems discussed in this chapter and rank them in order of importance to eBay's business.

4. Describe how eBay could leverage the power of a knowledge management system for its employees and for its customers.

Chapter Fifteen Case: DreamWorks Animation Collaboration

Hewlett-Packard (HP) and DreamWorks Animation SKG were the first to introduce a collaboration studio for simulating face-to-face business meetings across long distances. Vyomesh Joshi, executive vice president at HP, and Jeffrey Katzenberg, CEO of DreamWorks, officially unveiled the HP Halo Collaboration Studio in New York City in 2005. Halo enables people in different locations to communicate in a vivid, face-to-face environment in real time. Whether across a country or across the ocean, users can see and hear one another's physical and emotional reactions to conversation and information.

By giving participants the remarkable sense that they are in the same room, the Halo Collaboration Studio is already transforming the way businesses such as PepsiCo, Advanced Micro Devices, and DreamWorks communicate across the globe. Halo significantly increases team effectiveness, provides faster decision-making capabilities, and decreases the need for travel.

"The HP Halo Collaboration Studio enables remote teams to work together in a setting so lifelike that participants feel as though they are in the same room," said Joshi. "To create this experience, HP is harnessing its expertise in color science, imaging, and networking in this new category of innovation. It is something we believe will not only disrupt the traditional videoconferencing market, but will also change the way people work in a global market."

Early in the production of the animated film *Shrek 2*, DreamWorks realized a significant return on investment using the Halo technology. By connecting its California teams in Glendale and Redwood City, DreamWorks was able to speed up many aspects of the production.

"In 2002, while we were producing *Shrek 2*, we realized that DreamWorks needed face-to-face collaboration between key creative talent in different locations," said Katzenberg. "We weren't satisfied with the available videoconferencing systems, so we designed a collaboration solution that would fulfill our needs. HP took the system and turned it into Halo, which is now the only solution on the market that allows this kind of effective communication."

Halo Connection

To connect via Halo, organizations purchase at least two Halo rooms set up for six people each. Three plasma displays in each room enable participants to see those they are collaborating with in life-size images. The rooms come equipped with studio-quality audio and lighting, and participants use a simple on-screen user interface to begin collaborating with just a few mouse clicks.

An intricate software control system ensures Halo rooms work easily and seamlessly together. The control system also provides precise image and color calibration, so participants see each other as they appear in real life. A dedicated HP Halo Video Exchange Network provides a high-bandwidth experience with imperceptible delays between Halo studios worldwide.

To ensure a 24x7 connection and eliminate the need for enterprises to manage the operation and maintenance of a Halo room, services offered include network operations and management, remote diagnostics and calibration, concierge, equipment warranty, and ongoing service and repair.

Participants can easily share documents and data directly from their notebook PCs with individuals in other rooms using a collaboration screen mounted above the plasma displays. The rooms also contain a high-magnification camera that enables individuals to zoom in on objects on a table, revealing the finest of details and color shading, and a phone that opens a conference call line to those not in one of the Halo rooms.

"We believe there is a personal connection that comes with Halo that just clearly doesn't come from any other kind of technology we've used in the past," said Steve Reinemund, CEO of PepsiCo. "Halo is one of the best investments we've made to improve the effectiveness of our business and work/life balance for our people."[48]

Questions

1. How could companies use Halo to increase their business efficiency?
2. Explain how a company like PepsiCo can use Halo to gain a competitive advantage in its industry.
3. How can knowledge management be increased by using a product such as Halo?
4. Why would a company like DreamWorks, that is not IT focused, be interested in collaboration technology?

16 Integrating Wireless Technology in Business

Wireless Fidelity (Wi-Fi)

An hour's drive west of Toronto sits a 120,000-square-foot building where Mike Lazaridis's 20-year dream is coming to life. Seven 125-foot-long assembly lines are stamping out wallet-size BlackBerrys—the wireless handheld computers now in the hands of more than 1.3 million users worldwide—at a rate of about 230 an hour. Lazaridis, the co-CEO of Research in Motion (RIM), gave the go-ahead to ratchet up plant production from five days a week to seven. Orders are surging, so RIM's BlackBerry-making machine does not sleep.[49]

The Motley Fool

Wireless fidelity (wi-fi) is a means of linking computers using infrared or radio signals. Wi-fi is a type of Ethernet, which makes the wireless network a straightforward extension of the wired network. Wireless users can run the same network applications they use on an Ethernet local area network (LAN). Wireless communication can be installed using the existing network infrastructure with minimal retraining or system changes. Laptop users can roam throughout their locales while remaining in contact with the network via strategically placed access points that are plugged into the wired network. One of the biggest benefits of wireless communications is its ability to deliver real-time information.

Business Drivers for Wireless Technologies

United Parcel Service and FedEx have been using wireless technologies for years, making it possible for information about dispatching and deliveries to travel between couriers and central stations. FedEx's famous tracking system, which can find a package's location from its tracking number, uses a wireless courier-management system.[50]

The terms *mobile* and *wireless* are often used synonymously, but actually denote two different technologies. *Mobile technology* means the technology can travel with the user, but it is not necessarily in real time; users can download software, e-mail messages, and Web pages onto their personal digital assistant (PDA), laptop, or other mobile device for portable reading or reference. Information collected while on the road can be synchronized with a PC or corporate server.

Wireless technology, on the other hand, gives users a live (Internet) connection via satellite or radio transmitters. International Data Corporation forecasts that by 2010 nearly two-thirds of handheld devices will include integrated wireless networking.

Drivers of Wireless Technology Growth	
Universal access to information and applications	People are mobile and have more access to information than ever before, but they still need to get to the point where they can access all information anytime, anywhere, anyplace.
The automation of business processes	Wireless technologies have the ability to centralize critical information and eliminate redundant processes.
User convenience, timeliness, and ability to conduct business 24×7×365	People delayed in airports no longer have to feel cut off from the world or their office. Through wireless tools and wireless solutions such as a BlackBerry RIM device, they can access their information anytime, anywhere, anyplace.

FIGURE 16.1

Wireless Drivers

Number of U.S. Users	Wireless Device Technology
Less than 15,000	Smart phones
4,000,000	Web-enabled (WAP) phones
65,000,000	Digital cell phones

FIGURE 16.2

U.S. Wireless Device Users

For instance, newly announced PDAs integrate phones, text messaging, Web browsers, and organizers. Figure 16.1 displays the factors inspiring the growth of wireless technologies.[51]

State government agencies, such as transportation departments, use wireless devices to collect field information, tracking inventory, reporting times, monitoring logistics, and completing forms—all from a mobile environment. The transportation industry is using wireless devices to help determine current locations and alternate driving routes.

Wireless technology is rapidly evolving and is playing an increasing role in the lives of people throughout the world. The final key factor driving the increased use of wireless devices is the sheer number of U.S. wireless device users (see Figure 16.2). With such a large market, businesses simply must embrace wireless technologies or be left behind.[52]

Wireless technologies are transforming how we live, work, and play. Handheld devices continue to offer additional functionality, and cellular networks are advancing rapidly in their increased speed and throughput abilities. These enabling technologies fuel widespread adoption and creation of new and innovative ways to perform business. The big changes that will re-create workplaces, industries, and organizations are coming from wireless technologies. Figure 16.3 displays a few common examples of wireless technologies that are changing our world.

Networks

Advantages of Enterprise Mobility

Organizations have realized that while the value of electronic corporate information can be nearly limitless, it is worth nothing if employees cannot access it. Work does not always get done at an office desk, and the ability to connect remote workers to the information they require to perform their job provides benefits to an organization.

Wireless laptops facilitate emergency room registration so doctors can start working on the patients as soon as the medics wheel them into the hospital. High-end tractors equipped with wireless sensors help farmers monitor everything from the weather to the amount of seed released. Tractors that break down automatically e-mail the service department with the information for the repair. Roaming ticket sellers armed with wi-fi enabled devices and belt-mounted printers shorten

FIGURE 16.3

Wireless Technologies
Changing Business

Wireless Devices Changing Business
■ **Wireless local area network (wLAN):** uses radio waves rather than wires to transmit information across a local area network.
■ **Cellular phones and pagers:** provide connectivity for portable and mobile applications, both personal and business.
■ **Cordless computer peripherals:** connect wirelessly to a computer, such as a cordless mouse, keyboard, and printer.
■ **Satellite television:** allows viewers in almost any location to select from hundreds of channels.
■ **WiMax wireless broadband:** enables wireless networks to extend as far as 30 miles and transfer information, voice, and video at faster speeds than cable. It is perfect for Internet service providers (ISPs) that want to expand into sparsely populated areas, where the cost of bringing in cable wiring or DSL is too high.
■ **Security sensor:** alerts customers to break-ins and errant pop flies. Its dual sensors record vibration and acoustic disturbances—a shattered window—to help avoid false alarms.

the wait at the front gate at theme parks such as Universal Studios. Figure 16.4 lists the wireless technologies influencing business mobility, which are described in detail in the following section.[53]

BLUETOOTH

One challenge to wireless devices is their size. Everyone wants their mobile devices to be small, but many people also curse the tiny, cryptic keyboards that manufacturers squeeze into smart phones and PDAs. The laws of physics have proved a significant barrier to solving this problem, but VKB Inc.'s Bluetooth Virtual Keyboard offers a possible solution (see Figure 16.5). VKB's technology uses a red laser to illuminate a virtual keyboard outline on any surface. Despite its futuristic look, the laser is really just a visual guide to where users put their fingers. A separate illumination and sensor module invisibly tracks when and where each finger touches the surface, translating that into keystrokes or other commands.[54]

Wireless

Bluetooth is an omnidirectional wireless technology that provides limited-range voice and data transmission over the unlicensed 2.4-GHz frequency band, allowing connections with a wide variety of fixed and portable devices that normally would have to be cabled together. Bluetooth headsets allow users to cut the cord and make calls even while their cell phones are tucked away in a briefcase. Wireless Bluetooth printing allows users of a Bluetooth-enabled PDA or laptop to connect to any printer via a Bluetooth adapter connected to the printer's parallel port.[55]

Since Bluetooth's development in 1994 by the Swedish telecommunications company Ericsson, more than 1,800 companies worldwide have signed on to build

FIGURE 16.4

Wireless Technologies
Influencing Business
Mobility

Wireless Technlogies Influencing Business Mobility
■ **Bluetooth:** creating a niche market for traditionally cabled devices.
■ **Radio frequency identification (RFID) tags:** possessing the potential to reinvent the supply chain. Wal-Mart's suppliers must now use the tags for pallets and cases of merchandise.
■ **Satellite:** changing the way television and radio stations operate. Plus, global positioning systems (GPS) allow drivers of cars and trucks, captains of boats and ships, backpackers, hikers, skiers, and pilots of aircraft to ascertain their location anywhere on earth.

products to the wireless specification and promote the new technology in the marketplace. The engineers at Ericsson code-named the new wireless technology Bluetooth to honor a 10th-century Viking King, Harald Bluetooth, who is credited with uniting Denmark and bringing order to the country.

Bluetooth capability is enabled in a device by means of an embedded Bluetooth chip and supporting software. Although Bluetooth is slower than competing wireless LAN technologies, the Bluetooth chip enables Bluetooth networking to be built into a wide range of devices—even small devices such as cellular phones and PDAs. Bluetooth's maximum range is 30 feet, limiting it to gadget-to-gadget communication. There are more than 1,000 Bluetooth products on the market, with 10 more introduced each week.[56]

RADIO FREQUENCY IDENTIFICATION (RFID)

Radio frequency identification (RFID) technologies use active or passive tags in the form of chips or smart labels that can store unique identifiers and relay this information to electronic readers. At Starbucks, good service is nearly as important as good coffee to customer loyalty. But when a delivery person comes knocking on the back door to drop off muffins, it means employees may need to leave their countertop posts, jeopardizing customer service. To help solve the problem, Starbucks is considering using radio frequency identification technology as part of a proposed plan to let its 40,000 suppliers drop off pastries, milk, coffee beans, and other supplies at night, after stores have closed. This solution solves one problem while causing another: How does Starbucks ensure that delivery people do not walk out with as much stuff as they dropped off?[57]

To solve the problem, the company will distribute to its suppliers cards with RFID chips that give delivery people access to stores at night, while recording who is coming and going. *RFID tags* contain a microchip and an antenna, and typically work by transmitting a serial number via radio waves to an electronic reader, which confirms the identity of a person or object bearing the tag.

RFID technology is finally coming into its own. Wal-Mart, the nation's largest retailer, asked suppliers to attach RFID tags to product shipment pallets by the end of 2005 to automate tracking. However, drawbacks to RFID technology, including its high cost and concerns about consumer privacy, must be overcome before it finds widespread use. Figure 16.6 displays the three components of RFID, and Figure 16.7 shows how tracking with RFID tags is expected to work in the supply chain.

As many as 10,000 radio frequency identification tags are taking to the skies, affixed to everything from airline seats to brakes, as part of the Airbus A380, a 550-seat jet. The tags contain serial numbers, codes, and maintenance history that should make it easier to track, fix, and replace parts. Not to be outdone, Boeing is using tags on many of the parts in its upcoming 7E7 Dreamliner, a smaller commercial jet that is set to fly in 2008.

These initiatives are not the first use of RFID in the airline industry, but they represent aggressive plans to further leverage the real-time and detail capabilities of RFID. Boeing and Airbus are equipping all tools and toolboxes with RFID tags.[58]

Integrating RFID and Software

Integrating RFID with enterprise software is expected to change the way companies manage maintenance, combat theft, and even augment Sarbanes-Oxley Act IT initiatives. Oracle and SAP have begun adding RFID capability to their enterprise application suites. Oracle's RFID and Sensor-Based Services analyze and respond to data from RFID so the information can be integrated with Oracle's applications.

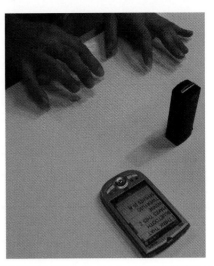

FIGURE 16.5

Bluetooth Virtual Keyboard

Beams of light, which detect the user's movements, make up this virtual keyboard. It can be integrated into mobile phones, laptops, tablet PCs, or even sterile medical environments.

RFID

FIGURE 16.6

Three RFID Components

The Three Components to an RFID System

Tag - A microchip holds data, in this case an EPC (electronic product code), a set of numbers unique to an item. The rest of the tag is an antenna that transmits data to a reader.
EPC example: 01-0000A77-000136BR5

Reader - A reader uses radio waves to read the tag and sends the EPC to computers in the supply chain.

Computer Network - Each computer in the supply chain recognizes the EPC and pulls up information related to the item, such as dates made and shipped, price, and directions for use, from a server maintained by the manufacturer. The computers track the item's location throughout the supply chain.

RFID tags are evolving, too, and the advances will provide more granular information to enterprise software. Today's tags can store an electronic product code. In time, tags could hold more information, making them portable mini-databases.

The possibilities of RFID are endless. Delta Air Lines recently completed a pilot project that used baggage tags incorporating RFID chips instead of the standard bar codes. With RFID readers installed at counters and key sorting locations, not a single duffel was misplaced.[59]

FIGURE 16.7

RFID in the Supply Chain

RFID in the Retail Supply Chain
RFID tags are added to every product and shipping box. At every step of an item's journey, a reader scans one of the tags and updates the information on the server.

The Manufacturer
A reader scans the tags as items leave the factory.

The Distribution Center
Readers in the unloading area scan the tags on arriving boxes and update inventory, avoiding the need to open packages.

The Store
Tags are scanned upon arrival to update inventory. At the racks, readers scan tags as shirts are stocked. At the checkout counter, a cashier can scan individual items with a handheld reader. As items leave the store, inventory is updated. Manufacturers and retailers can observe sales patterns in real time and make swift decisions about production, ordering, and pricing.

The Home
The consumer can have the tag disabled at the store for privacy or place readers in closets to keep track of clothes. With customers' approval, stores can follow purchasing patterns and notify them of sales.

SATELLITE

Microwave transmitters, especially satellite systems, are commonly used to transmit network signals over great distances. A microwave transmitter uses the atmosphere (or outer space) as the transmission medium to send the signal to a microwave receiver. The microwave receiver then either relays the signal to another microwave transmitter or translates the signal to some other form, such as digital impulses, as illustrated in Figure 16.8. Originally, this technology was used almost exclusively for satellite and long-range communication. Recently, however, developments in cellular technology allow complete wireless access to networks, intranets, and the Internet via microwave transmission.[60]

XM Satellite Radio made a tech-savvy decision when it decided to develop the chipsets for XM's radios in-house rather than outsourcing the job. The move allowed the XM service to launch faster and better, giving the company a lead over its archrival, Sirius Satellite Radio. Both companies are growing quickly.

GPS

Global Positioning Systems and Geographic Information Systems

The Department of Defense installed more than 30 satellites in space over the equator to help the military identify positions on Earth. In 1993, the Defense Department made this global positioning technology available for commercial use to anyone who has a GPS. A ***global positioning system (GPS)*** is a device that determines current latitude, longitude, speed, and direction of movement. GPS devices have special microprocessors that analyze satellite signals. Sirf Technology specializes in building GPS microprocessors and charges about $13 per device to put its GPS chipset in phones, electronics, and car navigation systems. Since going public, Sirf Technology has seen revenue climb 60 percent to $117 million with net profits of $30.7 million. With new federal regulation forcing wireless operators to include GPS in their phones and networking equipment, chip demand is sure to explode.[61]

The market for GPS services has grown to over $5 billion with expectations for demand to double over the next few years. Tracking, navigation, and hardware promise to be multibillion-dollar markets. UPS plans to outfit 75,000 drivers with GPS-enabled handhelds to help them reach destinations more efficiently. The handhelds will also trigger e-mail alerts if a company vehicle speeds or ventures into unauthorized areas. Steve Wozniak, Apple co-founder, started a company named Wheels of Zeus that combines GPS data with local wireless networking. The

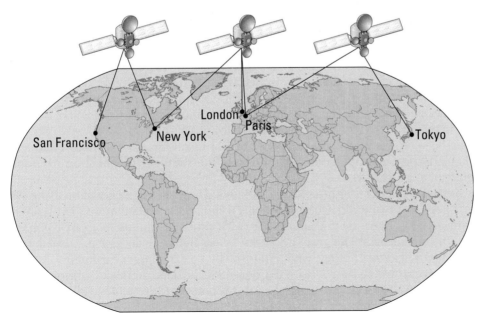

FIGURE 16.8

Satellite Microwave Link

technology helps parents keep tabs on their children or can alert IT managers when company-owned computers leave the premises. Zingo, in the United Kingdom, uses GPS-enabled cars and text messaging to help subscribers hail cabs.

A **geographic information system (GIS)** is designed to work with information that can be shown on a map. Companies that deal in transportation use GISs combined with database and GPS technology. Airlines and shipping companies can plot routes with up-to-the-second information on the location of all their transport vehicles. Hospitals can keep track of where personnel are located by using a GIS and sensors in the ceiling that pick up the transmission of badges worn by hospital staff.

Automobiles have GPSs linked to maps that display in a screen on the dashboard driving directions and exact location of the vehicle. GM offers the OnStar system, which sends a continuous stream of information to the OnStar center about the car's exact location. The new OnStar Vehicle Diagnostics automatically performs hundreds of diagnostic checks on four key operating systems—the engine/transmission, antilock brakes, air bags, and OnStar systems—in GM vehicles. The vehicle is programmed to send the results via e-mail to the owner each month. The unique e-mail report also provides maintenance reminders based on the current odometer reading, remaining engine oil life, and other relevant ownership information.[62]

Some cell phone providers equip their phones with GPS chips that enable users to be located to within a geographical location about the size of a tennis court. This allows emergency services such as 911 to find a cell phone user. Marketers are monitoring cell phone GPS development, hoping to be able to call potential customers when they are walking past their store to let them know of a special sale.[63]

The Future of Wireless

Cirque Du Soleil

One of the strangest Internet innovations in recent history was Microsoft's toilet project. It was a widely reported weird-news item in the spring of 2003, later revealed to be a hoax, and even later to be confirmed by Microsoft as an actual project, albeit a defunct one. The gist of the story was that Microsoft U.K. wanted to create a portable toilet, the iLoo, with a built-in high-speed Internet connection, wireless keyboard, and height-adjustable plasma monitor—a contraption, so they said, that would appeal to the British market.

Now it seems that the restroom and the Internet are converging yet again. A *hotspot* consists of one or more access points positioned on a ceiling, wall, or other strategic spot in a public place to provide maximum wireless coverage for a specific area. Users in range of the hotspot can then access the Internet from their wireless device. The latest front in the wireless hotspot movement is the interstate rest area. "I know it sounds strange at first, but when you think about it, rest areas are a great fit for wi-fi," said Mark Wheeler, CEO of I Spot Networks, a wireless Internet service provider. Wheeler noted that highway travelers often actively seek out an Internet connection because the Internet has become so integral to 21st century life.

Working in conjunction with state transportation departments, I Spot Networks is rolling out hotspots along interstates in Iowa, Missouri, and Nebraska. The company also targets more conventional hotspot locations, such as hotels and coffee shops, but it believes that heavily traveled interstate corridors are an overlooked hotspot opportunity.

Analysts predict that more than 120 million U.S. consumers will be using wireless devices for Internet access by 2008. Overall, there will be more than 1.4 billion wireless subscribers by the end of 2010, with about 500 million of those using wireless Internet access. The growth of the wireless market will drive the development of new wireless technology, which in turn will create a larger market for Bluetooth connectivity, which allows wireless handheld devices, personal computers, and laptops to work together. Analysts expect Bluetooth shipments to rise from fewer than 1 million in 2001 to 3 billion in 2010.[64]

Application	Western Europe	Eastern Europe	United States
On 6-point interest scale, 6 = high interest, and 1 = low interest:			
E-mail	4.5	4.7	4.3
Payment authorization/enablement	3.4	3.8	3.0
Banking/trading online	3.5	3.4	3.2
Shopping/reservations	3.0	3.1	2.9
Interactive games	2.0	2.2	2.4

FIGURE 16.9

Current Mobile Phone Users' Applications Interest

Gartner predicts that the future will belong to "The Real-Time Enterprise," the organization that thrives in uncertain times because it can detect sooner and respond faster. Wireless technologies clearly play a major role in increasing an organization's agility.

Wireless access to corporate e-mail systems, often the primary catalyst to an organization's first significant venture into wireless technology, has become the focus of much attention. E-mail is the foremost communication system in most organizations, surpassing voice mail in importance and interest (see Figure 16.9).

Organizations are fast approaching the point where they will have the technical wireless infrastructure to support an always-on connection that will let users roam seamlessly from Starbucks, to a customer site, to conference rooms, and even to a comfortable chair in front of the TV at home.[65]

OPENING CASE STUDY QUESTIONS

1. Why would eBay want to explore the wireless market for new opportunities?
2. With the emergence of mobile technologies, why would eBay be concerned with the lack of compatibility between wireless applications?
3. If eBay chose not to embrace wireless technologies would it be at a disadvantage? Explain your answer.
4. How can a wireless device add value for eBay customers?

Chapter Sixteen Case: UPS versus FedEx: Head-to-Head on Wireless

Federal Express and United Parcel Service are always seeking a competitive edge over one another. And as the two companies are encroaching on each other's primary businesses (UPS on overnight delivery and FedEx on ground delivery), they are concurrently stepping up their wireless deployments as well. The reason: operational efficiency—a critical business requirement aimed at shaving costs, increasing reach, and doing more with the same resources.

Their approaches to deploying wireless technologies over the past 15 years have been markedly different; FedEx has led the way with cutting-edge applications, while UPS has been slower and more deliberate. FedEx deploys new technologies as soon as it can justify the cost and demonstrate improved efficiencies and customer benefit. UPS refreshes its technology base roughly every five to seven years, when it rolls out a unified system in stages that it synchronizes with the life span of the older system. But the goal is the same for both companies: to use next-generation wireless technologies to better manage the delivery of millions of packages that flow through dozens of sorting facilities every day.

	UPS	FedEx
Main hub:	Louisville, Kentucky	Memphis, Tennessee
Total packages handled each day:	13.6 million	5 million
Number of air deliveries daily:	2 million	3.1 million
Wireless devices in field:	90,000	80,000
Wireless devices in sorting facilities:	55,000	70,000
Wireless access points:	9,000	5,000

The two companies are exploiting new wireless technologies in their differing attempts at aiding the two main components of their operations: pickup/delivery and packaging/sorting. Both are also looking ahead to potential applications of radio frequency identification and GPS wireless technologies.

Seeking New Benefits from Wireless

In addition to their major package-scanning retooling efforts, FedEx and UPS continue to investigate what business benefits they might gain from other wireless technologies. Two have gained particular attention: RFID tags, which could replace bar-code scanners, and GPS, which can precisely locate field units.

As UPS and FedEx are showing, wireless technology provides the medium through which dynamic exchange happens. Interconnectedness allows drivers to talk, computers to interact, and businesses to work together. Whether it is wireless routing or fueling of trucks, it is all happening dynamically. Although few companies have the scale of UPS and FedEx, they can adopt many of the wireless technologies scaled to their size, and use devices and network components that fit their operations.[66]

Questions

1. Explain the fundamentals of wireless fidelity.
2. Describe the differences between UPS's and FedEx's use of wi-fi.
3. Identify two types of wireless business opportunities the companies could use to gain a competitive advantage.
4. Describe how RFID could help the companies deal with potential security issues.
5. Develop a Bluetooth, GPS, or satellite product that the parcel delivery business could use to improve efficiencies.

BUSINESS PLUG-IN POINTER>>

Review the **Plug-In Pointer B12 "Emerging Trends and Technologies"** for a closer look at many emerging trends and new technologies such as wireless devices that can help an organization prepare for the future.

In a remarkably short time, the Internet has grown from a virtual playground into a vital, sophisticated medium for business, more specifically, e-business. Online consumers are flooding to the Internet, and they come with very high expectations and a degree of control that they did not have with traditional bricks-and-mortar companies. The enticement of doing business online must be strengthened by the understanding that, to succeed online, businesses will have to be able to deliver a satisfying and consistent customer experience, building brand loyalty and guaranteeing high rates of customer retention.

Strategic alliances enable businesses to gain competitive advantage(s) through access to a partner's resources, including markets, technologies, and people. Teaming up with another business adds complementary resources and capabilities, enabling participants to grow and expand more quickly and efficiently.

KEY TERMS

Application programming
    interforce (API) 193
Bluetooth, 216
Brick-and-mortar business, 191
Business-to-business
    (B2B), 190
Business-to-consumer
    (B2C), 190
Business wiki 206
Click-and-mortar business, 191
Collaboration system, 200
Consumer-to-business
    (C2B), 190
Consumer-to-consumer
    (C2C), 190
Content management
    system, 205
Core competency, 200
Core competency strategy, 200
Database-based workflow
    system, 207
Digital asset management
    system (DAM), 206
Digital Darwinism, 179
Digital divide, 183
Disruptive technology, 179
Document management system
    (DMS), 206
E-business, 178, 189

E-business model, 189
E-commerce, 189
Electronic marketplace
    (e-marketplace), 191
E-mall, 192
E-shop (e-store, e-tailer), 191
Explicit knowledge, 203
Geographic information system
    (GIS), 220
Global positioning system
    (GPS), 219
Groupware, 209
Hypertext transport protocol
    (HTTP), 182
Information partnership, 200
Information reach, 183
Information richness, 183
Instant messaging (IM or
    IMing), 211
Internet, 181
Knowledge management
    (KM), 202
Knowledge management
    system (KMS), 203
Messaging-based workflow
    system, 207
Mashup editor 194
Microwave transmitter, 219
Protocol, 182

Pure-play (virtual)
    business, 191
Radio frequency identification
    (RFID), 217
RFID tag, 217
Semantic Web 185
Service oriented architecture
    (SOA) 186
Social networking analysis
    (SNA), 205
Structured collaboration
    (process collaboration), 201
Sustaining technology, 179
Tacit knowledge, 203
Unstructured collaboration
    (information
    collaboration), 201
Videoconference 210
Web 2.0, 184
Web content management
    system (WCM), 206
Web conferencing 211
Web mashup 193
Wiki 206
Wireless fidelity (wi-fi), 214
Workflow, 207
Workflow management
    system, 207
World Wide Web (WWW), 182

Improving Highway Safety through Collaboration

Information on traffic-related deaths and accidents are two to three years out of date in some states, making it difficult to devise new safety regulations, rebuild unsafe roads, develop safer automobiles, and improve emergency services. Systems used by federal, state, and local agencies to collect and share information need to be overhauled, and the U.S. Department of Transportation's National Highway Traffic Safety Administration said it would ask Congress for $300 million over the next six years to upgrade them.

The goal is to eliminate antiquated paper-based reporting systems and implement a nation-wide initiative to automate and synchronize the collection and sharing of information. The information will include vehicle-related injuries, associated health care costs, safety stops, driver licenses, vehicle registration, and adjudicated violations.

Safer Driving

Federal highway safety officials want $300 million to finance:

- Wireless communications equipment to facilitate electronic information collection and transmission during traffic safety stops.
- Real-time information transfer and editing processes to update driver's license or vehicle registration information from traffic stops or crash sites.
- Centralized access to query all traffic record databases.
- Standardized search capabilities on common queries and information transmission using XML formats.

Few states have the capability to capture and transmit traffic record and crash information electronically, and those that do are limited, said Joseph Carra, director of the National Center for Statistics and Analysis at the highway safety agency. "Today, the information is written and stored in files. It's a paper process. The files are sent to the state office, whose clerks input the information into proprietary computer systems. And there it sits."

Collaborating

Better information will save lives and money, says the federal highway safety administration. About 43,220 people were killed on the nation's highways in 2003, and another 2.9 million suffered serious injuries. Traffic accidents in 2000, the latest year for which information is available, cost the U.S. economy about $230 billion, the agency says.

The wide-ranging proposal calls for standardized formats to improve information sharing among various government agencies and private groups, more sophisticated sensors in cars and along highways to gather detailed information on crashes, and wireless handheld devices to let police officers check for outstanding warrants on drivers, among other ideas. Federal funding will encourage states to adopt federal standards. Many states, suffering from a slow economy and declining tax revenues, have not been able to fund upgrades themselves. Some, however, have projects under way.

Revamping Texas

Texas is about halfway done with an IT project to build a crash-records information system, a joint initiative between its Department of Public Safety and the Texas Department of Transportation. When completed, police officers will be able to file accident reports via the Web, and other state agencies will be able to electronically link their systems with it and share information.

Texas has been working on the crash-records system for several years. The state has a $9.9 million contract with IBM to build an information warehouse using a DB2 Universal Database, WebSphere Application Server, Tivoli Storage Manager, and MQ-Series, its message-queuing product. IBM says Florida, Arizona, and New Mexico are considering similar systems.

The Texas system is replacing a decades-old one that is "archaic and in need of many changes," said Carol Rawson, deputy division director for the traffic operations division with the state transportation department. The old system requires time-consuming manual entry of around 850,000 accident forms a year, as well as manual cross-checking and validation to ensure the information is correct. Because the process took so long, the state's accident information is backlogged some 30 months. "This is all about safety," Rawson said. "The way you tell if a road is safe is you look at accident information. So that information is critical."[67]

Questions

1. How are collaboration tools helping to save lives in Texas?
2. How could a police department use groupware to help with collaboration on accident reports?
3. Describe how a police department could use workflow systems to help with accident reports and health-care-related issues.
4. What would be the impact on lives if a state fails to implement collaboration tools to help track and analyze highway accidents?
5. How could police departments use wireless technologies to operate more efficiently and effectively?

 UNIT CLOSING CASE TWO

Amazon.com—Not Your Average Bookstore

Jeffrey Bezos, CEO and founder of Amazon.com, is running what some people refer to as the "world's biggest bookstore." The story of Bezos's virtual bookstore teaches many lessons about online business. Out of nowhere, this digital bookstore turned an industry upside down.

What happened here was more than just creating a Web site. Bezos conceived and implemented an intelligent, global digital business. Its business is its technology; its technology is its business. Shocking traditional value chains in the book-selling industry, Amazon opened thousands of virtual bookstores in its first few months of operation.

Bezos graduated from Princeton and was the youngest vice president at Banker's Trust in New York. He had to decide if he would stay and receive his 1994 Wall Street bonus or leave and start a business on the Internet. "I tried to imagine being 80 years old, looking back on my life. I knew that I would hardly regret having missed the 1994 Wall Street bonus. But having missed being part of the Internet boom—that would have really hurt," stated Bezos. One evening he compiled a list of 20 products he believed would sell on the Internet. Books, being small-ticket items that are easy and inexpensive to ship, were on the top of the list. It was also apparent that no bookstore could conceivably stock more than a fraction of the 5 million books published annually. Bezos, who had never sold a book in his life, developed a strategic plan for selling books on the Internet. Amazon launched three years later. In the fall of 1994, Amazon filled its first book order—personally packaged by Bezos and his wife.

Amazon's E-Business Strategy

Amazon does not operate any physical stores. All of its sales occur through its Web site. It is consistently pushing the technological envelope in its search to provide a satisfying, personalized experience for its customers. What started as a human-edited list of product suggestions morphed into a sophisticated computer-generated recommendation engine. The company captures the comments and recommendations of buyers for site visitors to read—similar to the friendly salesperson in a store offering advice on which books to buy. The Web site tracks customer traffic, the number of visitors who access the site, how long they stay, what pages they click on, and so forth. The company uses the information to evaluate buying and selling patterns and the success of promotions. Amazon has quickly become a model success story for e-businesses around the globe.

Amazon retains customers with Web site features such as personalized recommendations, online customer reviews, and "1-click ordering"—the creation of a true one-stop shopping establishment where customers can find anything they want to buy online. Through the Amazon.com Auctions, zShops (independent third-party sellers), and more recently the Amazon.com Marketplace (where customers can sell used items), the company is able to offer its customers almost everything.

Shaping Amazon's Future

Amazon released a free Web service that enables its business partners (whom Amazon calls "associates") to interact with its Web site. More specifically, this Web service allows its partners to access catalog data, to create and populate an Amazon.com shopping cart, and even to initiate the checkout process. In 16 months, the company inspired 30,000 associates to invent new ways to extend Amazon's visibility on the Internet. With over 30 million customers, Amazon has become a household brand.[68]

Questions

1. How has Amazon used technology to revamp the book-selling industry?
2. Is Amazon using disruptive or sustaining technology to run its business?
3. What is Amazon's e-business model?
4. How is Amazon using collaboration to improve its business?
5. What are some of the business challenges facing Amazon?
6. How can Amazon use wireless technology to improve its business?

1. Everybody Needs an Internet Strategy

An Internet strategy addresses the reasons businesses want to "go online." "Going online" because it seems like the right thing to do now or because everyone else is doing it is not a good enough reason. A business must decide how it will best utilize the Internet for its particular needs. It must plan for where it wants to go and how best the Internet can help shape that vision. Before developing a strategy, a business should spend time on the Internet, see what similar businesses have, and what is most feasible, given a particular set of resources. Think of a new online business opportunity and answer the following questions:

a. Why do you want to put your business online?

b. What benefits will going online bring?

c. What effects will Internet connectivity have on your staff, suppliers, and customers?

2. Searching for Disruption

Scheduler.com is a large corporation that develops software that automates scheduling and record keeping for medical and dental practices. Scheduler.com currently holds 48 percent of its market share, has more than 8,700 employees, and operates in six countries. You are the vice president of product development at Scheduler.com. You have just finished reading *The Innovator's Dilemma* by Clayton Christensen and you are interested in determining what types of disruptive technologies you can take advantage of, or should watch out for, in your industry. Use the Internet to develop a presentation highlighting the types of disruptive technologies you have found that have the potential to give the company a competitive advantage or could cause the company to fail.

3. Leveraging the Competitive Value of the Internet

Physical inventories have always been a major cost component of business. Linking to suppliers in real time dramatically enhances the classic goal of inventory "turn." The Internet provides a multitude of opportunities for radically reducing the costs of designing, manufacturing, and selling goods and services. E-mango.com, a fruit e-marketplace, must take advantage of these opportunities or find itself at a significant competitive disadvantage. Identify the disadvantages that confront E-mango.com if it does not leverage the competitive value of the Internet.

4. Assessing Internet Capabilities

Hoover's Rentals is a small privately owned business that rents sports equipment in Denver, Colorado. The company specializes in winter rentals including ski equipment, snowboarding equipment, and snowmobile equipment. Hoover's has been in business for 20 years and, for the first time, it is experiencing a decline in rentals. Brian Hoover, the company's owner, is puzzled by the recent decreases. The snowfall for the last two years has been outstanding, and the ski resorts have opened earlier and closed later than most previous years. Reports say tourism in the Colorado area is up, and the invention of loyalty programs has significantly increased the number of local skiers. Overall, business should be booming. The only reason for the decrease in sales might be the fact that big retailers such as Wal-Mart and Gart Sports are now renting winter sports equipment. Brian would like your team's help in determining how he can use the Internet to help his company increase sales and decrease costs to compete with these big retailers.

5. Gaining Efficiency with Collaboration

During the past year, you have been working for a manufacturing firm to help improve its supply chain management by implementing enterprise resource planning and supply chain management systems. For efficiency gains, you are recommending that the manufacturing firm should be turning toward collaborative systems. The firm has a need to share intelligent plans and forecasts with supply chain partners, reduce inventory levels, improve working capital, and reduce manufacturing changeovers. Given the technologies presented to you in this unit, what type of system(s) would you recommend to facilitate your firm's future needs?

6. Collaboration on Intranets

MyIntranet.com is a worldwide leader providing online intranet solutions. The MyIntranet.com online collaboration tool is a solution for small businesses and groups inside larger organizations that need to organize information, share files and documents, coordinate calendars, and enable efficient collaboration, all in a secure, browser-based environment. MyIntranet.com has just added conferencing and group scheduling features to its suite of hosted collaboration software. Explain why infrastructure integration is critical to the suite of applications to function within this environment.

7. Finding Innovation

Along with disruptive technologies, there are also disruptive strategies. The following are a few examples of companies that use disruptive strategies to gain competitive advantages:

- Circuit City, Best Buy—These two disrupted the consumer electronics departments of full-service and discount department stores, which has sent them up-market into higher margin goods.
- Ford—Henry Ford's Model T was so inexpensive that he enabled a much larger population of people, who historically could not afford cars, to own one.
- JetBlue—Whereas Southwest Airlines initially followed a strategy of new-market disruption, JetBlue's approach is low-end disruption. Its long-range viability depends on the major airlines' motivation to run away from the attack, as integrated steel mills and full-service department stores did.
- McDonald's—The fast-food industry has been a hybrid disrupter, making it so inexpensive and convenient to eat out that it created a massive wave of growth in the "eating out" industry. McDonald's earliest victims were mom-and-pop diners.

There are numerous other examples of corporations that have used disruptive strategies to create competitive advantages. In a team, prepare a presentation highlighting three additional companies that used disruptive strategies to gain a competitive advantage.

8. Communicating with Instant Messages

You are working for a new start-up magazine, *Jabber Inc.,* developed for information professionals that provides articles, product reviews, case studies, evaluation, and informed opinions. You need to collaborate on news items and projects, and exchange data with a variety of colleagues inside and outside the *Jabber Inc.* walls. You know that many companies are now embracing the instant messaging technology. Prepare a brief report for the CIO that will explain the reasons IM is not just a teenage fad, but also a valuable communications tool that is central to everyday business.

★ APPLY YOUR KNOWLEDGE

1. Working Together

Upon execution of a business process, a workflow system dictates the presentation of the information, tracks the information, and maintains the information's status. For example, the following highlights the common steps performed during a team project:

1. Find out what information and deliverables are required for the project and the due date.
2. Divide the work among the team members.
3. Determine due dates for the different pieces of work.
4. Compile all the completed work together into a single project.

One of the hardest parts of a team project is getting team members to complete their work on time. Often one team member cannot perform his or her work until another team member has finished. This situation causes work to sit idle waiting for a team member to pick it up to either approve it, continue working on it, or reformat it. Workflow systems help to automate the process of presenting and passing information around a team.

Project Focus

You have just received an assignment to work on a group project with 10 other students. The project requires you to develop a detailed business plan for a business of your choice. The types of activities you will need to perform include market analysis, industry analysis, growth opportunities, Porter's Five Forces analysis, financial forecasts, competitive advantage analysis, and so on. For your project, determine the following:

1. How could you use collaboration tools to facilitate the sharing of information and the completion of the project?
2. What advantages can your group gain from using groupware?
3. What advantages can your group gain from using IM?
4. How could you use a workflow system to manage the tasks for the group members?
5. Describe a few of the biggest issues you anticipate experiencing during the group project. Identify ways that you can resolve these issues using collaboration tools.

2. Internet Groceries

E-Grocery, founded in 2007, is an online grocery shopping and delivery service. The company caters to thousands of customers in the Phoenix, Seattle, and Denver areas. Established on the idea that people will buy groceries over the Internet, e-Grocery offers over 25,000 items.

Ninety percent of e-Grocery's orders come in via computer; the rest are received by fax. Orders are received at the central office in Lakewood, Colorado, and then distributed by e-mail to a local affiliate store. The store receives the order, the delivery address, and a map to the order location. A store employee designated to online orders will fill, deliver, and collect for the order. E-Grocery members are charged actual shelf prices, plus a per-order charge of $5.00 or 5 percent of the order amount, whichever is greater. Members also receive additional benefits such as electronic coupons, customer discounts, recipes, and tips.

Project Focus

The company is using interactive technology to change the shopping experience. The success of e-Grocery lies within many areas. Analyze the e-Grocery business model using the questions below. Feel free to think outside the box to develop your own analysis of online grocery shopping and e-business models.

1. What is e-Grocery's e-business model?
2. How does e-Grocery compete with traditional retailers?
3. What value can e-Grocery offer as a true competitive advantage in this marketplace?
4. What is the threat of new entrants in this market segment?
5. How is e-Grocery using technology to change the shopping experience?

6. What are the logistics for making e-Grocery profitable?

7. How does e-Grocery profit from online customer interaction?

8. What kinds of e-business strategies can e-Grocery's marketing department use to help grow its business?

9. What are some of the benefits and challenges facing e-Grocery?

3. Getting Personal

Consider Sally Albright, the reigning queen of customization in the movie *When Harry Met Sally*. Take, for example, the scene where she orders pie a la mode: "I'd like the pie heated. And I don't want the ice cream on top; I want it on the side. And I'd like strawberry instead of vanilla if you have it. If not, then no ice cream, just whipped cream, but only if it's real." Particular, yes, but Sally knew what she liked—and was not afraid to ask for it.

Project Focus

A growing number of online retailers are letting you have it your way, too. Choose a company highlighted in Figure AYK.1 and create your own product. Was the Web site easy to use? Would this service entice you as a customer to make a purchase over a generic product? If you could personalize a product what would it be and how would the Web site work?

4. Express Yourself

One of the most popular Web sites among students is MySpace, a site that allows students to express themselves by personalizing their home page. What is your favorite band? Who is your favorite author? What is your favorite movie? You can find out a lot about a person by finding out the answers to these questions.

Project Focus

Build a Web site dedicated to your favorite band, book, or movie. Your Web site must contain all of the following:

- An image.
- Two different size headings.
- Different sizes and colors of text.

FIGURE AYK.1

Customization Companies

Company	Product
Tommy Hilfiger, custom.tomm.com	Premium-cotton chinos and jeans ($98)
Lands' End, www.landsend.com	Utilitarian jeans and chinos made of luxurious twill in traditional silhouettes ($59)
JCPenney, www.custom.jcpenney.com	Substantial twill pants in classic cuts ($44)
Ralph Lauren Polo, www.polo.com	Everything from basic polos to oxford shirts ($80)
TIMBUK2; www.timbuk2.com	Hip nylon messenger bags ($105)
L.L. Bean, www.llbean.com	Sturdy and colorful books, totes, and messenger bags ($70)
Nike, www.nikeid.com	Full range of athletic shoes and accessories ($90)
VANS, www.vans.com	Classic "Old Skool" lace-up or slip-on sneakers ($50)
Converse, www.converseone.com	Custom Chuck Taylors, the company's most classic style ($60)

- Two horizontal rules.
- Text that is bolded, underlined, and/or italicized.
- A textured background.
- A link to a Web site.
- A link to your e-mail.
- One numbered and one unnumbered list.

5. Creating a Presence

More than 1 billion people are on the Internet. Having an Internet presence is critical for any business that wants to remain competitive. Businesses need their Web sites to create a "buzz" to attract customers. E-business Web sites must be innovative, stimulating, add value, and provide useful information. In short, the site must build a sense of community and collaboration, eventually becoming the "port of entry" for business.

Project Focus

You are applying for a job at BagEm, a start-up e-business devoted to selling custom book bags that does not have any physical stores and only sells bags over the Internet. You are up against several other candidates for the job. BagEm has asked you to use your business expertise and Web site development skills to design and build a potential Web site. The candidate with the best Web site will be awarded the job. Good luck!

6. GoGo Gadgets

Now that wi-fi and other types of high-speed wireless networks are becoming common, devices using that technology are multiplying rapidly. Wireless gadgets run the gamut from cell phones to kitchen appliances and digital cameras. Here are some of the hottest new wireless broadband gadgets.

- Samsung's $3,499 POPCON refrigerator will feature a wi-fi enabled, detachable screen that can function as a TV. The fridge also can be programmed to remember products' expiration dates and generate alerts when the milk is getting old.
- The Nokia 770 Internet Tablet is small enough to fit in a pocket. It comes with a 4.13-inch-wide touch screen that can be used to access the Web over a wi-fi network. The $350 device can also access the Web via a cell phone with a Bluetooth connection.
- Motorola's latest E815 mobile phone operates over Verizon Wireless's new EVDO (Evolution Data Optimized) wireless network, offering speeds comparable to digital subscriber line (DSL). The phone can even record and play back video clips. It also features a built-in MP3 digital music player.
- Hop-On's just-announced HOP 1515 may look like a typical cell phone, but it actually makes calls over wi-fi networks. Typically sold with a $20 to $30 monthly service plan, the phone allows for unlimited over-the-Web international and long-distance calling. The $39 HOP 1515 is sold through wi-fi hotspot operators, wireless carriers, and retailers.
- Eastman Kodak's EasyShare-One is a digital camera with wi-fi capabilities, allowing users to share their snapshots wirelessly. You will be able to snap a photo and immediately show it to a friend on a wi-fi-enabled PC or TV.

Project Focus

A dizzying array of new wireless technologies now promises to make today's wi-fi networks seem like poky dial-up connections by comparison. These new technologies will extend the reach of wireless networks, not just geographically but also into new uses in the home and office.

1. Research the Internet and discover new wireless devices that entrepreneurs and established companies can use to improve their business.

2. Explain how businesses can use these devices to create competitive advantages, streamline production, and improve productivity.

7. WAP

Wireless Internet access is quickly gaining popularity among people seeking high-speed Internet connections when they are away from their home or office. The signal from a typical wireless access point (WAP) only extends for about 300 feet in any direction, so the user must find a "hotspot" to be able to access the Internet while on the road. Sometimes hotspots are available for free or for a small fee.

You work for a sales company, SalesTek, which has a salesforce of 25 representatives and customers concentrated in Denver, Colorado; Salt Lake City, Utah; and Santa Fe, New Mexico. Your sales representatives are constantly on the road and they require 24×7 Internet access.

Project Focus

You have been asked to find hotspots for your colleagues to connect to while they are on the road. It is critical that your salesforce can access the Internet 24×7 to connect with customers, suppliers, and the corporate office. Create a document detailing how your mobile workforce will be able to stay connected to the Internet while traveling. Here are a few tips to get you started:

1. Use Web sites such as www.wifinder.com and www.jiwire.com to determine which commercial hotspots would be the most appropriate for your salesforce and the commercial network service that these hotspots use.

2. Research the Web sites of two or three commercial networks that seem most appropriate to discover more about pricing and services. (Hint: T-Mobile is one example.)

3. Use www.wifinder.com and www.wififreespot.com to determine how many free public hotspots are available in these cities. Are there enough for your company to rely on them or should you use a commercial wi-fi system. If so, which one?

4. You might also research www.fon.com to see alternative methods of using home broadband connections to stay connected.

8. Securing Your Home Wireless Network

These days wireless networking products are so ubiquitous and inexpensive that anyone can easily build a wireless network with less than $100 worth of equipment. However, wireless networks are exactly that—wireless—they do not stop at walls. In fact, wireless networks often carry signals more than 300 feet from the wireless router. Living in an apartment, dorm, condominium, or house means that you might have dozens of neighbors who can access your wireless network.

It is one thing to let a neighbor borrow a lawn mower, but it is another thing to allow a neighbor to access a home wireless network. There are several good reasons for not sharing a home wireless network including:

- It may slow Internet performance.

- It allows others to view files on your computers and spread dangerous software such as viruses.

- It allows others to monitor the Web sites you visit, read your e-mail and instant messages as they travel across the network, and copy your user names and passwords.

- It allows others to send spam or perform illegal activities with your Internet connection.[69]

Project Focus

Securing a home wireless network is invaluable and allows you to enable security features that can make it difficult for uninvited guests to connect through your wireless network. Create a document detailing all of the features you can use to secure a home wireless network.

9. Weather Bots

Warren Jackson, an engineering graduate student at the University of Pennsylvania, was not interested in the weather until he started investigating how the National Weather Service collected weather data. The weather service has collected most of its information using weather balloons that carry a device to measure items such as pressure, wind speed, and humidity. When the balloon reaches about 100,000 feet and pressure causes it to pop, the device falls and lands a substantial distance from its launch point. The National Weather Service and researchers sometimes look for the $200 device, but of the 80,000 sent up annually, they write off many as lost.

Convinced there had to be a better way, Warren began designing a GPS-equipped robot that launches a parachute after the balloon pops and brings the device back down to Earth, landing it at a predetermined location set by the researchers. The idea is so inventive that the Penn's Weiss Tech House, a university organization that encourages students to innovate and bring their ideas to market, awarded Warren and some fellow graduate engineering students first prize in its third annual PennVention Contest. Warren won $5,000 and access to expert advice on prototyping, legal matters, and branding.[70]

Project Focus

GPS and GIS can be used in all sorts of devices, in many different industries, for multiple purposes. You want to compete, and win first prize, in the PennVention next year. Create a product, using a GPS or GIS, that is not currently in the market today that you will present at the fourth annual PennVention.

10. Wireless Networks and Streetlamps

Researchers at Harvard University and BBN Technologies have designed CitySense, a wireless network capable of reporting real-time sensor data across the entire city of Cambridge, Massachusetts. CitySense is unique because it solves a constraint on previous wireless networks—battery life. The network mounts each node on a municipal streetlamp, where it draws power from city electricity. Researchers plan to install 100 sensors on streetlamps throughout Cambridge by 2011, using a grant from the National Science Foundation. Each node will include an embedded PC running the Linux operating system, an 802.11 wi-fi interface, and weather sensors.

One of the challenges in the design was how the network would allow remote nodes to communicate with the central server at Harvard and BBN. CitySense will do that by letting each node form a mesh with its neighbors, exchanging data through multiple-hop links. This strategy allows a node to download software or upload sensor data to a distant server hub using a small radio with only a 1-kilometer range.[71]

Project Focus

You are responsible for deploying a CitySense network around your city. What goals would you have for the system besides monitoring urban weather and pollution? What other benefits could a CitySense network provide? How could local businesses and citizens benefit from the network? What legal and ethical concerns should you understand before deploying the network? What can you do to protect your network and your city from these issues?

11. Sharptooth Incorporated

Stephen Kern is the founder and CEO of Sharptooth, a small business that buys and sells comic strips to magazines and newspapers around the country. Some of Sharptooth's artists have made it big and are syndicated in hundreds of magazines and newspapers, while others are new to the industry. Stephen started in the business as an artist and began contracting with other artists when he realized he had a knack for promoting and marketing comic materials. His artistic background is great for spotting talented young artists, but not so great for running the business.

Project Focus

Stephen recently began selling comics to new forms of media such as blog sites, Web sites, and other online tools. Stephen has hired you to build him a new system to track all online comic sales. You quickly notice that Stephen has a separate system for each of his different lines of business including newspaper sources, magazine sources, billboard sources, and now online sources. You notice that each system works independently to perform its job of creating, updating, and maintaining sales information, but you are wondering how Stephen operates his business as a whole. Create a list of issues Stephen will encounter if he continues to run his business with four separate systems performing the same operations. What could happen to Stephen's business if he cannot correlate the details of each? Be sure to highlight at least 10 issues where separate systems could cause Stephen problems.

12. Wiki Debate

Wikipedia is a multilingual, Web-based, free content encyclopedia project. Wikipedia is written collaboratively by volunteers from all around the world. With rare exceptions, its articles can be edited by anyone with access to the Internet, simply by clicking a line to edit the page. The name Wikipedia is a portmanteau of the words *wiki* (a type of collaborative Web site) and *encyclopedia.* Since its creation in 2001, Wikipedia has grown rapidly into one of the largest reference Web sites.

In every article, links guide users to associated articles, often with additional information. Anyone is welcome to add information, cross-references, or citations, as long as they do so within Wikipedia's editing policies and to an appropriate standard. One need not fear accidentally damaging Wikipedia when adding or improving information, as other editors are always around to advise or correct obvious errors, and Wikipedia's software, known as MediaWiki, is carefully designed to allow easy reversal of editorial mistakes.[72]

Project Focus

A group of people believe the end of Wikipedia is close as people use the tool to self-promote. Some believe that Wikipedia will fail in four years, crushed under the weight of an automated assault by marketers and others seeking online traffic. Eric Goldman, a professor at the Santa Clara University School of Law, argues that Wikipedia will see increasingly vigorous efforts to subvert its editorial process, much as Digg has seen. As marketers become more determined and turn to automated tools to alter Wikipedia entries to generate online traffic, Goldman predicts Wikipedians will burn out trying to keep entries clean. Goldman writes that Wikipedia will enter a death spiral where the rate of junkiness will increase rapidly until the site becomes a wasteland. Alternatively, to prevent this death spiral, Wikipedia will change its core open-access architecture, increasing the database's vitality by changing its mission somewhat.

Create a paper discussing where you think the future of Wikipedia is headed.

13. Secure Collaboration

As the methods and modes of communication continue to evolve, challenges will mount for businesses trying to secure their data and for law enforcement looking to monitor communications as part of their investigations. That was the theme of the keynote speech that Sun Microsystems' chief security officer and renowned cryptographer Whitfield Diffie delivered at the AT&T Cyber Security Conference.

The growth of virtual communities across the Web as a communications channel creates a double-edged sword in this respect. Second Life and other virtual communities offer a growing abundance of information, although this information will ultimately need to be protected if virtual communities are to grow as meaningful channels of business-to-business and business-to-customer communication.

Diffie believes that with millions of people joining Second Life and companies building facilities there, it may be that virtual communities become the preferred medium of human communication. This growing volume of information opens the opportunity to use virtual communities as a source of intelligence, and communications will always be spied on.

Of course, the volume of businesses present in virtual communities such as Second Life will have to grow before they become a meaningful source of information. Once this happens, though, watch out. Diffie believes that communication always outstrips the ability to protect it. Who would be interested in gathering intelligence floating through virtual communities? The answer is businesses, governments (domestic and foreign), and reporters—the same entities that have adapted every other form of communication preceding the Web. Diffie feels the future will be a golden age for intelligence.[73]

Project Focus
As we create new and better ways to collaborate, what happens to information security?

5

UNIT

Transforming Organizations

The Digital Hospital

For years, health care has missed the huge benefits that information technology has bestowed upon the rest of the economy. During the 1990s, productivity in health care services declined, according to estimates from Economy.com Inc. That is a huge underachievement in a decade of strong gains from the overall economy. This is beginning to change as hospitals, along with insurers and the government, are stepping up their IT investments. Hospitals are finally discarding their clumsy, sluggish first-generation networks and are beginning to install laptops, software, and Internet technologies.

Hackensack University Medical Center in Hackensack, New Jersey, is one of the nation's most aggressive technology adopters, investing $72 million in IT projects since 1998. The IT investments are paying off for the hospital with patient mortality rates decreasing—down 16 percent in four years—and quality of care and productivity increasing. The most important piece of Hackensack's digital initiatives is the networked software that acts as the hospital's central nervous system. Using wireless laptops, nurses log in to the system to record patient information and progress. Doctors tap into the network via wireless devices to order prescriptions and lab tests. Everything is linked, from the automated pharmacy to the X-ray lab, eliminating the need for faxes, phone calls, and other administrative hassles. Figure Unit 5.1 displays the hospital's IT systems development projects.

Health care spending accounts for 15 percent of the U.S. economy, or $1.7 trillion. It is so gargantuan that any efficiency gains will affect the overall economy. Dr. David Brailer, President George W. Bush's point man on health IT initiatives, predicts that IT investments will lead to $140 billion a year in cost savings by 2014. More important than saving money is saving lives. Poor information kills some 7,000 Americans each year just by missing drug-interaction problems, according to the National Academy of Sciences

Hackensack University Medical Center's IT Projects

- Patients can use 37-inch plasma TVs in their rooms to surf the Internet for information about their medical conditions. They can also take interactive classes about their condition and find out how to take care of themselves after discharge.

- From virtually anywhere in the world, physicians can make their hospital rounds with the help of a life-size robot, Mr. Rounder. Using laptops with joysticks and Web links, doctors drive the robot around the hospital to confer by remote video with patients and other doctors. When a blizzard prevented Dr. Garth Ballantynes from reaching the hospital, he used Mr. Rounder to make his rounds from his home 82 miles away.

- Pocket-sized PCs that hook wirelessly into the hospital's network allow doctors the freedom to place pharmacy orders and pull up medical records from anywhere in the hospital.

- Nurses use wireless laptops to record patients' vitals signs, symptoms, and medications. Doctors can sign into the same central system from the laptops to order prescriptions and lab tests and read their patient's progress.

- The hospital's internal Web site stores all of its medical images. Doctors can view crystal-clear digital versions of their patients' X-rays, MRIs, and CT scans from any computer in or out of the hospital.

- A giant robot named Robbie, equipped with arms, reads prescriptions entered into the hospital's computer system and then grabs medications stored on pegs on the wall. The pills are then dropped into containers that are marked for each patient.

Institute of Medicine. Hospital errors result in 100,000 deaths annually. Early evidence indicates that proper technology can reduce this amount. Hospitals using electronic prescription systems have seen 80 percent fewer prescription errors.[1]

Introduction

In a competitive business climate, an organization's ability to efficiently align resources and business activities with strategic objectives can mean the difference between succeeding and just surviving. To achieve strategic alignment, organizations increasingly manage their systems development efforts and project planning activities to monitor performance and make better business decisions. Fast-growing companies outsource many areas of their business to extend their technical and operational resources. By outsourcing, they save time and boost productivity by not having to develop their own systems from scratch. They are then free to concentrate on innovation and their core business. The chapters in Unit 5 are:

- **Chapter Seventeen**—Building Software to Support an Agile Organization.
- **Chapter Eighteen**—Outsourcing in the 21st Century.
- **Chapter Nineteen**—Developing a 21st Century Organization.

17 Building Software to Support an Agile Organization

Systems Development

Archtv 2

Nike's SCM system failure, which spun out of control to the tune of $400 million, is legendary. Nike blamed the system failure on its SCM vendor i2 Technologies. Nike stated that i2 Technologies' demand and supply planning module created serious inventory problems. The i2 deployment, part of a multimillion-dollar e-business upgrade, caused Nike CEO Philip Knight to famously say, "This is what we get for our $400 million?" The SCM vendor saw its stock plummet with the Nike disaster, along with its reputation. I2's chief marketing officer, Katrina Roche, asserted that Nike failed to use the vendor's implementation methodology and templates, which contributed to the problem.[2]

Organizations must learn how to build and implement disruptive technologies, such as software for wireless devices, to remain competitive. Software that is built correctly can support agile organizations and can transform as the organization and its business transforms. Software that effectively meets employee needs will help an organization become more productive and enhance decision making. Software that does not meet employee needs may have a damaging effect on productivity and can even cause a business to fail. Employee involvement along with the right implementation methodology when developing software is critical to the success of an organization.

Software development problems often lead to high-profile disasters. Hershey Food's glitch in its ERP implementation made the front page of *The Wall Street Journal* and cost the company millions of dollars. Hershey said computer problems with its SAP software system created a backlog of orders, causing slower deliveries, and resulting in lower earnings. Statistics released in 2006 by the National Research Council show that U.S. companies spent $250 billion in 2005 to repair damage caused by software defects.[3]

If software does not work, the organization will not work. Traditional business risk models typically ignored software development, largely because most organizations considered the impact from software and software development on the business to be minor. In the digital age, however, software success, or failure, can lead directly to business success, or failure. Almost every large organization in the world relies on software, either to drive its business operations or to make its products work. As organizations' reliance on software grows, so do the business-related consequences of software successes and failures including:

- **Increase or decrease revenues**—Organizations have the ability to directly increase profits by implementing successful IT systems. Organizations can also lose millions when software fails or key information is stolen or compromised.

  Nike's poorly designed supply chain management software delayed orders, increased excess inventories, and caused third-quarter earnings to fall 24 percent below expectations.

- **Repair or damage to brand reputation**—Technologies such as CRM can directly enhance a company's brand reputation. Software can also severely damage a company's reputation if it fails to work as advertised or has security vulnerabilities that affect its customers' trust.

  H&R Block customers were furious when the company accidentally placed its customers' passwords and Social Security numbers on its Web site.

- **Prevent or incur liabilities**—Technology such as CAT scans, MRIs, and mammograms can save lives. Faulty technology used in airplanes, automobiles, pacemakers, or nuclear reactors can cause massive damage, injury, or death.

  The parent company of bankrupt pharmaceutical distributor FoxMeyer sued SAP for $500 million over ERP software failure that allegedly crippled its operations.

- **Increase or decrease productivity**—CRM and SCM software can directly increase a company's productivity. Large losses in productivity can also occur when software malfunctions or crashes.

  The Standish Group estimates that defective software code accounted for 45 percent of computer-system downtime and cost U.S. companies $100 billion in lost productivity in 2003 alone.[4]

The lucrative advantages of successful software implementations provide significant incentives to manage software development risks. But according to the Standish Group's Chaos report, more than half the software development projects undertaken in the United States come in late or over budget and the majority of successful projects maintain fewer features and functions than originally specified. Organizations also cancel around 33 percent of these projects during development. Understanding the basics of software development, or the systems development life cycle, will help organizations avoid potential software development pitfalls and ensure that software development efforts are successful.[5]

Developing Software—The Systems Development Life Cycle (SDLC)

Information systems are the support infrastructure that helps an organization change quickly when adapting to shifting business environments and markets. Many factors must come together to develop successful software. This chapter focuses on the *systems development life cycle (SDLC)*, also known as the software life cycle or the application life cycle, which is the overall process for developing information systems from planning and analysis through implementation and maintenance (see Figure 17.1).

1. **Planning**—The *planning phase* involves establishing a high-level plan of the intended project and determining project goals. Planning is the first and most critical phase of any systems development effort an organization undertakes, regardless of whether the effort is to develop a system that allows customers to

FIGURE 17.1

The Systems Development
Life Cycle

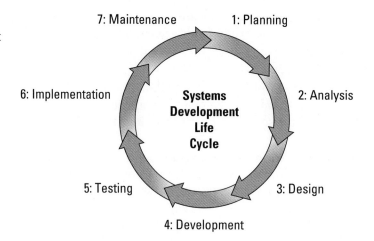

7: Maintenance   1: Planning

6: Implementation   **Systems Development Life Cycle**   2: Analysis

5: Testing   3: Design

4: Development

System
Development

order products over the Internet, determine the best logistical structure for warehouses around the world, or form a strategic information alliance with another organization. Organizations must carefully plan the activities (and determine why they are necessary) to be successful.

2. **Analysis**—The *analysis phase* involves analyzing end-user business requirements and refining project goals into defined functions and operations of the intended system. *Business requirements* are the detailed set of business requests that the system must meet in order to be successful. The analysis phase is obviously critical. A good start is essential, and the organization must spend as much time, energy, and resources as necessary to perform a detailed, accurate analysis.

3. **Design**—The *design phase* involves describing the desired features and operations of the system including screen layouts, business rules, process diagrams, pseudo code, and other documentation.

4. **Development**—The *development phase* involves taking all of the detailed design documents from the design phase and transforming them into the actual system. In this phase the project transitions from preliminary designs to the actual physical implementation.

5. **Testing**—The *testing phase* involves bringing all the project pieces together into a special testing environment to test for errors, bugs, and interoperability and verify that the system meets all of the business requirements defined in the analysis phase.

   According to a report issued in June 2003 by the National Institute of Standards and Technology (NIST), defective software costs the U.S. economy an estimated $59.5 billion each year. Of that total, software users incur 64 percent of the costs and software developers 36 percent. NIST suggests that improvements in testing could reduce this cost significantly—by about a third, or $22.5 billion—but that testing improvements would not eliminate most software errors.[6]

6. **Implementation**—The *implementation phase* involves placing the system into production so users can begin to perform actual business operations with the system.

7. **Maintenance**—Maintaining the system is the final sequential phase of any systems development effort. The *maintenance phase* involves performing changes, corrections, additions, and upgrades to ensure the system continues to meet the business goals. This phase continues for the life of the system because the system must change as the business evolves and its needs change, demanding constant monitoring, supporting the new system with frequent minor changes (for example, new reports or information capturing), and reviewing the system to be sure it is moving the organization toward its strategic goals.

The London Stock Exchange is among the most admired equity exchanges in the world, not only for its long-standing position in the financial community, but also for its technology deployment and infrastructure. The London Stock Exchange must have a solid architecture because it processes over 15 million real-time messages per day (with peaks of 2,000 messages per second). In choosing a new technology infrastructure on which to ride into the future, the London Stock Exchange focused a great deal of its efforts on requiring vendors to meet benchmarks across a broad range of metrics. Below are just a few.

- **Guaranteed performance**—In financial trading, information is valuable only if it reaches traders within the first second.

- **Development costs**—Reduced development costs and development cycle times mean more productivity. Ian Homan, head of technology for the London Stock Exchange, estimates that implementation of the new infrastructure occurred in one-fifth to one-third the time it would have taken to implement other vendor infrastructures.

- **Scalability**—According to David Lester, CIO for the London Stock Exchange, "We want to be able to extend it and make it richer. Investment decisions of this kind aren't made carelessly and the ability to scale to our future needs was a critical factor."[7]

Software Development Methodologies

Today, systems are so large and complex that teams of architects, analysts, developers, testers, and users must work together to create the millions of lines of custom-written code that drive enterprises. For this reason, developers have created a number of different system development life cycle methodologies including *waterfall; rapid application development (RAD); extreme programming;* and *agile.* The oldest of these, and the best known, is the waterfall methodology: a sequence of phases in which the output of each phase becomes the input for the next (see Figure 17.2).

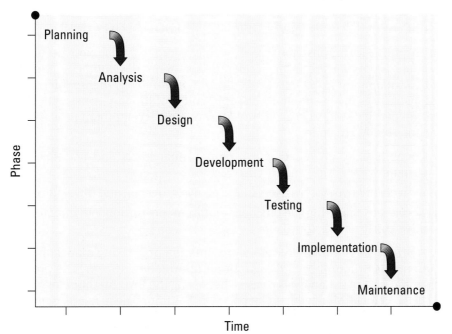

FIGURE 17.2

The Traditional Waterfall Methodology

WATERFALL METHODOLOGY

The traditional *waterfall methodology* is a sequential, activity-based process in which each phase in the SDLC is performed sequentially from planning through implementation and maintenance. The waterfall methodology is one of the oldest software development methods and has been around for more than 30 years. The success rate for software development projects that follow this approach is only about 1 in 10. One primary reason for such a low success rate is that the waterfall methodology does not sufficiently consider the level of uncertainty in new projects and the creativity required to complete software development projects in several aspects:

- **The business problem:** Any flaws in accurately defining and articulating the business problem in terms of what the business users actually require flow onward to the next phase.

- **The plan:** Managing costs, resources, and time constraints is difficult in the waterfall sequence. What happens to the schedule if a programmer quits? How will a schedule delay in a specific phase impact the total cost of the project? Unexpected contingencies may sabotage the plan.

- **The solution:** The waterfall methodology is problematic in that it assumes users can specify all business requirements in advance. Defining the appropriate IT infrastructure that is flexible, scalable, and reliable is a challenge. The final IT infrastructure solution must meet not only current but also future needs in terms of time, cost, feasibility, and flexibility. Vision is inevitably limited at the head of the waterfall.

Unfortunately, business requirements change as the business changes, which calls for considerable feedback and iterative consultation for all business requirements. Essentially, software is "soft" and it must be easily changed and manipulated to meet the changing dynamics of an organization. As people's understanding of the business problems evolve, so must the software. For this reason, it is counterproductive to define all requirements precisely upfront since, by the time the software goes into production, which can be several months or even years after completing the initial analysis phase, chances are the business problems have changed as well as the business.[8]

RAPID APPLICATION DEVELOPMENT METHODOLOGY (RAD)

In response to the faster pace of business, rapid application development has become a popular route for accelerating systems development. *Rapid application development (RAD) (*also called *rapid prototyping) methodology* emphasizes extensive user involvement in the rapid and evolutionary construction of working prototypes of a system to accelerate the systems development process. The fundamentals of RAD include:

- Focus initially on creating a prototype that looks and acts like the desired system.
- Actively involve system users in the analysis, design, and development phases.
- Accelerate collecting the business requirements through an interactive and iterative construction approach.[9]

A *prototype* is a smaller-scale representation or working model of the users' requirements or a proposed design for an information system. The prototype is an essential part of the analysis phase when using the RAD methodology.

PHH Vehicle Management Services, a Baltimore fleet-management company with over 750,000 vehicles, wanted to build an enterprise application that opened the entire vehicle information database to customers over the Internet. To build the application quickly, the company abandoned the traditional waterfall approach.

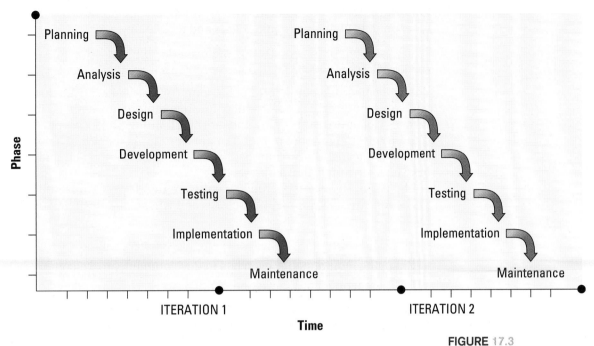

FIGURE 17.3

The Iterative Approach

Instead, a team of 30 developers began prototyping the Internet application, and the company's customers evaluated each prototype for immediate feedback. The development team released new prototypes that incorporated the customers' feedback every six weeks. The PHH Interactive Vehicle application went into production seven months after the initial work began. Over 20,000 customers, using a common browser, can now access the PHH Interactive site at any time from anywhere in the world to review their accounts, analyze billing information, and order vehicles.[10]

EXTREME PROGRAMMING METHODOLOGY

Extreme programming (XP) methodology breaks a project into tiny phases, and developers cannot continue on to the next phase until the first phase is complete. The primary difference between the waterfall and XP methodologies is that XP divides its phases into iterations with user feedback. The waterfall approach develops the entire system, whereas XP develops the system in iterations (see Figure 17.3). XP is a lot like a jigsaw puzzle; there are many small pieces. Individually the pieces make no sense, but when they are combined (again and again) an organization can gain visibility into the entire new system.

Microsoft Corporation developed Internet Explorer and Netscape Communications Corporation developed Communicator using extreme programming. Both companies did a nightly compilation (called a build) of the entire project, bringing together all the current components. They established release dates and expended considerable effort to involve customers in each release. The extreme programming approach allowed both Microsoft and Netscape to manage millions of lines of code as specifications changed and evolved over time. Most important, both companies frequently held user design reviews and strategy sessions to solicit and incorporate user feedback.[11]

XP is a significant departure from traditional software development methodologies, and many organizations in different industries have developed successful software using it. One reason for XP's success is its stress on customer satisfaction. XP empowers developers to respond to changing customer and business requirements, even late in the systems development life cycle, and XP emphasizes teamwork. Managers, customers, and developers are all part of a team dedicated to delivering quality software. XP implements a simple, yet effective way to enable groupware-style development. The XP methodology promotes quickly being able to respond to changing requirements and technology.

AGILE METHODOLOGY

The *agile methodology,* a form of XP, aims for customer satisfaction through early and continuous delivery of useful software components. Agile is similar to XP but with less focus on team coding and more on limiting project scope. An agile project sets a minimum number of requirements and turns them into a deliverable product. Agile means what it sounds like: fast and efficient; small and nimble; lower cost; fewer features; shorter projects.

The Agile Alliance is a group of software developers whose mission is to improve software development processes and whose manifesto includes the following tenets:

- Early and continuous delivery of valuable software will satisfy the customer.
- Changing requirements, even late in development, are welcome.
- Businesspeople and developers must work together daily throughout the project.
- Projects should be built around motivated individuals. Give them the environment and support they need, and trust them to get the job done.
- The best architectures, requirements, and designs emerge from self-organizing teams.
- At regular intervals, the team should reflect on how to become more effective, then tune and adjust behavior accordingly.[12]

Look for development and operational models that suit the organization's culture but move toward the perpetual beta. On the development side, use agile, iterative approaches, and on the operations side, consider best practice–centered models, such as the Information Technology Infrastructure Library (ITIL). The *Information Technology Infrastructure Library (ITIL)* is a framework of best practice approaches intended to facilitate the delivery of high quality IT services. ITIL outlines an extensive set of management procedures that are intended to support businesses in achieving both high financial quality and value in IT operations. These procedures are supplier-independent and have been developed to provide guidance across the breadth of IT infrastructure, development, and operations. ITIL is published in a series of books (hence the term *Library*), each of which covers a core area within IT management.

Developing Successful Software

The Gartner Group estimates that 65 percent of agile projects are successful. This success rate is extraordinary compared to the 10 percent success rate of waterfall projects. The following are the primary principles an organization should follow for successful agile software development.[13]

SLASH THE BUDGET

Small budgets force developers and users to focus on the essentials. Small budgets also make it easier to kill a failing project. For example, imagine that a project that has already cost $20 million is going down the tubes. With that much invested, it is tempting to invest another $5 million to rescue it rather than take a huge loss. All too often, the system fails and the company ends up with an even bigger loss.

Jim Johnson, chairman of The Standish Group, says he forced the CIO of one Fortune 500 company to set a $100,000 ceiling on all software development projects.

There were no exceptions to this business rule without approval from the CIO and CEO. Johnson claims the company's project success rate went from 0 percent to 50 percent.[14]

IF IT DOESN'T WORK, KILL IT

Bring all key stakeholders together at the beginning of a project and as it progresses bring them together again to evaluate the software. Is it doing what the business wants and, more important, requires? Eliminate any software that is not meeting business expectations. This is called triage, and it's "the perfect place to kill a software project," said Pat Morgan, senior program manager at Compaq's Enterprise Storage Group. He holds monthly triage sessions and says they can be brutal. "At one [meeting], engineering talked about a cool process they were working on to transfer information between GUIs. No one in the room needed it. We killed it right there. In our environment, you can burn a couple of million dollars in a month only to realize what you're doing isn't useful."[15]

KEEP REQUIREMENTS TO A MINIMUM

Start each project with what the software must absolutely do. Do not start with a list of everything the software should do. Every software project traditionally starts with a requirements document that will often have hundreds or thousands of business requirements. The Standish Group estimates that only 7 percent of the business requirements are needed for any given application. Keeping requirements to a minimum also means that scope creep and feature creep must be closely monitored. *Scope creep* occurs when the scope of the project increases. *Feature creep* occurs when developers add extra features that were not part of the initial requirements. Both scope creep and feature creep are major reasons software development fails.[16]

TEST AND DELIVER FREQUENTLY

As often as once a week, and not less than once a month, complete a part of the project or a piece of software. The part must be working and it must be bug-free. Then have the customers test and approve it. This is the agile methodology's most radical departure from traditional development. In some traditional software projects, the customers did not see any working parts or pieces for years.

ASSIGN NON-IT EXECUTIVES TO SOFTWARE PROJECTS

Non-IT executives should coordinate with the technical project manager, test iterations to make sure they are meeting user needs, and act as liaisons between executives and IT. Having the business side involved full-time will bring project ownership and a desire to succeed to all parties involved. SpreeRide, a Salt Lake City market research outfit, used the agile methodology to set up its company's Web site. The project required several business executives designated full-time. The company believes this is one of the primary reasons that the project was successfully deployed in less than three months.[17]

Project Managing the Systems Development Effort

No one would think of building an office complex by turning loose 100 different construction teams to build 100 different rooms, with no single blueprint or agreed-upon vision of the completed structure. Yet this is precisely the situation in which many large organizations find themselves when managing systems development

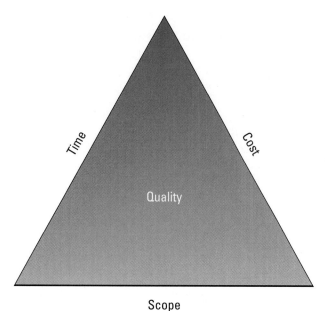

FIGURE 17.4

Project Management
Interdependent Variables

projects. Organizations routinely overschedule their resources (human and otherwise), develop redundant projects, and damage profitability by investing in nonstrategic efforts that do not contribute to the organization's bottom line. Project management offers a strategic framework for coordinating the numerous activities associated with organizational projects.

According to the Project Management Institute, **project management** is the application of knowledge, skills, tools, and techniques to project activities in order to meet or exceed stakeholder needs and expectations from a project. **Project management software** specifically supports the long-term and day-to-day management and execution of the steps in a project (such as building a new warehouse or designing and implementing a new IT system).

Project management is essential to the success of almost every aspect of IT. Without it, projects tend to be delayed, over budget, and often never reach completion. Horizon Blue Cross Blue Shield of New Jersey, a $6-billion-plus health insurance provider, allocated several hundred million dollars to IT over a five-year period to tackle tasks such as consolidating five enterprise software platforms, managing compliance with regulatory offices, and simplifying new product development. These IT initiatives involve hundreds of skilled people working on hundreds of concurrently developing projects. Horizon's executives needed to gain visibility into all projects, subsets of projects, and existing and planned projects collectively. The company considered a rigorous and formalized project management strategy fundamental to the project's success.

Horizon decided to implement IT project management software from Business Engine Inc. to manage its projects. The software collects information through standardized templates created for Microsoft Project, which are stored in an enterprise database and then fed into Business Engine's analytical tool, called Ben. Each user can then view and manipulate spreadsheets and graphs, share documents, track revisions, and run what-if scenarios in a personalized digital dashboard view. With the help from Business Engine, Horizon is managing IT projects and assets as if they were investments, tracking their performance against business goals, assessing their individual return and value to the company, and helping sort out which projects require greater attention and resources and which require reduced attention and resources. Horizon found itself ahead of schedule on over 70 percent of its IT projects.[18]

Figure 17.4 displays the relationships between the three primary variables in any project—(1) time, (2) cost, and (3) scope. These three variables are interdependent. For example, decreasing a project's time frame means either increasing the cost of the project or decreasing the scope of the project to meet the new deadline. Increasing a project's scope means either increasing the project's time frame or increasing the project's cost—or both—to meet the increased scope changes. Project management is the science of making intelligent trade-offs between time, cost, and scope. All three of the factors combined determine a project's quality.

Benjamin Franklin's timeless advice—by failing to prepare, you prepare to fail—especially applies to many of today's software development projects. A recent survey concluded that the failure rate of IT projects is much higher in organizations that do not exercise disciplined project management. Figure 17.5 displays the top six reasons IT projects fail, according to *Information Week*'s research survey of 150 IT managers.[19]

A successful project is typically on time, within budget, meets the business's requirements, and fulfills the customer's needs. The Hackett Group, an Atlanta-based

FIGURE 17.5

Why IT Projects Fall
Behind Schedule or Fail

consultancy, analyzed its client database (which includes 2,000 companies, including 81 Fortune 100 companies) and discovered:

- Three in 10 major IT projects fail.
- 21 percent of the companies state that they cannot adjust rapidly to market changes.
- One in four validate a business case for IT projects after completion.[20]

Nicolas Dubuc, collaborative project manager at Rhodia Inc., a $6 billion worldwide manufacturer of specialty chemicals, uses Microsoft's software to develop project management templates and methodologies for its 18 divisions. "We're designing a platform for rapid application development that will enhance opportunities for innovation," Dubuc said.

Today, the leaders in the project management software market include Microsoft, Primavera, Oracle, and SAP. Microsoft Project is the core project management tool for many organizations and dominates with more than 8 million users and over 80 percent of the market share. Figure 17.6 displays the growth in project management software. If an organization wants to deliver successful, quality software on time and under budget, it must take advantage of project management software.[21]

FIGURE 17.6

Growth for Project
Management Software

1. How are hospitals using new software to improve their operations?

2. List and describe the seven phases in the systems development life cycle and determine which phase is most important to a hospital when developing new systems.

3. Review the primary principles of successful software development and list them in order of importance for Hackensack University Medical Center's business strategy.

4. Why is building agile software important to Hackensack University Medical Center?

5. Assess the impact to a hospital if it decided to use the waterfall methodology to build its customers' information systems.

Chapter Seveenteen Case: Transforming the Entertainment Industry—Netflix

The online DVD rental pioneer Netflix is transforming the movie business with its unique business model and streamlined shipping strategy. Netflix is quickly becoming one of Hollywood's most promising new business partners and is experiencing staggering growth with over 1 million subscribers, accounting for 3 to 5 percent of all U.S. home video rentals.

Typically, traditional video rental stores focus on major films and ignore older movies and smaller titles with niche audiences. Netflix is turning that idea upside down by offering a serious market for every movie, not just blockbusters. How? Netflix attributes its success to its proprietary software, called the Netflix Recommendation System, which constantly suggests movies a customer might like, based on how the customer rates any of the 15,000 titles in the company's catalog. Beyond recommendations, Netflix has figured out how to get DVDs from one subscriber to the next with unbelievable efficiency.

Netflix operates by allowing its 3.5 million subscribers to rent unlimited videos for $9.99 a month, as long as they have no more than three DVDs rented at a time. Currently there are more than 5 million discs in the hands of its customers at any given time, with an average of 500,000 DVDs shipped out of the company's 36 leased distribution centers daily. To handle the rental logistics for its 10 million-DVD library the company created a proprietary supply chain management system.

As with any change or market advance, when new competition invades, existing competitors will not stand still. Walmart.com recently launched its own version of the Netflix model; it has already built six distribution centers, and is charging less per month for the same services offered by Netflix. Blockbuster purchased a similar service called FilmCaddy and is deciding how it will promote the service nationally. Other companies threatening to steal Netflix's market share are satellite and cable companies that now offer on-demand movies. To remain disruptive, Netflix will need to analyze its competition and strategize new ways to continue to increase subscriptions and revenues.

Netflix's Value Proposition

A crucial competitive weapon for maintaining its market share (estimated at two-thirds of online rentals) is new, homegrown software that improves upon the Oracle database the company uses to automate the DVD distribution process. The software consults the database to match a customer request with the movies in inventory. Based on algorithms devised to maximize delivery time by mail, the application decides which distribution center will fulfill each movie. The program then generates a "pull list" for workers at each center to fulfill the orders and ship them to customers.

Blockbuster, with 1 million online subscribers and 5,700 retail stores, is attacking with similar technology to orchestrate DVD delivery by mail from the chain's stores. Central to the Blockbuster strategy is the integration of 28 systems into one that feeds data about online orders to retail locations quickly.[22]

Questions

1. Assess the business-related consequences of a failure in Netflix's proprietary supply chain management system.

2. List and describe the seven phases in the systems development life cycle and determine which phase you think is most important to Netflix when it is developing software.

3. Determine the primary differences between the waterfall development methodology and the agile development methodology. Which methodology would you recommend Netflix use and why?

4. Why would prototyping be a good idea for Netflix if it decides to build a CRM system?

5. Given $10,000, would you recommend purchasing Netflix or Blockbuster stock?

BUSINESS PLUG-IN POINTER

Review **Business Plug-In B14 "Systems Development"** for in-depth coverage of the SDLC and its associated activities including performing feasibility studies, gathering business requirements, analyzing a buy versus build decision, designing and building systems, writing and performing testing, supporting users, etc.

Review **Business Plug-In B15 "Project Management"** for an overview of the fundamentals of project management including prioritizing projects and developing project plans, along with a detailed look at risk management and change management.

TECHNOLOGY PLUG-IN POINTER

Review **Technology Plug-In T11 "Creating Web Pages Using Dreamweaver"** for a tour of using Dreamweaver to create Web pages. Dreamweaver allows anyone with limited Web page design experience to create, modify, and maintain full-featured, professional-looking pages without having to learn how to code all the functions and features from scratch.

Review **Technology Plug-In T12 "Creating Gantt Charts with Excel and Microsoft Project"** for a quick and efficient way to manage projects. Excel and Microsoft Project are great for managing all phases of a project, creating templates, collaborating on planning processes, tracking project progress, and sharing information with all interested parties.

18

Outsourcing in the 21st Century

18.1. Describe the advantages and disadvantages of insourcing, outsourcing, and offshore outsourcing.

18.2. Describe why outsourcing is a critical business decision.

18.3. Assess the reasons for developing strategic outsourcing partnerships.

Outsourcing Development

Outsourcing

More than 400 people from Merrill Lynch, Thomson Financial (a large market data vendor), and a number of other vendors worked feverishly on Merrill Lynch's biggest outsourcing initiative ever. This highly complex $1 billion makeover of its wealth management system is designed to improve the efficiency of Merrill's financial advisers. With the new system, Merrill Lynch advisers can manage more of the assets of their high-net-worth customers.

The new system also represents a major shift in the way Merrill approaches IT initiatives. In the 1990s, Merrill developed its previous system, Trusted Global Advisor (TGA), as it did any other major system—it developed it in-house. The thought of outsourcing a critical business system to a vendor was viewed as highly unfavorable by most financial services organizations. In 2004, Merrill Lynch signed a contract that outsourced much of the responsibility for its new platform to Thomson Financial.[23]

In the high-speed global business environment, an organization needs to maximize its profits, enlarge its market share, and restrain its ever-increasing costs. Businesses need to make every effort to rethink and adopt new processes, especially the prospective resources regarding insourcing, outsourcing, and offshore outsourcing.

Insourcing

Insourcing or *in-house development* is a common approach using the professional expertise within an organization to develop and maintain the organization's information technology systems. Insourcing has been instrumental in creating a viable supply of IT professionals and in creating a better quality workforce combining both technical and business skills.

Michael Palmer, the COO (and former CIO) of Allied Office Products, decided to bring in-house nearly all of the IT functions that had been outsourced. Palmer calculated that he could cut the $24,000-a-month hardware monitoring and maintenance costs by two-thirds and save several hundred thousand dollars on development by insourcing. Since Palmer turned to insourcing 85 percent of the IT work, he is now saving nearly $500,000 a year.[24]

Outsourcing

Outsourcing is an arrangement by which one organization provides a service or services for another organization that chooses not to perform them in-house. In some cases, the entire information technology department is outsourced, including planning and business analysis as well as the installation, management, and servicing of the network and workstations. Outsourcing can range from a large contract under which an organization like IBM manages IT services for a company such as Xerox, to the practice of hiring contractors and temporary office workers on an individual basis. Figure 18.1 compares the functions companies have outsourced.

Ever since Eastman Kodak announced that it was outsourcing its information systems function in 1988 to IBM, DEC, and Businessland, large organizations have found it acceptable to transfer their IT assets, leases, and staff to outsourcers. In view of the changes in sourcing, the key question now is not "should we outsource IT?" but rather "where and how can we take advantage of the rapidly developing market of IT services providers?" Organizations should consider outsourcing in order to achieve the following benefits:

- Financial savings
- Increased technical abilities
- Market agility[25]

FINANCIAL SAVINGS

Cost competitiveness drove the Big Three automakers—Ford, Chrysler, and General Motors—to collaborate in a unique way by building an IT service. Automotive Network eXchange (ANX) joins suppliers and buyers across the automotive supply chain and allows the sharing of CAD/CAM drawings, as well as exchanging trade e-mail messages and shipping communications. Ironing out such inefficiencies across the supply chain alone could decrease the cost of producing a car as much as $1,200.[26]

INCREASED TECHNICAL ABILITIES

Rapid technological change has become an issue for many businesses throughout all industries, resulting in more expense to upgrade systems, more time to install, and increased complexity to master. For a business whose IT department is a non-core function, maintaining a "best-of-breed" status under these conditions is next to impossible, especially for small and medium-sized enterprises where cost is a critical factor.

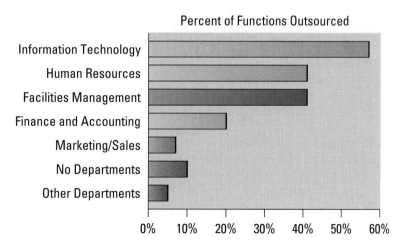

FIGURE 18.1

Common Departments Outsourced by Organizations

Nike's footwear business generates $6 billion in revenues per year. It requires global communication to keep its Nike designers, product developers, marketing teams, sales staff, distributors, and dealers in line with product developments and marketing plans. Nike uses a system called GPIN (Global Product Information Network), an innovative IT service that allows Nike's employees to collaborate throughout their processes and keeps every partner up-to-date with developments.[27]

MARKET AGILITY

Market agility includes the ability to expand core businesses more rapidly depending on the outsourcer's capabilities to provide efficient transitions to new systems, better information management for decision making, and expansion to new geographical markets.

Kodak is over 100 years old. So is chemical-based photography. Therefore, Kodak moved its focus from being in the film business to being in the picture-processing business, and from this developed Kodak's e-service, Photonet, a password-protected application that allows users to post photographs on the Internet, order copies, send picture postcards, and customize postcard greetings.[28]

IT outsourcing is a fast-growing industry since it provides access to state-of-the-art technologies with expert guidance, thus curtailing the need to open up expensive in-house departments. According to a report by IDC, global spending on IT services was expected to reach $700 billion by 2005, an increase from $440 billion in 2002. Many factors have converged to prompt firms to outsource. Figure 18.2 displays the reasons many organizations outsource key departments.[29]

Focusing a company's resources on core business functions allows outsourcing noncore functions. Outsourcing can give the right combination of people, processes, and technology to operate efficiently and effectively in the global marketplace without burdening time and budget. Some of the influential drivers affecting the growth of the outsourcing market include:

- **Core competencies**—Many companies have recently begun to consider outsourcing as a means to fuel revenue growth rather than just a cost-cutting measure. Outsourcing enables an organization to maintain an up-to-date technology infrastructure while freeing it to focus on revenue growth goals by reinvesting cash and human capital in areas offering the greatest return on investment.

FIGURE 18.2

Reasons Companies Have Outsourced

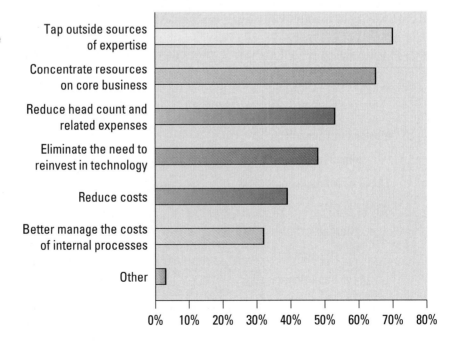

- **Rapid growth**—A company's sustainability depends on both speed to market and ability to react quickly to changes in market conditions. By taking advantage of outsourcing, an organization is able to acquire best practices process expertise. This facilitates the design, building, training, and deployment of business processes or functions.

- **Industry changes**—High levels of reorganization across industries have increased demand for outsourcing to better focus on core competencies. The significant increase in merger and acquisition activity created a sudden need to integrate multiple core and noncore business functions into one business, while the deregulation of the utilities and telecom industries created a need to ensure compliance with government rules and regulations. Companies in either situation turned to outsourcing so they could better focus on industry changes at hand.

- **The Internet**—The pervasive nature of the Internet as an effective sales channel has allowed clients to become more comfortable with outsourcing.[30]

Developing Strategic Outsourcing Partnerships

Business process outsourcing (BPO) is the contracting of a specific business task, such as payroll, to a third-party service provider. Business process outsourcing is increasingly becoming the strategic choice of companies looking to achieve cost reductions while improving their service quality, increasing shareholder value, and focusing on their core business capabilities. Many organizations are looking beyond traditional IT outsourcing to business process outsourcing as the next logical step.

Implementing BPO can save costs for tasks that an organization requires but does not depend upon to maintain its position in the marketplace. BPO is divided into two categories: (1) back-office outsourcing that includes internal business functions such as billing or purchasing, and (2) front-office outsourcing, which includes customer-related services such as marketing or technical support.

Business process outsourcing is not a new field. Paychex, based in Rochester, New York, for example, has been outsourcing payroll processing for small businesses since 1971. However, the market is heating up these days, as companies' need for strategic cost cutting, desire to improve business methods, and comfort with outsourcing arrangements grow.

The Gartner Group estimated that the worldwide market for business process outsourcing would grow to $178 billion in 2005. Management consulting and technology services company Accenture is a BPO player. Accenture's first BPO deal came in the early 1990s, when it outsourced finance and accounting functions for British Petroleum. Accenture now handles a variety of outsourcing tasks, such as airline ticket processing and call center staffing for AT&T.[31]

Sourcing's New Surge—Offshoring

Offshore outsourcing is using organizations from developing countries to write code and develop systems. Numerous countries have substantially well-trained IT professionals and clerical staff who have lower salary expectations compared to their U.S. counterparts. Offshore outsourcing has become a small but rapidly growing sector in the overall outsourcing market. Nearly half of all businesses use offshore providers, and two-thirds plan to send work overseas in the near future, according to Forrester Research. India receives most of the outsourcing functions from all over the world. However, as more American companies seek to source globally, more countries are emerging to benefit from that demand—from Canada to Malaysia—each with its own particular strengths and weaknesses. Organizations have much to gain from offshore outsourcing.[32]

Chapter Eighteen Case: UPS in the Computer Repair Business

When people think of UPS they usually think of brown delivery trucks and employees in shorts dropping off and picking up packages. This image is about to change. UPS has now entered the laptop repair business. Toshiba is handing over its entire laptop repair operation to UPS Supply Chain Solutions, the shipper's $2.4 billion logistics outsourcing division. Toshiba's decision to allow a shipping company to fix its laptops might appear odd. However, when you understand that the primary challenge of computer repair is more logistical than technical, Toshiba's business decision seems brilliant. "Moving a unit around and getting replacement parts consumes most of the time," explained Mark Simons, general manager at Toshiba's digital products division. "The actual service only takes about an hour."

UPS sends broken Toshiba laptops to its facility in Louisville, Kentucky, where UPS engineers diagnose and repair defects. In the past, repairs could take weeks, depending on whether Toshiba needed components from Japan. Since the UPS repair site is adjacent to its air hub, customers should get their machines back, as good as new, in just a matter of days. UPS has been servicing Lexmark and Hewlett-Packard printers since 1996 and has been performing initial inspections on laptops being returned to Toshiba since 1999.

The expanded Toshiba relationship is another step in UPS's strategy to broaden its business beyond package delivery into commerce services. The company works with clients to manage inventory, ordering, and custom processes. It recently introduced a service to dispose of unwanted electrical devices. To take on laptop repair, UPS put 50 technicians through a Toshiba-certified training course.[33]

Questions

1. Do you think UPS's entrance into the laptop repair business was a good business decision? Why or why not?

2. Explain why Toshiba decided to outsource its computer repair business to UPS.

3. What are some advantages UPS can offer Toshiba in the outsourcing arrangement?

4. Explain the advantages of forming an outsourcing relationship with a parcel delivery company such as UPS.

<<BUSINESS PLUG-IN POINTER

Review **Business Plug-In B13 "Strategic Outsourcing"** for an in-depth review of the reasons American companies seek to source globally.

19

Developing a 21st Century Organization

19.1. List and describe the four 21st century trends that businesses are focusing on and rank them in order of business importance.

19.2. Explain how the integration of business and technology is shaping 21st century organizations.

Developing Organizations

Organizations face changes more extensive and far reaching in their implications than anything since the modern industrial revolution occurred in the early 1900s. Technology is one of the primary forces driving these changes. Organizations that want to survive in the 21st century must recognize the immense power of technology, carry out required organizational changes in the face of it, and learn to operate in an entirely different way. Figure 19.1 displays a few examples of the way technology is changing the business arena.[34]

21st Century Organization Trends

On the business side, 21st century organization trends are:

- Uncertainty in terms of future business scenarios and economic outlooks.
- Emphasis on strategic analysis for cost reduction and productivity enhancements.
- Focus on improved business resiliency via the application of enhanced security.

Trends

On the technology side, there has been a focus on improved business management of IT in order to extract the most value from existing resources and create-alignment between business and IT priorities. Today's organizations focus on defending and safeguarding their existing market positions in addition to targeting new market growth. The four primary information technology areas where organizations are focusing are:

- IT infrastructures
- Security
- E-business
- Integration

INCREASED FOCUS ON IT INFRASTRUCTURE

A significant trend for the 21st century is to increase the focus on *IT infrastructure*—the hardware, software, and telecommunications equipment that, when combined, provide the underlying foundation to support the organization's goals.

Industry	Business Changes Due to Technology
Travel	Travel site Expedia.com is now the biggest leisure-travel agency, with higher profit margins than even American Express. Thirteen percent of traditional travel agencies closed in 2002 because of their inability to compete with online travel.
Entertainment	The music industry has kept Napster and others from operating, but $35 billion annual online downloads are wrecking the traditional music business. U.S. music unit sales are down 20 percent since 2000. The next big entertainment industry to feel the effects of e-business will be the $67 billion movie business.
Electronics	Using the Internet to link suppliers and customers, Dell dictates industry profits. Its operating margins have risen from 7.3 percent in 2002 to 8 percent in 2003, even as it takes prices to levels where rivals cannot make money.
Financial services	Nearly every public e-finance company remaining makes money, with online mortgage service LendingTree growing 70 percent a year. Processing online mortgage applications is now 40 percent cheaper for customers.
Retail	Less than 5 percent of retail sales occur online, but eBay was on track in 2003 to become one of the nation's top 15 retailers, and Amazon.com will join the top 40. Wal-Mart's e-business strategy is forcing rivals to make heavy investments in technology.
Automobiles	The cost of producing vehicles is down because of SCM and Web-based purchasing. Also, eBay has become the leading U.S. used-car dealer, and most major car sites are profitable.
Education and training	Cisco saved $133 million in 2002 by moving training sessions to the Internet, and the University of Phoenix online college classes please investors.

FIGURE 19.1

Examples of How Technology Is Changing Business

Architecture

Organizations in the past underestimated the importance that IT infrastructures have for the many functional areas of an organization.

In the early days of the Internet, the basic infrastructure in terms of protocols and standards was unsophisticated (and still is), but software companies managed to enhance the Internet and offer compelling applications for functional business areas. The original design for the Internet and the Web was for simple e-mail, document exchange, and the display of static content, not for sophisticated and dynamic business applications that require access to back-end systems and databases.

Organizations today are looking to Internet-based cross-functional systems such as CRM, SCM, and ERP to help drive their business success. The days of implementing independent functional systems are gone. Creating an effective organization requires a 360-degree view of all operations. For this reason, ownership of the IT infrastructure now becomes the responsibility of the entire organization and not just the individual users or functional department. This is primarily because the IT infrastructure has a dramatic influence on the strategic capabilities of an organization (see Figure 19.2).

INCREASED FOCUS ON SECURITY

With war and terrorist attacks on many people's minds, security is a hot topic. For businesses, too, security concerns are widespread. Increasingly opening up their networks and applications to customers, partners, and suppliers using an ever more diverse set of computing devices and networks, businesses can benefit from deploying the latest advances in security technologies. These benefits include fewer

FIGURE 19.2

The Position of the
Infrastructure within the
Organization

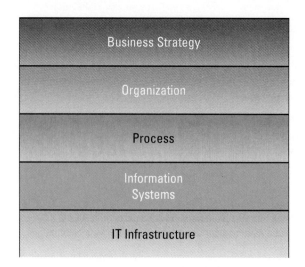

Hurricane
Katrina
Recovery

Threats

disruptions to organizational systems, increased productivity of employees, and greater advances in administration, authorization, and authentication techniques. For businesses it is important to have the appropriate levels of authentication, access control, and encryption in place, which help to ensure (1) that only authorized individuals can gain access to the network, (2) that they have access to only those applications for which they are entitled, and (3) that they cannot understand or alter information while in transit. Figure 19.3 displays a recent survey concerning both the level of physical security integration and the current security practices used by most organizations.

Security breaches not only inconvenience business users and their customers and partners, but can also cost millions of dollars in lost revenues or lost market capitalization. The business cost of inadequate security does not stop at inconvenience and loss of revenues or market valuation. It can even force a business out of existence. For example, in early 2002 British Internet service provider Cloud-Nine Communications was the victim of a distributed denial-of-service (DDoS) attack that forced the company to close operations and to eventually transfer over 2,500 customers to a rival organization. While "disruptive technologies" can help a company to gain competitive advantage and market share (and avoid real business disruptions), lack of security can have the opposite effect, causing profitable companies to lose market share or even their entire business within hours or days of an attack.[35]

It is now more important than ever for an organization to have well-rehearsed and frequently updated processes and procedures to insure against a variety of adverse scenarios—Internet e-mail and denial-of-service attacks from worms and viruses, loss of communications, loss of documents, password and information theft, fire, flood, physical attacks on property, and even terrorist attacks.

FIGURE 19.3

Physical Security
Integration and Best
Security Practices

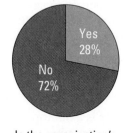

Is the organization's
physical security integrated
with IT security?

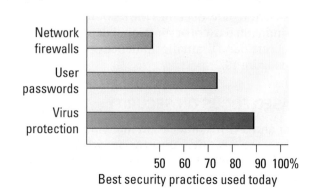

Best security practices used today

INCREASED FOCUS ON E-BUSINESS

Mobility and wireless are the new focus in e-business, and some upcoming trends are mobile commerce, telematics, electronic tagging, and RFID.

- *Mobile commerce (m-commerce)*—the ability to purchase goods and services through a wireless Internet-enabled device.
- *Telematics*—blending computers and wireless telecommunications technologies with the goal of efficiently conveying information over vast networks to improve business operations. The most notable example of telematics may be the Internet itself, since it depends on a number of computer networks connected globally through telecommunication devices.[36]
- *Electronic tagging*—a technique for identifying and tracking assets and individuals via technologies such as radio frequency identification and smart cards.
- *Radio frequency identification (RFID)*—technologies use active or passive tags in the form of chips or smart labels that can store unique identifiers and relay this information to electronic readers. Within the supply chain, RFID can enable greater efficiencies in business processes such as inventory, logistics, distribution, and asset management. On the mobile commerce side, RFID can enable new forms of e-business through mobile phones and smart cards. This can increase loyalty by streamlining purchases for the consumer. For example, RFID readers are being embedded in store shelving to help retailers, including Marks & Spencer and The Gap, to better manage their assets and inventories and understand customer behavior.[37]

These are all interesting subcategories within mobile business that open up new opportunities for mobility beyond simple employee applications. Electronic tagging and RFID are especially interesting because they extend wireless and mobile technologies not just to humans, but also to a wide range of objects such as consumer and industrial products. These products will gain intelligence via electronic product codes, which are a (potential) replacement for universal product code (UPC) bar codes, and via RFID tags with two-way communication capabilities.

Mobile employees will soon have the ability to leverage technology just as if they were in the office. Improvements in devices, applications, networks, and standards over the past few years have made this far more practical than it was when introduced. The drivers for adoption are finally starting to outweigh the barriers. For example, major vendors such as IBM, Microsoft, Oracle, and Sybase are all playing a larger role and taking a greater interest in mobile business than they had previously. These vendors all have mature, proven offerings for enterprise mobility.

Mobile technology will help extend an organization out to its edges in areas such as sales automation and enterprise operations. Benefits can include improved information accuracy, reduced costs, increased productivity, increased revenues, and improved customer service. Beyond being an additional channel for communications, mobile business will enable an organization to think about the powerful combination of business processes, e-business, and wireless communications.[38]

INCREASED FOCUS ON INTEGRATION

Information technology has penetrated the heart of organizations and will stay there in the future. The IT industry is one of the most dynamic in the global economy. As a sector, it not only creates millions of high-level jobs, but also helps organizations to be more efficient and effective, which in turn stimulates innovation. The integration of business and technology has allowed organizations to increase

FIGURE 19.4

The Integration of
Business and Technology

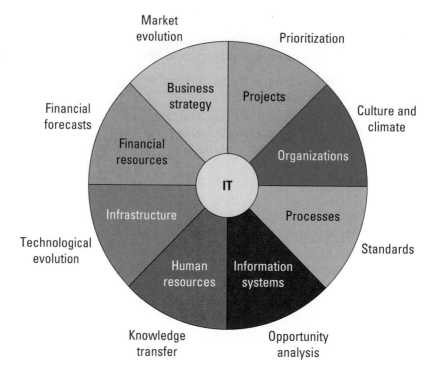

ilities

their share of the global economy, transform the way they conduct business, and become more efficient and effective (see Figure 19.4).

The past few years have produced a confluence of events that has reshaped the global economy. Around the world, free-market competition has flourished and a new globally interdependent financial system has emerged. Reflecting these changes, core business relationships and models are dramatically changing, including shifts from:

- Product-centricity to customer-centricity.
- Mass production to mass customization.
- The value in material things to the value of knowledge and intelligence.

In concert with these trends, a new series of business success factors and challenges has emerged that is helping to determine marketplace winners and losers:

- Organization agility, often supported by a "plug and play" IT infrastructure (with a flexible and adaptable applications architecture).
- A focus on core competencies and processes.
- A redefinition of the value chain.
- Instantaneous business response.
- The ability to scale resources and infrastructure across geographic boundaries.

These developments add up to an environment that is vastly more complex than even five years ago. This in turn has resulted in organizations increasingly embracing new business models. The new environment requires organizations to focus externally on their business processes and integration architectures. The virtually integrated business model will cause a sharp increase in the number of business partners and the closeness of integration between them.

Never before have IT investments played such a critical role in business success. As business strategies continue to evolve, the distinction between "the business" and IT will virtually disappear.

1. How might a hospital define its IT infrastructure when developing its 21st century strategy?

2. How might a hospital define security when developing its 21st century strategy?

3. How might a hospital define its e-business infrastructure when developing its 21st century strategy?

4. How might a hospital define its integrations when developing its 21st century strategy?

Chapter Nineteen Case: Creating a Clearer Picture for Public Broadcasting Service (PBS)

One of the leaders in the transformation of the broadcasting industry is André Mendes, chief technology integration officer, or CTIO, at Public Broadcasting Service (PBS). Mendes oversees the company's technology organization, a 50-person group created by melding PBS's IT and broadcast-engineering departments. The new CTIO position replaces the formerly separate jobs of CIO and CTO at the nonprofit television network.

Mendes encountered a few roadblocks during his first few months as CTIO including resistance from the broadcast engineering staff, his limited knowledge of broadcast engineering, and breaking down barriers between the two departments. Mendes managed through the change with finesse and now refers to it as a "bidirectional learning experience" for him and his staff. "Once you're in a new environment, you start asking a lot of questions," he says. "Every question requires the responder to think about the answer. That helped the process of evaluating why procedures and practices are done a certain way—and identifying possible improvements."

Michael Hunt, PBS's vice president of enterprise applications, states that Mendes broke down many barriers and offered his employees a way to address and respond to change. The united team is currently working on large, sophisticated projects that are improving the efficiency of PBS and its member stations. "Projects are getting bigger and bigger, with more and more collaboration, with a more global picture," says Marilyn Pierce, director of PBS digital assets, who came from the broadcast-engineering side of the company.

"The broadcast environment is becoming an IT environment," states Mendes in reference to the fact that as the worlds of broadcast and traditional information technologies converge, this uncovers new ways to improve quality of service and increase opportunities for innovation through new digitized formats, which replace traditional analog video. The primary drivers of this convergence are advances in digital technologies and the Internet. Though those changes are unique to the television industry, it is not the first—or last—time that welding together different technology organizations has been responsible for advances in technology. For instance, companies pursuing voice-over-IP (VOIP) initiatives are combining their IT and telecommunications groups, and other industries face similar integration challenges as everything from automobiles to appliances becomes increasingly technology dependent.

The integration of broadcast and information technologies is raising the visibility of technology as an organizational infrastructure enabler and a strategic partner for new business models. PBS is launching several projects that are revamping the way the company does business. One project allows producers to send program content digitally rather than on videotapes. In the past, PBS rejected and returned 60 percent of the video content because it did not contain key technical information such as the number of frames in a program to allow for seamless merging of programs. "From a supply chain standpoint, that was highly inefficient," Mendes says.

Another project is saving PBS tens of millions of dollars a year by transporting its programs to TV stations as e-mail files via TCP/IP over satellite. This delivery vehicle greatly improves quality by avoiding weather-related interference that can arise in transmitting programs by streaming signals over satellite. "The change in broadcast is similar to the transformation in the telecom industry as companies moved from switch circuitry to packet circuits," Mendes says. For PBS the business lines are blurring as the industry responds to technology changes, which is making the overall picture much clearer.[39]

Questions

1. Assess the impact to PBS's business if it failed to focus on IT infrastructures when determining its 21st century business strategy.

2. Assess the impact to PBS's business if it failed to focus on security when determining its 21st century business strategy.

3. Assess the impact to PBS's business if it failed to focus on e-business when determining its 21st century business strategy.

4. Assess the impact to PBS's business if it failed to focus on integrations when determining its 21st century business strategy.

An organization must remain competitive in this quick-paced, constantly changing, global business environment. It must implement technology that is adaptive, disruptive, and transformable to meet new and unexpected customer needs. Focusing on the unexpected and understanding disruptive technologies can give an organization a competitive advantage.

Organizations need software that users can transform quickly to meet the requirements of the rapidly changing business environment. Software that effectively meets employee needs will help an organization become more productive and make better decisions. Software that does not meet employee needs may have a damaging effect on productivity. Employee involvement along with using the right implementation methodology in developing software is critical to the success of an organization.

Four areas of focus for organizations heading into the 21st century are IT infrastructure, security, e-business (mobility), and integration. Information technology has rapidly expanded from a backroom resource providing competitive advantage (e.g., cost, time, quality) to a front-office resource (e.g., marketing, sales) that is a competitive necessity. The dynamic business and technical environment of the 21st century is driving the need for technology infrastructures and applications architecture that are increasingly flexible, integrated, and maintainable (while always providing functionality, cost effectiveness, timeliness, and security).

KEY TERMS

Agile methodology, 246
Analysis phase, 242
Business process outsourcing (BPO), 255
Business requirement, 242
Design phase, 242
Development phase, 242
Electronic tagging, 261
Extreme programming (XP) methodology, 245
Feature creep, 247
Implementation phase, 242
Information Technology Infrastructure Library (ITIL), 246

Insourcing (in-house development), 252
IT infrastructure, 258
Maintenance phase, 242
Mobile commerce (m-commerce), 261
Offshore outsourcing 255
Outsourcing 253
Planning phase, 241
Project management, 248
Project management software, 248
Prototype, 244

Radio frequency identification (RFID), 261
Rapid application development (RAD) (also called rapid prototyping) methodology, 244
Scope creep, 247
Systems development life cycle (SDLC), 241
Telematics, 261
Testing phase, 242
Waterfall methodology, 244

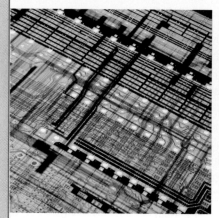  

RFID—Future Tracking

The elementary school that required students to wear radio frequency identification (RFID) tags to track their movements ended the program because the company that developed the technology pulled out. "I'm disappointed; that's about all I can say at this point," stated Ernie Graham, the superintendent and principal of Brittan Elementary School. "I think I let my staff down."

The tags, developed by California-based technology company InCom Corp., were introduced in January 2005. Students were required to wear identification cards around their necks with their picture, name, and grade and a wireless transmitter that beamed ID numbers to a teacher's handheld computer when the children passed under an antenna posted above a classroom door. The school instituted the system, without parental input, to simplify attendance-taking and potentially reduce vandalism and improve student safety. "I'm happy for now that kids are not being tagged, but I'm still fighting to keep it out of our school system," said parent Dawn Cantrall, who filed a complaint with the American Civil Liberties Union. "It has to stop here."

While many parents criticized the tags for violating privacy and possibly endangering children's health, some parents supported the plan. "Technology scares some people; it's a fear of the unknown," parent Mary Brower said. "Any kind of new technology has the potential for misuse, but I feel confident the school is not going to misuse it."

Tracking Children

Children's sleepwear with radio frequency identification tags sewn into the seams hit stores in early 2006. Made by Lauren Scott California, the nightgowns and pajamas will be one of the first commercial RFID-tagged clothing lines sold in the United States.

The PJs are designed to keep kids safe from abductions, says proprietor Lauren Scott, who licensed the RFID technology from SmartWear Technologies Inc., a maker of personal-security systems. Readers positioned in doorways and windows throughout a house scan tags within a 30-foot radius and trigger an alarm when boundaries are breached.

A pamphlet attached to the garment informs customers that the sleepwear is designed to help prevent child abductions. It directs parents to a Web site that explains how to activate and encode the RFID tag with a unique digital identification number. The site also provides information on a $500 home-installed system that consists of RFID readers and a low-frequency encoder that connects through a USB port to a computer. Parents can sign up to include data about their children, including photos, in the SmartWear database. That information can be shared with law enforcement agencies or the Amber Alert system if a child disappears.

SmartWear has several other projects in the works including an extended-range RFID tag that can transmit signals up to 600 feet. The tag could be inserted into law enforcement and military uniforms or outerwear, such as ski jackets, and used to find a missing or lost person or to recover and identify a body.

Plastic RFID

A typical RFID tag costs 40 cents, making price a barrier for many potential applications. Start-up OrganicID is creating a plastic RFID tag that it expects will reduce the price to a penny or less. CEO Klaus Dimmler hopes to market the plastic tags, which will operate in the 13.56-MHz range, by 2008.[40]

Questions

1. What are some advantages and disadvantages of tagging students with RFID tags?
2. What are some advantages and disadvantages of tagging children's pajamas with RFID tags?
3. Do you agree or disagree that tagging students with RFID tags is a violation of privacy rights? Explain why.
4. Do you agree or disagree that tagging children's pajamas with RFID tags is a violation of privacy rights? Explain why.
5. Describe the relationship between privacy rights and RFID.
6. Determine a way that schools could use RFID tags without violating privacy rights.

 UNIT CLOSING CASE TWO

Masters of Innovation, Technology, and Strategic Vision

Several companies are emerging as leaders on the intensely competitive playing field of e-business. *Wired* magazine highlights The Wired 40—companies driven by innovative thinking, not marketplace brawn, that demonstrate a mastery of tomorrow's business essentials including innovation, technology, strategic vision, global reach, and networked communication.

BusinessWeek magazine highlights The Web Smart 50—companies that are using technology to develop new e-business opportunities in the areas of collaboration, customer service, customization, streamlining, management, and cutting-edge technology. Cross-referencing the two lists reveals seven outstanding companies that are included in both The Wired 40 and The Web Smart 50:

■ Amazon.com
■ Charles Schwab

- Cisco
- Dell
- IBM
- Sony
- Wal-Mart

Amazon.com—It's a Mall World after All

- Ranked seventh on The Wired 40.
- Featured on The Web Smart 50 under "Cutting Edge."

"Amazon.com and you're done!" was the e-business pioneer's slogan. Critics of Amazon.com said that CEO Jeff Bezos should have stuck with books; his online store would soon crumple under the debt it had taken on to expand into other goods. Jeff Bezos proved the critics wrong by reducing Amazon.com's debt while doubling its revenue growth rate.

In 2003, Amazon.com opened its site to independent developers, allowing merchants to use its gold-standard e-business technology to build their own stores on top of Amazon's. To date, over 35,000 software developers have created programs from building customized Web stores to checking prices from handheld devices. Currently, other retailers now account for 22 percent of all items sold on Amazon.com. Amazon.com continues to prove critics wrong and is demonstrating that a Web site can be the best storefront location of all.

Charles Schwab—Trading Places

- Ranked 37th on The Wired 40.
- Featured on The Web Smart 50 under "Customer Service."

Charles Schwab, the full-service investment firm, continues to shock the investment industry by using technology innovations to transform its business. The company invested $20 million on Web technology to build the Schwab Equity Rating System, a computer-generated online service that offers recommendations for the buying and selling of over 3,000 stocks. The system allows Schwab to avoid the $20-million-a-year cost of hiring new analysts and avoid conflicts of interest between analysts and business, something to watch in the wake of Wall Street scandals.

Charles Schwab also rolled out Web-based services for financial advisers. Collaboration between Schwab and independent financial advisers gives retail investors the best of both worlds.

Cisco—The Network Connection

- Ranked 11th on The Wired 40.
- Featured on The Web Smart 50 under "Cutting Edge."

Cisco, with its flat revenue and steady profit, has become a cash machine in less than two decades. The company is continuing to transform to ensure it is evolving as the Internet evolves. First, it is switching 35,000 employees and consultants to Voice-over-IP (VOIP) Internet-enabled telephone systems. Cisco workers worldwide now use Internet phones, cutting down on telephony services by $300,000 monthly.

Second, the company is changing its lines of business. John Chambers, the CEO of Cisco, understands that the market for routers and switches, which account for 70 percent of Cisco's sales, is headed for stagnation. To combat this, the company is investing 40 percent of its research and development dollars into areas that constitute a mere 15 percent of sales: optical and storage networking, wireless communications, security software, and VOIP. Cisco promises to be ready for companies that want to start investing in next-generation networks.

Dell—Just-in-Time Hardware

- Ranked 15th on The Wired 40.
- Featured on The Web Smart 50 under "Cutting Edge."

Dell's core PC business is still "disruptive" (cutting edge) as the company installs robots to automate its e-business network. By installing robots on the assembly lines that process orders from the Web, the company can build 900 computers an hour, increasing output by over 40 percent. At Dell's plant in Nashville, assembly line robots retrieve online orders and fetch all of the required components to build the custom PCs. This new setup requires half as many workers and operates at three times the speed. The plant churns out one computer every four seconds.

Dell has a reputation for shattering every industry it targets. When the personal computer went from branded gizmo to commodity, Dell polished its famous strategy—assemble on demand, deliver high value at low cost, sell directly to customers—and drove IBM out of the PC market and Compaq into HP's arms. Dell is now focusing on attacking the server sector (of which it claims nearly a quarter), the workstation niche (where it has Sun on the run), the networking arena (where Cisco is looking vulnerable), and the consulting business specializing in systems integration.

IBM—The Ultimate IT Outsource

- Ranked fourth on The Wired 40.
- Featured on The Web Smart 50 under "Collaboration."

Perhaps IBM's acronym should stand for It's Been Morphing. The 92-year-old company proved as nimble as a start-up by supporting Linux and promoting it as an enterprise-friendly solution. IBM is now promoting "e-business on demand," which envisions computing as a utility: Switch it on when needed and pay only for what is used. The services will allow everything including offering organizations the ability to expand at will.

IBM is also creating an online collaboration system for employees that has cut training costs by $375 million annually and travel expenses by $20 million annually. IBM's intranet allows its 300,000 workers to brainstorm. Web jams, big sessions with over 1,000 employees, encourage the free flow of ideas. Many organizations are now looking to IBM for expertise in the area of intranet development. IBM hopes to become to computing what "Ma Bell" once was to telephones.

Sony—That's Home Entertainment!

- Ranked 16th on The Wired 40.
- Featured on The Web Smart 50 under "Collaboration."

CEO Nobuyuki Idei sees Sony's future in home networks that beam files among PCs, TVs, and portables. That means melding the company's music and video departments, which currently deliver more than half the company's profit. Nobuyuki Idei is restructuring the organization by moving away from departmental silos into a more seamless organization.

Wal-Mart—Retail-o-rama

- Ranked 13th on The Wired 40.
- Featured on The Web Smart 50 under "Collaboration."

Wal-Mart squeezes big brands for low prices and passes the savings on to consumers. Then it pumps suppliers for information that will help it give shoppers what they want, when they want it. The newest technology innovation the company is pursuing to help streamline its supply chain is "smart tags," which will be placed in every product case for its top 100 suppliers.

The tags will track product in every phase of the supply chain, allowing the company to know exactly where every product is and increase its ability to keep its shelves stocked. Analysts expect Wal-Mart to reap pretax savings of as much as $8 billion by 2007.

CEO Lee Scott is focusing on several other new investments including branding products like dog food and moving into pharmaceuticals, financial services, and DVD rentals. Global expansion continues: Wal-Mart has more stores in Mexico (551) than in its two biggest states, Texas and Florida, combined, plus 486 others in the United Kingdom, Brazil, China, and South Korea. Wal-Mart promises to continue to redefine efficiency in retailing.[41]

Questions

1. Which one of the seven companies has the most disruptive technology that is capable of making the greatest impact on business?
2. How has Amazon used technology to change the bookselling industry in the 21st century?
3. Choose one of the seven companies and create a Porter's Five Forces analysis to highlight potential issues the company might face in the 21st century.
4. List and describe the seven phases in the systems development life cycle and determine which phase is most important to Cisco when it is developing software.
5. Review the primary principles of successful software development and prioritize them in order of importance for Sony.
6. Why is building agile software important for all seven companies?
7. What potential systems might Dell want to outsource?
8. Discuss the pitfalls Wal-Mart might encounter if it decided to outsource its SCM system.

✱ MAKING BUSINESS DECISIONS

1. Selecting a Systems Development Methodology

Exus Incorporated is an international billing outsourcing company. Exus currently has revenues of $5 billion, over 3,500 employees, and operations on every continent. You have recently been hired as the CIO. Your first task is to increase the software development project success rate, which is currently at 20 percent. To ensure that future software development projects are successful, you want to standardize the systems development methodology across the entire enterprise. Currently, each project determines which methodology it uses to develop software.

Create a report detailing three additional system development methodologies that were not covered in this text. Compare each of these methodologies to the traditional waterfall approach. Finally, recommend which methodology you want to implement as your organizational standard. Be sure to highlight any potential roadblocks you might encounter when implementing the new standard methodology.

2. Transforming an Organization

Your college has asked you to help develop the curriculum for a new course titled "Building a 21st Century Organization." Use the materials in this text, the Internet, and any other resources to outline the curriculum that you would suggest the course cover. Be sure to include your reasons why the material should be covered and the order in which it should be covered.

3. **Approving a Project**

You are working in the IT development team for Gear International, a privately held sports and recreational equipment manufacturer. To date, you have spent the majority of your career developing applications for your corporate intranet. Your team has an idea to add an application that allows employees to learn about corporate athletic teams, register online, determine team schedules, post team statistics, etc. Your supervisor likes your idea and would like your team to prepare a short presentation with 5 to 10 slides that she can use to convince senior management to approve the project. Be sure to list benefits of the project along with your suggested methodology to help guarantee the project's development success.

4. **Patrolling by Remote**

Today's gadgets offer all-weather, all-knowing, anytime, anyplace. Whether you are trying to keep tabs on your children, your new home theater, or your streaming audio, here are a few wireless tools you can use around your house.

- **Wi-fi camera**—A five-inch-high Wireless Observer lets you take pictures at regular intervals or in response to motion and you can access it anytime through a Web browser (www.veo.com).

- **Security sensor**—This detector system alerts you to break-ins and errant pop flies. Its dual sensors record vibration and acoustic disturbances—signs of a shattered window—to help avoid false alarms. (www.getintellisense.com).

- **GPS tracking device**—Total Parental Information Awareness is here. Lock this GPS locator to your kids' wrist and whenever you want to check on them just query Wherify's Web page. It pinpoints their location on a street map and displays an aerial photo (www.wherify.com).

- **Wireless speakers**—Sony's versatile 900-MHz speakers connect the RF receiver to your stereo, TV, or PC, and get crystal-clear audio anywhere within 150 feet (www.sonystyle.com).

In a group, create a document discussing how these new wireless technologies could potentially change the business arena and list at least one company for each technology that should view these new products as potential threats.

5. **Saving Failing Systems**

Signatures Inc. specializes in producing personalized products for companies, such as coffee mugs and pens with company logos. The company generates over $40 million in annual revenues and has more than 300 employees. The company is in the middle of a large multimillion-dollar SCM implementation and has just hired your Project Management Outsourcing firm to take over the project management efforts. On your first day, your team is told that the project is failing for the following reasons:

- The project is using the traditional waterfall methodology.
- The SDLC was not followed and the developers decided to skip the testing phase.
- A project plan was developed during the analysis phase, but the old project manager never updated or followed the plan.

In a group determine what your first steps would be to get this project back on track.

1. Connecting Components

Components of a solid enterprise architecture include everything from documentation to business concepts to software and hardware. Deciding which components to implement and how to implement them can be a challenge. New IT components are released daily, and business needs continually change. An enterprise architecture that meets your organization's needs today may not meet those needs tomorrow. Building an enterprise architecture that is scalable, flexible, available, accessible, and reliable is key to your organization's success.

Project Focus

You are the enterprise architect for a large clothing company called Xedous. You are responsible for developing the initial enterprise architecture. Create a list of questions you will need answered to develop your architecture. Below are examples of a few questions you might ask.

- What are the company's growth expectations?
- Will systems be able to handle additional users?
- How long will information be stored in the systems?
- How much customer history must be stored?
- What are the organization's business hours?
- What are the organization's backup requirements?

2. Back on Your Feet

You are working for GetSmart, a document creation company for legal professionals. Due to the highly sensitive nature of the industry, employees must store all work on the network drive and are not allowed to back up the data to a CD, flash drive, or any other type of external storage including home computers. The company has been following this policy for the last three years without any issues. You return to work Monday morning after a long weekend to find that the building was struck by lightning destroying several servers. Unfortunately, the backup strategy failed and all of the data from your department has been lost.

When the head of the company demanded an explanation as to why there were no individual backups, he was shown the company policy he had signed not once but three times. The head of IT along with four of his cronies who had developed this ridiculous policy were fired.

Project Focus

You have been placed on a committee with several of your peers to revamp the backup and recovery policies and create a new disaster recovery plan. You must create policies and procedures that will preserve the sensitive nature of the documents, while ensuring the company is safe from disasters. Be sure to address a worst-case scenario where the entire building is lost.

3. GEM Athletic Center

First Information Corporation is a large consulting company that specializes in systems analysis and design. The company has over 2,000 employees and first-quarter revenues reached $15 million. The company prides itself on maintaining an 85 percent success rate for all project implementations. The primary reason attributed to the unusually high project success rate is the company's ability to define accurate, complete, and high quality business requirements.

The GEM Athletic Center located in Cleveland, Ohio, is interested in implementing a new payroll system. The current payroll process is manual and takes three employees two days each month to complete. The GEM Athletic Center does not have an IT department and is outsourcing the entire procurement, customization, and installation of the new payroll system to First Information Corporation.

Project Focus

You have been working for First Information for a little over one month. Your team has just been assigned the GEM Athletic Center project and your first task is to define the initial business requirements for the development of the new payroll system.

1. Review the testimony of three current GEM Athletic Center accounting employees who detail the current payroll process along with their wish list for the new system. Use the files MaggieCleaver.doc, AnneLogan.doc, JimPoulos.doc.
2. Review the Characteristics of Good Business Requirements document (Business-Requirements.doc) that highlights several techniques you can use to develop solid business requirements.
3. After careful analysis, create a report detailing the business requirements for the new system. Be sure to list any assumptions, issues, or questions in your document.

Data Folder: Chapter 19_AYK 3

4. Confusing Coffee

Business requirements are the detailed set of business requests that any new system must meet in order to be successful. A sample business requirement might state, "The system must track all customer sales by product, region, and sales representative." This requirement states what the system must do from the business perspective, giving no details or information on how the system is going to meet this requirement.

Project Focus

You have been hired to build an employee payroll system for a new coffee shop. Review the following business requirements and highlight any potential issues.

- All employees must have a unique employee ID.
- The system must track employee hours worked based on employee's last name.
- Employees must be scheduled to work a minimum of eight hours per day.
- Employee payroll is calculated by multiplying the employee's hours worked by $7.25.
- Managers must be scheduled to work morning shifts.
- Employees cannot be scheduled to work more than eight hours per day.
- Servers cannot be scheduled to work morning, afternoon, or evening shifts.
- The system must allow managers to change and delete employees from the system.

5. Picking Projects

You are a project management contractor attempting to contract work at a large telecommunications company, Hex Incorporated. Your interview with Debbie Fernandez, the senior vice president of IT, went smoothly. The last thing Debbie wants to see from you before she makes her final hiring decision is a prioritized list of the projects below. You are sure to land the job if Debbie is satisfied with your prioritization.

Project Focus

Create a report for Debbie prioritizing the following projects and be sure to include the business justifications for your prioritization.

- Upgrade accounting system.
- Develop employee vacation tracking system.

- Enhance employee intranet.
- Cleanse and scrub data warehouse information.
- Performance test all hardware to ensure 20 percent growth scalability.
- Implement changes to employee benefits system.
- Develop backup and recovery strategy.
- Implement supply chain management system.
- Upgrade customer relationship management system.
- Build executive information system for CEO.

6. Keeping Time

Time Keepers Inc. is a small firm that specializes in project management consulting. You are a senior project manager, and you have recently been assigned to the Tahiti Tanning Lotion account. The Tahiti Tanning Lotion company is currently experiencing a 10 percent success rate (90 percent failure rate) on all internal IT projects. Your first assignment is to analyze one of the current project plans being used to develop a new CRM system (see Figure AYK.1).

Project Focus

1. Review the project plan and create a document listing the numerous errors in the plan. Be sure to also provide suggestions on how to fix the errors.
2. If you have access to Microsoft Project, open the file BadProject.mpp. Fix the errors you found in question 1 directly to BadProject.mpp. (If you are new to using Microsoft Project, review the document MSProjectGuidelines.doc for an overview of several tips for using Microsoft Project.)

FIGURE AYK.1

Sample Project Plan

Data Folder: Chapter 19_AYK 6

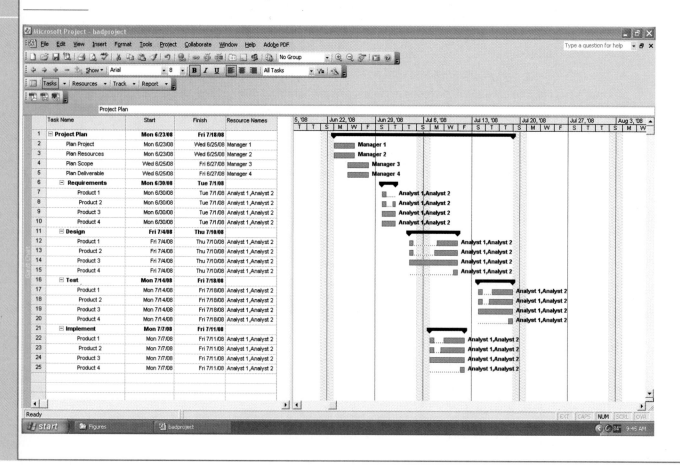

7. Growing, Growing, Gone

You are the founder of Black Pearl, a small comic book start-up. The good news is Black Pearl has found tremendous success. You have 34 employees in a creative, yet functional, office in downtown Chicago. The comics you produce are of extremely high quality. The artwork is unmatched and the story lines are compelling, gripping, and addictive, according to your customers. Your comics are quickly becoming a cult classic and Black Pearl customers are extremely loyal. You produce all of the comics and sell them in your store and via the Internet to individuals all over the United States.

Project Focus

You had vision when you started Black Pearl. You knew the potential of your business model to revamp the comic industry. You purchased high-end computers and customizable software to support your operations. Now, you are faced with a new dilemma. You have a large international following and you have decided to pursue international opportunities. You would like to open stores in Japan, France, and Brazil during the next year. To determine if this is possible, you need to evaluate your current systems to see if they are flexible and scalable enough to perform business internationally. You know that you are going to run into many international business issues. Create a list of questions you need to answer to determine if your systems are capable of performing international business.

8. The Virtualization Opportunity

Virtualization makes good business sense. Organizations recognize the opportunity to use virtualization to break down the silos that keep applications from sharing infrastructure and that contribute to chronic underutilization of IT resources. Virtualization can help an organization simultaneously reduce costs, increase agility, and make IT more responsive to the needs of the business. So for many organizations, the question is not, "Should we virtualize?" Instead, the question is, "How can we transition to a virtualized environment in a predictable, cost-effective manner?"

Project Focus

You are the CFO for Martello's, a food distribution organization with locations in Chicago, New York, and San Francisco. Your CIO, Jeff Greenwald, has given you a proposal for a budget of $2 million to convert the organization to a virtualized environment. You are unfamiliar with virtualization, how it works, and the long-term goals it will satisfy for the company. You have a meeting with Jeff tomorrow and you want to be able to discuss his proposal. Use the Internet to research virtualization to prepare for your meeting. Once you have a solid understanding of virtualization, create a report detailing your decision to grant or deny Jeff's budget proposal.

Business Basics

LEARNING OUTCOMES

1. Define the three common business forms.
2. List and describe the seven departments commonly found in most organizations.
3. Describe a transaction and its importance to the accounting department.
4. Identify the four primary financial statements used by most organizations.
5. Define the relationship between sales and marketing, along with a brief discussion of the marketing mix.
6. Define business process reengineering and explain how an organization can use it to transform its business.

Introduction

A sign posted beside a road in Colorado states, "Failing to plan is planning to fail." Playnix Toys posted the sign after successfully completing its 20th year in the toy business in Colorado. The company's mission is to provide a superior selection of high-end toys for children of all ages. When the company began, it generated interest by using unique marketing strategies and promotions. The toy business has a lot of tough competition. Large chain stores such as Wal-Mart and Target offer toys at deep discount prices. Finding the right strategy to remain competitive is difficult in this industry, as FAO Schwarz discovered when it filed for bankruptcy after 143 years in the toy business.[1]

This plug-in introduces basic business fundamentals beginning with the three most common business structures—sole proprietorship, partnership, and corporation. It then focuses on the internal operations of a corporation including accounting, finance, human resources, sales, marketing, operations/production, and management information systems.

Types of Business

Businesses come in all shapes and sizes and exist to sell products or perform services. Businesses make profits or incur losses. A **profit** occurs when businesses sell products or services for more than they cost to produce. A **loss** occurs when businesses sell products or services for less then they cost to produce. Businesses typically organize in one of the following types:

1. Sole proprietorship
2. Partnership
3. Corporation

SOLE PROPRIETORSHIP

The **sole proprietorship** is a business form in which a single person is the sole owner and is personally responsible for all the profits and losses of the business. The sole proprietorship is the quickest and easiest way to set up a business operation. No prerequisites or specific costs are associated with starting a sole proprietorship. A simple business license costing around $25 from the local county clerk is all that is required to start a sole proprietorship. The person who starts the sole proprietorship is the sole owner.[2]

PARTNERSHIP

Partnerships are similar to sole proprietorships, except that this legal structure allows for more than one owner. Each partner is personally responsible for all the profits and losses of the business. Similar to the sole proprietorship, starting a partnership is a relatively easy process since there are no prerequisites or specific costs required. When starting a partnership, it is wise to have a lawyer draft a partnership agreement. A **partnership agreement** is a legal agreement between two or more business partners that outlines core business issues. Partnership agreements typically include:

- Amount of capital each partner expects to contribute. **Capital** represents money whose purpose is to make more money, for example, the money used to buy a rental property or a business.
- Duties and responsibilities expected from each partner.
- Expectations for sharing profits and losses.
- Partners' salary requirements.
- Methods for conflict resolution.
- Methods for dissolving the partnership.[3]

Limited Partnership

A **limited partnership** is much like a general partnership except for one important fundamental difference; the law protects the limited partner from being responsible for all of the partnership's losses. The limited partner's legal liability in the business is limited to the amount of his or her investment. The limited partnership enables this special type of investor to share in the partnership profits without being exposed to its losses in the event the company goes out of business. However, this protection exists only as long as the limited partner does not play an active role in the operation of the business.

CORPORATION

The corporation is the most sophisticated form of business entity and the most common among large companies. The **corporation** (also called **organization, enterprise,** or **business**) is an artificially created legal entity that exists separate and apart from those individuals who created it and carry on its operations. In a corporation, the business entity is separate from the business owners. **Shareholder** is another term for business owners. An important advantage of using a corporation as a business form is

that it offers the shareholders limited liability. ***Limited liability*** means that the share-holders are not personally liable for the losses incurred by the corporation. In most instances, financial losses incurred by a corporation are limited to the assets owned by the corporation. Shareholders' personal assets, such as their homes or invest-ments, cannot be claimed to pay off debt or losses incurred by the corporation.

There are two general types of corporations—for profit and not for profit. ***For profit corporations*** primarily focus on making money and all profits and losses are shared by the business owners. ***Not for profit*** (or ***nonprofit***) ***corporations*** usually exist to accomplish some charitable, humanitarian, or educational purpose, and the profits and losses are not shared by the business owners. Donations to non-profit businesses may be tax deductible for the donor. Typical examples include hospitals, colleges, universities, and foundations.[4]

Eleanor Josaitis is a tiny 72-year-old woman who co-founded the Detroit civil-rights group Focus: HOPE. Focus: HOPE, founded in 1968, began as a food pro-gram serving pregnant women, new mothers, and their children. Josaitis has built the nonprofit organization from a basement operation run by a handful of friends into a sprawling 40-acre campus in Detroit that now employs over 500 people, boasts more than 50,000 volunteers and donors, and has helped over 30,000 people become gainfully employed.

Josaitis and her team developed a technical school to help job seekers gain cer-tifications in IT support. They operate a machinists' training program that funnels people into the employment pipeline at local automotive companies. The organi-zation also teams up with local universities to help disadvantaged students receive college educations, and it runs a child care center to make sure all these opportuni-ties are available to working and single parents. Josaitis states that the most coura-geous act she has performed in her life occurred 36 years ago when she turned off her television, got up off the couch, and decided to do something. "You have to have the guts to try something, because you won't change a thing by sitting in front of the TV with the clicker in your hand," Josaitis said.[5]

Forming a corporation typically costs several hundred dollars in fees, and the own-ers must file a charter within the respective state. The charter typically includes:

- Purpose of the intended corporation.
- Names and addresses of the incorporators.
- Amount and types of stock the corporation will be authorized to issue.
- Rights and privileges of the shareholders.

FIGURE B1.1

Reasons Businesses Choose to Incorporate

Reasons Businesses Choose to Incorporate	
Limited liability	In most instances, financial losses or judgments against the corporation are limited to the assets owned by the corporation.
Unlimited life	Unlike sole proprietorships and partnerships, the life of the corporation is not dependent on the life of a particular individual or individuals. It can continue indefinitely until it accomplishes its objective, merges with another business, or goes bankrupt. Unless stated otherwise, it could go on indefinitely.
Transferability of shares	It is easy to sell, transfer, or give the ownership interest in a corporation to another person. The process of divesting sole proprietorships or partnerships can be cumbersome and costly. Property has to be re-titled, new deeds drawn, and other administrative steps taken any time the slightest change of ownership occurs. With a corporation, all of the individual owners' rights and privileges are represented by the shares of stock they own. Corporations can quickly transfer ownership by simply having the shareholders endorse the back of each stock certificate to another party.
Ability to raise investment capital	It is easy to attract new investors into a corporate entity because of limited liability and the easy transferability of ownership.

	Sole Proprietorship	Partnership	Corporation
Licensing	Local license, $25–$100	Partnership agreement, legal fees	Articles of incorporation through the Secretary of State
Income	Business flows directly into personal income	Distributions taken by partners, as agreed by partners	Business and personal earnings separate, depending on corporate structure
Liability	Owner is liable	Owners are liable	Only business is liable

FIGURE B1.2

Comparison of Business
Structures

The most common reason for incurring the cost of setting up a corporation is the recognition that the shareholder is not legally liable for the actions of the corporation. Figure B1.1 displays the primary reasons businesses choose to incorporate.

The Limited Liability Corporation (LLC)

The *limited liability corporation (LLC)* is a hybrid entity that has the legal protections of a corporation and the ability to be taxed (one time) as a partnership. A company can form an LLC for any lawful business as long as the nature of the business is not banking, insurance, and certain professional service operations. By simply filing articles of organization with the respective state agency, an LLC takes on a separate identity similar to a corporation, but without the tax problems of the corporation. Figure B1.2 summarizes the primary differences between the three most common business structures.[6]

Internal Operations of a Corporation

The majority of corporations use different specialized departments to perform the unique operations required to run the business. These departments commonly include accounting, finance, human resources, sales, marketing, operations/production, and management information systems (see Figure B1.3).

Accounting

The *accounting department* provides quantitative information about the finances of the business including recording, measuring, and describing financial information. People tend to use the terms *accounting* and *bookkeeping* synonymously;

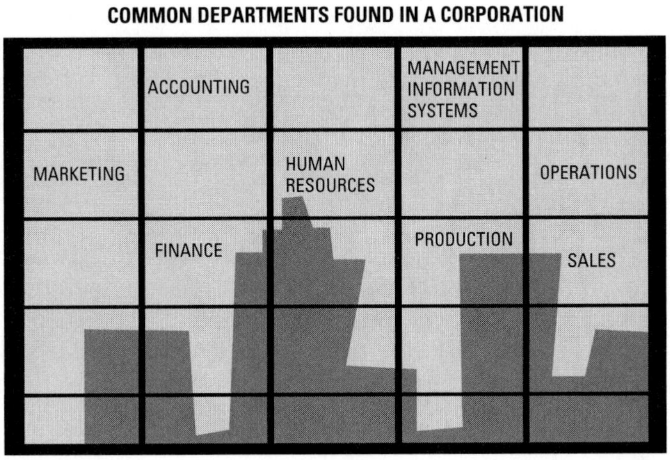

COMMON DEPARTMENTS FOUND IN A CORPORATION

FIGURE B1.3

Departmental Structure of
a Typical Organization

however, the two are different. ***Bookkeeping*** is the actual recording of the business's transactions, without any analysis of the information. ***Accounting*** analyzes the transactional information of the business so the owners and investors can make sound economic decisions.

The two primary types of accounting are financial and managerial. ***Financial accounting*** involves preparing financial reports that provide information about the business's performance to external parties such as investors, creditors, and tax authorities. Financial accounting must follow strict guidelines known as Generally Accepted Accounting Principles (GAAP). ***Managerial accounting*** involves analyzing business operations for internal decision making and does not have to follow any rules issued by standard-setting bodies such as GAAP.[7]

FINANCIAL STATEMENTS

All businesses operate using the same basic element, the transaction. A ***transaction*** is an exchange or transfer of goods, services, or funds involving two or more people. Each time a transaction occurs a source document captures all of the key data involved with the transaction. The ***source document*** describes the basic transaction data such as its date, purpose, and amount and includes cash receipts, canceled checks, invoices, customer refunds, employee time sheet, etc. The source document is the beginning step in the accounting process and serves as evidence that the transaction occurred. ***Financial statements*** are the written records of the financial status of the business that allow interested parties to evaluate the profitability and solvency of the business. ***Solvency*** represents the ability of the business to pay its bills and service its debt. The financial statements are the final product of the accountant's analysis of the business transactions. Preparing the financial statements is a major undertaking and requires a significant amount of effort. Financial statements must be understandable, timely, relevant, fair, and objective in order to be useful. The four primary financial statements include:

- Balance sheet.
- Income statement.
- Statement of owner's equity.
- Statement of cash flows.[8]

Balance Sheet

The ***balance sheet*** gives an accounting picture of property owned by a company and of claims against the property on a specific date. The balance sheet is based on the fundamental accounting principle that assets = liabilities + owner's equity. An ***asset*** is anything owned that has value or earning power. A ***liability*** is an obligation to make financial payments. ***Owner's equity*** is the portion of a company belonging to the owners. The left (debit) side of a balance sheet states assets. The right (credit) side shows liabilities and owners' equity. The two sides must be equal (balance). The balance sheet is like a snapshot of the position of an individual or business at one point in time (see Figure B1.4).[9]

Income Statement

The ***income statement*** (also referred to as ***earnings report, operating statement,*** and ***profit-and-loss (P&L) statement***) reports operating results (revenues minus expenses) for a given time period ending at a specified date. ***Revenue*** refers to the amount earned resulting from the delivery or manufacture of a product or from the rendering of a service. Revenue can include sales from a product or an amount received for performing a service. ***Expenses*** refer to the costs incurred in operating and maintaining a business. The income statement reports a company's ***net income,*** or the amount of money remaining after paying taxes (see Figure B1.5).[10]

ASSETS		LIABILITIES	
Current Assets		**Current Liabilities**	
Cash	$ 250,000	Accounts Payable	$ 150,000
Securities	$ 30,000	Loans (due < 1 year)	$ 750,000
Accounts Receivable	$ 1,500,000	Taxes	$ 200,000
Inventory	$ 2,920,000		
		Long-term Liabilities	
Fixed Assets	$ 7,500,000	Loans (due > 1 year)	$ 2,500,000
		Total Liabilities	$ 3,600,000
		Owner's Equity	$ 8,600,000
Total Assets	**$12,200,000**	**Total Liabilities + Owner's Equity**	**$12,200,000**

ASSETS = LIABILITIES + OWNER'S EQUITY

Income Statement	
Revenue (Sales)	$60,000,000
Cost of Goods Sold	$30,000,000
Gross Profit (Sales – Cost of Goods Sold)	$30,000,000
Operating Expenses	$7,000,000
Profit Before Taxes (Gross Profit – Operating Expenses)	$23,000,000
Taxes	$18,000,000
Net Profit (or Loss)	**$5,000,000**

Statement of Owner's Equity

The *statement of owner's equity* (also called the *statement of retained earnings* or *equity statement*) tracks and communicates changes in the shareholder's earnings. Profitable organizations typically pay the shareholders dividends. *Dividends* are a distribution of earnings to shareholders.

Statement of Cash Flows

Cash flow represents the money an investment produces after subtracting cash expenses from income. The *statement of cash flows* summarizes sources and uses of cash, indicates whether enough cash is available to carry on routine operations, and offers an analysis of all business transactions, reporting where the firm obtained its cash and how it chose to allocate the cash. The cash flow statement shows where money comes from, how the company is going to spend it, and when the company will require additional cash. Companies typically project cash flow statements on a monthly basis for the current year and a quarterly basis for the next two to five years. A *financial quarter* indicates a three-month period (four quarters per year). Cash flow statements become less valid over time since numerous assumptions are required to project into the future.[11]

When it comes to decreasing expenses and managing a company's cash flow, managers need to look at all costs. Ben Worthen, executive vice president and CIO of Manufacturers Bank in Los Angeles, states that everyone notices the million-dollar negotiation; however, a couple of thousand dollars here and there are just as important. When attempting to cut costs, Worthen listed every contract the bank had. He saved $5,000 by renegotiating a contract with the vendor who watered the plants, a vendor that most employees did not even know existed. He also saved $50,000 by renegotiating the contract with the bank's cleaning agency. "You need to think of everything when cutting costs," Worthen said. "$5,000 buys three or four laptops for salespersons."[12]

Finance

Finance deals with the strategic financial issues associated with increasing the value of the business while observing applicable laws and social responsibilities. Financial decisions include such things as:

- How the company should raise and spend its capital.
- Where the company should invest its money.
- What portion of profits will be paid to shareholders in the form of dividends.
- Whether the company should merge with or acquire another business.

Financial decisions are short term (usually up to one year), medium term (one to seven years), or long term (more than seven years). The typical forms of financing include loans (debt or equity) or grants. Financing may be required for immediate use in business operations or for an investment.[13]

FINANCIAL ANALYSIS

Different financial ratios are used to evaluate a company's performance. Companies can gain additional insight into their performance by comparing financial ratios against other companies in their industry. A few of the more common financial ratios include:

- **Internal rate of return (IRR)**—the rate at which the net present value of an investment equals zero.
- **Return on investment (ROI)**—indicates the earning power of a project and is measured by dividing the benefits of a project by the investment.
- **Cash flow analysis**—a means to conduct a periodic check on the company's financial health. A projected cash flow statement estimates what the stream of money will be in coming months or years, based on a history of sales and expenses. A monthly cash flow statement reveals the current state of affairs. The ability to perform a cash flow analysis is an essential skill for every business owner; it can be the difference between being able to open a business and being able to stay in business.
- **Break-even analysis**—a way to determine the volume of business required to make a profit at the current prices charged for the products or services. For example, if a promotional mailing costs $1,000 and each item generates $50 in revenue, the company must generate 20 sales to break even and cover the cost of the mailing. The *break-even point* is the point at which revenues equal costs. The point is located by performing a break-even analysis. All sales over the break-even point produce profits; any drop in sales below that point will produce losses (see Figure B1.6).[14]

Human Resources

Human resources (HR) includes the policies, plans, and procedures for the effective management of employees (human resources). HR typically focuses on the following:

- Employee recruitment.
- Employee selection.

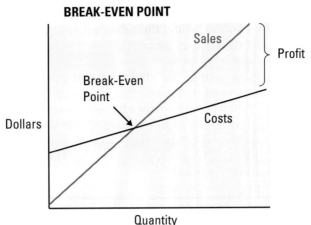

BREAK-EVEN POINT

- Employee training and development.
- Employee appraisals, evaluations, and rewards.
- Employee communications.

The primary goal of HR is to instill employee commitment by creating an environment of shared values, innovation, flexibility, and empowerment. Most organizations recognize that focusing on strong HR practices that foster employee growth and satisfaction can significantly contribute to achieving business success. The most obvious way HR practices create business success is through quality employee selection. Hiring the right employee who suits the company's culture is difficult. Organizations create employee value by implementing employment practices such as training, skill development, and rewards. An organization that focuses on HR creates valuable employees with strategic business competencies.[15]

MANAGEMENT TECHNIQUES

There may be no such thing as a best practice for managing people. Numerous management techniques are used by all different types of managers in a variety of industries. For example, Sears and Nordstrom are legends in the retailing industry; however, their approaches to HR are completely different. Sears is one of the pioneering companies in the science of employee selection, relying on some of the most sophisticated selection tests in American industry. Sears employees receive extensive training in company practices; management tracks employee attitudes and morale through frequent and rigorous employee surveys. The company provides its sales representatives, who work on salary rather than commission, with intensive training in Sears products, the company's operating systems, and sales techniques.

Nordstrom operates with virtually no formal personnel practices. Its hiring is decentralized, using no formal selection tests. Managers look for applicants with experience in customer contact, but the main desirable quality appears to be pleasant personalities and motivation. The company has only one rule in its personnel handbook: "Use your best judgment at all times." Individual salesclerks virtually run their areas as private stores. Nordstrom maintains a continuous stream of programs to motivate employees to provide intensive service, but it offers very little training. Its commission-based payroll system makes it possible for salesclerks to earn sizable incomes. Nordstrom sales personnel are ranked within each department according to their monthly sales; the most successful are promoted (almost all managers are promoted from within the company) and the least successful are terminated.[16]

Sears and Nordstrom are both highly successful retailers, yet they operate using widely different recruitment policies. One of the biggest success factors for any business is the company's management and personnel. Employees must possess certain critical skills for the company to succeed. The HR department takes on the important task of hiring, training, evaluating, rewarding, and terminating employees. Effective HR goes far beyond executing a standard set of policies and procedures; it requires questioning and understanding the relationships between choices in managing people, the strategies and goals of the organization, and the possibilities presented by the external environment. Today's competitive environment features rapid technological change, increasingly global markets, and a diverse workforce comprising not just men and women with different sorts of career objectives, but also potential workers from diverse cultural and ethnic backgrounds. HR must ensure that the choices made in managing people are made sensibly and with clear purposes in mind.

Sales

Sales is the function of selling a good or service and focuses on increasing customer sales, which increases company revenues. A salesperson has the main activity of selling a product or service. Many industries require a license before a salesperson can sell the products, such as real estate, insurance, and securities.

A common view of the sales department is to see the salespersons only concerned with making the sale now, without any regard to the cost of the sale to the business. This is called the hard sell, where the salesperson heavily pushes a product (even when the customer does not want the product) and where price cuts are given even if they cause financial losses for the company. A broader view of the sales department sees it as taking on the task of building strong customer relationships where the primary emphasis is on securing new customers and keeping current customers satisfied. Many sales departments are currently focusing on building strong customer relationships.

THE SALES PROCESS

FIGURE B1.7

The Sales Process

Figure B1.7 depicts the typical sales process, which begins with an opportunity and ends with billing the customer for the sale. An opportunity is a name of a potential customer who might be interested in making a purchase (opportunities are also

Sales Process

Opportunity generated → Lead sent to salesperson → Potential customer contacted → Potential customer meeting → Problems and solutions identified → Customer sales quote generated → Sales order placed → Order fulfilled → Customer billed

called *leads*). The company finds opportunities from a variety of sources such as mailing lists and customer inquiries. The name is sent to a salesperson who contacts the potential customer and sets up a meeting to discuss the products. During the meeting, all problems and issues are identified and resolved, and the salesperson generates a quote for the customer. If the customer decides to accept the quote, a sales order is placed. The company fulfills the order and delivers the product, and the process ends when the customer is billed.

MARKET SHARE

Sales figures offer a good indication of how well a company is performing. For example, high sales volumes typically indicate that a company is performing well. However, they do not always indicate how a firm is performing relative to its competitors. For example, changes in sales might simply reflect shifts in market size or in economic conditions. A sales increase might occur because the market increased in size, not because the company is performing better.

Measuring the proportion of the market that a firm captures is one way to measure a firm's performance relative to its competitors. This proportion is the firm's *market share* and is calculated by dividing the firm's sales by the total market sales for the entire industry. For example, if a firm's total sales (revenues) were $2 million and the sales for the entire industry were $10 million, the firm would have captured 20 percent of the total market, or have a 20 percent market share.

Many video game products launch with great enthusiasm and die a quick death such as Sega's GameGear and DreamCast, Atari's Lynx, and Nintendo's Virtual Boy. Video game consoles die quickly when only a limited number of game publishers sign up to supply games for the particular product. Producing video game products is a tough competitive business in a finicky market.

Sony released its first handheld video game player, the PSP (for PlayStation Portable), to go up against the market leader Nintendo's GameBoy, which uses pricey cartridges for games. Instead of pricey cartridges, the PSP plays inexpensive mini disks to bring PlayStation2-quality graphics to the relatively primitive handheld market. When Sony announced the PSP, game publishers raced to get a piece of the action, and Sony had 89 companies contracted to build games within a few weeks. In contrast, when Nokia launched its N-Gage game device, it struggled to land five game publishers. Electronic Arts, the world's biggest game publisher, has declared that the PSP will be the biggest driver of growth in the video game market for the next five years. For a new video game product heading into an uncertain and high-stakes market, that is the ultimate vote of confidence.[17]

Reasons to Increase Market Share

Many organizations seek to increase their market share because many individuals associate market share with profitability. Figure B1.8 indicates the primary reasons organizations seek to increase their market share.

Reasons to Increase Market Share
Economies of scale—An organization can develop a cost advantage by selling additional products or higher volumes.
Sales growth in a stagnant industry—If an industry stops growing, an organization can increase its sales by increasing its market share.
Reputation—A successful organization with a solid reputation can use its clout to its advantage.
Increased bargaining power—Larger organizations have an advantage in negotiating with suppliers and distributors.

FIGURE B1.8

Reasons to Increase Market Share

Ways to Increase Market Share
Product—An organization can change product attributes to provide more value to the customer. Improving product quality is one example.
Price—An organization can decrease a product's price to increase sales. This strategy will not work if competitors are willing to match discounts.
Place (Distribution)—An organization can add new distribution channels. This allows the organization to increase the size of its market, which should increase sales.
Promotion—An organization can increase spending on product advertising, which should increase sales. This strategy will not work if competitors also increase advertising.

Reasons Not to Increase Market Share
If an organization is near its production capacity and it experiences an increase in market share, it could cause the organization's supply to fall below its demand. Not being able to deliver products to meet demand could damage the organization's reputation.
Profits could decrease if an organization gains market share by offering deep discounts or by increasing the amount of money it spends on advertising.
If the organization is not prepared to handle the new growth, it could begin to offer shoddy products or less attentive customer service. This could result in the loss of its professional reputation and valuable customers.

Ways to Increase Market Share

A primary way to increase market share is by changing one of the following variables: product, price, place, or promotion (see Figure B1.9). It is common to refer to these four variables as the marketing mix, discussed in detail below.[18]

Reasons Not to Increase Market Share

Surprisingly, it is not always a good idea to increase an organization's market share. Figure B1.10 offers a few reasons increasing an organization's market share can actually decrease an organization's revenues.[19]

Marketing

Marketing is the process associated with promoting the sale of goods or services. The marketing department supports the sales department by creating promotions that help sell the company's products. *Marketing communications* seek to build product or service awareness and to educate potential consumers on the product or service.

Jenny Ming, president of Old Navy, a division of Gap Inc., believes that unique marketing ideas for Old Navy's original designs heavily contributed to the success of the $6.5 billion brand. Ideas come from anywhere, and Ming found one of the company's most successful products when she was dropping her daughter off at school. It was pajama day at school, and all of the girls were wearing pajama bottoms with a tank top. Ming began wondering why they even created and sold pajama tops; nobody seemed to wear them. The company, having problems selling pajama sets, quickly introduced "just bottoms," a line of pajama bottoms selling at $15. A full pajama set cost $25. Along with the bottoms, the company offered tank tops in different colors so the customer could mix and match the items. The company built a huge business from the "just bottoms" line. Ming encourages her staff to look for marketing and product opportunities everywhere, even in the most unlikely of places.[20]

MARKETING MIX

The classic components of marketing include the four Ps in the marketing mix: product, price, place, and promotion. The ***marketing mix*** includes the variables that marketing managers can control in order to best satisfy customers in the target market (see Figure B1.11). The organization attempts to generate a positive response in the target market by blending these four marketing mix variables in an optimal manner.

Figure B1.12 summarizes the primary attributes involved with each decision made in the marketing mix.[21]

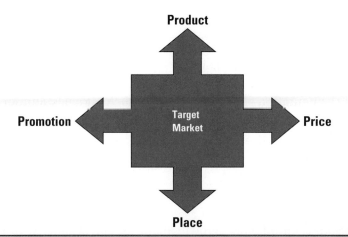

FIGURE B1.11

The Marketing Mix

1. **Product** — the physical product or service offered to the consumer. Product decisions include function, appearance, packaging, service, warranty, etc.

2. **Price** — takes into account profit margins and competitor pricing. Pricing includes list price, discounts, financing, and other options such as leasing.

3. **Place** (distribution) — associated with channels of distribution that serve as the means for getting the product to the target customers. Attributes involved in place decisions include market coverage, channel member selection, logistics, and levels of service.

4. **Promotion** — related to communication to and selling to potential consumers. An organization can perform a break-even analysis when making promotion decisions. If an organization knows the value of each customer, it can determine whether additional customers are worth the coast of acquisition. Attributes involved in promotion decisions involve advertising, public relations, media types, etc.

Product	Price	Place (Distribution)	Promotion
Quality	Discount	Channel	Advertising
Brand	Financing	Market	Sales
Appearance	Lease	Location	Public relations
Package		Logistics	Marketing message
Function		Service Level	Media type
Warranty			Budget
Service/Support			

FIGURE B1.12

Common Attributes Involved with Each P in the Marketing Mix

CUSTOMER SEGMENTATION

Market segmentation is the division of a market into similar groups of customers. It is not always optimal for an organization to offer the same marketing mix to vastly different customers. Market segmentation makes it possible for organizations to tailor the marketing mix for specific target markets, hence better satisfying its customer needs. Not all attributes of the marketing mix need to be changed for each market segment. For example, one market segment might require a discounted price, while another market segment might require better customer service. An organization uses marketing research, market trends, and managerial judgment when deciding the optimal way to segment a market. Market segmentation typically includes:

- **Geographic segmentation**—based on regional variables such as region, climate, population density, and population growth rate.
- **Demographic segmentation**—based on variables such as age, gender, ethnicity, education, occupation, income, and family status.
- **Psychographic segmentation**—based on variables such as values, attitudes, and lifestyles.
- **Behavioral segmentation**—based on variables such as usage rate, usage patterns, price sensitivity, and brand loyalty.[22]

THE PRODUCT LIFE CYCLE

The ***product life cycle*** includes the four phases a product progresses through during its life cycle including introduction, growth, maturity, and decline. An organization's marketing of a product will change depending on its stage in the product life cycle. An organization can plot a product's profits as a function of the product life cycle (see Figure B1.13).

Joanne Bischmann, vice president, Harley-Davidson Inc., is still awed by the lengths customers will go to display their commitment to Harley-Davidson products. Recently, she saw a man who had tattooed a portrait of the four founding fathers along with their 100th anniversary logo on his back. When Bischmann was hired, her manager told her the following, "This will be the best job you're ever going to have because it isn't just about working at a company that makes motorcycles. The founding fathers actually seep out of the walls here." After 15 years with the company, Bischmann agrees with that statement. She always receives calls asking for the Harley-Davidson manual on how to keep customers passionate. Unfortunately, there is no manual. According to Bischmann, Harley-Davidson is a brand that none can own individually; it is more like a tribe, and its members carry on its traditions so it will be here for future generations.[23]

Operations/Production

Operations management (also called ***production management***) includes the methods, tasks, and techniques organizations use to produce goods and services. The operations department oversees the transformation of input resources (i.e., labor, materials, and machines) into output resources (i.e., products and services). The operations department is critical because it manages the physical processes by which companies take in raw materials, convert them into products, and distribute them to customers. The operations department generally ranks high in the responsibilities of general management.

BUSINESS PROCESS REENGINEERING

A ***business process*** is a standardized set of activities that accomplishes a specific task, such as processing a customer's order. ***Business process reengineering (BPR)*** is the analysis and redesign of workflow within and between enterprises. In

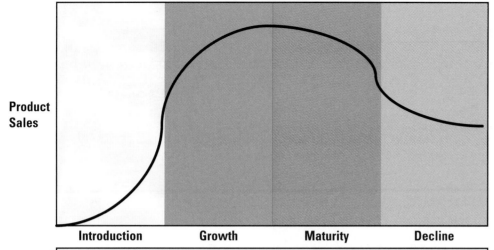

Product
Sales

| Introduction | Growth | Maturity | Decline |

- **Introduction Stage**—The organization seeks to build product awareness and develop the product's market. The organization will use the marketing mix to help impact the target market. Product branding and quality level are established.

- **Growth Stage**—The organization seeks to build brand preference and increase market share. The organization maintains or increases the quality of the product and might add additional features or better customer service. The organization typically enjoys increases in demand with little competition allowing the price to remain constant.

- **Maturity Stage**—The strong growth in sales diminishes. Competition begins to appear with similar products. The primary objective at this point is to defend market share while maximizing profits. Some companies enhance product features to differentiate the product in the market.

- **Decline Stage**—Sales begin to decline. At this point, the organization has several options. It can maintain the product, possibly rejuvenating it by adding new features and finding new uses. It can reduce costs and continue to offer it, possibly to a loyal niche segment. It can discontinue the product, liquidating remaining inventory or selling it to another firm that is willing to continue the product.

business process reengineering, the project team starts with a clean sheet of paper and redesigns the process to increase efficiency and effectiveness. The project team does not take anything for granted and questions all the aspects of the process and the business. The reengineering project team obtains dramatic process improvement by redesigning processes that cross departments.

Most of the major opportunities for process improvement exist in cross-departmental processes. Information technology usually plays a key role in process improvement by making possible a radically faster and almost paperless process. However, IT is only an enabling factor. A classic reengineering project example is the accounts payable process at Ford. Through BPR, Ford reduced the number of people required to perform the process from 500 to 125.[24]

TRANSFORMING CORPORATIONS

Complete transformation of an organization, or an entire industry, is the ultimate goal of successful business process reengineering. Figure B1.14 displays a matrix that has project scope on one axis and project speed on the other. For a project with a relatively narrow scope where the speed is fast, reengineering occurs. Fast speed with broad scope may be a turnaround situation requiring downsizing and tough decision making. A project with a relatively slow speed and narrow scope results in continuous improvement. In the upper right-hand corner of Figure B1.14, where the project scope is broad and the time frame for achieving that change is longer, the term *transformation* is appropriate.

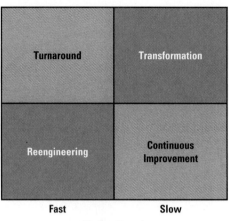

Progressive Insurance offers a great example of a corporation that transformed its entire industry by reengineering the insurance claims process. Progressive Insurance has seen phenomenal growth in an otherwise staid auto insurance market. Progressive's growth came not through acquisitions or mergers—the stuff that puts CEOs on the front page of *The Wall Street Journal*—but through substantial innovations in everyday operations. Progressive reengineered the insurance claim process. When a customer has an auto accident, Progressive representatives are on hand 24 hours a day to take the call and schedule a claims adjustor. The claims adjustor works out of a mobile van, enabling a nine-hour turnaround rather than the industry standard of 10 to 17 days. The Progressive adjustor prepares an estimate on the spot and will, in most cases, write the customer a check immediately and even offer a ride home.

What provoked this innovation? Progressive says it was the strong connection it has to its customers, its willingness to listen to customers' frustrations, and the common sense to act on those frustrations by changing the core of its business operations. As a result of customer feedback, the company did not merely tweak the details of the claims adjustment process. It dramatically rewrote the process, resulting in significant cost savings for the company. More important, however, the hassle-free claims process keeps customers happy and loyal, reducing the significant burden of constantly replacing lapsed customers with new ones.[25]

Management Information Systems

Information technology (IT) is a field concerned with the use of technology in managing and processing information. Information technology is a broad subject concerned with technology and other aspects of managing and processing information, especially in large organizations. In particular, IT deals with the use of electronic computers and computer software to convert, store, protect, process, transmit, and retrieve information. For that reason, computer professionals are often called IT specialists, and the division that deals with software technology is often called the IT department.

Management information systems is a business function just as marketing, finance, operations, and human resources management are business functions. Formally defined, *management information systems (MIS)* is a general name for the business function and academic discipline covering the application of people technologies, and procedures—collectively called information systems—to solve business problems. Other names for MIS include information services (IS), management information services (MIS), or managed service provider (MSP). In business, MIS supports business processes and operations, decision making, and competitive strategies. MIS involves collecting, recording, storing, and basic processing of information including:

- Accounting records such as sales, purchase, investment, and payroll information, processed into financial statements such as income statements, balance sheets, ledgers, management reports, and so on.

- Operations records such as inventory, work-in-process, equipment repair and maintenance, supply chain, and other production/operations information, processed into production schedules, production controllers, inventory systems, and production monitoring systems.

- Human resources records such as personnel, salary, and employment history information, processed into employee expense reports and performance-based reports.

- Marketing records such as customer profiles, customer purchase histories, marketing research, advertising, and other marketing information, processed into advertising reports, marketing plans, and sales activity reports.

- Strategic records such as business intelligence, competitor analysis, industry analysis, corporate objectives, and other strategic information, processed into industry trends reports, market share reports, mission statements, and portfolio models.

The bottom line is that management information systems use all of the above to implement, control, and monitor plans, strategies, tactics, new products, new business models, or new business ventures. Unit 1 covers IT and MIS in detail.

The study of business begins with understanding the different types of businesses including a sole proprietorship, partnership, or a corporation. Figure B1.15 highlights seven departments found in a typical business.

All of these departments must be able to execute activities specific to their business function and also be able to work with the other departments to create synergies throughout the entire business.

- **Accounting** provides quantitative information about the finances of the business including recording, measuring, and describing financial information.

- **Finance** deals with the strategic financial issues associated with increasing the value of the business, while observing applicable laws and social responsibilities.

- **Human resources (HR)** includes the policies, plans, and procedures for the effective management of employees (human resources).

- **Sales** is the function of selling a good or service and focuses on increasing customer sales, which increases company revenues.

- **Marketing** is the process associated with promoting the sale of goods or services. The marketing department supports the sales department by creating promotions that help sell the company's products.

- **Operations management** (also called **production management**) includes the methods, tasks, and techniques organizations use to produce goods and services. Transportation (also called logistics) is part of operations management.

- **Management information systems (MIS)** is a general name for the business function and academic discipline covering the application of people technologies, and procedures—collectively called information systems—to solve business problems.

FIGURE B1.15

Common Departments in a Business

Accounting, 280
Accounting department, 279
Asset, 280
Balance sheet, 280
Bookkeeping, 280
Break-even point, 282
Business process, 283
Business process reengineering
   (BPR), 288
Capital, 277
Corporation (also called,
   organization, enterprise, or
   business), 277
Dividend, 281
Expense, 280
Finance, 282
Financial accounting, 280
Financial quarter, 281
Financial statement, 280
For profit corporation, 278
Human resources (HR), 282
Income statement (also
   referred to as earnings
   report, operating statement,

and profit-and-loss (P&L)
   statement), 280
Information technology (IT), 290
Liability, 280
Limited liability, 278
Limited liability corporation
   (LLC), 279
Limited partnership, 277
Loss, 276
Management information
   systems (MIS), 290
Managerial accounting, 280
Marketing, 286
Marketing communication, 286
Marketing mix, 287
Market segmentation, 288
Market share, 285
Net income, 280
Not for profit (or nonprofit)
   corporation, 278
Operations management
   (also called production
   management), 288
Owner's equity, 280

Partnership, 277
Partnership agreement, 277
Product life cycle, 288
Profit, 276
Revenue, 280
Sales, 284
Shareholder, 277
Sole proprietorship, 277
Solvency, 280
Source document, 280
Statement of cash flow, 281
Statement of owner's equity
   (also called the statement of
   retained earnings or equity
   statement), 281
Transaction, 280

 CLOSING CASE ONE

Battle of the Toys—FAO Schwarz Is Back!

German immigrant Frederick Schwarz established FAO Schwarz, a premier seller of fine toys, in 1862. After moving between several store locations in Manhattan, the growing company settled at 745 Fifth Avenue in 1931. FAO Schwarz soon became a toy institution, despite the impending Depression.

Unfortunately, the New York institution closed its doors in 2004 after its owner, FAO Inc., filed for bankruptcy twice in 2003. The company ran into trouble because it could not compete with the deep discounts offered on toys at chain stores like Wal-Mart and Target. All the stores in the FAO chain were closed.

Some people believe that FAO Schwarz was its own worst enemy. The company sold Sesame Street figures for $9 while the same figure at a discount store went for less than $3.

In 2004, the New York investment firm D. E. Shaw & Co. bought the rights to the FAO Schwarz name and reopened the Manhattan and Las Vegas stores. The grand reopening of the New York store occurred on November 25, 2004, during the Macy's Thanksgiving Day parade. It appears that the company has learned from its previous mistakes and is moving forward with a new business strategy of offering high-end, hard-to-find toys and products along with outstanding customer service.

Jerry Welch, FAO chief executive officer, states the company based its new business strategy on offering customers—local, visitors, and Internet—a unique shopping experience in which they can spend thousands of dollars or just twenty, but still purchase an exclusive item. The store no longer carries any items from top toymakers Hasbro Inc. or Lego. The only toys it carries from Mattel Inc. are Hot Wheels and limited-edition Barbie dolls, starting at $130 for the Bridal Barbie dressed in a Badgley Mischka designer wedding gown and chandelier earrings. A few of the items the store is offering include:

- $20 made-to-order Hot Wheels car that a child can custom design via a computer.
- $50,000 miniature Ferrari with a full leather interior, fiberglass body, three-speed transmission, and working sound system that travels up to 24 kilometers an hour and is not recommended for children six and under.
- $15,000 stuffed elephant.
- $150,000 6.7-meter-long piano keyboard, which premiered in the Tom Hanks movie *Big*.
- Baby dolls that are arranged in incubators and sold by staff wearing nurses' uniforms.

Welch said, "FAO is a 142-year-old brand that, because of our location on Fifth Avenue, people all over the world know. So we start out with great recognition and what we've done here is pull together something that you just can't find anywhere else in the world. Everything here is made by small, unique manufacturers from all over the world." Welch is confident the stores will be richly profitable for its new owners because they have stopped offering mainstream products found in rival stores to generate sales volume. The new owners have returned to a business strategy focusing on quality and exclusivity that were the hallmark of the original store.

The Future of the Toy Store Playing Field

Toys 'R' Us began slashing prices during the 2004 holiday season in a last-ditch effort to fight off intense price competition from big discounters like Wal-Mart and Target. Toys 'R' Us CEO John Eyler stated the company would not be outdone on pricing, during the holiday sales rush, though he cautioned he was not planning to engage in a price war. There have been several reports that the company might leave the toy business to focus on its more profitable Babies 'R' Us unit. Toys 'R' Us lost $25 million for the three months ended in October 2004. The company lost $46 million in the same period the year earlier. The decrease in losses can be attributed to a big cost-cutting effort.

Kurt Barnard of Barnard's *Retail Trend Report* stated that Toys 'R' Us is destined for oblivion—it cannot stand up to the discounters. Toymakers like Mattel and Hasbro, whose profits have also suffered from Wal-Mart's market power, have given Toys 'R' Us a hand by offering it 21 exclusive items not available at other stores.

Toy manufacturers fear that greater monopoly power from Wal-Mart will force them to slash their profit margins. Wal-Mart carries fewer items than toy stores like Toys 'R' Us, which could lead to fewer choices for consumers.

FAO's new owners believe that Wal-Mart cannot compare with the atmosphere now offered at FAO Schwarz, a true toy heaven. The company is hoping that its new business strategy will allow it to move beyond the battle of the toy stores. Toys 'R' Us will need to find new ways to compete with discounters like Wal-Mart and Target.[26]

Questions

1. Why did FAO Inc. have to declare bankruptcy?
2. Describe the issues with FAO's original business model.
3. Identify the toy retailer's new business model. Do you believe it will keep the new company in business? Why or why not?
4. What strategy can Toys 'R' Us follow that will help it compete with big discount chains like Wal-Mart and Target?

Innovative Managers	
Jeffrey Immelt, General Electric (GE)	■ Repositioned GE's portfolio with major acquisitions in health care, entertainment, and commercial finance ■ Created a more diverse, global, and customer-driven culture
Steven Reinemund, PepsiCo	■ Developed strong and diverse leadership that helped PepsiCo tap new markets ■ Attained consistent double-digit growth through product innovation and smart marketing
Steven Spielberg, Jeffrey Katzenberg, and David Geffen, DreamWorks SKG	■ Computer-animated *Shrek 2* set a record with a gross of $437 million ■ IPO pulled in $812 million
Robert Nardelli, Home Depot	■ Turned a $46 billion company focused on big stores into a $70 billion chain with urban, suburban, and international outlets ■ Drive for efficiency, such as centralizing purchasing and investing in technology, pushed margins above 30 percent
John Henry, Boston Red Sox	■ Broke the most fabled curse in sports, when the Boston Red Sox won the team's first World Championship since 1918 ■ Sold out all 81 home games for the first time in team history
Phil Knight, Nike	■ Transformed a volatile, fad-driven marketing and design icon into a more shareholder-friendly company

FIGURE B1.16

Innovative Business Managers

Innovative Business Managers

BusinessWeek magazine recognized several innovative managers who have demonstrated talent, vision, and the ability to identify excellent opportunities (see Figure B1.16).

Jeffrey Immelt, General Electric (GE)

When Jeffrey Immelt took over as CEO of General Electric, he had big shoes to fill. The former CEO, Jack Welch, had left an unprecedented record as one of the top CEOs of all time. Immelt proved his ability to run the company by creating a customer-driven global culture that spawns innovation and embraces technology. The company was forecasting earnings to increase 17 percent in 2005.

Steven Reinemund, PepsiCo

Steven Reinemund has turned PepsiCo into a $27 billion food and beverage giant. "To be a leader in consumer products, it's critical to have leaders who represent the population we serve," states Reinemund, who created a diverse leadership group that defines the strategic vision for the company. Reinemund also takes a major role in mentoring and teaching his employees and demands that all senior executives do the same. The payoff: consistent double-digit earnings and solid sales at a time when many of the company's staple products—potato chips and soft drinks—are under attack for fears about childhood obesity and health concerns.

Steven Spielberg, Jeffrey Katzenberg, and David Geffen, DreamWorks

The DreamWorks studio, founded in 1994 by Steven Spielberg, Jeffrey Katzenberg, and David Geffen, suffered through its share of early bombs. Finally, the studio discovered a green ogre named Shrek and quickly became the hottest studio this side of Pixar Animation. DreamWorks Animation turned a $187 million loss in 2003 into a $196 million profit in 2004, with revenues of $1.1 billion. DreamWorks plans to release two animation films per year, each taking almost four years to produce.

Robert Nardelli, Home Depot

Robert Nardelli took several risks when he became CEO of Home Depot. First, he allocated $14 billion into upgrading merchandise, renovating outdated stores, and investing in new technology such as self-checkout lanes and cordless scan guns. Second, Nardelli expanded into Mexico, China, and other regions, tapping the growing homeowner market. Finally, Nardelli bet big on carrying products for aging baby boomers who wanted to spruce up their empty nests. The moves are paying off. The company sits on $3.4 billion in cash. With 2005 revenues headed to $80 billion, Home Depot is the number two U.S. retailer after Wal-Mart.

John Henry, Boston Red Sox

John Henry earned his fortune in the global futures market by developing a proprietary futures-trading system that consistently produced double-digit returns. Henry's new system, Sabermetrics, helped him reverse the most fabled curse in sports history by leading the Boston Red Sox to the team's first World Championship since 1918. Sabermetrics mines baseball statistics to find undervalued players while avoiding long contracts for aging stars whose performance is likely to decline. With the help of Sabermetrics, Henry has built one of the most effective teams in baseball.

Philip Knight, Nike

Philip Knight, who got his start by selling Japanese sneakers from the trunk of his car, built the $12 billion sports behemoth Nike. Knight and his team transformed high-performance sports equipment into high-fashion gear and forever changed the rules of sports marketing with huge endorsement contracts and in-your-face advertising. Then, just as suddenly, Nike lost focus. In early 2000, kids stopped craving the latest sneaker, the company's image took a huge hit from its labor practices, sales slumped, and costs soared.

Thus began Knight's second act. He revamped management and brought in key outsiders to oversee finances and apparel lines. Knight devoted more energy to developing new information systems. Today, Nike's earnings are less volatile and less fad-driven. In 2004, Nike's earnings increased $1 billion.[27]

Questions

1. Choose one of the companies listed above and explain how it has achieved business success.
2. Why is it important for all of DreamWorks' functional business areas to work together? Provide an example of what might happen if the DreamWorks marketing department failed to work with its sales department.
3. Why is marketing important to an organization like the Boston Red Sox? Explain where Major League Baseball is in the product life cycle.
4. Which types of financial statements are most important to Home Depot's business?
5. Identify the marketing mix and why customer segmentation is critical to PepsiCo's business strategy.
6. Explain business process reengineering and how a company like GE can use it to improve operations.

1. **Setting Up a Business**

   Your friend, Lindsay Harvey, is going to start her own chocolate shop, called Chocolate-By-Design. Lindsay is an expert candy maker and one of the city's top pastry chefs. Lindsay has come to you for advice on what type of business Chocolate-By-Design should be—a sole proprietorship, partnership, or corporation. Create a report comparing the three different types of businesses, along with your recommendation for Chocolate-By-Design's business structure.

2. **Guest Lecturing on Business**

   As a recent college graduate, your favorite professor, Dr. Henning, has asked you to come back and guest lecture at his introduction to business course. Create a presentation defining the different departments in a typical business, what roles each play, and why it is important that they all work together.

3. **Expanding Markets**

   J. R. Cash created a small business selling handmade cowboy boots, and within a year his business is booming. J. R. currently builds all of the boots in his store and takes orders over the phone and from walk-in customers. There is currently a three-month waiting list for boots. J. R. is not sure how to grow his business and has come to you for advice. Describe the reasons and ways some businesses increase market share and why J. R. might choose not to increase his market share.

4. **Segmenting Customers**

   Due to your vast marketing experience, you have been hired by a new company, Sugar, to perform a strategic analysis on chewing gum. The company wants to understand the many market segments for the different brands, flavors, sizes, and colors of gum. Create an analysis of the different market segments for chewing gum. What market segment would you recommend Sugar pursue?

5. **Product Life Cycle**

   An associate, Carl Grotenhuis, has developed a new brand of laundry detergent called Clean. Carl wants your opinion on his potential to enter and dominate the laundry detergent market. Using the product life cycle create a recommendation for Carl's new product.

6. **Redesigning a Business**

   Tom Walton is the new CEO for Lakeside, a large cereal manufacturing company. Tom's predecessor had run the company for 50 years and did little in terms of process improvement; in fact, his motto was "if it isn't broke, why fix it." Tom wants to take advantage of technology to create new processes for the entire company. He believes that improving operations will increase efficiency and lower costs.

   Tom has a major hurdle to overcome before he can begin revamping the company—its employees. Many of the employees have worked at the company for decades and are comfortable with the motto "if it isn't broke, why fix it." Develop a plan Tom can use to communicate to his employees the potential value gained from business process reengineering.

Business Process

Introduction

The benefits of business process improvement vary, but a rough rule of thumb is that it will, at a minimum, double the gains of a project by streamlining outdated practices, enhancing efficiency, promoting compliance and standardization, and making an organization more agile. Business process improvement involves three key steps:

1. Measure what matters to most customers.
2. Monitor the performance of key business processes.
3. Assign accountability for process improvement.

Comprehensive business process management systems help organizations model and define complete business processes, implement those processes integrated with existing systems, and provide business leaders with the ability to analyze, manage, and improve the execution of processes in real time.[1]

Examining Business Processes

Waiting in line at a grocery store is a great example of the need for process improvement. In this case, the "process" is called checkout, and the purpose is to pay for and bag groceries. The process begins when a customer steps into line and ends when the customer receives the receipt and leaves the store. The *process* steps are the activities the customer and store personnel do to complete the transaction. A **business process** is a standardized set of activities that accomplish a specific task, such as processing a customer's order. Business processes transform a set of inputs into a set of outputs (goods or services) for another person or process by using people and tools. This simple example describes a customer checkout process. Imagine other business processes: developing new products, building a new home, ordering clothes from mail-order companies, requesting new telephone service from a telephone company, administering Social Security payments, and so on.

Examining business processes helps an organization determine bottlenecks and identify outdated, duplicate, and smooth running processes. To stay competitive, organizations must optimize and automate their business processes. To identify which business processes need to be optimized, the organization must clearly understand its business processes, which typically have the following important characteristics:

- The processes have internal and external users.
- A process is cross-departmental. Departments are functional towers of expertise, but processes cut across departments.
- The processes occur across organizations.
- The processes are based on how work is done in the organization.
- Every process should be documented and fully understood by everyone participating in the process.
- Processes should be modeled to promote complete understanding.[2]

A business process can be viewed as a "value chain." By contributing to the creation or delivery of a product or service, each step in a process should add value to the preceding step. For example, one step in the product development process consists of conducting market acceptance tests. This step adds value by ensuring that the product meets the needs of the market before the product or service is finalized. A tremendous amount of learning and improvement can result from the documentation and examination of the input-output linkages. However, between every input and every output is a process. Knowledge and improvement can only be completed by peeling the layers of the onion and examining the processes through which inputs are converted into outputs. Figure B2.1 displays several sample business processes.[3]

Some processes (such as a programming process) may be contained wholly within a single department. However, most processes (such as ordering a product) are cross-departmental, spanning the entire organization. Figure B2.2 (on page 302) displays the different categories of cross-departmental business processes. **Customer facing processes** result in a product or service that is received by an organization's external customer. **Business facing processes** are invisible to the external customer but essential to the effective management of the business and include goal setting, day-to-day planning, performance feedback, rewards, and resource allocation.[4]

UNDERSTANDING THE IMPORTANCE OF BUSINESS PROCESSES

Organizations are only as effective as their business processes. Developing logical business processes can help an organization achieve its goals. For example, an automobile manufacturer might have a goal to reduce the time it takes to deliver a car to a customer. The automobile manufacturer cannot hope to meet this goal with an inefficient ordering process or a convoluted distribution process. Sales representatives might be making mistakes when completing order forms, data-entry clerks might not accurately code order information, and dock crews might be inefficiently loading cars onto trucks. All of these errors increase the time it will take

Sample Business Processes

ACCOUNTING BUSINESS PROCESSES
- Accounts payable
- Accounts receivable
- Bad/NSF checks
- Bank account reconciliation
- Cash receipts
- Check requests
- Check signing authority
- Depreciation
- Invoice billings
- Petty cash
- Month-end closing procedures

CUSTOMER SERVICE BUSINESS PROCESSES
- Customer satisfaction survey
- Customer service contact/complaint handling
- Guarantee customer service satisfaction
- Postsale customer follow-up
- Warranty and service policies

ENVIRONMENTAL BUSINESS PROCESSES
- Environmental protection
- Hazardous waste management
- Air/water/soil resource management

FINANCE BUSINESS PROCESSES
- Account collection
- Bank loan applications
- Banking policy and relations
- Business plans and forecasts
- Customer credit approval and credit terms
- Exercise of incentive stock options
- Property tax assessments
- Release of financial or confidential information
- Stock transactions
- Weekly financial and six-week cash flow reports

HUMAN RESOURCES BUSINESS PROCESSES
- Board of directors and shareholders meetings, minutes, and protocol
- Disabilities employment policies
- Drug-free workplace employment policies
- Employee hiring policies
- Employee orientation
- Family and medical leave act
- Files and records management
- Health care benefits
- Paid and unpaid time off
- Pay and payroll matters
- Performance appraisals and salary adjustments
- Resignations and terminations
- Sexual harassment policies
- Training/tuition reimbursement
- Travel and entertainment
- Workplace rules and guidelines
- Workplace safety

Sample Business Processes

MANAGEMENT INFORMATION SYSTEMS BUSINESS PROCESSES
- Disaster recovery procedures
- Backup/recovery procedures
- Service agreements, emergency services, and community resources
- Emergency notification procedures
- Office and department recovery
- User workstation standards
- Use of personal software
- Computer security incident reporting
- Control of computer virus programs
- Computer user/staff training plan
- Internet use policy
- E-mail policy
- Computer support center

MANUFACTURING BUSINESS PROCESSES
- Assembly manuals
- Bill of materials
- Calibration for testing and measuring equipment
- FDA inspections
- Manufacturing change orders
- Master parts list and files
- Serial number designation
- Quality control for finished goods
- Quality assurance audit procedure

SALES AND MARKETING BUSINESS PROCESSES
- Collection of sales tax
- Copyrights and trademarks
- Marketing plans model number
- Designation public relations
- Return of goods from customers
- Sales leads
- Sales order entry
- Sales training
- Trade shows

SHIPPING, PURCHASING, AND INVENTORY CONTROL BUSINESS PROCESSES
- Packing, storage, and distribution
- Physical inventory procedures
- Purchasing procedures
- Receiving, inspection, and stocking of parts and materials
- Shipping and freight claims
- Vendor selection, files, and inspections

---

to get the car to the customer. Improving any one of these business processes can have a significant effect on the total distribution process, made up of the order entry, production scheduling, and transportation processes.

IBM Business Consulting Services helped Bank of America's card services division identify $40 million of simplification and cost savings projects over two years by improving business processes to identify opportunities, eliminate redundancies, consolidate systems/applications, and remove duplicate processes. Within the card services and e-commerce division were several fragmented strategies and IT architectures. These were consolidated and simplified to streamline the business area and provide better and faster response to customer demand.

The scope of the IT strategy and architecture business process realignment project included all consumer card segments (including military, school, airlines, etc.), ATM cards and services, and e-commerce.[5]

Customer Facing Processes	Industry-Specific Customer Facing Processes	Business Facing Processes
Marketing and sales	Banking—loan processing	Strategic planning
Product development	Insurance—claims processing	Tactical planning
Service development	Government—grant allocation	Budgeting
Manufacturing	Retail—merchandise return	Training
Distribution	Restaurant—food preparation	Purchasing
Billing	Airline—baggage handling	
Order processing	Hotel—reservation handling	
Customer service		

Business Process Improvement

Improving business processes is paramount for businesses to stay competitive in today's marketplace. Over the past 10 to 15 years, companies have been forced to improve their business processes because customers are demanding better products and services; if they do not receive what they want from one supplier, they have many others to choose from (hence the competitive issue for businesses). Figure B2.3 displays several opportunities for business process improvement.

Many organizations began business process improvement with a continuous improvement model. A *continuous process improvement model* attempts to understand and measure the current process, and make performance improvements accordingly. Figure B2.4 illustrates the basic steps for continuous process improvement. Organizations begin by documenting what they do today, establish some way to measure the process based on what customers want, perform the process, measure the results, and then identify improvement opportunities based on the collected information. The next step is to implement process improvements, and then measure the performance of the new process. This loop repeats over and over again and is called continuous process improvement. It might also be called business process improvement or functional process improvement.[6]

This method for improving business processes is effective to obtain gradual, incremental improvement. However, several factors have accelerated the need to improve business processes. The most obvious is technology. New technologies (like the Internet and wireless) rapidly bring new capabilities to businesses, thereby raising the competitive bar and the need to improve business processes dramatically.

Another apparent trend is the opening of world markets and increased free trade. Such changes bring more companies into the marketplace, adding to the competition. In today's marketplace, major changes are required just to stay in the game. As a result, companies have requested methods for faster business process improvement. Also, companies want breakthrough performance changes, not just incremental

Business Process Improvement Examples
Eliminate duplicate activities
Combine related activities
Eliminate multiple reviews and approvals
Eliminate inspections
Simplify processes
Reduce batch sizes
Process in parallel
Implement demand pull
Outsource inefficient activities
Eliminate movement of work
Organize multifunctional teams
Design cellular workplaces
Centralize/decentralize

FIGURE B2.3

Opportunities for Business
Process Improvement

FIGURE B2.4

Continuous Process
Improvement Model

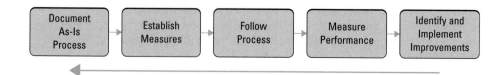

changes, and they want it now. Because the rate of change has increased for everyone, few businesses can afford a slow change process. One approach for rapid change and dramatic improvement is business process reengineering (BPR).

BUSINESS PROCESS REENGINEERING (BPR)

An organization must continuously revise and reexamine its decisions, goals, and targets to improve its performance. A bank may have many activities, such as investing, credit cards, loans, and so on, and it may be involved in cross-selling (e.g., insurance) with other preferred vendors in the market. If the credit card department is not functioning in an efficient manner, the bank might reengineer the credit card business process. This activity, ***business process reengineering (BPR),*** is the analysis and redesign of workflow within and between enterprises. BPR relies on a different school of thought than continuous process improvement. *In the extreme,* BPR assumes the current process is irrelevant, does not work, or is broken and must be overhauled from scratch. Such a clean slate enables business process designers to disassociate themselves from today's process and focus on a new process. It is like the designers projecting themselves into the future and asking: What should the process look like? What do customers want it to look like? What do other employees want it to look like? How do best-in-class companies do it? How can new technology facilitate the process?[7]

Figure B2.5 displays the basic steps in a business process reengineering effort. It begins with defining the scope and objectives of the reengineering project, then goes through a learning process (with customers, employees, competitors, non-competitors, and new technology). Given this knowledge base, the designers can create a vision for the future and design new business processes by creating a plan of action based on the gap between current processes, technologies, and structures, and process vision. It is then a matter of implementing the chosen solution. The Department of Defense (DoD) is an expert at reengineering business process. Figure B2.6 highlights the Department of Defense's best-in-class suggestions for a managerial approach to a reengineering effort.[8]

Managerial Approach to Reengineering Projects
1. **Define the scope.** Define functional objectives; determine the management strategy to be followed in streamlining and standardizing processes; and establish the process, data, and information systems baselines from which to begin process improvement.
2. **Analyze.** Analyze business processes to eliminate non-value-added processes; simplify and streamline processes of little value; and identify more effective and efficient alternatives to the process, data, and system baselines.
3. **Evaluate.** Conduct a preliminary, functional, economic analysis to evaluate alternatives to baseline processes and select a preferred course of action.
4. **Plan.** Develop detailed statements of requirements, baseline impacts, costs, benefits, and schedules to implement the planned course of action.
5. **Approve.** Finalize the functional economic analysis using information from the planning data, and present to senior management for approval to proceed with the proposed process improvements and any associated data or system changes.
6. **Execute.** Execute the approved process and data changes, and provide functional management oversight of any associated information system changes.

Business Process Design

After choosing the method of business process improvement that is appropriate for the organization, the process designers must determine the most efficient way to begin revamping the processes. To determine whether each process is appropriately structured, organizations should create a cross-functional team to build process models that display input-output relationships among process-dependent operations and departments. They should create business process models documenting a step-by-step process sequence for the activities that are required to convert inputs to outputs for the specific process.

Business process modeling (or *mapping*) is the activity of creating a detailed flow chart or process map of a work process showing its inputs, tasks, and activities, in a structured sequence. A *business process model* is a graphic description of a process, showing the sequence of process tasks, which is developed for a specific purpose and from a selected viewpoint. A set of one or more process models details the many functions of a system or subject area with graphics and text and its purpose is to:

- Expose process detail gradually and in a controlled manner.
- Encourage conciseness and accuracy in describing the process model.
- Focus attention on the process model interfaces.
- Provide a powerful process analysis and consistent design vocabulary.[9]

A process model typically displays activities as boxes and uses arrows to represent data and interfaces. Process modeling usually begins with a functional process representation of *what* the process problem is or an As-Is process model. **As-Is process models** represent the current state of the operation that has been mapped, without any specific improvements or changes to existing processes. The next step is to build a To-Be process model that displays *how* the process problem will be solved or implemented. **To-Be process models** show the results of applying change improvement opportunities to the current (As-Is) process model. This approach ensures that the process is fully and clearly understood before the details of a process solution are decided. The To-Be process model shows *how* the *what* is to be realized. Figure B2.7 displays the As-Is and To-Be process models for ordering a hamburger.

Analyzing As-Is business process models leads to success in business process reengineering since these diagrams are very powerful in visualizing the activities, processes, and data flow of an organization. As-Is and To-Be process models are integral in process reengineering projects. Figure B2.8 illustrates an As-Is process model of an order-filling process developed by a process modeling team representing all departments that contribute to the process. The process modeling team traces the process of converting the input (orders) through all the intervening steps until the final required output (payment) is produced. The map shows how all departments are involved as the order is processed.[10]

It is easy to become bogged down in excessive detail when creating an As-Is process model. The objective is to aggressively eliminate, simplify, or improve the

FIGURE B2.7

As-Is and To-Be Process Model for Ordering a Hamburger

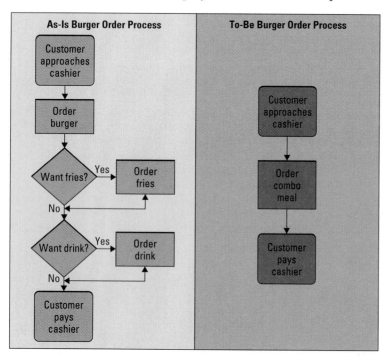

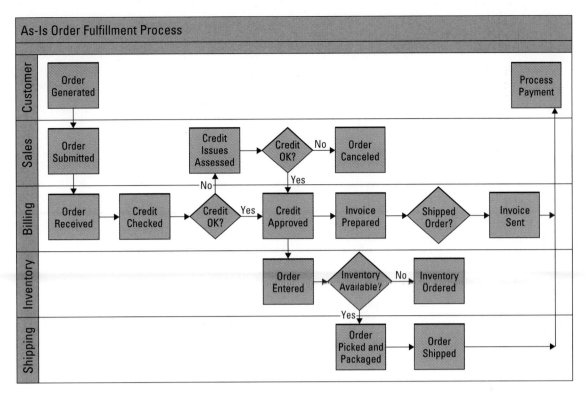

As-Is Order Fulfillment Process

FIGURE B2.8

As-Is Process Model for
Order Entry

To-Be processes. Successful process improvement efforts result in positive answers to the key process design or improvement question: Is this the most efficient and effective process for accomplishing the process goals? This process modeling structure allows the team to identify all the critical interfaces, overlay the time to complete various processes, start to define the opportunities for process simulation, and identify disconnects (illogical, missing, or extraneous steps) in the processes. Figure B2.9 displays sample disconnects in the order filling process in Figure B2.8.

The team then creates a To-Be process model, which reflects a disconnect-free order fulfillment process (see Figure B2.10). Disconnects fixed by the new process include

- Direct order entry by sales, eliminating sales administration.
- Parallel order processing and credit checking.
- Elimination of multiple order-entry and order-logging steps.[11]

The consulting firm KPMG Peat Marwick uses process modeling as part of its business reengineering practice. Recently the firm helped a large financial services company slash costs and improve productivity in its Manufactured Housing Finance Division. Turnaround time for loan approval was reduced by half, using 40 percent fewer staff members.

Issues in the As-Is Order Process Model
■ Sales representatives take too long to submit orders.
■ There are too many process steps.
■ Sales administration slows down the process by batch-processing orders.
■ Credit checking is performed for both old and new customers.
■ Credit checking holds up the process because it is done before (rather than concurrently with) order picking.

FIGURE B2.9

Issues in the As-Is
Process Model for
Order Entry

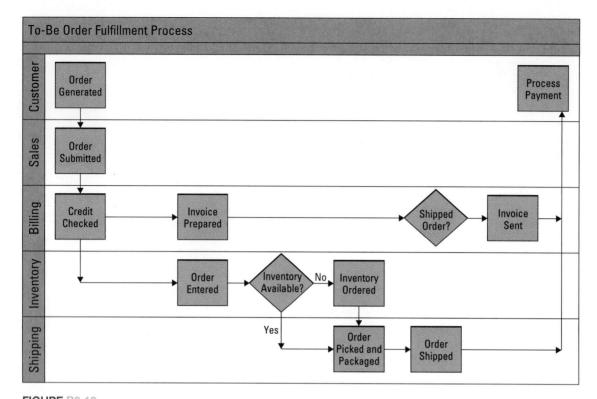

FIGURE B2.10

To-Be Process Model for Order Entry

Modeling helped the team analyze the complex aspects of the project. "In parts of the loan origination process, a lot of things happen in a short period of time," according to team leader Bob Karrick of KPMG. "During data capture, information is pulled from a number of different sources, and the person doing the risk assessment has to make judgment calls at different points throughout the process. There is often a need to stop, raise questions, make follow-up calls, and so on and then continue with the process modeling effort. Modeling allows us to do a thorough analysis that takes into account all these decision points and variables."[12]

SELECTING A PROCESS TO REENGINEER

An organization can reengineer its cross-departmental business processes or an individual department's business processes according to its needs. When selecting a business process to reengineer, wise organizations will focus on those core processes that are critical to their performance, rather than marginal processes that have little impact. Reengineering practitioners can use several criteria to determine the importance of the process:

- Is the process broken?
- Is it feasible that reengineering of this process will succeed?
- Does it have a high impact on the agency's strategic direction?
- Does it significantly impact customer satisfaction?
- Is it antiquated?
- Does it fall far below best-in-class?
- Is it crucial for productivity improvement?
- Will savings from automation be clearly visible?
- Is the return on investment from implementation high and preferably immediate?[13]

Business Process Management (BPM)

A key advantage of technology is its ability to improve business processes. Working faster and smarter has become a necessity for companies. Initial emphasis was given to areas such as production, accounting, procurement, and logistics. The next big areas to discover technology's value in business process were sales and marketing automation, customer relationship management, and supplier relationship management. Some of these processes involve several departments of the company and some are the result of real-time interaction of the company with its suppliers, customers, and other business partners. The latest area to discover the power of technology in automating and reengineering business process is business process management. **Business process management (BPM)** integrates all of an organization's business process to make individual processes more efficient. BPM can be used to solve a single glitch or to create one unifying system to consolidate a myriad of processes.

Many organizations are unhappy with their current mix of software applications and dealing with business processes that are subject to constant change. These organizations are turning to BPM systems that can flexibly automate their processes and glue their enterprise applications together. Figure B2.11 displays the key reasons organizations are embracing BPM technologies.

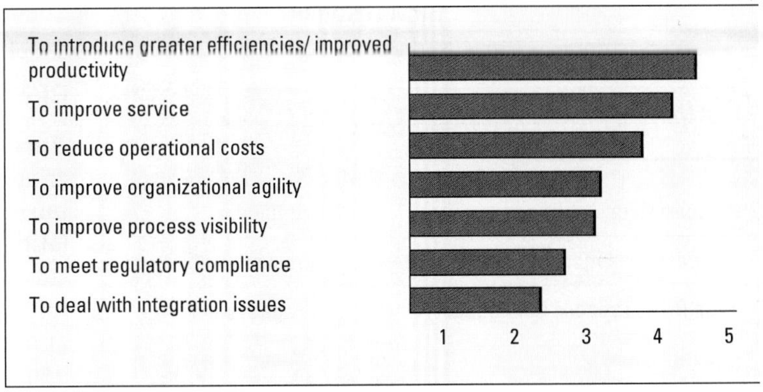

BPM technologies effectively track and orchestrate the business process. BPM can automate tasks involving information from multiple systems, with rules to define the sequence in which the tasks are performed as well as responsibilities, conditions, and other aspects of the process (see Figure B2.12 for BPM benefits). BPM not only allows a business process to be executed more efficiently, but it also provides the tools to measure performance and identify opportunities for improvement—as well as to easily make changes in processes to act upon those opportunities such as:

- Bringing processes, people, and information together.
- Identifying the business processes is relatively easy. Breaking down the barriers between business areas and finding owners for the processes are difficult.
- Managing business processes within the enterprise and outside the enterprise with suppliers, business partners, and customers.
- Looking at automation horizontally instead of vertically.[14]

IS BPM FOR BUSINESS OR IT?

A good BPM solution requires two great parts to work together as one. Since BPM solutions cross application and system boundaries, they often need to be sanctioned and implemented by the IT organization, while at the same time BPM products are business tools that business managers need to own. Therefore, confusion often arises in companies as to whether business or IT managers should be responsible for driving the selection of a new BPM solution.

The key requirement for BPM's success in an organization is the understanding that it is a collaboration of business and IT, and thus both parties need to be involved in evaluating, selecting, and implementing a BPM solution. IT managers need to understand the business

To introduce greater efficiencies/ improved productivity
To improve service
To reduce operational costs
To improve organizational agility
To improve process visibility
To meet regulatory compliance
To deal with integration issues

Scale 1 to 5 where 1 = not important and 5 = very important

FIGURE B2.11

Key Reasons for BPM

FIGURE B2.12

Benefits of BPM

BPM Benefits
■ Update processes in real time
■ Reduce overhead expenses
■ Automate key decisions
■ Reduce process maintenance cost
■ Reduce operating cost
■ Improve productivity
■ Improve process cycle time
■ Improve forecasting
■ Improve customer service

drivers behind the processes, and business managers need to understand the impact the BPM solution may have on the infrastructure. Generally, companies that have successfully deployed BPM solutions are those whose business and IT groups have worked together as a cohesive team.

All companies can benefit from a better understanding of their key business processes, analyzing them for areas of improvement and implementing improvements. BPM applications have been successfully developed to improve complex business issues of some medium- to large-sized companies. Like many large-scale implementation projects, BPM solutions are most successful in companies with a good understanding of their technology landscape and management willing to approach business in a new way. BPM solutions are truly driven by the business process and the company's owners.

Effective BPM solutions allow business owners to manage many aspects of the technology through business rules they develop and maintain. Companies that cannot support or manage cultural and organizational changes may lack positive BPM results.[15]

Tool Name	Company Name
BPM Suite	Ultimus
Process Suite	Stalfware
Business Manager	Savvion
Pega Rules Process Commander	PegaSystem
E Work Vision	MetaStorm
Team Works	Lombardi Software
Intalio	Intalio
Bizflow	Handysoft
FugeoBPM	Fugeo
Business Process Manager	Filenet

FIGURE B2.13

Popular BPM Tools

BPM TOOLS

Business process management tools are used to create an application that is helpful in designing business process models and also helpful in simulating, optimizing, monitoring, and maintaining various processes that occur within an organization. Many tasks are involved in achieving a goal, and these tasks are done either manually or with the help of software systems. For example, if an organization needs to buy a software application that costs $6 million, then a request has to be approved by several authorities and managers. The request approval may be done manually. However, when a person applies for a loan of $300,000, several internal and external business processes are triggered to find out details about that person before approving the loan. For these activities the BPM tool creates an application that coordinates the manual and automated tasks. Figure B2.13 displays several popular BPM tools.[16]

BPM RISKS AND REWARDS

If an organization is considering BPM, it must be aware of the risks involved in implementing these systems. One factor that commonly derails a BPM project has nothing to do with technology and everything to do with people. BPM projects involve cultural and organizational changes that companies must make to support the new management approach required for success. Where 10 area leaders once controlled 10 pieces of an end-to-end process, now a new group is involved in implementing a BPM solution across all these areas. Suddenly the span of control is consolidated and all are accountable to the whole process, not just one piece of the puzzle.

The added benefit of BPM is not only a technology solution, but also a business solution. BPM is a new business architecture and approach to managing the process and enabling proactive, continuous improvement. The new organizational structure and roles created to support BPM help maximize the continuous benefits to ensure success.

An IT director from a large financial services company gave this feedback when asked about his experience in using a BPM solution to improve the company's

Critical Success Factors for BPM Projects

1. Understand reengineering.
- Understand business process fundamentals.
- Know what reengineering is.
- Differentiate and integrate process improvement approaches.

2. Build a business and political case.
- Have necessary and sufficient business (mission delivery) reasons for reengineering.
- Have the organizational commitment and capacity to initiate and sustain reengineering.
- Secure and sustain political support for reengineering projects.

3. Adopt a process management approach.
- Understand the organizational mandate and set mission strategic directions and goals cascading to process-specific goals and decision making across and down the organization.
- Define, model, and prioritize business processes important for mission performance.
- Practice hands-on senior management ownership of process improvement through personal involvement, responsibility, and decision making.
- Adjust organizational structure to better support process management initiatives.
- Create an assessment program to evaluate process management.

4. Measure and track performance continuously.
- Create organizational understanding of the value of measurement and how it will be used.
- Tie performance management to customer and stakeholder current and future expectations.

5. Practice change management and provide central support.
- Develop human resource management strategies to support reengineering.
- Build information resources management strategies and a technology framework to support process change.
- Create a central support group to assist and integrate reengineering efforts and other improvement efforts across the organization.
- Create an overarching and project-specific internal and external communication and education program.

6. Manage reengineering projects for results.
- Have a clear criterion to select what should be reengineered.
- Place the project at the right level with a defined reengineering team purpose and goals.
- Use a well-trained, diversified, expert team to ensure optimum project performance.
- Follow a structured, disciplined approach for reengineering.

FIGURE B2.14

Critical Success Factors for BPM Projects

application help desk process. "Before BPM, the company's application help desk was a manual process, filled with inefficiencies, human error, and no personal accountability. In addition, the old process provided no visibility into the process. There was absolutely no way to track requests, since it was all manual. Business user satisfaction with the process was extremely low. A BPM solution provided a way for the company to automate, execute, manage, and monitor the process in real time. The biggest technical challenge in implementation was ensuring that the user group was self-sufficient. While the company recognized that the IT organization is needed, it wanted to be able to maintain and implement any necessary process changes with little reliance on IT. It views process management as empowering the business users to maintain, control, and monitor the process. BPM goes a long way to enable this process."[17]

CRITICAL SUCCESS FACTORS

In a publication for the National Academy of Public Administration, Dr. Sharon L. Caudle identified six critical success factors that ensure government BPM initiatives achieve the desired results (see Figure B2.14).[18]

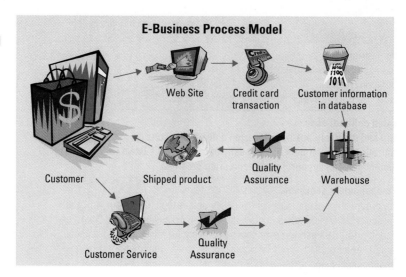

Business Process Modeling Examples

A picture is worth a thousand words. Just ask Wayne Kendrick, a system analyst for Mobil Oil Corporation in Dallas, Texas. Kendrick, whose work involves planning and designing complex processes, was scheduled to make a presentation to familiarize top management with a number of projects his group was working on. "I was given 10 minutes for my presentation, and I had 20 to 30 pages of detailed documentation to present. Obviously, I could not get through it all in the time allocated." Kendrick turned to business process models to help communicate his projects. "I think people can relate to pictures better than words," Kendrick said. He applied his thinking to his presentation by using Microsoft's Visio to create business process models and graphs to represent the original 30 pages of text. "It was an effective way to get people interested in my projects and to quickly see the importance of each project," he stated. The process models worked and Kendrick received immediate approval to proceed with all of his projects. Figures B2.15 through B2.21 offer examples of business process models.[19]

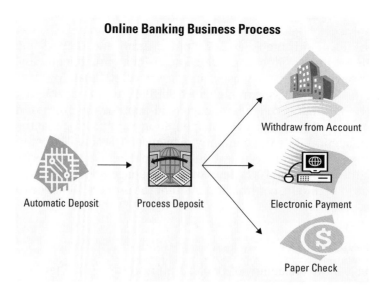

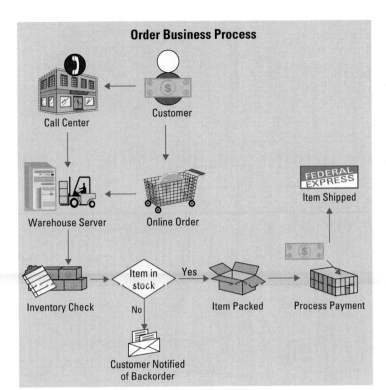

Order Business Process

Call Center

Customer

Warehouse Server

Online Order

FEDERAL EXPRESS
Item Shipped

Inventory Check → Item in stock → Yes → Item Packed → Process Payment

No ↓

Customer Notified of Backorder

FIGURE B2.17

Customer Order Business Process Model

Purchase an Item on eBay Business Process

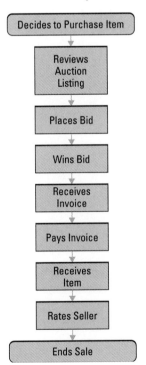

Decides to Purchase Item

Reviews Auction Listing

Places Bid

Wins Bid

Receives Invoice

Pays Invoice

Receives Item

Rates Seller

Ends Sale

FIGURE B2.18

eBay Buyer Business Process Model

Sell an Item on eBay Business Process

Decides to Sell Item

Lists Item on eBay

Sets Initial Price

Sets Auction Length

Invoices Winning Bid

Receives Payment

Ships Item

Rates Buyer

Ends Sale

FIGURE B2.19

eBay Seller Business Process Model

Customer Service Business Process

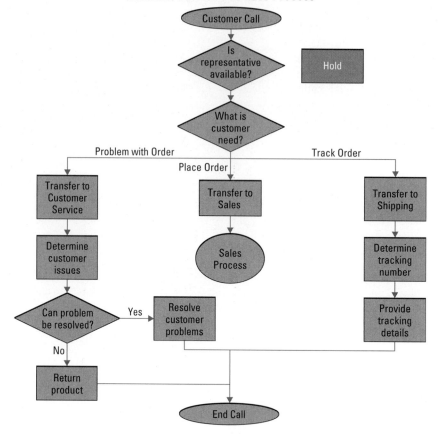

Process Improvement Model

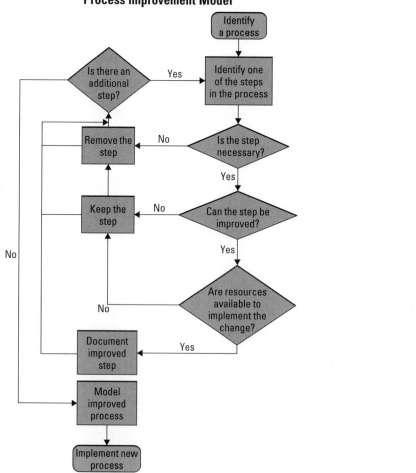

Investment in continuous process improvement, business process reengineering, or business process management is the same as any other technology-related investment. Planning the project properly, setting clear goals, educating those people who have to change their mind-set once the system is implemented, and retaining strong management support will help with a successful implementation generating a solid return on investment.

Organizations must go beyond the basics when implementing business process improvement and realize that it is not a one-time project. Management and improvement of end-to-end business processes is difficult and requires more than a simple, one-time effort. Continuously monitoring and improving core business processes will guarantee performance improvements across an organization.

KEY TERMS

As-Is process model, 304
Business facing process, 299
Business process, 299
Business process management (BPM), 307
Business process management tool, 308

Business process model, 304
Business process modeling (or mapping), 304
Business process reengineering (BPR), 303

Continuous process improvement model, 302
Customer facing process, 299
To-Be process model, 304

 CLOSING CASE ONE

Streamlining Processes at Adidas

The Adidas name resonates with athletes and retail consumers worldwide. Registered as a company in 1949, the company differentiated itself during the 1960s by supporting all athletes who were committed to raising performance levels, including athletes in what some considered fringe sports such as high jumping. During a banner year in 1996, the "three stripes company" equipped 6,000 Olympic athletes from 33 countries. Those athletes won 220 medals, including 70 gold, and helped increase immediate apparel sales by 50 percent.

In 1997, Adidas acquired the Salomon Group, which included the Salomon, Taylor Made, and Bonfire brands. Today, Adidas-Salomon strives to be the global leader in the sporting goods industry with a wide range of products that promote a passion for competition and a sports-oriented lifestyle. Its strategy is simple: continuously strengthen its brands and products to improve its competitive position and financial performance.

Adidas-Salomon competes in an environment as relentless as that of the Olympics. Staying in the forefront requires the support of world-class technology. Over the past 15 years, Adidas-Salomon transformed itself from a manufacturing organization to a global sports brand manager with 14,000 employees located around the world. Previously, Adidas-Salomon operated in a decentralized manner, and each operating unit chose software that suited its geography and internal preferences. The company believed that implementing and creating common processes, especially in its sales organization, would help it establish global direction. With common processes, the company could streamline and automate its business operations—improving flexibility, scalability, and visibility across the extended enterprise. Overall, system integration would translate into faster time to market, higher revenue, and lower costs.

Adidas-Salomon reviewed its IT systems and associated information. One finding was that the company needed to develop a better solution for business process integration and establish an easy way to automate new applications throughout the enterprise. Such an infrastructure required Adidas-Salomon to impose a common business process platform that would allow the company's operating units to remain flexible in meeting their own particular needs and goals.

Adidas-Salomon identified several major business requirements for the project. First, it wanted to automate business events and reduce the manual effort required to exchange data between internal and external parties. Second, Adidas-Salomon needed to develop a cost-effective solution that would be simple to use, maintain, and update in the future. Last, the company wanted to enable real-time data exchange among the key Adidas-Salomon business processes.

"We considered many metrics, and it was clear that TIBCO Software had the breadth and depth of product offering backed by a strong reputation," said Garry Semetka, head of development and integration services in global application development at Adidas-Salomon. With its desired infrastructure in place, Adidas-Salomon standardized on TIBCO products and moved toward real-time business process management of its internal supply chain. The company now publishes and makes the most of events when they occur on key systems, giving the most current, valuable information to business processes and decision makers.[20]

Questions

1. Describe business processes and their importance for Adidas-Salomon.
2. Identify a few examples of customer facing processes and business facing processes at Adidas-Salomon.
3. How could Adidas-Salomon use continuous process improvement and business process reengineering to remain competitive?
4. How can a business process management tool help Adidas-Salomon remain at the top of its game?

 CLOSING CASE TWO

3Com Optimizes Product Promotion Processes

Product promotions, such as rebates or subsidized promotional items, can serve as excellent marketing and sales tools to drive increased revenues by providing incentives for customers to purchase select items. However, when you are a leading global networking provider like 3Com that serves thousands of channel partners and customers, such promotions must be easily managed and executed.

To gain better control over the creation and execution of its product promotions, 3Com used Savvion's business process automation and management platform to build a Web-based system that streamlines the approval and management workflow of product promotions offered to distributors and resellers. "We needed to ensure that our product promotions were attractive to our channel partners while also being manageable in terms of execution," said Ari

Bose, CIO at 3Com. "Using Savvion BusinessManager, we were able to quickly put a process in place that speeds approval and enhances awareness of product promotions to generate opportunities for increased revenue."

Promoting Effective Promotions

The Savvion BusinessManager-based promotions system provides significant time and cost savings by replacing former inefficient and uncontrollable e-mail processes. Instead of informally sending promotion ideas around for approval, employees now use the automated system as a centralized location to manage the workflow involved in proposing new promotions and ensuring all needed approvals are in place before promotion details are shared on the 3Com partner and reseller Web site.

The promotions system automatically routes proposed promotions to each department that is required to sign off on the promotion, including marketing, promotions communications, and claims administration. The streamlined system also immediately notifies all key parties once new promotions are approved, increasing visibility and revenue opportunities through improved communication with 3Com sales representatives, distributors, and resellers.

Adding Muscle to Management

An important feature of the new system is the automatic auditing of each step taken. The company can easily establish an audit trail, increasing accountability as approvals are given. The structured process also ensures that approved promotions are manageable from an administrative perspective.

In addition, the system tracks promotion fulfillment, enforcing associated terms and conditions such as purchasing limits or available supplies—tracking that was previously almost impossible to do, creating numerous management headaches. The promotions system is also integrated with another BusinessManager-developed process that generates special price quotes (SPQs) for 3Com channel partners, creating built-in checks and balances to prevent the approval of an SPQ while a promotion is being offered for the same product.

The system also provides extensive reporting capabilities that 3Com now uses to gain a better understanding of all offered promotions, authorizations, and potential financial impacts. These online reports replace manually created Excel spreadsheets, enabling departments to generate reports on the fly for enhanced strategic planning.

Bottom-Line Benefits

Greater visibility of product promotions is yielding significant opportunities for increased revenue at 3Com. Sales representatives are immediately notified when promotions are approved, improving internal communications and enabling representatives to share promotion details with resellers and distributors more quickly to foster increased sales. Other business benefits delivered by the automated promotions system include the following:

- Real-time monitoring features enable 3Com employees to check the status of a promotion's approval at any time.
- Greater efficiency in the approval cycle and streamlined communications increase employee productivity, providing significant time and cost savings.
- Claims processing is also more effective because of the structured approval process, delivering additional savings.
- Increased visibility enables 3Com to reduce reserve spending by having a clearer idea of channel response to each promotion.
- Order and efficiency come to previously chaotic manual processes.[21]

Questions

1. Describe business processes and their importance to 3Com's business model.
2. How can 3Com use continuous process improvement to become more efficient?
3. How can 3Com use business process reengineering to become more efficient?
4. Describe the importance of business process modeling (or mapping) and business process models for 3Com.
5. How did 3Com use business process management software to revamp its business?

★ MAKING BUSINESS DECISIONS

1. Discovering Reengineering Opportunities

In an effort to increase efficiency, your college has hired you to analyze its current business processes for registering for classes. Analyze the current business processes from paying tuition to registering for classes and determine which steps in the process are:

- Broken
- Redundant
- Antiquated

Be sure to define how you would reengineer the processes for efficiency.

2. Modeling a Business Process

Do you hate waiting in line at the grocery store? Do you find it frustrating when you go to the movie store and cannot find the movie you wanted to rent? Do you get annoyed when the pizza delivery person brings you the wrong order? This is your chance to reengineer the annoying process that drives you crazy. Choose a problem you are currently experiencing and reengineer the process to make it more efficient. Be sure to provide an As-Is and To-Be process model.

3. Revamping Business Processes

The following is the sales order business process for MusicMan. Draw the As-Is process model based on the following narrative:

1. A customer submits an order for goods to MusicMan, a music retailer, through an online mechanism such as a browser-based order form. The customer supplies his or her name, the appropriate e-mail address, the state to which the order will be shipped, the desired items (IDs and names), and the requested quantities.
2. The order is received by a processing system, which reads the data and appends an ID number to the order.
3. The order is forwarded to a customer service representative, who checks the customer's credit information.
4. If the credit check fails, the customer service representative is assigned the task of notifying the customer to obtain correct credit information, and the process becomes manual from this point on.
5. If the credit check passes, the system checks a database for the current inventory of the ordered item, according to the item ID, and it compares the quantity of items available with the quantity requested.

6. If the amount of stock is not sufficient to accommodate the order, the order is placed on hold until new inventory arrives. When the system receives notice of new incoming inventory, it repeats step 5 until it can verify that the inventory is sufficient to process the order.

7. If the inventory is sufficient, the order is forwarded simultaneously to a shipping agent who arranges shipment and an accounting agent who instructs the system to generate an invoice for the order.

8. If the system encounters an error in processing the input necessary to calculate the total price for the invoice, including state sales tax, the accounting agent who initiated the billing process is notified and prompted to provide the correct information.

9. The system calculates the total price of the order.

10. The system confirms that the order has been shipped and notifies the customer via e-mail.

11. At any point in the transaction before shipping, the order can be canceled by notification from the customer.

4. Revamping Accounts

The accounting department at your company deals with the processing of critical documents. These documents must arrive at their intended destination in a secure and efficient manner. Such documents include invoices, purchase orders, statements, purchase requisitions, financial statements, sales orders, and quotes.

The current processing of documents is done manually, which causes a negative ripple effect. Documents tend to be misplaced or delayed through the mailing process. Unsecured documents are vulnerable to people making changes or seeing confidential documents. In addition, the accounting department incurs costs such as preprinted forms, inefficient distribution, and storage. Explain BPM and how it can be used to revamp the accounting department.

PLUG-IN

B3

Hardware and Software

1. Describe the six major categories of hardware and provide an example of each.
2. Identify the different computer categories and explain their potential business uses.
3. Explain the difference between primary and secondary storage.
4. List the common input, output, storage, and communication devices.
5. Describe the eight categories of computers by size.
6. Define the relationship between operating system software and utility software.

Introduction

Managers need to determine what types of hardware and software will satisfy their current and future business needs, the right time to buy the equipment, and how to protect their IT investments. This does not imply that managers need to be experts in all areas of technology; however, building a basic understanding of hardware and software can help them make the right IT investment choices.

Information technology (IT) is a field concerned with the use of technology in managing and processing information. Information technology can be composed of the Internet, a personal computer, a cell phone that can access the Web, a personal digital assistant, or presentation software. All of these technologies help to perform specific information processing tasks. There are two basic categories of information technology: hardware and software. *Hardware* consists of the physical devices associated with a computer system. *Software* is the set of instructions that the hardware executes to carry out specific tasks. Software, such as Microsoft Excel, and various hardware devices, such as a keyboard and a monitor, interact to create a spreadsheet or a graph. This plug-in covers the basics of computer hardware and software including terminology, business uses, and common characteristics.

Hardware Basics

In many industries, exploiting computer hardware is key to gaining a competitive advantage. Frito-Lay gained a competitive advantage by using handheld devices

Six Hardware Components	
Central processing unit (CPU)	The actual hardware that interprets and executes the program (software) instructions and coordinates how all the other hardware devices work together.
Primary storage	The computer's main memory, which consists of the random access memory (RAM), the cache memory, and the read-only memory (ROM) that is directly accessible to the central processing unit (CPU).
Secondary storage	The equipment designed to store large volumes of data for long-term storage (e.g., diskette, hard drive, memory card, CD).
Input devices	The equipment used to capture information and commands (e.g., keyboard, scanner).
Output devices	The equipment used to see, hear, or otherwise accept the results of information processing requests (e.g., monitor, printer).
Communication devices	The equipment used to send information and receive it from one location to another (e.g., modem).

FIGURE B3.1

Hardware Components of a Computer System

to track the strategic placement and sale of items in convenience stores. Sales representatives could track sale price, competitor information, the number of items sold, and item location in the store all from their handheld device.[1]

A **computer** is an electronic device operating under the control of instructions stored in its own memory that can accept, manipulate, and store data. A computer system consists of six hardware components (see Figure B3.1). Figure B3.2 displays how these components work together to form a computer system.

CENTRAL PROCESSING UNIT

The dominant manufacturers of CPUs today include Intel (with its Celeron and Pentium lines for personal computers) and Advanced Micro Devices (AMD) (with its Athlon series). AMD was initially dismissed as a company that simply cloned current chips, producing processors that mimic the features and capabilities of those from industry leader Intel. However, over the past few years, AMD has begun introducing innovative CPUs that are forcing Intel into the unfamiliar position of reacting to competition. AMD led the way in transforming the processor market by creating chips that handle 64 bits of data at a time, up

from 32 bits. It also broke new territory when it became the first provider of dual-core processors for the server market. Hector Ruiz, chairman and CEO of AMD, stated, "In our position there is only one thing we can do: Stay close to our customers and end users, understand what they need and want, and then simply out-innovate the competition. Innovation is at the center of our ability to succeed. We cannot win by just copying the competition."[2]

The **central processing unit (CPU)** (or **microprocessor**) is the actual hardware that interprets and executes the program (software) instructions and coordinates how all the other hardware devices work together. The CPU is built on a small flake of silicon and can contain the equivalent of several million transistors. CPUs are unquestionably one of the 20th century's greatest technological advances.

A CPU contains two primary parts: control unit and arithmetic/logic unit. The **control unit** interprets software instructions and literally tells the other hardware

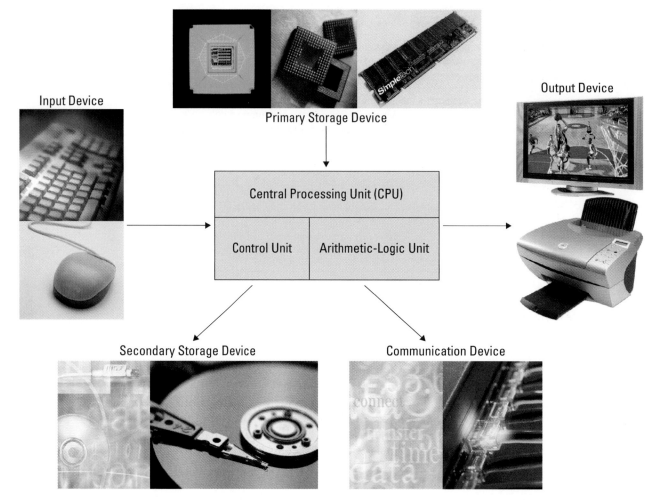

Input Device

Primary Storage Device

Output Device

Central Processing Unit (CPU)

Control Unit | Arithmetic-Logic Unit

Secondary Storage Device

Communication Device

FIGURE B3.2

How the Hardware
Components Work
Together

devices what to do, based on the software instructions. The ***arithmetic-logic unit (ALU)*** performs all arithmetic operations (for example, addition and subtraction) and all logic operations (such as sorting and comparing numbers). The control unit and ALU perform different functions. The control unit obtains instructions from the software. It then interprets the instructions, decides which tasks other devices perform, and finally tells each device to perform the task. The ALU responds to the control unit and does whatever it dictates, performing either arithmetic or logic operations.

The number of CPU cycles per second determines how fast a CPU carries out the software instructions; more cycles per second means faster processing, and faster CPUs cost more than their slower counterparts. CPU speed is usually quoted in megahertz and gigahertz. ***Megahertz (MHz)*** is the number of millions of CPU cycles per second. ***Gigahertz (GHz)*** is the number of billions of CPU cycles per second. Figure B3.3 displays the factors that determine CPU speed.

Advances in CPU Design

Chip makers are pressing more functionality into CPU technology. Most CPUs are ***complex instruction set computer (CISC) chips,*** which is a type of CPU that can recognize as many as 100 or more instructions, enough to carry out most computations directly. ***Reduced instruction set computer (RISC) chips*** limit the number of instructions the CPU can execute to increase processing speed. The idea of RISC is to reduce the instruction set to the bare minimum, emphasizing the instructions used most of the time and optimizing them for the fastest possible execution. A RISC processor runs faster than a CISC processor.

CPU Speed Factors
Clock speed—the speed of the internal clock of a CPU that sets the pace at which operations proceed within the computer's internal processing circuitry. Clock speed is measured in megahertz (MHz) and gigahertz (GHz). Faster clock speeds bring noticeable gains in microprocessor-intensive tasks, such as recalculating a spreadsheet.
Word length—number of bits (0s and 1s) that can be processed by the CPU at any one time. Computers work in terms of bits and bytes using electrical pulses that have two states: on and off. A *binary digit (bit)* is the smallest unit of information that a computer can process. A bit can be either a 1 (on) or a 0 (off). A group of eight bits represents one natural language character and is called a *byte*.
Bus width—the size of the internal electrical pathway along which signals are sent from one part of the computer to another. A wider bus can move more data, hence faster processing.
Chip line width—the distance between transistors on a chip. The shorter the chip line width the faster the chip since more transistors can be placed on a chip and the data and instructions travel short distances during processing.

FIGURE B3.3

Factors That Determine CPU Speed

In the next few years, better performance, systems management capabilities, virtualization, security, and features to help track computer assets will be built directly into the CPU (see Figure B3.4). *Virtualization* is a protected memory space created by the CPU allowing the computer to create virtual machines. Each virtual machine can run its own programs isolated from other machines.

PRIMARY STORAGE

Primary storage is the computer's main memory, which consists of the random access memory (RAM), cache memory, and the read-only memory (ROM) that is directly accessible to the CPU.

Random Access Memory

Random access memory (RAM) is the computer's primary working memory, in which program instructions and data are stored so that they can be accessed directly by the CPU via the processor's high-speed external data bus.

RAM is often called read/write memory. In RAM, the CPU can write and read data. Most programs set aside a portion of RAM as a temporary work space for data so that one can modify (rewrite) as needed until the data are ready for printing or storage on secondary storage media, such as a hard drive or memory key. RAM does not retain its contents when the power to the computer is switched off, hence individuals should save their work frequently. When the computer is turned off, everything in RAM is wiped clean. *Volatility* refers to RAM's

Chip Advancements
AMD: Security, virtualization, and advanced power-management technology.
IBM: Cryptography for additional security and floating point capability for faster graphics processing.
Intel: Cryptography for additional security, hardware-assisted virtualization, and Active Management Technology for asset tracking, patching, and software updates.
Sun Microsystems: Cryptography for additional security, increased speed for data transmission and receipt, and ability to run 32 computations simultaneously.

FIGURE B3.4

Chip Advancements by Manufacturer

complete loss of stored information if power is interrupted. RAM is volatile and its contents are lost when the computer's electric supply fails.

Cache Memory

Cache memory is a small unit of ultra-fast memory that is used to store recently accessed or frequently accessed data so that the CPU does not have to retrieve this data from slower memory circuits such as RAM. Cache memory that is built directly into the CPU's circuits is called primary cache. Cache memory contained on an external circuit is called secondary cache.

Read Only Memory (ROM)

Read-only memory (ROM) is the portion of a computer's primary storage that does not lose its contents when one switches off the power. ROM contains essential system programs that neither the user nor the computer can erase. Since the computer's internal memory is blank during start-up, the computer cannot perform any functions unless given start-up instructions. These instructions are stored in ROM.

Flash memory is a special type of rewriteable read-only memory (ROM) that is compact and portable. ***Memory cards*** contain high-capacity storage that holds data such as captured images, music, or text files. Memory cards are removable; when one is full the user can insert an additional card. Subsequently, the data can be downloaded from the card to a computer. The card can then be erased and used again. Memory cards are typically used in digital devices such as cameras, cellular phones, and personal digital assistants (PDA). ***Memory sticks*** provide nonvolatile memory for a range of portable devices including computers, digital cameras, MP3 players, and PDAs.

SECONDARY STORAGE

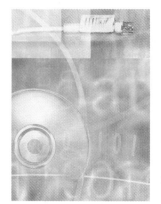

Storage is a hot area in the business arena as organizations struggle to make sense of exploding volumes of data. Storage sales grew more than 16 percent to nearly $8 billion in 2004, according to IDC market research. ***Secondary storage*** consists of equipment designed to store large volumes of data for long-term storage. Secondary storage devices are nonvolatile and do not lose their contents when the computer is turned off. Some storage devices, such as a hard disk, offer easy update capabilities and a large storage capacity. Others, such as CD-ROMs, offer limited update capabilities but possess large storage capacities.

Storage capacity is expressed in bytes, with megabytes being the most common. A ***megabyte (MB or M or Meg)*** is roughly 1 million bytes. Therefore, a computer with 256 MB of RAM translates into the RAM being able to hold roughly 256 million characters of data and software instructions. A ***gigabyte (GB)*** is roughly 1 billion bytes. A ***terabyte (TB)*** is roughly 1 trillion bytes (refer to Figure B3.5).

Most standard desktops have a hard drive with storage capacity in excess of 80 GB. Hard drives for large organizational computer systems can hold in excess of 100 TB of information. For example, a typical double-spaced page of pure text is roughly 2,000 characters. Therefore, a 40 GB (40 gigabyte or 40 billion characters) hard drive can hold approximately 20 million pages of text.

Common storage devices include:

- Magnetic medium
- Optical medium

Term	Size
Kilobyte (KB)	1,024 Bytes
Megabyte (MB)	1,024 KB 1,048,576 Bytes
Gigabyte (GB)	1,024 MB (10^9 bytes)
Terabyte (TB)	1,024 GB (10^{12} bytes) 1 TB = Printing of 1 TB would require 50,000 trees to be made into paper
Petabyte (PB)	1,024 TB (10^{15} bytes) 200 PB = All production of digital magnetic tape in 1995
Exabyte (EB)	1,024 PB (10^{18} bytes) 2 EB = total volume of information generated worldwide annually 5 EB = all words ever spoken by human beings

FIGURE B3.5

Binary Terms

Magnetic Medium

Magnetic medium is a secondary storage medium that uses magnetic techniques to store and retrieve data on disks or tapes coated with magnetically sensitive materials. Like iron filings on a sheet of waxed paper, these materials are reoriented when a magnetic field passes over them. During write operations, the read/write heads emit a magnetic field that orients the magnetic materials on the disk or tape to represent encoded data. During read operations, the read/write heads sense the encoded data on the medium.

One of the first forms of magnetic medium developed was magnetic tape. *Magnetic tape* is an older secondary storage medium that uses a strip of thin plastic coated with a magnetically sensitive recording medium. The most popular type of magnetic medium is a hard drive. A *hard drive* is a secondary storage medium that uses several rigid disks coated with a magnetically sensitive material and housed together with the recording heads in a hermetically sealed mechanism. Hard drive performance is measured in terms of access time, seek time, rotational speed, and data transfer rate.

Optical Medium

Optical medium is a secondary storage medium for computers on which information is stored at extremely high density in the form of tiny pits. The presence or absence of pits is read by a tightly focused laser beam. Optical medium types include:

- **Compact disk-read-only memory (CD-ROM) drive**—an optical drive designed to read the data encoded on CD-ROMs and to transfer this data to a computer.
- **Compact disk-read-write (CD-RW) drive**—an optical drive that enables users to erase existing data and to write new data repeatedly to a CD-RW.
- **Digital video disk (DVD)**—a CD-ROM format capable of storing up to a maximum of 17 GB of data; enough for a full-length feature movie.
- **DVD-ROM drive**—a read-only drive designed to read the data encoded on a DVD and transfer the data to a computer.
- **Digital video disk-read/write (DVD-RW)**—a standard for DVD discs and player/recorder mechanisms that enables users to record in the DVD format.

CD-ROMs and DVDs offer an increasingly economical medium for storing data and programs. The overall trend in secondary storage is toward more direct-access methods, higher capacity with lower costs, and increased portability.

INPUT DEVICES

An *input device* is equipment used to capture information and commands. A keyboard is used to type in information, and a mouse is used to point and click on buttons and icons. Numerous input devices are available in many different environments, some of which have applications that are more suitable in a personal setting than a business setting. A keyboard, mouse, and scanner are the most common forms of input devices (see Figures B3.6 and B3.7).

New forms of input devices allow people to exercise and play video games at the same time. The Kilowatt Sport from Powergrid Fitness lets people combine strength training with their favorite video games. Players can choose any PlayStation or Xbox game that uses a joystick to run the elliptical trainer. After loading the game, participants stand on a platform while pushing and pulling a resistance rod in all directions to control what happens in the game. The varied movement targets muscle groups on the chest, arms, shoulders, abdomen, and back. The machine's display shows information such as pounds lifted and current resistance level, and players can use one-touch adjustment to vary the degree of difficulty.[3]

Another new input device is a stationary bicycle. A computer design team of graduate and undergraduate students at MIT built the Cyclescore, an integrated video game and bicycle. The MIT students tested current games on the market but found users would stop pedaling to concentrate on the game. To engage users, the team is designing games that interact with the experience of exercise itself, for example, monitoring heart rate and adjusting the difficulty of the game according to the user's bicycling capabilities. In one game, the player must pedal to make a hot-air balloon float over mountains, while collecting coins and shooting at random targets.[4]

OUTPUT DEVICES

An *output device* is equipment used to see, hear, or otherwise accept the results of information processing requests. Among output devices, printers and monitors are the most common; however, speakers and plotters (special printers that draw output on a page) are widely used (see Figure B3.8). In addition, output devices are responsible for converting computer-stored information into a form that can be understood.

Manual Input Devices
Joystick—widely used as an alternative to the keyboard for computer games and some professional applications, such as computer-aided design
Keyboard—provides a set of alphabetic, numeric, punctuation, symbol, and control keys
Microphone—captures sounds such as a voice for voice recognition software
Mouse—one or more control buttons housed in a palm-sized case and designed so that one can move it about on the table next to the keyboard
Pointing stick—causes the pointer to move on the screen by applying directional pressure (popular on notebooks and PDAs)
Touch screen—allows the use of a finger to point at and touch a particular function to perform
Touch pad—a form of a stationary mouse on which the movement of a finger causes the pointer on the screen to move

FIGURE B3.6

Manual Input Devices

Automated Input Devices
Bar code scanner—captures information that exists in the form of vertical bars whose width and distance apart determine a number
Digital camera—captures still images or video as a series of 1s and 0s
Magnetic ink character reader—reads magnetic ink numbers printed on checks that identify the bank, checking account, and check number
Optical-character recognition—converts text into digital format for computer input
Optical-mark recognition (OMR)—detects the presence or absence of a mark in a predetermined place (popular for multiple-choice exams)
Point-of-sale (POS)—captures information at the point of a transaction, typically in a retail environment
Radio frequency identification (RFID)—uses active or passive tags in the form of chips or smart labels that can store unique identifiers and relay this information to electronic readers

FIGURE B3.7

Automated Input Devices

Output Devices
Cathode-ray tube (CRT)—a vacuum tube that uses an electron gun (cathode) to emit a beam of electrons that illuminates phosphors on a screen as the beam sweeps across the screen repeatedly; a monitor is often called a CRT
Liquid crystal display (LCDs)—a low-powered display technology used in laptop computers where rod-shaped crystal molecules change their orientation when an electrical current flows through them
Laser printer—a printer that forms images using an electrostatic process, the same way a photocopier works
Ink-jet printer—a printer that makes images by forcing ink droplets through nozzles
Plotter—a printer that uses computer-directed pens for creating high-quality images, blueprints, schematics, etc.

FIGURE B3.8

Output Devices

A new output device based on sensor technology aims to translate American Sign Language (ASL) into speech, enabling the millions of people who use ASL to better communicate with those who do not know the rapid gesturing system. The AcceleGlove is a glove lined on the inside with sensors embedded in rings. The sensors, called accelerometers, measure acceleration and can categorize and translate finger and hand movements. Additional, interconnected attachments for the elbow and shoulder capture ASL signs that are made with full arm motion. When users wear the glove while signing ASL, algorithms in the glove's software translate the hand gestures into words. The translations can be relayed through speech synthesizers or read on a PDA-size computer screen. Inventor Jose L. Hernandez-Rebollar started with a single glove that could translate only the ASL alphabet. Now, the device employs two gloves that contain a 1,000-word vocabulary.[5]

Other new output devices are being developed every day. Needapresent.com, a British company, has developed a vibrating USB massage ball, which plugs into a computer's USB port to generate a warm massage for sore body parts during those long evenings spent coding software or writing papers. Needsapresent.com also makes a coffee cup warmer that plugs into the USB port.[6]

COMMUNICATION DEVICES

A **communication device** is equipment used to send information and receive it from one location to another. A telephone modem connects a computer to a phone line in order to access another computer. The computer works in terms of digital signals, while a standard telephone line works with analog signals. Each digital signal represents a bit (either 0 or 1). The modem must convert the digital signals of a computer into analog signals so they can be sent across the telephone line. At the other end, another modem translates the analog signals into digital signals, which can then be used by the other computer. Figure B3.9 displays the different types of modems.

Computer Categories

Supercomputers today can hit processing capabilities of well over 200 teraflops—the equivalent of everyone on earth performing 35,000 calculations per second (see Figure B3.10). For the past 20 years, federally funded supercomputing research has given birth to some of the computer industry's most significant technology breakthroughs including:

- Clustering, which allows companies to chain together thousands of PCs to build mass-market systems.
- Parallel processing, which provides the ability to run two or more tasks simultaneously and is viewed as the chip industry's future.
- Mosaic browser, which morphed into Netscape and made the Web a household name.

Federally funded supercomputers have also advanced some of the country's most dynamic industries, including advanced manufacturing, gene research in the life sciences, and real-time financial-market modeling.[7]

Carrier Technology	Description	Speed	Comments
Dial-up Access	On demand access using a modem and regular telephone line (POT).	2400 bps to 56 Kbps	■ Cheap but slow.
Cable	Special cable modem and cable line required.	512 Kbps to 20 Mbps	■ Must have existing cable access in area. ■ Bandwidth is shared.
DSL Digital Subscriber Line	This technology uses the unused digital portion of a regular copper telephone line to transmit and receive information. A special modem and adapter card are required.	128 Kbps to 8 Mbps	■ Doesn't interfere with normal telephone use. ■ Bandwidth is dedicated. ■ Must be within 5 km (3.1 miles) of telephone company switch.
Wireless (LMCS)	Access is gained by connection to a high-speed cellular like local multipoint communications system (LMCS) network via wireless transmitter/receiver.	30 Mbps or more	■ Can be used for high-speed data, broadcast TV, and wireless telephone service.
Satellite	Newer versions have two-way satellite access, removing need for phone line.	6 Mbps or more	■ Bandwidth is not shared. ■ Some connections require an existing Internet service account. ■ Setup fees can range from $500 to $1,000.

FIGURE B3.9

Comparing Modems

Computers come in different shapes, sizes, and colors. Some are small enough to carry around, while others are the size of a telephone booth. Size does not always correlate to power, speed, and price (see Figure B3.11).

MIT's Media Lab is developing a laptop that it will sell for $100 each to government agencies around the world for distribution to millions of underprivileged schoolchildren. Using a simplified sales model and some reengineering of the device helped MIT reach the $100 price point. Almost half the price of a current laptop comprises marketing, sales, distribution, and profit. Of the remaining costs, the display panel and backlight account for roughly half while the rest covers the operating system.

FIGURE B3.10

Supercomputer

Computer Category	Description	Size
Personal digital assistant (PDA)	A small handheld computer that performs simple tasks such as taking notes, scheduling appointments, and maintaining an address book and a calendar. The PDA screen is touch-sensitive, allowing a user to write directly on the screen, capturing what is written.	Fits in a person's hand
Laptop	A fully functional computer designed to be carried around and run on battery power. Laptops come equipped with all of the technology that a personal desktop computer has, yet weigh as little as two pounds.	Similar to a textbook
Tablet	A pen-based computer that provides the screen capabilities of a PDA with the functional capabilities of a laptop or desktop computer. Similar to PDAs, tablet PCs use a writing pen or stylus to write notes on the screen and touch the screen to perform functions such as clicking on a link while visiting a Web site.	Similar to a textbook
Desktop	Available with a horizontal system box (the box is where the CPU, RAM, and storage devices are held) with a monitor on top, or a vertical system box (called a tower) usually placed on the floor within a work area.	Fits on a desk
Workstation	Similar to a desktop but has more powerful mathematical and graphics processing capabilities and can perform more complicated tasks in less time. Typically used for software development, Web development, engineering, and e-business tools.	Fits on a desk
Minicomputer (midrange computer)	Designed to meet the computing needs of several people simultaneously in a small to medium-size business environment. A common type of minicomputer is a server and is used for managing internal company networks and Web sites. Minicomputers are more powerful than desktop computers but also cost more, ranging in price from $5,000 to several hundred thousand dollars.	Ranges from fitting on a desk to the size of a filing cabinet
Mainframe computer	Designed to meet the computing needs of hundreds of people in a large business environment. Mainframe computers are a step up in size, power, capability, and cost from minicomputers. Mainframes can cost in excess of $1 million. With processing speeds greater than 1 trillion instructions per second (compared to a typical desktop that can process about 2.5 billion instructions per second), mainframes can easily handle the processing requests of hundreds of people simultaneously.	Similar to a refrigerator
Supercomputer	The fastest, most powerful, and most expensive type of computer. Organizations such as NASA that are heavily involved in research and number crunching employ supercomputers because of the speed with which they can process information. Other large, customer-oriented businesses such as General Motors and AT&T employ supercomputers just to handle customer information and transaction processing.	Similar to a car

FIGURE B3.11

Computer Categories

The low-cost laptop will use a display system that costs less than $25, a 500 MHz processor from AMD, a wireless LAN connection, 1 GB of storage, and the Linux operating system. The machine will automatically connect with others. China and Brazil have already ordered 3 million and 1 million laptops, respectively. MIT's goal is to produce around 150 million laptops per year.[8]

Software Basics

Hardware is only as good as the software that runs it. Over the years, the cost of hardware has decreased while the complexity and cost of software have increased. Some large software applications, such as customer relationship management systems, contain millions of lines of code, take years to develop, and cost millions of dollars. The two main types of software are system software and application software.

SYSTEM SOFTWARE

System software controls how the various technology tools work together along with the application software. System software includes both operating system software and utility software.

Operating System Software

Linus Torvalds, a shy Finnish programmer, may seem an unlikely choice to be one of the world's top managers. However, Linux, the software project he created while a university student, is now one of the most powerful influences on the computer world. Linux is an operating system built by volunteers and distributed for free and has become one of the primary competitors to Microsoft. Torvalds coordinates Linux development with a few dozen volunteer assistants and more than 1,000 programmers scattered around the globe. They contribute code for the kernel—or core piece—of Linux. He also sets the rules for dozens of technology companies that have lined up behind Linux, including IBM, Dell, Hewlett-Packard, and Intel.

While basic versions of Linux are available for free, Linux is having a considerable financial impact. According to market researcher IDC, the total market for Linux devices and software will increase from $11 billion in 2004 to $35.7 billion by 2008.[9]

Operating system software controls the application software and manages how the hardware devices work together. When using Excel to create and print a graph, the operating system software controls the process, ensures that a printer is attached and has paper, and sends the graph to the printer along with instructions on how to print it.

Operating system software also supports a variety of useful features, one of which is multitasking. *Multitasking* allows more than one piece of software to be used at a time. Multitasking is used when creating a graph in Excel and simultaneously printing a word processing document. With multitasking, both pieces of application software are operating at the same time. There are different types of operating system software for personal environments and for organizational environments (see Figure B3.12).

Utility Software

Utility software provides additional functionality to the operating system. Utility software includes antivirus software, screen savers, and anti-spam software. Figure B3.13 displays a few types of available utility software.

Operating System Software	
Linux	An open source operating system that provides a rich environment for high-end workstations and network servers. Open source refers to any program whose source code is made available for use or modification as users or other developers see fit.
Mac OS X	The operating system of Macintosh computers.
Microsoft Windows	Generic name for the various operating systems in the Microsoft Windows family, including Microsoft Windows CE, Microsoft Windows 98, Microsoft Windows ME, Microsoft Windows 2000, Microsoft Windows XP, Microsoft Windows NT, and Microsoft Windows Server 2003.
MS-DOS	The standard, single-user operating system of IBM and IBM-compatible computers, introduced in 1981. MS-DOS is a command-line operating system that requires the user to enter commands, arguments, and syntax.
UNIX	A 32-bit multitasking and multiuser operating system that originated at AT&T's Bell Laboratories and is now used on a wide variety of computers, from mainframes to PDAs.

APPLICATION SOFTWARE

Application software is used for specific information processing needs, including payroll, customer relationship management, project management, training, and many others. Application software is used to solve specific problems or perform specific tasks. From an organizational perspective, payroll software, collaborative software such as videoconferencing (within groupware), and inventory management software are all examples of application software (see Figure B3.14).

Types of Utility Software	
Crash-proof	Helps save information if a computer crashes.
Disk image for data recovery	Relieves the burden of reinstalling and tweaking scores of applications if a hard drive crashes or becomes irretrievably corrupted.
Disk optimization	Organizes information on a hard disk in the most efficient way.
Encrypt data	Protects confidential information from unauthorized eyes. Programs such as BestCrypt simply and effectively apply one of several powerful encryption schemes to hard drive information. Users unlock the information by entering a password in the BestCrypt control panel. The program can also secure information on rewritable optical disks or any other storage media that is assigned a drive letter.
File and data recovery	Retrieves accidental deletion of photos or documents in Windows XP by utilities such as Free Undelete, which searches designated hard drive deletion areas for recognizable data.
Text protect	In Microsoft Word, prevents users from typing over existing text after accidentally hitting the Insert key. Launch the Insert Toggle Key program, and the PC will beep whenever a user presses the Insert key.
Preventative security	Through programs such as Window Washer, erases file histories, browser cookies, cache contents, and other crumbs that applications and Windows leave on a hard drive.
Spyware	Removes any software that employs a user's Internet connection in the background without the user's knowledge or explicit permission.
Uninstaller	Can remove software that is no longer needed.

Types of Application Software	
Browser	Enables the user to navigate the World Wide Web. The two leading browsers are Netscape Navigator and Microsoft Internet Explorer.
Communication	Turns a computer into a terminal for transmitting data to and receiving data from distant computers through the telephone system.
Data management	Provides the tools for data retrieval, modification, deletion, and insertion; for example, Access, MySQL, and Oracle.
Desktop publishing	Transforms a computer into a desktop publishing workstation. Leading packages include Adobe FrameMaker, Adobe PageMaker, and QuarkXpress.
E-mail	Provides e-mail services for computer users, including receiving mail, sending mail, and storing messages. Leading e-mail software includes Microsoft Outlook, Microsoft Outlook Express, and Eudora.
Groupware	Increases the cooperation and joint productivity of small groups of co-workers.
Presentation graphics	Creates and enhances charts and graphs so that they are visually appealing and easily understood by an audience. A full-features presentation graphics package such as Lotus Freelance Graphics or Microsoft PowerPoint includes facilities for making a wide variety of charts and graphs and for adding titles, legends, and explanatory text anywhere in the chart or graph.
Programming	Possesses an artificial language consisting of a fixed vocabulary and a set of rules (called syntax) that programmers use to write computer programs. Leading programming languages include Java, C + +, C#, and .NET.
Spreadsheet	Simulates an accountant's worksheet onscreen and lets users embed hidden formulas that perform calculations on the visible data. Many spreadsheet programs also include powerful graphics and presentation capabilities to create attractive products. The leading spreadsheet application is Microsoft Excel.
Word processing	Transforms a computer into a tool for creating, editing, proofreading, formatting, and printing documents. Leading word processing applications include Microsoft Word and WordPerfect.

FIGURE B3.14

Application Software

Information technology (IT) is a field concerned with the use of technology in managing and processing information. IT includes cell phones, PDAs, software such as spreadsheet software, and printers. There are two categories of IT: hardware and software. The six hardware components include CPU, primary storage, secondary storage, input devices, output devices, and communication devices. Computer categories include PDAs, laptops, tablets, desktops, workstations, minicomputers, mainframe computers, and supercomputers.

Software includes system software and application software. Operating system software and utility software are the two primary types of system software. There are many forms of application software from word processing to databases.

Application software, 330
Arithmetic-logic unit (ALU), 320
Binary digit (bit), 321
Byte, 321
Cache memory, 322
Central processing unit (CPU)
   (or microprocessor), 319
Communication device, 326
Complex instruction set
   computer (CISC) chip, 320
Computer, 319
Control unit, 319
Flash memory, 322
Gigabyte (GB), 322

Gigahertz (GHz), 320
Hard drive, 323
Hardware, 318
Information technology (IT), 318
Input device, 324
Magnetic medium, 323
Magnetic tape, 323
Megabyte (MB, M, or
   Meg), 322
Megahertz (MHz), 320
Memory card, 322
Memory stick, 322
Multitasking, 329
Operating system software, 329

Output device, 324
Primary storage, 321
Random access memory
   (RAM), 321
Read-only memory (ROM), 322
Reduced instruction set
   computer (RISC) chip, 320
Secondary storage, 322
Software, 318
System software, 329
Terabyte (TB), 322
Utility software, 329
Virtualization, 321
Volatility, 321

Changing Circuits at Circuit City

When Circuit City expanded the big-box warehouse format to consumer electronics retailing in the 1980s, the company was on its way to becoming the place to go for TVs and stereos. By the late 1980s, it had sidestepped its then top competitor, Silo, and it soon put the squeeze on the likes of Tweeter and RadioShack. Circuit City was doing so well in the 1990s that business consultant Jim Collins, in his best seller *Good to Great*, wrote: "From 1982 to 1999, Circuit City generated cumulative stock returns 22 times better than the market, handily beating Intel, Wal-Mart, GE, Hewlett-Packard and Coca-Cola."

Today, Circuit City is in a markedly different position. By 2001, Best Buy had raced past the Richmond, Virginia-based chain, usurping its position as the number one consumer electronics retailer. Best Buy now has 608 stores compared with Circuit City's 599 and nearly $25 billion in revenue to Circuit City's $9.7 billion. Circuit City is ranked by consultancy Retail Forward as the number three seller of consumer electronics, behind Best Buy and Wal-Mart. "Circuit City was the 800-pound gorilla," said Joseph Feldman, a research analyst with the investment bank SG Cowen & Co. However, "they woke up one morning and Best Buy had doubled its size with the same number of stores."

Catching Best Buy

Circuit City has been trying to catch up to Best Buy, or at least cement its position as a serious contender in consumer electronics retailing. Its top executives announced plans to turn the company into a customer-focused business that delivers a personalized experience to all customers across all its channels (stores, Web, and call centers). Michael Jones, who took over as Circuit City's CIO in January 2004, speaks passionately about the high-profile role technology will play in delivering personalized customer experiences. However, before he can achieve his vision of store associates recognizing customers through their loyalty cards as soon as they enter the store, he has a lot of unglamorous groundwork to lay. Circuit City's strategy hinges on a robust IT infrastructure that makes information readily accessible to decision makers. Everything the company is doing to improve its business—from developing more effective promotions to deciding which products should be displayed at the ends of aisles in stores—hinges on data. "This is heavy analytical work. It's fact-based, data-driven," said Philip Schoonover, Circuit City's new president who was hired in October 2004 from Best Buy.

Circuit City is just starting to invest heavily in the technology needed to act on this strategy. It is upgrading its mostly proprietary point-of-sale (POS) system and building an enterprise data warehouse to replace siloed databases. However, some analysts say Circuit City's turnaround effort has been hampered by a stodgy, overly complacent leadership that lacks vision. Top executives saw the Best Buy locomotive coming but failed to react as it steamed past them. Indeed, some analysts say they doubt Circuit City will ever catch up.

Bottom-Up Changes

As part of its turnaround effort over the past few years, Circuit City has sold all of its noncore businesses to focus on its core: consumer electronics. It also has changed the pay structure for in-store employees, begun relocating stores (it closed 19), and hired new management. In addition, the company is finally starting to hone its customer-centric strategy. Circuit City is already improving the customer experience in its stores by, among other things, locating accessories and services close to big-ticket items so that customers can see more quickly what they might need to furnish their home office or outfit a home theater. For example, when a customer is looking at a high-definition television, nearby is a selection of furniture to hold the TV, the cables needed to hook it up, and DirectTV or digital cable service products. Circuit City is also making merchandising decisions based on what is important to the customer. For example, its stores are beginning to feature products deemed most important to customers on the displays at the ends of aisles. The company is trying to nail the basics of customer service by making sure that items are not out of stock.[10]

Questions

1. How would anticipating Best Buy's growth have helped Circuit City remain as an industry leader?
2. Why is keeping up with technology critical to a global company such as Circuit City?
3. Highlight some of the potential risks facing Circuit City's new business model.
4. Why is Circuit City benefiting from implementing strategic product placement techniques?

Electronic Breaking Points

What happens when someone accidentally spills a cup of hot coffee on a laptop, puts a USB memory key in a washing machine, or drops an iPod in the sand? How much abuse can electronic products take and keep on working? *PC World* tested several products to determine their breaking points.[11]

Laptop

A Gateway laptop was placed in a shoulder bag and smashed into several doors and walls. It was also dropped off a six-foot-high bookcase to simulate a drop from an airplane's overhead bin. Finally, it was knocked off a desk onto a carpeted floor without the bag. After all the abuse, the Gateway consistently rebooted and recognized the wireless network; however, the battery did become slightly dislodged and the optical drive opened.

Severe physical damage was caused when the laptop was dropped onto a hardwood floor. The laptop's screen cracked, and the black plastic molding above the keyboard cracked. Plastic splinters littered the floor, and the optical drive refused to open.

Spilling coffee in a travel-size mug onto the keyboard caused a slight sizzle, after which the Gateway's blue light winked out. The machine was quickly turned off, the battery removed, the liquid drained, the keys mopped, and the unit set aside. Unfortunately, the laptop never recovered.

Smart Phone

The PalmOne Treo 600 smart phone was stepped on, buried in the sand, bounced around in a car, and dropped off a desk onto carpeted and hardwood floors. Even though the Treo 600 was not protected by a shock-absorbent case or plastic screen cover, there were no signs of failure. Repeatedly knocking it off the desk onto a carpeted floor also left it undamaged, although the unit did turn off on several occasions.

The desk-to-hardwood-floor test produced scratches but nothing else. If dropped when in phone mode, the Treo automatically turned off. If an application was running—the calculator, for example—the device stayed on and the data remained on the screen, though a mysterious extra numeral nine appeared every time it was dropped.

MP3 Player

A 6 GB silver iPod Mini went for a bouncy car ride, was dropped on wet grass and dry pavement, was knocked off a desk onto carpeted and hardwood floors, and was finally dropped in dry sand. Bouncing inside the car caused a couple of skips. Drops on soft wet grass and carpet had no ill effect. Dropping it from the car seat to the curb and off a desk onto a hardwood floor produced a few nicks and caused songs to skip and the device to shut down repeatedly. Still, all the unit's features continued to work after the abuse, and songs played.

However, the Mini did not like the beach. Without the benefit of a protective case or plastic display covering on the unit, sand wedged under the scroll wheel, affecting all controls. Feature settings could be seen and highlighted, but the crunching sand prevented the Mini from launching them. The unit turned on but could not turn off until the iPod's automatic shutdown feature took over.

Protecting Electronic Products
Bag it. Place your product in a cushioned case or shock-absorbent travel bag. The secret is to make sure it has plenty of padding.
Get protection. Almost every technology manufacturer offers some type of warranty and equipment-replacement program. For example, Sprint provides the PCS Total Equipment Protection service, which costs $5 per month and covers loss, theft, and accidental damage to a cell phone.
Clean up spills. Try these tips to bring a laptop and data back from the dead after a spill.
1. **Disconnect the battery.** The faster the battery is disconnected the less likely components will burn out.
2. **Empty it.** Turn over the device and pour out as much liquid as possible.
3. **Open it up.** Remove the optical drive and keyboard. This can be tricky, so check the user manual for instructions. Once open, use a towel to soak up as much liquid as possible. According to Herman De Hoop, HP's technical marketing manager, you can even use a hair dryer set on cool (not hot) to dry the liquid.
4. **Leave it alone.** Let the device sit for at least 12 to 24 hours. Robert Enochs, IBM's worldwide product manager for the ThinkPad Series, warns that you should not turn the device on until all the liquid is gone and it is completely dry.
5. **Plug and pray.** Reassemble the device, and if it powers up, copy off important data, and then call the manufacturer. Even if the unit works, a professional cleaning is recommended.
6. **Enter a recovery program.** For an average price of $900, enlist the help of data recovery services like DriveSavers to rescue data from drowned hard disks.

FIGURE B3.15

How to Protect
Electronic Products

Memory Stick

Lexar claims that its JumpDrive Sport 256 MB USB 2.0 Flash Drive is "built for the rugged life." A rubber cap protects the device, absorbing shock from any drops. For these experiments, the device was used without its cap. It was dropped, stepped on, buried in the sand, and knocked off a desk onto a hardwood floor. It also took a spin through the washing machine and dryer and was even run over by a car.

There is truth in advertising. Neither water, heat, sand, nor car could keep the memory stick from its appointed storage rounds. The car did squeeze the metal USB connector tip a tad tighter, but the device was still able to make contact with the USB port, and it worked perfectly.

Memory Card

The SanDisk SD 64 MB memory card is easy to misplace, but not easy to break. It was swatted off a desk onto a hardwood floor, dropped, stepped on, and buried in the sand. It also underwent a two-rinse cycle in the wash in a jeans pocket and then tumbled in the dryer for an hour on a high-heat setting. The SanDisk memory card aced every torture test.

For tips on how to protect electronic products, review Figure B3.15.

Questions

1. Identify the six hardware categories and place each product listed in the case in its appropriate category.
2. Describe the CPU and identify which products would use a CPU.
3. Describe the relationship between memory sticks and laptops. How can a user employ one to help protect information loss from the other?
4. Identify the different types of software each of the products listed in the case might use.

1. Purchasing a Computer

Dell is considered the fastest company on earth and specializes in computer customization. Connect to Dell's Web site at www.dell.com. Go to the portion of Dell's site that allows you to customize either a laptop or a desktop computer. First, choose an already prepared system and note its price and capability in terms of CPU speed, RAM size, monitor quality, and storage capacity. Now, customize that system to increase CPU speed, add more RAM, increase monitor size and quality, and add more storage capacity. What is the difference in price between the two? Which system is more in your price range? Which system has the speed and capacity you need?

2. Web-Enabled Cell Phones

When categorizing computers by size for personal needs, we focused on PDAs, laptops, and desktop computers. Other variations include Web-enabled cell phones that include instant text messaging and Web computers. For this project, you will need a group of four people, which you will then split into two groups of two. Have the first group research Web-enabled cell phones, their capabilities and costs. Have that group make a purchase recommendation based on price and capability. Have the second group do the same for Web computers. What is your vision of the future? Will we ever get rid of clunky laptops and desktops in favor of more portable and cheaper devices such as Web-enabled cell phones and Web computers? Why or why not?

3. Small Business Computers

Many different types of computers are available for small businesses. Use the Internet to find three different vendors of laptops or notebooks that are good for small businesses. Find the most expensive and the least expensive that the vendor offers and create a table comparing the different computers based on the following:

- CPU
- Memory
- Hard drive
- Optical drive
- Operating system
- Utility software
- Application software
- Support plan

Determine which computer you would recommend for a small business looking for an inexpensive laptop. Determine which computer you would recommend for a small business looking for an expensive laptop.

4. PDA Software

The personal digital assistant (PDA) market is ferocious, dynamic, and uncertain. One of the uncertainties is which operating system for PDAs will become dominant. Today, Microsoft operating systems dominate the laptop and desktop market. Research the more popular PDAs available today. What are the different operating systems? What different functionality do they offer? Are they compatible with each other? Determine which one will dominate in the future.

PLUG-IN
B4

Enterprise Architectures

LEARNING OUTCOMES

1. Explain the three components of an enterprise architecture.
2. Describe how an organization can implement a solid information architecture.
3. List and describe the five qualities of an infrastructure architecture.
4. Compare Web services and open systems.

Enterprise Architectures

A 66-hour failure of an FBI database that performed background checks on gun buyers was long enough to allow criminals to buy guns. The database failed at 1:00 p.m. on a Thursday and was not restored until 7:30 a.m. Sunday. The FBI must complete a gun check within three days; if it fails to do so, a merchant is free to make the sale. During this outage, any gun checks that were in progress were not finished, allowing merchants to complete those gun sales at their own discretion.[1]

To support the volume and complexity of today's user and application requirements, information technology needs to take a fresh approach to enterprise architectures by constructing smarter, more flexible environments that protect from system failures and crashes. ***Enterprise architectures*** include the plans for how an organization will build, deploy, use, and share its data, processes, and IT assets. A unified enterprise architecture will standardize enterprisewide hardware and software systems, with tighter links to the business strategy. A solid enterprise architecture can decrease costs, increase standardization, promote reuse of IT assets, and speed development of new systems. The end result is that the right enterprise architecture can make IT cheaper, strategic, and more responsive. The primary business goals of enterprise architectures are displayed in Figure B4.1.[2]

Enterprise architectures are never static; they continually change. Organizations use enterprise architects to help manage change. An ***enterprise architect (EA)*** is a person grounded in technology, fluent in business, a patient diplomat, and provides the important bridge between IT and the business. An EA is expensive and generally

FIGURE B4.1

Primary Business Goals of Enterprise Architectures

Reduce costs/improve productivity	81%
Improve customer satisfaction	71%
Create competitive advantages	66%
Generate growth	54%
Generate new revenue streams	43%
Optimize the supply chain	37%

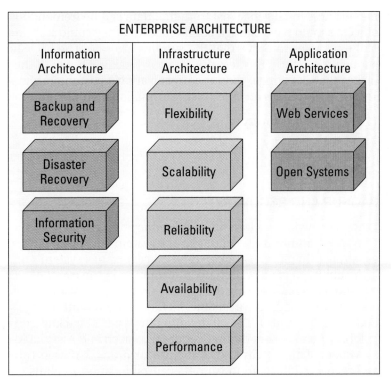

receives a salary upward of $150,000 per year. T-Mobile International's enterprise architects review projects to ensure they are soundly designed, meet the business objectives, and fit in with the overall enterprise architecture. One T-Mobile project was to create software that would let subscribers customize the ring sounds on their cell phones. The project group assumed it would have to create most of the software from scratch. However, T-Mobile's EAs found software already written elsewhere at T-Mobile that could be reused to create the new application. The reuse reduced the development cycle time by eight months, and the new application was available in less than six weeks.[3]

Companies that have created solid enterprise architectures, such as T-Mobile, are reaping huge rewards in savings, flexibility, and business alignment. Basic enterprise architectures contain three components (see Figure B4.2).

1. *Information architecture* identifies where and how important information, like customer records, is maintained and secured.

2. *Infrastructure architecture* includes the hardware, software, and telecommunications equipment that, when combined, provide the underlying foundation to support the organization's goals.

3. *Application architecture* determines how applications integrate and relate to each other.

Information Architecture

Information architecture identifies where and how important information, like customer records, is maintained and secured. A single backup or restore failure can cost an organization more than time and money; some data cannot be re-created, and the business intelligence lost from that data can be tremendous. Chief information officers should have enough confidence that they could walk around and randomly pull out cables to prove that the systems are safe. The CIO should also be secure enough to perform this test during peak business hours. If the thought of this test makes the CIO cringe, then the organization's customers should be cringing also. Three primary areas an enterprise information architecture should focus on are:

1. Backup and recovery
2. Disaster recovery
3. Information security

BACKUP AND RECOVERY

Each year businesses lose time and money because of system crashes and failures. One way to minimize the damage of a system crash is to have a backup and recovery strategy in place. A **backup** is an exact copy of a system's information. **Recovery** is the ability to get a system up and running in the event of a system crash or failure and includes restoring the information backup. Many different types of backup and recovery media are available, including redundant storage servers, tapes, disks, and even CDs and DVDs. All the different types of backup and recovery media are reliable; their primary differences are the speed and associated costs.

A chain of more than 4,000 franchise locations, 7-Eleven Taiwan uploads backup and recovery information from its central location to all its chain locations daily. The company implemented a new technology solution by Digital Fountain that could quickly and reliably download and upload backup and recovery information to all its stores. In addition, when a connection fails during the download or upload, the technology automatically resumes the download without having to start over, saving valuable time.[4]

Organizations should choose a backup and recovery strategy that is in line with business goals. If the organization deals with large volumes of critical information, it will require daily backups, perhaps even hourly backups, to storage servers. If the organization deals with small amounts of noncritical information, then it might require only weekly backups to tapes, CDs, or DVDs. Deciding how often to back up information and what media to use is a critical business decision. If an organization decides to back up on a weekly basis, then it is taking the risk that, if a total system crash occurs, it could lose a week's worth of work. If this risk is acceptable, then a weekly backup strategy will work. If this risk is unacceptable, then the organization needs to move to a daily backup strategy. Some organizations find the risk of losing a day's worth of work too high and move to an hourly backup strategy.

Two techniques used to help in case of system failure are fault tolerance and failover. **Fault tolerance** is a computer system designed that in the event a component fails, a backup component or procedure can immediately take its place with no loss of service. Fault tolerance can be provided with software, or embedded in hardware, or provided by some combination. **Failover** is a backup operational mode in which the functions of a computer component (such as a processor, server, network, or database) are assumed by secondary system components when the primary component becomes unavailable through either failure or scheduled down time. A failover procedure involves automatically offloading tasks to a standby system component so that the procedure is as seamless as possible to the end user. Used to make systems more fault tolerant, failover is typically an integral part of mission-critical systems that must be constantly available.[5]

DISASTER RECOVERY

A northern Ohio power company, FirstEnergy, missed signs that there were potential problems in its portion of North America's electrical grid. The events that followed left an estimated 50 million people in the Northeast and Canada in the dark. The failings are laid out in the widely reported findings of a joint U.S./Canada task force that investigated the causes of the blackout and recommended what to do to avoid big-scale outages in the future. The report detailed many procedures or best practices including:

- Mind the enterprise architectures.
- Monitor the quality of computer networks that provide data on power suppliers and demand.
- Make sure the networks can be restored quickly in the case of downtime.
- Set up disaster recovery plans.
- Provide adequate staff training, including verbal communication protocols "so that operators are aware of any IT-related problems that may be affecting their situational awareness of the power grid."[6]

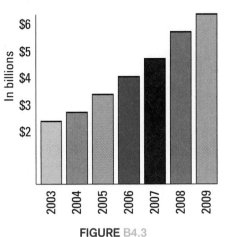

FIGURE B4.3

Financial Institutions Worldwide Spending on Disaster Recovery

Disasters such as power outages, floods, and even harmful hacking strike businesses every day. Organizations must develop a disaster recovery plan to prepare for such occurrences. A ***disaster recovery plan*** is a detailed process for recovering information or an IT system in the event of a catastrophic disaster such as a fire or flood. Spending on disaster recovery is rising worldwide among financial institutions (see Figure B4.3).[7]

A comprehensive disaster recovery plan takes into consideration the location of the backup information. Many organizations store backup information in an off-site facility. StorageTek specializes in providing off-site information storage and disaster recovery solutions. A comprehensive disaster recovery plan also foresees the possibility that not only the computer equipment but also the building where employees work may be destroyed. A ***hot site*** is a separate and fully equipped facility where the company can move immediately after a disaster and resume business. A ***cold site*** is a separate facility that does not have any computer equipment, but is a place where employees can move after a disaster.

A ***disaster recovery cost curve*** charts (1) the cost to the organization of the unavailability of information and technology and (2) the cost to the organization of recovering from a disaster over time. Figure B4.4 displays a disaster recovery cost curve and shows that where the two lines intersect is the best recovery plan in terms of cost and time. Creating an organization's disaster recovery cost curve is no small task. It must consider the cost of losing information and technology within each department or functional area, and the cost of losing information and technology across the whole enterprise. During the first few hours of a disaster, those costs will be low but become increasingly higher over time. With those costs in hand, an organization must then determine the costs of recovery. Cost of recovery during the first few hours of a disaster is exceedingly high and diminishes over time.

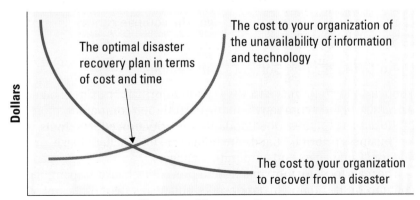

FIGURE B4.4

The Disaster Recovery Cost Curve

Marshall & Swift, which provides property valuation services, may be located in sunny Los Angeles, but the company barely averted a major disaster when Hurricane Charley ripped through southwest Florida. Many of the nation's largest insurance companies rely on Marshall & Swift's 200-plus servers to process claims and calculate the costs of rebuilding commercial and residential properties. Within one month of the Florida hurricane, the number of claims jumped from 20,000 to a whopping 180,000. This sudden surge in server utilization could have spelled disaster.

Fortunately, Marshall & Swift used an application performance management solution called ProactiveNet that identifies when an application or system is operating outside of its normal parameters and pinpoints the most likely source of the problem. ProactiveNet alerted the company's IT department to an improper balance of application, Web, and database servers. Some servers were being underutilized while others were being overburdened, thereby causing degradations in overall system performance. Marshall & Swift quickly began monitoring the usage patterns of each server and moved certain servers to ensure that all requests were processed in a timely matter.[8]

INFORMATION SECURITY

Security professionals are under increasing pressure to do the job right and cost-effectively as networks extend beyond organizations to remote users, partners, and customers, and to cell phones, PDAs, and other mobile devices. Regulatory requirements to safeguard data have increased. Concerns about identity theft are at an all-time high. Hacking and other unauthorized access contribute to the approximately 10 million instances of identity theft each year, according to the Federal Trade Commission. A good information architecture includes a strong information security plan, along with managing user access and up-to-date antivirus software and patches.[9]

Managing User Access

Managing user access to information is a critical piece of the information architecture. Passwords may still be the weakest link in the security chain. At Vitas Healthcare Corporation, with a workforce of 6,000 and operations across 15 states, authorized employees enter as many as a half-dozen passwords a day to access multiple systems. While it is important to maintain password discipline to secure customers' health care data, maintaining and managing the situation creates a drag on the IT department. "Our help desk spends 30 percent of their time on password management and provisioning," says John Sandbrook, senior IT director.

The company began using Fischer International Corporation's Identity Management Suite to manage passwords and comply with data-access regulations such as the Sarbanes-Oxley Act. The ID-management product includes automated audit, reporting, and compliance capabilities, plus a common platform for password management, provisioning, and self-service. With the software, Vitas can enforce stronger passwords with seven, eight, or nine characters, numbers, and capital letters that frequently change. The company anticipates curbing help-desk password time by 50 percent.[10]

Up-to-Date Antivirus Software and Patches

There is little doubt that security is a top priority for business managers, regardless of the size of their company. Among Fortune 500 companies, more than 80 percent of those surveyed described updating security procedures, tools, and services as a key business priority. That desire holds true for small, midsize, or large companies and for IT managers and corporate managers.

The main focus for most managers is preventing hackers, spammers, and other malcontents from entering their networks, and nearly two-thirds are looking to enhance their network-security-management, intrusion-detection, content-filtering, and anti-spam software. More than half also plan to upgrade their encryption software.[11]

Microsoft issues patches for its software on the second Tuesday of every month. These patches must be downloaded and installed on all systems across the entire enterprise if the company wants to keep its systems protected. At OMD, a media buying and planning subsidiary of Omnicom Group Inc., the network administrator had to manually install critical patches on all 100 servers, taking more than a week to deploy the patch across the company. Now, OMD uses automated installation software for patches and upgrades. The company purchased Altiris Management Suite for Dell servers, which let it move ahead with applying patches without taking down entire systems and balancing patch-deployment timing among servers so that all departments were not down at once during a patch install. Given everything else that security professionals need to think about, automated installation software is a welcome relief.[12]

Infrastructure Architecture

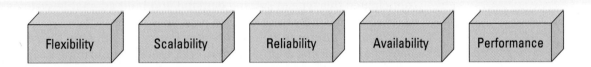

Gartner Inc. estimates that the typical Web application goes down 170 hours per year. At Illinois-based online brokerage OptionsXpress, application performance problems can have a serious impact on livelihoods. Nearly 7,000 options traders visit the OptionsXpress Web site at any given time, completing nearly 20,000 transactions a day. With all this online traffic, the brokerage's IT administrators were always up against the clock when re-creating troublesome applications offline in the development environment. The company struggled to unlock the mystery behind a troublesome trading application that was forcing traders to resubmit orders. Sometimes the application would just die and then restart itself for no apparent reason.[13]

Infrastructure architecture includes the hardware, software, and telecommunications equipment that, when combined, provide the underlying foundation to support the organization's goals. As an organization changes, its systems must be able to change to support its operations. If an organization grows by 50 percent in a single year, its systems must be able to handle a 50 percent growth rate. Systems that cannot adapt to organizational changes can severely hinder the organization's ability to operate. The future of an organization depends on its ability to meet its partners and customers on their terms, at their pace, any time of the day, in any geographic location. The following are the five primary characteristics of a solid infrastructure architecture:

1. Flexibility
2. Scalability
3. Reliability
4. Availability
5. Performance

FLEXIBILITY

Organizations must watch today's business, as well as tomorrow's, when designing and building systems. Systems must be flexible enough to meet all types of business changes. For example, a system might be designed to include the ability to handle multiple currencies and languages, even though the company is not currently performing business in other countries. When the company starts growing and performing business in new countries, the system will already have the flexibility to handle multiple currencies and languages. If the company failed to recognize that its business would someday be global, it would need to redesign all its systems to handle multiple currencies and languages, not easy once systems are up and running.

SCALABILITY

Estimating organizational growth is a challenging task. Growth can occur in a number of different forms including more customers and product lines and expansion into new markets. *Scalability* refers to how well a system can adapt to increased demands. A number of factors can create organizational growth including market, industry, and economy factors. If an organization grows faster than anticipated, it might experience all types of performance degradations, ranging from running out of disk space to a slowdown in transaction speeds. Anticipating expected—and unexpected—growth is key to building scalable systems that can support that growth.

MSNBC's Web site typically received moderate traffic. On September 11, 2001, the site was inundated with more than 91 million page views as its customers were trying to find out information about the terrorist attacks. Fortunately, MSNBC had anticipated this type of surging demand and built adaptable systems accordingly, allowing it to handle the increased page view requests.[15]

Capacity planning determines the future IT infrastructure requirements for new equipment and additional network capacity. Performing a capacity plan is one way to ensure the IT infrastructure is scalable. It is cheaper for an organization to implement an IT infrastructure that considers capacity growth at the beginning of a system launch than to try to upgrade equipment and networks after the system has been implemented. Not having enough capacity leads to performance issues and hinders the ability of knowledge workers to perform their jobs. If 100 workers are using the Internet to perform their jobs and the company purchases bandwidth that is too small and the network capacity is too small, the workers will spend a great deal of time just waiting to get information from the Internet. Waiting for an Internet site to return information is not very productive.

A computer glitch caused Delta Air Lines subsidiary Comair to cancel 1,100 flights on Christmas Day. The problem occurred when snowstorms caused the airline to ground flights, and the resulting quagmire overwhelmed its aging crew-scheduling system, causing further cancellations. Delta's crew-scheduling system is being replaced by one that can scale to handle more transactions.[16]

RELIABILITY

Reliability ensures all systems are functioning correctly and providing accurate information. Reliability is another term for accuracy when discussing the correctness of systems within the context of efficiency IT metrics. Inaccurate information processing occurs for many reasons, from the incorrect entry of data to information corruption. Unreliable information puts the organization at risk when making decisions based on the information.

AVAILABILITY

Availability (an efficiency IT metric) addresses when systems can be accessed by employees, customers, and partners. *High availability* refers to a system or component that is continuously operational for a desirably long length of time. Availability is typically measured relative to "100 percent operational" or "never failing." A widely held but difficult-to-achieve standard of availability for a system or product is known as "five 9s" (99.999 percent) availability.

Some companies have systems available 24x7 to support business operations and global customer and employee needs. With the emergence of the Web, companies expect systems to operate around the clock. A customer who finds that a Web site closes at 9:00 p.m. is not going to be a customer long.

Systems, however, must come down for maintenance, upgrades, and fixes. One challenge organizations face is determining when to schedule system downtime if the system is expected to operate continually. Exacerbating the negative impact of scheduled system downtime is the global nature of business. Scheduling maintenance during the evening might seem like a great idea, but the evening in one city is the morning somewhere else in the world, and global employees may not be able to perform their jobs if the system is down. Many organizations overcome this problem by having redundant systems, allowing the organization to take one system down by switching over to a redundant, or duplicate, system.[17]

PERFORMANCE

Performance measures how quickly a system performs a certain process or transaction (in terms of efficiency IT metrics of both speed and throughput). Not having enough performance capacity can have a devastating, negative impact on a business. A customer will wait only a few seconds for a Web site to return a request before giving up and moving on to another Web site. To ensure adaptable systems performance, capacity planning helps an organization determine future IT infrastructure requirements for new equipment and additional network capacity. It is cheaper for an organization to design and implement an IT infrastructure that envisions performance capacity growth than to update all the equipment after the system is already operational.

Abercrombie & Fitch (A&F) uses the Internet to market its distinctive image of being a fashion trendsetter to one of its largest customer segments, college students. The company designed its enterprise architecture with the help of IBM, which ensured www.abercrombie.com paralleled the same sleek but simple design of *A&F Quarterly,* the company's flagship magazine. Abercrombie & Fitch knew that its Web site had to be accessible, available, reliable, and scalable to meet the demands of its young customers. Young customers tend to be Internet savvy, and their purchasing habits vary from customers who only shop for sale items at midnight to customers who know exactly what they want immediately. The highly successful Web site gives customers not only an opportunity to shop online, but also a taste of the Abercrombie & Fitch lifestyle through downloadable MP3s, calendars, and desktop accessories.[18]

Application Architecture

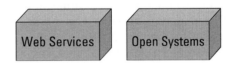

Gartner Inc. research indicates that application problems are the single largest source of downtime, causing 40 percent of annual downtime hours and 32 percent of average downtime costs. ***Application architecture*** determines how applications integrate and relate to each other. Advances in integration technology—primarily Web services and open systems—are providing new ways for designing more agile, more responsive enterprise architectures that provide the kind of value businesses need. With these new architectures, IT can build new business capabilities faster, cheaper, and in a vocabulary the business can understand.[19]

WEB SERVICES

Web services promise to be the next major frontier in computing. ***Web services*** contain a repertoire of Web-based data and procedural resources that use shared protocols and standards permitting different applications to share data and services. The major application of Web services is the integration among different applications. Before Web services, organizations had trouble with interoperability. *Interoperability* is the capability of two or more computer systems to share data and resources, even though they are made by different manufacturers. If a supply chain management (SCM) system can talk to (share information with) a customer relationship management (CRM) system, interoperability exists between the two systems. The traditional way that organizations achieved interoperability was to build integrations. Now, an organization can use Web services to perform the same task.

Verizon's massive enterprise architecture includes three different companies GTE, Bell Atlantic, and Nynex, each with its own complex systems. To find a customer record in any of the three companies' systems, Verizon turns to its search engine, called Spider. Spider is Verizon's version of Google, and it's helping Verizon's business to thrive.

Spider contains a vital customer information Web service that encapsulates Verizon's business rules, which help it to access the correct data repository when looking for customer information. Whenever a new system is built that needs to link to customer information, all the developer has to do is reuse the Web service that will link to the customer records. Because Verizon has the Web service in place as part of its enterprise architecture, development teams can build new applications within a month, as opposed to six months.[20]

Web services encompass all the technologies that are used to transmit and process information on and across a network, most specifically the Internet. It is easiest to think of an individual Web service as software that performs a specific task, with that task being made available to any user who needs its service. For example, a "Deposit" Web service for a banking system might allow customers to perform the task of depositing money to their accounts. The Web service could be used by a bank teller, by the customer at an ATM, and/or by the customer performing an online transaction through a Web browser.

The "Deposit" Web service demonstrates one of the great advantages of using the Web service model to develop applications. Developers do not have to reinvent the wheel every time they need to incorporate new functionality. A Web service is really a piece of reusable software code. A software developer can quickly build a new application by using many of these pieces of reusable code. The two primary parts of Web services are events and services.[21]

Events

Events are the eyes and ears of the business expressed in technology—they detect threats and opportunities and alert those who can act on the information. Pioneered by telecommunication and financial services companies, this involves using IT systems to monitor a business process for events that matter—a stock-out in the warehouse or an especially large charge on a consumer's credit card—and automatically alert the people best equipped to handle the issue. For example, a credit monitoring system automatically alerts a credit supervisor and shuts down an account when the system processes a $7,000 charge on a credit card with a $6,000 limit.[22]

Services

Services are more like software products than they are coding projects. They must appeal to a broad audience, and they need to be reusable if they are going to have an impact on productivity. Early forms of services were defined at too low a level in the architecture to interest the business, such as simple "Print" and "Save" services. The new services are being defined at a higher level; they describe such things as "Credit Check," "Customer Information," and "Process Payment." These services describe a valuable business process. For example, "Credit Check" has value not just for programmers who want to use that code in another application, but also for businesspeople who want to use it across multiple products—say, auto loans and mortgages—or across multiple businesses.[23]

The trick to building services is finding the right level of granularity. T-Mobile builds services starting at the highest level and then works its way down to lower levels, helping to ensure it does not build services that no one uses. The company first built a "Send Message" Web service and then built a "Send SMS Message" Web service that sends messages in special formats to different devices such as cell phones and pagers.

Lydian Trust's enterprise architects designed a Web service called "Get Credit" that is used by several different business units for loan applications. "Get Credit" seeks out credit ratings over the Internet from the major credit bureaus. One day, one of the credit bureaus' Web servers crashed, and Lydian Trust's "Get Credit" Web service could not make a connection. Since the connection to the server was loosely linked, the system did not know what to do. "Get Credit" was not built to make more than one call. So, while it waited for a response, hundreds of loan applications sat idle.

Lydian Trust's loan officers had to work overnight to ensure that all of the applications were completed within 24 hours as promised by the company. Fortunately, Lydian Trust's customers never felt the pain; however, its employees did. Systems must be designed to deal with the existence of certain events, or the lack of an event, in a way that does not interrupt the overall business. The "Get Credit" Web service has been modified to include an automatic e-mail alert to a supervisor whenever the Web service encounters a delay.[24]

OPEN SYSTEMS

Microsoft Internet Explorer's share of the Web browser market has dipped below 90 percent because of Mozilla's Firefox, an open source Web browser. According to WebSideStory, which has been tracking the Firefox versus Internet Explorer numbers, the Mozilla-made open source browser had captured 5 percent of the U.S. market in January 2005, an increase of almost a full percentage point in a month. Firefox claimed more than 25 million copies of the browser had been downloaded in its first 15 weeks of release.[25]

An **open system** is a broad, general term that describes nonproprietary IT hardware and software made available by the standards and procedures by which their products work, making it easier to integrate them. Amazon.com embraced open source technology converting from Sun's proprietary operating system to Linux. The switch to an open source operating system, such as Linux, is simplifying the process by which Amazon.com associates can build links to Amazon.com applications into their Web sites.[26]

The designs of open systems allow for information sharing. In the past, different systems were independent of each other and operated as individual islands of control. The sharing of information was accomplished through software drivers and devices that routed data allowing information to be translated and shared between systems. Although this method is still widely used, its limited capability and added cost are not an effective solution for most organizations. Another drawback to the stand-alone system is it can communicate only with components developed by a single manufacturer. The proprietary nature of these systems usually results in costly repair, maintenance, and expansion because of a lack of competitive forces. On the other hand, open system integration is designed to:

- Allow systems to seamlessly share information. The sharing of information reduces the total number of devices, resulting in an overall decrease in cost.

- Capitalize on enterprise architectures. This avoids installing several independent systems, which creates duplication of devices.

- Eliminate proprietary systems and promote competitive pricing. Often a sole-source vendor can demand its price and may even provide the customer with less than satisfactory service. Utilization of open systems allows users to purchase systems competitively.

Companies that have created solid enterprise architectures are reaping huge rewards in savings, flexibility, and business alignment. Basic enterprise architectures contain three components:

1. Information architecture identifies where and how important information, like customer records, are maintained and secured.

2. Infrastructure architecture includes the hardware, software, and telecommunications equipment that, when combined, provide the underlying foundation to support the organization's goals.

3. Application architecture determines how applications integrate and relate to each other.

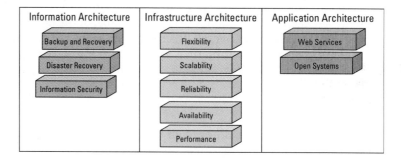

Chicago *Tribune*'s Server Consolidation a Success

The *Chicago Tribune* is the seventh-largest newspaper in the country. Overhauling its data center and consolidating servers was a difficult task; however, the payoff was tremendous. The *Chicago Tribune* successfully moved its critical applications from a mishmash of mainframes and older Sun Microsystems servers to a new dual-site enterprise architecture, which has resulted in lower costs and increased reliability throughout the company.

The paper's new enterprise architecture clustered its servers over a two-mile distance, lighting up a 1Gbps dark-fiber link—an optical fiber that is in place but not yet being used—between two data centers. This architecture lets the newspaper spread the processing load between the servers while improving redundancy and options for disaster recovery.

The transfer to the new architecture was not smooth. A small piece of software written for the transition contained a coding error that caused the *Tribune*'s editorial applications to experience intermittent processing failures. As a result, the paper was forced to delay delivery to about 40 percent of its 680,000 readers and cut 24 pages from a Monday edition, costing the newspaper nearly $1 million in advertising revenue.

After editorial applications were stabilized, the *Tribune* proceeded to migrate applications for operations—the physical production and printing of the newspaper—and circulation to the new enterprise architecture. "As we gradually took applications off the mainframe, we realized that we were incurring very high costs in maintaining underutilized mainframes at two different locations," says Darko Dejanovic, vice president and CTO of the Tribune Co., which owned the *Chicago Tribune,* the *Los Angeles Times,* Long Island's *Newsday,* and about a dozen other metropolitan newspapers. "By moving from two locations to one, we've achieved several million dollars in cost savings. There's no question that server consolidation was the right move for us."

The company is excited about its new enterprise architecture and is looking to consolidate software across its newspapers. Currently, each newspaper maintains its own applications for classified advertising and billing, which means the parent company must support about 10 billing packages and the same number of classified-ad programs. Most of the business processes can be standardized. So far, the company has standardized about 95 percent of classified-ad processes and about 90 percent of advertising-sales processes. Over three years, the company will replace the disparate billing and ad applications with a single package that will be used by all business units. The different newspapers will not necessarily share the same data, but they will have the same processes and the same systems for accessing them. Over time, that will allow some of the call centers to handle calls for multiple newspapers; East Coast centers will handle the early-morning calls and West Coast centers the late-day and evening calls.

The company is looking at a few additional projects including the implementation of hardware that will allow its individual applications to run on partial CPUs, freeing up processor power and making more efficient use of disk space.[27]

Questions

1. Review the five characteristics of infrastructure architecture and rank them in order of their potential impact on the Tribune Co.'s business.
2. What is the disaster recovery cost curve? Where should the Tribune Co. operate on the curve?
3. Define backups and recovery. What are the risks to the Tribune's business if it fails to implement an adequate backup plan?
4. Why is a scalable and highly available enterprise architecture critical to current operations and future growth?
5. Identify the need for information security at the Tribune Co.
6. How could the Tribune Co. use a classified ad Web service across its different businesses?

Fear the Penguin

Linux has proved itself the most revolutionary software of the past decade. Spending on Linux was reported to reach $280 million by 2006. Linus Torvalds, who wrote the kernel (the core) of the Linux operating system at age 21, posted the operating system on the Internet and invited other programmers to improve his code and users to download his operating system for free. Since then, tens of thousands of people have, making Linux perhaps the single largest collaborative project in the planet's history.

Today, Linux, if not its penguin mascot, is everywhere. You can find Linux inside a boggling array of computers, machines, and devices. Linux is robust enough to run the world's most powerful supercomputers, yet sleek and versatile enough to run inside consumer items like TiVo, cell phones, and handheld portable devices. Even more impressive than Linux's increasing prevalence in living rooms and pockets is its growth in the market for corporate computers.

Since its introduction in 1991, no other operating system in history has spread as quickly across such a broad range of systems as Linux, and it has finally achieved critical mass. According to studies by market research firm IDC, Linux is the fastest-growing server operating system, with shipments expected to grow by 34 percent per year over the next four years. With its innovative open source approach, strong security, reliability, and scalability, Linux can help companies achieve the agility they need to respond to changing consumer needs and stay ahead of the game.

Thanks to its unique open source development process, Linux is reliable and secure. A "meritocracy," a team specifically selected for their competence by the technical developer community, governs the entire development process. Each line of code that makes up the Linux kernel is extensively tested and maintained for a variety of different platforms and application scenarios.

This open collaborative approach means the Linux code base continually hardens and improves itself. If vulnerabilities appear, they get the immediate attention of experts from around the world, who quickly resolve the problems. According to Security Portal, which tracks vendor response times, it takes an average of 12 days to patch a Linux bug compared to an average of three months for some proprietary platforms. With the core resilience and reliability of Linux, businesses can minimize downtime, which directly increases their bottom line.

The Spread of Open Systems

Businesses and governments are opting for open source operating systems like Linux instead of Windows. One attendee at the Linux Desktop Consortium in 2004 was Dr. Martin Echt, a cardiologist from Albany, New York. Dr. Echt, chief operating officer of Capital Cardiology Associates, an eight-office practice, discussed his decision to shift his business from Microsoft's Windows to Linux. Dr. Echt is not your typical computer geek or Linux supporter, and he is not the only one switching to Linux.

The State Council in China has mandated that all ministries install the local flavor of Linux, dubbed Red Flag, on their PCs. In Spain, the government has installed a Linux operating system that incorporates the regional dialect. The city of Munich, despite a personal visit from Microsoft CEO Steve Ballmer, is converting its 14,000 PCs from Windows to Linux.

"It's open season for open source," declared Walter Raizner, general manager of IBM Germany. One of the biggest corporate backers of Linux, IBM has more than 75 government customers worldwide, including agencies in France, Spain, Britain, Australia, Mexico, the United States, and Japan.

The move toward Linux varies for each country or company. For Dr. Echt, it was a question of lower price and long-term flexibility. In China, the government claimed national security as a reason to move to open source code because it permitted engineers to make sure there were no security leaks and no spyware installed on its computers. In Munich, the move was largely political. Regardless of the reason, the market is shifting toward Linux.

Microsoft versus Linux

Bill Gates has openly stated that Linux is not a threat to Microsoft. According to IDC analysts, Microsoft's operating systems ship with 93.8 percent of all desktops worldwide. Ted Schadler, IDC research principal analyst, states that despite the push of lower cost Linux players into the market, Microsoft will maintain its desktop market share for the following three reasons:

1. Linux adds features to its applications that most computer users have already come to expect.
2. Linux applications might not be compatible with Microsoft applications such as Microsoft Word or Microsoft Excel.
3. Microsoft continues to innovate, and the latest version of Office is beginning to integrate word processing and spreadsheet software to corporate databases and other applications.

The Future of Linux

IDC analyst Al Gillen predicts that an open source operating system will not enjoy explosive growth on the desktop for at least six or eight years. Still, even Gillen cannot deny that Linux's penetration continues to rise, with an estimated 18 million users. Linux's market share increased from 1.5 percent at the end of 2000 to 4.2 percent at the beginning of 2004. According to IDC, by the end of 2005 it surpassed Apple's Mac OS, which has 2.9 percent of the market, as the second most popular operating system. Gartner Dataquest estimates Linux's server market share will grow seven times faster than Windows.[28]

Questions

1. How does Linux differ from traditional software?
2. Should Microsoft consider Linux a threat? Why or why not?
3. How is open source software a potential trend shaping organizations?
4. How can you use Linux as an emerging technology to gain a competitive advantage?
5. Research the Internet and discover potential ways that open source software might revolutionize business in the future.

 MAKING BUSINESS DECISIONS

1. Planning for Disaster Recovery

You are the new senior analyst in the IT department at Beltz, a large snack food manufacturing company. The company is located on the beautiful shoreline in Charleston, North Carolina. The company's location is one of its best and also worst features. The weather and surroundings are beautiful, but the threat of hurricanes and other natural disasters is high. Compile a disaster recovery plan that will minimize any risks involved with a natural disaster.

2. Comparing Backup and Recovery Systems

Research the Internet to find three different vendors of backup and recovery systems. Compare and contrast the three systems and determine which one you would recommend if you were installing a backup and recovery system for a medium-sized business with 3,500 employees that maintains information on the stock market. Compile your findings in a presentation that you can give to your class that details the three systems' strengths and weaknesses, along with your recommendation.

3. Ranking the -ilities

In a group, review the following list of IT infrastructure qualities and rank them in order of their impact on an organization's success. Use a rating system of 1 to 7, where 1 indicates the biggest impact and 7 indicates the least impact.

IT Infrastructure Qualities	Business Impact
Availability	
Accessibility	
Reliability	
Scalability	
Flexibility	
Performance	
Capacity Planning	

4. Designing an Enterprise Architecture

Components of a solid enterprise architecture include everything from documentation to business concepts to software and hardware. Deciding which components to implement and how to implement them can be a challenge. New IT components are released daily, and business needs continually change. An enterprise architecture that meets your organization's needs today may not meet those needs tomorrow. Building an enterprise architecture that is scalable, flexible, available, accessible, and reliable is key to your organization's success.

You are the enterprise architect (EA) for a large clothing company called Xedous. You are responsible for developing the initial enterprise architecture. Create a list of questions you will need answered to develop your architecture. Below is an example of a few of the questions you might ask.

- What are the company's growth expectations?
- Will systems be able to handle additional users?
- How long will information be stored in the systems?
- How much customer history must be stored?
- What are the organization's business hours?
- What are the organization's backup requirements?

B5

Networks and Telecommunications

1. Compare LANs, WANs, and MANs.
2. List and describe the four components that differentiate networks.
3. Compare the two types of network architectures.
4. Explain topology and the different types found in networks.
5. Describe TCP/IP along with its primary purpose.
6. Identify the different media types found in networks.

Networks and Telecommunications

Telecommunication systems enable the transmission of data over public or private networks. A *network* is a communications, data exchange, and resource-sharing system created by linking two or more computers and establishing standards, or protocols, so that they can work together. Telecommunication systems and networks are traditionally complicated and historically inefficient. However, businesses can benefit from today's modern network infrastructures that provide reliable global reach to employees and customers. Businesses around the world are moving to network infrastructure solutions that allow greater choice in how they go to market—solutions with global reach. Plug-In B5 takes a detailed look at key network and telecommunication technologies being integrated into businesses around the world.

Network Basics

Music is the hottest new product line at ubiquitous coffee retailer Starbucks. In Starbucks stores, customers can burn CDs while sipping coffee, thanks to the company's own online music library and increasingly sophisticated in-store network. Networks range from small two-computer networks to the biggest network of all, the Internet. A network provides two principal benefits: the ability to communicate and the ability to share. E-mail is the most popular form of network communication. Figure B5.1 highlights the three different types of networks, and Figure B5.2 graphically depicts each network type.

Network Types	
Local area network (LAN)	A computer network that uses cables or radio signals to link two or more computers within a geographically limited area, generally one building or a group of buildings. A networked office building, school, or home usually contains a single LAN. The linked computers are called workstations.
Wide area network (WAN)	A computer network that provides data communication services for business in geographically dispersed areas (such as across a country or around the world). The Internet is a WAN that spans the world.
Metropolitan area network (MAN)	A computer network that provides connectivity in a geographic area or region larger than that covered by a local area network, but smaller than the area covered by a wide area network. A college or business may have a MAN that joins the different LANs across its campus.

FIGURE B5.1

Network Types

FIGURE B5.2

LAN, WAN, and MAN

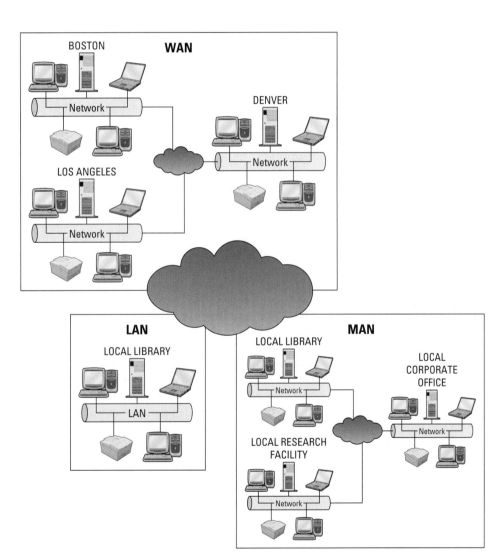

Networks are differentiated by the following:

- Architecture—peer-to-peer, client/server.
- Topology—bus, star, ring, hybrid, wireless.
- Protocols—Ethernet, Transmission Control Protocol/Internet Protocol (TCP/IP).
- Media—coaxial, twisted-pair, fiber-optic.

Architecture

The two primary types of network architectures are: peer-to-peer networks and client/server networks.

PEER-TO-PEER NETWORKS

A *peer-to-peer (P2P) network* is any network without a central file server and in which all computers in the network have access to the public files located on all other workstations, as illustrated in Figure B5.3. Each networked computer can allow other computers to access its files and use connected printers while it is in use as a workstation without the aid of a server.

While Napster may be the most widely known example of a P2P implementation, it may also be one of the most narrowly focused since the Napster model takes advantage of only one of the many capabilities of P2P computing: file sharing. The technology has far broader capabilities, including the sharing of processing, memory, and storage, and the supporting of collaboration among vast numbers of distributed computers. Peer-to-peer computing enables immediate interaction among people and computer systems.[1]

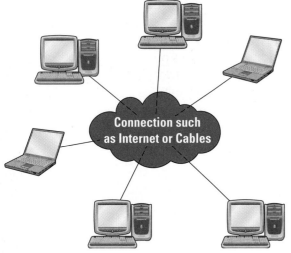

FIGURE B5.3

Peer-to-Peer (P2P) Networks

CLIENT/SERVER NETWORKS

A *client* is a computer that is designed to request information from a server. A *server* is a computer that is dedicated to providing information in response to external requests. A *client/server network* is a model for applications in which the bulk of the back-end processing, such as performing a physical search of a database, takes place on a server, while the front-end processing, which involves communicating with the users, is handled by the clients (see Figure B5.4). A *network operating system (NOS)* is the operating system that runs a network, steering information between computers and managing security and users. The client/server model has become one of the central ideas of network computing. Most business applications written today use the client/server model.

A fundamental part of client/server architecture is packet-switching. *Packet-switching* occurs when the sending computer divides a message into a number of efficiently sized units called packets, each of which contains the address of the destination computer. Each packet is sent on the network and intercepted by routers. A *router* is an intelligent connecting device that examines each packet of data it receives and then decides which way to send it onward toward its destination. The packets arrive at their intended destination, although some may have actually traveled by different physical paths, and the receiving computer assembles the packets and delivers the message to the appropriate application. The number of network routers being installed by businesses worldwide is booming (see Figure B5.5).[2]

Eva Chen, CIO at Trend Micro, built a router that helps prevent worms and viruses from entering networks. The problem with most existing antivirus software is that it starts working after a destructive sequence of code is identified, meaning it starts doing its job only after the virus or worm has been unleashed inside

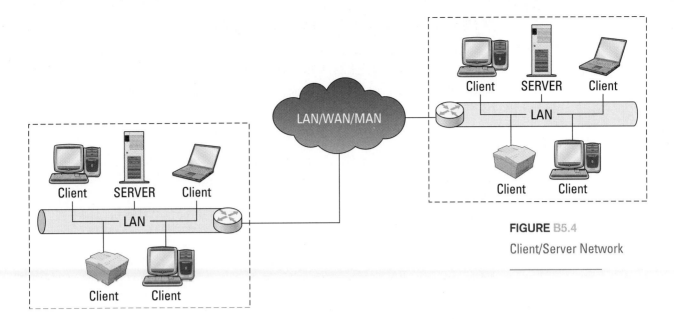

FIGURE B5.4

Client/Server Network

the network. Chen's router, the Network VirusWall, sits on the edge of a corporate network, scanning data packets and detaining those that might contain viruses or worms. Any suspicious packets are compared with up-to-the-second information from Trend Micro's virus-tracking command center. Viruses and worms are then deleted and refused entry to the network, allowing the company to perform a pre-emptive strike.[3]

Topology

Networks are assembled according to certain rules. Cables, for example, have to be a certain length; each cable strand can support only a certain amount of network traffic. A **network topology** refers to the geometric arrangement of the actual physical organization of the computers (and other network devices) in a network. Topologies vary depending on cost and functionality. Figure B5.6 highlights the five common topologies used in networks, and Figure B5.7 displays each topology.[4]

Protocols

A **protocol** is a standard that specifies the format of data as well as the rules to be followed during transmission. Simply put, for one computer (or computer program) to talk to another computer (or computer program) they must both be talking the same language, and this language is called a protocol.

A protocol is based on an agreed-upon and established standard, and this way all manufacturers of hardware and software that are using the protocol do so in a similar fashion to allow for interoperability. **Interoperability** is the capability of two or more computer systems to share data and resources, even though they are made by different manufacturers. The most popular network protocols used are Ethernet and Transmission Control Protocol/Internet Protocol (TCP/IP).

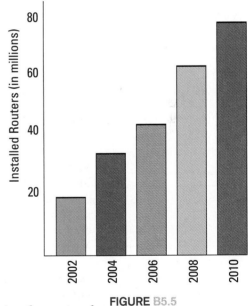

FIGURE B5.5

Worldwide Router Growth

ETHERNET

Ethernet is a physical and data layer technology for LAN networking (see Figure B5.8). Ethernet is the most widely installed LAN access method, originally developed by Xerox and then developed further by Xerox, Digital Equipment Corporation, and

Network Topologies	
Bus	All devices are connected to a central cable, called the bus or backbone. Bus networks are relatively inexpensive and easy to install for small networks.
Star	All devices are connected to a central device, called a hub. Star networks are relatively easy to install and manage, but bottlenecks can occur because all data must pass through the hub.
Ring	All devices are connected to one another in the shape of a closed loop, so that each device is connected directly to two other devices, one on either side of it. Ring topologies are relatively expensive and difficult to install, but they offer high bandwidth and can span large distances.
Hybrid	Groups of star-configured workstations are connected to a linear bus backbone cable, combining the characteristics of the bus and star topologies.
Wireless	Devices are connected by a receiver/transmitter to a special network interface card that transmits signals between a computer and a server, all within an acceptable transmission range.

Intel. When it first began to be widely deployed in the 1980s, Ethernet supported a maximum theoretical data transfer rate of 10 megabits per second (Mbps). More recently, Fast Ethernet has extended traditional Ethernet technology to 100 Mbps peak, and Gigabit Ethernet technology extends performance up to 1,000 Mbps.[5]

Ethernet has survived as the major LAN technology—it is currently used for approximately 85 percent of the world's LAN-connected PCs and workstations—because its protocol has the following characteristics:

- Is easy to understand, implement, manage, and maintain.
- Allows low-cost network implementations.

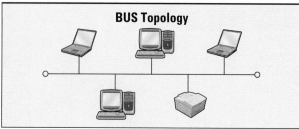

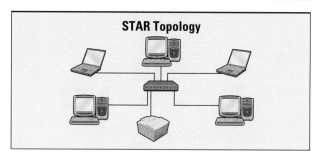

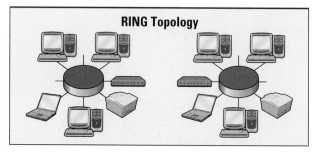

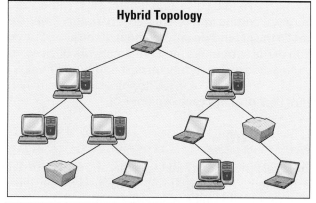

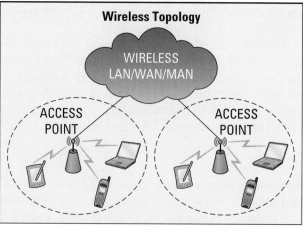

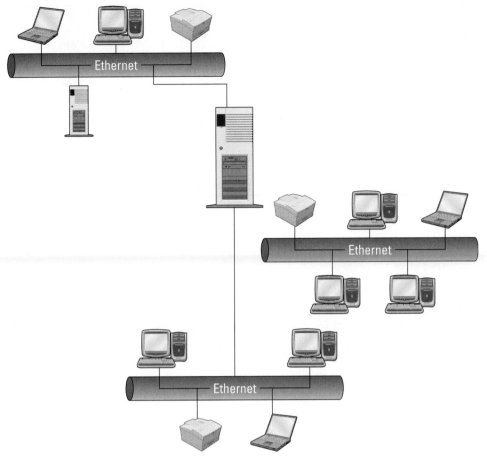

- Provides extensive flexibility for network installation.
- Guarantees successful interconnection and operation of standards-compliant products, regardless of manufacturer.[6]

TRANSMISSION CONTROL PROTOCOL/INTERNET PROTOCOL

The most common telecommunication protocol is Transmission Control Protocol/ Internet Protocol (TCP/IP), which was originally developed by the Department of Defense to connect a system of computer networks that became known as the Internet. *Transmission Control Protocol/Internet Protocol (TCP/IP)* provides the technical foundation for the public Internet as well as for large numbers of private networks. The key achievement of TCP/IP is its flexibility with respect to lower-level protocols. TCP/IP uses a special transmission method that maximizes data transfer and automatically adjusts to slower devices and other delays encountered on a network. Although more than 100 protocols make up the entire TCP/IP protocol suite, the two most important of these are TCP and IP. **TCP** provides transport functions, ensuring, among other things, that the amount of data received is the same as the amount transmitted. **IP** provides the addressing and routing mechanism that acts as a postmaster. Figure B5.9 displays TCP/IP's four-layer reference model:

- Application layer—serves as the window for users and application processes to access network services.
- Transport layer—handles end-to-end packet transportation.
- Internet layer—formats the data into packets, adds a header containing the packet sequence and the address of the receiving device, and specifies the services required from the network.
- Network interface layer—places data packets on the network for transmission.[7]

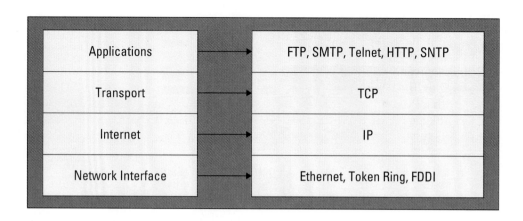

Applications	FTP, SMTP, Telnet, HTTP, SNTP
Transport	TCP
Internet	IP
Network Interface	Ethernet, Token Ring, FDDI

FIGURE B5.10

TCP/IP Applications

TCP/IP Applications	
File Transfer Protocol (FTP)	Allows files containing text, programs, graphics, numerical data, and so on to be downloaded off or uploaded onto a network.
Simple Mail Transfer Protocol (SMTP)	TCP/IP's own messaging system for e-mail.
Telnet Protocol	Provides terminal emulation that allows a personal computer or workstation to act as a terminal, or access device, for a server.
Hypertext Transfer Protocol (HTTP)	Allows Web browsers and servers to send and receive Web pages.
Simple Network Management Protocol (SNMP)	Allows the management of networked nodes to be managed from a single point.

The TCP/IP suite of applications includes five protocols—file transfer, simple mail transfer, telnet, hypertext transfer, and simple network management (see Figure B5.10).

Another communication reference model is the seven-layer Open System Interconnection (OSI) reference model. Figure B5.11 show the OSI model's seven layers.[8]

The lower layers (1 to 3) represent local communications, while the upper layers (4 to 7) represent end-to-end communications. Each layer contributes protocol functions that are necessary to establish and maintain the error-free exchange of information between network users.

FIGURE B5.11

Open System
Interconnection Model

For many years, users thought the OSI model would replace TCP/IP as the preferred technique for connecting multivendor networks. But the slow pace of OSI standards as well as the expense of implementing complex OSI software and having products certified for OSI interoperability will preclude this from happening.

OSI Model
7. Application
6. Presentation
5. Session
4. Transport
3. Network
2. Data Link
1. Physical

Voice over IP (VoIP)

Originally, phone calls made over the Internet had a reputation of offering poor call quality, lame user interfaces, and low call-completion rates. With new and improved technology and IT infrastructures, Internet phone calls now offer similar quality to traditional telephone calls. Today, many consumers are making phone calls over the Internet by using voice over Internet protocol (VoIP). **_Voice over IP (VoIP)_** uses TCP/IP technology to transmit voice calls over long-distance telephone lines. In fact, VoIP transmits over 10 percent of all phone calls and this number is growing exponentially.

VoIP and e-mail work in similar ways. The user sends a call over the Internet in packets of audio data tagged with the same destination. VoIP reassembles the packets once they arrive at their final destination.

Numerous vendors offer VoIP services; however, the service works differently depending on the vendor's IT infrastructure. Skype pairs P2P (peer-to-peer) technology with a PC's sound card to create a voice service, which the user can use to call other Skype users. Unfortunately, the user can talk only to other Skype users. Vonage lets the user place calls to any person who has a mobile or landline (regular telephone) number. Vonage sends the call over a cable via a digital-to-analog converter. A few providers even offer an adapter for a traditional handset that plugs into a broadband modem. All of these vendors are providing VoIP, but the service and its features can vary significantly.[9]

The telecom industry expects great benefits from combining VoIP with emerging standards that allow for easier development, interoperability among systems, and application integration. This is a big change for an industry that relies on proprietary systems to keep customers paying for upgrades and new features. The VoIP and open-standards combo should produce more choices, lower prices, and new applications.

Writing voice applications may never be as common as writing computer applications. But the spread of VoIP will make it easier to manage applications and add capabilities to the voice feature set. In a decade, the telecom network "will be like getting water out of the tap," predicts Stef van Aarle, vice president of marketing and strategy at Lucent Worldwide Services. "The only time you think of it will be when it doesn't work. And software is the glue that makes it all easy to use."

Upstarts like Vonage and Skype are bringing VoIP to the masses. But a bigger opportunity lurks in the $2 billion corporate phone market. New York-based start-up Popular Telephony is offering a new VoIP technology that dramatically cuts corporate phone costs while letting workers take their office phones anywhere. Its secret: peer-to-peer software called Peerio that is built right into handsets.

CEO Dmitry Goroshevsky founded the company to bring PC economics to the office telephone system. A traditional workplace setup requires a dedicated voice network and a private branch exchange, or PBX, to connect to the outside world and can cost up to $1 million (see Figure B5.12). Cisco has been selling an IP PBX, which uses a data network for voice calls. But Popular Telephony eliminates pricey hardware. Using an ordinary PC, network administrators assign an extension to each phone. Peerio-enabled handsets, which will be sold through discount retailers and office supply stores, plug directly into a company's data network, where calls are routed through a gateway and then out. Since Peerio is based on Internet protocol, office workers can use their phones wherever there is a broadband connection. And though companies pay the usual rates to call conventional landline and mobile phone numbers, ringing up other Peerio and VoIP users will not cost a dime. A handful of licensees are manufacturing the phones.[10]

Telephone System	Typical Telecom System	IP-Based System	Peerio
Requirements	■ Phones ■ Private branch exchange (PBX) ■ Voice switches network ■ Dedicated voice network	■ Phones ■ IP PBX ■ Existing data network ■ Gateway	■ Phones ■ PC ■ Existing data ■ Gateway
Total Cost	$1,000,000	$500,000	$100,000

FIGURE B5.12

Typical Telephone Start-up Costs for a 1,000-Person Office

Media

Network transmission media refers to the various types of media used to carry the signal between computers. When information is sent across the network, it is converted into electrical signals. These signals are generated as electromagnetic waves (analog signaling) or as a sequence of voltage pulses (digital signaling). To be sent from one location to another, a signal must travel along a physical path. The physical path that is used to carry a signal between a signal transmitter and a signal receiver is called the transmission media. The two types of transmission media are wire (guided) and wireless (unguided).

WIRE MEDIA

Wire media are transmission material manufactured so that signals will be confined to a narrow path and will behave predictably. The three most commonly used types of guided media are (see Figure B5.13):

- Twisted-pair wiring
- Coaxial cable
- Fiber-optic cable

Twisted-Pair Wiring

Twisted-pair wiring refers to a type of cable composed of four (or more) copper wires twisted around each other within a plastic sheath. The wires are twisted to reduce outside electrical interference. Twisted-pair cables come in shielded and unshielded varieties. Shielded cables have a metal shield encasing the wires that acts as a ground for electromagnetic interference. Unshielded twisted-pair (UTP) is the most popular and is generally the best option for LAN networks. The quality of UTP may vary from telephone-grade wire to high-speed cable. The cable has four pairs of wires inside the jacket. Each pair is twisted with a different number of twists per inch to help eliminate interference from adjacent pairs and other electrical devices. The RJ-45 connectors on twisted-pair cables resemble large telephone connectors.[11]

Coaxial Cable

Coaxial cable is cable that can carry a wide range of frequencies with low signal loss. It consists of a metallic shield with a single wire placed along the center of a shield and isolated from the shield by an insulator. This type of cable is referred to as coaxial because it contains one copper wire (or physical data channel) that carries the signal and is surrounded by another concentric physical channel consisting of a

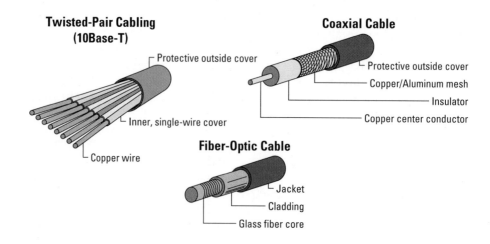

wire mesh. The outer channel serves as a ground for electrical interference. Because of this grounding feature, several coaxial cables can be placed within a single conduit or sheath without significant loss of data integrity.

Fiber-Optic Cable

Fiber optic (or **optical fiber**) refers to the technology associated with the transmission of information as light impulses along a glass wire or fiber. The 10Base-FL and 100Base-FX optical fiber cable are the same types of cable used by most telephone companies for long-distance service. Optical fiber cable can transmit data over long distances with little loss in data integrity. In addition, because data are transferred as a pulse of light, optical fiber is not subject to interference. The light pulses travel through a glass wire or fiber encased in an insulating sheath.

Optical fiber's increased maximum effective distance comes at a price. Optical fiber is more fragile than wire, difficult to split, and labor intensive to install. For these reasons, optical fiber is used primarily to transmit data over extended distances where the hardware required to relay the data signal on less expensive media would exceed the cost of optical fiber installation. It is also used where large amounts of data need to be transmitted on a regular basis.[12]

WIRELESS MEDIA

Wireless media are natural parts of the Earth's environment that can be used as physical paths to carry electrical signals. The atmosphere and outer space are examples of wireless media that are commonly used to carry signals. These media can carry such electromagnetic signals as microwave, infrared light waves, and radio waves.

Network signals are transmitted through all media as a type of waveform. When transmitted through wire and cable, the signal is an electrical waveform. When transmitted through fiber-optic cable, the signal is a light wave, either visible or infrared light. When transmitted through the Earth's atmosphere, the signal can take the form of waves in the radio spectrum, including microwaves, infrared, or visible light.

Recent advances in radio hardware technology have produced significant advancements in wireless networking devices: the cellular telephone, wireless modems, and wireless LANs. These devices use technology that in some cases has been around for decades but until recently was too impractical or expensive for widespread use.[13]

E-Business Networks

To set up an e-business even a decade ago would have required an individual organization to assume the burden of developing the entire network infrastructure. Today, industry-leading companies have developed Internet-based products and services to handle many aspects of customer and supplier interactions.

"In today's retail market, you cannot be a credible national retailer without having a robust Web site," says Dennis Bowman, senior vice president and CIO of Circuit City, who adds that customers now expect seamless retailing just as they expect stores that are clean and well stocked. For this reason, retailers are working furiously to integrate their e-business sites with their inventory and point-of-sale (POS) systems so that they can accept in-store returns of merchandise bought online and allow customers to buy on the Web and pick up in the store.[14]

Some companies, such as Best Buy, Circuit City, Office Depot, and Sears, already have their physical and online stores integrated. These companies have been the fast movers because they already had an area in their stores for merchandise pickup (usually for big, bulky items like TVs and appliances), and because long before the

E-Business Network Characteristics
■ Provide for the transparent exchange of information with suppliers, trading partners, and customers.
■ Reliably and securely exchange information internally and externally via the Internet or other networks.
■ Allow end-to-end integration and provide message delivery across multiple systems, in particular, databases, clients, and servers.
■ Respond to high demands with scalable processing power and networking capacity.
■ Serve as the integrator and transaction framework for both digital businesses and traditional brick-and-mortar businesses that want to leverage the Internet for any type of business.

Web they had systems and processes in place that facilitated the transfer of a sale from one store to another. Other retailers are partially integrated. Ann Taylor, Bed Bath & Beyond, Eddie Bauer, Linens 'n' Things, Macy's, REI, Target, The Gap, and others let customers return but not pick up online-ordered merchandise in stores. To take on the challenge of e-business integration, an organization needs a secure and reliable IT infrastructure for mission-critical systems (see Figure B5.14).[15]

A *virtual private network (VPN)* is a way to use the public telecommunication infrastructure (e.g., Internet) to provide secure access to an organization's network (see Figure B5.15). A *valued-added network (VAN)* is a private network, provided by a third party, for exchanging information through a high capacity connection. To date, organizations engaging in e-business have relied largely on VPNs, VANs, and other dedicated links handling electronic data interchange transactions. These traditional solutions are still deployed in the market and for many companies will likely hold a strategic role for years to come. However, conventional technologies present significant challenges:

■ By handling only limited kinds of business information, these contribute little to a reporting structure intended to provide a comprehensive view of business operations.

■ They offer little support for the real-time business process integration that will be essential in the digital marketplace.

■ Relatively expensive and complex to implement, conventional technologies make it difficult to expand or change networks in response to market shifts.[16]

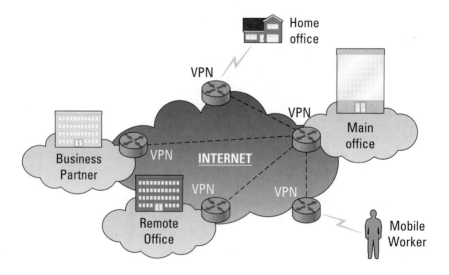

Networks come in all sizes, from two computers connected to share a printer, to the Internet, which is the largest network of all, joining millions of computers of all types all over the world. In between are business networks, which vary in size from a dozen or fewer computers to many thousands. There are three primary types of networks: local area network (LAN), wide area network (WAN), and metropolitan area network (MAN). The following differentiate networks:

- Architecture—peer-to-peer, client/server.
- Topology—bus, star, ring, hybrid, wireless.
- Protocols—Ethernet, Transmission Control Protocol/Internet Protocol (TCP/IP).
- Media—coaxial, twisted-pair, fiber-optic.

Client, 356
Client/server network, 356
Coaxial cable, 362
Ethernet, 357
Fiber optic (or optical fiber), 363
Interoperability, 357
Local area network (LAN), 355
Metropolitan area network (MAN), 355
Network, 354
Network operating system (NOS), 356

Network topology, 357
Network transmission media, 362
Packet-switching, 356
Peer-to-peer (P2P) network, 356
Protocol, 357
Router, 356
Server, 356
Telecommunication system, 354
Transmission Control Protocol/

Internet Protocol (TCP/IP), 359
Twisted-pair wiring, 362
Valued-added network (VAN), 364
Virtual private network (VPN), 364
Voice over Internet Protocol (VoIP), 360
Wide area network (WAN), 355
Wire media, 362
Wireless media, 363

Watching Where You Step—Prada

Prada estimates its sales per year at $22 million. The luxury retailer recently spent millions on IT for its futuristic "epicenter" store—but the flashy technology turned into a high-priced hassle. The company needed to generate annual sales of $75 million by 2007 to turn a profit on its new high-tech investment.

When Prada opened its $40 million Manhattan flagship, hotshot architect Rem Koolhaas promised a radically new shopping experience. And he kept the promise—though not quite according to plan. Customers were soon enduring hordes of tourists, neglected technology, and the occasional thrill of getting stuck in experimental dressing rooms. A few of the problems associated with the store:

1. **Fickle fitting rooms**—Doors that turn from clear to opaque confuse shoppers and frequently fail to open on cue.
2. **Failed RFID**—Touch screens meant to spring to life when items are placed in the RFID "closets" are often just blank.
3. **Pointless PDAs**—Salesclerks let the handheld devices gather dust and instead check the stockroom for inventory.
4. **Neglected network**—A lag between sales and inventory systems makes the wireless network nearly irrelevant.

This was not exactly the vision for the high-end boutique when it debuted in December 2001. Instead, the 22,000-square-foot SoHo shop was to be the first of four "epicenter" stores around the world that would combine cutting-edge architecture and 21st century technology to revolutionize the luxury shopping experience. Prada poured roughly 25 percent of the store's budget into IT, including a wireless network to link every item to an Oracle inventory database in real-time using radio frequency identification (RFID) tags on the clothes. The staff would roam the floor armed with PDAs to check whether items were in stock, and customers could do the same through touch screens in the dressing rooms.

But most of the flashy technology today sits idle, abandoned by employees who never quite embraced computing chic and are now too overwhelmed by large crowds to assist shoppers with handhelds. On top of that, many gadgets, such as automated dressing-room doors and touch screens, are either malfunctioning or ignored. Packed with experimental technology, the clear-glass dressing-room doors were designed to open and close automatically at the tap of a foot pedal, then turn opaque when a second pedal sent an electric current through the glass. Inside, an RFID-aware rack would recognize a customer's selections and display them on a touch screen linked to the inventory system.

In practice, the process was hardly that smooth. Many shoppers never quite understood the pedals and disrobed in full view, thinking the door had turned opaque. That is no longer a problem, since staff members usually leave the glass opaque, but often the doors get stuck. Some of the chambers are open only to VIP customers during peak traffic times.

With the smart closets and handhelds out of commission, the wireless network in the store is nearly irrelevant, despite its considerable expense. As Prada's debt reportedly climbed to around $1 billion in late 2001, the company shelved plans for the fourth epicenter store, in San Francisco. A second store opened in Tokyo to great acclaim, albeit with different architects in a different market. Though that store incorporates similar cutting-edge concepts, architect Jacques Herzog emphasized that avant-garde retail plays well only in Japan. "This building is clearly a building for Tokyo," he told *The New York Times.* "It couldn't be somewhere else."

The multimillion-dollar technology is starting to look more like technology for technology's sake than an enhancement of the shopping experience, and the store's failings have prompted Prada to reevaluate its epicenter strategy.[17]

Questions

1. Explain how Prada was anticipating using its wireless network to help its stores operate more efficiently. What prevented the system from working correctly?
2. What could Prada have done to help its employees embrace the wireless network?
3. Would Prada have experienced the same issues if it had used a wire (guided) network instead of a wireless (unguided) network?
4. What security issues would Prada need to be aware of concerning its wireless network?
5. What should Prada do differently when designing its fourth store to ensure its success?

✳ CLOSING CASE TWO

Banks Banking on Network Security

Bank of America, Commerce Bancorp, PNC Financial Services Group, and Wachovia were victims of a crime involving a person trying to obtain customer data and sell it to law firms and debt-collection agencies. New Jersey police seized 13 computers from the alleged mastermind with 670,000 account numbers and balances. There is no indication the data were used for identity theft, but it highlights how increasingly difficult it is to protect information against such schemes as the market value of personal information grows. In the past, banks were wary of the cost or customer backlash from adopting network security technologies. Today, banks are beefing up network security as more customers begin to view security as a key factor when choosing a bank.

Bank of America

Bank of America is moving toward a stronger authentication process for its 13 million online customers. Bank of America's new SiteKey service is designed to thwart scams in which customers think they are entering data on the bank's Web site, when they are actually on a thief's site built to steal data. This occurs when a worm tells a computer to reroute the bank's URL into a browser to another site that looks exactly like the bank's.

SiteKey offers two-factor authentication. When enrolling in SiteKey, a customer picks an image from a library and writes a brief phrase. Each time the customer signs on, the image and phrase are displayed, indicating that the bank recognizes the computer the customer is using and letting the customer know that he or she is at the bank's official Web site. The customer then enters a password and proceeds. When signing on from a different computer than usual, the customer must answer one of three prearranged questions.

Wells Fargo & Company

"Out-of-wallet" questions contain information that is not found on a driver's license or ATM card. Wells Fargo is implementing a security strategy that operates based on "out-of-wallet" questions as a second factor for network password enrollment and maintenance. It is also offering network security hardware such as key fobs that change passwords every 60 seconds. Last fall, it launched a two-factor authentication pilot in which small businesses making electronic funds transfers need a key fob to complete transactions.

E-Trade Financial Corporation

E-Trade Financial Corporation provides customers holding account balances of more than $50,000 with a free Digital Security ID for network authentication. The device displays a new six-digit code every 60 seconds, which the customer must use to log on. Accounts under $50,000 can purchase the Digital Security ID device for $25.

Barclays Bank

Barclays Bank instituted online-transfer delays of between several hours and one day. The delays, which apply the first time a transfer is attempted between two accounts, are intended to give the bank time to detect suspicious activity, such as a large number of transfers from multiple accounts into a single account. The online-transfer delay was adopted in response to a wave of phishing incidents in which thieves transferred funds from victims' bank accounts into accounts owned by "mules." Mules are people who open bank accounts based on e-mail solicitations, usually under the guise of a business proposal. From the mule accounts, the thieves withdraw cash, open credit cards, or otherwise loot the account.

Barclays also offers account monitoring of customers' actions to compare them with historical profile data to detect unusual behavior. For instance, the service would alert the bank to contact the customer if the customer normally logs on from England and suddenly logs on from New York and performs 20 transactions.[18]

Questions

1. What reason would a bank have for not wanting to adopt an online-transfer delay policy?
2. Why is network security critical to financial institutions?

3. Explain the differences between the types of network security offered by the banks in the case. Which bank would you open an account with and why?

4. What additional types of network security, not mentioned in the case, would you recommend a bank implement?

5. Identity three policies a bank should implement to help it improve network information security.

✳ MAKING BUSINESS DECISIONS

1. Secure Access

Organizations that have traditionally maintained private, closed systems have begun to look at the potential of the Internet as a ready-made network resource. The Internet is inexpensive and globally pervasive: Every phone jack is a potential connection. However, the Internet lacks security. What obstacles must organizations overcome to allow secure network connections?

2. Rolling Out with Networks

As organizations begin to realize the benefits of adding a wireless component to their network, they must understand how to leverage this emerging technology. Wireless solutions have come to the forefront for many organizations with the rollout of more standard, cost-effective, and secure wireless protocols. With wireless networks, increased business agility may be realized by continuous data access and synchronization. However, with the increased flexibility comes many challenges. Develop a report detailing the benefits an organization could obtain by implementing wireless technology. Also, include the challenges that a wireless network presents along with recommendations for any solutions.

3. Wireless Fitness

Sandifer's Fitness Club is located in beautiful South Carolina. Rosie Sandifer has owned and operated the club for 20 years. The club has three outdoor pools, two indoor pools, 10 racquetball courts, 10 tennis courts, an indoor and outdoor track, along with a four-story exercise equipment and massage therapy building. Rosie has hired you as a summer intern specializing in information technology. The extent of Rosie's current technology includes a few PCs in the accounting department and two PCs with Internet access for the rest of the staff. Your first assignment is to create a report detailing networks and wireless technologies. The report should explain how the club could gain a business advantage by implementing a wireless network. If Rosie likes your report, she will hire you as the full-time employee in charge of information technology. Be sure to include all of the different uses for wireless devices the club could implement to improve its operations.

Information Security

1. Describe the relationship between information security policies and an information security plan.
2. Summarize the five steps to creating an information security plan.
3. Provide an example of each of the three primary security areas: (1) authentication and authorization, (2) prevention and resistance, and (3) detection and response.
4. Describe the relationships and differences between hackers and viruses.

Introduction

The core units introduced **information security,** which is a broad term encompassing the protection of information from accidental or intentional misuse by persons inside or outside an organization. With current advances in technologies and business strategies such as CRM, organizations are able to determine valuable information such as who are the top 20 percent of the customers that produce 80 percent of all revenues. Most organizations view this type of information as valuable intellectual capital, and they are implementing security measures to prevent the information from walking out the door or falling into the wrong hands. This plug-in discusses how an organization can implement information security lines of defense through people first and through technology second.

The First Line of Defense—People

Adding to the complexity of information security is the fact that organizations must enable employees, customers, and partners to access information electronically to be successful in this electronic world. Doing business electronically automatically creates tremendous information security risks for organizations. Surprisingly, the biggest issue surrounding information security is not a technical issue, but a people issue.

The CSI/FBI Computer Crime and Security Survey reported that 38 percent of respondents indicated security incidents originated within the enterprise. **Insiders** are legitimate users who purposely or accidentally misuse their access to the environment and cause some kind of business-affecting incident. Most information security breaches result from people misusing an organization's information either advertently or inadvertently. For example, many individuals freely give up their passwords or write them on sticky notes next to their computers, leaving the door wide open to intruders.[1]

The director of information security at a large health care company discovered how easy it was to create an information security breach when she hired outside auditors to test her company's security awareness. In one instance, auditors found that staff members testing a new system had accidentally exposed the network to outside hackers. In another, auditors were able to obtain the passwords of 16 employees when the auditors posed as support staff; hackers frequently use such "social engineering" to obtain passwords. **Social engineering** is using one's social skills to trick people into revealing access credentials or other information valuable to the attacker. Dumpster diving, or looking through people's trash, is another way social engineering hackers obtain information.[2]

Information security policies identify the rules required to maintain information security. An **information security plan** details how an organization will implement the information security policies. Figure B6.1 is an example of the University of Denver's Information Security Plan.

FIGURE B6.1

Sample Information
Security Plan

Interim Information Security Plan

This Information Security Plan ("Plan") describes the University of Denver's safeguards to protect information and data in compliance ("Protected Information") with the Financial Services Modernization Act of 1999, also known as the Gramm Leach Bliley Act, 15 U.S.C. Section 6801. These safeguards are provided to:

- Ensure the security and confidentiality of Protected Information;
- Protect against anticipated threats or hazards to the security or integrity of such information; and
- Protect against unauthorized access to or use of Protected Information that could result in substantial harm or inconvenience to any customer.

This Information Security Plan also provides for mechanisms to:

- Identify and assess the risks that may threaten Protected Information maintained by the University of Denver;
- Develop written policies and procedures to manage and control these risks;
- Implement and review the plan; and
- Adjust the plan to reflect changes in technology, the sensitivity of covered data and information and internal or external threats to information security.

Identification and Assessment of Risks to Customer Information

The University of Denver recognizes that it has both internal and external risks. These risks include, but are not limited to:

- Unauthorized access of Protected Information by someone other than the owner of the covered data and information
- Compromised system security as a result of system access by an unauthorized person
- Interception of data during transmission
- Loss of data integrity
- Physical loss of data in a disaster
- Errors introduced into the system
- Corruption of data or systems
- Unauthorized access of covered data and information by employees
- Unauthorized requests for covered data and information
- Unauthorized access through hardcopy files or reports
- Unauthorized transfer of covered data and information through third parties

The University of Denver recognizes that this may not be a complete list of the risks associated with the protection of Protected Information. Since technology growth is not static, new risks are created regularly. Accordingly, the Information Technology Department and the Office of Student Affairs will actively participate with and seek advice from an advisory committee made up of university representatives for identification of new risks. The University of Denver believes current safeguards used by the Information Technology Department are reasonable and, in light of current risk assessments, are sufficient to provide security and confidentiality to Protected Information maintained by the University.

(Continued)

Interim Information Security Plan

Information Security Plan Coordinators

The University CIO and the Vice President for Student Affairs, in consultation with an advisory committee, have been appointed as the coordinators of this Plan. They are responsible for assessing the risks associated with unauthorized transfers of covered data and information and implementing procedures to minimize those risks to the University of Denver.

Design and Implementation of Safeguards Program

Employee Management and Training

During employee orientation, each new employee in departments that handle Protected Information will receive proper training on the importance of confidentiality of Protected Information.

Physical Security

The University of Denver has addressed the physical security of Protected Information by limiting access to only those employees who have a business reason to know such information.

Information Systems

The University of Denver has policies governing the use of electronic resources and firewall and wireless policies. The University of Denver will take reasonable and appropriate steps consistent with current technological developments to make sure that all Protected Information is secure and to safeguard the integrity of records in storage and transmission. The University of Denver will develop a plan to ensure that all electronic Protected Information is encrypted in transit.

Selection of Appropriate Service Providers

Due to the specialized expertise needed to design, implement, and service new technologies, vendors may be needed to provide resources that the University of Denver determines not to provide on its own. In the process of choosing a service provider that will maintain or regularly access Protected Information, the evaluation process shall include the ability of the service provider to safeguard Protected Information. Contracts with service providers may include the following provisions:

- A stipulation that the Protected Information will be held in strict confidence and accessed only for the explicit business purpose of the contract;
- An assurance from the contract partner that the partner will protect the Protected Information it receives.

Continuing Evaluation and Adjustment

This Information Security Plan will be subject to periodic review and adjustment, especially when due to the constantly changing technology and evolving risks. The Coordinators, in consultation with the Office of General Counsel, will review the standards set forth in this policy and recommend updates and revisions as necessary. It may be necessary to adjust the plan to reflect changes in technology, the sensitivity of student/customer data and internal or external threats to information security.

FIGURE B6.1
(Continued)

The first line of defense an organization should follow is to create an information security plan detailing the various information security policies. A detailed information security plan can alleviate people-based information security issues. Figure B6.2 displays the five steps for creating an information security plan. Figure B6.3 provides the top 10 questions from Ernst & Young that managers should ask to ensure their information is secure.

The Second Line of Defense—Technology

Arkansas State University (ASU) recently completed a major network upgrade that brought gigabit-speed network capacity to every dorm room and office on its campus. The university was concerned that the new network would be a tempting playground for hackers. To reduce its fear the university decided to install intrusion detection software (IDS) from Cisco Systems to stay on top of security and potential network abuses. Whenever the IDS spots a potential security threat, such as a virus or a hacker, it alerts the central management system. The system automatically pages the IT staff, who deal with the attack by shutting off access to the system, identifying the hacker's location, and calling campus security.[3]

Five Steps for Creating an Information Security Plan	
1. **Develop the information security policies**	Identify who is responsible and accountable for designing and implementing the organization's information security policies. Simple, yet highly effective types of information security policies include requiring users to log off of their systems before leaving for lunches or meetings, never sharing passwords with anyone, and changing personal passwords every 60 days. The chief security officer (CSO) will typically be responsible for designing these information security policies.
2. **Communicate the information security policies**	Train all employees on the policies and establish clear expectations for following the policies. For example, let all employees know that they will receive a formal reprimand for leaving a computer unsecured.
3. **Identify critical information assets and risks**	Require the use of user IDs, passwords, and antivirus software on all systems. Ensure any systems that contain links to external networks have the appropriate technical protections such as firewalls or intrusion detection software. A *firewall* is hardware and/or software that guards a private network by analyzing the information leaving and entering the network. *Intrusion detection software (IDS)* searches out patterns in information and network traffic to indicate attacks and quickly responds to prevent any harm.
4. **Test and reevaluate risks**	Continually perform security reviews, audits, background checks, and security assessments.
5. **Obtain stakeholder support**	Gain the approval and support of the information security polices from the board of directors and all stakeholders.

Once an organization has protected its intellectual capital by arming its people with a detailed information security plan, it can begin to focus its efforts on deploying the right types of information security technologies such as the IDS installed at Arkansas State.

Organizations can deploy numerous technologies to prevent information security breaches. When determining which types of technologies to invest in, it helps to understand the three primary information security areas:

1. Authentication and authorization.
2. Prevention and resistance.
3. Detection and response.[4]

FIGURE B6.2

Creating an Information Security Plan

Top 10 Questions Managers Should Ask Regarding Information Security
1. Does the board of directors recognize information security is a board-level issue that cannot be left to the IT department alone?
2. Is there clear accountability for information security in the organization?
3. Do the board members articulate an agreed-upon set of threats and critical assets? How often do they review and update these?
4. How much is spent on information security and what is it being spent on?
5. What is the impact on the organization of a serious security incident?
6. Does the organization view information security as an enabler? (For example, by implementing effective security, could the organization increase business over the Internet?)
7. What is the risk to the business of getting a reputation for low information security?
8. What steps have been taken to ensure that third parties will not compromise the security of the organization?
9. How does the organization obtain independent assurance that information security is managed effectively?
10. How does the organization measure the effectiveness of its information security activities?

FIGURE B6.3

Top 10 Questions Managers Should Ask Regarding Information Security

AUTHENTICATION AND AUTHORIZATION

Authentication is a method for confirming users' identities. Once a system determines the authentication of a user, it can then determine the access privileges (or authorization) for that user. *Authorization* is the process of giving someone permission to do or have something. In multiple-user computer systems, user access or authorization determines such things as file access, hours of access, and amount of allocated storage space. Authentication and authorization techniques are broken down into three categories, and the most secure type involves a combination of all three:

1. Something the user knows such as a user ID and password.

2. Something the user has such as a smart card or token.

3. Something that is part of the user such as a fingerprint or voice signature.

Something the User Knows such as a User ID and Password

The first type of authentication, using something the user knows, is the most common way to identify individual users and typically consists of a unique user ID and password. However, this is actually one of the most *ineffective* ways for determining authentication because passwords are not secure. All it typically takes to crack a password is enough time. More than 50 percent of help-desk calls are password related, which can cost an organization significant money, and passwords are vulnerable to being coaxed out of somebody by a social engineer.

Identity theft is the forging of someone's identity for the purpose of fraud. The fraud is often financial fraud, to apply for and use credit cards in the victim's name or to apply for a loan. Figure B6.4 displays several examples of identity theft.

Phishing is a common way to steal identities online. *Phishing* is a technique to gain personal information for the purpose of identity theft, usually by means of fraudulent e-mail. One way to accomplish phishing is to send out e-mail messages that look as though they came from legitimate businesses such as AOL, MSN, or Amazon. The messages appear to be genuine with official-looking formats and logos. These e-mails typically ask for verification of important information like passwords and account numbers. The reason given is often that this personal

FIGURE B6.4

Examples of Identity Theft

Identity Theft Examples
An 82-year-old woman in Fort Worth, Texas, discovered that her identity had been stolen when the woman using her name was involved in a four-car collision. For 18 months, she kept getting notices of lawsuits and overdue medical bills that were really meant for someone else. It took seven years for her to get her financial good name restored after the identity thief charged over $100,000 on her 12 fraudulently acquired credit cards.
A 42-year-old retired Army captain in Rocky Hill, Connecticut, found that an identity thief had spent $260,000 buying goods and services that included two trucks, a Harley-Davidson motorcycle, and a time-share vacation home in South Carolina. The victim discovered his problem only when his retirement pay was garnished to pay the outstanding bills.
In New York, members of a pickpocket ring forged the driver's licenses of their victims within hours of snatching the women's purses. Stealing a purse typically results in around $200, if not less. But stealing the person's identity can net on average between $4,000 and $10,000.
A crime gang took out $8 million worth of second mortgages on victims' homes. It turned out the source of all the instances of identity theft came from a car dealership.
The largest identity-theft scam to date in U.S. history was broken up by police in 2002 when they discovered that three men had downloaded credit reports using stolen passwords and sold them to criminals on the street for $60 each. Many millions of dollars were stolen from people in all 50 states.

information is required for accounting or auditing purposes. Since the e-mails look authentic, up to one in five recipients respond with the information, and subsequently become victim of identity theft and other fraud. [5]

Something the User Has such as a Smart Card or Token

The second type of authentication, using something that the user has, offers a much more effective way to identify individuals than a user ID and password. Tokens and smart cards are two of the primary forms of this type of authentication. **Tokens** are small electronic devices that change user passwords automatically. The user enters his/her user ID and token displayed password to gain access to the network. A **smart card** is a device that is around the same size as a credit card, containing embedded technologies that can store information and small amounts of software to perform some limited processing. Smart cards can act as identification instruments, a form of digital cash, or a data storage device with the ability to store an entire medical record.

Something That Is Part of the User such as a Fingerprint or Voice Signature

The third kind of authentication, using something that is part of the user, is by far the best and most effective way to manage authentication. **Biometrics** (narrowly defined) is the identification of a user based on a physical characteristic, such as a fingerprint, iris, face, voice, or handwriting. Unfortunately, biometric authentication can be costly and intrusive. For example, iris scans are expensive and considered intrusive by most people. Fingerprint authentication is less intrusive and inexpensive but is also not 100 percent accurate.

PREVENTION AND RESISTANCE

Prevention and resistance technologies stop intruders from accessing intellectual capital. A division of Sony Inc., Sony Pictures Entertainment (SPE), defends itself from attacks by using an intrusion detection system to detect new attacks as they occur. SPE develops and distributes a wide variety of products including movies, television, videos, and DVDs. A compromise to SPE security could result in costing the company valuable intellectual capital as well as millions of dollars and months of time. The company needed an advanced threat management solution that would take fewer resources to maintain and require limited resources to track and respond to suspicious network activity. The company installed an advanced intrusion detection system allowing it to monitor all of its network activity including any potential security breaches.[6]

The cost of downtime or network operation failures can be devastating to any business. For example, eBay experienced a 22-hour outage that caused the company's market cap to plunge an incredible $5.7 billion. Downtime costs for businesses can vary from $100 to $1 million per hour. An organization must prepare for and anticipate these types of outages resulting most commonly from hackers and viruses. Technologies available to help prevent and build resistance to attacks include (1) content filtering, (2) encryption, and (3) firewalls.[7]

Content Filtering

Content filtering occurs when organizations use software that filters content to prevent the transmission of unauthorized information. Organizations can use content filtering technologies to filter e-mail and prevent e-mails containing sensitive information from transmitting, whether the transmission was malicious or accidental. It can also filter e-mails and prevent any suspicious files from transmitting such as potential virus-infected files. E-mail content filtering can also filter for **spam,** a form of unsolicited e-mail. Organizational losses from spam were estimated to be about $198 billion in 2007 (see Figure B6.5).[8]

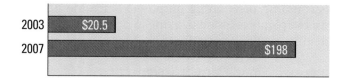

2003	$20.5
2007	$198

Encryption

Encryption scrambles information into an alternative form that requires a key or password to decrypt the information. If there is an information security breach and the information was encrypted, the person stealing the information will be unable to read it. Encryption can switch the order of characters, replace characters with other characters, insert or remove characters, or use a mathematical formula to convert the information into some sort of code. Companies that transmit sensitive customer information over the Internet, such as credit card numbers, frequently use encryption.

Some encryption technologies use multiple keys like public key encryption. *Public key encryption (PKE)* is an encryption system that uses two keys: a public key that everyone can have and a private key for only the recipient (see Figure B6.6). When implementing security using multiple keys, the organization provides the public key to all of its customers (end consumers and other businesses). The customers use the public key to encrypt their information and send it along the Internet. When it arrives at its destination, the organization would use the private key to unscramble the encrypted information.

Firewalls

One of the most common defenses for preventing a security breach is a firewall. A *firewall* is hardware and/or software that guards a private network by analyzing the information leaving and entering the network. Firewalls examine each message that wants entrance to the network. Unless the message has the correct markings, the firewall prevents it from entering the network. Firewalls can even detect computers communicating with the Internet without approval. As Figure B6.7 illustrates, organizations typically place a firewall between a server and the Internet.

DETECTION AND RESPONSE

The final area where organizations can allocate resources is in detection and response technologies. If prevention and resistance strategies fail and there is a

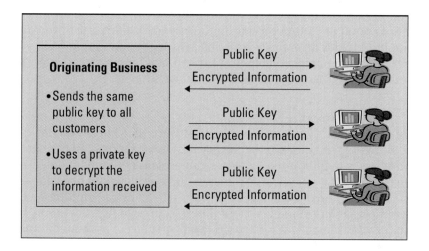

Originating Business

• Sends the same public key to all customers

• Uses a private key to decrypt the information received

Public Key
Encrypted Information

Public Key
Encrypted Information

Public Key
Encrypted Information

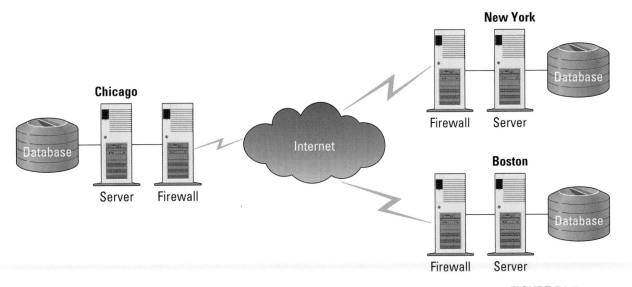

FIGURE B6.7

Sample Firewall
Architecture Connecting
Systems Located in
Chicago, New York, and
Boston

security breach, an organization can use detection and response technologies to mitigate the damage. The most common type of defense within detection and response technologies is antivirus software.

A single worm can cause massive damage. The "Blaster worm" infected over 50,000 computers worldwide. Jeffrey Lee Parson, 18, was arrested by U.S. cyber investigators for unleashing the damaging worm on the Internet. The worm replicated itself repeatedly, eating up computer capacity, but did not damage information or programs. The worm generated so much traffic that it brought entire networks down.

The FBI used the latest technologies and code analysis to find the source of the worm. Prosecutors said Microsoft suffered financial losses that significantly exceeded $5,000, the statutory threshold in most hacker cases. Parson, charged with intentionally causing or attempting to cause damage to a computer, was sentenced to 18 months in prison, three years of supervised release, and 100 hours of community service. "What you've done is a terrible thing. Aside from injuring people and their computers, you shook the foundation of technology," U.S. District Judge Marsha Pechman told Parson.

"With this arrest, we want to deliver a message to cyber-hackers here and around the world," said U.S. Attorney John McKay in Seattle. "Let there be no mistake about it, cyber-hacking is a crime. We will investigate, arrest, and prosecute cyber-hackers."[9]

Typically, people equate viruses (the malicious software) with hackers (the people). While not all types of hackers create viruses, many do. Figure B6.8 provides an overview of the most common types of hackers and viruses.

Some of the most damaging forms of security threats to e-business sites include malicious code, hoaxes, spoofing, and sniffers (see Figure B6.9).

Hackers—people very knowledgeable about computers who use their knowledge to invade other people's computers.
■ **White-hat hackers**—work at the request of the system owners to find system vulnerabilities and plug the holes.
■ **Black-hat hackers**—break into other people's computer systems and may just look around or may steal and destroy information.
■ **Hactivists**—have philosophical and political reasons for breaking into systems and will often deface the Web site as a protest.
■ **Script kiddies** or **script bunnies**—find hacking code on the Internet and click-and-point their way into systems to cause damage or spread viruses.
■ **Cracker**—a hacker with criminal intent.
■ **Cyberterrorists**—seek to cause harm to people or to destroy critical systems or information and use the Internet as a weapon of mass destruction.

Viruses—software written with malicious intent to cause annoyance or damage.
■ **Worm**—a type of virus that spreads itself, not only from file to file, but also from computer to computer. The primary difference between a virus and a worm is that a virus must attach to something, such as an executable file, in order to spread. Worms do not need to attach to anything to spread and can tunnel themselves into computers.
■ **Denial-of-service attack (DoS)**—floods a Web site with so many requests for service that it slows down or crashes the site.
■ **Distributed denial-of-service attack (DDoS)**—attacks from multiple computers that flood a Web site with so many requests for service that it slows down or crashes. A common type is the Ping of Death, in which thousands of computers try to access a Web site at the same time, overloading it and shutting it down.
■ **Trojan-horse virus**—hides inside other software, usually as an attachment or a downloadable file.
■ **Backdoor programs**—viruses that open a way into the network for future attacks.
■ **Polymorphic viruses and worms**—change their form as they propagate.

FIGURE B6.8

Hackers and Viruses

FIGURE B6.9

Security Threats to
E-Business

Security Threats to E-Business
Elevation of privilege is a process by which a user misleads a system into granting unauthorized rights, usually for the purpose of compromising or destroying the system. For example, an attacker might log on to a network by using a guest account, and then exploit a weakness in the software that lets the attacker change the guest privileges to administrative privileges.
Hoaxes attack computer systems by transmitting a virus hoax, with a real virus attached. By masking the attack in a seemingly legitimate message, unsuspecting users more readily distribute the message and send the attack on to their co-workers and friends, infecting many users along the way.
Malicious code includes a variety of threats such as viruses, worms, and Trojan horses.
Spoofing is the forging of the return address on an e-mail so that the e-mail message appears to come from someone other than the actual sender. This is not a virus but rather a way by which virus authors conceal their identities as they send out viruses.
Spyware is software that comes hidden in free downloadable software and tracks online movements, mines the information stored on a computer, or uses a computer's CPU and storage for some task the user knows nothing about. According to the National Cyber Security Alliance, 91 percent of the study had spyware on their computers that can cause extremely slow performance, excessive pop-up ads, or hijacked home pages.
A **sniffer** is a program or device that can monitor data traveling over a network. Sniffers can show all the data being transmitted over a network, including passwords and sensitive information. Sniffers tend to be a favorite weapon in the hacker's arsenal.
Packet tampering consists of altering the contents of packets as they travel over the Internet or altering data on computer disks after penetrating a network. For example, an attacker might place a tap on a network line to intercept packets as they leave the computer. The attacker could eavesdrop or alter the information as it leaves the network.

PLUG-IN SUMMARY

Implementing information security lines of defense through people first and through technology second is the best way for an organization to protect its vital intellectual capital. The first line of defense is securing intellectual capital by creating an information security plan detailing the various information security policies. The second line of defense is investing in technology to help secure information through authentication and authorization, prevention and resistance, and detection and response.

KEY TERMS

Authentication, 374
Authorization, 374
Backdoor program, 378
Biometrics, 375
Black-hat hacker, 378
Content filtering, 375
Cracker, 378
Cyberterrorist, 378
Denial-of-service attack
    (DoS), 378
Distributed denial-of-service
    attack (DDoS), 378
Encryption, 376
Elevation of privilege, 378
Firewall, 373, 376

Hacker, 378
Hactivist, 378
Hoaxes, 378
Identify theft, 374
Information security, 370
Information security plan, 371
Information security policy, 371
Insider, 370
Intrusion detection software
    (IDS), 373
Malicious code, 378
Packet tampering, 378
Phishing, 374
Polymorphic virus and
    worm, 378

Public key encryption
    (PKE), 376
Script kiddies or script
    bunnies, 378
Smart card, 375
Sniffer, 378
Social engineering, 371
Spam, 375
Spoofing, 378
Spyware, 378
Token, 375
Trojan-horse virus, 378
Virus, 378
White-hat hacker, 378
Worm, 378

CLOSING CASE ONE

Thinking Like the Enemy

David and Barry Kaufman, the founders of the Intense School, recently added several security courses, including the five-day "Professional Hacking Boot Camp" and "Social Engineering in Two Days."

Information technology departments must know how to protect organizational information. Therefore, organizations must teach their IT personnel how to protect their systems, especially in light of the many new government regulations, such as the Health Insurance Portability and Accountability Act (HIPAA), that demand secure systems. The concept of sending IT professionals to a hacking school seems counterintuitive; it is somewhat similar to sending accountants to an Embezzling 101 course. The Intense School does not strive to breed the next generation of hackers, however, but to teach its students how to be "ethical" hackers: to use their skills to build better locks, and to understand the minds of those who would attempt to crack them.

The main philosophy of the security courses at the Intense School is simply "To know thy enemy." In fact, one of the teachers at the Intense School is none other than Kevin Mitnick, the famous hacker who was imprisoned from 1995 to 2000. Teaching security from the hacker's perspective, as Mitnick does, is more difficult than teaching hacking itself: A hacker just needs to know one way into a system, David Kaufman notes, but a security professional needs to know *all* of the system's vulnerabilities. The two courses analyze those vulnerabilities from different perspectives.

The hacking course, which costs $3,500, teaches ways to protect against the mischief typically associated with hackers: worming through computer systems through vulnerabilities that are susceptible to technical, or computer-based, attacks. Mitnick's $1,950 social engineering course, by contrast, teaches the more frightening art of worming through the vulnerabilities of the people using and maintaining systems—getting passwords and access through duplicity, not technology. People that take this class, or read Mitnick's book, *The Art of Deception*, never again think of passwords or the trash bin the same way.

So how does the Intense School teach hacking? With sessions on dumpster diving (the unsavory practice of looking for passwords and other bits of information on discarded papers), with field trips to case target systems, and with practice runs at the company's in-house "target range," a network of computers set up to thwart and educate students.

One feature of the Intense School that raises a few questions is that the school does not check on morals at the door: Anyone paying the tuition can attend the school. Given the potential danger that an unchecked graduate of a hacking school could represent, it is surprising that the FBI does not collect the names of the graduates. But perhaps it gets them anyhow—several governmental agencies have sent students to the school.[10]

Questions

1. How could an organization benefit from attending one of the courses offered at the Intense School?

2. What are the two primary lines of security defense and how can organizational employees use the information taught by the Intense School when drafting an information security plan?

3. Determine the differences between the two primary courses offered at the Intense School, "Professional Hacking Boot Camp" and "Social Engineering in Two Days." Which course is more important for organizational employees to attend?

4. If your employer sent you to take a course at the Intense School, which one would you choose and why?

5. What are the ethical dilemmas involved with having such a course offered by a private company?

 CLOSING CASE TWO

Hacker Hunters

Hacker hunters are the new breed of crime-fighter. They employ the same methodology used to fight organized crime in the 1980s—informants and the cyberworld equivalent of wiretaps. Daniel Larking, a 20-year veteran who runs the FBI's Internet Crime Complaint Center, taps online service providers to help track down criminal hackers. Leads supplied by the FBI and eBay helped Romanian police round up 11 members of a gang that set up fake eBay accounts and auctioned off cell phones, laptops, and cameras they never intended to deliver.

On October 26, 2004, the FBI unleashed Operation Firewall, targeting the ShadowCrew, a gang whose members were schooled in identity theft, bank account pillage, and selling illegal goods on the Internet. ShadowCrew's 4,000 gang members lived in a dozen countries and across the United States. For months, agents had been watching their every move through a clandestine gateway into their Web site, shadowcrew.com. One member turned informant called a group meeting, ensuring the members would be at home on their computers during a certain time. At 9 p.m. the Secret Service issued orders to move in on the gang. The move was synchronized around the globe to prevent gang members from warning each other via instant messages. Twenty-eight gang members in eight states and six countries were arrested, most still at their computers. Authorities seized dozens of computers and found 1.7 million credit card numbers and more than 18 million e-mail accounts.

ShadowCrew's Operations

The alleged ringleaders of ShadowCrew included Andres Mantovani, 23, a part-time community college student in Arizona, and David Appleyard, 45, a former New Jersey mortgage broker. Mantovani and Appleyard allegedly were administrators in charge of running the Web site and recruiting members. The site created a marketplace for over 4,000 gang members who bought and sold hot information and merchandise. The Web site was open for business 24 hours a day, but since most of the members held jobs, the busiest time was from 10 p.m. to 2 a.m. on Sundays. Hundreds of gang members would meet online to trade credit card information, passports, and even equipment to make fake identity documents. Platinum credit cards cost more than gold ones and discounts were offered for package deals. One member known as "Scarface" sold 115,695 stolen credit card numbers in a single trade. Overall, the gang made more than $4 million in credit card purchases over two years. ShadowCrew was equivalent to an eBay for the underworld. The site even posted crime tips on how to use stolen credit cards and fake IDs at big retailers.

The gang stole credit card numbers and other valuable information through clever tricks. One of the favorites was sending millions of phishing e-mails—messages that appeared to be from legitimate companies such as Yahoo!— designed to steal passwords and credit card numbers. The gang also hacked into corporate databases to steal account data. According to sources familiar with the investigation, the gang cracked the networks of 12 unidentified companies that were not even aware their systems had been breached.

Police Operations

Brian Nagel, an assistant director at the Secret Service, coordinated the effort to track the ShadowCrew. Allies included Britain's National High-Tech Crimes unit, the Royal Canadian Mounted Police, and the Bulgarian Interior Ministry. Authorities turned one of the high-ranking members of the gang into a snitch and had the man help the Secret Service set up a new electronic doorway for ShadowCrew members to enter their Web site. The snitch spread the word that the new gateway was a more secure way to the Web site. It was the first-ever tap of a private computer network. "We became shadowcrew.com," Nagel said. [11]

Questions

1. What types of technology could big retailers use to prevent identity thieves from purchasing merchandise?
2. What can organizations do to protect themselves from hackers looking to steal account data?
3. Authorities frequently tap online service providers to track down hackers. Do you think it is ethical for authorities to tap an online service provider and read people's e-mail? Why or why not?
4. Do you think it was ethical for authorities to use one of the high-ranking officials to trap other gang members? Why or why not?
5. In a team, research the Internet and find the best ways to protect yourself from identity theft.

1. Firewall Decisions

You are the CEO of Inverness Investments, a medium-sized venture capital firm that specializes in investing in high-tech companies. The company receives over 30,000 e-mail messages per year. On average, there are two viruses and three successful hackings against the company each year, which result in losses to the company of about $250,000. Currently, the company has antivirus software installed but does not have any firewalls.

Your CIO is suggesting implementing 10 firewalls for a total cost of $80,000. The estimated life of each firewall is about three years. The chances of hackers breaking into the system with the firewalls installed are about 3 percent. Annual maintenance costs on the firewalls is estimated around $15,000. Create an argument for or against supporting your CIO's recommendation to purchase the firewalls.

2. Drafting an Information Security Plan

Making The Grade is a nonprofit organization that helps students learn how to achieve better grades in school. The organization has 40 offices in 25 states and over 2,000 employees. The company is currently building a Web site to offer its services online. You have recently been hired by the CIO as the director of information security. Your first assignment is to develop a document discussing the importance of creating information security policies and an information security plan. Be sure to include the following:

- The importance of educating employees on information security.
- A few samples of employee information security policies.
- Other major areas the information security plan should address.
- Signs the company should look for to determine if the new site is being hacked.
- The major types of attacks the company should expect to experience.

3. Discussing the Three Areas of Security

Great Granola Inc. is a small business operating out of northern California. The company specializes in selling unique homemade granola, and its primary sales vehicle is through its Web site. The company is growing exponentially and expects its revenues to triple this year to $12 million. The company also expects to hire 60 additional employees to support its growing number of customers. Joan Martin, the CEO, is aware that if her competitors discover the recipe for her granola, or who her primary customers are, it could easily ruin her business. Joan has hired you to draft a document discussing the different areas of information security, along with your recommendations for providing a secure e-business environment.

4. College Security

Computer and online security is a growing concern for businesses of all sizes. Computer security issues range from viruses to automated Internet attacks to outright theft, the result of which is lost information and lost time. Security issues pop up in news articles daily, and most business owners understand the need to secure their businesses. Your college is no different from any other business when it comes to information security. Draft a document identifying the questions you should ask your college's CIO to ensure information security across your campus.

PLUG-IN

B7

Ethics

1. Summarize the guidelines for creating an information privacy policy.
2. Identify the differences between an ethical computer use policy and an acceptable use policy.
3. Describe the relationship between an e-mail privacy policy and an Internet use policy.
4. Explain the effects of spam on an organization.
5. Summarize the different monitoring technologies and explain the importance of an employee monitoring policy.

Introduction

The core units introduced *ethics,* which are the principles and standards that guide our behavior toward other people. Technology has created many new ethical dilemmas in our electronic society. The following are a few important concepts and terms related to ethical issues stemming from advances in technology:

- *Intellectual property*—intangible creative work that is embodied in physical form.
- *Copyright*—the legal protection afforded an expression of an idea, such as a song, video game, and some types of proprietary documents.
- *Fair use doctrine*—in certain situations, it is legal to use copyrighted material.
- *Pirated software*—the unauthorized use, duplication, distribution, or sale of copyrighted software.
- *Counterfeit software*—software that is manufactured to look like the real thing and sold as such.

The core units also introduced *privacy,* which is the right to be left alone when you want to be, to have control over your own personal possessions, and not to be observed without your consent. Privacy is related to *confidentiality,* which is the assurance that messages and information are available only to those who are authorized to view them. This plug-in takes a detailed look at *ePolicies*—policies and procedures that address the ethical use of computers and Internet usage in the business environment. These ePolicies typically address information privacy and confidentiality issues and include the following:

- Ethical computer use policy.
- Information privacy policy.
- Acceptable use policy.
- E-mail privacy policy.
- Internet use policy.
- Anti-spam policy.

Ethics

Individuals form the only ethical component of an IT system. They determine how they use IT, and how they are affected by IT. How individuals behave toward each other, how they handle information and technology, are largely influenced by their ethics. Ethical dilemmas usually arise not in simple, clear-cut situations but out of a clash between competing goals, responsibilities, and loyalties. Ethical decisions are complex judgments that balance rewards against responsibilities. Inevitably, the decision process is influenced by uncertainty about the magnitude of the outcome, by the estimate of the importance of the situation, by the perception of conflicting "right reactions," when there is more than one socially acceptable "correct" decision. Figure B7.1 contains examples of ethically questionable or unacceptable uses of information technology.

People make arguments for or against—justify or condemn—the behaviors in Figure B7.1. Unfortunately, there are few hard and fast rules for always determining what is and is not ethical. Knowing the law will not always help because what is legal might not always be ethical, and what might be ethical is not always legal. For example, Joe Reidenberg received an offer for cell phone service from AT&T Wireless. The offer revealed that AT&T Wireless had used Equifax, a credit reporting agency, to identify Joe Reidenberg as a potential customer. Overall, this strategy seemed like good business. Equifax could generate additional revenue by selling information it already owned and AT&T Wireless could identify target markets, thereby increasing response rates to its marketing campaigns. Unfortunately, by law, credit information cannot be used to sell anything. The Fair Credit Reporting Act (FCRA) forbids repurposing credit information except when the information is used for "a firm offer of credit or insurance." In other words, the only product that can be sold based on credit information is credit. A spokesman for Equifax stated that "as long as AT&T Wireless (or any company for that matter) is offering the cell

Examples of Questionable Information Technology Use
Individuals copy, use, and distribute software.
Employees search organizational databases for sensitive corporate and personal information.
Organizations collect, buy, and use information without checking the validity or accuracy of the information.
Individuals create and spread viruses that cause trouble for those using and maintaining IT systems.
Individuals hack into computer systems to steal proprietary information.
Employees destroy or steal proprietary organization information such as schematics, sketches, customer lists, and reports.

FIGURE B7.1

Ethically Questionable or Unacceptable Information Technology Use

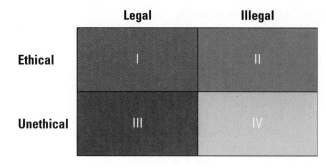

	Legal	Illegal
Ethical	I	II
Unethical	III	IV

FIGURE B7.2

Acting Ethically and
Legally Are Not Always
the Same

phone service on a credit basis, such as allowing the use of the service before the consumer has to pay, it is in compliance with the FCRA."[1] But is it ethical?

This is a good example of the ethical dilemmas facing many organizations today; because technology is so new and pervasive in unexpected ways, the ethics surrounding information have not been all worked out. Figure B7.2 displays the four quadrants of ethical and legal behavior. The ideal goal for organizations is to make decisions within quadrant I that are both legal and ethical.

INFORMATION HAS NO ETHICS

Jerry Rode, CIO of Saab Cars USA, realized he had a public relations fiasco on his hands when he received an e-mail from an irate customer. Saab had hired four Internet marketing companies to distribute electronic information about Saab's new models to its customers. Saab specified that the marketing campaign be *opt-in,* implying that it would contact only the people who had agreed to receive promotions and marketing material via e-mail. Unfortunately, one of the marketing companies apparently had a different definition of opt-in and was e-mailing all customers regardless of their opt-in decision.

Rode fired the errant marketing company and immediately developed a formal policy for the use of customer information. "The customer doesn't see ad agencies and contracted marketing firms. They see Saab USA spamming them," Rode said. "Finger-pointing after the fact won't make your customers feel better."[2]

Information has no ethics. Information does not care how it is used. It will not stop itself from spamming customers, sharing itself if it is sensitive or personal, or revealing details to third parties. Information cannot delete or preserve itself. Therefore, it falls on the shoulders of those who lord over the information to develop ethical guidelines on how to manage it. Figure B7.3 provides an overview of some of the important laws that individuals must follow when they are attempting to manage and protect information.[3]

FIGURE B7.3

Established Information-
Related Laws

Established Information-Related Laws	
Privacy Act—1974	Restricts what information the federal government can collect; allows people to access and correct information on themselves; requires procedures to protect the security of personal information; and forbids the disclosure of name-linked information without permission.
Family Education Rights and Privacy Act—1974	Regulates access to personal education records by government agencies and other third parties and ensures the right of students to see their own records.
Cable Communications Act—1984	Requires written or electronic consent from viewers before cable TV providers can release viewing choices or other personally identifiable information.
Electronic Communications Privacy Act—1986	Allows the reading of communications by a firm and says that employees have no right to privacy when using the companies' computers.
Computer Fraud and Abuse Act—1986	Prohibits unauthorized access to computers used for financial institutions, the U.S. government, or interstate and international trade.

(Continued)

Established Information-Related Laws	
The Bork Bill (officially known as the Video Privacy Protection Act)—1988	Prohibits the use of video rental information on customers for any purpose other than that of marketing goods and services directly to the customer.
Communications Assistance for Law Enforcement Act—1994	Requires that telecommunications equipment be designed so that authorized government agents are able to intercept all wired and wireless communications being sent or received by any subscriber. The act also requires that subscriber call-identifying information be transmitted to a government when and if required.
Freedom of Information Act—1967, 1975, 1994, and 1998	Allows any person to examine government records unless it would cause an invasion of privacy. It was amended in 1974 to apply to the FBI, and again in 1994 to allow citizens to monitor government activities and information gathering, and once again in 1998 to allow access to government information on the Internet.
Health Insurance Portability and Accountability Act (HIPAA)—1996	Requires that the health care industry formulate and implement regulations to keep patient information confidential.
Identity Theft and Assumption Deterrence Act—1998	Strengthened the criminal laws governing identity theft making it a federal crime to use or transfer identification belonging to another. It also established a central federal service for victims.
USA Patriot Act—2001 and 2003	Allows law enforcement to get access to almost any information, including library records, video rentals, bookstore purchases, and business records when investigating any act of terrorist or clandestine intelligence activities. In 2003, Patriot II broadened the original law.
Homeland Security Act—2002	Provided new authority to government agencies to mine data on individuals and groups including e-mails and Web site visits; put limits on the information available under the Freedom of Information Act; and gave new powers to government agencies to declare national health emergencies.
Sarbanes-Oxley Act—2002	Sought to protect investors by improving the accuracy and reliability of corporate disclosures and requires companies to (1) implement extensive and detailed policies to prevent illegal activity within the company, and (2) to respond in a timely manner to investigate illegal activity.
Fair and Accurate Credit Transactions Act—2003	Included provisions for the prevention of identity theft including consumers' right to get a credit report free each year, requiring merchants to leave all but the last five digits of a credit card number off a receipt, and requiring lenders and credit agencies to take action even before a victim knows a crime has occurred when they notice any circumstances that might indicate identity theft.
CAN-Spam Act—2003	Sought to regulate interstate commerce by imposing limitations and penalties on businesses sending unsolicited e-mail to consumers. The law forbids deceptive subject lines, headers, return addresses, etc., as well as the harvesting of e-mail addresses from Web sites. It requires businesses that send spam to maintain a do-not-spam list and to include a postal mailing address in the message.

Developing Information Management Policies

Treating sensitive corporate information as a valuable resource is good management. Building a corporate culture based on ethical principles that employees can understand and implement is responsible management. In an effort to provide guidelines for ethical information management, *CIO* magazine (along with over 100 CIOs) developed six principles for ethical information management displayed in Figure B7.4.

To follow *CIO*'s six principles for ethical information management, a corporation should develop written policies establishing employee guidelines, personnel procedures, and organizational rules. These policies set employee expectations about the organization's practices and standards and protect the organization from misuse of computer systems and IT resources. If an organization's employees use computers at work, the organization should, at a minimum, implement ePolicies. Such *ePolicies* are policies and procedures that address the ethical use of computers and Internet usage in the business environment. They typically embody the following:

- Ethical computer use policy.
- Information privacy policy.
- Acceptable use policy.
- E-mail privacy policy.
- Internet use policy.
- Anti-spam policy.[4]

ETHICAL COMPUTER USE POLICY

One of the essential steps in creating an ethical corporate culture is establishing an ethical computer use policy. An *ethical computer use policy* contains general principles to guide computer user behavior. For example, the ethical computer use policy might explicitly state that users should refrain from playing computer games during working hours. This policy ensures that the users know how to behave at work and that the organization has a published standard by which to deal with user infractions—for example, after appropriate warnings, terminating an employee who spends significant amounts of time playing computer games at work.

There are variations in how organizations expect their employees to use computers, but in any approach the overriding principle when seeking appropriate computer use should be informed consent. The users should be *informed* of the rules and, by agreeing to use the system on that basis, *consent* to abide by the rules.[5]

An organization should make a conscientious effort to ensure that all users are aware of the policy through formal training and other means. If an organization were to have only one policy, it would want it to be an ethical computer use policy since it is the starting point and the umbrella for any other policies that the organization might establish.

FIGURE B7.4

CIO Magazine's Six Principles for Ethical Information Management

Six Principles for Ethical Information Management
1. Information is a valuable corporate asset like cash, facilities, or any other corporate asset and should be managed as such.
2. The CIO is steward of corporate information and is responsible for managing it over its life cycle—from its generation to its appropriate destruction.
3. The CIO is responsible for controlling access to and use of information, as determined by governmental regulation and corporate policy.
4. The CIO is responsible for preventing the inappropriate destruction of information.
5. The CIO is responsible for bringing technological knowledge to the development of information management practices and policies.
6. The CIO should partner with executive peers to develop and execute the organization's information management policies.

INFORMATION PRIVACY POLICY

Scott Thompson is the executive vice president of Inovant, the company Visa set up to handle its technology. Thompson errs on the side of caution in regard to Visa's information: He bans the use of Visa's customer information for anything outside its intended purpose—billing.

Visa's customer information details such things as what people are spending their money on, in which stores, on which days, and even at what time of day. Sales and marketing departments around the country no doubt are salivating at any prospect of gaining access to Thompson's databases. "They would love to refine the information into loyalty programs, target markets, or even partnerships with Visa. There are lots of creative people coming up with these ideas," Thompson says. "This whole area of information sharing is enormous and growing. For the marketers, the sky's the limit." Thompson, along with privacy specialists, developed a strict credit card information policy, which the company follows. The question now is can Thompson guarantee that some unethical use of his information will not occur? Many experts do not believe that he can.[6]

In fact, in a large majority of cases, the unethical use of information happens not through the malicious scheming of a rogue marketer, but rather unintentionally. For example, information is collected and stored for some purpose, such as record keeping or billing. Then, a sales or marketing professional figures out another way to use it internally, share it with partners, or sell it to a trusted third party. The information is "unintentionally" used for new purposes. The classic example of this type of unintentional information reuse is the Social Security number, which started simply as a way to identify government retirement benefits and is now used as a sort of universal personal ID, found on everything from drivers' licenses to savings accounts.

An organization that wants to protect its information should develop an information privacy policy. An ***information privacy policy*** contains general principles regarding information privacy. Figure B7.5 highlights a few guidelines an organization can follow when creating an information privacy policy.[7]

FIGURE B7.5

Organizational Guidelines for Creating an Information Privacy Policy

---

Creating an Information Privacy Policy

1. **Adoption and implementation of a privacy policy.** An organization engaged in online activities or e-business has a responsibility to adopt and implement a policy for protecting the privacy of personal information. Organizations should also take steps that foster the adoption and implementation of effective online privacy policies by the organizations with which they interact, for instance, by sharing best practices with business partners.

2. **Notice and disclosure.** An organization's privacy policy must be easy to find, read, and understand. The policy must clearly state:
   - What information is being collected.
   - The use of information being collected.
   - Possible third-party distribution of that information.
   - The choices available to an individual regarding collection, use, and distribution of the collected information,
   - A statement of the organization's commitment to information security.
   - What steps the organization takes to ensure information quality and access.

3. **Choice and consent.** Individuals must be given the opportunity to exercise choice regarding how personal information collected from them online may be used when such use is unrelated to the purpose for which the information was collected. At a minimum, individuals should be given the opportunity to opt out of such use.

4. **Information security.** Organizations creating, maintaining, using, or disseminating personal information should take appropriate measures to assure its reliability and should take reasonable precautions to protect it from loss, misuse, or alteration.

5. **Information quality and access.** Organizations should establish appropriate processes or mechanisms so that inaccuracies in material personal information, such as account or contact information, may be corrected. Other procedures to assure information quality may include use of reliable sources, collection methods, appropriate consumer access, and protection against accidental or unauthorized alteration.

Acceptable Use Policy Stipulations
1. Not using the service as part of violating any law.
2. Not attempting to break the security of any computer network or user.
3. Not posting commercial messages to groups without prior permission.
4. Not performing any nonrepudiation.
5. Not attempting to send junk e-mail or spam to anyone who does not want to receive it.
6. Not attempting to mail bomb a site. A *mail bomb* is sending a massive amount of e-mail to a specific person or system resulting in filling up the recipient's disk space, which, in some cases, may be too much for the server to handle and may cause the server to stop functioning.

ACCEPTABLE USE POLICY

An *acceptable use policy (AUP)* is a policy that a user must agree to follow in order to be provided access to a network or to the Internet. *Nonrepudiation* is a contractual stipulation to ensure that e-business participants do not deny (repudiate) their online actions. A nonrepudiation clause is typically contained in an AUP.

It is common practice for many businesses and educational facilities to require that employees or students sign an acceptable use policy before being granted a network ID. When signing up with an Internet service provider (ISP), each customer is typically presented with an AUP, which states that they agree to adhere to certain stipulations (see Figure B7.6).[8]

E-MAIL PRIVACY POLICY

E-mail is so pervasive in organizations that it requires its own specific policy. In a recent survey, 80 percent of professional workers identified e-mail as their preferred means of corporate communications. Trends also show a dramatic increase in the adoption rate of instant messaging (IM) in the workplace. While e-mail and IM are terrific business communication tools, there are risks associated with using them.

For instance, a sent e-mail is stored on at least three or four different computers (see Figure B7.7). Simply deleting an e-mail from one computer does not delete it off the other computers. Companies can mitigate many of the risks of using electronic messaging systems by implementing and adhering to an e-mail privacy policy.[9]

One of the major problems with e-mail is the user's expectations of privacy. To a large extent, this exception is based on the false assumption that there exists e-mail privacy protection somehow analogous to that of U.S. first-class mail. This is simply not true. Generally, the organization that owns the e-mail system can operate the system as openly or as privately as it wishes. That means that if the organization wants to read everyone's e-mail, it can do so. If it chooses not to read any, that is allowable too. Hence, it is up to the organization to decide how much, if any, e-mail it is going to read. Then, when it decides, it must inform the users, so that they can consent to this level of intrusion. In other words, an *e-mail privacy policy* details the extent to which e-mail messages may be read by others.[10]

Organizations are urged to have some kind of e-mail privacy policy and to publish it no matter what the degree of intrusion. Figure B7.8 displays a few of the key stipulations generally contained in an e-mail privacy policy.

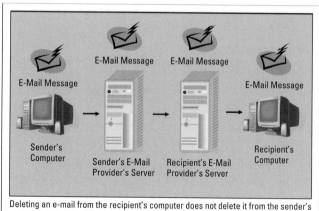

E-Mail Message — E-Mail Message — E-Mail Message — E-Mail Message

Sender's Computer → Sender's E-Mail Provider's Server → Recipient's E-Mail Provider's Server → Recipient's Computer

Deleting an e-mail from the recipient's computer does not delete it from the sender's computer or the provider's computers.

E-mail Privacy Policy Stipulations	
1.	The policy should be complementary to the ethical computer use policy.
2.	It defines who legitimate e-mail users are.
3.	It explains the backup procedure so users will know that at some point, even if a message is deleted from their computer, it will still be on the backup tapes.
4.	It describes the legitimate grounds for reading someone's e-mail and the process required before such action can be taken.
5.	It informs that the organization has no control of e-mail once it is transmitted outside the organization.
6.	It explains what will happen if the user severs his or her connection with the organization.
7.	It asks employees to be careful when making organizational files and documents available to others.

INTERNET USE POLICY

Similar to e-mail, the Internet has some unique aspects that make it a good candidate for its own policy. These include the large amounts of computing resources that Internet users can expend, thus making it essential that such use be legitimate. In addition, the Internet contains numerous materials that some might feel are offensive and, hence, some regulation might be required in this area. An *Internet use policy* contains general principles to guide the proper use of the Internet. Figure B7.9 displays a few important stipulations that might be included in an Internet use policy.

ANTI-SPAM POLICY

Chief technology officer (CTO) of the law firm Fenwick and West, Matt Kesner reduced incoming spam by 99 percent and found himself a corporate hero. Before the spam reduction, the law firm's partners (whose time is worth $350 to $600 an hour) found themselves spending hours each day sifting through 300 to 500 spam messages. The spam blocking engineered by Kesner traps between 5,000 and 7,000 messages a day.[11]

Spam is unsolicited e-mail. An *anti-spam policy* simply states that e-mail users will not send unsolicited e-mails (or spam). Spam plagues all levels of employees within an organization from receptionists to CEOs. Estimates indicate that spam accounts for 40 percent to 60 percent of most organizations' e-mail traffic. Ferris Research says spam costs U.S. businesses over $15 billion per year and Nucleus Research stated that companies forfeit $874 per employee annually in lost productivity from spam alone. Spam clogs e-mail systems and siphons IT resources away from legitimate business projects.[12]

Internet Use Policy Stipulations	
1.	The policy should describe available Internet services because not all Internet sites allow users to access all services.
2.	The policy should define the organization's position on the purpose of Internet access and what restrictions, if any, are placed on that access.
3.	The policy should complement the ethical computer use policy.
4.	The policy should describe user responsibility for citing sources, properly handling offensive material, and protecting the organization's good name.
5.	The policy should clearly state the ramifications if the policy is violated.

Spam Prevention Tips
■ **Disguise e-mail addresses posted in a public electronic place.** When posting an e-mail address in a public place, disguise the address through simple means such as replacing "jsmith@domain.com" with "jsmith at domain dot com." This prevents spam from recognizing the e-mail address.
■ **Opt-out of member directories that may place an e-mail address online.** Choose not to participate in any activities that place e-mail addresses online. If an e-mail address is placed online be sure it is disguised in some way.
■ **Use a filter.** Many ISPs and free e-mail services now provide spam filtering. While filters are not perfect, they can cut down tremendously on the amount of spam a user receives.

It is difficult to write anti-spam policies, laws, or software because there is no such thing as a universal litmus test for spam. One person's spam is another person's newsletter. End users have to be involved in deciding what spam is because what is unwanted can vary widely not just from one company to the next, but from one person to the next. What looks like spam to the rest of the world could be essential business communications for certain employees.

John Zarb, CIO of Libbey, a manufacturer of glassware, china, and flatware, tested Guenivere (a virus and subject-line filter) and SpamAssassin (an open source spam filter). He had to shut them off after 10 days because they were rejecting important legitimate e-mails. As Zarb quickly discovered, once an organization starts filtering e-mail, it runs the risk of blocking legitimate e-mails because they look like spam. Avoiding an unacceptable level of "false positives" requires a delicate balancing act. The IT team tweaked the spam filters and today the filters block about 70 percent of Libbey's spam. Zarb says the "false positive" rate is far lower but not zero. Figure B7.10 presents a few methods an organization can follow to prevent spam.[13]

Ethics in the Workplace

Concern is growing among employees that infractions of corporate policies—even accidental ones—will be a cause for disciplinary action. The Whitehouse.gov Internet site displays the U.S. president's official Web site and updates on bill signings and new policies. Whitehouse.com, however, leads to a trashy site that capitalizes on its famous name. A simple mistype from .gov to .com could potentially cost someone her or his job if the company has a termination policy for viewing illicit Web sites. Monitoring employees is one of the largest issues facing CIOs when they are developing information management policies.

The question of whether to monitor what employees do on company time with corporate resources has been largely decided by legal precedents that are already holding businesses financially responsible for their employees' actions. Increasingly, employee monitoring is not a choice; it is a risk-management obligation.

A recent survey of workplace monitoring and surveillance practices by the American Management Association (AMA) and the ePolicy Institute showed the degree to which companies are turning to monitoring:

- 82 percent of the study's 1,627 respondents acknowledged conducting some form of electronic monitoring or physical surveillance.
- 63 percent of the companies stated that they monitor Internet connections.
- 47 percent acknowledged storing and reviewing employee e-mail messages.[14]

MONITORING TECHNOLOGIES

Many employees use their company's high-speed Internet access to shop, browse, and surf the Web. Fifty-nine percent of all Web purchases in the United States are made from the workplace, according to ComScore Networks. Vault.com determined that 47 percent of employees spend at least half an hour a day surfing the Web.[15]

Employee Monitoring Effects
1. Employee absenteeism is on the rise, almost doubling in 2004 to 21 percent. The lesson here might be that more employees are missing work to take care of personal business. Perhaps losing a few minutes here or there—or even a couple of hours—is cheaper than losing entire days.
2. Studies indicate that electronic monitoring results in lower job satisfaction, in part because people begin to believe the quantity of their work is more important than the quality.
3. Electronic monitoring also induces what psychologists call "psychological reactance": the tendency to rebel against constraints. If you tell your employees they cannot shop, they cannot use corporate networks for personal business, and they cannot make personal phone calls, then their desire to do all these things will likely increase.

FIGURE B7.11

Employee Monitoring Effects

This research indicates that managers should monitor what their employees are doing with their Web access. Most managers do not want their employees conducting personal business during working hours. For these reasons many organizations have increasingly taken the Big Brother approach to Web monitoring with software that tracks Internet usage and even allows the boss to read employees' e-mail. Figure B7.11 highlights a few reasons the effects of employee monitoring are worse than the lost productivity from employee Web surfing.

This is the thinking at SAS Institute, a private software company consistently ranked in the top 10 on many "Best Places to Work" surveys. SAS does not monitor its employees' Web usage. The company asks its employees to use company resources responsibly, but does not mind if they occasionally check sports scores or use the Web for shopping.

Many management gurus advocate that organizations whose corporate cultures are based on trust are more successful than those whose corporate cultures are based on distrust. Before an organization implements monitoring technology it should ask itself, "What does this say about how the organization feels about its employees?" If the organization really does not trust its employees, then perhaps it should find new ones. If an organization does trust its employees, then it might want to treat them accordingly. An organization that follows its employees' every keystroke is unwittingly undermining the relationships with its employees.[16]

Information technology monitoring is tracking people's activities by such measures as number of keystrokes, error rate, and number of transactions processed. Figure B7.12 displays different types of monitoring technologies currently available.

Employee Monitoring Policies

The best path for an organization planning to engage in employee monitoring is open communication surrounding the issue. A recent survey discovered that communication about monitoring issues is weak for most organizations. One in five companies did not even have an acceptable use policy and one in four companies did not have an Internet use policy.

Companies that did have policies usually tucked them into the rarely probed recesses of the employee handbook, and then the policies tended to be of the vague and legal jargon variety: "XYZ company reserves the right to monitor or review any information stored or transmitted on its equipment." Reserving the right to monitor is materially different from clearly stating that the company does monitor, listing what is tracked, describing what is looked for, and detailing the consequences for violations.

An organization must formulate the right monitoring policies and put them into practice. *Employee monitoring policies* explicitly state how, when, and where the company monitors its employees. CSOs that are explicit about what the company does in the way of monitoring and the reasons for it, along with actively educating

Common Monitoring Technologies	
Key logger, or key trapper, software	A program that, when installed on a computer, records every keystroke and mouse click.
Hardware key logger	A hardware device that captures keystrokes on their journey from the keyboard to the motherboard.
Cookie	A small file deposited on a hard drive by a Web site containing information about customers and their Web activities. Cookies allow Web sites to record the comings and goings of customers, usually without their knowledge or consent.
Adware	Software that generates ads that install themselves on a computer when a person downloads some other program from the Internet.
Spyware (sneakware or stealthware)	Software that comes hidden in free downloadable software and tracks online movements, mines the information stored on a computer, or uses a computer's CPU and storage for some task the user knows nothing about.
Web log	Consists of one line of information for every visitor to a Web site and is usually stored on a Web server.
Clickstream	Records information about a customer during a Web surfing session such as what Web sites were visited, how long the visit was, what ads were viewed, and what was purchased.

their employees about what unacceptable behavior looks like, will find that employees not only acclimate quite quickly to a policy, but also reduce the CSO's burden by policing themselves. Figure B7.13 displays several common stipulations an organization can follow when creating an employee monitoring policy.[17]

Employee Monitoring Policy Stipulations	
1.	Be as specific as possible.
2.	Always enforce the policy.
3.	Enforce the policy in the same way for everyone.
4.	Expressly communicate that the company reserves the right to monitor all employees.
5.	Specifically state when monitoring will be performed.
6.	Specifically state what will be monitored (e-mail, IM, Internet, network activity, etc.).
7.	Describe the types of information that will be collected.
8.	State the consequences for violating the policy.
9.	State all provisions that allow for updates to the policy.
10.	Specify the scope and manner of monitoring for any information system.
11.	When appropriate, obtain a written receipt acknowledging that each party has received, read, and understood the monitoring policies.

Advances in technology have made ethics a concern for many organizations. Consider how easy it is for an employee to e-mail large amounts of confidential information, change electronic communications, or destroy massive amounts of important company information all within seconds. Electronic information about customers, partners, and employees has become one of corporate America's most valuable assets. However, the line between the proper and improper use of this asset is at best blurry. Should an employer be able to search employee files without employee consent? Should a company be able to sell customer information without informing the customer of its intent? What is a responsible approach to document deletion?

The law provides guidelines in many of these areas, but how a company chooses to act within the confines of the law is up to the judgment of its officers. Since CIOs are responsible for the technology that collects, maintains, and destroys corporate information, they sit smack in the middle of this potential ethical quagmire.

One way an organization can begin dealing with ethical issues is to create a corporate culture that encourages ethical considerations and discourages dubious information dealings. Not only is an ethical culture an excellent idea overall, but it also acts as a precaution, helping prevent customer problems from escalating into front-page news stories. The establishment of and adherence to well-defined rules and policies will help organizations create an ethical corporate culture. These policies include:

- Ethical computer use policy.
- Information privacy policy.
- Acceptable use policy.
- E-mail privacy policy.
- Internet use policy.
- Anti-spam policy.
- Employee monitoring policy.

✱ KEY TERMS

Acceptable use policy
(AUP), 390
Adware, 394
Anti-spam policy, 391
Clickstream, 394
Confidentiality, 384
Cookie, 394
Copyright, 384
Counterfeit software, 384
E-mail privacy policy, 390
Employee monitoring
policy, 393
ePolicies, 384, 388

Ethical computer use
policy, 388
Ethics, 384
Fair use doctrine, 384
Hardware key logger, 394
Information privacy policy, 389
Information technology
monitoring, 393
Intellectual property, 384
Internet use policy, 391
Key logger or key trapper
software, 394
Mail bomb, 390

Nonrepudiation, 390
Opt-in, 386
Pirated software, 384
Privacy, 384
Spam, 391
Spyware (sneakware or
stealthware), 394
Web log, 394

Sarbanes-Oxley: Where Information Technology, Finance, and Ethics Meet

The Sarbanes-Oxley Act (SOX) of 2002 was enacted in response to the high-profile Enron and WorldCom financial scandals to protect shareholders and the general public from accounting errors and fraudulent practices by organizations. One primary component of the Sarbanes-Oxley Act is the definition of which records are to be stored and for how long. For this reason, the legislation not only affects financial departments, but also IT departments whose job it is to store electronic records. The Sarbanes-Oxley Act states that all business records, including electronic records and electronic messages, must be saved for "not less than five years." The consequences for noncompliance are fines, imprisonment, or both. The following are the three rules of Sarbanes-Oxley that affect the management of electronic records.

1. The first rule deals with destruction, alteration, or falsification of records and states that persons who knowingly alter, destroy, mutilate, conceal, or falsify documents shall be fined or imprisoned for not more than 20 years or both.

2. The second rule defines the retention period for records storage. Best practices indicate that corporations securely store all business records using the same guidelines set for public accountants, which state that organizations shall maintain all audit or review work-papers for a period of five years from the end of the fiscal period in which the audit or review was concluded.

3. The third rule specifies all business records and communications that need to be stored, including electronic communications. IT departments are facing the challenge of creating and maintaining a corporate records archive in a cost-effective fashion that satisfies the requirements put forth by the legislation.

Essentially, any public organization that uses IT as part of its financial business processes will find that it must put in place IT controls in order to be compliant with the Sarbanes-Oxley Act. The following are a few practices you can follow to begin to ensure organizational compliance with the Sarbanes-Oxley Act.

- Overhaul or upgrade your financial systems in order to meet regulatory requirements for more accurate, detailed, and speedy filings.

- Examine the control processes within your IT department and apply best practices to comply with the act's goals. For example, segregation of duties within the systems development staff is a widely recognized best practice that helps prevent errors and outright fraud. The people who code program changes should be different from the people who test them, and a separate team should be responsible for changes in production environments.

- Homegrown financial systems are fraught with potential information-integrity issues. Although leading ERP systems offer audit-trail functionality, customizations of these systems often bypass those controls. You must work with internal and external auditors to ensure that customizations are not overriding controls.

- Work with your CIO, CEO, CFO, and corporate attorneys to create a document-retention-and-destruction policy that addresses what types of electronic documents should be saved, and for how long.

Ultimately, Sarbanes-Oxley compliance will require a great deal of work among all of your departments. Compliance starts with running IT as a business and strengthening IT internal controls.[18]

Questions

1. Define the relationship between ethics and the Sarbanes-Oxley Act.
2. Why is records management an area of concern for the entire organization?
3. What are two policies an organization can implement to achieve Sarbanes-Oxley compliance? Be sure to elaborate on how these policies can achieve compliance.
4. Identify the biggest roadblock for organizations that are attempting to achieve Sarbanes-Oxley compliance.
5. What types of information systems might facilitate SOX compliance?
6. How will electronic monitoring affect the morale and performance of employees in the workplace?
7. What do you think an unethical accountant or manager at Enron thought were the rewards and responsibilities associated with his or her job?

 CLOSING CASE TWO

Invading Your Privacy

Can your employer invade your privacy through monitoring technologies? Numerous lawsuits have been filed by employees who believed their employer was wrong to invade their privacy with monitoring technologies. Below are a few cases highlighting lawsuits over employee privacy and employer rights to monitor.

Smyth versus Pillsbury Company

An employee was terminated for sending inappropriate and unprofessional messages over the company's e-mail system. The company had repeatedly assured its employees that e-mail was confidential, that it would not be intercepted, and that it would not be used as a basis for discipline or discharge. Michael Smyth retrieved, from his home computer, e-mail sent from his supervisor over Pillsbury's e-mail system. Smyth allegedly responded with several comments concerning the sales management staff, including a threat to "kill the backstabbing bastards" and a reference to an upcoming holiday party as "the Jim Jones Kool-aid affair." Pillsbury intercepted the e-mail and terminated Smyth, who then sued the company for wrongful discharge and invasion of privacy.

The court dismissed the case in 1996, finding that Smyth did not have a reasonable expectation of privacy in the contents of his e-mail messages, despite Pillsbury's assurances, because the messages had been voluntarily communicated over the company's computer system to a second person. The court went on to find that, even if some reasonable expectation of privacy existed, that expectation was outweighed by Pillsbury's legitimate interest in preventing inappropriate or unprofessional communications over its e-mail system.

Bourke versus Nissan Motor Corporation

While training new employees on the e-mail system, a message sent by Bonita Bourke was randomly selected and reviewed by the company. The message turned out to be a personal e-mail of a sexual nature. Once Bourke's e-mail was discovered, the company decided to review the e-mails of the rest of Bourke's workgroup. As a result of this investigation, several other personal e-mails were discovered. Nissan gave the employees who had sent the personal messages written warnings for violating the company's e-mail policy.

The disciplined employees sued Nissan for invasion of privacy. The employees argued that although they signed a form acknowledging the company's policy that company-owned hardware and software was restricted for company business use only, their expectation of privacy was reasonable because the company gave the plaintiffs passwords to access the computer system and told them to guard their passwords. However, a California court in 1993 held that this was not an objectively reasonable expectation of privacy because the plaintiffs knew that e-mail messages "were read from time to time by individuals other than the intended recipient."

McLaren versus Microsoft Corporation

The Texas Court of Appeals in 1999 dismissed an employee's claim that his employer's review and dissemination of e-mail stored in the employee's workplace personal computer constituted an invasion of privacy. The employee argued that he had a reasonable expectation of privacy because the e-mail was kept in a personal computer folder protected by a password. The court found this argument unconvincing because the e-mail was transmitted over his employer's network.

However, according to a news account of one case, a court held that an employer's use of a supervisor's password to review an employee's e-mail may have violated a Massachusetts state statute against interference with privacy. In that case, Burk Technology allowed employees to use the company's e-mail system to send personal messages, but prohibited "excessive chatting." To use the e-mail system, each employee used a password. The employer never informed employees that their messages would or could be monitored by supervisors or the company president. The president of the company reviewed the e-mails of two employees who had referred to him by various nicknames and discussed his extramarital affair. The two employees were fired by the company president, who claimed the terminations were for their excessive e-mail use and not because of the messages' content. The court denied the company's attempt to dismiss the suit and allowed the matter to be set for trial on the merits. The court focused on the fact that the employees were never informed that their e-mail could be monitored.

This case illustrates the importance of informing employees that their use of company equipment to send e-mail and to surf the Internet is subject to monitoring to prevent subsequent confusion, and a possible future defense, on the part of employees.[19]

Questions

1. Pick one of the above cases and create an argument on behalf of the employee.
2. Pick one of the above cases and create an argument against the employee.
3. Pick one of the above cases and create an argument on behalf of the employer's use of monitoring technologies.
4. Pick one of the above cases and create an argument against the employer's use of monitoring technologies.

★ MAKING BUSINESS DECISIONS

1. Information Privacy

A study by the Annenberg Public Policy Center at the University of Pennsylvania shows that 95 percent of people who use the Internet at home think they should have a legal right to know everything about the information that Web sites collect from them. Research also shows that 57 percent of home Internet users incorrectly believe that when a Web site has an information privacy policy it will not share personal information with other Web sites or companies. In fact, the research found that after showing the users how companies track, extract, and share Web site information to make money, 85 percent found the methods unacceptable, even for a highly valued site. Write a short paper arguing for or against an organization's right to use and distribute personal information gathered from its Web site.

2. Acting Ethically

Describe how you would react to the following scenarios:

- A senior marketing manager informs you that one of her employees is looking for another job and she wants you to give her access to look through her e-mail.
- A vice president of sales informs you that he has made a deal to provide customer information to a strategic partner and he wants you to burn all of the customer information onto a CD.
- You start monitoring one of your employees' e-mail and discover that he is having an affair with one of the other employees in the office.
- You install a video surveillance system in your office and discover that employees are taking office supplies home with them.

3. Spying on E-Mail

Technology advances now allow individuals to monitor computers that they do not even have physical access to. New types of software can capture an individual's incoming and outgoing e-mail and then immediately forward that e-mail to another person. For example, if you are at work and your child is home from school and she receives an e-mail from John at 3:00 p.m., at 3:01 p.m. you will receive a copy of that e-mail sent to your e-mail address. A few minutes later, if she replies to John's e-mail, within seconds you will again receive a copy of what she sent to John. Describe two scenarios (other than the above) for the use of this type of software: (1) where the use would be ethical, (2) where the use would be unethical.

4. Stealing Software

The issue of pirated software is one that the software industry fights on a daily basis. The major centers of software piracy are in places like Russia and China where salaries and disposable income are comparatively low. People in developing and economically depressed countries will fall behind the industrialized world technologically if they cannot afford access to new generations of software. Considering this, is it reasonable to blame someone for using pirated software when it could potentially cost him or her two months' salary to purchase a legal copy? Create an argument for or against the following statement: "Individuals who are economically less fortunate should be allowed access to software free of charge in order to ensure that they are provided with an equal technological advantage."

B8

Supply Chain Management

1. List and describe the four drivers of supply chain management.
2. Explain supply chain management strategies focused on efficiency.
3. Explain supply chain management strategies focused on effectiveness.
4. Summarize the future of supply chain management.

Introduction

The core units introduced the supply chain and supply chain management. A *supply chain* consists of all parties involved, directly or indirectly, in the procurement of a product or raw material. *Supply chain management (SCM)* involves the management of information flows between and among stages in a supply chain to maximize total supply chain effectiveness and profitability.

This plug-in takes a detailed look at how an organization can create a supply chain strategy focusing on *efficiency* and *effectiveness*. *Efficiency IT metrics* measure the performance of the IT system including throughput, speed, and availability. *Effectiveness IT metrics* measure the impact IT has on business processes and activities including customer satisfaction, conversion rates, and sell-through increases. Once an organization determines its supply chain strategy it can begin to estimate the impact that its supply chain will have on its business and ultimately the performance of the organization. The payoff for a successful supply chain strategy can be tremendous. A study by Peter J. Metz, executive director of the MIT Center for e-business, found that companies have achieved impressive bottom-line results from managing their supply chains—on average a 50 percent reduction in inventory and a 40 percent increase in timely deliveries.[1]

Supply Chain Drivers

An organization's goals and strategic objectives should determine its overall supply chain management strategy. The SCM strategy in turn determines how the supply chain will perform with respect to efficiency and effectiveness. The four primary drivers of supply chain management are:

1. Facilities
2. Inventory
3. Transportation
4. Information

An organization can use these four drivers in varying measure to push it toward either a supply chain strategy focusing on efficiency or a supply chain strategy focusing on effectiveness. The organization must decide on the trade-off it desires between efficiency and effectiveness for each driver. The selected combined impact of the various drivers then determines the efficiency and effectiveness of the entire supply chain. Figure B8.1 provides an overview of the four supply chain drivers in terms of their effect on overall efficiency and effectiveness.[2]

FACILITIES DRIVER

A facility processes or transforms inventory into another product or it stores the inventory before shipping it to the next facility. Toyota is an example of a company that stresses effectiveness in its facilities. Toyota's goal is to open a facility in every major market where it does business. These local facilities protect the company from currency fluctuations and trade barriers and thus are more effective for Toyota's customers. An organization should consider three primary components when determining its facilities strategy:

1. Location
2. Capacity
3. Operational design[3]

Location

An organization must determine where it will locate its facilities, an important decision that constitutes a large part of its supply chain strategy. The two primary options when determining facilities location are: (1) centralize the location to gain economies of scale, which increases efficiency or (2) decentralize the locations to be closer to the customers, which increases effectiveness.

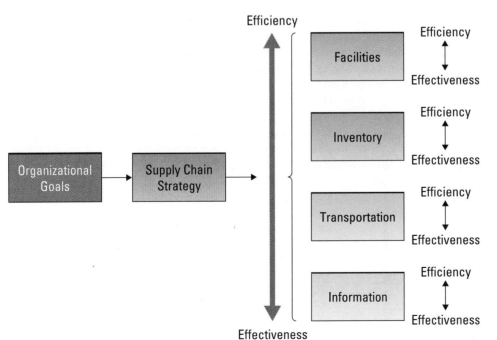

FIGURE B8.1

Analyzing the Design of a Supply Chain in Terms of Efficiency and Effectiveness

The combination of efficiency and effectiveness for all four supply chain drivers determines total supply chain efficiency or effectiveness.

A company can gain economies of scale when it centralizes its facilities. However, this cost reduction decreases the company's effectiveness, since many of its customers may be located far away from the facility. The opposite is also true; having a number of different facilities located closer to customers reduces efficiency because of the increased costs associated with the additional facilities. Many other factors will influence location decisions including facility costs, employee expense, exchange rates, tax effects, and so on.

UPS uses package flow SCM systems at each of its locations. The custom-built software combines operations research and mapping technology to optimize the way boxes are loaded and delivered. The goal is to use the package flow software to cut the distance that delivery trucks travel by more than 100 million miles each year. The project will also help UPS streamline the profitability of each of its facility locations.[4]

Capacity

Demand planning SCM software can help an organization determine capacity. An organization must determine the performance capacity level for each of its facilities. If it decides a facility will have a large amount of excess capacity, which provides the flexibility to respond to wide swings in demand, then it is choosing an effectiveness strategy. Excess capacity, however, costs money and can therefore decrease efficiency.[5]

Operational Design

An organization must determine if it wants a product focus or a functional focus for its facilities operational design. If it chooses a product focus design, it is anticipating that the facility will produce only a certain type of product. All operations, including fabrication and assembly, will focus on developing a single type of product. This strategy allows the facility to become highly efficient in producing a single product.

If it chooses a functional design, the facility will perform a specific function (e.g., fabrication only or assembly only) on many different products. This strategy allows the facility to become more effective since it can use a single process on many different types of products (see Figure B8.2).[6]

FIGURE B8.2

The Facilities Driver's Effect on Efficiency and Effectiveness

Facilities Driver

Efficiency

Increases Efficiency
- Low number of facilities
- Centralized facilities
- Minimal amounts of excess capacity
- Single product focus

Increases Effectiveness
- High number of facilities
- Decentralized facilities
- Large amounts of excess capacity
- Multiple product focus

Effectiveness

INVENTORY DRIVER

For most of business history, inventory has been a form of security. A warehouse bulging with components, or a distribution center packed with finished products, meant that even when a customer forecast went wildly awry, there would still be enough supply on hand to meet demand. Ever since the 1980s, when General Motors began adopting Toyota's pioneering methods in lean manufacturing, fast companies have delayered, reengineered, and scrubbed the waste from their assembly lines and supply chains by slashing lead time and stripping inventory and spare capacity from their operations.

Dillard's department store's competitive strategy is to appeal to higher-end customers who are willing to pay a premium to obtain products immediately. Dillard's carries large amounts of inventory to ensure products are always available for its customers. In return, its customers are willing to pay extra for the products.[7]

Companies require inventory to offset any discrepancies between supply and demand, but inventory is a major cost in any supply chain. Inventory's impact on a company's effectiveness versus efficiency can be enormous. Effectiveness results from more inventory, and efficiency results from less inventory. If a company's strategy requires a high level of customer effectiveness, then the company will locate large amounts of inventory in many facilities close to its customers, such as Dillard's strategy demands. If a company's strategy requires a high level of efficiency, the strategy of a low-cost producer, for instance, then the company will maintain low levels of inventory in a single strategic location.

Inventory management and control software provides control and visibility to the status of individual items maintained in inventory. The software maintains inventory record accuracy, generates material requirements for all purchased items, and analyzes inventory performance. Inventory management and control software provides the supply chain with information from a variety of sources including:

- Current inventory and order status.
- Cost accounting.
- Sales forecasts and customer orders.
- Manufacturing capacity.
- New product introductions.[8]

Inventory management and control software provides an organization with information when making decisions in regard to two primary inventory strategies:

1. Cycle inventory
2. Safety inventory

Cycle Inventory

Cycle inventory is the average amount of inventory held to satisfy customer demands between inventory deliveries. A company can follow either of two approaches regarding cycle inventory. The first approach is to hold a large amount of cycle inventory and receive inventory deliveries only once a month. The second approach is to hold a small amount of inventory and receive orders weekly or even daily. The trade-off is the cost comparison between holding larger lots of inventory for an effective supply chain and ordering products frequently for an efficient supply chain.[9]

Safety Inventory

Safety inventory is extra inventory held in the event demand exceeds supply. For example, a toy store might hold safety inventory for the Christmas season. The risk a company faces when making a decision in favor of safety inventory is that in addition to the cost of holding it, if it holds too much, some of its products may go unsold and it may have to discount them—after the Christmas season, in the toy store example. However, if it holds too little inventory it may lose sales and risk losing customers. The company must decide if it wants to risk the expense of carrying too much inventory or to risk losing sales and customers (see Figure B8.3).[10]

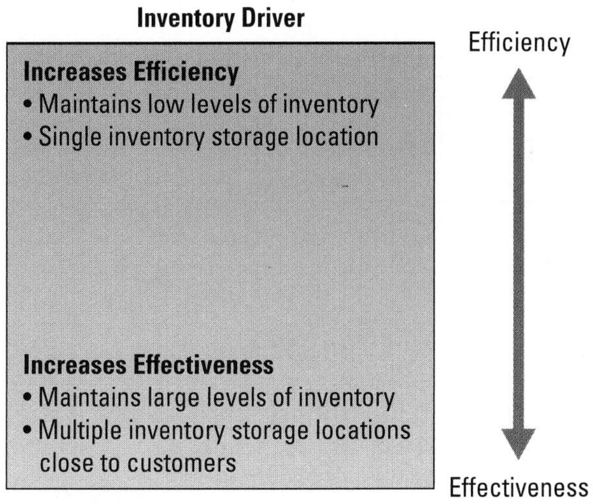

TRANSPORTATION DRIVER

Organizations use IT-enabled supply chain management systems that use quantitative analysis, decision support systems, and intelligent systems for configuring shipping plans. FedEx's entire business strategy focuses on its customers' need for highly effective transportation

FIGURE B8.3

The Inventory Driver's Effect on Efficiency and Effectiveness

Inventory Driver

Efficiency

Increases Efficiency
- Maintains low levels of inventory
- Single inventory storage location

Increases Effectiveness
- Maintains large levels of inventory
- Multiple inventory storage locations close to customers

Effectiveness

methods. Any company that uses FedEx to transport a package is focusing primarily on a safe and timely delivery and not on the cost of delivery. Many businesses even locate their facilities near FedEx hubs so that they can quickly transport inventory overnight to their customers.

An organization can use many different methods of transportation to move its inventories between the different stages in the supply chain. Like the other supply chain drivers, transportation cost has a large impact either way on effectiveness and efficiency. If an organization focuses on a highly effective supply chain, then it can use transportation to increase the price of its products by using faster, more costly transportation methods. If the focus is a highly efficient supply chain, the organization can use transportation to decrease the price of its products by using slower, less costly transportation methods. There are two primary facets of transportation an organization should consider when determining its strategy:

1. Method of transportation
2. Transportation route[11]

Method of Transportation

An organization must decide how it wants to move its inventory through the supply chain. There are six basic methods of transportation it can choose from: truck, rail, ship, air, pipeline, and electronic. The primary differences between these methods are the speed of delivery and price of delivery. An organization might choose an expensive method of transportation to ensure speedy delivery if it is focusing on a highly effective supply chain. On the other hand, it might choose an inexpensive method of transportation if it is focusing on a highly efficient supply chain.

Some organizations will use a *global inventory management system* that provides the ability to locate, track, and predict the movement of every component or material anywhere upstream or downstream in the supply chain. So regardless of the chosen method of transportation, the organization can find its inventory anywhere in the supply chain.[12]

FIGURE B8.4

The Transportation Driver's Effect on Efficiency and Effectiveness

Transportation Route

An organization will also need to choose the transportation route for its products. Two supply chain software modules can aid in this decision. *Transportation planning software* tracks and analyzes the movement of materials and products to ensure the delivery of materials and finished goods at the right time, the right place, and the lowest cost. *Distribution management software* coordinates the process of transporting materials from a manufacturer to distribution centers to the final customer.[13]

Transportation route directly affects the speed and cost of delivery. For example, an organization might decide to use an effectiveness route and ship its products directly to its customers, or it might decide to use an efficiency route and ship its products to a distributor that ships the products to customers (see Figure B8.4).

INFORMATION DRIVER

Information is a driver whose importance has grown as companies use it to become both more efficient and more effective. An organization must decide what information is most valuable in efficiently reducing costs or

Transportation Driver

Increases Efficiency
- Reduced speed of delivery
- Reduced cost of delivery
- Ship products to a distributor

Efficiency

Increases Effectiveness
- Increased speed of delivery
- Increased cost of delivery
- Ship products directly to customers

Effectiveness

in improving effectiveness. This decision will vary depending on a company's strategy and the design and organization of the supply chain. Two things to consider about information in the supply chain include:

1. Information sharing.
2. Push versus pull information strategy.[14]

Information Sharing

An organization must determine what information it wants to share with its partners throughout the stages of the supply chain. Information sharing is a difficult decision since most organizations do not want their partners to gain insight into strategic or competitive information. However, they do need to share information so they can coordinate supply chain activities such as providing suppliers with inventory order levels to meet production forecasts. Building trusting relationships is one way to begin to understand how much information supply chain partners require.

If an organization chooses an efficiency focus for information sharing then it will freely share lots of information to increase the speed and decrease the costs of supply chain processing. If an organization chooses an effectiveness focus for information sharing, then it will share only selected information with certain individuals, which will decrease the speed and increase the costs of supply chain processing.

Push vs. Pull Information Strategy

In a ***push technology*** environment, organizations send information. In a ***pull technology*** environment, organizations receive or request information. An organization must decide how it is going to share information with its partners. It might decide that it wants to push information out to partners by taking on the responsibility of sending information to them. On the other hand, it might decide that it wants its partners to take on the responsibility of getting information by having them directly access the information from the systems and pull the information they require.

Again, an organization must determine how much it trusts its partners when deciding on a push versus pull information sharing strategy. Using a push information sharing strategy is more effective because the organization has control over exactly what information is shared and when the information is shared. However, a push strategy is less efficient because there are costs associated with sending information such as computer equipment, applications, time, resources, and so forth.

Using a pull information sharing strategy is more efficient since the organization does not have to undertake the costs associated with sending information. However, the pull strategy is less effective since the organization has no control over when the information is pulled. For example, if the company needs inventory there is no guarantee that the suppliers will pick up the information. Hence, an organization could find itself in trouble if its partners forget to obtain the information and fail to deliver the required products (see Figure B8.5).[15]

Applying a Supply Chain Design

Figure B8.6 displays Wal-Mart's supply chain management design and how it correlates to its competitive strategy to be a reliable, low-cost retailer for a wide variety of mass consumption goods. Wal-Mart's supply chain emphasizes efficiency, but also maintains an adequate level of effectiveness.

FIGURE B8.5

The Information Driver's Effect on Efficiency and Effectiveness

Information Driver

Increases Efficiency
- Openly shares information with all individuals
- Pull information strategy

Increases Effectiveness
- Selectively shares certain information with certain individuals
- Push information strategy

Efficiency

Effectiveness

Wal-Mart uses its four primary supply chain drivers to drive supply chain efficiency.

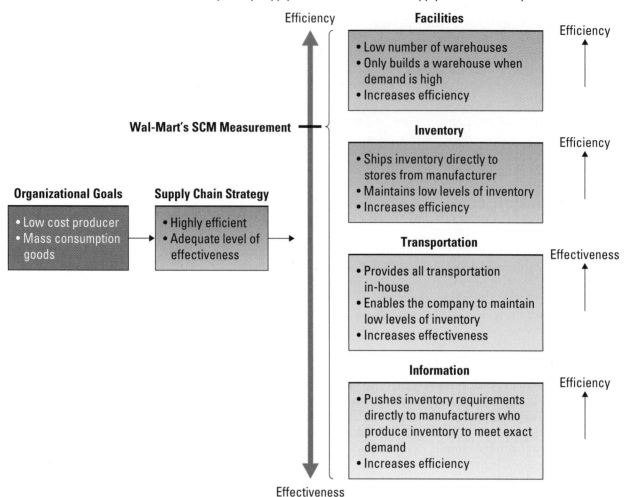

FIGURE B8.6

Wal-Mart's Supply Chain Management Drivers

- **Facilities focus—efficiency:** Wal-Mart maintains few warehouses and will build a new warehouse only when demand is high enough to justify one.

- **Inventory focus—efficiency:** Wal-Mart ships directly to its stores from the manufacturer. This significantly lowers inventory levels because stores maintain inventory, not stores and warehouses.

- **Transportation focus—effectiveness:** Wal-Mart maintains its own fleet of trucks. The benefits in terms of overall supply chain efficiency justify the expense of maintaining its own trucks because effective transportation allows Wal-Mart to keep low levels of inventory.

- **Information focus—efficiency:** Wal-Mart invests heavily in technology and the flow of information throughout its entire supply chain. Wal-Mart pushes inventory information all the way back up the supply chain to its suppliers who then manufacture only enough inventories to meet demand. The cost to build the information flows between its supply chain partners has been tremendous. However, the result of this investment is a highly successful and efficient supply chain.[16]

Future Trends

A television commercial shows a man in a uniform quietly moving through a family home. The man replaces the empty cereal box with a full one just before a hungry child opens the cabinet; he then opens a new sack of dog food as the hungry bulldog eyes him warily, and finally hands a full bottle of shampoo to the man in the shower who had just run out. The next wave in supply chain management will be home-based supply chain fulfillment.

Walgreens is differentiating itself from other national chains by marketing itself as the family's just-in-time supplier. Consumers today are becoming incredibly comfortable with the idea of going online to purchase products when they want, how they want, and at the price they want. Walgreens is developing custom Web sites for each household that allow families to order electronically and then at their convenience go to the store to pick up their goods at a special self-service counter or the drive-through window. Walgreens is making a promise that goes beyond low prices and customer service and extends right into the home.[17]

The functionality in supply chain management systems is becoming more and more sophisticated as supply chain management matures. Now and in the future, the next stages of SCM will incorporate more functions such as marketing, customer service, and product development. This will be achieved through more advanced communication, adoption of more user-friendly decision support systems, and availability of shared information to all participants in the supply chain. SCM is an ongoing development as technology makes it possible to acquire information ever more accurately and frequently from all over the world, and introduces new tools to aid in the analytical processes that deal with the supply chain's growing complexity.

According to Forrester Research, Inc., U.S. firms will spend $35 billion over the next five years to improve business processes that monitor, manage, and optimize their extended supply chains. Figure B8.7 displays the fastest growing SCM components because they have the greatest potential impact on an organization's bottom line.[18]

New technologies are also going to improve the supply chain. Radio frequency identification (RFID) technologies use active or passive tags in the form of chips or smart labels that can store unique identifiers and relay this information to electronic readers. RFID will become an effective tool for tracking and monitoring inventory movement in a real-time SCM environment. The real-time information will provide managers with an instant and accurate view of inventories within the supply chain. Using current SCM systems, the RFID will check the inventory

Growing SCM Components	
Supply chain event management (SCEM)	Enables an organization to react more quickly to resolve supply chain issues. SCEM software increases real-time information sharing among supply chain partners and decreases their response time to unplanned events. SCEM demand will skyrocket as more and more organizations begin to discover the benefits of real-time supply chain monitoring.
Selling chain management	Applies technology to the activities in the order life cycle from inquiry to sale.
Collaborative engineering	Allows an organization to reduce the cost and time required during the design process of a product.
Collaborative demand planning	Helps organizations reduce their investment in inventory, while improving customer satisfaction through product availability.

FIGURE B8.7

Growing SCM Components

status and then trigger the replenishment process. Organizations using RFIDs will be able to quickly and accurately provide current inventory levels (in real-time) at any point in the supply chain as long as there are readers to detect their location. As inventory levels are reduced to their reorder points, replenishment orders can then be electronically generated. With quick and accurate information about inventories, the use of safety stock levels guarding against uncertainty can also be reduced. Hence, the potential benefits of RFIDs include a reduction of human intervention (or required labor) and holding fewer inventories, which nets a reduction in operating costs.

SCM applications have always been expensive, costing between $1 million and $10 million. As the industry matures and competition increases, vendors will continue adapting their pricing models to attract midsize and smaller companies.[19]

The fundamental decisions an organization needs to make regarding its supply chain strategy concern:

- **Facilities**—An organization must decide between the cost of the number, location, and type of facilities (efficiency) and the level of effectiveness that these facilities provide.
- **Inventory**—An organization can increase inventory levels to make its supply chain more effective for its customers. This choice, however, comes at a cost as added inventory significantly decreases efficiency.
- **Transportation**—An organization can choose between the cost of transporting inventory (efficiency) and the speed of transporting inventory (effectiveness). Transportation choices also influence other drivers such as inventory levels and facility locations.
- **Information**—A focus on information can help improve both supply chain effectiveness and efficiency. The information driver also improves the performance of other drivers.

Collaborative demand
   planning, 407
Collaborative engineering, 407
Cycle inventory, 403
Distributions management
   software, 404
Effectiveness IT metric, 400
Efficiency IT metric, 400

Global inventory management
   system, 404
Inventory management and
   control software, 403
Pull technology, 405
Push technology, 405
Safety inventory, 403
Selling chain management, 407

Supply chain, 400
Supply chain event
   management (SCEM), 407
Supply chain management
   (SCM), 400
Transportation planning
   software, 404

Listerine's Journey

When you use Listerine antiseptic mouthwash, you are experiencing the last step in a complex supply chain spanning several continents and requiring months of coordination by countless businesses and individuals. The resources involved in getting a single bottle of Listerine to a consumer are unbelievable. As raw material is transformed to finished product, what will be Listerine travels around the globe and through multiple supply chains and information systems.

The Journey Begins

A farmer in Australia is harvesting a crop of eucalyptus for eucalyptol, the oil found in its leathery leaves. The farmer sells the crop to an Australian processing company, which spends about four weeks extracting the eucalyptol from the eucalyptus.

Meanwhile, in New Jersey, Warner-Lambert (WL) partners with a distributor to buy the oil from the Australian company and transport it to WL's Listerine manufacturing and distribution facility in Lititz, Pennsylvania. The load will arrive at Lititz about three months after the harvest.

At the same time, in Saudi Arabia, a government-owned operation is drilling deep under the desert for the natural gas that will yield the synthetic alcohol that gives Listerine its 43-proof punch. Union Carbide Corp. ships the gas via tanker to a refinery in Texas, which purifies it and converts it into ethanol. The ethanol is loaded onto another tanker, then transported from Texas through the Gulf of Mexico to New Jersey, where it is transferred to storage tanks and transported via truck or rail to WL's plant. A single shipment of ethanol takes about six to eight weeks to get from Saudi Arabia to Lititz.

SPI Polyols Inc., a manufacturer of ingredients for the confectionery, pharmaceutical, and oral-care industries, buys corn syrup from farmers in the Midwest. SPI converts the corn syrup into sorbitol solution, which sweetens and adds bulk to the Cool Mint Listerine. The syrup is shipped to SPI's New Castle, Delaware, facility for processing and then delivered on a tank wagon to Lititz. The whole process, from the time the corn is harvested to when it is converted into sorbitol, takes about a month.

By now the ethanol, eucalyptol, and sorbitol have all arrived at WL's plant in Lititz, where employees test them, along with the menthol, citric acid, and other ingredients that make up Listerine, for quality assurance before authorizing storage in tanks. To mix the ingredients, flow meters turn on valves at each tank and measure out the right proportions, according to the Cool Mint formula developed by WL R&D in 1990. (The original amber mouthwash was developed in 1879.)

Next, the Listerine flows through a pipe to fillers along the packaging line. The fillers dispense the product into bottles delivered continuously from a nearby plastics company for just-in-time manufacturing. The bottles are capped, labeled, and fitted with tamper-resistant safety bands, then placed in shipping boxes that each hold one dozen 500-milliliter bottles. During this process, machines automatically check for skewed labels, missing safety bands, and other problems. The entire production cycle, from the delivery via pipe of the Listerine liquid to the point where bottles are boxed and ready to go, takes a matter of minutes. The line can produce about 300 bottles per minute—a far cry from the 80 to 100 bottles that the line produced per minute before 1994.

Each box travels on a conveyor belt to the palletizer, which organizes and shrink-wraps the boxes into 100-case pallets. Stickers with identifying bar codes are affixed to the pallets. Drivers forklift the pallets to the distribution center, located in the same Lititz facility, from which the boxes are shipped around the world.

Finally, the journey is completed when a customer purchases a bottle of Listerine at a local drugstore or grocery store. In a few days, the store will place an order for a replacement bottle of Listerine. And so begins the cycle again.[20]

Questions

1. Summarize SCM and describe Warner-Lambert's supply chain strategy. Diagram the SCM components.
2. Detail Warner-Lambert's facilities strategy.
3. Detail Warner-Lambert's inventory strategy.
4. Detail Warner-Lambert's transportation strategy.
5. Detail Warner-Lambert's information strategy.
6. What would happen to Warner-Lambert's business if a natural disaster in Saudi Arabia depleted its natural gas resources?

Katrina Shakes Supply Chains

How do corporations cope with the realities of risk, uncertainty, and crisis? Many businesses prepared well for Hurricane Katrina, responded quickly, and did so because Katrina was exactly the kind of event for which well-run corporations ready themselves. Corporations donated more than $500 million for relief for the hurricane that hit New Orleans in 2005 and were the first to provide help to Katrina victims.

Home Depot

As the residents of shattered Gulf Coast towns began returning home or crawling from the wreckage in the days after Hurricane Katrina hit, many found their way to the big concrete box with the battered orange sign. Home Depot stores were among the first to reopen in the storm's wake, offering rebuilding supplies plus the even more precious commodities of electricity and normalcy.

Home Depot had started mobilizing four days before Katrina slammed into the coast. Two days before landfall, maintenance teams battened down stores in the hurricane's projected path, while it moved electrical generators and hundreds of extra workers into place. A day after the storm, all but 10 of the company's 33 stores in Katrina's impact zone were open. Within a week, only four of its nine stores in metropolitan New Orleans were closed. "We always take tremendous pride in being able to be among the first responders," Home Depot CEO Bob Nardelli said.

Wal-Mart

Jessica Lewis could not believe her eyes. Her entire community of Waveland, Mississippi, a Gulf Coast resort town of 7,000, had been laid waste by the storm, and Lewis, co-manager of the local Wal-Mart, was assessing the damage to her store. The fortresslike big box on Highway 90 still stood, but Katrina's floodwaters had surged through the entrance, knocking over freezers full of frozen pizza, shelves of back-to-school items, and racks of clothing. Trudging through nearly two feet of water in the fading light, Lewis wondered how they would ever clean up the mess.

That quickly became the least of Lewis's worries. As the sun set on Waveland, a nightmarish scene unfolded on Highway 90. She saw neighbors wandering around with bloody feet because they had fled their homes with no shoes. Some wore only underwear. "It broke my heart to see them like this," Lewis recalled. "These were my kids' teachers. Some of them were my teachers. They were the parents of the kids on my kids' sports teams. They were my neighbors. They were my customers."

Lewis felt there was only one thing to do. She had her stepbrother clear a path through the mess in the store with a bulldozer. Then she salvaged everything she could and handed it out in the parking lot. She gave socks and underwear to shivering Waveland police officers who had climbed into trees to escape the rising water. She handed out shoes to her barefoot neighbors and diapers for their babies. She gave people bottled water to drink and sausages, stored high in the warehouse, which had not been touched by the flood. She even broke into the pharmacy and got insulin and drugs for AIDS patients. "This is the right thing to do," she recalled thinking. "I hope my bosses aren't going to have a problem with that."

The hurricane was a pivotal moment for Wal-Mart, one that it nearly fumbled. The company dispatched armored cars to the region before the storm hit to remove cash from stores, but it left behind guns that ended up in the hands of looters. As the extent of the devastation became clear, however, Wal-Mart did a remarkable about-face. At the urging of CEO Lee Scott, its truckers hauled $3 million of supplies to the ravaged zone, arriving days before the Federal Emergency Management Agency in many cases. The company also contributed $17 million in cash to relief efforts. Wal-Mart also demonstrated how efficient it could be. Katrina shut down 126 Wal-Mart facilities in the Gulf Coast area, and within weeks all but 13 of the facilities were up and running again. The company located 97 percent of the employees displaced by the storm and offered them jobs at any Wal-Mart operation in the country.

FedEx

Watching TV in Memphis, Mike Mitchell did not get it. Day after day, the FedEx Express senior technical adviser heard reporters describe how desperately New Orleans rescuers needed communications. Nobody seemed able to fix the problem. Finally, on the Thursday after Katrina hit, Mitchell spied a way to help: an aerial shot of a 54-story building near the convention center showed the intact base for a FedEx radio antenna, part of a system he had visited in 2004 on a maintenance check. That led him to hope that part of the installation had survived. He thought if they could get a generator to the roof and radios to the rescuers, they would have a way of talking to one another. Mitchell shot an e-mail to his boss the next day. It made its way up the ranks. FedEx called FEMA. FEMA called the 82nd Airborne Division. They all liked the idea.

Five days later Mitchell arrived in New Orleans with 125 walkie-talkies, a few changes of clothes, and a sleeping bag. He did not know how he would get to the top of the building or exactly what he would find there. However, he was determined to make the radios work. "I didn't want to let all those people down," he said. There turned out to be just enough fuel in the building's emergency generator for a couple of elevator rides to the top. An Army helicopter dropped in a half-ton of gear, including a nine-foot antenna to replace the one Katrina had sheared off. With help from eight soldiers, Mitchell fixed it. "Radio check," he called into a walkie-talkie after they had finished. "Lima Charlie," a soldier shot back. (Translation: loud and clear.) Thanks to FedEx, members of the 82nd and other rescuers finally had a reliable radio network.

Impressive as Mitchell's radio rescue was, such dramas are almost routine for FedEx. "That's the nature of our business," said Dave Bronczek, who heads FedEx's Express division. "We're used to dealing with crisis." Every day of the year, FedEx must cope with some sort of local disruption. In 2005, the company had to activate contingency plans on 37 tropical storms. Add to that such events as an air-traffic-controller strike in France and a blackout in Los Angeles, and it is no wonder that FedEx gets so much practice in flexibility. FedEx conducts disaster drills several times a year—for everything from big earthquakes to bioterrorism to a monster typhoon hitting the company's hub in the Philippines. Eight disaster kits, each containing two tons of such supplies as fuel and communications gear, stand ready in Memphis in case a facility is in need of repair. Each night, five empty FedEx flights roam the skies, standing by to replace a broken-down plane or assist with an unexpected surge in volume.

All this makes FedEx a national resource during a crisis like Katrina. Before the storm hit, FedEx positioned 30,000 bags of ice, 30,000 gallons of water, and 85 home generators outside Baton Rouge and Tallahassee so that it could move in quickly after the storm to relieve employees. In addition, FedEx dispatched in advance four 4,000-pound facility repair kits. FedEx also made preparations on behalf of the Red Cross, which keeps shipping containers filled with bandages, blankets, batteries, and such at FedEx hubs to be dispatched around the globe at a moment's notice. Before Katrina, FedEx staged 60 tons of Red Cross provisions (it has since delivered another 440 tons of relief supplies, mostly at no charge).

Like Hurricane Andrew before her, Katrina has taught FedEx a thing or two about disaster preparation. Lesson one: Arrange for temporary housing in advance for employees who might be displaced. Lesson two: Do not count on cell phones. The local networks were down for days after the storm; the company is increasing the number of satellite phones it deploys.[21]

Questions

1. How did Home Depot manage its supply chain to be one of the first stores to reopen after Katrina?

2. How could Wal-Mart have revamped its transportation driver to handle Katrina more efficiently?

3. Why is it critical to FedEx's success to be able to handle all types of global disasters? Highlight FedEx's use of the information driver.

4. How can the government learn from big business in dealing with disasters such as Katrina?

5. What can companies do in terms of facilities, inventory, transportation, and information to prepare themselves for disasters such as Katrina?

✱ MAKING BUSINESS DECISIONS

1. Focusing on Facilities

Focus is a large distributor of films and is owned and operated by Lauren O'Connell. The company has been in business for over 50 years and distributes motion pictures to theaters all over the United States and Canada. Focus is in the middle of a supply chain overhaul and is currently deciding its supply chain strategy. Lauren has asked you to create a report discussing the company's options for its facilities including location, capacity, and operational design. The report should include two primary focuses: one on efficiency and one on effectiveness.

2. Investing in Inventory

Poppa's Toy Store Inc. has more than 150 stores in 38 states. The chain has been owned and operated for the last 30 years by CEO Taylor Coombe. Taylor has been reading reports on supply chain management and is particularly interested in updating the company's current supply chain. It is the beginning of April and Taylor wants a new SCM system up and running before the Christmas season starts in November. Taylor is particularly interested in demand planning and forecasting for the entire company's inventory during its busiest season—Christmas. Taylor has asked you to create a report discussing the company's options for its inventory management strategy including cycle and safety inventory. The report should include two primary focuses: one on efficiency and one on effectiveness.

3. Targeting Transportation

Extra Express Co. is an overnight freight and parcel delivery business that operates on a global level and has annual revenues in excess of $400 million. You have just been hired as the company's director of transportation. The CEO, Jeff Brewer, has asked you to put together a report detailing how the company can gain efficiencies by streamlining its transportation methods and routes.

4. Increasing Information

Galina's is a high-end auction house located in New York City. Galina's specializes in selling jewelry, art, and antique furniture primarily from estate sales. The owner, Galina Bucrya, would like to begin offering certain items for auction over the Internet. Galina is unfamiliar with the Internet and not quite sure how to pursue her new business strategy. You are working for Information Inc., a small business consulting company that specializes in e-business strategies. Galina has hired you to help her create her supply chain e-business strategy. Compile a report describing supply chain management, the potential benefits her company can receive from an SCM strategy, your recommendation for an efficient or effective SCM strategy, and your views on the future of SCM.

5. Increasing Revenues with SCM

Cold Cream is one of the premier beauty supply stores in the metro New York area. People come from all over to sample the store's unique creams, lotions, makeup, and perfumes. The company receives its products from manufacturers around the globe. The company would like to implement an SCM system to help it better understand its customers and their purchasing habits. Create a report summarizing SCM systems and explain how an SCM system can directly influence Cold Cream's revenues.

Customer Relationship Management

1. Describe the three CRM technologies used by marketing departments.
2. Describe and differentiate the CRM technologies used by sales departments and customer service departments.
3. Compare customer relationship management, supplier relationship management, partner relationship management, and employee relationship management.
4. Summarize the future of customer relationship management.

Introduction

The core units introduced *customer relationship management (CRM),* which involves managing all aspects of a customer's relationship with an organization to increase customer loyalty and retention and an organization's profitability. The two primary components of a CRM strategy are operational CRM and analytical CRM. *Operational CRM* supports traditional transactional processing for day-to-day front-office operations or systems that deal directly with the customers. *Analytical CRM* supports back-office operations and strategic analysis and includes all systems that do not deal directly with the customers. The primary difference between operational CRM and analytical CRM is the degree of direct interaction between the organization and its customers. Figure B9.1 provides an overview of operational CRM and analytical CRM.

Using IT to Drive Operational CRM

Figure B9.2 displays the different technologies marketing, sales, and customer service departments can use to perform operational CRM.

MARKETING AND OPERATIONAL CRM

Companies are no longer trying to sell one product to as many customers as possible; instead, they are trying to sell one customer as many products as possible. Marketing departments are able to transform to this new way of doing business by

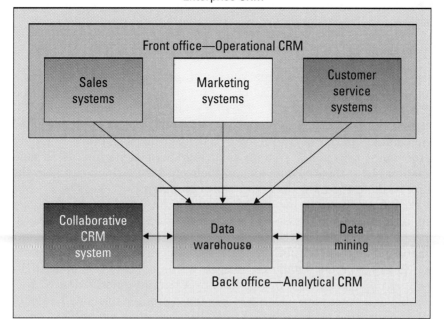

Enterprise CRM

Front office—Operational CRM

| Sales systems | Marketing systems | Customer service systems |

Collaborative CRM system | Data warehouse | Data mining

Back office—Analytical CRM

FIGURE B9.1

Operational CRM and Analytical CRM

using CRM technologies that allow them to gather and analyze customer information to deploy successful marketing campaigns. In fact, a marketing campaign's success is directly proportional to the organization's ability to gather and analyze the right information. The three primary operational CRM technologies a marketing department can implement to increase customer satisfaction are:

1. List generator.
2. Campaign management.
3. Cross-selling and up-selling.

List Generator

List generators compile customer information from a variety of sources and segment the information for different marketing campaigns. Information sources include Web site visits, Web site questionnaires, online and off-line surveys, fliers, toll-free numbers, current customer lists, and so on. After compiling the customer list, an organization can use criteria to filter and sort the list for potential customers. Filter and sort criteria can include such things as household income, education level, and age. List generators provide the marketing department with a solid understanding of the type of customer it needs to target for marketing campaigns.

Campaign Management

Campaign management systems guide users through marketing campaigns performing such tasks as campaign definition, planning, scheduling, segmentation, and

Operational CRM Technologies		
Marketing	**Sales**	**Customer Service**
1. List generator	1. Sales management	1. Contact center
2. Campaign management	2. Contact management	2. Web-based self-service
3. Cross-selling and up-selling	3. Opportunity management	3. Call scripting

FIGURE B9.2

Operational CRM Technologies for Sales, Marketing, and Customer Service Departments

success analysis. These advanced systems can even calculate quantifiable results for return on investment (ROI) for each campaign and track the results in order to analyze and understand how the company can fine-tune future campaigns.

Cross-Selling and Up-Selling

Two key sales strategies a marketing campaign can deploy are cross-selling and up-selling. **Cross-selling** is selling *additional* products or services to a customer. **Up-selling** is *increasing* the value of the sale. For example, McDonald's performs cross-selling by asking customers if they would like an apple pie with their meal. McDonald's performs up-selling by asking customers if they would like to super-size their meals. CRM systems offer marketing departments all kinds of information about their customers and their products, which can help them identify cross-selling and up-selling marketing campaigns.

California State Automobile Association (CSAA) had to take advantage of its ability to promote and cross-sell CSAA automotive, insurance, and travel services to beat its competition. Accomplishing this task was easy once the company implemented E.piphany's CRM system. The system integrated information from all of CSAA's separate databases, making it immediately available to all employees through a Web-based browser. Employees could quickly glance at a customer's profile and determine which services the customer currently had and which services the customer might want to purchase based on her or his needs as projected by the software.[1]

SALES AND OPERATIONAL CRM

Siebel, one of the largest providers of CRM software, had 33,000 subscribers in January 2005. Salesforce.com, provider of on-demand Web-based customer relationship management software, added 40,000 subscribers during the first three months of 2005, more than all of Siebel's subscribers. Salesforce.com's total number of subscribers is over 300,000. Merrill Lynch, one of the biggest customers in the sales force market, signed on for 5,000 subscriptions for its global private client division, making the brokerage firm Salesforce.com's largest customers. Salesforce.com's Customforce includes tools for adding data analysis capabilities, spreadsheet-style mathematical formulas, business processes, and forecasting models.[2]

The sales department was the first to begin developing CRM systems. Sales departments had two primary reasons to track customer sales information electronically. First, sales representatives were struggling with the overwhelming amount of customer account information they were required to maintain and track. Second, companies were struggling with the issue that much of their vital customer and sales information remained in the heads of their sales representatives. One of the first CRM components built to help address these issues was the sales force automation component. **Sales force automation (SFA)** is a system that automatically tracks all of the steps in the sales process. SFA products focus on increasing customer satisfaction, building customer relationships, and improving product sales by tracking all sales information.

Serving several million guests each year, Vail Resorts Inc. maintains dozens of systems across all seven of its properties. These systems perform numerous tasks including recording lift ticket, lodging, restaurant, conference, retail, and ski rental sales. Since a significant percentage of the company's revenue results from repeat guests, building stronger, more profitable relationships with its loyal customers is Vail Resorts first priority.

To improve its customer service and marketing campaign success, Vail deployed the Ascential CRM system, which integrated the customer information from its many disparate systems. The CRM system is providing Vail Resorts with a detailed level of customer insight, which helps the company personalize its guest offerings and promotions. By using a CRM system that integrates information from across all of its resorts and business lines, the company can determine what, where, and how its guests behave across all of its properties. For example, the company can now offer discounts on lift ticket and ski rentals for customers staying in its resorts.[3]

The three primary operational CRM technologies a sales department can implement to increase customer satisfaction are:

1. Sales management
2. Contact management
3. Opportunity management

Sales Management CRM Systems

Figure B9.3 depicts the typical sales process, which begins with an opportunity and ends with billing the customer for the sale. Leads and potential customers are the lifeblood of all sales organizations, whether the products they are peddling are computers, clothing, or cars. How the leads are handled can make the difference between revenue growth or decline. *Sales management CRM systems* automate each phase of the sales process, helping individual sales representatives coordinate and organize all of their accounts. Features include calendars to help plan customer meetings, alarm reminders signaling important tasks, customizable multimedia presentations, and document generation. These systems even have the ability to provide an analysis of the sales cycle and calculate how each individual sales representative is performing during the sales process.

Contact Management CRM Systems

A *contact management CRM system* maintains customer contact information and identifies prospective customers for future sales. Contact management systems include such features as maintaining organizational charts, detailed customer notes, and supplemental sale information. For example, a contact management system can take an incoming telephone number and display the caller's name along with notes detailing previous conversations. This allows the sales representative to

FIGURE B9.3

Overview of the Sales Process

Sales Process

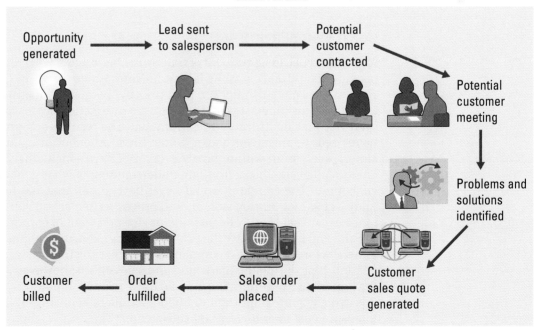

answer the telephone and say, "Hi, Sue, how is your new laptop working? How was your vacation to Florida?" without receiving any reminders of such details first from the customer. The customer feels valued since the sales associate knows her name and even remembers details of their last conversation!

The $16 billion 3M is a leader in the health care, safety, electronics, telecommunications, office, and consumer markets. The company began to focus on streamlining and unifying its sales processes with the primary goals of better customer segmentation and more reliable lead generation and qualification. To achieve these goals the company implemented a CRM system and soon found itself receiving the following benefits:

- Cutting the time it takes to familiarize sales professionals with new territories by 33 percent.
- Increasing management's visibility of the sales process.
- Decreasing the time it takes to qualify leads and assign sales opportunities by 40 percent.

One of the more successful campaigns driven by the CRM system allowed 3M to quickly deliver direct mail to targeted government agencies and emergency services in response to the anthrax attacks in 2002. All inquiries to the mail campaign were automatically assigned to a sales representative who followed up with a quote. In little more than a week, the company had received orders for 35,000 respirator masks.[4]

Opportunity Management CRM Systems

Opportunity management CRM systems target sales opportunities by finding new customers or companies for future sales. Opportunity management systems determine potential customers and competitors and define selling efforts including budgets and schedules. Advanced opportunity management systems can even calculate the probability of a sale, which can save sales representatives significant time and money when attempting to find new customers. The primary difference between contact management and opportunity management is that contact management deals with existing customers and opportunity management deals with prospective customers. Figure B9.4 displays six CRM pointers a sales representative can use to increase prospective customers.

CUSTOMER SERVICE AND OPERATIONAL CRM

Andy Taylor became president of Enterprise, his father's $76 million rental-car company, in 1980. Today, it is the largest in North America, with $7 billion in revenue. How has he kept customer service a priority? By quantifying it. Enterprise surveys 1.7 million customers a year. If a branch's satisfaction scores are low, employees, even vice presidents, cannot be promoted. The result is self-propagating. Seeking better scores, managers make better hires. And because Enterprise promotes almost solely from within, nearly every executive—including Taylor, who started out washing cars—has a frontline understanding of what it takes to keep customers happy. "The company would never have gotten that 100-fold growth without Andy's knack for putting systems and processes in place so you can deliver consistent service," said Sandy Rogers, senior vice president of corporate strategy.

Sales and marketing are the primary departments that interact directly with customers before a sale. Most companies recognize the importance of building strong relationships during the marketing and sales efforts; however, many fail to realize the importance of continuing to build these relationships after the sale is complete. It is actually more important to build postsale relationships if the company wants to ensure customer loyalty and satisfaction. The best way to implement postsale CRM strategies is through the customer service department.

CRM Pointers for Gaining Prospective Customers	
1. **Get their attention**	If you have a good prospect, chances are that he or she receives dozens of offers from similar companies. Be sure your first contact is professional and gets your customer's attention.
2. **Value their time**	When you ask for a meeting, you are asking for the most valuable thing a busy person has—time. Many companies have had great success by offering high-value gifts in exchange for a meeting with a representative. Just be careful because some organizations frown on expensive gifts. Instead, offer these prospective customers a report that can help them perform their jobs more effectively.
3. **Overdeliver**	If your letter offered a free DVD in exchange for a meeting, bring a box of microwave popcorn along with the movie. Little gestures like these tell customers that you not only keep your word, but also can be counted on to overdeliver.
4. **Contact frequently**	Find new and creative ways to contact your prospective customers frequently. Starting a newsletter and sending out a series of industry updates are excellent ways to keep in contact and provide value.
5. **Generate a trustworthy mailing list**	If you are buying a mailing list from a third party be sure that the contacts are genuine prospects, especially if you are offering an expensive gift. Be sure that the people you are meeting have the power to authorize a sale.
6. **Follow up**	One of the most powerful prospecting tools is a simple thank-you note. Letting people know that their time was appreciated may even lead to additional referrals.

FIGURE B9.4

CRM Pointers for Gaining Prospective Customers

One of the primary reasons a company loses customers is bad customer service experiences. Providing outstanding customer service is a difficult task, and many CRM technologies are available to assist organizations with this important activity. For example, by rolling out Lotus Instant Messaging to its customers, Avnet Computer Marketing has established an efficient, direct route to push valuable information and updates out to its customers. The company uses Lotus Instant Messaging to provide real-time answers to customer questions by listing its support specialists' status by different colors on its Web site: green if they are available, red if they are not, or blue if they are out of the office. The customer simply clicks on a name to begin instant messaging or a chat session to get quick answers to questions.

Before access to Lotus Instant Messaging, customers had to wait in "1-800" call queues or for e-mail responses for answers. The new system has increased customer satisfaction along with tremendous savings from fewer long-distance phone charges. Avnet also estimates that Lotus Instant Messaging saves each of its 650 employees 5 to 10 minutes a day.[5]

The three primary operational CRM technologies a customer service department can implement to increase customer satisfaction are:

1. Contact center.
2. Web-based self-service.
3. Call scripting.

Contact Center

Knowledge-management software, which helps call centers put consistent answers at customer-service representatives' fingertips, is often long on promise and short on delivery. The problem? Representatives have to take time out from answering calls to input things they've learned, putting the "knowledge" in knowledge management.

Brad Cleveland, who heads the Incoming Calls Management Institute, said, "Software is just a tool. It doesn't do any good unless people across the organization are using it to its potential." Sharp Electronics is making it happen. Sharp's frontline representatives built the system from scratch. And as Sharp rolled out its network over the past four years, representatives' compensation and promotions were tied directly to the system's use. As a result, the customer call experience at Sharp has improved dramatically: The proportion of problems resolved by a single call has soared from 76 percent to 94 percent since 2000.[6]

A *contact center* (or *call center*) is where customer service representatives (CSRs) answer customer inquiries and respond to problems through a number of different customer touchpoints. A contact center is one of the best assets a customer-driven organization can have because maintaining a high level of customer support is critical to obtaining and retaining customers. Numerous systems are available to help an organization automate its contact centers. Figure B9.5 displays a few of the features available in contact center systems.

Contact centers also track customer call history along with problem resolutions—information critical for providing a comprehensive customer view to the CSR. CSRs who can quickly comprehend and understand all of a customer's products and issues provide tremendous value to the customer and the organization. Nothing makes frustrated customers happier than not having to explain their problems to yet another CSR.

New emotion-detection software called Perform, created by Nice Systems, is designed to help companies improve customer service by identifying callers who are upset. When an elderly man distressed over high medical premiums hung up during his phone call to the Wisconsin Physician Services Insurance Corp.'s call center, an IT system detected the customer's exasperation and automatically e-mailed a supervisor. The supervisor listened to a digital recording of the conversation, called the customer, and suggested ways to lower the premium. The system uses algorithms to determine a baseline of emotion during the first 5 to 10 seconds of a call; any deviation from the baseline triggers an alert.[7]

Web-Based Self-Service

Web-based self-service systems allow customers to use the Web to find answers to their questions or solutions to their problems. FedEx uses Web-based self-service systems to allow customers to track their own packages without having to talk to a CSR. FedEx customers can simply log on to FedEx's Web site and enter their tracking number. The Web site quickly displays the exact location of the package and the estimated delivery time.

Another great feature of Web-based self-service is click-to-talk buttons. *Click-to-talk* buttons allow customers to click on a button and talk with a CSR via the Internet. Powerful customer-driven features like these add tremendous value to any organization by providing customers with real-time information without having to contact company representatives.[8]

Call Scripting

Being a CSR is not an easy task, especially when the CSR is dealing with detailed technical products or services. *Call scripting systems* access organizational databases that track similar issues or questions and automatically generate the details

FIGURE B9.5

Common Features Included in Contact Centers

Common Features Included in Contact Centers	
Automatic call distribution	A phone switch routes inbound calls to available agents.
Interactive voice response (IVR)	Directs customers to use touch-tone phones or keywords to navigate or provide information.
Predictive dialing	Automatically dials outbound calls and when someone answers, the call is forwarded to an available agent.

for the CSR who can then relay them to the customer. The system can even provide a list of questions that the CSR can ask the customer to determine the potential problem and resolution. This feature helps CSRs answer difficult questions quickly while also presenting a uniform image so two different customers do not receive two different answers.

Documedics is a health care consulting company that provides reimbursement information about pharmaceutical products to patients and health care professionals. The company currently supports inquiries for 12 pharmaceutical companies and receives over 30,000 customer calls per month. Originally, the company had a data file for each patient and for each pharmaceutical company. This inefficient process resulted in the potential for a single patient to have up to 12 different information files if the patient was a client of all 12 pharmaceutical companies. To answer customer questions, a CSR had to download each customer file causing tremendous inefficiencies and confusion.

The company implemented a CRM system with a call scripting feature to alleviate the problem by providing its CSRs with a comprehensive view of every customer, regardless of the pharmaceutical company. The company anticipated 20 percent annual growth primarily because of the successful implementation of its new system.[9]

Analytical CRM

Maturing analytical CRM and behavioral modeling technologies are helping numerous organizations move beyond legacy benefits like enhanced customer service and retention to systems that can truly improve business profitability. Unlike operational CRM that automates call centers and sales forces with the aim of enhancing customer transactions, analytical CRM solutions are designed to dig deep into a company's historical customer information and expose patterns of behavior on which a company can capitalize. Analytical CRM is primarily used to enhance and support decision making and works by identifying patterns in customer information collected from the various operational CRM systems.

For many organizations, the power of analytical CRM solutions provides tremendous managerial opportunities. Depending on the specific solution, analytical CRM tools can slice-and-dice customer information to create made-to-order views of customer value, spending, product affinities, percentile profiles, and segmentations. Modeling tools can identify opportunities for cross-selling, up-selling, and expanding customer relationships.

Personalization occurs when a Web site can know enough about a person's likes and dislikes that it can fashion offers that are more likely to appeal to that person. Many organizations are now utilizing CRM to create customer rules and templates that marketers can use to personalize customer messages.

The information produced by analytical CRM solutions can help companies make decisions about how to handle customers based on the value of each and every one. Analytical CRM can reveal information about which customers are worth investing in, which should be serviced at an average level, and which should not be invested in at all.

Data gained from customers can also reveal information about employees. When Wachovia Bank surveys customers—25,000 every month—for feedback on their service experience, it asks about individual employees and uses those answers in one-on-one staff coaching. A recent 20-minute coaching session at a Manhattan branch made clear how this feedback—each customer surveyed rates 33 employee behaviors—can improve service. The branch manager urged an employee to focus on sincerity rather than on mere friendliness, to "sharpen her antenna" so she would listen to customers more intuitively, and to slow down rather than

Analytical CRM Information Examples	
1. **Give customers more of what they want**	Analytical CRM can help an organization go beyond the typical "Dear Mr. Smith" salutation. An organization can use its analytical CRM information to make its communications more personable. For example, if it knows a customer's shoe size and preferred brand it can notify the customer that there is a pair of size 12 shoes set aside to try on the next time the customer visits the store.
2. **Find new customers similar to the best customers**	Analytical CRM might determine that an organization does a lot of business with women 35 to 45 years old who drive SUVs and live within 30 miles of a certain location. The company can then find a mailing list that highlights this type of customer for potential new sales.
3. **Find out what the organization does best**	Analytical CRM can determine what an organization does better than its competitors. For example, if a restaurant caters more breakfasts to midsized companies than its competition does, it can purchase a specialized mailing list of midsized companies in the area and send them a mailing that features the breakfast catering specials.
4. **Beat competitors to the punch**	Analytical CRM can determine sales trends allowing an organization to offer the best customers deals before the competition has a chance to. For example, a clothing store might determine its best customers for outdoor apparel and send them an offer to attend a private sale right before the competition runs its outdoor apparel sale.
5. **Reactivate inactive customers**	Analytical CRM can highlight customers who have not done any business with the organization in a while. The organization can then send them a personalized letter along with a discount coupon. It will remind them of the company and may help spark a renewed relationship.
6. **Let customers know they matter**	Analytical CRM can determine what customers want and need, so an organization can contact them with this information. Anything from a private sale to a reminder that the car is due for a tune-up is excellent customer service.

FIGURE B9.6

Analytical CRM
Information Examples

hurry up. That focus on careful, sincere, intuitive service has paid off: Wachovia has held the top score among banks in the American Customer Satisfaction Index since 2001.[10]

Analytical CRM relies heavily on data warehousing technologies and business intelligence to glean insights into customer behavior. These systems quickly aggregate, analyze, and disseminate customer information throughout an organization. Figure B9.6 displays a few examples of the kind of information insights analytical CRM can help an organization gain.

UPS's data-intensive environment is supported by the largest IBM DB2 database in the world, consisting of 236 terabytes of data related to its analytical CRM tool. The shipping company's goal is to create one-to-one customer relationships, and it is using Quantum View tools that allow it to let customers tailor views of such things as shipment history and receive notices when a package arrives or is delayed. UPS has built more than 500 customer relationship management applications that run off of its data warehouse.[11]

Sears, Roebuck and Company is the third-largest U.S. retailer. Over the past two decades, Sears has experienced a well-publicized encroachment by discount mass merchandisers. Even though Sears does not know exactly "who" its customers are (by name and address) since many customers use cash or non-Sears credit cards, it can still benefit from analytical CRM technologies. Sears uses these technologies to determine what its generic customers prefer to buy and when they buy it, which enables the company to predict what they will buy. Using analytical CRM, Sears can view each day's sales by region, district, store, product line, and individual item. Sears can now monitor the precise impact of advertising, weather, and other factors on sales of specific items. For the first time, Sears can even group together, or "cluster," widely divergent types of items. For example, merchandisers can track sales of a store display marked "Gifts under $25" that might include sweatshirts, screwdrivers, and other unrelated items. The advertising department can then follow the sales of "Gifts under $25" to determine which products to place in its newspaper advertisements.[12]

Current Trends: SRM, PRM, and ERM

Organizations are discovering a wave of other key business areas where it is beneficial to take advantage of building strong relationships. These emerging areas include supplier relationship management (SRM), partner relationship management (PRM), and employee relationship management (ERM).

SUPPLIER RELATIONSHIP MANAGEMENT

Supplier relationship management (SRM) focuses on keeping suppliers satisfied by evaluating and categorizing suppliers for different projects, which optimizes supplier selection. SRM applications help companies analyze vendors based on a number of key variables including strategy, business goals, prices, and markets. The company can then determine the best supplier to collaborate with and can work on developing strong relationships with that supplier. The partners can then work together to streamline processes, outsource services, and provide products that they could not provide individually.

With the merger of the Bank of Halifax and Bank of Scotland, the new company, HBOS, implemented an SRM system to supply consistent information to its suppliers. The system integrates procurement information from the separate Bank of Halifax and Bank of Scotland operational systems, generating a single repository of management information for consistent reporting and analysis. Other benefits HBOS derived from the SRM solution include:

- A single consolidated view of all suppliers.
- Consistent, detailed management information allowing multiple views for every executive.
- Elimination of duplicate suppliers.[13]

PARTNER RELATIONSHIP MANAGEMENT

Organizations have begun to realize the importance of building relationships with partners, dealers, and resellers. ***Partner relationship management (PRM)*** focuses on keeping vendors satisfied by managing alliance partner and reseller relationships that provide customers with the optimal sales channel. PRM's business strategy is to select and manage partners to optimize their long-term value to an organization. In effect, it means picking the right partners, working with them to help them be successful in dealing with mutual customers, and ensuring that partners and the ultimate end customers are satisfied and successful. Many of the features of a PRM application include real-time product information on availability, marketing materials, contracts, order details, and pricing, inventory, and shipping information.

PRM is one of the smaller segments of CRM that has superb potential. PRM has grown to more than a $1 billion industry. This is a direct reflection of the growing interdependency of organizations in the new economy. The primary benefits of PRM include:

- Expanded market coverage.
- Offerings of specialized products and services.
- Broadened range of offerings and a more complete solution.

EMPLOYEE RELATIONSHIP MANAGEMENT

Jim Sinegal runs Costco, one of the largest wholesale club chains, but there are two things he does not discount: employee benefits and customer service. Average hourly wages trounce those of rival Sam's Club, and 86 percent of workers have health insurance (versus a reported 47 percent at Sam's). Sinegal is not just being nice. Happy employees, he believes, make for happier customers. Low prices (he caps per-item profits at 14 percent) and a generous return policy certainly help. Although Wall Street has long been arguing for smaller benefits, a stingier return policy, and bigger profits, Sinegal sides with customers and staff. "We're trying to run Costco in a fashion that is not just going to satisfy our shareholders this year or this month," he said, "but next year and on into the future."[14]

Employee relationship management (ERM) provides employees with a subset of CRM applications available through a Web browser. Many of the ERM applications assist the employee in dealing with customers by providing detailed information on company products, services, and customer orders.

At Rackspace, a San Antonio-based Web-hosting company, customer focus borders on the obsessive. Joey Parsons, 24, won the Straightjacket Award, the most coveted employee distinction at Rackspace. The award recognizes the employee who best lives up to the Rackspace motto of delivering "fanatical support," a dedication to customers that is so intense it borders on the loony. Rackspace motivates its staff by treating each team as a separate business, which is responsible for its own profits and losses and has its own ERM Web site. Each month, employees can earn bonuses of up to 20 percent of their monthly base salaries depending on the performance of their units by both financial and customer-centric measurements such as customer turnover, customer expansion, and customer referrals. Daily reports are available through the team's ERM Web site.[15]

Future Trends

CRM revenue forecast for 2008 is $11.5 billion. In the future, CRM applications will continue to change from employee-only tools to tools used by suppliers, partners, and even customers. Providing a consistent view of customers and delivering timely and accurate customer information to all departments across an organization will continue to be the major goal of CRM initiatives.

As technology advances (intranet, Internet, extranet, wireless), CRM will remain a major strategic focus for companies, particularly in industries whose product is difficult to differentiate. Some companies approach this problem by moving to a low-cost producer strategy. CRM will be an alternative way to pursue a differentiation strategy with a nondifferentiable product.

CRM applications will continue to adapt wireless capabilities supporting mobile sales and mobile customers. Sales professionals will be able to access e-mail, order details, corporate information, inventory status, and opportunity information all from a PDA in their car or on a plane. Real-time interaction with human CSRs over the Internet will continue to increase.

CRM suites will also incorporate PRM and SRM modules as enterprises seek to take advantage of these initiatives. Automating interactions with distributors, resellers, and suppliers will enhance the corporation's ability to deliver a quality experience to its customers.

A s organizations migrate from the traditional product-focused organization toward customer-driven organizations, they are recognizing their customers as experts, not just revenue generators. Organizations are quickly realizing that without customers they simply would not exist and it is critical they do everything they can to ensure their customers' satisfaction. In an age when product differentiation is difficult, CRM is one of the most valuable assets a company can acquire.

Sales, marketing, and customer service departments can implement many different types of CRM technologies that can assist in the difficult tasks of customer identification, segmentation, and prediction (see Figure B9.7).

Analytical CRM relies on data warehousing and business intelligence to find insights into customer information in order to build stronger relationships. Organizations are also discovering a wave of other key business areas where it is beneficial to take advantage of building strong relationships including supplier relationship management (SRM), partner relationship management (PRM), and employee relationship management (ERM). The sooner a company embraces CRM the better off it will be and the harder it will be for competitors to steal loyal and devoted customers.

Operational CRM Technologies		
Marketing	**Sales**	**Customer Service**
1. List generator	1. Sales management	1. Contact center
2. Campaign management	2. Contact management	2. Web-based self-service
3. Cross-selling and up-selling	3. Opportunity management	3. Call scripting

FIGURE B9.7

Operational CRM Technologies for Sales, Marketing, and Customer Service Departments

Analytical CRM, 416
Automatic call distribution, 422
Call scripting system, 422
Campaign management
    system, 417
Click-to-talk, 422
Contact center (Call center), 422
Contact management CRM
    system, 419
Cross-selling, 418
Customer relationship
    management (CRM), 416

Employee relationship
    management (ERM), 426
Interactive voice response
    (IVR), 422
List generator, 417
Operational CRM, 416
Opportunity management CRM
    system, 420
Partner relationship
    management (PRM), 425
Personalization, 423
Predictive dialing, 422

Sales force automation
    (SFA), 418
Sales management CRM
    system, 419
Supplier relationship
    management (SRM), 425
Up-selling, 418
Web-based self-service
    system, 422

Fighting Cancer with Information

"The mission of the American Cancer Society (ACS) is to cure cancer and relieve the pain and suffering caused by this insidious disease," states Zachary Patterson, chief information officer, ACS.

The ACS is a nationwide voluntary health organization dedicated to eliminating cancer as a major health problem by supporting research, education, advocacy, and volunteer service. Headquartered in Atlanta, Georgia, with 17 divisions and more than 3,400 local offices throughout the United States, the ACS represents the largest source of private nonprofit cancer research funds in the United States.

To support its mission, the ACS must perform exceptionally well in three key areas. First, it must be able to provide its constituents—more than 2 million volunteers, patients, and donors—with the best information available regarding the prevention, detection, and treatment of cancer. Second, ACS must be able to demonstrate that it acts responsibly with the funds entrusted to it by the public. "Among other things, that means being able to provide exceptional service when someone calls our call center with a question about mammography screening or our latest antismoking campaign," says Terry Music, national vice president for Information Delivery at the ACS. Third, ACS must be able to continually secure donations of time and money from its constituent base. Its success in this area is directly related to providing excellent information and service, as well as having an integrated view of its relationship with constituents. "To succeed, we need to understand the full extent of each constituent's relationship with us so we can determine where there might be opportunities to expand that relationship," says Music.

The ACS was experiencing many challenges with its current information. "Our call center agents did not know, for example, if a caller was both a donor and a volunteer, or if a caller was volunteering for the society in multiple ways," he says. "This splintered view made it challenging for American Cancer Society representatives to deliver personalized service and make informed recommendations regarding other opportunities within the society that might interest a caller."

The ACS chose to implement a customer relationship management solution to solve its information issues. Critical to the CRM system's success was consolidating information from various databases across the organization to provide a single view of constituents and all information required to serve them. After an evaluation process that included participation from individuals across the organization, the ACS chose Siebel Systems as its CRM solution provider. The society wanted to work with a company that could address both its immediate needs with a best-in-class e-business solution and its future requirements.

The Siebel Call Center is specifically designed for the next generation of contact centers, enabling organizations to provide world-class customer service, generate increased revenue, and create a closed-loop information flow seamlessly over multichannel sales, marketing, and customer service operations. Siebel Call Center empowers agents at every level by providing up-to-the-minute information and in-depth customer and product knowledge. This approach enables quick and accurate problem resolution and generates greater relationship opportunities. The ACS has received numerous benefits from the system including:

1. Increased constituent satisfaction and loyalty by supporting personalized interactions between constituents and cancer information specialists.
2. Improved productivity of cancer information specialists by consolidating all information required to serve constituents into a single view.
3. Increased donations of time and money by helping call center agents identify callers who are likely to be interested in expanding their relationship with the ACS.[16]

Questions

1. How could the ACS's marketing department use operational CRM to strengthen its relationships with its customers?
2. How could the ACS's customer service department use operational CRM to strengthen its relationships with its customers?
3. Review all of the operational CRM technologies and determine which one would add the greatest value to ACS's business.
4. Describe the benefits ACS could gain from using analytical CRM.
5. Summarize SRM and describe how ACS could use it to increase efficiency in its business.

 CLOSING CASE TWO

Calling All Canadians

With multiple communication channels available and so many CRM failures, many companies are concluding that the best method for providing customer service is good old-fashioned customer service provided by a live person. At the same time companies consider outsourcing their customer service departments to other countries in order to save money, many worry about foreign accents as well as time-zone issues related to offshore outsourcing.

Canada has become one of the primary targets for outsourcing customer service centers by U.S. companies. Not only are accent and time-zone issues nonexistent, but companies also receive a favorable exchange rate. The Bank of Canada estimates that over the past five years, the currency exchange rate between the United States and Canada favors Americans by 44 percent. For every dollar an American business spends in Canada, it receives over a dollar and a half in goods and services.

Additional factors that make Canada even more attractive include a high Canadian unemployment rate estimated at 7.5 percent in 2003, while the U.S. unemployment rate was 5.9 percent. Canadians also have high education rates with 63 percent of Canadians over the age of 15 being high school graduates. The country's predominantly rural population and strong work ethic along with a declining industrial base have made call center outsourcing an attractive solution for Canada, too.

Canada has been a leader in the call center industry for over a decade. Since the early 1990s, "the Canadian call center industry has grown at an annual rate of 20 percent," according to Steve Demmings, president of Site Selection Canada of Winnipeg, Manitoba. Site Selection Canada promotes and assists site selection for American and Canadian firms. Demmings estimates there are 14,000 call centers in Canada with six or more agents employing 500,000 people, contributing about $36 billion (Canadian) in annual salaries.

In 1994, two Canadian provinces—Manitoba and New Brunswick—made a concerted effort to develop a local call center industry, recognizing the area's high unemployment with little native industry, says Demmings. The other provinces soon followed. Then the call center industry "made a big move" to bring educational institutions on board. "Many colleges have set up call center training programs," Demmings reports. The result has been an established industry with a highly skilled labor pool. "American companies come up here to go shopping, and we need to have the tableware on the table," states Demmings.

What is important to outsourcing buyers is that many Canadian call center customer service representatives have made it their career. Consequently, there is a much lower turnover rate for call centers than in the United States. Demmings reports the CSR turnover rate in the Province of Ontario was 18.3 percent last year. Compare that to the United States, where call center staffing can be a problem. Christopher Fletcher, vice president and research director of CRM for the Aberdeen Group, states, "It is tough to find people to staff a call center. Turnover ranges from 25 percent to 50 percent annually or above. The skill sets of the people you have available are often equivalent to McDonald's."[17]

Questions

1. What are the two different types of CRM and how can they be used to help an organization gain a competitive advantage?
2. Explain how a contact center (or call center) can help an organization achieve its CRM goals.
3. Describe three ways an organization can perform CRM functions over the Internet.
4. How will outsourcing contact centers (call centers) to Canada change as future CRM technologies replace current CRM technologies?
5. Do you believe that call centers in the future will be replaced by robot technology? Why or why not.

✳ MAKING BUSINESS DECISIONS

1. Driving Up Profits with Successful Campaigns (or Driving Down?)

The Butterfly Café is a local hot spot located in downtown San Francisco that offers specialty coffee, teas, and organic fruits and vegetables. The café holds a number of events to attract customers such as live music venues, poetry readings, book clubs, charity events, and local artists' nights. A listing of all participants attending each event is tracked in the café's database. The café uses the information for marketing compaigns and offers customers who attend multiple events additional discounts. A maketing database company, InTheKnow.com, has offered to pay the Butterfly Café a substantial amount of money for access to its customer database, which it will then sell to other local businesses. The owner of the Butterfly Café, Mary Conzachi, has come to you for advice. Mary is not sure if her customers would appreciate her selling their personal information and how it might affect her business. However, the amount of money InTheKnow.com is offering is enough to finance her much needed new patio for the back of the café. InTheKnow.com has promised Mary that the sale will be completely confidential. What should Mary do?

2. Searching for Employee Loyalty

You are the CEO of Razz, a start-up Web-based search company, which is planning to compete directly with Google. The company had an exceptional first year and is currently receiving over 500,000 hits a day from customers all over the world. You have hired 250 people in the last four months, doubling the size of your organization. With so many new employees starting so quickly you are concerned about how your company's culture will evolve and whether your employees are receiving enough attention. You are already familiar with customer relationship management and how CRM systems can help an organization create strong customer relationships. However, you are unfamiliar with employee relationship management and you are wondering what ERM systems might be able to offer your employees and your company. Research the Web, create a report detailing features and functions of ERM systems, and determine what value will be added to your organization if you decide to implement an ERM solution.

3. Increasing Revenues with CRM

Cold Cream is one of the premier beauty supply stores in the metro New York area. People come from all over to sample the store's unique creams, lotions, makeup, and perfumes. The store is four stories high with each department located on a separate floor. The company would like to implement a CRM system to help it better understand its customers and their purchasing habits. Create a report summarizing CRM systems and detail how such a system can directly influence Cold Cream's revenues.

4. Employee Relationship Management

All new employees at the Shinaberry Inn & Spa wear bathing suits during orientation to experience the spa's exfoliating showers and hot mineral baths. At the Shinaberry San Francisco, new employees get the same penthouse champagne toast the hotel uses to woo meeting planners. And at many properties, employees arriving for their first day have their cars parked by the valet or get vouchers for a free night's stay. This innovative orientation program, which lets employees experience what guests experience, began two years ago after focus groups pointed to empathy as a service differentiator. As a result, the company added empathy to the attributes for which it screens and a training program that involves listening to recorded guest phone calls. Even its discounted employee travel program gives employees yet another way to understand the guest experience. Design an ERM system that would help Shinaberry further its employee-centered culture. The ERM system must take into account all employee needs.

5. Supporting Customers

Creative.com is an e-business that sells craft materials and supplies over the Internet. You have just started as the vice president of customer service, and you have a team of 45 customer service representatives. Currently, the only form of customer service is the 1-800 number, and the company is receiving a tremendous number of calls regarding products, orders, and shipping information. The average wait time for a customer to speak to a customer service representative is 35 minutes. Orders are being canceled and Creative.com is losing business due to its lack of customer service. Create a strategy to revamp the customer service center at Creative.com and get the company back on track.

Enterprise Resource Planning

1. Compare core enterprise resource planning components and extended enterprise resource planning components.
2. Describe the three primary components found in core enterprise resource planning systems.
3. Describe the four primary components found in extended enterprise resource planning systems.
4. Explain the benefits and risks associated with enterprise resource planning systems.
5. Assess the future of enterprise resource planning systems.

Introduction

Enterprise resource planning (ERP) integrates all departments and functions throughout an organization into a single IT system (or integrated set of IT systems) so that employees can make decisions by viewing enterprisewide information on all business operations.

SAP, the leading ERP vendor, boasts 20,000 installations and 10 million users worldwide. These figures represent only 30 percent of the overall ERP market. Figure B10.1 highlights a few reasons ERP solutions have proven to be such a powerful force.

ERP as a business concept resounds as a powerful internal information management nirvana: Everyone involved in sourcing, producing, and delivering the company's product works with the same information, which eliminates redundancies, reduces wasted time, and removes misinformation.

Core and Extended ERP Components

Turner Industries grew from $300 million in sales to $800 million in sales in less than 10 years thanks to the implementation of an ERP system. Ranked number 369 on the Forbes 500 list of privately held companies, Turner Industries is a leading industrial services firm. Turner Industries develops and deploys advanced software

Reasons ERP Systems Are Powerful Organizational Tools
ERP is a logical solution to the mess of incompatible applications that had sprung up in most businesses.
ERP addresses the need for global information sharing and reporting.
ERP is used to avoid the pain and expense of fixing legacy systems.

FIGURE B10.1

Reasons ERP Systems Are Powerful Organizational Tools

applications designed to maximize the productivity of its 25,000 employees and construction equipment valued at more than $100 million.

The company considers the biggest challenges in the industrial services industry to be completing projects on time, within budget, while fulfilling customers' expectations. To meet these challenges the company invested in an ERP system and named the project Interplan. Interplan won Constructech's Vision award for software innovation in the heavy construction industry. Interplan runs all of Turner's construction, turnaround, shutdown, and maintenance projects and is so adept at estimating and planning jobs that Turner Industries typically achieves higher profit margins on projects that use Interplan. As the ERP solution makes the company more profitable, the company can pass on the cost savings to its customers, giving the company an incredible competitive advantage.[1]

Figure B10.2 provides an example of an ERP system with its core and extended components. *Core ERP components* are the traditional components included in most ERP systems and they primarily focus on internal operations. *Extended ERP components* are the extra components that meet the organizational needs not covered by the core components and primarily focus on external operations.

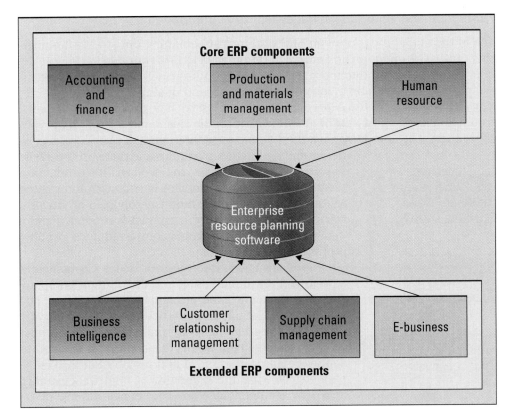

FIGURE B10.2

Core ERP Components and Extended ERP Components

CORE ERP COMPONENTS

The three most common *core* ERP components focusing on internal operations are:

1. Accounting and finance.
2. Production and materials management.
3. Human resources.

Accounting and Finance ERP Components

Deeley Harley-Davidson Canada (DHDC), the exclusive Canadian distributor of Harley-Davidson motorcycles, has improved inventory, turnaround time, margins, and customer satisfaction—all with the implementation of a financial ERP system. The system has opened up the power of information to the company and is helping it make strategic decisions when it still has the time to change things. The ERP system provides the company with ways to manage inventory, turnaround time, and warehouse space more effectively.[2]

Accounting and finance ERP components manage accounting data and financial processes within the enterprise with functions such as general ledger, accounts payable, accounts receivable, budgeting, and asset management. One of the most useful features included in an ERP accounting/finance component is its credit-management feature. Most organizations manage their relationships with customers by setting credit limits, or a limit on how much a customer can owe at any one time. The company then monitors the credit limit whenever the customer places a new order or sends in a payment. ERP financial systems help to correlate customer orders with customer account balances determining credit availability. Another great feature is the ability to perform product profitability analysis. ERP financial components are the backbone behind product profitability analysis and allow companies to perform all types of advanced profitability modeling techniques.

Production and Materials Management ERP Components

One of the main functions of an ERP system is streamlining the production planning process. **Production and materials management ERP components** handle the various aspects of production planning and execution such as demand forecasting, production scheduling, job cost accounting, and quality control. Companies typically produce multiple products, each of which has many different parts. Production lines, consisting of machines and employees, build the different types of products. The company must then define sales forecasting for each product to determine production schedules and materials purchasing. Figure B10.3 displays the typical ERP production planning process. The process begins with forecasting sales in order to plan operations. A detailed production schedule is developed if the product is produced and a materials requirement plan is completed if the product is purchased.

Grupo Farmanova Intermed, located in Costa Rica, is a pharmaceutical marketing and distribution company that markets nearly 2,500 products to approximately 500 customers in Central and South America. The company identified a need for software that could unify product logistics management in a single country. It decided to deploy PeopleSoft financial and distribution ERP components allowing the company to improve customer data management, increase confidence among internal and external users, and coordinate the logistics of inventory. With the software the company enhanced its capabilities for handling, distributing, and marketing its pharmaceuticals.[3]

FIGURE B10.3

The Production Planning Process

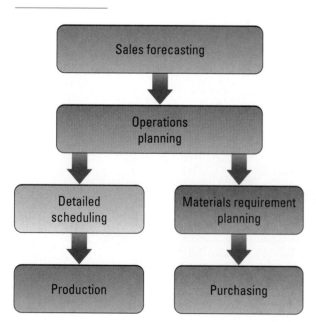

Human Resources ERP Components

Human resources ERP components track employee information including payroll, benefits, compensation, and performance assessment, and assure compliance with the legal requirements of multiple jurisdictions and tax authorities. Human resources components even offer features that allow the organization to perform detailed analysis on its employees to determine such things as the identification of individuals who are likely to leave the company unless additional compensation or benefits are provided. These components can also identify which employees are using which resources, such as online training and long-distance telephone services. They can also help determine whether the most talented people are working for those business units with the highest priority—or where they would have the greatest impact on profit.

EXTENDED ERP COMPONENTS

Extended ERP components are the extra components that meet the organizational needs not covered by the core components and primarily focus on external operations. Many of the numerous extended ERP components are Internet enabled and require interaction with customers, suppliers, and business partners outside the organization. The four most common extended ERP components are:

1. Business intelligence.
2. Customer relationship management.
3. Supply chain management.
4. E-business.

Business Intelligence Components

ERP systems offer powerful tools that measure and control organizational operations. Many organizations have found that these valuable tools can be enhanced to provide even greater value through the addition of powerful business intelligence systems. *Business intelligence* describes information that people use to support their decision-making efforts. The business intelligence components of ERP systems typically collect information used throughout the organization (including data used in many other ERP components), organize it, and apply analytical tools to assist managers with decisions. Data warehouses are one of the most popular extensions to ERP systems, with over two-thirds of U.S. manufacturers adopting or planning such systems.[4]

Customer Relationship Management Components

ERP vendors are expanding their functionality to provide services formerly supplied by customer relationship management (CRM) vendors such as Siebel. *Customer relationship management (CRM)* involves managing all aspects of a customer's relationship with an organization to increase customer loyalty and retention and an organization's profitability. CRM components provide an integrated view of customer data and interactions allowing organizations to work more effectively with customers and be more responsive to their needs. CRM components typically include contact centers, sales force automation, and marketing functions. These improve the customer experience while identifying a company's most (and least) valuable customers for better allocation of resources.

Supply Chain Management Components

ERP vendors are expanding their functionality to provide services formerly supplied by supply chain management vendors such as i2 Technologies and Manugistics. *Supply chain management (SCM)* involves the management of information flows between and among stages in a supply chain to maximize total supply chain effectiveness and profitability. SCM components help an organization plan, schedule, control, and optimize the supply chain from its acquisition of raw materials to the receipt of finished goods by customers.

E-Business Components

The original focus of ERP systems was the internal organization. In other words, ERP systems are not fundamentally ready for the external world of e-business. The newest and most exciting extended ERP components are the e-business components. *E-business* means conducting business on the Internet, not only buying and selling, but also serving customers and collaborating with business partners. Two of the primary features of e-business components are e-logistics and e-procurement. *E-logistics* manages the transportation and storage of goods. *E-procurement* is the business-to-business (B2B) purchase and sale of supplies and services over the Internet.

E-business and ERP complement each other by allowing companies to establish a Web presence and fulfill orders expeditiously. A common mistake made by many businesses is deploying a Web presence before the integration of back-office systems or an ERP system. For example, one large toy manufacturer announced less than a week before Christmas that it would be unable to fulfill any of its Web orders. The company had all the toys in the warehouse, but it could not organize the basic order processing function to get the toys delivered to the consumers on time.

Customers and suppliers are now demanding access to ERP information including order status, inventory levels, and invoice reconciliation. Plus, the customers and partners want all this information in a simplified format available through a Web site. This is a difficult task to accomplish because most ERP systems are full of technical jargon, which is why employee training is one of the hidden costs associated with ERP implementations. Removing the jargon to accommodate untrained customers and partners is one of the more difficult tasks when Web-enabling an ERP system. To accommodate the growing needs of the e-business world, ERP vendors need to build two new channels of access into the ERP system information—one channel for customers (B2C) and one channel for businesses, suppliers, and partners (B2B).[5]

ERP Benefits and Risks (Cost)

There is no guarantee of success for an ERP system. ERPs focus on how a corporation operates internally, and optimizing these operations takes significant time and energy. According to Meta Group, it takes the average company 8 to 18 months to see any benefits from an ERP system. The good news is that the average savings from new ERP systems are $1.6 million per year. Figure B10.4 displays a list of the five most common benefits an organization can expect to achieve from a successful ERP implementation.[6]

Along with understanding the benefits an organization can gain from an ERP system, it is just as important to understand the primary risk associated with an ERP implementation—cost. ERP systems do not come cheap. Meta Group studied the total cost of ownership (TCO) for an ERP system. The study included hardware, software, professional services, and internal staff costs. Sixty-three companies were surveyed ranging in size from small to large over a variety of industries. The average TCO was $15 million (highest $300 million and lowest $400,000). The price tag for an ERP system can easily start in the multiple millions of dollars and implementation can take an average of 23 months.[7] Figure B10.5 displays a few of the costs associated with an ERP system.

Common ERP Benefits
1. **Integrate financial information:** To understand an organization's overall performance, managers must have a single financial view.
2. **Integrate customer order information:** With all customer order information in a single system it is easier to coordinate manufacturing, inventory, and shipping to send a common message to customers regarding order status.
3. **Standardize and speed up manufacturing processes:** ERP systems provide standard methods for manufacturing companies to use when automating steps in the manufacturing process. Standardizing manufacturing processes across an organization saves time, increases production, and reduces head count.
4. **Reduce inventory:** With improved visibility in the order fulfillment process, an organization can reduce inventories and streamline deliveries to its customers.
5. **Standardize human resource information:** ERPs provide a unified method for tracking employees' time, as well as communicating HR benefits and services.

FIGURE B10.4

Common Benefits Received from ERP Systems

The Future of ERP

ERP places new demands not only on support and delivery information technology, but also on the way business processes have to be designed, implemented, monitored, and maintained. For example, several persons in different locations and with different hardware and software resources may simultaneously initiate a purchase process for the same product but with different selection criteria. Reliability, efficiency, and scalability are among the features that have to be embedded in e-business processes in ERP systems. Despite the rapid growth in the number of ERP installations, conducting ERP operations is still challenging.

Understanding the many different types of core and extended ERP components can help an organization determine which components will add the most value. The two biggest vendors in the ERP market are Oracle, which purchased PeopleSoft in 2005, and SAP. Figure B10.6 is an overview of a few of the components offered by each ERP vendor.

In the future, the line between ERP, SCM, and CRM will continue to blur as ERP vendors broaden the functionality of their product suites and redefine the packaging of their products. ERP vendors with comprehensive but modular components

Associated ERP Risks (Cost)
Software cost: Purchasing the software.
Consulting fees: Hiring external experts to help implement the system correctly.
Process rework: Redefining processes in order to ensure the company is using the most efficient and effective processes.
Customization: If the software package does not meet all of the company's needs, customizing the software may be required.
Integration and testing: Ensuring all software products, including disparate systems not part of the ERP system, are working together or are integrated. Testing the ERP system includes testing all integrations.
Training: Training all new users.
Data warehouse integration and data conversion: Moving data from an old system into the new ERP system.

FIGURE B10.5

Associated ERP Risks (Cost)

PeopleSoft (Purchased by Oracle)	
Component	**Description**
Application Integration	Integrate PeopleSoft and non-PeopleSoft applications at all levels with Portal Solutions, AppConnect, and Data Warehousing and Analytic Solutions.
Customer Relationship Management	Get immediate, seamless integration among customer, financial, supply chain, and employee management systems.
Enterprise Performance Management	Enable customers, suppliers, and employees to connect to set goals, develop plans, and measure progress with our integrated, scalable applications.
Financial Management	Get the power to compete in the business world with a comprehensive suite of pure Internet financial applications.
Human Capital Management (including Human Resources Management Solutions)	Manage and mobilize a unified, global workforce, and align workforce contribution with business objectives.
Service Automation	Optimize project investments, reduce project delivery costs, and maximize resources to increase utilization and value to the organization.
Supplier Relationship Management	Manage all aspects of supplier relationships including indirect and direct goods, as well as services procurement.
Supply Chain Management	Take advantage of solutions that promote business-to-business interaction throughout the supply chain, from customer to supplier.

Oracle	
Component	**Description**
Oracle Financials	Financial applications manage the flow of cash and assets into, out of, and within the enterprise: tracking thousands of transactions, setting fiscal goals for various departments, and allowing managers to project future financial health as they record today's profits.
Oracle Human Resources Management	Oracle Human Resources Management System (HRMS) empowers businesses with the tools to find, extract, and analyze data related to human capital. This intelligence readies a company to rapidly deploy the best resources for maximum employee productivity, satisfaction, and retention.
Oracle Intelligence	Oracle Daily Business Intelligence accesses and shares unified information and analysis across the enterprise with a single definition of customers, suppliers, employees, and products.
Oracle Learning Management	Oracle Learning Management (Oracle iLearning, Oracle Training Management, and Oracle Human Resources Management System) provides a complete infrastructure that lets organizations manage, deliver, and track training, in both online and classroom environments.
Oracle Supply Chain Management	Oracle Supply Chain Management lets organizations gain global visibility, automate internal processes, and readily collaborate with suppliers, customers, and partners.
Oracle Manufacturing	Oracle Manufacturing optimizes production capacity beginning with raw materials through final products.
Oracle Order Management	Oracle's support of the complete fulfillment process from order to cash.
Oracle Marketing	Oracle Marketing drives profit by intelligently marketing to the most profitable customers. By leveraging a single repository of customer information, marketing professionals can better target and personalize their campaigns, and refine them in real time with powerful analytical tools.
Oracle Projects	To consistently deliver on time and on budget, an organization must fine-tune execution, align global organization with projects, and assign the right resources to the most important initiatives at the right time.
Oracle Sales	Oracle Sales allows an organization to learn more about its entire business to identify and target profitable opportunities.

(Continued)

SAP	
Component	**Description**
mySAP™ Customer Relationship Management	The fully integrated CRM solution that facilitates world-class service across all customer touchpoints.
mySAP™ Financials	The leading solution for operational, analytical, and collaborative financial management.
mySAP™ Human Resources (mySAP HR)	The HR resource that helps more than 7,800 organizations worldwide maximize their return on human capital.
mySAP™ Marketplace	An online marketplace solution that allows a company to buy, sell, and conduct business around the clock and around the world.
mySAP™ Product Lifecycle Management	The collaborative solution that helps designers, engineers, and suppliers achieve new levels of innovation.
mySAP™ Supplier Relationship Management	Covers the full supply cycle—from strategic sourcing for lower costs to faster process cycles.
mySAP™ Supply Chain Management	Gives an organization the power to dramatically improve its planning, responsiveness, and execution to suppliers, customers, and partners.

FIGURE B10.6

(Continued)

will dominate the next high-growth phase of the enterprise applications market. Since core functionality is virtually the same for all vendors, a vendor's success will primarily depend upon how quickly it incorporates other kinds of functionality such as the Internet, interface, and wireless technology.

INTERNET

The adoption of the Internet is one of the single most important forces reshaping the architecture and functionality of ERP systems and is responsible for the most important new developments in ERP. The Internet serves as a basis for extending ERP's traditional vision of integrating data and processes across an organization's functional departments to include sharing data and processes among multiple enterprises.

INTERFACE

Most ERP suites offer a customizable browser that allows each employee to configure his or her own view of the system. A manager can also customize each employee's view of the system. This feature allows managers to control access to highly sensitive information such as payroll and performance appraisals. The same customizable browser will be used in the future to allow customers and partners to see only select ERP information via the Internet.

WIRELESS TECHNOLOGY

Wireless technologies provide a means for users with handheld devices, such as PDAs and Web-enabled telephones, to connect to and interact with ERP systems. Most large ERP vendors will acquire smaller companies that specialize in wireless access. If they fail to do so, they will need to develop their own expertise in this area to build wireless access packages.

Wireless technologies will enable users to carry out the same transactions from their mobile devices as they used to do from any fixed device. Being able to buy and sell goods and services over mobile devices is an important step toward achieving the anywhere-anytime paradigm. In the future, location and time will no longer constrain organizations from completing their operations.

Core ERP components are the traditional components included in most ERP systems and they primarily focus on internal operations:

- Accounting and finance components.
- Production and materials management components.
- Human resources components.

Extended ERP components are the extra components that meet the organizational needs not covered by the core components and primarily focus on external operations:

- Business intelligence.
- Customer relationship management.
- Supply chain management.
- E-business.

ERP vendors with comprehensive but modular components will dominate the next high-growth phase of the enterprise applications market. Since core functionality is virtually the same for all vendors, a vendor's success will primarily depend upon how quickly it incorporates other kinds of functionality such as the Internet, interfaces, and wireless technologies.

✳ KEY TERMS

Accounting and finance ERP
    component, 434
Business intelligence, 435
Core ERP component, 433
Customer relationship
    management
    (CRM), 435

E-business, 436
E-logistics, 436
Enterprise resource planning
    (ERP), 432
E-procurement, 436
Extended ERP
    component, 433, 435

Human resources ERP
    component, 435
Production and materials
    management ERP
    component, 434
Supply chain management
    (SCM), 435

✳ CLOSING CASE ONE

PepsiAmericas' Enterprises

Headquartered in Rolling Meadows, Illinois, PepsiAmericas generates $2.97 billion in revenues yearly. The supplier of PepsiCo products has over 15,000 employees and 365,000 customers. The challenge facing PepsiAmericas was the integration of its enterprise systems. The company chose to implement a PeopleSoft ERP solution to enable it to deliver top-line growth and superior customer service through improved selling and delivery methods using standard processes along with proven technology.

With the introduction of numerous products, distribution gaps, and lost promotion opportunities, PepsiAmericas realized it needed a new strategy for managing its enterprise. It needed real-time access to enterprise information and seamless integration between its systems. The company especially required real-time customer information for its telemarketing agents to be able to effectively do their jobs. "It's important for a tel-sell (telemarketing) agent to understand if the customer has any issues or needs based on what's going on with the account.

An error in credit status, a balance history, issues they've logged with the company—all of this will have an impact on how they interact with the customer," said John Kreul, director of enterprise applications for PepsiAmericas.

One of the biggest benefits of the PeopleSoft ERP solution was that it provided complete integration between PepsiAmericas' front-office and back-office systems. This integration allowed tel-sell agents to gain a clear picture of customers and their relationship with the company. "We can more readily see additional sales opportunities. For example, if the customer ordered certain products in the past and there's a promotion going on for a similar product, the agents can offer that to the customer," Kreul said.

PepsiAmericas also implemented PeopleSoft's supply chain management component to automate its inventory accounting. Before implementing PeopleSoft SCM, portions of the company's monthly inventory accounting were done manually and took two weeks to conduct. "Now product inventory accounting is done at period end automatically. It provides us much greater control of the data and has shaven one to two days off our close," said Dave Van Volkenburg, manager of IT applications. Transferring products from one division to another was also a problem with the old system. Differences in product quantities shipped and received would create bottlenecks and result in days spent going back and forth between divisions to determine the accurate amount of products transferred. The SCM component changed all that. "Now our divisions have to send and receive product transfers within the system—so there's much tighter control on the activity, and the data is more accurate," Van Volkenburg said.

The following are the overall benefits PepsiAmericas received from its PeopleSoft ERP solution:

- Convert disparate sales systems to a single, integrated Internet application solution.
- Integrate computer telephony for tel-sell/pre-sell methodology.
- Deliver a 360-degree view of entire customer base.
- Improve customer distribution and profit potential.
- Simplify the issue resolution process.
- Provide more accurate and timely deliveries of products.
- Reduce product inventory close time by one to two days.[8]

Questions

1. How have core ERP components helped PepsiAmericas improve its business?
2. How have extended ERP components helped PepsiAmericas improve its business?
3. Explain how future ERP systems will help PepsiAmericas increase revenues.
4. Assess the impact on PepsiAmericas' business if it failed to implement the CRM component of its ERP system.
5. Review the different components in Figure B10.6. Which component would you recommend PepsiAmericas implement if it decided to purchase an additional component?
6. Compare PepsiAmericas' experience with other ERP cases you can find in most business articles.

★ CLOSING CASE TWO

Campus ERP

When Stefanie Fillers returned to college she needed to log in to the school's new online registration system to make certain that the courses she was taking would allow her to graduate. She also wanted to waive her participation in her college's health insurance plan. When the system crashed the day before classes began, Fillers, a senior, was annoyed. But at least she knew where her classes were—unlike most first-year students.

Several colleges around the country have experienced problems with nonfunctioning Web portals that prevented students from finding out where their classes were. At one college, financial aid was denied to 3,000 students by a buggy new ERP system, even though they had already received loan commitments. The college provided short-term loans for the cash-strapped students while the IT department and financial aid administrators scrambled to fix the complex system.

Disastrous ERP implementations have given more than a few colleges black eyes. These recent campus meltdowns illustrate how the growing reliance on expensive ERP systems has created nightmare scenarios for some colleges. In every case, the new systems were designed to centralize business processes in what historically has been a hodgepodge of discrete legacy systems. College administrators are drawn to ERP systems offering integrated views of finance, HR, student records, financial aid, and more.

ERP implementations are difficult, even in very top-down corporate environments. Getting them to work in colleges, which are essentially a conglomeration of decentralized fiefdoms, has been nearly impossible. Staff members in the largely autonomous departments do not like the one-size-fits-all strategy of an ERP implementation. Plus, these nonprofit organizations generally lack the talent and financial resources to create and manage a robust enterprise system. Representatives from Oracle, which dominates the higher education market for ERP, say that a large part of the problem results from the inexperience of college IT departments and their tendency to rush implementations and inadequately test the new systems.

Standardizing at Stanford

Stanford University bought into the late 1990s enterprise software pitch and never slowed down its implementation engine. "In hindsight, we tried to do too much in too little time," said Randy Livingston, Stanford's vice president of business affairs and CFO.

Starting in 2001, Stanford implemented student administration systems, PeopleSoft HR, Oracle financials, and several other ancillary applications. Years later, users still complain that they have lower productivity with the new systems than with the previous ones, which were supported by a highly customized mainframe. Users also have had difficulty accessing critical information on a timely basis. Livingston said many transactions, such as initiating a purchase requisition or requesting a reimbursement, now take longer for users than with the prior legacy system.

Stanford has also not realized any of the projected savings the vendors promised. "We are finding that the new ERP applications cost considerably more to support than our legacy applications," Livingston said. He does not know how much it will cost to get the enterprise systems working at acceptable user levels.

Stanford's IT department is still trying to get campuswide buy-in for the enterprise applications, which have necessitated new ways of doing business, which leads to nonuse of the new systems and costly customizations to keep all users satisfied. For example, Stanford's law school operates on a semester schedule, while the other six schools operate on a trimester schedule. "This means that every aspect of the student administration system needs to be configured differently for the law school," Livingston said. Within the schools, some faculty members are paid a 12-month salary; other schools pay by 9 months, 10 months, or 11 months. "The standard HR payroll system is not designed to handle all these unusual pay schedules," Livingston said.

To resolve the issues, Livingston has reorganized the IT department, which he hopes will be better able to manage the enterprise projects going forward. He also created a separate administrative systems group that reports directly to him, with responsibility for development, integration, and support of the major ERP systems.

The hurdles Stanford and other colleges face with ERP systems are largely cultural ones. For instance, lean staffs and tight budgets at most university campuses usually lead to a lack of proper training and systems testing. At Stanford, plenty of training was offered, but many users did not take it, Livingston said. He has set up new training programs, including a group of trainers who sit side by side with users to help them learn how to do complex tasks; periodic user group meetings; Web site and e-mail lists that offer more help; and expert users embedded in the various departments who aid their colleagues.

Stanford's IT was still struggling with integrating the enterprise systems when the newly launched PeopleSoft Web portal (called Axess) crashed in 2004. Axess could not handle the load of all the returning students trying to log in to the untested Web-based system at the same time, Livingston said. Stanford was able to fix those problems relatively quickly, but the struggle with the enterprise projects continued. The university's departments remain "highly suspicious and resistant" of his efforts to standardize and centralize business processes, Livingston said.[9]

Questions

1. How could core ERP components help improve business operations at your college?
2. How could extended ERP components help improve business operations at your college?
3. How can integrating SCM, CRM, and ERP help improve business operations at your college?
4. Review the different components in Figure B10.6. Which components would you recommend your college implement if it decided to purchase three components?

✳ MAKING BUSINESS DECISIONS

1. CRM, SCM, and ERP Vendors

Health Caring Inc. recently purchased 12 hospitals in the Denver, Colorado, area. Three of the 12 hospitals currently use SAP products for their CRM and SCM systems. The other nine hospitals use systems from a variety of vendors including Oracle, IBM, and Microsoft. With so many separate systems it is currently impossible to track patients, nurses, doctors, inventory, food services, etc. Health Caring Inc. wants to be able to leverage economies of scale by using its buying clout to drive down prices of such things as inventory and food service, along with creating an environment for flexible staffing in the hospitals for its nurses and doctors. The company's mission is to become known as the "Hospital That Cares." Treating its patients with understanding, care, and high quality service is vitally important to the company's success.

You are the newly appointed CIO and the board of directors is expecting you to develop a plan for moving Health Caring Inc. into the future. The plan should include details of the issues the company is likely to experience with so many disparate systems, along with your recommendation and reasons for implementing an ERP solution.

2. Building an ERP Solution—Cirris Minerals

You are working for Cirris Minerals, a multibillion-dollar mining company, which operates over 3,000 mines in 25 countries. The company is currently looking at implementing an ERP system to help streamline its operations and manage its 150,000 employees. You are leading the team that has to make the decision as to whether the company should buy or build an ERP solution. For the most part, your company's system requirements are similar to other companies in your industry. Compile a list of questions you would require answers to in order to make your buy versus build decision.

3. Building an ERP Solution—Cirris Minerals (continued)

You (in the decision above) have recommended that Cirris Minerals implement an Oracle ERP solution. The CEO is on board with your recommendation. However, she wants you to use a phased approach to implementation. This means you must implement the new system in phases until it is evident that the new system performs correctly. The company will implement the remaining phases as soon as the first phase is completed successfully. You must now recommend which components the company should implement first. From the table below, choose the first two components that Cirris Minerals should implement. Be sure to include the justifications for the implementation of these components.

Oracle	
Component	**Description**
Application Integration	Integrate Oracle and non-Oracle applications at all levels with Portal Solutions, AppConnect, and Data Warehousing and Analytic Solutions.
Customer Relationship Management	Get immediate, seamless integration among customer, financial, supply chain, and employee management systems.
Enterprise Performance Management	Enable customers, suppliers, and employees to connect to set goals, develop plans, and measure progress with our integrated, scalable applications.
Financial Management	Get the power to compete in the business world with a comprehensive suite of pure Internet financial applications.
Human Capital Management (including Human Resources Management Solutions)	Manage and mobilize a unified, global workforce, and align workforce contribution with business objectives.
Service Automation	Optimize project investments, reduce project delivery costs, and maximize resources to increase utilization and value to your organization.
Supplier Relationship Management	Manage all aspects of supplier relationships including indirect and direct goods, as well as services procurement.
Supply Chain Management	Take advantage of solutions that promote business-to-business interaction throughout the supply chain, from customer to supplier.

4. Most Popular ERP Component

Mackenzie Coombe is currently thinking about implementing an ERP solution in her online music company, The Burford Beat. The company is generating over $12 million in revenues and is growing by 150 percent a year. Create a one-page document explaining the advantages and disadvantages of ERP systems, why ERP systems include CRM and SCM components, and why the most popular ERP component in today's marketplace is the accounting and finance core component.

5. Value-Added ERP

Pirate's Pizza is a large pizza chain that operates 700 franchises in 15 states. The company is contemplating implementing a new ERP system, which is expected to cost $7 million and take 18 months to implement. Once the system is completed, it is expected to generate $12 million a year in decreased costs and increased revenues. You are working in the finance department for the company and your boss has asked you to compile a report detailing the different financial metrics you can use to assess the business value of the new ERP system. Once your report is completed, the company will make a decision about purchasing the ERP system.

6. **Increasing Revenues with ERP**

Cold Cream is one of the premier beauty supply stores in the metro New York area. People come from all over to sample the store's unique creams, lotions, makeup, and perfumes. The company receives its products from manufacturers around the globe. The company would like to implement an ERP system to help it better understand its customers and their purchasing habits. Create a report summarizing ERP systems and explain how an ERP system can directly influence Cold Cream's revenues.

PLUG-IN

B11

E-Business

PLUG-IN

LEARNING OUTCOMES

1. Describe the four common tools an organization can use to access Internet information.
2. Compare ISPs, OSPs, and ASPs. Be sure to include an overview of common services offered by each.
3. Describe how marketing, sales, financial services, and customer service departments can use e-business to increase revenues or reduce costs.
4. Explain why an organization would use metrics to determine a Web site's success.
5. Identify the different types of e-government business models.
6. Define m-commerce and explain how an e-government could use it to increase its efficiency and effectiveness.

Introduction

As organizations, governments, and academia embrace the Internet to conduct business, new approaches in the way they reach their target customers have resulted in numerous e-business opportunities. A *pure play (virtual) business* is a business that operates on the Internet only without a physical store, such as Expedia.com and Amazon.com. New technologies, competition, and cost savings along with the global nature of the Internet have significantly transformed traditional businesses into e-businesses. The core units introduced the concepts of e-business as well as e-business models. This plug-in will build on the units' discussion, providing specific details on the functions of e-business as well as current and future trends.

Accessing Internet Information

Many restaurant and franchise experts believe that Cold Stone Creamery's franchisee intranet is what keeps the company on the fast track. Franchisee owners communicate with other owners through Creamery Talk, the company's intranet-based chat room. Since it launched, Creamery Talk has turned into a franchisee's black book, with tips on everything from storefront design to equipment repair. When one owner's freezer broke recently, a post to the chat room turned up an easy fix involving a $21 motor fan.[1]

Four common tools for accessing Internet information include:

- Intranet
- Extranet
- Portal
- Kiosk

INTRANET

An ***intranet*** is an internalized portion of the Internet, protected from outside access, that allows an organization to provide access to information and application software to only its employees. An intranet is an invaluable tool for presenting organizational information as it provides a central location where employees can find information. It can host all kinds of company-related information such as benefits, schedules, strategic directions, and employee directories. At many companies, each department has its own Web page on the intranet for departmental information sharing. An intranet is not necessarily open to the external Internet and enables organizations to make internal resources available using familiar Internet clients, such as Web browsers, newsreaders, and e-mail.

Intranet publishing is the ultimate in electronic publishing. Companies realize significant returns on investment (ROI) simply by publishing information, such as employee manuals or telephone directories, on intranets rather than printed media.

Citigroup's Global Corporate and Investment Banking division uses an intranet to provide its entire IT department with access to all IT projects including information on project owners, delivery dates, key resources, budget information, and project metrics. Providing this information via an intranet, or one convenient location, has enabled Citigroup to gain a 15 percent improvement in IT project delivery.[2]

EXTRANET

An ***extranet*** is an intranet that is available to strategic allies (such as customers, suppliers, and partners). Many companies are building extranets as they begin to realize the benefit of offering individuals outside the organization access to intranet-based information and application software such as order processing. Having a common area where employees, partners, vendors, and customers access information can be a major competitive advantage for an organization.

Wal-Mart created an extranet for its suppliers, which can view detailed product information at all Wal-Mart locations. Suppliers log on to Wal-Mart's extranet and view metrics on products such as current inventory, orders, forecasts, and marketing campaigns. This helps Wal-Mart's suppliers maintain their supply chains and ensure Wal-Mart never runs out of products.[3]

PORTAL

Portal is a very generic term for what is in essence a technology that provides access to information. A ***portal*** is a Web site that offers a broad array of resources and services, such as e-mail, online discussion groups, search engines, and online shopping malls. There are general portals and specialized or niche portals. Leading general portals include Yahoo!, Netscape, Microsoft, and America Online. Examples of niche portals include Garden.com (for gardeners), Fool.com (for investors), and SearchNetworking.com (for network administrators).

Pratt & Whitney, one of the largest aircraft-engine manufacturers in the world, has saved millions of dollars with its field service portal initiative. Pratt & Whitney's sales and service field offices are geographically scattered around the globe and were connected via expensive dedicated lines. The company saved $2.6 million

annually by replacing the dedicated lines with high-speed Internet access to its field service portal. Field staff can find information they need in a fraction of the time it took before. The company estimates this change will save another $8 million per year in "process and opportunity" savings.[4]

KIOSK

A *kiosk* is a publicly accessible computer system that has been set up to allow interactive information browsing. In a kiosk, the computer's operating system has been hidden from view, and the program runs in a full-screen mode, which provides a few simple tools for navigation.

Jason Suker walked into the Mazda showroom in Bountiful, Utah, and quickly found what he was looking for in a car dealership—a Web kiosk, one of six stationed around the showroom. Using the Web kiosk, he could track down the latest pricing information from sites like Kelley Blue Book and Edmunds.com. Suker, eyeing a four-year-old limited-edition Miata in mint condition, quickly pulled up the average retail price on Kelley Blue Book. At $16,000, it was $500 more than the dealer's price. Then, on eBay, Suker checked bids for similar models and found they were going for far less. With a sales representative looking over his shoulder to confirm his findings, the skeptical Suker made a lowball offer and expected the worst: endless haggling over price. However, the sales representative, after commending Suker for his research talent, eventually compromised and offered up the Miata for $13,300.

It was an even better deal for Bountiful Mazda. By using a kiosk to help Suker find the bargain price he wanted, the dealership moved a used car (with a higher profit margin than a new model) and opened the door to the unexpected up-sell with a $1,300, 36,000-mile service warranty.[5]

Providing Internet Information

British Airways, the $11.9 billion airline, outsourced the automation of its FAQ (frequently asked questions) Web pages. The airline needed to automatically develop, manage, and post different sets of FAQs for British Airway's loyalty program customers, allowing the company to offer special promotions based on the customer's loyalty program status (gold, silver, bronze). The company outsourced the project to application service provider RightNow Technologies. The new system is helping British Airways create the right marketing programs for the appropriate customer tier.[6]

There are three common forms of service providers including:

1. Internet service provider (ISP).
2. Online service provider (OSP).
3. Application service provider (ASP).

INTERNET SERVICE PROVIDER

An *Internet service provider (ISP)* is a company that provides individuals and other companies access to the Internet along with additional related services, such as Web site building. An ISP has the equipment and the telecommunication line access required to have a point of presence on the Internet for different geographic areas. Larger ISPs have their own high-speed leased lines so they are less dependent on telecommunication providers and can deliver better service to their customers. Among the largest national and regional ISPs are AT&T WorldNet, IBM Global Network, MCI, Netcom, UUNet, and PSINet.

Navigating the different options for an ISP can be daunting and confusing. There are more than 7,000 ISPs in the United States; some are large with household names, and others are literally one-person operations. Although Internet access is

Common ISP Services
■ **Web hosting**. Housing, serving, and maintaining files for one or more Web sites is a widespread offering.
■ **Hard-disk storage space**. Smaller sites may need only 300 to 500 MB (megabytes) of Web site storage space, whereas other e-business sites may need at least 10 GB (gigabytes) of space or their own dedicated Web server.
■ **Availability**. To run an e-business, a site must be accessible to customers 24×7. ISPs maximize the availability of the sites they host using techniques such as load balancing and clustering many servers to reach 100 percent availability.
■ **Support**. A big part of turning to an ISP is that there is limited worry about keeping the Web server running. Most ISPs offer 24×7 customer service.

viewed as a commodity service, in reality features and performance can differ tremendously among ISPs. Figure B11.1 highlights common ISP features.

Another member of the ISP family is the ***wireless Internet service provider (WISP),*** an ISP that allows subscribers to connect to a server at designated hotspots or access points using a wireless connection. This type of ISP offers access to the Internet and the Web from anywhere within the zone of coverage provided by an antenna. This is usually a region with a radius of one mile. Figure B11.2 displays a brief overview of how this technology works.

One example of a WISP is T-Mobile International, a company that provides access to wireless laptop users in more than 2,000 locations including airports, airline clubs, Starbucks coffeehouses, and Borders Books. A wireless service called T-Mobile HotSpot allows customers to access the Internet and T-Mobile's corporate intranet via a wireless network from convenient locations away from their home or office. T-Mobile International is the first mobile communications company to extend service on both sides of the Atlantic, offering customers the advantage of using their wireless services when traveling worldwide.[7]

ONLINE SERVICE PROVIDER

An ***online service provider (OSP)*** offers an extensive array of unique services such as its own version of a Web browser. The term *online service provider* helps to distinguish ISPs that offer Internet access and their own online content, such as America

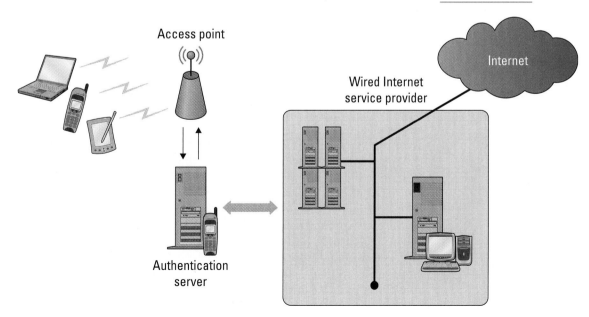

Online (AOL), from ISPs that simply connect users directly with the Internet, such as EarthLink. Connecting to the Internet through an OSP is an alternative to connecting through one of the national ISPs, such as AT&T or MCI, or a regional or local ISP.

APPLICATION SERVICE PROVIDER

An *application service provider (ASP)* is a company that offers an organization access over the Internet to systems and related services that would otherwise have to be located in personal or organizational computers. Employing the services of an ASP is essentially outsourcing part of a company's business logic. Hiring an ASP to manage a company's software allows the company to hand over the operation, maintenance, and upgrade responsibilities for a system to the ASP.

One of the most important agreements between the customer and the ASP is the service level agreement. *Service level agreements (SLAs)* define the specific responsibilities of the service provider and set the customer expectations. SLAs include such items as availability, accessibility, performance, maintenance, backup/recovery, upgrades, equipment ownership, software ownership, security, and confidentiality. For example, an SLA might state that the ASP must have the software available and accessible from 7:00 a.m. to 7:00 p.m. Monday through Friday. It might also state that if the system is down for more than 60 minutes, there will be no charge for that day. Most industry analysts agree that the ASP market is growing rapidly. International Data Corporation (IDC) estimates the worldwide ASP market will grow from around $25 billion by 2008 to $40 billion by 2011.[8] Figure B11.3 displays the top ISPs, OSPs, and ASPs.

Organizational Strategies for E-Business

To be successful in e-business, an organization must master the art of electronic relationships. Traditional means of customer acquisition such as advertising, promotions, and public relations are just as important with a Web site. Primary business areas taking advantage of e-business include:

- Marketing/sales
- Financial services
- Procurement
- Customer service
- Intermediaries

MARKETING/SALES

Direct selling was the earliest type of e-business and has proven to be a stepping-stone to more complex commerce operations. Successes such as eBay, Barnes and Noble, Dell Inc., and Travelocity have sparked the growth of this segment, proving customer acceptance of e-business direct selling. Marketing and sales departments are initiating some of the most exciting e-business innovations (see Figure B11.4).

Cincinnati's WCPO-TV once was a ratings blip and is now the number three ABC affiliate in the nation. WCPO-TV credits its success largely to digital billboards that promote different programming depending on the time of day. The billboards are updated directly from a Web site. The station quickly noticed that when current events for the early-evening news were plugged during the afternoon, ratings spiked.

The digital billboards let several companies share one space and can change messages directly from the company's computer. In the morning, a department store can advertise a sale, and in the afternoon, a restaurant can advertise its specials. Eventually customers will be able to buy billboard sign time in hour or minute increments. Current costs to share a digital billboard are $40,000 a month, compared with $10,000 for one standard billboard.[9]

Company	Description	Specialty
Appshop www.appshop.com	Application Service Provider	Oracle 11i e-business suite applications
BlueStar Solutions www.bluestarsolutions.com	Application Service Provider	Managing ERP solutions with a focus on SAP
Concur www.concur.com	Internet Service Provider	Integrates B2B procurement
Corio www.corio.com	Application Service Provider	Specializes in Oracle applications
Employease www.employease.com	Online service provider	Human resource application services
Intacct www.intacct.com	Online service provider	Online general ledger service
LivePerson www.liveperson.com	Online service provider	Real-time chat provider
NetLedger www.netledger.com	Online service provider	Web-based accounting platform
Outtask www.outtask.com	Application Service Provider	Integration of budgeting, customer service, sales management, and human resources applications
RightNow www.rightnow.com	Online service provider, Internet Service Provider	Suite of customer service applications
Salesforce.com www.salesforce.com	Online service provider	Suite of customer service applications
Salesnet www.salesnet.com	Online service provider	Suite of sales force automation products and services
Surebridge www.surebridge.com	Application Service Provider	High-tech manufacturing, distribution, health care applications
UpShot www.upshot.com	Online service provider	Sales force automation products and services
USi www.usinternetworking.com	Application Service Provider	Ariba, Siebel, Microsoft, and Oracle customer base

E-business provides an easy way to penetrate a new geographic territory and extend global reach. Large, small, or specialized businesses can use their online sales sites to sell on a worldwide basis with little extra cost. This ability to tap into expanded domestic or even international markets can be an immediate revenue boost to artists, jewelry makers, wineries, and the like, for initial orders and especially for reorders.

The Hotel Gatti (www.hotel-gatti.com) is a small hotel in northern Italy catering primarily to Italian travelers. By introducing its own Web site with English-language options, it significantly extended its geographic reach. Now, at very little cost, the hotel communicates with and takes reservations from potential customers in the United States and other English-speaking countries. The bottom line is that e-business now allows any company to market and sell products globally, regardless of its size.[10]

Marketing and Sales E-Business Innovations
■ An *online ad* is a box running across a Web page that is often used to contain advertisements. The banner generally contains a link to the advertiser's Web site. Web-based advertising services can track the number of times users click the banner, generating statistics that enable advertisers to judge whether the advertising fees are worth paying. Online ads are like living, breathing classified ads.
■ A *pop-up ad* is a small Web page containing an advertisement that appears on the Web page outside of the current Web site loaded in the Web browser. A *pop-under ad* is a form of a pop-up ad that users do not see until they close the current Web browser screen.
■ *Associate programs (affiliate programs)* allow businesses to generate commissions or royalties from an Internet site. For example, a business can sign up as an associate of a major commercial site such as Amazon. The business then sends potential buyers to the Amazon site using a code or banner ad. The business receives a commission when the referred customer makes a purchase on Amazon.
■ *Viral marketing* is a technique that induces Web sites or users to pass on a marketing message to other Web sites or users, creating exponential growth in the message's visibility and effect. One example of successful viral marketing is Hotmail, which promotes its service and its own advertisers' messages in every user's e-mail notes. Viral marketing encourages users of a product or service supplied by an e-business to encourage friends to join. Viral marketing is a word-of-mouth type advertising program.
■ *Mass customization* is the ability of an organization to give its customers the opportunity to tailor its products or services to the customers' specifications. For example, customers can order M&M's with customized sayings such as "Marry Me."
■ *Personalization* occurs when a Web site can know enough about a person's likes and dislikes that it can fashion offers that are more likely to appeal to that person. Personalization involves tailoring a presentation of an e-business Web site to individuals or groups of customers based on profile information, demographics, or prior transactions. Amazon uses personalization to create a unique portal for each of its customers.
■ A *blog* (the contraction of the phrase "Web log") is a Web site in which items are posted on a regular basis and displayed in reverse chronological order. Like other media, blogs often focus on a particular subject, such as food, politics, or local news. Some blogs function as online diaries. A typical blog combines text, images, and links to other blogs, Web pages, and other media related to its topic. Since its appearance in 1995, blogging has emerged as a popular means of communication, affecting public opinion and mass media around the world.
■ *Real simple syndications (RSS)* is a family of Web feed formats used for Web syndication of programs and content. RSS is used by (among other things) news Web sites, blogs, and podcasting, which allows consumers and journalists to have news constantly fed to them instead of searching for it. In addition to facilitating syndication, RSS allows a Web site's frequent readers to track updates on the site.
■ *Podcasting* is the distribution of audio or video files, such as radio programs or music videos, over the Internet to play on mobile devices and personal computers. Podcasting's essence is about creating content (audio or video) for an audience that wants to listen when they want, where they want, and how they want. Podcasters' Web sites also may offer direct download of their files, but the subscription feed of automatically delivered new content is what distinguishes a podcast from a simple download or real-time streaming. Usually, the podcast features one type of show with new episodes either sporadically or at planned intervals such as daily, weekly, etc.
■ *Search engine optimization (SEO)* is a set of methods aimed at improving the ranking of a Web site in search engine listings. Search engines display different kinds of listings in the search engine results pages (SERPs), including: pay-per-click advertisements, paid inclusion listings, and organic search results. SEO is primarily concerned with advancing the goals of Web sites by improving the number and position of organic search results for a wide variety of relevant keywords. SEO strategies can increase the number of visitors and the quality of visitors, where quality means visitors who complete the action the site intends (e.g., purchase, sign up, learn something). SEO, or "white hat SEO," is distinguished from "black hat SEO," or spamdexing by methods and objectives. *Spamdexing* uses a variety of deceptive techniques in an attempt to manipulate search engine rankings, whereas legitimate SEO focuses on building better sites and using honest methods of promotion. What constitutes an honest, or ethical, method is an issue that has been the subject of numerous debates.

Online Consumer Payments	
Financial cybermediary	A ***financial cybermediary*** is an Internet-based company that facilitates payments over the Internet. PayPal is the best-known example of a financial cybermediary.
Electronic check	An ***electronic check*** is a mechanism for sending a payment from a checking or savings account. There are many implementations of electronic checks, with the most prominent being online banking.
Electronic bill presentment and payment (EBPP)	An ***electronic bill presentment and payment (EBPP)*** is a system that sends bills over the Internet and provides an easy-to-use mechanism (such as clicking on a button) to pay the bill. EBPP systems are available through local banks or online services such as Checkfree and Quicken.
Digital wallet	A ***digital wallet*** is both software and information—the software provides security for the transaction and the information includes payment and delivery information (for example, the credit card number and expiration date).

FIGURE B11.5

Types of Online Consumer Payments

FINANCIAL SERVICES

Financial services Web sites are enjoying rapid growth as they help consumers, businesses, and financial institutions distribute information with greater convenience and richness than is available in other channels. Consumers in e-business markets pay for products and services using a credit card or one of the methods outlined in Figure B11.5. Online business payments differ from online consumer payments because businesses tend to make large purchases (from thousands to millions of dollars) and typically do not pay with a credit card. Businesses make online payments using electronic data interchange (EDI) (see Figure B11.6). Transactions between businesses are complex and typically require a level of system integration between the businesses.

Many organizations are now turning to providers of electronic trading networks for enhanced Internet-based network and messaging services. Electronic trading networks are service providers that manage network services. They support business-to-business integration information exchanges, improved security, guaranteed service levels, and command center support (see Figure B11.7). As electronic trading networks expand their reach and the number of Internet businesses continues to grow, so will the need for managed trading services. Using these services allows organizations to reduce time to market and the overall development, deployment, and maintenance costs associated with their integration infrastructures.

Traders at Vanguard Petroleum Corporation spent most days on the phone, patrolling the market for pricing and volume information in order to strike the best

Online Business Payments
Electronic data interchange (EDI) is a standard format for exchanging business data. One way an organization can use EDI is through a value-added network. A ***value-added network (VAN)*** is a private network, provided by a third party, for exchanging information through a high-capacity connection. VANs support electronic catalogs (from which orders are placed), EDI-based transactions (the actual orders), security measures such as encryption, and EDI mailboxes.
Financial EDI (financial electronic data interchange) is a standard electronic process for B2B market purchase payments. National Cash Management System is an automated clearinghouse that supports the reconciliation of the payments.

FIGURE B11.6

Types of Online Business Payments

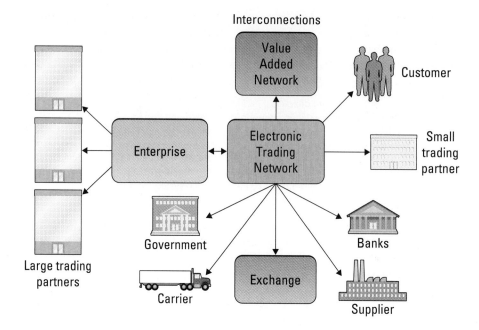

possible deal. The process was slow and tied up traders on one negotiation at a time, making it inherently difficult to stay on top of quickly changing prices. One winter, for example, the weather got cold and stayed cold, causing propane prices to increase dramatically. The price was moving so fast that Vanguard was missing opportunities to buy, sell, and execute deals since it was able to complete only one deal at a time.

To bridge these shortcomings and speed the process, Vanguard became one of the first users of Chalkboard, a commodity markets electronic trading network that is now part of ChemConnect, a B2B e-marketplace. Vanguard uses Chalkboard to put bids and offers in front of hundreds of traders and complete various trades at multiple delivery points simultaneously. Vanguard now completes deals in real time and is able to access a broader audience of buyers and sellers.[11]

PROCUREMENT

Web-based procurement of maintenance, repair, and operations (MRO) supplies is expected to reach more than $200 billion worldwide by the year 2009. ***Maintenance, repair, and operations (MRO) materials*** (also called ***indirect materials***) are materials necessary for running an organization but do not relate to the company's primary business activities. Typical MRO goods include office supplies (such as pens and paper), equipment, furniture, computers, and replacement parts. In the traditional approach to MRO purchasing, a purchasing manager would receive a paper-based request for materials. The purchasing manager would need to search a variety of paper catalogs to find the right product at the right price. Not surprisingly, the administrative cost for purchasing indirect supplies often exceeded the unit value of the product itself. According to the Organization for Economic Cooperation and Development (OECD), companies with more than $500 million in revenue spend an estimated $75 to $150 to process a single purchase order for MRO supplies.[12]

E-Procurement

E-procurement is the B2B purchase and sale of supplies and services over the Internet. The goal of many e-procurement applications is to link organizations directly to preapproved suppliers' catalogs and to process the entire purchasing transaction online. Linking to electronic catalogs significantly reduces the need to check the timeliness and accuracy of supplier information.

An *electronic catalog* presents customers with information about goods and services offered for sale, bid, or auction on the Internet. Some electronic catalogs manage large numbers of individual items, and search capabilities help buyers navigate quickly to the items they want to purchase. Other electronic catalogs emphasize merchandise presentation and special offers, much as a retail store is laid out to encourage impulse or add-on buying. As with other aspects of e-business, it is important to match electronic catalog design and functionality to a company's business goals.

CUSTOMER SERVICE

E-business enables customers to help themselves by combining the communications capability of a traditional customer response system with the content richness only the Web can provide—all available and operating 24×7. As a result, conducting business via the Web offers customers the convenience they want while freeing key support staff to tackle more complex problems. The Web also allows an organization to provide better customer service through e-mail, special messages, and private password-Web access to special areas for top customers.

Vanguard manages $690 billion in assets and charges the lowest fees in the industry: 0.26 percent of assets versus an industry average of 0.81 percent. Vanguard keeps fees down by teaching its investors how to better use its Web site. For good reason: A Web log-on costs Vanguard mere pennies, while each call to a service rep is a $9 expense.[13]

Customer service is the business process where the most human contact occurs between a buyer and a seller. Not surprisingly, e-business strategists are finding that customer service via the Web is one of the most challenging and potentially lucrative areas of e-business. The primary issue facing customer service departments using e-business is consumer protection.

Consumer Protection

An organization that wants to dominate by using superior customer service as a competitive advantage must not only consider how to service its customers, but also how to protect its customers. Organizations must recognize that many consumers are unfamiliar with their digital choices, and some e-businesses are well aware of these vulnerabilities. For example, 17-year-old Miami high school senior Francis Cornworth offered his "Young Man's Virginity" for sale on eBay. The offer attracted a $10 million phony bid. Diana Duyser of Hollywood, Florida, sold half of a grilled cheese sandwich that resembles the Virgin Mary to the owners of an online casino for $28,000 on eBay. Figure B11.8 highlights the different protection areas for consumers.[14]

Regardless of whether the customers are other businesses or end consumers, one of their greatest concerns is the security level of their financial transactions. This includes all aspects of electronic information, but focuses mainly on the information associated with payments (e.g., a credit card number) and the payments themselves, that is, the "electronic money." An organization must consider such issues as encryption, secure socket layers (SSL), and secure electronic transactions (SET), as explained in Figure B11.9.

FIGURE B11.8

Consumer Protection

Issues for Consumer Protection
■ Unsolicited goods and communication
■ Illegal or harmful goods, services, and content
■ Insufficient information about goods or their suppliers
■ Invasion of privacy
■ Cyberfraud

INTERMEDIARIES

Intermediaries are agents, software, or businesses that bring buyers and sellers together that provide a trading infrastructure to enhance e-business. With the introduction

FIGURE B11.9

E-Business Security

_____

E-Business Security
Encryption scrambles information into an alternative form that requires a key or password to decrypt the information. Encryption is achieved by scrambling letters, replacing letters, replacing letters with numbers, and other ways.
A **secure socket layer (SSL)** (1) creates a secure and private connection between a client and server computer, (2) encrypts the information, and (3) sends the information over the Internet. SSL is identified by a Web site address that includes an "s" at the end—https.
A **secure electronic transaction (SET)** is a transmission security method that ensures transactions are secure and legitimate. Similar to SSL, SET encrypts information before sending it over the Internet. However, SET also enables customer authentication for credit card transaction. SETs are endorsed by major e-commerce players including MasterCard, American Express, Visa, Netscape, and Microsoft.

FIGURE B11.10

Types of Intermediaries

_____

Type of Intermediary	Description	Example
Internet service providers	Make money selling a service, not a product	Earthlink.com Comcast.com AOL.com
Portals	Central hubs for online content	Yahoo!.com MSN.com Google.com
Content providers	Use the Internet to distribute copyrighted content	wsj.com cnn.com espn.com
Online brokers	Intermediaries between buyers and sellers of goods and services	charlesschwab.com fidelity.com datek.com
Market makers	Aggregate three services for market participants: a place, rules, and infrastructure	amazon.com ebay.com priceline.com
Online service providers	Extensive online array of services	xdrive.com lawinfo.com
Intelligent agents	Software applications that follow instructions and learn independently	Sidestep.com WebSeeker.com iSpyNOW.com
Application service providers	Sell access to Internet-based software applications to other companies	ariba.com commerceone.com ibm.com
Infomediaries	Provide specialized information on behalf of producers of goods and services and their potential customers	autobytel.com BizRate.com

of e-commerce there was much discussion about disintermediation of middle people/organizations; however, recent developments in e-business have seen more reintermediation. **Reintermediation** refers to using the Internet to reassemble buyers, sellers, and other partners in a traditional supply chain in new ways. Examples include New York-based e-Steel Corp. and Philadelphia-based PetroChemNet Inc. bringing together producers, traders, distributors, and buyers of steel and chemicals, respectively, in Web-based marketplaces. Figure B11.10

lists intermediaries and their functions, including the more commonly applied, such as the following:

- **Content providers** are companies that use the Internet to distribute copyrighted content, including news, music, games, books, movies, and many other types of information. Retrieving and paying for content is the second largest revenue source for B2C e-business.

- **Online brokers** act as intermediaries between buyers and sellers of goods and services. Online brokers, who usually work for commission, provide many services. For example, travel agents are information brokers who pass information from product suppliers to customers. They also take and process orders, collect money, and provide travel assistance, including obtaining visas.

- **Market makers** are intermediaries that aggregate three services for market participants: (1) a place to trade, (2) rules to govern trading, and (3) an infrastructure to support trading. For example, eBay's e-business model focuses on creating a digital electronic environment for buyers and sellers to meet, agree on a price, and conduct a transaction.

Measuring E-Business Success

Traffic on the Internet retail site for Wal-Mart has grown 66 percent in the last year. The site receives over 500,000 visitors daily (6.5 million per week), downloads 2 million Web pages daily, and averages 60,000 users logged on simultaneously. Wal-Mart's primary concern is maintaining optimal performance for online transactions. A disruption to the Web site directly affects the company's bottom line and customer loyalty. The company monitors and tracks the hardware, software, and network running the company's Web site to ensure high quality of service.[15]

The Yankee Group reports that 66 percent of companies determine Web site success solely by measuring the amount of traffic. Unfortunately, heavy Web site traffic does not necessarily indicate large sales. Many Web sites with lots of traffic have minimal sales. The best way to measure a Web site's success is to measure such things as the revenue generated by Web traffic, the number of new customers acquired by Web traffic, or any reductions in customer service calls resulting from Web traffic.[16]

WEB SITE METRICS

Figure B11.11 displays a few metrics an organization can use to measure Web site effectiveness.

Effectiveness Web Site Metrics
■ **Cookie**—a small file deposited on a hard drive by a Web site containing information about customers and their Web activities. Cookies allow Web sites to record the comings and goings of customers, usually without their knowledge or consent.
■ **Click-through**—a count of the number of people who visit one site and click on an advertisement that takes them to the site of the advertiser. Tracking effectiveness based on click-throughs guarantees exposure to target ads; however, it does not guarantee that the visitor liked the ad, spent any substantial time viewing the ad, or was satisfied with the information contained in the ad.
■ **Online ad**—a box running across a Web page that is often used to contain advertisements. An online ad advertises the products and services of another business, usually another dot-com business. Advertisers can track how often customers click on online ads resulting in a click-through to their Web site. Often the cost of the online ad depends on the number of customers who click on the online ad. Tracking the number of online ad clicks is one way to understand the effectiveness of the ad on its target audience.

FIGURE B11.11

Web Site Effectiveness Metrics

To help understand advertising effectiveness, interactivity measures are tracked and monitored. **Interactivity** measures the visitor interactions with the target ad. Such interaction measures include the duration of time the visitor spends viewing the ad, the number of pages viewed, and even the number of repeat visits to the target ad. Interactivity measures are a giant step forward for advertisers, since traditional methods of advertising—newspapers, magazines, radio, and television—provide few ways to track effectiveness metrics. Interactivity metrics measure actual consumer activities, something that was impossible to do in the past, and provides advertisers with tremendous amounts of business intelligence.

The ultimate outcome of any advertisement is a purchase. Tying purchase amounts to Web site visits makes it easy to communicate the business value of the Web site. Organizations use metrics to tie revenue amounts and new customer creation numbers directly back to the Web sites or banner ads. Organization can observe through **clickstream data** the exact pattern of a consumer's navigation through a site. Clickstream data can reveal a number of basic data points on how consumers interact with Web sites. Figure B11.12 displays different types of clickstream metrics.

Marc Barach is the co-inventor and chief marketing officer of Ingenio, a start-up company that specializes in connecting people in real time. When the Internet first emerged, banner ads were the prevalent marketing tools. Next came pay-per-click where the company pays the search engine each time its Web site is accessed from a search. Today 35 percent of online spending occurs through pay-per-clicks. Unfortunately, pay-per-clicks are not suitable for all businesses. Roofers, plumbers, auto repair people, and cosmetic surgeons rarely have Web sites and do not generate business via pay-per-clicks. Barach believes that the next line of Internet advertising will be pay-per-call, and Ingenio has invested five years and $50 million in building the platform to run the business. Here is how pay-per-call works:

- The user types a keyword into a search engine.
- The search engine passes the keyword to Ingenio.
- Ingenio determines the category and sends back the appropriate merchant's unique, traceable 800 telephone number.
- The 800 number routes through Ingenio's switches, and Ingenio charges the merchant when a customer calls.

A Jupiter Research study discovered that businesses were willing to pay between $2 and $35 for each call lead.[17]

FIGURE B11.12

Clickstream Data Metrics

Clickstream Data Metrics
■ The number of page views (i.e., the number of times a particular page has been presented to a visitor).
■ The pattern of Web sites visited, including most frequent exit page and most frequent prior Web site.
■ Length of stay on the Web site.
■ Dates and times of visits.
■ Number of registrations filled out per 100 visitors.
■ Number of abandoned registrations.
■ Demographics of registered visitors.
■ Number of customers with shopping carts.
■ Number of abandoned shopping carts.

Figure B11.13 provides definitions of common metrics based on clickstream data. To interpret such data properly, managers try to benchmark against other companies. For instance, consumers seem to visit their preferred Web sites regularly, even checking back to the Web site multiple times during a given session. Consumers tend to become loyal to a small number of Web sites, and they tend to revisit those Web sites a number of times during a particular session.

Visitor	Visitor Metrics
Unidentified visitor	A visitor is an individual who visits a Web site. An "unidentified visitor" means that no information about that visitor is available.
Unique visitor	A unique visitor is one who can be recognized and counted only once within a given period of time. An accurate count of unique visitors is not possible without some form of identification, registration, or authentication.
Session visitor	A session ID is available (e.g., cookie) or inferred by incoming address plus browser type, which allows a visitor's responses to be tracked within a given visit to a Web site.
Tracked visitor	An ID (e.g., cookie) is available, which allows a user to be tracked across multiple visits to a Web site. No information, other than a unique identifier, is available for a tracked visitor.
Identified visitor	An ID is available (e.g., cookie or voluntary registration), which allows a user to be tracked across multiple visits to a Web site. Other information (name, demographics, possibly supplied voluntarily by the visitor) can be linked to this ID.
Exposure	**Exposure Metrics**
Page exposures (page-views)	The number of times a particular Web page has been viewed by visitors in a given time period, without regard to duplication.
Site exposures	The number of visitor sessions at a Web site in a given time period, without regard to visitor duplication.
Visit	**Visit Metrics**
Stickiness (visit duration time)	The length of time a visitor spends on a Web site. Can be reported as an average in a given time period, without regard to visitor duplication.
Raw visit depth (total Web pages exposure per session)	The total number of pages a visitor is exposed to during a single visit to a Web site. Can be reported as an average or distribution in a given time period, without regard to visitor duplication.
Visit depth (total unique Web pages exposure per session)	The total number of unique pages a visitor is exposed to during a single visit to a Web site. Can be reported as an average or distribution in a given time period, without regard to visitor duplication.
Hit	**Hit Metrics**
Hits	When visitors reach a Web site, their computer sends a request to the site's computer server to begin displaying pages. Each element of a requested page (including graphics, text, interactive items) is recorded by the Web site's server log file as a "hit."
Qualified hits	Exclude less important information recorded in a log file (such as error messages, etc.).

FIGURE B11.13

Definitions of Web Site Metrics

New Trends in E-Business: E-Government and M-Commerce

Recent business models that have arisen to enable organizations to take advantage of the Internet and create value are within e-government. *E-government* involves the use of strategies and technologies to transform government(s) by improving the delivery of services and enhancing the quality of interaction between the citizen-consumer within all branches of government (refer to Figure B11.14).

One example of an e-government portal, FirstGov.gov, the official U.S. gateway to all government information, is the catalyst for a growing electronic government. Its powerful search engine and ever-growing collection of topical and customer-focused links connect users to millions of Web pages, from the federal government, to local and tribal governments, to foreign nations around the world. Figure B11.15 highlights specific e-government models.

M-COMMERCE

In a few years, Internet-enabled mobile devices will outnumber PCs. *Mobile commerce,* or *m-commerce,* is the ability to purchase goods and services through a wireless Internet-enabled device. The emerging technology behind m-commerce is a mobile device equipped with a Web-ready micro-browser. To take advantage of the m-commerce market potential, handset manufacturers Nokia, Ericsson, Motorola, and Qualcomm are working with telecommunication carriers AT&T Wireless and Sprint to develop smartphones. Using new forms of technology, smartphones offer fax, e-mail, and phone capabilities all in one, paving the way for m-commerce to be accepted by an increasingly mobile workforce. Figure B11.16 gives a visual overview of m-commerce.

Amazon.com has collaborated with Nokia to pioneer a new territory. With the launch of its Amazon.com Anywhere service, it has become one of the first major online retailers to recognize and do something about the potential of Internet-enabled wireless devices. As content delivery over wireless devices becomes faster, more secure, and scalable, m-commerce will surpass landline e-business (traditional telephony) as the method of choice for digital commerce transactions. According to the research firm Strategy Analytics, the global m-commerce market was expected to be worth more than more than $400 million by 2010, with 800 million customers generating almost 30 billion transactions annually. Additionally, information activities like e-mail, news, and stock quotes will progress to personalized transactions, "one-click" travel reservations, online auctions, and videoconferencing.[18]

FIGURE B11.14

Extended E-Business Models

	Business	Consumer	Government
Business	B2B conisint.com	B2C dell.com	B2G lockheedmartin.com
Consumer	C2B priceline.com	C2C ebay.com	C2G eGov.com
Government	G2B export.gov	G2C medicare.gov	G2G disasterhelp.gov

E-Government Models	
Consumer-to-government (C2G)	C2G will mainly constitute the areas where a consumer (or citizen) interacts with the government. It will include areas like elections, when citizens vote for government officials; census, where the consumer provides demographic information to the government; and taxation, where the consumer is paying taxes to the government.
Government-to-business (G2B)	This model includes all government interaction with business enterprises whether it is procurement of goods and services from suppliers or information regarding legal and business issues that is transmitted electronically.
Government-to-consumer (G2C)	Governments around the world are now dealing with consumers (or citizens) electronically, providing them with updated information. Governments are also processing applications for visas, renewal of passports and driver's licenses, advertising of tender notices, and other services online.
Government-to-government (G2G)	Governments around the world are now dealing with other governments electronically. Still at an inception stage, this e-business model will enhance international trade and information retrieval, for example, on criminal records of new migrants. At the state level, information exchange and processing of transactions online will enable enhanced efficiencies.

FIGURE B11.15

E-Government Models

Organizations face changes more extensive and far reaching in their implications than anything since the modern industrial revolution occurred in the early 1900s. Technology is a primary force driving these changes. Organizations that want to survive must recognize the immense power of technology, carry out required organizational changes in the face of it, and learn to operate in an entirely different way.

FIGURE B11.16

M-Commerce Technology Overview

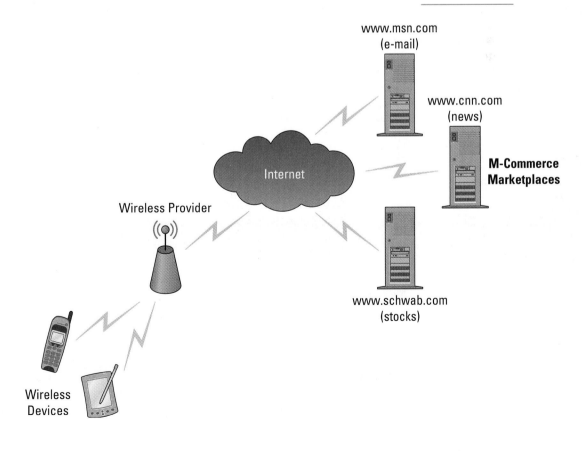

www.msn.com (e-mail)

www.cnn.com (news)

M-Commerce Marketplaces

Internet

Wireless Provider

www.schwab.com (stocks)

Wireless Devices

With the advent of the Internet and e-commerce, e-business is booming. To capitalize on e-business and create new channels that cut expenses, speed delivery time, and open new markets, new strategic e-businesses are emerging daily. To establish an environment conducive to e-business, companies are required to change their strategies, realign their organizations with emerging opportunities, and articulate the new strategies to partners.

Merely deciding to adopt a new e-business model does not guarantee success. Organizations must embrace ASPs, OSPs, intranets, extranets, online bill payments, and so on, all of which involve considerable disruption to current business processes. Technical adjustments, such as integration, debugging, software integration, and effective Web site management, are necessary. Effectively managing the changes associated with the implementation of a new e-business will help an organization find the path to electronic success.

✳ KEY TERMS

Application service provider (ASP), 450
Associate program (affiliate program), 452
Blog, 452
Clickstream data, 458
Click-through, 457
Content provider, 457
Cookie, 457
Digital wallet, 453
E-government, 460
Electronic bill presentment and payment (EBPP), 453
Electronic catalog, 455
Electronic check, 453
Electronic data interchange (EDI), 453
Encryption, 456
E-procurement, 454
Extranet, 447
Financial cybermediary, 453
Financial EDI (financial

electronic data interchange), 453
Interactivity, 458
Intermediary, 455
Internet service provider (ISP), 448
Intranet, 447
Kiosk, 448
Maintenance, repair, and operations (MRO) materials (also called indirect materials), 454
Market maker, 457
Mass customization, 452
Mobile commerce, or m-commerce, 460
Online ad, 452, 457
Online broker, 457
Online service provider (OSP), 449
Personalization, 452
Podcasting, 452

Pop-under ad, 452
Pop-up ad, 452
Portal, 447
Pure play (virtual) business, 446
Real simple syndication (RSS), 452
Reintermediation, 456
Search engine optimization (SEO), 452
Secure electronic transaction (SET), 456
Secure socket layer (SSL), 456
Service level agreements (SLA), 450
Spamdexing, 452
Value-added network (VAN), 453
Viral marketing, 452
Wireless Internet service provider (WISP), 449

✳ CLOSING CASE ONE

Mail with PostalOne

Despite billions of dollars invested in automation and information technology since the early 1970s, the 226-year-old United States Postal Service's (USPS) productivity grew by only 11 percent over the past three decades. The 800,000 employees at USPS faced a fiscal deficit of $2.4 billion in 2001. Factors in the shortfall included the slow economy, rising fuel costs, and electronic alternatives to paper mail.

Agency leaders maintain that technology is one of the keys to making the USPS more competitive, as they have started a heavy campaign to combat declining revenues using a series of Web technology projects. One of the most significant projects for the USPS is a Web front-end for PostalOne, a system that seeks to eliminate the administrative paperwork for bulk mail, which accounts for 70 percent of total mail volume and 50 percent of the agency's $65 billion in revenue. More than 770,000 businesses use the USPS to send bulk mail.

PostalOne is one of the main customer-facing portions of the USPS's plan to build the Information Platform, which comprises the core IT systems that receive, process, transport, and deliver the mail. A tremendous amount of paperwork is associated with verifying a mailing to receive a discounted postage rate and creating related documentation. Business customers will install a USPS application that will reside on their server and manage the online paperwork, validate and encrypt files, and handle communications with PostalOne servers.

The Information Platform will include a Web interface to the agency's Processing Operations Information System (POIS), which collects, tracks, and ultimately delivers performance data on the agency's more than 350 processing and distribution facilities. These efforts follow several e-business projects:

- **NetPost Mailing Online** lets small businesses transmit documents, correspondence, newsletters, and other first-class, standard, and nonprofit mail over the Web to the USPS. Electronic files are transmitted to printing contractors, which print the documents, insert them into addressed envelopes, sort the mail pieces, and then add postage. The finished pieces are taken to a local post office for processing and delivery. Customers get the automated first-class rate, which is a few cents less per piece than the first-class rate.

- **Post Electronic Courier Service, or PosteCS**, a secure messaging product, allows mailers to send documents by e-mail or over the Web to recipients via a secure communication session. PosteCS has an electronic postmark, an electronic time and date stamp developed by USPS, embedded for proof of delivery. PosteCS is used mainly to transfer large files, such as financial statements. Cost is based on the security option chosen and file size.

- **NetPost.Certified,** a secure messaging product, was developed to help federal agencies comply with the Government Paperwork Elimination Act. NetPost.Certified is used, for example, by the Social Security Administration to receive notification from prisons when inmates are no longer eligible for benefits. NetPost.Certified includes an electronic postmark. The service costs 50 cents per transaction.

- **EBillPay** lets customers receive, view, and pay their bills via the agency's Web site. The Postal Service partners with CheckFree, which offers its service on the USPS site and performs back-end processing. Some enhancements to this service are being developed, including an embedded electronic postmark, person-to-person payments, and the ability to receive and pay bills via e-mail. The ability to offer businesses and consumers online bill payment options is vital for the Postal Service, which estimates that $17 billion in annual revenue is at risk from first-class mail going through electronic alternatives for bill payment and presentment.

Despite its problems, the USPS has been resilient over the years, in large part because of its enormous resources. It is the nation's second largest employer behind Wal-Mart, and its revenue would rank it eighth in the Fortune 500.[19]

Questions

1. Do you think the steps by the USPS are far-reaching enough to ensure its relevance in e-business?

2. What other strategic alliances, akin to its partnership with CheckFree, can the USPS develop to stay competitive?

3. Why would the USPS compete in a market that private companies already serve well?
4. How can the USPS use portals to help grow its business?
5. How can the USPS use e-business sales and marketing techniques such as blogs, podcasts, and SEO to improve its business?
6. How can the USPS use ASPs to improve its business?

✱ CLOSING CASE TWO

Made-to-Order Businesses

In the past, customers had two choices for purchasing products: (1) purchase a mass-produced product like a pair of jeans or a candy bar, or (2) commission a custom-made item that was perfect but cost a lot more. Mass customization is a new trend in the retail business. Mass customization hits that sweet spot between harnessing the cost efficiencies of mass production and offering so many different options that customers feel the product has been designed just for them. Today, strategic information systems help many companies implement mass customization business strategies.

Lands' End

Lands' End built a decision support system that could pinpoint a person's body size by taking just a few of their measurements and running a series of algorithms. The process begins when the customer answers questions on Lands' End's Web site about everything from waist size to inseam. Lands' End saves the data in its customer relationship management system, which is used for reorders, promotions, and marketing campaigns. When a customer places an order, the order is sent to San Francisco where supply chain management software determines which one of five contracted manufacturers should receive the order. The chosen manufacturer then cuts and sews the material and ships the finished garment directly to the customer.

Over 40 percent of Lands' End shoppers prefer a customized garment to the standard-sized equivalent, even though each customized garment costs at least $20 more and takes four weeks to deliver. Customized clothes account for a growing percentage of Lands' End's $511 million online business. Reorder rates for Lands' End custom-clothing buyers are 34 percent higher than for buyers of its standard-sized clothing.

Nike

The original business model for Nike iD concentrated on connecting with consumers and creating customer loyalty. Nike iD's Web site allows customers to build their own running shoes. The process begins when customers choose from one of seven styles and a multitude of color combinations. Think dark-pink bottoms, red mesh, bright yellowing lining, purple laces, blue swoosh, and a eucalyptus green accent. Customers can even place eight-character personalized messages on the side of the shoe. The cost averages about $30 more than buying the regular shoes in a store.

Once Nike receives the custom order, its supply chain management system sends it to one of 15 plants depending on production availability. Customers receive their shoes within four weeks. The program has experienced triple-digit annual growth for two years.

Stamps.com

Stamps.com, which provides online stamp purchases, made an agreement with the U.S. Postal Service to sell customized stamps. Customers could put pictures of their choice on an actual

U.S. postage stamp. Pictures ranged from dogs to fiancées. The response was phenomenal: Within seven weeks, Stamps.com processed and sold more than 2 million PhotoStamps at $1 each (37 cents for a regular stamp). Unfortunately, pranksters managed to slip controversial photos through the system, and the U.S. Postal Service temporarily canceled the agreement.

Making mass customization a goal changes the way businesses think about their customers. Using supply chain management and customer relationship management to implement mass customization can have a direct impact on a business's bottom line.[20]

Questions

1. What role does e-business play in a mass customization business strategy?

2. How can Lands' End use additional sales and marketing e-business techniques to improve its business?

3. How can Nike use e-business financial services to improve its business?

4. How can Stamps.com use ASPs and electronic bill payment to improve its business?

5. Choose one of the examples above and analyze its e-business approach. Would you invest $20,000 in the company?

6. Choose one of the examples above and explain how the company is attempting to gain a competitive advantage with mass customization and personalization. How could this company use podcasts, blogs, and SEO to improve its business?

 MAKING BUSINESS DECISIONS

1. Analyzing Web Sites

Stars Inc. is a large clothing corporation that specializes in reselling clothes worn by celebrities. The company's four Web sites generate 75 percent of its sales. The remaining 25 percent of sales occur directly through the company's warehouse. You have recently been hired as the director of sales. The only information you can find on the success of the four Web sites follows:

Web Site	Classic	Contemporary	New Age	Traditional
Traffic analysis	5,000 hits/day	200 hits/day	10,000 hits/day	1,000 hits/day
Stickiness (average)	20 min.	1 hr.	20 min.	50 min.
Number of abandoned shopping carts	400/day	0/day	5,000/day	200/day
Number of unique visitors	2,000/day	100/day	8,000/day	200/day
Number of identified visitors	3,000/day	100/day	2,000/day	800/day
Average revenue per sale	$1,000	$1,000	$50	$1,300

You decide that maintaining four separate Web sites is expensive and adds little business value. You want to propose consolidating to one Web site. Create a report detailing the business value gained by consolidating to a single Web site, along with your recommendation for consolidation. Be sure to include your Web site profitability analysis.

2. A Portal into Saab

Saab Cars USA, a marketing and distribution arm for the Swedish automaker, knew it had to improve communication with dealerships. Specifically, Saab wanted to ensure that dealers could communicate more reliably and easily access all the business systems and tools they needed. That meant upgrading the current system so dealers could tap into several of the company's legacy systems without having to install any Saab-specific hardware or software onsite. In addition, the refined system had to be reliable and inexpensive to maintain, easily support future upgrades, work within existing network and hardware designs, and integrate with existing systems. The portal was designed to make it easy for dealers across the United States to instantly access remote inventory, order parts, conduct online training sessions or research, and submit warranty claims. Identify the specific technological services Saab is looking to integrate into its new portal.

3. Online Auction Sites

You are working for a new Internet start-up company, eMart.com, an online marketplace for the sale of goods and services. The company offers a wide variety of features and services that enable online members to buy and sell their goods and services quickly and conveniently. Its mission is to provide a global trading platform where anyone can trade practically anything. Suggest some ways that eMart.com can gain business efficiencies in its marketing, sales, customer service, financial service, and purchasing departments. Be sure to include intranets, extranets, portals, ASPs, and OSPs.

4. Brewing Marketplace

Founded in 2003, the Foothills Brewing Company, foothillsbrew.com, is a pure play Internet brewing master. In its first year, the brewery sold 1,500 barrels of beer online. Its lagers and ales are brewed in small batches, handcrafted by a team of dedicated workers with high ideals of quality. Identify the advantages and disadvantages foothillsbrew.com will experience if it continues to operate as a pure play in the midst of a highly competitive marketplace.

5. E-Business Metrics

The Razor is a revolutionary mountain bike with full-suspension and shock-adjustable forks that is being marketed via the Internet. The Razor needs an e-business solution that will easily enable internal staff to deliver fresh and relevant product information through its Web site. To support its large audience, it also needs the ability to present information in multiple languages and serve more than 1 million page-views per month to global visitors. Identify the many different Web site metrics Razor should be evaluating to ensure its e-business solution is as efficient and effective as possible.

B12 Emerging Trends and Technologies

1. Identify the trends that will have the greatest impact on future business.
2. Identify the technologies that will have the greatest impact on future business.
3. Explain why understanding trends and new technologies can help an organization prepare for the future.

Introduction

The core units brought out how important it is for organizations to anticipate and prepare for the future by studying emerging trends and new technologies. Having a broad view of emerging trends and new technologies as they relate to business can provide an organization with a valuable strategic advantage. Those organizations that can most effectively grasp the deep currents of technological evolution can use their knowledge to protect themselves against sudden and fatal technological obsolescence.

This plug-in identifies several emerging trends and new technologies that can help an organization prepare for future opportunities and challenges.

Reasons to Watch Trends

Organizations anticipate, forecast, and assess future events using a variety of rational, scientific methods including:

- **Trend analysis:** A trend is examined to identify its nature, causes, speed of development, and potential impacts.
- **Trend monitoring:** Trends viewed as particularly important in a specific community, industry, or sector are carefully monitored, watched, and reported to key decision makers.
- **Trend projection:** When numerical data are available, a trend can be plotted to display changes through time and into the future.
- **Computer simulation:** Complex systems, such as the U.S. economy, can be modeled by means of mathematical equations and different scenarios can be run against the model to determine "what if" analysis.

Top Reasons to Study Trends	
1. Generate ideas and identify opportunities	Find new ideas and innovations by studying trends and analyzing publications.
2. Identify early warning signals	Scan the environment for potential threats and risks.
3. Gain confidence	A solid foundation of awareness about trends can provide an organization with the confidence to take risks.
4. Beat the competition	Seeing what is coming before others can give an organization the lead time it requires to establish a foothold in the new market.
5. Understand a trend	Analyzing the details within a trend can help separate truly significant developments from rapidly appearing and disappearing fads.
6. Balance strategic goals	Thinking about the future is an antidote to a "profit now, worry later" mentality that can lead to trouble in the long term.
7. Understand the future of specific industries	Organizations must understand everything inside and outside their industry.
8. Prepare for the future	Any organization that wants to compete in this hyperchanging world needs to make every effort to forecast the future.

FIGURE B12.1

Top Reasons to Study Trends

- *Historical analysis:* Historical events are studied to anticipate the outcome of current developments.

Foresight is one of the secret ingredients of business success. Foresight, however, is increasingly in short supply because almost everything in our world is changing at a faster pace than ever before. Many organizations have little idea what type of future they should prepare for in this world of hyperchange. Figure B12.1 displays the top reasons organizations should look to the future and study trends.[1]

Trends Shaping Our Future

According to the World Future Society, the following trends have the potential to change our world, our future, and our lives.[2]

- The world's population will double in the next 40 years.
- People in developed countries are living longer.
- The growth in information industries is creating a knowledge-dependent global society.
- The global economy is becoming more integrated.
- The economy and society are dominated by technology.
- The pace of technological innovation is increasing.
- Time is becoming one of the world's most precious commodities.

THE WORLD'S POPULATION WILL DOUBLE IN THE NEXT 40 YEARS

The countries that are expected to have the largest increases in population between 2000 and 2050 are:

- Palestinian Territory—217 percent increase.
- Niger—205 percent increase.
- Yemen—168 percent increase.

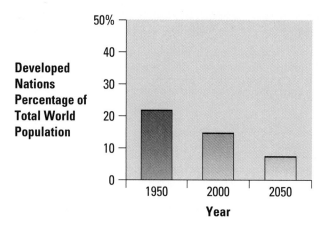

**Developed
Nations
Percentage of
Total World
Population**

- Angola—162 percent increase.
- Democratic Republic of the Congo—161 percent increase.
- Uganda—133 percent increase.

In contrast, developed and industrialized countries are expected to see fertility rates decrease below population replacement levels, leading to significant declines in population (see Figure B12.2).

Potential Business Impact

- Global agriculture will be required to supply as much food as has been produced during all of human history to meet human nutritional needs over the next 40 years.
- Developed nations will find that retirees will have to remain on the job to remain competitive and continue economic growth.
- Developed nations will begin to increase immigration limits.

PEOPLE IN DEVELOPED COUNTRIES ARE LIVING LONGER

New pharmaceuticals and medical technologies are making it possible to prevent and cure diseases that would have been fatal to past generations. This is one reason that each generation lives longer and remains healthier than the previous generation. On average, each generation in the United States lives three years longer than the previous. An 80-year-old in 1950 could expect to live 6.5 years longer today. Many developed countries are now experiencing life expectancy over 75 years for males and over 80 years for females (see Figure B12.3).

Rising Life Expectancy in Developed Countries		
Country	Life Expectancy (Born 1950–1955)	Life Expectancy (Born 1995–2000)
United States	68.9	76.5
United Kingdom	69.2	77.2
Germany	67.5	77.3
France	66.5	78.1
Italy	66.0	78.2
Canada	69.1	78.5
Japan	63.9	80.5

Potential Business Impact

- Global demand for products and services for the elderly will grow quickly in the coming decades.
- The cost of health care is destined to skyrocket.
- Pharmaceutical companies will be pushed for advances in geriatric medicine.

THE GROWTH IN INFORMATION INDUSTRIES IS CREATING A KNOWLEDGE-DEPENDENT GLOBAL SOCIETY

Estimates indicate that 90 percent of American management personnel will be knowledge workers by 2008. Estimates for knowledge workers in Europe and Japan are not far behind. A typical large organization in 2010 will have fewer than half the management levels of its counterpart in 1990, and about one-third the number of managers. Soon, large organizations will be composed of specialists who rely on information from co-workers, customers, and suppliers to guide their actions. Employees will gain new power as they are provided with the authority to make decisions based on the information they acquire.

Potential Business Impact

- Top managers must be computer-literate to retain their jobs and achieve success.
- Knowledge workers are generally higher paid and their proliferation is increasing overall prosperity.
- Entry-level and unskilled positions are requiring a growing level of education.
- Information now flows from front-office workers to higher management for analysis. Thus, in the future, fewer midlevel managers will be required, flattening the corporate pyramid.
- Downsizing, restructuring, reorganization, outsourcing, and layoffs will continue as typical large organizations struggle to reinvent and restructure themselves for greater flexibility.

THE GLOBAL ECONOMY IS BECOMING MORE INTEGRATED

International outsourcing is on the rise as organizations refuse to pay high salaries for activities that do not contribute directly to the bottom line. The European Union has relaxed its borders and capital controls making it easier for companies to outsource support functions throughout the continent.

The Internet is one of the primary tools enabling our global economy. Internet users numbered 1 billion in 2005 and are anticipated to grow to 3 billion by 2010. One of the primary reasons for the increase in Internet use is the increase in connectivity technology. China's Internet users are growing by 6 percent each month, to 111 million in 2005. India's Internet users reached 50 million in 2005 (see Figure B12.4 for India's statistics). The increase in Internet use is increasing revenues for e-businesses.

FIGURE B12.4

Growth of Internet Users in India

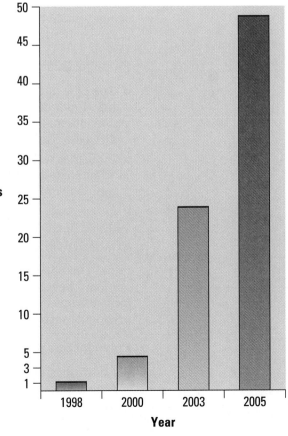

Potential Business Impact

- Demand for personnel in distant countries will increase the need for foreign-language training, employee incentives suited to other cultures, and many other aspects of performing business globally.
- The growth of e-business and the use of the Internet to shop globally for raw materials and supplies will reduce the cost of doing business.
- The Internet will continue to enable small companies to compete with worldwide giants with relatively little investment.
- Internet-based operations require sophisticated knowledge workers and thus people with the right technical skills will be heavily recruited over the next 15 years.

THE ECONOMY AND SOCIETY ARE DOMINATED BY TECHNOLOGY

Computers are becoming a part of our environment. Mundane commercial and service jobs, environmentally dangerous jobs, standard assembly jobs, and even the repair of inaccessible equipment such as space stations will be increasingly performed by robots. Personal robots will appear in the home by 2010. By 2009, artificial intelligence and expert systems will help most companies and government agencies assimilate data and solve problems beyond the range of today's computers including energy prospecting, automotive diagnostics, insurance underwriting, and law enforcement.

Superconductors operating at economically viable temperatures are expected to be in commercial use by 2015. Products eventually will include supercomputers the size of a three-pound coffee can, electronic motors 75 percent smaller and lighter than those in use today, and power plants.

Potential Business Impact

- New technologies provide dozens of new opportunities to create businesses and jobs.
- Automation will continue to decrease the cost of products and services, making it possible to reduce prices while improving profits.
- The Internet is expected to push prices of most products to the commodity level.
- The demand for scientists, engineers, and technicians will continue to grow.

PACE OF TECHNOLOGICAL INNOVATION IS INCREASING

Technology is advancing at a phenomenal pace. Medical knowledge is doubling every eight years. Half of what students learn in their freshman year of college about innovative technology is obsolete, revised, or taken for granted by their senior year. In fact, all of today's technical knowledge will represent only 1 percent of the knowledge that will be available in 2050.

Potential Business Impact

- The time to get products and services to market is being shortened by technology. Products must capture their market quickly before the competition can copy them. During the 1940s the average time to get a product to market was 40 weeks. Today, a product's entire life cycle seldom lasts 40 weeks.
- Industries will face tighter competition based on new technologies. Those who adopt state-of-the-art technology first will prosper, while those who ignore it eventually will fail.

TIME IS BECOMING ONE OF THE WORLD'S MOST PRECIOUS COMMODITIES

In the United States, workers today spend around 10 percent more time on the job than they did a decade ago. European executives and nonunionized workers face the same trend. This high-pressure environment is increasing the need for any product or service that saves time or simplifies life.

Potential Business Impact

- Companies must take an active role in helping their employees balance their time at work with their family lives and need for leisure.
- Stress-related problems affecting employee morale and wellness will continue to grow.

- As time for shopping continues to evaporate, Internet and mail-order marketers will have a growing advantage over traditional stores.

Technologies Shaping Our Future

The following technologies are changing our world, our future, and our lives.[3]

- Digital ink
- Digital paper
- Teleliving
- Alternative energy sources
- Autonomic computing

FIGURE B12.5

Digital Ink

DIGITAL INK

Digital ink (or *electronic ink*) refers to technology that digitally represents handwriting in its natural form (see Figure B12.5). E Ink Corporation, headquartered in Cambridge, Massachusetts, has developed a proprietary technology called electronic ink, which provides significant advantages over other display technologies. E Ink was founded in 1997 to advance electronic ink, develop applications, and create markets for displays based on this unique technology.

Potential Business Impact

- Digital ink has broad usage in many applications, from point-of-sale signs in retail stores, to next generation displays in mobile devices and PDAs, to thin, portable electronic books and newspapers. E Ink has collaborated with various companies like Lucent Technologies to produce reusable paper with digital ink.

- The ultimate dream of E Ink is *RadioPaper,* a dynamic high-resolution electronic display that combines a paperlike reading experience with the ability to access information anytime, anywhere. RadioPaper will be thin and flexible and could be used to create an electronic book or newspaper with real pages.

DIGITAL PAPER

Digital paper (or *electronic paper*) is any paper that is optimized for any type of digital printing. In some ways, digital paper is produced much like a sheet of paper. It comes from a pulp and the finished product has the flexibility to be rolled into scrolls of "paper." However, the major difference between paper produced from a tree and paper produced in a laboratory is that information on a digital paper sheet can be altered thousands of times and not degrade over time (see Figure B12.6). Digital paper offers excellent resolution and high contrast under a wide range of viewing angles, requires no external power to retain its image, is extremely lightweight, costs less, and is remarkably flexible, unlike computer displays.

Macy's department store was the first company to experiment by placing digital paper signs in the children's section at a New Jersey store. As the company spends more than $250,000 a week changing its in-store signs, such renewable signage could prove highly desirable. A networked programmable sign will run for two years on three AA batteries (see Figure B12.7).[4]

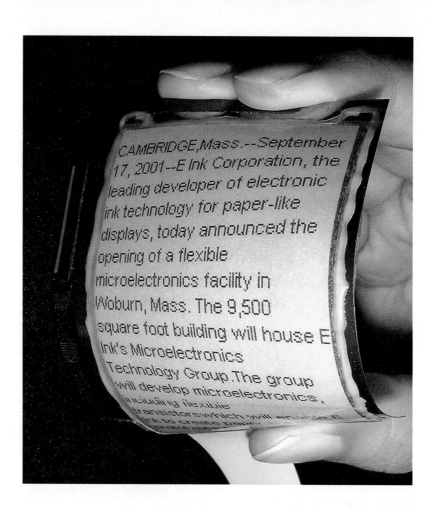

Date	Technology
April 1996	MIT's Media Lab starts work on electronic paper prototype.
April 1997	E Ink is founded to commercialize MIT's electronic paper displays.
May 1999	E Ink debuts Immedia electronic paper display products.
November 2000	E Ink and Lucent Technologies demonstrate first flexible electronic products.
December 2000	Gyricon Media is spun off from Xerox PARC.
February 2001	E Ink teams with Philips Components to develop a high-resolution display for smart handhelds.
March 2001	Gyricon introduces digital paper technology.
June 2001	Macy's is scheduled to test digital paper for in-store signage use.
Late 2001	E Ink/Philips handheld prototype is delivered.
2004/2005	E Ink electronic paper handheld devices becomes available to users.
Mid-2000s	Possible debut of E Ink's RadioPaper wireless electronic publishing technology.

FIGURE B12.8

Digital Ink and Digital Paper Past, Present, and Future

As a laboratory prototype, digital ink and digital paper have been around for some time with demonstration of the technologies often leading to wild predictions about e-books and e-newspapers (see Figure B12.8).

Potential Business Impact

- Digital paper is driving a new wave of innovation in the content distribution field. Paperlike displays will replace newspapers, magazines, and books since they will be almost as manageable as paper and allow display resolution close to print.

- The concept of a reusable paper product is an environmentally sound idea considering that a major portion of the world's paper goes to printing newspapers, magazines, pamphlets, and so on.

TELELIVING

Lifestyle changes will emerge as computers develop capabilities that are more sophisticated. *Teleliving* refers to using information devices and the Internet to conduct all aspects of life seamlessly. This can include such things as shopping, working, learning, playing, healing, and praying. Even today, homes, autos, and work environments are wired into intelligent networks that interact with one another. Each year, 4 billion chips are embedded in everything from coffeemakers to Cadillacs.

Potential Business Impact

- In the future, people will move through a constant stream of information summoned at the touch of a finger. They will interact with life-size images, data, and text in homes and offices. The days of hunching over a computer will be gone.

- The *virtual assistant (VA)* will be a small program stored on a PC or portable device that monitors e-mails, faxes, messages, and phone calls. Virtual assistants will help individuals solve problems in the same way a real assistant would. In time, the VA will take over routine tasks such as writing a letter, retrieving a file, and making a phone call.

- Robotic salespeople will take on human appearances and have the ability to perform all tasks associated with a sales job.

ALTERNATIVE ENERGY SOURCES

By the end of the decade, wind, geothermal, hydroelectric, solar, and other alternative energy sources will increase from their present level of 10 percent of all energy use to about 30 percent. Worldwide wind-power generating capacity grew by 6,500 megawatts in 2003, the fastest rate of growth yet recorded and 50 percent more than the previous year (see Figure B12.9). Nuclear plants will supply 16 percent of the energy in Russia and Eastern Europe by 2010. New sources of carbon fuels are frequently being discovered and more-powerful extraction methods are being developed, thereby keeping supply up and costs down.

Potential Business Impact

- China, Asia, India, South America, and Russia are modernizing their economies, which increasingly use large amounts of energy.

- The cost of alternative energy sources is dropping with technical advances. This growing competition from other energy sources will help limit the price of oil.

- The imminent deregulation of the energy industry is expected to create a huge spurt of innovative entrepreneurship, fostering a wide variety of new energy sources.

- Oil will remain the world's most important energy resource. However, in two or three decades a declining reliance on oil will help reduce air and water pollution. By 2060, a costly but pollution-free hydrogen economy may become possible.

FIGURE B12.9

Wind Power—An Alternative Energy Source

AUTONOMIC COMPUTING

Autonomic computing is a self-managing computing model named after, and patterned on, the human body's autonomic nervous system. Autonomic computing is one of the building blocks of widespread computing, an anticipated future computing model in which small—even invisible—computers will be all around us, communicating through increasingly interconnected networks. Many industry leaders, including IBM, HP, Sun, and Microsoft, are researching various components of autonomic computing. However, autonomic computing is not an overnight revolution in which systemwide, self-managing environments suddenly appear. As described in Figure B12.10, autonomic computing is a gradual evolution that delivers new technologies that are adopted and implemented at various stages and levels.[5]

Potential Business Impact

- The complex IT infrastructures of the future will require more computer automation than ever before. Autonomic computing will be used in a variety of areas that include security, storage, network management, and new redundancy and fail-over capabilities.

- Autonomic computers will continuously seek out ways to optimize computing. In the autonomic environment, computers will monitor components and fine-tune workflows to achieve system performance goals.

- Autonomic computers will be able to "self-heal." In the event of a component failure, an autonomic computer will be able to diagnose the failure and develop a workaround that allows the computer to continue with its functions.

Level	Technologies Implemented
Level 1: Basic	The starting point where most systems are today, this level represents manual computing in which all system elements are managed independently by an extensive, highly skilled IT staff. The staff sets up, monitors, and eventually replaces system elements.
Level 2: Managed	Systems management technologies can be used to collect and consolidate information from disparate systems onto fewer consoles, reducing administrative time. There is greater system awareness and improved productivity.
Level 3: Predictive	The system monitors and correlates data to recognize patterns and recommends actions that are approved and initiated by the IT staff. This reduces the dependency on deep skills and enables faster and better decision making.
Level 4: Adaptive	In addition to monitoring and correlating data, the system takes action based on the information, thereby enhancing IT agility and resiliency with minimal human interaction.
Level 5: Autonomic	Fully integrated systems and components are dynamically managed by business rules and policies, enabling IT staff to focus on meeting business needs with true business agility and resiliency.

FIGURE B12.10

Evolutionary Process of Autonomic Computing

- Autonomic computers will be able to "self-protect." Protection for computing resources primarily takes the form of fighting off invasive viruses and security intrusion attempts.

O
rganizations that can think ahead will be prepared to take advantage of all the new opportunities that rapid social and technological progress is creating. Trends shaping our future include:

- The world's population will double in the next 40 years.
- People in developed countries are living longer.
- The growth in information industries is creating a knowledge-dependent global society.
- The global economy is becoming more integrated.
- The economy and society are dominated by technology.
- The pace of technological innovation is increasing.
- Time is becoming one of the world's most precious commodities.

Technologies shaping our future include:

- Digital ink
- Digital paper
- Teleliving
- Alternative energy sources
- Autonomic computing

✳ KEY TERMS

Autonomic
   computing, 476
Computer simulation, 468
Digital ink (or electronic
   ink), 473

Digital paper (or electronic
   paper), 473
Historical analysis, 469
RadioPaper, 473
Teleliving, 475

Trend analysis, 468
Trend monitoring, 468
Trend projection, 468
Virtual assistant (VA), 475

✳ CLOSING CASE ONE

Autonomic Railways

Canadian Pacific Railway (CPR), based in Calgary, Alberta, Canada, is one of the largest railway systems in North America. With more than 14,400 miles of rail line in Canada and the United States, this $2.6 billion (U.S.) transportation company serves virtually every major industry, from the resource-based industries of the West to the manufacturing bases and consumer markets in central Canada and the northern United States.

Shippers expect fast, reliable services and on-time delivery of goods. As a result, CPR designed many programs—from improving asset management, to strengthening service reliability, to accounting for fluctuating costs—to help it respond to market forces with agility and ease. Val King, manager of IT security for CPR, explains that security management is an essential element in the delivery of these on-demand services. King said, "We must protect our operations from technology attacks, while providing our customers easy, reliable access to information and services online."

The goal of the company's IT security team is simple: minimize risk while optimizing user satisfaction. Yet the team's greatest challenges are lack of resources and tight budgets. "We had to look to technology to help us accomplish our goals," explained King. CPR collaborated with IBM to deliver solutions that are both automated (they can control a defined process without human intervention) and autonomic (they can sense and respond to conditions in accordance with business policies). As a result, IT employees can deliver consistent, reliable service levels at reduced costs since they collaborated with IBM using autonomic computing resources such as Tivoli Risk Manager, Tivoli Access Manager, Tivoli Identity Manager, and Tivoli Decision Support. "The automation of processes through the intelligent self-managing features of Tivoli software can help companies respond to threats more quickly," King said. "The benefit is that organizations can strengthen the resiliency of their environments even as the number of security events increases."

CPR is realizing measurable results from its implementation of Tivoli Security Management solutions and King sees the already-realized benefits as only the "tip of the iceberg." Some of the notable ROI from CPR's investment in Tivoli Security Management solutions include:

1. **Improved productivity**—The IT security team spends less time managing security incidents with Tivoli Risk Manager. The IT staff also expects to spend less time on reporting because data from the various security monitors will be integrated.

2. **Reduced costs**—The application development team estimates that a centralized security model helps accelerate development time. The help desk organization reports a reduction in user calls, due to the password-reset capabilities of Tivoli Identity Manager.

3. **Increased business resiliency**—Using Tivoli Risk Manager, Tivoli Enterprise Console, Tivoli Decision Support, and Tripwire, a data integrity assurance solution from Tripwire, Inc., CPR tests show that if an attack shuts down a service, administrators can get systems back online much faster.

4. **Improved audit compliance**—Before the implementation of Tivoli Access Manager for e-business, security staff would need to look at each system or application to see if it properly applied security policy. Now, security policies are consistent enterprisewide.[6]

Questions

1. Which of the trends shaping our future discussed in this plug-in will have the greatest impact on CPR's business?
2. Which of the trends will have the least impact on CPR's business?
3. How are the functions of autonomic computing providing CPR with a competitive advantage?
4. How can CPR take advantage of other technological advances to improve security?

 CLOSING CASE TWO

Wireless Progression

Progressive Corporation is the fourth-largest automobile insurer in the United States with more than 8 million policyholders and net premiums of $6.1 billion. Progressive offers wireless Web access to holders of its auto insurance policies, a move that analysts have said fits the company's reputation as a technology leader in the insurance industry and its emphasis on customer service.

Customers can use their Web-enabled phones to get price quotes, report claims, locate nearby independent agents by ZIP code, and access real-time account information through the company's Web site. Progressive also has the ability to push time-sensitive data to policyholders via wireless connections, instantly delivering information about an auto-recall notice to a customer's cell phone.

As a cost-saving measure, and in keeping with a corporate tradition of internal development, Ohio-based Progressive decided to build its own wireless applications. Policyholders simply have to type Progressive's Web address into their phones or connect to the site through search engines that specialize in wireless e-business.

Stephen Williams, president of the Insurance Institute of Indiana, a nonprofit trade association that represents insurers in that state, said it's "not uncommon for Progressive to be on the cutting edge with its use of technology." If Progressive is starting to take advantage of the wireless Web, other companies could follow its lead, he added. Jeffrey Kagan, an Atlanta-based wireless technology analyst, called Progressive "the Nordstrom's of insurance because of its emphasis on customer service." The addition of wireless access to its Web site "is a simple but smart way to use technology" to further improve the company's service, Kagan said. Progressive.com leads the insurance industry in consumer-friendly innovations. It was the first auto insurance Web site (1995), first to offer online quoting and comparison rates (1996), first to offer instantaneous online purchase of an auto policy (1997), and first to offer after-the-sale service (1998).

The Progressive.com Web site leads the insurance industry in consumer-friendly innovations and functionality. Progressive.com was recognized as one of the "top 10 Web sites that work" by *InfoWeek Magazine* and was named to the Smart Business 50 by *Smart Business Magazine* for successful use of the Internet to enhance and expand its business.[7]

Questions

1. Which of the trends shaping our future discussed in this plug-in will have the greatest impact on Progressive's business?
2. Which of the trends will have the least impact on Progressive's business?
3. What other forms of advanced technology would you expect Progressive to deploy in the near future?

✱ MAKING BUSINESS DECISIONS

1. Identifying and Following Trends

What's Hot.com is a new business that specializes in helping companies identify and follow significant trends in their industries. You have recently been hired as a new business analyst and your first task is to highlight current trends in the e-business industry. Using the Internet and any other resources you have available, highlight five significant trends not discussed in this text. Prepare a PowerPoint presentation that lists the trends and discusses the potential business impacts for each trend.

2. Reading the Ink on the Wall

IPublish.com is an e-book-only imprint publisher. While large publishers find that e-books are not selling as expected, IPublish.com continues to report positive growth. However, IPublish.com feels threatened by digital ink and digital paper inventions that seem to be revolutionizing the publishing environment and endangering the global paper industry. You have been hired by IPublish.com to develop a strategy to embrace this new technology. Create a detailed report listing the reasons IPublish.com needs to support these two new technologies.

3. Pen Pal

StyleUs is a digital pen that writes on ordinary paper printed with a unique dot pattern almost invisible to the naked eye. A tiny camera in the pen registers the pen's movement across a printed grid and stores it as a series of map coordinates. These coordinates correspond to the exact location of the page that is being written on. The dot pattern makes up a huge map of tiny distinctive squares, so small portions of it can also be given specific functions, such as "send," "store," or "synchronize." When a mark is made in the send box with the digital pen, it is instructed to send the stored sequence of map coordinates, which are translated into an image. The result is an exact copy of the handwriting displayed on the computer, mobile phone, or received as a fax anywhere in the world.

Analyze this new technology and identify how it might affect the digital ink or digital paper market. Be sure to include a Porter's Five Forces analysis of the market.

4. Less Is More

Your organization is teetering on the edge of systems chaos. Your systems administrator is stressed beyond tolerance by too many systems, too many applications, too few resources, and too little time. The scope, frequency, and diversity of demand are causing greater risk than anyone dares to admit. Automating (and reducing complexity of) the operating environment is critical for your business to survive. Research autonomic computing and write a report discussing how this technology can help an organization gain control over its systems.

5. Fly Pentop Computer

BusinessED specializes in creating new and innovative software for education in the business market. Danny Henningson, founder and president of BusinessED, is interested in developing educational products using digital paper and digital ink. Danny has hired you as the vice president of research and development and is excited to hear your ideas for new products. Your first assignment is to study the Fly Pentop computer (www.flypentop.com) and decide how you can apply this type of technology to the business arena.

6. Alternative Energy

With energy costs on the rise, many U.S. homes are turning to homegrown energy solutions. Your friend Cole Lazarus has decided to start a business offering such solutions. Cole would like your help developing his business. Begin by researching the Internet and find different ways that you could design a home with its own energy sources. Create a document listing the different sources along with advantages and disadvantages of each source.

PLUG-IN

B13

Strategic Outsourcing

1. Explain the business benefits and challenges of outsourcing.
2. Identify the three primary outsourcing options.
3. Summarize a list of leading offshore outsourcing countries.
4. Summarize a list of up-and-coming offshore outsourcing countries.
5. Summarize a list of rookie offshore outsourcing countries.
6. Describe the future trend of multisourcing and how it can support a business need for outsourcing.

Introduction

The core units introduced the concept of *outsourcing,* an arrangement by which one organization provides a service or services for another organization that chooses not to perform them in-house. Typically, the outsourced process or function is a noncore business activity; what is outsourced can range from high-volume, repetitive processes such as electronic transaction processing to more customized services such as a help desk.

This plug-in describes outsourcing as a strategic mechanism that aligns technology initiatives and business goals, manages technology operations in a difficult business environment, and reduces operating costs. Often, companies begin the process by outsourcing nonessential business operations, which may include applications, assets, people, and other resources. As organizations realize the benefits of outsourcing, they extend this approach to other business functions or processes.

Yet outsourcing carries risks: loss of control, inflexibility, and geopolitical uncertainty. Not all functions and processes can or should be outsourced, at least not without careful analysis of the advantages and disadvantages.

The Outsourcing Phenomenon

The outsourcing market has experienced strong growth over the last several years because of businesses' need to focus on core competencies, Web implementation initiatives, consolidation across industries, and a tight labor pool. The outsourcing of noncore, transaction-based processes has gained significant momentum over the last few years as organizations have become more comfortable with the concept of outsourcing and its advantages.

Organizations elect to outsource for a variety of reasons. Some of these reasons are tactical, while others are strategic. In the past, outsourcing was often used tactically, as a quick-fix, short-term solution to a particular need or problem that did not form part of an overall business strategy. In recent years, many companies have begun to use strategic outsourcing where an organization works with suppliers in order to make a significant improvement in business performance.

No one would seriously expect an oil company to outsource its exploration and refining functions; pharmaceutical companies probably would not outsource their research and development; and few, if any, major automakers would consider outsourcing their production planning or marketing campaigns. These activities are core to their businesses and often the means for differentiation in the marketplace and a source of competitive advantage. Businesses outsource their noncore functions, such as payroll and IT. By outsourcing IT, most organizations can cut costs, improve service, and focus on their core business.

Best Buy Co. Inc. is the number one U.S. specialty retailer for consumer electronics, personal computers, entertainment software, and appliances. Best Buy needed to find a strategic IT partner that could help the company leverage its IT functions in order to meet its business objectives. Best Buy further wanted to integrate its disparate enterprise systems and minimize its operating expenses. Best Buy outsourced these functions to Accenture, a global management consulting, technology services, and outsourcing company. The comprehensive outsourcing relationship that drove Best Buy's transformation produced spectacular results that were measurable in every key area of its business, such as a 20 percent increase in key category revenue that translated into a $25 million profit improvement.[1]

According to PricewaterhouseCoopers' survey of CEOs from 452 of the fastest growing U.S. companies, "Businesses that outsource are growing faster, larger, and more profitably than those that do not. In addition, most of those involved in outsourcing say they are saving money and are highly satisfied with their outsourcing service providers." Figure B13.1 lists common areas for outsourcing opportunities across industries.[2]

The drivers behind the rapid growth of the outsourcing industry include the following:

- **Globalization:** As markets open worldwide, competition heats up. Companies may engage outsourcing service providers to deliver international services.
- **The Internet:** Barriers to entry, such as lack of capital, are dramatically reduced in the world of e-business. New competitors enter the market daily.

Industry	Outsourcing Opportunities
Banking and finance	Check and electronic payment processing, credit report issuance, delinquency management, securities, and trades processing
Insurance	Claims reporting and investigation, policy administration, check processing, risk assessment
Telecommunications	Invoice and bill production, transaction processing
Health care	Electronic data interchange, database management, accounting
Transportation	Ticket and order processing
Government	Loan processing, Medicaid processing
Retail	Electronic payment processing

FIGURE B13.1

Outsourcing Opportunities

- **Growing economy and low unemployment rate:** Building a competitive workforce is much harder and more expensive.
- **Technology:** Technology is advancing at such an accelerated rate that companies often lack the resources, workforce, or expertise to keep up.
- **Deregulation:** As private industries such as telecommunications and energy deregulate, markets open and competition increases.

OUTSOURCING BENEFITS

The many benefits associated with outsourcing include:

- Increased quality and efficiency of a process, service, or function.
- Reduced operating expenses.
- Focusing resources on core profit-generating competencies.
- Reduced exposure to risks involved with large capital investments.
- Access to outsourcing service provider's economies of scale.
- Access to outsourcing service provider's expertise and best-in-class practices.
- Access to advanced technologies.
- Increased flexibility with the ability to respond quickly to changing market demands.
- Avoiding costly outlay of capital funds.
- Reduced head count and associated overhead expense.
- Reduced frustration and expense related to hiring and retaining employees in an exceptionally tight job market.
- Reduced time to market for products or services.

Outsourcing Options

In the early 1990s, British Petroleum (BP) began looking at IT outsourcing as a way to radically reduce costs and gain more flexible and higher quality IT resources that directly improve the overall business. Over the past decade, all companies within the global BP Group have incorporated outsourcing initiatives in their business plans. BP's information technology costs were reduced by 40 percent globally over the first three years of the outsourcing engagement and have continued at a 10 percent reduction year after year, leading to hundreds of millions of dollars in savings to BP.

Information technology outsourcing enables organizations to keep up with market and technology advances—with less strain on human and financial resources and more assurance that the IT infrastructure will keep pace with evolving business priorities (see Figure B13.2). Planning, deploying, and managing IT environments is both a tactical and a strategic challenge that must take into account a company's organizational, industrial, and technological concerns. There are three different forms of outsourcing options:

1. *Onshore outsourcing* is the process of engaging another company within the same country for services.
2. *Nearshore outsourcing* refers to contracting an outsourcing arrangement with a company in a nearby country. Often this country will share a border with the native country.
3. *Offshore outsourcing* is using organizations from developing countries to write code and develop systems. In offshore outsourcing the country is geographically far away.

FIGURE B13.2

Outsourcing Models and Cost Savings

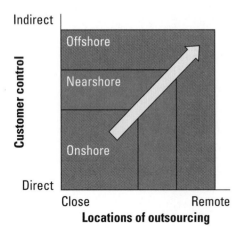

For many companies, certain IT services, such as application development, maintenance, and help desk support, fall within the category of functions that are ideal for outsourcing, including offshore outsourcing.

OFFSHORE OUTSOURCING

Since the mid-1990s, major U.S. companies have been sending significant portions of their software development work offshore—primarily to vendors in India, but also to vendors in China, Eastern Europe (including Russia), Ireland, Israel, and the Philippines. The big selling point for offshore outsourcing to these countries is "inexpensive good work." A programmer who earns as much as $63,000 per year in the United States is paid as little as $5,000 per year overseas (see Figure B13.3). Companies can easily realize cost savings of 30 percent to 50 percent through offshore outsourcing and still get the same, if not better, quality of service.[3]

Developed and developing countries throughout Europe and Asia offer some IT outsourcing services, but most are hampered to some degree by language, telecommunications infrastructure, or regulatory barriers. The first and largest offshore marketplace is India, whose English-speaking and technologically advanced population have built its IT services business into a $4 billion industry. Infosys, NIIT, Satyam, TCS, and Wipro are among the biggest Indian outsourcing service providers, each with a significant presence in the United States. There are currently three categories of outsourcing countries (see Figure B13.4):

1. The leaders—countries that are leading the outsourcing industry.

2. The up-and-comers—countries that are beginning to emerge as solid outsourcing options.

3. The rookies—countries that are just entering the outsourcing industry.[4]

Country	Salary Range Per Year
China	$ 5,000–$9,000
India	6,000–10,000
Philippines	6,500–11,000
Russia	7,000–13,000
Ireland	21,000–28,000
Canada	25,000–50,000
United States	60,000–90,000

FIGURE B13.3

Typical Salary Ranges for Computer Programmers

FIGURE B13.4

Categories of Outsourcing Countries

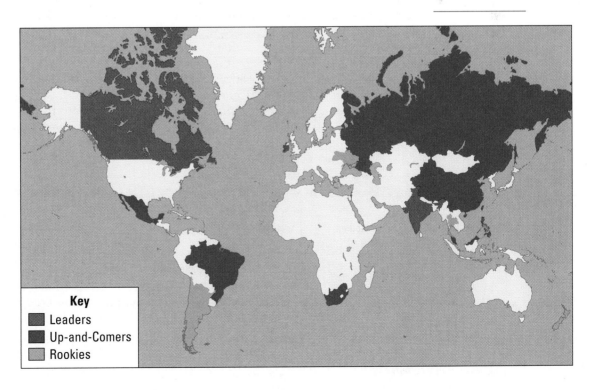

Key
- Leaders
- Up-and-Comers
- Rookies

The Leaders

The following countries are leaders in the outsourcing industry:

- Canada
- India
- Ireland
- Israel
- Philippines

CANADA

Expertise	■ Software development/maintenance, contact centers, technical support.
Major Customers	■ Allmerica, Agilent.
Advantages	■ Though labor costs are high, geographic proximity and cultural affinity with the United States make it highly desirable. ■ Contact center turnover is low.
Disadvantage	■ High cost of labor pool, but still less expensive than outsourcing in the United States.

INDIA

Expertise	■ Software development/maintenance, contact centers, financial processing.
Major Customers	■ Citigroup, GE Capital, American Express.
Advantages	■ India is the leader in business process and IT services outsourcing. ■ Two million English-proficient speakers graduate every year from more than 1,000 colleges that offer information technology education. ■ Strong history of software development. ■ Highly skilled labor pool. ■ Favorable cost structure.
Disadvantages	■ Political instability. ■ Labor costs are rising as demand for IT workers begins to exceed supply. ■ High turnover, particularly in contact centers, is becoming an issue.

IRELAND

Expertise	■ European shared-services centers, software development, contact centers.
Major Customers	■ Intel, Dell, Microsoft.
Advantages	■ Reputation for producing highly skilled IT professionals. ■ Strong cultural affinity with the United States. ■ Low political or financial risk. ■ Solid telecommunications infrastructure. ■ Strong educational system.
Disadvantage	■ High cost of IT salaries, however, labor costs are still lower than in the United States.

Expertise	■ Software development/maintenance, packaged software implementation, application integration, security, e-business.
Major Customers	■ Merrill Lynch, Shaw Industries.
Advantages	■ Highly skilled workforce including scientists and engineers from Eastern Europe and Russia. ■ Excellent educational system. ■ Hotbed for IT innovation.
Disadvantages	■ Political instability. ■ Employee safety is a cause for concern. ■ High cost of IT salaries.

PHILIPPINES

Expertise	■ Accounting, finance, contact centers, human resources.
Major Customers	■ Procter & Gamble, American International Group, Citigroup.
Advantages	■ The population boasts a high percentage of English speakers with American accents. ■ Culture dictates aim-to-please attitude. ■ Estimated 15,000 technology students graduate from universities annually.
Disadvantages	■ Filipinos are not nearly as strong in software development and maintenance as other outsourcing countries. ■ Political instability.

The Up-and-Comers

The following countries are up-and-coming in the outsourcing industry:

- Brazil
- China
- Malaysia
- Mexico
- Russia
- South Africa

BRAZIL

Expertise	■ Software development/maintenance.
Major Customers	■ General Electric, Goodyear, Xerox.
Advantages	■ Big cost savings from a large supply of IT labor. ■ Brazil is Latin America's largest economy with a strong industrial base. ■ Brazil's national focus is on growing small and midsize businesses, including IT services. ■ Affinity with U.S. culture including minimal time zone differences.
Disadvantage	■ Remains on priority watch list of International Intellectual Property Alliance for copyright infractions.

CHINA

Expertise	■ Transaction processing, low-end software development/maintenance.
Major Customers	■ HSBC Bank, Microsoft.
Advantages	■ Large pool of educated IT workers with broad skill sets. ■ Government provides strong support for IT outsourcing industry. ■ Telecommunications infrastructure is improving. ■ Entry into World Trade Organization winning confidence of foreign investors. ■ Government has established 15 national software industrial parks.
Disadvantages	■ English proficiency low. ■ Workers lack knowledge of Western business culture. ■ Workers lack project management skills. ■ Intellectual property protections weak. ■ Piracy. ■ Red tape and corruption from a highly bureaucratic government.

MALAYSIA

Expertise	■ Wireless applications.
Major Customers	■ IBM, Shell, DHL, Motorola, Electronic Data Systems Corporation.
Advantages	■ Good business environment with strong government support for IT and communications industries. ■ Workforce has strong global exposure. ■ World-class telecommunications infrastructure. ■ Over half of the 250,000 students in higher education major in scientific or technical disciplines.
Disadvantages	■ Labor costs higher than India. ■ Few suppliers, which limits business choices. ■ Shortage of skilled IT talent.

MEXICO

Expertise	■ Software development, contact centers.
Major Customers	■ AOL Time Warner, General Motors, IBM.
Advantages	■ Solid telecommunications infrastructure. ■ Shares cultural affinity and time zones with the United States. ■ Second-largest U.S. trading partner. ■ Programmers highly proficient on latest technologies.
Disadvantages	■ English proficiency low. ■ Government corruption.

RUSSIA

Expertise	■ Web design, complex software development, aerospace engineering.
Major Customer	■ Boeing.
Advantages	■ Large number of highly skilled workers with degrees in science, engineering, and math. ■ Strong venue for research and development. ■ Programmers have skills for both cutting-edge projects and working with legacy applications. ■ European-based companies benefit from historic cultural affinity and geographic proximity.
Disadvantages	■ English proficiency not as widespread as in India or the Philippines, making contact centers impractical. ■ Government corruption and red tape. ■ Copyright piracy. ■ Outsourcing industry is fragmented and many firms have 20 programmers or less, making them unattractive to companies with large IT projects. ■ Telecommunications infrastructure needs work.

SOUTH AFRICA

Expertise	■ Contact centers, e-business, software development, IT security.
Major Customers	■ AIG, Old Mutual, Sage Life, Swissair.
Advantages	■ Time zone compatibility with Europe. ■ English is a native language. ■ Solid telecommunications infrastructure.
Disadvantages	■ Small pool of IT skilled workers. ■ IT talent tends to emigrate. ■ Crime.

The Rookies

The following countries are just beginning to offer outsourcing and are considered rookies in the industry:

■ Argentina
■ Chile
■ Costa Rica
■ New Zealand
■ Thailand
■ Ukraine

ARGENTINA

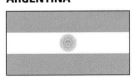

Expertise	■ Software development/maintenance, contact centers.
Major Customers	■ BankOne, Citibank, Principal Financial Group.
Advantages	■ Low costs resulting from an economic collapse in 2001. ■ Economy began to rebound in 2003, growing more than 8 percent, but unemployment remains high. ■ Large labor pool, including solid base of engineering talent.
Disadvantages	■ Country has yet to reach agreement with creditors on restructuring debt. ■ Foreign investors are cautious.

CHILE

Expertise	■ Software development/maintenance.
Major Customer	■ Compaq.
Advantages	■ Large highly skilled pool of IT talent. ■ State-of-the-art telecommunications infrastructure. ■ Good satellite connectivity and digital network. ■ Government actively supports business process and software development sectors. ■ Government plans to begin offering English classes to technical workers.
Disadvantages	■ English proficiency lacking. ■ Slightly higher costs than neighboring countries.

COSTA RICA

Expertise	■ Contact centers, e-business.
Major Customer	■ Unisys.
Advantages	■ Business-friendly environment. ■ Highly skilled pool of engineering talent. ■ Well-educated workforce. ■ Favorable cost structure. ■ English and Spanish widely spoken.
Disadvantage	■ Relatively small labor supply.

NEW ZEALAND

Expertise	■ Contact centers, e-business, Web hosting, Web design.
Major Customers	■ IBM, Microsoft, Cisco.
Advantages	■ Stable political and economic environment. ■ Well-established telecommunications infrastructure. ■ Thriving contact center industry. ■ Limited supply of domestic labor. To meet demand, the government has eased visa restrictions allowing entry of workers from countries such as Bangladesh.
Disadvantage	■ New Zealand cannot compete on costs with India and the Philippines.

THAILAND

Expertise	■ Software development/maintenance.
Major Customers	■ Dell, Glovia, Sungard.
Advantages	■ Reasonable telecommunications infrastructure. ■ Cost structure is slightly lower than Malaysia.
Disadvantages	■ Demand for skilled IT labor exceeds supply. ■ Population is not as educated as in neighboring countries. ■ English is not widely spoken.

Expertise	■ Software development, Web site development.
Major Customers	■ Sears, Roebuck and Company, Target Corporation.
Advantages	■ History of training highly educated scientists and engineers. (The Soviet Union based the majority of its space and aviation technology work here.) ■ Information technology outsourcing growth predicted to double over the next couple of years.
Disadvantages	■ Unstable political climate. ■ Fears that the country is drifting away from democracy and pro-Western stance.

UKRAINE

In summary, many countries are racing to participate in the outsourcing phenomenon. When an organization outsources, it needs to analyze all of its options and weigh all of the advantages and disadvantages. When faced with an outsourcing decision, be sure to evaluate the countries on such things as geopolitical risk, English proficiency, and salary cost (see Figure B13.5).

THE CHALLENGES OF OUTSOURCING

There are several challenges in outsourcing. These arguments are valid and should be considered when a company is thinking about outsourcing. Many challenges can be avoided with proper research on the outsourcing service provider. Some challenges of outsourcing include:

■ **Contract length**—Most of the outsourced IT contracts are for a relatively long time period (several years). This is because of the high cost of transferring assets and employees as well as maintaining technological investment. The long time period of the contract causes three particular problems:

1. Difficulties in getting out of a contract if the outsourcing service provider turns out to be unsuitable.

2. Problems in foreseeing what the business will need over the next 5 or 10 years (typical contract lengths), hence creating difficulties in establishing an appropriate contract.

3. Problems in reforming an internal IT department after the contract period is finished.

■ **Competitive edge**—Effective and innovative use of IT can give an organization a competitive edge over its rivals. A competitive business advantage provided by an internal IT department that understands the organization and is committed to its goals can be lost in an outsourced arrangement. In an outsourced arrangement, IT staff are striving to achieve the goals and objectives of the outsourcing service provider, which may conflict with those of the organization.

■ **Confidentiality**—In some organizations, the information stored in the computer systems is central to the enterprise's success or survival, such as information about pricing policies, product mixing formulas, or sales analysis. Some companies decide against outsourcing for fear of placing confidential information in the hands of the outsourcing service provider, particularly if the provider offers services to companies competing in the same marketplace. Although the organization usually dismisses this threat, claiming it is covered by confidentiality clauses in a contract, the organization must assess the potential risk and costs of a confidentiality breach in determining the net benefits of an outsourcing agreement.

THE LEADERS			
Country	**Geopolitical Risk**	**English Proficiency**	**Average Programmer Salary**
Canada	Low	Good	> $12K
India	Moderate	Good	$4K–$12K
Ireland	Low	Good	> $12K
Israel	Moderate	Good	> $12K
Philippines	Moderate	Good	$4K–12K

THE UP-AND-COMERS			
Country	**Geopolitical Risk**	**English Proficiency**	**Average Programmer Salary**
Brazil	Moderate	Poor	$4K–$12K
China	Low	Poor	$4K–$12K
Malaysia	Low	Fair	$4K–$12K
Mexico	Moderate	Poor	> $12K
Russia	Moderate	Poor	$4K–$12K
South Africa	Moderate	Good	> $12K

THE ROOKIES			
Country	**Geopolitical Risk**	**English Proficiency**	**Average Programmer Salary**
Argentina	Moderate	Fair	$4K–$12K
Chile	Low	Poor	< $4K
Costa Rice	Moderate	Good	$4K–$12K
New Zealand	Low	Good	> $12K
Thailand	Low	Poor	$4K–$12K
Ukraine	Moderate	Poor	$4K–$12K

■ **Scope definition**—Most IT projects suffer from problems associated with defining the scope of the system. The same problem afflicts outsourcing arrangements. Many difficulties result from contractual misunderstandings between the organization and the outsourcing service provider. In such circumstances, the organization believes that the service required is within the contract scope while the service provider is sure it is outside the scope and so is subject to extra fees.

Future Trends

Companies are getting smarter about outsourcing and about aligning efficiency with core business priorities. As businesses become increasingly networked (for instance, via the Internet)—global, commoditized, 24 × 7, and collaborative—outsourcing is becoming less of a cost-saving strategy and more an overall context for business.

Outsourcing is rapidly approaching commodity status, and this will transform the outsourcing value equation from high margins and vendor control into a classic buyers' market with competition driving down margins, adding features and services, and increasing buyer choices. U.S. companies should consider Mexico and Canada for nearshore outsourcing since those countries often provide very competitive pricing. Vendors in these countries can be viable alternatives, such as IBM Global Services (Mexico and Canada), Softtek (Mexico), CGI (Canada), and Keane (Canada).[5]

Companies should look for value-based pricing rather than the lowest possible price. The emerging trend of companies using reverse auction bidding to select offshore vendors is a dangerous one—it could result in low prices, but also low value and low customer satisfaction.

MULTISOURCING

For many years, outsourcing has predominantly been a means to manage and optimize businesses' ever-growing IT infrastructures and ensure return on IT investments—or at a minimum, more cost-effective operations. As businesses move to Internet-based models, speed and skill have become more important than cost efficiencies, giving way to a "utility" service provider model called multisourcing. *Multisourcing* is a combination of professional services, mission-critical support, remote management, and hosting services that are offered to customers in any combination needed. Like the general contractor model, multisourcing brings together a wide set of specialized IT service providers, or "subcontractors," under one point of accountability. The goal of multisourcing is to integrate a collection of IT services into one stable and cost-effective system. Therefore, multisourcing helps companies achieve the advantages of a best-of-breed strategy.

A multisourcing service provider can offer a seamless, inexpensive migration path to whatever delivery model makes sense at that time. For instance, HR processes are outsourced to one best-of-breed outsourcing service provider. Logistics are outsourced to another, and IT development and maintenance to another. Although multisourcing mitigates the risk of choosing a single outsourcing service provider, additional resources and time are required to manage multiple service providers.

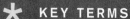
Outsourcing IT services and business functions is becoming an increasingly common global practice among organizations looking for competitive advantage. The guiding principle is that noncore and critical activities of an enterprise can be handed over to companies with expertise in those activities, thereby freeing internal resources to focus on enhancing the added-value of the organization's core business.

Outsourcing is no longer a simple matter of cutting costs and improving service levels. As more companies consider the benefits of outsourcing their IT functions and their business processes, they will find new ways to create business value. Companies that succeed will find innovative solutions to help drive costs down, select only the problem areas to outsource, and more important, learn to use outsourcing as a strategic weapon.

Companies continue to outsource at an increasing rate, despite reports of organizations disappointed and disillusioned by the process. The ultimate goal is multisourcing, combining professional services, mission-critical support, remote management, and hosting services.

 KEY TERMS

Multisourcing, 493

Nearshore outsourcing, 484

Offshore outsourcing, 484

Onshore outsourcing, 484

Outsourcing, 482

CLOSING CASE ONE

Mobil Travel Guide

For the past 45 years, the *Mobil Travel Guide* has been providing information on destinations, route planning, resorts, accommodations, restaurant reviews, and other travel-related subjects for people traveling in the United States and Canada. Print versions of the *Mobil Travel Guide* are created and updated annually at the company's Park Ridge, Illinois, headquarters, and are sold at most major booksellers and other publishing outlets.

Mobil Travel Guide, a well-known name in the travel industry, wanted to leverage its brand recognition by providing a highly responsive, real-time online service for leisure travelers that include customized travel planning, an around-the-clock customer service center, and a variety of privileges and rewards at a linked network of hotels and restaurants.

Mobil's existing online solution offered only a limited amount of static Web content that ran on just four servers, which were unable to process the site's considerable traffic, resulting in downtime for customers. Mobil needed a more robust solution that would provide real-time services such as route planning and fast access to the company's vast travel information database. The solution also had to be flexible and resilient enough to handle seasonal usage fluctuations, including anticipated spikes during the summertime and over major holidays. Mobil Travel Guide's internal goals also created a challenge for any solution. The site was expected to grow rapidly, but the company did not want to invest in an infrastructure capable of supporting its vision for the Web site.

Instead of using stand-alone Web, application, and database servers, Mobil Travel Guide decided to outsource all these functions to IBM. Because IBM delivers e-business infrastructure capacity as a utility, Mobil Travel Guide pays only for the processing, storage, and networking capacity it needs and can scale its virtual infrastructure up to meet demand spikes.

By avoiding up-front capital investment without sacrificing scalability, reliability, or flexibility, Mobil Travel Guide is positioned for success. The company can optimize its spending by scaling its infrastructure dynamically to meet demands and channeling resources toward generating new business and revenue. "Otherwise, we would have to buy enough infrastructure to handle the biggest day we could imagine, but typically it would sit unused. Now, we can take advantage of any market sweet spot we find, because we can scale with minimal lead time and capital dollars," explained Paul Mercurio, chief information officer for Mobil Travel Guide.

What is more, this capability moves portions of the Web-serving workload from Mobil Travel Guide's site onto servers located at strategic network points, so end users get faster responses even while Mobil Travel Guide lowers its per-transaction costs. "Because our service level ramps up or down dynamically in response to peaks and valleys in demand, we pay only for the capacity we need at any given moment in time," Mercurio said.

The on-demand delivery has already benefited Mobil Travel Guide in an unexpected way. After initially setting a committed capacity level that was too high, the company was able to leverage the flexibility of its IBM solution to "right-size" its capacity by reducing its contracted capacity level.

By outsourcing the solution to IBM, Mobil anticipates it will save about 35 percent in overall maintenance and software costs, while deploying an excellent e-business infrastructure solution that guarantees high availability, rapid scalability, and easy management of usage fluctuations.[6]

Questions

1. What are the main reasons Mobil Travel Guide used an outsourcing option?
2. What other areas would you recommend Mobil Travel Guide outsource?
3. What advantages and disadvantages would offshore outsourcing or nearshore outsourcing have for Mobil Travel Guide?
4. List the countries where Mobil could outsource its *Travel Guide*.

 CLOSING CASE TWO

Outsourcing Brew

Coors Brewing Company, the third-largest brewer in the United States, manufactures and markets more than a dozen varieties of beer and malt beverages in 30 markets around the world. In a rapidly consolidating industry, Coors had a choice: keep growing or be acquired. To create the optimal conditions for growth, the company needed to improve access to information, consolidate systems, and reduce costs.

In less than a decade, Coors Brewing Company had more than doubled in size. Managing that growth became increasingly difficult for the company's internal IT staff. The company wanted to maintain responsibility for the technologies directly related to making and selling beer. Therefore, Coors was looking for a partner with deep industry expertise, mature application experience, and global reach to help revitalize its technology to support its business goals—including bringing new acquisitions online quickly.

The company decided to outsource its day-to-day management of its technical operations, conversion of legacy applications, and systems. Coors outsourced these functions to EDS in order to create a globally integrated enterprise solution, helping to optimize the supply chain from beginning to end. EDS is an experienced outsourcing services company with more than 130,000 employees and 2003 revenues of $21.5 billion, ranked 80th on the Fortune 500.

EDS offered Coors an infrastructure "on demand." Coors avoids a huge up-front investment in infrastructure, but is able to access increased capacity when business volumes increase. Now IT costs are predictable, and additional infrastructure is instantly available when the company needs it. Coors also controls costs by using EDS's Best ShoreSM Services, which enables Coors to reduce the cost of applications management by as much as 40 percent through a combination of offshore, nearshore, and local service centers and personnel.

EDS's solutions at Coors deliver much more than lower costs and increased reliability. As EDS assumed control of Coors's help desk, staff increased service levels while identifying patterns that let Coors focus training where it was most needed and kept the company aware of where potential problems lay. Standardizing the company's desktop environment has allowed Coors to get rid of many obsolete applications.

EDS is much more than an information technology outsourcing service provider; it is Coors's business partner. "They work with us on project management and root-cause analysis, which have helped us to add a lot of discipline in our organization," said CIO Virginia Guthrie. With a modernized and efficient information environment taking shape, EDS and Coors have ambitious plans for the future, from improving manufacturing processes to enhancing Coors's global presence. Guthrie said, "What we really want here is for this partnership to be a poster child for how outsourcing partnerships should work."

With the help of EDS, Coors was able to:

- Within just 60 days, reduce cost of application maintenance by 70 percent.
- Save more than $1.2 million on project resources related to SAP implementation.
- Reduce applications in use by 48 percent.
- Work to retire 70 percent of legacy systems.[7]

Questions

1. Describe an alternative approach that Coors could have used instead of outsourcing to EDS.
2. What would be the advantages of offshore outsourcing the Coors IT department?
3. What are some other reasons Coors outsourced its information technology functions that were not mentioned in the case?
4. Describe some of the factors causing Coors to be "forced" to outsource its information technology functions.

★ MAKING BUSINESS DECISIONS

1. Sports Sourcing

Sierra Sports Network launched its Web site SierraSports.com in 2001. With a huge influx of new visitors expected this football season, it is critical that SierraSports.com attracts, retains, and handles its Web traffic. It needs an overhaul of its existing Web site. Since Sierra Sports Network does not have the in-house skills to support the needed changes, it must look at outsourcing its Web development. Some of the company's needs are working with an outsourcing service provider who is proficient in English, has a solid telecommunications infrastructure, and operates in a similar time zone. List the outsourcing countries that could assist Sierra Sports for Web development needs, in addition to the advantages that each country could give to the company.

2. Ops.com

Contact center Ops.com provides information to those who are involved in real-time customer service. Contact centers have emerged as *the* critical link between a company and its customers. The growth in contact centers has resulted in a strong demand for Ops.com's services; so much that it now needs to outsource part of its operation. One main reason for the move to an outsourcing service provider is its need to develop a new service to collect information, such as account numbers, via an automated attendant and tie it back to a database. Ops.com can tap the database information to give callers automated access to more information, such as account balances, and create priority queuing for their most important customers. Describe the advantages that outsourcing would give Ops.com and list the outsourcing options along with a recommendation of prospective countries that have the resources available to be considered.

3. The Travel Store

In 2004, The Travel Store faced a dilemma. The retailer had tripled in size over a three-year period to $1 billion in sales, but it had done so despite operational deficiencies. The company's inability to evolve its business processes as it grew was causing problems. Within a year, sales and profits fell below expectations, and its stock price plummeted from approximately $10 a share to less than $2 a share. The Travel Store is determined to take quick and decisive action to restore profitability and improve its credibility in the marketplace. One of its top priorities is to overhaul its inventory management system in an effort to create optimal levels of inventory to support sales demand. This would prevent higher volume stores from running out of key sale items while also ensuring that lower sales stores would not be burdened with excess inventory that could only be moved at closeout prices. The company would like to outsource this function but is worried about the challenges of transferring the responsibility of this important business function, as well as the issues surrounding confidentiality, and scope definition. Make a list of the competitive advantages outsourcing could give to The Travel Store, along with recommendations for addressing the company's outsourcing concerns.

4. Software Solutions

Founded in 2003, Gabster Software provides innovative search software, Web site demographics, and testing software. All serve as part of its desktop and enterprise resource planning solutions for government, corporate, educational, and consumer markets. Web site publishers, digital media publishers, content managers, document managers, business users, consumers, software companies, and consulting services companies use Gabster's solutions. The company is currently thinking about offshore outsourcing its call center functions, its e-business strategies, and its application development. Describe how Gabster could use multisourcing along with the potential advantages it might receive.

Systems Development

1. Summarize the activities associated with the planning phase in the SDLC.
2. Summarize the activities associated with the analysis phase in the SDLC.
3. Summarize the activities associated with the design phase in the SDLC.
4. Summarize the activities associated with the development phase in the SDLC.
5. Summarize the activities associated with the testing phase in the SDLC.
6. Summarize the activities associated with the implementation phase in the SDLC.
7. Summarize the activities associated with the maintenance phase in the SDLC.

Introduction

Today, systems are so large and complex that teams of architects, analysts, developers, testers, and users must work together to create the millions of lines of custom-written code that drive enterprises. For this reason, developers have created a number of different system development methodologies including waterfall, prototyping, rapid application development (RAD), extreme programming, agile, and others. All these methodologies are based on the ***systems development life cycle (SDLC),*** which is the overall process for developing information systems from planning and analysis through implementation and maintenance (see Figure B14.1).

The systems development life cycle is the foundation for all systems development methodologies, and there are literally hundreds of different activities associated with each phase in the SDLC. Typical activities include determining budgets, gathering system requirements, and writing detailed user documentation. The activities performed during each systems development project will vary. This plug-in takes a detailed look at a few of the more common activities performed during the systems development life cycle, along with common issues facing software development projects (see Figure B14.2).

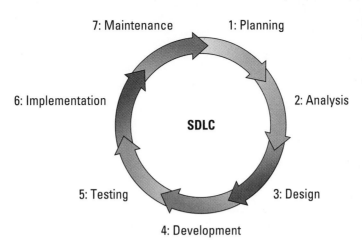

FIGURE B14.1

The Systems Development
Life Cycle (SDLC)

SDLC Phase	Activities
1. Planning	■ Identify and select the system for development ■ Assess project feasibility ■ Develop the project plan
2. Analysis	■ Gather business requirements ■ Create process diagrams ■ Perform a buy versus build analysis
3. Design	■ Design the IT infrastructure ■ Design system models
4. Development	■ Develop the IT infrastructure ■ Develop the database and programs
5. Testing	■ Write the test conditions ■ Perform the system testing
6. Implementation	■ Determine implementation method ■ Provide training for the system users ■ Write detailed user documentation
7. Maintenance	■ Build a help desk to support the system users ■ Perform system maintenance ■ Provide an environment to support system changes

FIGURE B14.2

Common Activities
Performed During
Systems Development

Systems Development Life Cycle

PHASE 1: PLANNING

The *planning phase* involves establishing a high-level plan of the intended project and determining project goals. The three primary activities involved in the planning phase are:

1. Identify and select the system for development.

2. Assess project feasibility.

3. Develop the project plan.

Evaluation Criteria	Description
Value chain analysis	The value chain determines the extent to which the new system will add value to the organization. Systems with greater value are given priority over systems with less value.
Strategic alignment	Projects that are in line with the organization's strategic goals and objectives are given priority over projects not in line with the organization's strategic goals and objectives.
Cost-benefit analysis	A cost-benefit analysis determines which projects offer the organization the greatest benefits with the least amount of cost.
Resource availability	Determine the amount and type of resources required to complete the project and determine if the organization has these resources available.
Project size, duration, and difficulty	Determine the number of individuals, amount of time, and technical difficulty of the project.

Identify and Select the System for Development

Systems are successful only when they solve the right problem or take advantage of the right opportunity. Systems development focuses on either solving a problem or taking advantage of an opportunity. Determining which systems are required to support the strategic goals of an organization is one of the primary activities performed during the planning phase. Typically, employees generate proposals to build new information systems when they are having a difficult time performing their jobs. Unfortunately, most organizations have limited resources and cannot afford to develop all proposed information systems. Therefore, they look to critical success factors to help determine which systems to build.

A *critical success factor (CSF)* is a factor that is critical to an organization's success. To determine which system to develop, an organization tracks all the proposed systems and prioritizes them by business impact or critical success factors. This allows the business to prioritize which problems require immediate attention and which problems can wait. Figure B14.3 displays possible evaluation criteria for determining which projects to develop.

Assess Project Feasibility

A *feasibility study* determines if the proposed solution is feasible and achievable from a financial, technical, and organizational standpoint. Typically, an organization will define several alternative solutions that it can pursue to solve a given problem. A feasibility study is used to determine if the proposed solution is achievable, given the organization's resources and constraints in regard to technology, economics, organizational factors, and legal and ethical considerations. Figure B14.4 displays the many different types of feasibility studies an organization can perform.

Develop the Project Plan

Developing a project plan is one of the final activities performed during the planning phase and it is one of the hardest and most important activities. The project plan is the guiding force behind on-time delivery of a complete and successful system. It logs and tracks every single activity performed during the project. If an activity is missed, or takes longer than expected to complete, the project plan must be updated to reflect these changes. Updating of the project plan must be performed in every subsequent phase during the systems development effort.

Types of Feasibility Studies	
Economic feasibility study (often called a **cost-benefit analysis**)	Identifies the financial benefits and costs associated with the systems development project.
Legal and contractual feasibility study	Examines all potential legal and contractual ramifications of the proposed system.
Operational feasibility study	Examines the likelihood that the project will attain its desired objectives.
Schedule feasibility study	Assesses the likelihood that all potential time frames and completion dates will be met.
Technical feasibility study	Determines the organization's ability to build and integrate the proposed system.

FIGURE B14.4

Types of Feasibility Studies

PHASE 2: ANALYSIS

The *analysis phase* involves analyzing end-user business requirements and refining project goals into defined functions and operations of the intended system. The three primary activities involved in the analysis phase are:

1. Gather business requirements.
2. Create process diagrams.
3. Perform a buy versus build analysis.

Gather Business Requirements

Business requirements are the detailed set of business requests that the system must meet to be successful. At this point, there is little or no concern with any implementation or reference to technical details. For example, the types of technology used to build the system, such as an Oracle database or the Java programming language, are not yet defined. The only focus is on gathering the true business requirements for the system. A sample business requirement might state, "The system must track all customer sales by product, region, and sales representative." This requirement states what the system must do from the business perspective, giving no details or information on how the system is going to meet this requirement.

Gathering business requirements is basically conducting an investigation in which users identify all the organization's business needs and take measurements of these needs. Figure B14.5 displays a number of ways to gather business requirements.

The *requirements definition document* contains the final set of business requirements, prioritized in order of business importance. The system users review the requirements definition document and determine if they will sign off on the business requirements. *Sign-off* is the system users' actual signatures indicating they approve all of the business requirements. One of the first major milestones on the project plan is usually the users' sign-off on business requirements.

A large data storage company implemented a project called Python whose purpose was to control all the company's information systems. Seven years, tens of millions of dollars, and 35 programmers later Python was canceled. At the end of the project, Python had over 1,800 business requirements of which 900 came from engineering and were written in order to make the other 900 customer requirements work. By the time the project was canceled, it was unclear what the primary goals, objectives, and needs of the project were. Management should have realized Python's issues when the project's requirements phase dragged on, bulged, and took years to complete. The sheer number of requirements should have raised a red flag.[1]

Methods for Gathering Business Requirements
Perform a *joint application development (JAD)* session where employees meet, sometimes for several days, to define or review the business requirements for the system.
Interview individuals to determine current operations and current issues.
Compile questionnaires to survey employees to discover issues.
Make observations to determine how current operations are performed.
Review business documents to discover reports, policies, and how information is used throughout the organization.

Create Process Diagrams

Once a business analyst takes a detailed look at how an organization performs its work and its processes, the analyst can recommend ways to improve these processes to make them more efficient and effective. *Process modeling* involves graphically representing the processes that capture, manipulate, store, and distribute information between a system and its environment. One of the most common diagrams used in process modeling is the data flow diagram. A *data flow diagram (DFD)* illustrates the movement of information between external entities and the processes and data stores within the system (see Figure B14.6). Process models and data flow diagrams establish the specifications of the system. *Computer-aided software engineering (CASE)* tools are software suites that automate systems analysis, design, and development. Process models and data flow diagrams can provide the basis for the automatic generation of the system if they are developed using a CASE tool.

FIGURE B14.6

Sample Data Flow Diagram

Automated Course Registration

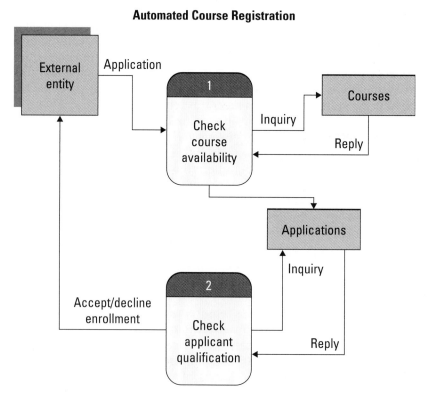

Perform a Buy versus Build Analysis

An organization faces two primary choices when deciding to develop an information system: (1) it can *buy* the information system from a vendor or (2) it can *build* the system itself. ***Commercial off-the-shelf (COTS)*** software is a software package or solution that is purchased to support one or more business functions and information systems. Most customer relationship management, supply chain management, and enterprise resource planning solutions are COTS. Typically, a cost-benefit analysis forms the basis of the buy versus build decision. Organizations must consider the questions displayed in Figure B14.7 during the buy versus build decision.

Three key factors an organization should also consider when contemplating the buy versus build decision are: (1) time to market, (2) corporate resources, and (3) core competencies. Weighing the complex relationship between each of these three variables will help an organization make the right choice (see Figure B14.8).

When making the all-important buy versus build decision consider when the product must be available, how many resources are available, and how the organization's core competencies affect the product. If these questions can be definitely answered either yes or no, then the answer to the buy versus build question is easy. However, most organizations cannot answer these questions with a solid yes or no. Most organizations need to make a trade-off between the lower cost of buying a system and the need for a system that meets all of their requirements. Finding a system to buy that meets all an organization's unique business requirements is next to impossible.

Buy versus Build Decision Questions
Do any currently available products fit the organization's needs?
Are unavailable features important enough to warrant the expense of in-house development?
Can the organization customize or modify an existing COTS to fit its needs?
Is there a justification to purchase or develop based on the cost of acquisition?

FIGURE B14.7

Buy versus Build Decision Questions

Three Key Factors in Buy versus Build Decisions	
1. **Time to market**	If time to market is a priority, then purchasing a good base technology and potentially building on to it will likely yield results faster than starting from scratch.
2. **Availability of corporate resources**	The buy versus build decision is a bit more complex to make when considering the availability of corporate resources. Typically, the costs to an organization to buy systems such as SCM, CRM, and ERP are extremely high. These costs can be so high—in the multiple millions of dollars—that acquiring these technologies might make the entire concept economically unfeasible. Building these systems, however, can also be extremely expensive, take indefinite amounts of time, and constrain resources.
3. **Corporate core competencies**	The more an organization wants to build a technical core competency, the less likely it will want to buy.

FIGURE B14.8

Key Factors in Buy versus Build Decisions

PHASE 3: DESIGN

The **design phase** involves describing the desired features and operations of the system including screen layouts, business rules, process diagrams, pseudo code, and other documentation. The two primary activities involved in the design phase are:

1. Design the IT infrastructure.
2. Design system models.

Design the IT Infrastructure

The system must be supported by a solid IT infrastructure or chances are the system will crash, malfunction, or not perform as expected. The IT infrastructure must meet the organization's needs in terms of time, cost, technical feasibility, and flexibility. Most systems run on a computer network with each employee having a client and the application running on a server. During this phase, the IT specialists recommend what types of clients and servers to buy including memory and storage requirements, along with software recommendations. An organization typically explores several different IT infrastructures that must meet current as well as future system needs. For example, databases must be large enough to hold the current volume of customers plus all new customers that the organization expects to gain over the next several years (see Figure B14.9).

Design System Models

Modeling is the activity of drawing a graphical representation of a design. An organization should model everything it builds including reports, programs, and

FIGURE B14.9

Sample IT Infrastructure

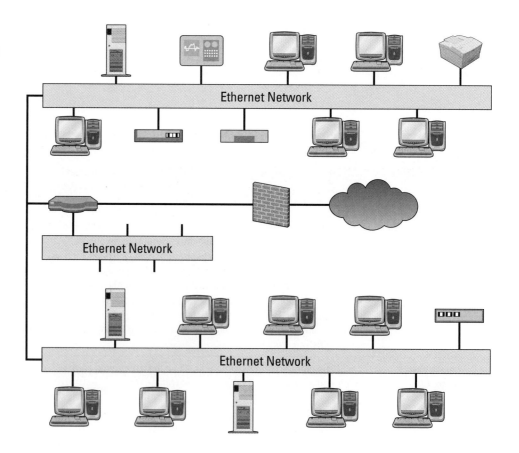

databases. Many different types of modeling activities are performed during the design phase, including:

- The **graphical user interface (GUI)** is the interface to an information system. **GUI screen design** is the ability to model the information system screens for an entire system using icons, buttons, menus, and submenus.
- **Data models** represent a formal way to express data relationships to a database management system (DBMS).
- **Entity relationship diagram (ERD)** is a technique for documenting the relationships between entities in a database environment (see Figure B14.10).

FIGURE B14.10

Sample Entity Relationship Diagram

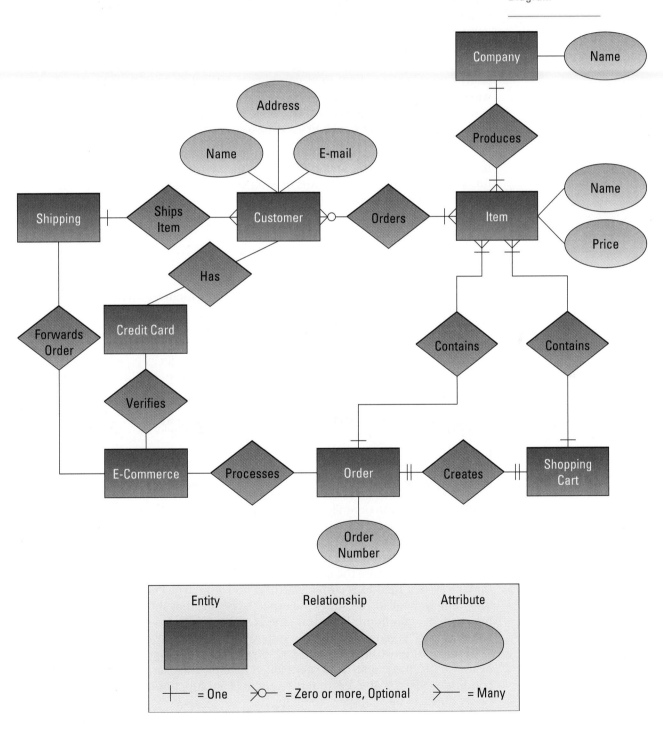

PHASE 4: DEVELOPMENT

The **development phase** involves taking all of the detailed design documents from the design phase and transforming them into the actual system. The two primary activities involved in the development phase are:

1. Develop the IT infrastructure.
2. Develop the database and programs.

Develop the IT Infrastructure

The platform upon which the system will operate must be built before building the actual system. In the design phase, an organization creates a blueprint of the proposed IT infrastructure displaying the design of the software, hardware, and telecommunication equipment. In the development phase, the organization purchases and implements the required equipment to support the IT infrastructure.

Most new systems require new hardware and software. It may be as simple as adding memory to a client or as complex as setting up a wide area network across several states.

Develop the Database and Programs

Once the IT infrastructure is built, the organization can begin to create the database and write the programs required for the system. IT specialists perform these functions and it may take months or even years to design and create all the needed elements to complete the system.

PHASE 5: TESTING

According to a report issued in June 2007 by the National Institute of Standards and Technology (NIST), defective software costs the U.S. economy an estimated $87.5 billion each year. Of that total, software users incurred 64 percent of the costs and software developers 36 percent. NIST suggests that improvements in testing could reduce this cost by about a third, or $30 billion, but that unfortunately testing improvements would not eliminate all software errors.[2]

The **testing phase** involves bringing all the project pieces together into a special testing environment to test for errors, bugs, and interoperability, in order to verify that the system meets all the business requirements defined in the analysis phase. The two primary activities involved in the testing phase are:

1. Write the test conditions.
2. Perform the system testing.

Write the Test Conditions

Testing is critical. An organization must have excellent test conditions to perform an exhaustive test. **Test conditions** are the detailed steps the system must perform along with the expected results of each step. Figure B14.11 displays several test conditions for testing user log-on functionality in a system. The tester will execute each test condition and compare the expected results with the actual results in order to verify that the system functions correctly. Notice in Figure B14.11 how each test condition is extremely detailed and states the expected results that should occur when executing each test condition. Each time the actual result is different from the expected result, a "bug" is generated and the system goes back to development for a bug fix.

Test condition 6 in Figure B14.11 displays a different actual result than the expected result because the system failed to allow the user to log on. After this test condition fails, it is obvious that the system is not functioning correctly and it must be sent back to development for a bug fix.

Test Condition Number	Date Tested	Tested	Test Condition	Expected Result	Actual Result	Pass/ Fail
1	1/1/09	Emily Hickman	Click on System Start Button	Main Menu appears	Same as expected result	Pass
2	1/1/09	Emily Hickman	Click on Log-on Button in Main Menu	Log-on Screen appears asking for User name and Password	Same as expected result	Pass
3	1/1/09	Emily Hickman	Type Emily Hickman in the User Name Field	Emily Hickman appears in the User Name Field	Same as expected result	Pass
4	1/1/09	Emily Hickman	Type Zahara123 in the password field	XXXXXXXXX appears in the password field	Same as expected result	Pass
5	1/1/09	Emily Hickman	Click on O.K. button	User log-on request is sent to database and user name and password are verified	Same as expected result	Pass
6	1/1/09	Emily Hickman	Click on Start	User name and password are accepted and the system main menu appears	Screen appeared stating log-on failed and user name and password were incorrect	Fail

FIGURE B14.11

Sample Test Conditions

A typical system development effort has hundreds or thousands of test conditions. Every single test condition must be executed to verify that the system performs as expected. Writing all the test conditions and performing the actual testing of the software takes a tremendous amount of time and energy. Testing is critical to the successful development of any system.

Perform the System Testing

System developers must perform many different types of testing to ensure that the system works as expected. Figure B14.12 displays a few of the more common types of tests performed during this phase.

PHASE 6: IMPLEMENTATION

The *implementation phase* involves placing the system into production so users can begin to perform actual business operations with the system. The three primary activities involved in the implementation phase are:

1. Write detailed user documentation.
2. Determine implementation method.
3. Provide training for the system users.

Write Detailed User Documentation

System users require *user documentation* that highlights how to use the system. This is the type of documentation that is typically provided along with the new system. System users find it extremely frustrating to have a new system without documentation.

Types of Tests Performed During the Testing Phase	
Application (or system) testing	Verifies that all units of code work together and the total system satisfies all of its functional and operational requirements.
Backup and recovery testing	Tests the ability of an application to be restarted after failure.
Documentation testing	Verifies that the instruction guides are helpful and accurate.
Integration testing	Exposes faults in the integration of software components or software units.
Regression testing	Determines if a functional improvement or repair to the system has affected the other functional aspects of the software.
Unit testing	Tests each unit of code as soon as the unit is complete to expose faults in the unit regardless of its interaction with other units.
User acceptance testing (UAT)	Determines whether a system satisfies its acceptance criteria, enabling the customer to decide whether or not to accept a system.

Determine Implementation Method

An organization must choose the right implementation method to ensure a successful system implementation. Figure B14.13 highlights the four primary implementation methods an organization can choose from.

Provide Training for the System Users

An organization must provide training for the system users. The two most popular types of training are online training and workshop training. *Online training* runs over the Internet or off a CD-ROM. System users perform the training at any time, on their own computers, at their own pace. This type of training is convenient for system users because they can set their own schedule for the training. *Workshop training* is set in a classroom-type environment and led by an instructor. Workshop training is recommended for difficult systems where the system users require one-on-one time with an individual instructor.

PHASE 7: MAINTENANCE

The *maintenance phase* involves performing changes, corrections, additions, and upgrades to ensure the system continues to meet the business goals. Once a system

Primary Implementation Methods	
1. **Parallel implementation**	Using both the old and new systems until it is evident that the new system performs correctly.
2. **Phased implementation**	Implementing the new system in phases (e.g., accounts receivables then accounts payable) until it is evident that the new system performs correctly and then implementing the remaining phases of the new system.
3. **Pilot implementation**	Having only a small group of people use the new system until it is evident that the new system performs correctly and then adding the remaining people to the new system.
4. **Plunge implementation**	Discarding the old system completely and immediately using the new system.

is in place, it must change as the organization changes. The three primary activities involved in the maintenance phase are:

1. Build a help desk to support the system users.
2. Perform system maintenance.
3. Provide an environment to support system changes.

Build a Help Desk to Support the System Users

A *help desk* is a group of people who respond to internal system user questions. Typically, internal system users have a phone number for the help desk they call whenever they have issues or questions about the system. Staffing a help desk that answers internal user questions is an excellent way to provide comprehensive support for new systems.

Perform System Maintenance

Maintenance is fixing or enhancing an information system. Many different types of maintenance must be performed on the system to ensure it continues to operate as expected. These include:

- **Adaptive maintenance**—making changes to increase system functionality to meet new business requirements.
- **Corrective maintenance**—making changes to repair system defects.
- **Perfective maintenance**—making changes to enhance the system and improve such things as processing performance and usability.
- **Preventive maintenance**—making changes to reduce the chance of future system failures.

Provide an Environment to Support System Changes

As changes arise in the business environment, an organization must react to those changes by assessing the impact on the system. It might well be that the system needs to adjust to meet the ever-changing needs of the business environment. If so, an organization must modify its systems to support the business environment.

A *change management system* includes a collection of procedures to document a change request and define the steps necessary to consider the change based on the expected impact of the change. Most change management systems require that a change request form be initiated by one or more project stakeholders (users, customers, analysts, developers). Ideally, these change requests are reviewed by a *change control board (CCB)* responsible for approving or rejecting all change requests. The CCB's composition typically includes a representative for each business area that has a stake in the project. The CCB's decision to accept or reject each change is based on an impact analysis of the change. For example, if one department wants to implement a change to the software that will increase both deployment time and cost, then the other business owners need to agree that the change is valid and that it warrants the extended time frame and increased budget.

Software Problems Are Business Problems

Only 28 percent of projects are developed within budget and delivered on time and as promised, says a report from the Standish Group, a Massachusetts-based consultancy. The primary reasons for project failure are:

- Unclear or missing business requirements.
- Skipping SDLC phases.
- Failure to manage project scope.

- Failure to manage project plan.
- Changing technology.[3]

UNCLEAR OR MISSING BUSINESS REQUIREMENTS

The most common reason systems fail is because the business requirements are either missing or incorrectly gathered during the analysis phase. The business requirements drive the entire system. If they are not accurate or complete, the system will not be successful.

It is important to discuss the relationship between the SDLC and the cost for the organization to fix errors. An error found during the analysis and design phase is relatively inexpensive to fix. All that is typically required is a change to a Word document. However, exactly the same error found during the testing or implementation phase is going to cost the organization an enormous amount to fix because it has to change the actual system. Figure B14.14 displays how the cost to fix an error grows exponentially the later the error is found in the SDLC.

SKIPPING SDLC PHASES

The first thing individuals tend to do when a project falls behind schedule is to start skipping phases in the SDLC. For example, if a project is three weeks behind in the development phase, the project manager might decide to cut testing down from six weeks to three weeks. Obviously, it is impossible to perform all the testing in half the time. Failing to test the system will lead to unfound errors, and chances are high that the system will fail. It is critical that an organization perform all phases in the SDLC during every project. Skipping any of the phases is sure to lead to system failure.

FAILURE TO MANAGE PROJECT SCOPE

As the project progresses, the project manager must track the status of each activity and adjust the project plan if an activity is added or taking longer than expected. *Scope creep* occurs when the scope of the project increases. *Feature creep* occurs when developers add extra features that were not part of the initial requirements. Scope creep and feature creep are difficult to manage and can easily cause a project to fall behind schedule.

FIGURE B14.14

The Cost of Finding Errors

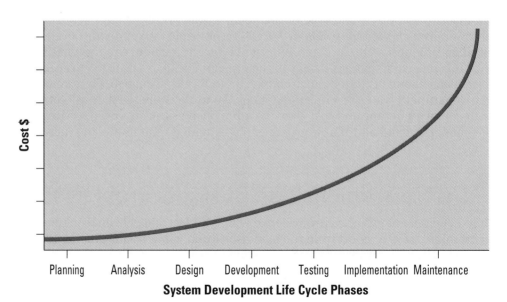

FAILURE TO MANAGE PROJECT PLAN

Managing the project plan is one of the biggest challenges during systems development. The project plan is the road map the organization follows during the development of the system. Developing the initial project plan is the easiest part of the project manager's job. Managing and revising the project plan is the hard part. The project plan is a living document since it changes almost daily on any project. Failing to monitor, revise, and update the project plan can lead to project failure.

CHANGING TECHNOLOGY

Many real-world projects have hundreds of business requirements, take years to complete, and cost millions of dollars. Gordon Moore, co-founder of Intel Corporation, observed in 1965 that chip density doubles every 18 months. This observation, known as Moore's law, simply means that memory sizes, processor power, and so on, all follow the same pattern and roughly double in capacity every 18 months. As Moore's law states, technology changes at an incredibly fast pace; therefore, it is possible to have to revise an entire project plan in the middle of a project as a result of a change in technology. Technology changes so fast that it is almost impossible to deliver an information system without feeling the pain of changing technology.

T he systems development life cycle (SDLC) is the foundation for all systems development methodologies. Understanding the phases and activities involved in the systems development life cycle is critical when developing information systems regardless of which methodology is being used. The SDLC contains the following phases:

1. The *planning phase* involves establishing a high-level plan of the intended project and determining project goals.

2. The *analysis phase* involves analyzing end-user business requirements and refining project goals into defined functions and operations of the intended system.

3. The *design phase* involves describing the desired features and operations of the system including screen layouts, business rules, process diagrams, pseudo code, and other documentation.

4. The *development phase* involves taking all the detailed design documents from the design phase and transforming them into the actual system.

5. The *testing phase* involves bringing all the project pieces together into a special testing environment to test for errors, bugs, and interoperability, in order to verify that the system meets all the business requirements defined in the analysis phase.

6. The *implementation phase* involves placing the system into production so users can begin to perform actual business operations with the system.

7. The *maintenance phase* involves performing changes, corrections, additions, and upgrades to ensure the system continues to meet the business goals.

Analysis phase, 501
Business requirement, 501
Change control board
  (CCB), 509
Change management
  system, 509
Commercial off-the-shelf
  (COTS), 503
Computer-aided software
  engineering (CASE), 502
Critical success factor
  (CSF), 500
Data flow diagram (DFD), 502
Data model, 505
Design phase, 504

Development phase, 506
Entity relationship diagram
  (ERD), 505
Feasibility study, 500
Feature creep, 510
Graphical user interface
  (GUI), 505
GUI screen design, 505
Help desk, 509
Implementation phase, 507
Joint application development
  (JAD), 502
Maintenance, 509
Maintenance phase, 508
Modeling, 504

Online training, 508
Planning phase, 499
Process modeling, 502
Requirements definition
  document, 501
Scope creep, 510
Sign-off, 501
Systems development life cycle
  (SDLC), 498
Test condition, 506
Testing phase, 506
User documentation, 507
Workshop training, 508

Disaster at Denver International Airport

One good way to learn how to develop successful systems is to review past failures. One of the most infamous system failures is Denver International Airport's (DIA) baggage system. When the automated baggage system design for DIA was introduced, it was hailed as the savior of modern airport design. The design relied on a network of 300 computers to route bags and 4,000 telecars to carry luggage across 21 miles of track. Laser scanners were to read bar-coded luggage tags, while advanced scanners tracked the movement of toboggan-like baggage carts.

When DIA finally opened its doors for reporters to witness its revolutionary baggage handling system the scene was rather unpleasant. Bags were chewed up, lost, and misrouted in what has since become a legendary systems nightmare.

One of the biggest mistakes made in the baggage handling system fiasco was that not enough time was allowed to properly develop the system. In the beginning of the project, DIA assumed it was the responsibility of individual airlines to find their own way of moving the baggage from the plane to the baggage claim area. The automated baggage system was not involved in the initial planning of the DIA project. By the time the developers of DIA decided to create an integrated baggage system, the time frame for designing and implementing such a complex and huge system was not possible.

Another common mistake that occurred during the project was that the airlines kept changing their business requirements. This caused numerous issues including the implementation of power supplies that were not properly updated for the revised system design, which caused overloaded motors and mechanical failures. Besides the power supplies design problem, the optical sensors did not read the bar codes correctly, causing issues with baggage routing.

Finally, BAE, the company that designed and implemented the automated baggage system for DIA, had never created a baggage system of this size before. BAE had created a similar system in an airport in Munich, Germany, where the scope was much smaller. Essentially, the baggage system had an inadequate IT infrastructure since it was designed for a much smaller system.

DIA simply could not open without a functional baggage system so the city had no choice but to delay the opening date for over 16 months, costing taxpayers roughly $1 million per day, which totaled around $500 million.[4]

Questions

1. One of the problems with DIA's baggage system was inadequate testing. Describe the different types of tests DIA could have used to help ensure its baggage system's success.

2. Evaluate the different implementation approaches. Which one would have most significantly increased the chances of the project's success?

3. Explain the cost of finding errors. How could more time spent in the analysis and design phase have saved Colorado taxpayers hundreds of millions of dollars?

4. Why could BAE not take an existing IT infrastructure and simply increase its scale and expect it to work?

Reducing Ambiguity in Business Requirements

The number one reason projects fail is bad business requirements. Business requirements are considered "bad" because of ambiguity or insufficient involvement of end users during analysis and design.

A requirement is unambiguous if it has the same interpretation for all parties. Different interpretations by different participants will usually result in unmet expectations. Here is an example of an ambiguous requirement and an example of an unambiguous requirement:

- **Ambiguous requirement:** The financial report must show profits in local and U.S. currencies.
- **Unambiguous requirement:** The financial report must show profits in local and U.S. currencies using the exchange rate printed in *The Wall Street Journal* for the last business day of the period being reported.

Ambiguity is impossible to prevent completely because it is introduced into requirements in natural ways. For example:

- Requirements can contain technical implications that are obvious to the IT developers but not to the customers.
- Requirements can contain business implications that are obvious to the customer but not to the IT developers.
- Requirements may contain everyday words whose meanings are "obvious" to everyone, yet different for everyone.
- Requirements are reflections of detailed explanations that may have included multiple events, multiple perspectives, verbal rephrasing, emotion, iterative refinement, selective emphasis, and body language—none of which are captured in the written statements.

Tips for Reviewing Business Requirements

When reviewing business requirements always look for the following words to help dramatically reduce ambiguity:

- **"And"** and **"or"** have well-defined meanings and ought to be completely unambiguous, yet they are often understood only informally and interpreted inconsistently. For example, consider the statement "The alarm must ring if button T is pressed and if button F is pressed." This statement may be intended to mean that to ring the alarm, both buttons must be pressed or it may be intended to mean that either one can be pressed. A statement like this should never appear in a requirement because the potential for misinterpretation is too great. A preferable approach is to be very explicit, for example, "The alarm must ring if both buttons T and F are pressed simultaneously. The alarm should not ring in any other circumstance."
- **"Always"** might really mean "most of the time," in which case it should be made more explicit. For example, the statement "We always run reports A and B together" could be challenged with "In other words, there is never any circumstance where you would run A without B and B without A?" If you build a system with an "always" requirement, then you are actually building the system to never run report A without report B. If a user suddenly wants report B without report A, you will need to make significant system changes.

- **"Never"** might mean "rarely," in which case it should be made more explicit. For example, the statement "We never run reports A and B in the same month" could be challenged with, "So that means that if I see that A has been run, I can be absolutely certain that no one will want to run B." Again, if you build a system that supports a "never" requirement then the system users can never perform that requirement. For example, the system would never allow a user to run reports A and B in the same month, no matter what the circumstances.

- **Boundary conditions** are statements about the line between true and false and do and do not. These statements may or may not be meant to include end points. For example, "We want to use method X when there are up to 10 pages, but method Y otherwise." If you were building this system, would you include page 10 in method X or in method Y? The answer to this question will vary causing an ambiguous business requirement.[5]

Questions

1. Why are ambiguous business requirements the leading cause of system development failures?

2. Why do the words *and* and *or* tend to lead to ambiguous requirements?

3. Research the Web and determine other reasons for "bad" business requirements.

4. What is wrong with the following business requirement: "The system must support employee birthdays since every employee always has a birthday every year."

✷ MAKING BUSINESS DECISIONS

1. Understanding Project Failure

You are the director of project management for Stello, a global manufacturer of high-end writing instruments. The company sells to primarily high-end customers, and the average price for one of its fine writing instruments is about $350. You are currently implementing a new customer relationship management system and you want to do everything you can to ensure a successful systems development effort. Create a document summarizing the five primary reasons this project could fail, along with your strategy to eliminate the possibility of system development failure on your project.

2. Missing Phases in the Systems Development Life Cycle

Hello Inc. is a large concierge service for executives operating in Chicago, San Francisco, and New York. The company performs all kinds of services from dog walking to airport transportation. Your manager, Dan Martello, wants to skip the testing phase during the company's financial ERP implementation. Dan feels that since the system came from a vendor it should work correctly. To meet the project's looming deadline he wants to skip the testing phase. Draft a memo explaining to Dan the importance of following the SDLC and the ramifications to the business if the financial system is not tested.

3. Saving Failing Systems

Crik Candle Company manufactures low-end candles for restaurants. The company generates over $40 million in annual revenues and has over 300 employees. You are in the middle of a large multimillion-dollar supply chain management implementation. Your project manager has just come to you with the information that the project might fail for the following reasons:

- Several business requirements were incorrect and the scope has to be doubled.
- Three developers recently quit.
- The deadline has been moved up a month.

Develop a list of options that your company can follow to ensure the project remains on schedule and within budget.

4. Refusing to Sign Off

You are the primary client on a large extranet development project. After carefully reviewing the requirements definition document, you are positive that there are missing, ambiguous, inaccurate, and unclear requirements. The project manager is pressuring you for your sign-off since he has already received sign-off from five of your co-workers. If you fail to sign off on the requirements, you are going to put the entire project at risk since the time frame is nonnegotiable. What would you do? Why?

5. Feasibility Studies

John Lancert is the new managing operations director for a large construction company, LMC. John is currently looking for an associate who can help him prioritize the 60 proposed company projects. You are interested in working with John and have decided to apply for the job. John has asked you to compile a report detailing why project prioritization is critical for LMC, along with the different types of feasibility studies you would recommend that LMC use when determining which projects to pursue.

B15

Project Management

LEARNING OUTCOMES

1. Describe the three primary activities performed by a project manager.
2. Explain change management and how an organization can prepare for change.
3. Explain risk management and how an organization can mitigate risk.
4. Summarize the strategies a project manager can use to ensure a successful project.

Introduction

The core units introduced project management. A **project** is a temporary endeavor undertaken to create a unique product or service. According to the Project Management Institute, **project management** is the application of knowledge, skills, tools, and techniques to project activities in order to meet or exceed stakeholder needs and expectations from a project. This plug-in takes a detailed look at the fundamentals of project management, along with change management and risk management.

Project Management Fundamentals

Project deliverables are any measurable, tangible, verifiable outcome, result, or item that is produced to complete a project or part of a project. Examples of project deliverables include design documents, testing scripts, and requirements documents. **Project milestones** represent key dates when a certain group of activities must be performed. For example, completing the planning phase might be a project milestone. If a project milestone is missed, then chances are the project is experiencing problems. A **project manager** is an individual who is an expert in project planning and management, defines and develops the project plan, and tracks the plan to ensure all key project milestones are completed on time. The art and science of project management must coordinate numerous activities as displayed in Figure B15.1. Project managers perform numerous activities, and three of these primary activities are:

1. Choosing strategic projects.
2. Setting the project scope.
3. Managing resources and maintaining the project plan.

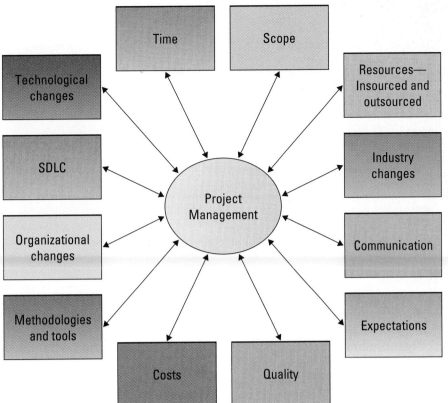

CHOOSING STRATEGIC PROJECTS

Calpine Corp., a large energy producer, uses project management software to look at its IT investments from a business perspective. The company classifies projects in one of three ways: (1) run the business, (2) grow the business, and (3) transform the business. Calpine splits its $100 million in assets accordingly: 60 percent for running the business, 20 percent for growing the business, and 20 percent for transforming the business. Calpine evaluates each of its 30 to 35 active projects for perceived business value against project costs. For the company to pursue a project it must pass a return on investment (ROI) hurdle. A business project must minimally provide two times ROI, and a transformation project must provide five times ROI.[1]

One of the most difficult decisions organizations make is determining the projects in which to invest time, energy, and resources. An organization must identify what it wants to do and how it is going to do it. The "what" part of this question focuses on issues such as justification for the project, definition of the project, and expected results of the project. The "how" part of the question deals with issues such as project approach, project schedule, and analysis of project risks. Determining which projects to focus corporate efforts on is as necessary to projects as each project is to an organization. The three common techniques an organization can use to select projects include:

1. Focus on organizational goals.
2. Categorize projects.
3. Perform a financial analysis (see Figure B15.2).

Before its merger with Hewlett-Packard, Compaq decided to analyze and prioritize its system development projects. Knowing that the CIO wanted to be able to view every project, project management leaders quickly identified and removed nonstrategic projects. At the end of the review process, the company canceled 39 projects, saving the organization $15 million. Most Fortune 100 companies are

Techniques for Choosing Strategic Projects
1. **Focus on organizational goals**—Managers are finding tremendous value in choosing projects that align with the organization's goals. Projects that address organizational goals tend to have a higher success rate since they are important to the entire organization.
2. **Categorize projects**—There are various categories that an organization can group projects into to determine a project's priority. One type of categorization includes problem, opportunity, and directives. Problems are undesirable situations that prevent an organization from achieving its goals. Opportunities are chances to improve the organization. Directives are new requirements imposed by management, government, or some other external influence. It is often easier to obtain approval for projects that address problems or directives because the organization must respond to these categories to avoid financial losses.
3. **Perform a financial analysis**—A number of different financial analysis techniques can be performed to help determine a project's priority. A few of these include net present value, return on investment, and payback analysis. These financial analysis techniques help determine the organization's financial expectations for the project.

receiving bottom-line benefits similar to Compaq's from implementing a project management solution.[2]

Organizations also need to choose and prioritize projects in such a way that they can make responsible decisions as to which projects to eliminate. Jim Johnson, chairman of the Standish Group, has identified project management as the process that can make the difference in project success. According to Johnson, "Companies need a process for taking a regular look at their projects and deciding, again and again, if the investment is going to pay off. As it stands now, for most companies, projects can take on a life of their own."[3]

An organization must build in continuous self-assessment, which allows earlier termination decisions on failing projects, with the associated cost savings. This frees capital and personnel for dedication to projects that are worth pursuing. The elimination of a project should be viewed as successful resource management, not as an admission of failure.

SETTING THE PROJECT SCOPE

Once an organization defines the projects it wants to pursue, it must set the project scope. *Project scope* defines the work that must be completed to deliver a product with the specified features and functions. The project scope statement is important because it specifies clear project boundaries. The project scope typically includes the following:

- *Project product*—a description of the characteristics the product or service has undertaken.

- *Project objectives*—quantifiable criteria that must be met for the project to be considered a success.

- *Project deliverables*—any measurable, tangible, verifiable outcome, result, or item that is produced to complete a project or part of a project.

- *Project exclusions*—products, services, or processes that are not specifically a part of the project.

The project objectives are one of the most important areas to define because they are essentially the major elements of the project. When an organization achieves the project objectives, it has accomplished the major goals of the project and the project scope is satisfied. Project objectives must include metrics so that the project's success can be measured. The metrics can include cost, schedule, and quality metrics along with a number of other metrics. Figure B15.3 displays the SMART criteria—useful reminders on how to ensure that the project has created understandable and measurable objectives.

MANAGING RESOURCES AND MAINTAINING THE PROJECT PLAN

FIGURE B15.3

SMART Criteria for Successful Objective Creation

Managing people is one of the hardest and most critical efforts a project manager undertakes. How to resolve conflicts within the team and how to balance the needs of the project with the personal/professional needs of the team are a few of the challenges facing project managers. More and more project managers are the main (and sometimes sole) interface with the client during the project. As such, communication, negotiation, marketing, and salesmanship are just as important to the project manager as financial and analytical acumen. There are many times when the people management side of project management made the difference in pulling off a successful project.

A *project plan* is a formal, approved document that manages and controls project execution. A well-defined project plan is characterized by the following:

- Easy to understand.
- Easy to read.
- Communicated to all key participants (key stakeholders).
- Appropriate to the project's size, complexity, and criticality.
- Prepared by the team, rather than by the individual project manager.

The most important part of the plan is communication. The project manager must communicate the plan to every member of the project team and to any key stakeholders and executives. The project plan must also include any project assumptions and be detailed enough to guide the execution of the project. A key to achieving project success is earning consensus and buy-in from all key stakeholders. By including key stakeholders in project plan development, the project manager allows them to have ownership of the plan. This often translates to greater commitment, which in turn results in enhanced motivation and productivity.

The two primary diagrams most frequently used in project planning are PERT and Gantt charts. A *PERT (Program Evaluation and Review Technique) chart* is a graphical network model that depicts a project's tasks and the relationships between those tasks. A *dependency* is a logical relationship that exists between the project tasks, or between a project task and a milestone. PERT charts define dependency between project tasks before those tasks are scheduled (see Figure B15.4). The boxes in Figure B15.4 represent project tasks, and the project manager can adjust the contents of the boxes to display various project attributes such as schedule and actual start and finish times. The arrows indicate that one task is dependent on the start or completion of another task. The *critical path* is a path from the start to the finish that passes through all the tasks that are critical to completing the project in the shortest amount of time. PERT charts frequently display a project's critical path.

A *Gantt chart* is a simple bar chart that depicts project tasks against a calendar. In a Gantt chart, tasks are listed vertically and the project's time frame is listed horizontally. A Gantt chart works well for representing the project schedule. It also shows actual progress of tasks against the planned duration. Figure B15.5 displays a software development project using a Gantt chart.

Change Management and Risk Management

Business leaders face a rapidly moving and unforgiving global marketplace that will force them to use every possible tool to sustain competitiveness. A good project manager understands not only the fundamentals of project management, but also how to effectively deal with change management and risk management.

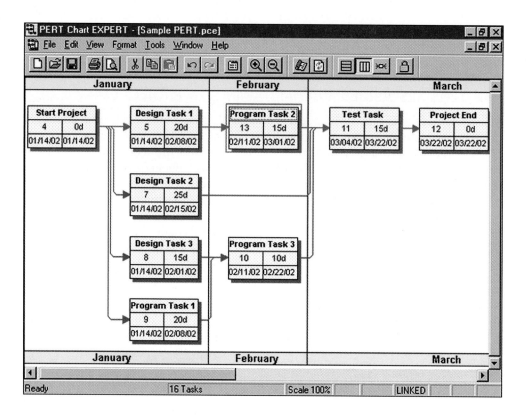

CHANGE MANAGEMENT

What works at Snap-on, a maker of tools and equipment for specialists such as car mechanics, is the organization's ability to manage change. The company recently increased profits by 12 percent while sales were down 6.7 percent. Dennis Leitner, vice president of IT, runs the IT group on a day-to-day basis and leads

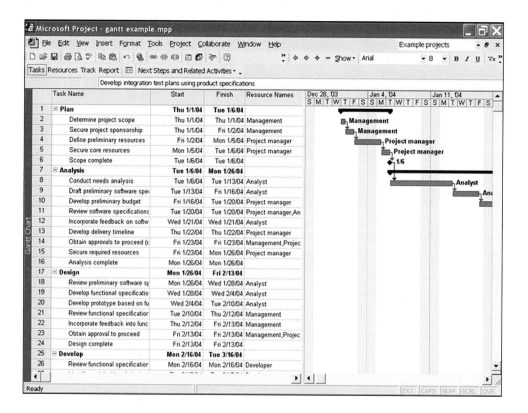

Common Reasons Change Occurs
1. An omission in defining initial scope
2. A misunderstanding of the initial scope
3. An external event such as government regulations that create new requirements
4. Organizational changes, such as mergers, acquisitions, and partnerships, that create new business problems and opportunities
5. Availability of better technology
6. Shifts in planned technology that force unexpected and significant changes to the business organization, culture, and/or processes
7. The users or management simply wanting the system to do more than they originally requested or agreed to
8. Management reducing the funding for the project or imposing an earlier deadline

the implementation of all major software development initiatives. Each software development initiative is managed by both the business and IT. In fact, business resources are on the IT group's payroll and they spend as much as 80 percent of their time learning what a business unit is doing and how IT can help make it happen. Leitner's role focuses primarily on strategic planning, change management, and setting up metrics to track performance.[4]

Dynamic organizational change is inevitable and an organization must effectively manage change as it evolves. With the numerous challenges and complexities that organizations face in today's rapidly changing environment, effective change management thus becomes a critical core competency. ***Change management*** is a set of techniques that aid in evolution, composition, and policy management of the design and implementation of a system. Figure B15.6 displays a few of the more common reasons change occurs.

A ***change management system*** includes a collection of procedures to document a change request and define the steps necessary to consider the change based on the expected impact of the change. Most change management systems require that a change request form be initiated by one or more project stakeholders (systems owners, users, customers, analysts, developers). Ideally, these change requests are considered by a ***change control board (CCB)*** that is responsible for approving or rejecting all change requests. The CCB's composition typically includes a representative from each business area that has a stake in the project. The CCB's decision to accept or reject each change is based on an impact analysis of the change. For example, if one department wants to implement a change to the software that will increase both deployment time and cost, then the other business owners need to agree that the change is valid and that it warrants the extended time frame and increased budget.

PREPARING FOR CHANGE

Change is an opportunity, not a threat. Realizing that change is the norm rather than the exception will help an organization stay ahead. Becoming a change leader and accepting the inevitability of change can help ensure that an organization can survive and even thrive in times of change. Change leaders make change effective both inside and outside their organization by following three important guidelines:

1. Institute change management policies.
2. Anticipate change.
3. Seek change (see Figure B15.7).

Three Important Guidelines for Effectively Dealing with Change Management
1. **Institute change management polices**—Create clearly defined policies and procedures that must be followed each time a request for change is received.
2. **Anticipate change**—View change as an opportunity and embrace it.
3. **Seek change**—Every 6 to 12 months look for changes that may be windows of opportunity. Review successes and failures to determine if there are any opportunities for innovation.

General Electric has successfully tackled change management through an innovative program trademarked "Work Out." Work Out is shorthand for the idea of taking excess work out of the system. The purpose is to eliminate bureaucracy and free people's time for more productive activities. The positive time-saving and productivity-enhancing results of the Work Out change management program include:

■ **Reports:** Teams calculated the time it took to prepare routine reports and compared it with the value generated from the reports. It quickly became apparent that much more effort went into preparing the reports than their comparative value to the recipients warranted. Valuable time was freed when those reports were eliminated or scaled back.

■ **Approvals:** The approval process was questioned and adjusted accordingly. One instance discovered that a simple purchase order request required 12 approval signatures.

■ **Meetings:** Teams evaluated the need for meetings and changed the way they were conducted to take advantage of technologies like teleconferencing.[5]

Change, whether it comes in the form of a crisis, a market shift, or a technological development, is challenging for all organizations. Successful organizations and successful people learn to anticipate and react appropriately to change.

RISK MANAGEMENT

Altria Group, Inc., the tobacco and food-products conglomerate, has a well-defined process for choosing projects based on project risk. The company gathers project information such as cash flow, return on investment, interfaces, and regulatory-compliance issues and creates a risk-based score of each project. The company then plots them on a grid with risk on the horizontal axis and value on the vertical axis. Managers then choose projects based on an optimal balance of risk and return.[6]

Project risk is an uncertain event or condition that, if it occurs, has a positive or negative effect on a project objective(s). ***Risk management*** is the process of proactive and ongoing identification, analysis, and response to risk factors. The best place to address project risk is during the project plan creation. Elements of risk management are outlined in Figure B15.8.

Elements of Risk Management
Risk identification—Determining which risks might affect the project and documenting their characteristics
Qualitative risk analysis—Performing a qualitative analysis of risks and conditions to prioritize their effects on project objectives
Quantitative risk analysis—Measuring the probability and consequences of risks as well as estimating their implications for the project objectives
Risk response planning—Developing procedures and techniques to enhance opportunities and reduce threats to the project's objectives

Common Project Risk Factors
Changing business circumstances that undermine expected benefits
Reluctance to report negative information or to "blow the whistle" on a project
Significant change management issues including resistance to change
The rush to get a project done quickly, often compromising the end result and desired outcome
Executives who are strongly wedded to a project and unwilling to admit that it may have been a mistake
A common tendency in IT projects to overengineer technology solutions, stemming from a belief in the superiority of technical solutions over simpler, people-based solutions
Building the project plan in conjunction with the budget or to validate some basic assumptions about the project's fiscal requirements and business base payback calculations

FIGURE B15.9

Common Project Risk Factors

Risks vary throughout a project and in general are more significant at the later phases of a project. Risk factors that may not be immediately obvious and are often the root causes of IT project success or failure are displayed in Figure B15.9.

MITIGATING RISK

An organization must devise strategies to reduce or mitigate risk. A wide range of strategies can be applied, with each risk category necessitating different mitigation strategies. When considering risk mitigation, the importance of choice, opportunities, and inexactitude should be kept clearly in mind. Organizations should take several actions at the enterprise level to improve risk management capabilities; these are displayed in Figure B15.10.

Audit and tax firm KPMG LLP and software maker SeeCommerce unveiled a service, called SeeRisk, to help companies assess supply chain management risk. SeeRisk helps a company establish common metrics and measure performance against them by identifying operational problems and risks. The SeeRisk system is integrated with operational and transactional systems along with external vendor systems. The goal of the system is to improve revenue as well as reduce costs by increasing visibility of inventory, and by knowing what is on the shelf and what is downstream in production. SeeRisk can calculate the implications that defective components would have on revenue, operating costs, what it would cost to start production over, and ultimately the effect on corporate profitability.[7]

Actions to Improve Risk Management Capabilities
Promote project leadership skills—Hire individuals with strong project management and project leadership skills as well as business management skills. These individuals can be extremely helpful in advisory and steering committee roles as well as coaching roles.
Learn from previous experience—Over many years of collective experiences, organizations have encountered hundreds of large IT projects. Document and revisit development methodologies, software tools, and software development best practices in order to share this vital information across the organization.
Share knowledge—Working in team or group environments tends to yield the most successful projects since individuals can share their unique learning experiences.
Create a project management culture—Orient people from day one on the importance of project management, change management, and risk management. Be sure to measure and reward project management skills and promote individuals based on successful projects.

FIGURE B15.10

Actions to Improve Risk Management Capabilities

Successful Project Management Strategies

Recreational Equipment, Inc. (REI) needs to consistently develop quality products and decrease the time to deliver them to market. To do that, REI needs to efficiently manage product development processes, projects, and information. The REI Gear and Apparel division takes an integrated project management approach to designing, managing, and tracking its product development projects, while collaborating and managing its workflow. REI's strategy entails combining Microsoft.NET technology, the Microsoft Office Enterprise Project Management (EPM) Solution, and software based on Microsoft Office Visio to create an integrated business solution it can use to model as-is business processes, experiment with what-if scenarios, and then convert the optimized processes into detailed project plans.

Project managers can further develop these plans, assign resources divisionwide, manage projects online, and collaborate globally. REI predicts this integrated solution will help it improve its efficiency, consistency, and scalability so it can deliver its products to market more quickly.[8] Figure B15.11 displays the top five successful project management strategies outlined in *CIO* magazine.

FIGURE B15.11

Top Five Successful Project Management Strategies

Top Five Successful Project Management Strategies
1. **Define project success criteria.** At the beginning of the project, make sure the stakeholders share a common understanding of how they will determine whether the project is successful. Too often, meeting a predetermined schedule is the only apparent success factor, but there are certainly others. Some examples are increasing market share, reaching a specified sales volume or revenue, achieving specific customer satisfaction measures, retiring a high-maintenance legacy system, and achieving a particular transaction processing volume and correctness.
2. **Develop a solid project plan.** The hard part of developing a plan is the thinking, negotiating, balancing, and communication project managers will have to do to develop a solid and realistic plan. The time they spend analyzing what it will take to solve the business problem will reduce the number of changes later in the project.
3. **Divide and conquer.** Break all large tasks into multiple small tasks to provide more accurate estimates, reveal hidden work activities, and allow for more accurate, fine-grained status tracking.
4. **Plan for change.** Things never go precisely as planned on a project; therefore, the budget and schedule should include some contingency buffers at the end of major phases to accommodate change.
5. **Manage project risk.** Failure to identify and control risks will allow the risks to control the project. Be sure to spend significant time during project planning to brainstorm possible risk factors, evaluate their potential threat, and determine the best way to mitigate or prevent them.

L arge IT projects require significant investment of time and resources. Successful software development projects have proven challenging and often elusive, wasting many resources and jeopardizing the goodwill of stakeholders, including customers and employees. Bringing strong, effective project, change, and risk management disciplines to large IT projects is essential to successful organizations. The days when a project manager could just concentrate on bringing a project in on time, on budget, and with agreed-upon deliverables are fading.

Change control board
   (CCB), 523
Change management, 523
Change management
   system, 523
Critical path, 521
Dependency, 521
Gantt chart, 521

PERT (Program Evaluation
   and Review Technique)
   chart, 521
Project, 518
Project deliverable, 518, 520
Project exclusion, 520
Project management, 518
Project manager, 518

Project milestone, 518
Project objective, 520
Project plan, 521
Project product, 520
Project risk, 524
Project scope, 520
Risk management, 524

Staying on Track—Toronto Transit

Schedules are at the heart of Toronto Transit Commission's (TTC) celebrated transit system, which services over 1 million customers daily. More than 50 large engineering and construction projects are under way to expand, upgrade, and maintain Toronto's transit systems and structures. One such project is the Sheppard project, which consists of constructing the new six-kilometer line north of the city. Sheppard is estimated to take more than five years to complete, with a total cost of $875 million.

TTC's challenge is to keep its 50 individual projects, most of which fall within the $2 million to $100 million price range and span an average of five years, on schedule and under budget. Staying on top of so many multifaceted, multiyear, and often interdependent projects adds additional complexity for the commission. TTC uses Primavera Project Planner (P3) to create a single master schedule for all of its engineering and construction projects.

TTC's 50 individual projects average 100 to 150 activities each, with some projects encompassing as many as 500 to 600 activities. "Seeing the big picture is important, not only for the 300 people who work in the Engineering and Construction branch of the TTC, but for the entire 9,000-person organization," said Vince Carroll, head scheduler for the Engineering and Construction branch. "Engineering managers need to see how other projects may impact their own. Materials and procurement managers need to track project progress. Senior managers need to be able to communicate with city government to secure funding. Marketing and public relations people need the latest information to set public expectations. And most important of all," said Carroll, "the operations group needs to stay informed of what is happening so that they can adjust the schedules that run the trains."

Carroll and his team of 25 people create, update, and publish a master schedule that summarizes the individual status of each project, shows the logical links between projects, and provides an integrated overview of all projects. The master schedule helps the team effectively and regularly communicate the status of all projects currently under way throughout the Toronto Transit system.

The master schedule organizes projects according to their location in the capital budget. For example, projects can be organized according to those that have been allotted funding for expansion, state of good repair, legislative reasons, or environmental reasons. Each project is organized by its logical flow—from planning, analysis, and design, through the maintenance phase. The final report shows positive and negative balances for each project and a single overview of the status of all the engineering and construction projects. Carroll and his team use PERT charts to create time-scaled logic diagrams and then convert this information to bar charts for presentation purposes in the master schedule. TTC is currently linking its master schedule directly to its payroll system, enabling it to track the number of hours actually worked versus hours planned.[9]

Questions

1. Describe Gantt charts and explain how TTC could use one to communicate project status.
2. Describe PERT charts and explain how TTC could use one to communicate project status.
3. How could TTC use its master schedule to gain efficiencies in its supply chain?
4. How could TTC use its master schedule to identify change management and risk management issues?

 CLOSING CASE TWO

Change at Toyota

At Toyota Motor Sales USA's headquarters in Torrance, California, a circular patch of manicured earth separates the IS building and corporate headquarters. A brook winds its way through lush flowers and pine trees, and a terraced path connects the two buildings. For many years, this was about the only thing the two groups shared with each other.

For the business executives at Toyota Motor Sales (TMS) peering across the courtyard at the Data building, the deep black windows were a symbol of IS's opacity. These executives felt that IS was unresponsive, and they had little clue where the money was going. "One of the complaints was that we spent a lot of money on IT projects, and the business was frequently disappointed with the results," recalled Bob Daly, group vice president of Toyota Customer Services. Daly says badly handled projects, such as a delayed PeopleSoft ERP implementation and a protracted parts inventory initiative, led to finger-pointing between the two factions.

Meanwhile, behind the darkened windows of the Data building, CIO Barbra Cooper's IS staff was buried under the weight of six enterprisewide projects. Called the Big Six, they included a new extranet for Toyota dealers and the PeopleSoft ERP rollout, as well as four new systems for order management, parts forecasting, advanced warranty and financial document management. Feeling besieged, the IS group made the mistake of not explaining to the business side all the things it was doing and how much it all cost. It was a classic case of mismanaged expectations and fractured alignment.

By late 2002, Cooper realized that if she wanted to win back the respect of the business managers—and remain in her post—she would have to make some radical changes. A conversation with Toyota Motor Sales CEO, in which he questioned the sharp incline of IS's spending curve, stopped her in her tracks. In her 30 years in IT, Cooper had developed something of a reputation for coming in to clean up other CIOs' messes. Now, she had to take a long look in the mirror and fix herself.

Cooper's Path to Success

Cooper could no longer ignore the rumblings from across the courtyard that had worked their way into the rank-and-file business staff. To them, IS had become an unresponsive, bureaucratic machine.

Cooper started soliciting informal feedback from a wide range of businesspeople. What she discovered was an accumulation of "very painful projects for both IT and the business," she said. "Clearly there was not enough communication and education on our part."

In late 2002, Cooper hired an outside consultancy to interview TMS's top 20 executives. She wanted their honest opinions of how IS was doing. The results did not provide all the answers to the ailments, but she certainly saw the trouble spots. "Parts of the survey results were stinging," Cooper said. "But you can't be a CIO and not face that."

Cooper spent many introspective weeks in 2003 formulating her vision for a new IT department. What she developed was a strategy for a decentralized and transparent IS organization that focused all of its energy on the major business segments. In the summer of 2003, she presented her vision to her senior IS staffers. Some of the managers were excited by the prospect of change; others were less so.

The first thing Cooper did was set up the Toyota Value Action Program, a team of eight staffers responsible for translating her vision into actionable items for the department and her direct reports. Using the survey results and Cooper's direction, the team winnowed the list to 18 initiatives, including increasing employee training and development, gaining cost savings, making process improvements, overcoming IS inefficiencies, and implementing a metrics program. Each initiative got a project owner and a team. Cooper insisted that each initiative have a mechanism to check its success. The most significant initiative called for improved alignment with the business side. At the heart of this new effort would be a revamped Office of the CIO structure—with new roles, reporting lines, and responsibilities.

As part of the overhaul, Cooper took top-flight personnel out of the Data building and embedded them as divisional information officers, or DIOs, in all of the business units. These DIOs are accountable for IT strategy, development, and services, and they sit on the management committees headed by top business executives. The DIOs' goal is to forge relationships with tier-one executives and executives at the vice president level.

The DIOs were not alone. Business operation managers and relationship managers from IS sat alongside the business folks. "I still believe in managing IT centrally, but it was incumbent on us to physically distribute IT into the businesses," Cooper said. "They could provide more local attention while keeping the enterprise vision alive."

Cooper upended the structure of Toyota's IS department in six months in a bid to weave IT functions more closely into the daily business operations. The process was painful: She changed IS employees' jobs, exposed all of IS's shortcomings, and forced her staff into the business offices. However, just over a year into the new plan, IS and the businesses were standing shoulder-to-shoulder when planning and implementing IT projects. And Cooper was still CIO of Toyota Motor Sales.

A Little Kicking and Screaming

Change can be scary for anyone, especially during an upheaval of an entire 400-person IS department. Cooper changed the jobs of 50 percent of her staffers within six months, yet no one left or was let go. Some took on new responsibilities; others took on expanded or new roles. Cooper said some mid- and upper-level staffers were initially uncomfortable with their new roles, but she spent a lot of time fostering a new attitude about the change. "I dragged them into the conversations kicking and screaming," Cooper said. "But I said to them, 'Unless you think of what it means to change on this level, you will never make it happen.' " The key, Cooper said, is that all IS staffers were brought into the development of the new organization early.[10]

Questions

1. What would be the impact on Toyota's business if it failed to implement a project management solution and managed its projects using a myriad of spreadsheets and Word documents?

2. Why would Toyota find it important to focus on implementing good project management techniques?

3. Why are project management, change management, and risk management critical to a global company such as Toyota?

4. Describe the ramifications to Toyota's business if it failed to anticipate change.

★ MAKING BUSINESS DECISIONS

1. Explaining Project Management

Prime Time Inc. is a large consulting company that specializes in outsourcing people with project management capabilities and skills. You are in the middle of an interview for a job with Prime Time. The manager performing the interview asks you to explain why managing a project plan is critical to a project's success. The manager also wants you to explain scope creep and feature creep and your tactics for managing them on a project. Finally, the manager wants you to elaborate on your strategies for delivering successful projects and reducing risks.

2. Applying Project Management Techniques

You have been hired by a medium-sized airline company, Sun Best. Sun Best currently flies over 300 routes in the East. The company is experiencing tremendous issues coordinating its 3,500 pilots, 7,000 flight attendants, and 2,000 daily flights. Determine how Sun Best could use a Gantt chart to help it coordinate its pilots, flight attendants, and daily flights. Using Excel, create a sample Gantt chart highlighting the different types of activities and resources Sun Best could track with the tool.

3. Prioritizing Projects

Nick Zele is the new managing operations director for a large construction company, CMA. Nick is looking for a project manager who can help him manage the 60 ongoing company projects. You are interested in working with Nick and have decided to apply for the job. Nick has asked you to compile a report detailing why project prioritization is critical for CMA, along with the different types of prioritization techniques you would recommend CMA use when determining which projects to pursue.

4. Managing Expectations

Trader is the name for a large human resource project that is currently being deployed at your organization. Your boss, Pam Myers, has asked you to compile an expectations management matrix for the project. The first thing you need to determine is management's expectations. Compile a list of questions you would ask to help determine management's expectations for the Trader project.

5. **Mitigating Risk**

Alicia Fernandez owns and operates a chain of nine seafood restaurants in the Boston area. Alicia is currently considering purchasing one of her competitors, which would give her an additional six restaurants. Alicia's primary concerns with the purchase are the constantly changing seafood prices and high staff turnover rate in the restaurant industry. Explain to Alicia what risk management is and how she can use it to mitigate the risks for the potential purchase of her competitor.

The overall goal of the Technology Plug-Ins is to provide additional information not covered in the text such as personal productivity using information technology, problem solving using Excel, and decision making using Access. These plug-ins also offer an all-in-one text to faculty, avoiding their having to purchase an extra book to support Microsoft Office. These plug-ins offer integration with the core chapters and provide critical knowledge using essential business applications, such as Microsoft Excel, Microsoft Access, and Microsoft Project with hands-on tutorials for comprehension and mastery. Plug-Ins T1 to T12 are located on this textbook's Web site at www.mhhe.com/baltzan.

PLUG-IN	DESCRIPTION
T1. Personal Productivity Using IT	This plug-in covers a number of things to do to keep a personal computer running effectively and efficiently. The 12 topics covered in this plug-in are: ■ Creating strong passwords. ■ Performing good file management. ■ Implementing effective backup and recovery strategies. ■ Using Zip files. ■ Writing professional e-mails. ■ Stopping spam. ■ Preventing phishing. ■ Detecting spyware. ■ Threads to instant messaging. ■ Increasing PC performance. ■ Using anti-virus software. ■ Installing a personal firewall.
T2. Basic Skills Using Excel	This plug-in introduces the basics of using Microsoft Excel, a spreadsheet program for data analysis, along with a few fancy features. The six topics covered in this plug-in are: ■ Workbooks and worksheets. ■ Working with cells and cell data. ■ Printing worksheets. ■ Formatting worksheets. ■ Formulas. ■ Working with charts and graphics.
T3. Problem Solving Using Excel	This plug-in provides a comprehensive tutorial on how to use a variety of Microsoft Excel functions and features for problem solving. The five areas covered in this plug-in are: ■ Lists ■ Conditional Formatting ■ AutoFilter ■ Subtotals ■ PivotTables
T4. Decision Making Using Excel	This plug-in examines a few of the advanced business analysis tools used in Microsoft Excel that have the capability to identify patterns, trends, and rules, and create "what-if" models. The four topics covered in this plug-in are: ■ IF ■ Goal Seek ■ Solver ■ Scenario Manager
T5. Designing Database Applications	This plug-in provides specific details on how to design relational database applications. One of the most efficient and powerful information management computer-based applications is the relational database. The four topics covered in this plug-in are: ■ Entities and data relationships. ■ Documenting logical data relationships. ■ The relational data model. ■ Normalization.

T6. Basic Skills Using Access	This plug-in focuses on creating a Microsoft Access database file. One of the most efficient information management computer-based applications is Microsoft Access. Access provides a powerful set of tools for creating and maintaining a relational database. The two topics covered in this plug-in are: ■ Create a new database file. ■ Create and modify tables.
T7. Problem Solving Using Access	This plug-in provides a comprehensive tutorial on how to query a database in Microsoft Access. Queries are essential for problem solving, allowing a user to sort information, summarize data (display totals, averages, counts, and so on), display the results of calculations on data, and choose exactly which fields are shown. The three topics in this plug-in are: ■ Create simple queries using the simple query wizard. ■ Create advanced queries using calculated fields. ■ Format results displayed in calculated fields.
T8. Decision Making Using Access	This plug-in provides a comprehensive tutorial on entering data in a well-designed form and creating functional reports using Microsoft Access. A form is essential to use for data entry and a report is an effective way to present data in a printed format. The two topics in this plug-in are: ■ Creating, modifying, and running forms. ■ Creating, modifying, and running reports.
T9. Designing Web Pages	This plug-in provides a comprehensive assessment into the functional aspects of Web design. Web sites are beginning to look more alike and to employ the same metaphors and conventions. The Web has now become an everyday thing whose design should not make users think. The six topics in this plug-in are: ■ The World Wide Web. ■ Designing for the unknown(s). ■ The process of Web design. ■ HTML basics. ■ Web fonts. ■ Web graphics.
T10. Creating Web Pages Using HTML	This plug-in provides an overview of creating Web pages using the HTML language. HTML is a system of codes that you use to create interactive Web pages. It provides a means to describe the structure of text-based information in a document—by denoting certain text as headings, paragraphs, lists, and so on. The five topics in this plug-in are: ■ An introduction to HTML. ■ HTML tools. ■ Creating, saving, and viewing HTML documents. ■ Applying style tags and attributes. ■ Using fancy formatting. ■ Creating hyperlinks. ■ Displaying graphics.
T11. Creating Web Pages Using Dreamweaver	This plug-in provides a tour of using Dreamweaver to create Web pages. Dreamweaver allows anyone with limited Web page design experience to create, modify, and maintain full-featured, professional-looking pages without having to learn how to code all the functions and features from scratch. The five topics in this plug-in are: ■ Navigation in Dreamweaver. ■ Adding content. ■ Formatting content. ■ Using cascading style sheets. ■ Creating tables.
T12. Creating Gantt Charts with Excel and Microsoft Project	This plug-in offers a quick and efficient way to manage projects. Excel and Microsoft Project are great for managing all phases of a project, creating templates, collaborating on planning processes, tracking project progress, and sharing information with all interested parties. The two topics in this plug-in are: ■ Creating Gantt Charts with Excel. ■ Creating Gantt Charts with Microsoft Project.

Apply Your Knowledge Project Overview

Project Number	Project Name	Project Type	Plug-In	Focus Area	Project Level	Skill Set	Page Number
1	Financial Destiny	Excel	T2	Personal Budget	Introductory	Formulas	536
2	Cash Flow	Excel	T2	Cash Flow	Introductory	Formulas	536
3	Technology Budget	Excel	T1, T2	Hardware and Software	Introductory	Formulas	536
4	Tracking Donations	Excel	T2	Employee Relationships	Introductory	Formulas	537
5	Convert Currency	Excel	T2	Global Commerce	Introductory	Formulas	537
6	Cost Comparison	Excel	T2	Total Cost of Ownership	Introductory	Formulas	537
7	Time Management	Excel or Project	T12	Project Management	Introductory	Gantt Charts	538
8	Maximize Profit	Excel	T2, T4	Strategic Analysis	Intermediate	Formulas or Solver	538
9	Security Analysis	Excel	T3	Filtering Data	Intermediate	Conditional Formatting, Autofilter, Subtotal	539
10	Gathering Data	Excel	T3	Data Analysis	Intermediate	Conditional Formatting, PivotTable	540
11	Scanner System	Excel	T2	Strategic Analysis	Intermediate	Formulas	540
12	Competitive Pricing	Excel	T2	Profit Maximization	Intermediate	Formulas	541
13	Adequate Acquisitions	Excel	T2	Break-Even Analysis	Intermediate	Formulas	541
14	Customer Relations	Excel	T3	CRM	Intermediate	PivotTable	541
15	Shipping Costs	Excel	T4	SCM	Advanced	Solver	542
16	Formatting Grades	Excel	T3	Data Analysis	Advanced	If, LookUp	543
17	Moving Dilemma	Excel	T2, T3	SCM	Advanced	Absolute versus Relative Values	543
18	Operational Efficiencies	Excel	T3	SCM	Advanced	PivotTable	544

(*Continued*)

Project Number	Project Name	Project Type	Plug-In	Focus Area	Project Level	Skill Set	Page Number
19	Too Much Information	Excel	T3	CRM	Advanced	PivotTable	545
20	Turnover Rates	Excel	T3	Data Mining	Advanced	PivotTable	545
21	Vital Information	Excel	T3	Data Mining	Advanced	PivotTable	546
22	Breaking Even	Excel	T4	Business Analysis	Advanced	Goal Seek	546
23	Profit Scenario	Excel	T4	Sales Analysis	Advanced	Scenario Manager	547
24	Electronic Résumés	HTML	T9, T10, T11	Electronic Personal Marketing	Introductory	Structural Tags	547
25	Gathering Feedback	Dreamweaver	T9, T10, T11	Data Collection	Intermediate	Organization of Information	547
26	Daily Invoice	Access	T5, T6, T7, T8	Business Analysis	Introductory	Entities, Relationships, and Databases	548
27	Billing Data	Access	T5, T6, T7, T8	Business Intelligence	Introductory	Entities, Relationships, and Databases	550
28	Inventory Data	Access	T5, T6, T7, T8	SCM	Intermediate	Entities, Relationships, and Databases	551
29	Call Center	Access	T5, T6, T7, T8	CRM	Intermediate	Entities, Relationships, and Databases	552
30	Sales Pipeline	Access	T5, T6, T7, T8	Business Intelligence	Advanced	Entities, Relationships, and Databases	553
31	Second Life—Virtual Networking	N/A	N/A	Collaboration	Introductory	The Digital Economy	554
32	Creating a Podcast	N/A	N/A	Collaboration	Introductory	The Digital Economy	555
33	Google Earth—Geographic Information	N/A	N/A	Geographic Web	Intermediate	The Digital Economy	556
34	Photo Story 3—Show-n-Tell	N/A	N/A	Electronic Personal Marketing	Intermediate	The Digital Workforce	557
35	Sticky Wiki	N/A	N/A	Collaboration	Intermediate	The Digital Workforce	558

NOTE: Many of the Excel projects support multiple data files. Therefore the naming convention that you see in the text may not be the same as what you see in a data folder. As an example, in the text we reference data files as AYK1_Data.xlsx; however, you may see a file named AYK1_Data_Version_1.xlsx, or AYK1_Data_Version_2.xlsx.

Project 1:
Financial Destiny

You have been introduced to Microsoft Excel and are ready to begin using it to help track your monthly expenses and take charge of your financial destiny. The first step is to create a personal budget so you can see where you are spending money and if you need to decrease your monthly expenses or increase your monthly income.

Project Focus

Create a template for a monthly budget of your income and expenditures, with some money set aside for savings (or you can use the data file, AYK1_Data.xlsx, we created). Create variations of this budget to show how much you could save if you cut back on certain expenses, found a roommate, or got a part-time job. Compare the costs of a meal plan to costs of groceries. Consider how much interest would be earned if you saved $100 a month, or how much debt paid on student loans or credit card bills. To expand your data set, make a fantasy budget for 10 years from now, when you might own a home, have student loan payments, and have a good salary.

Data File: AYK1_Data.xlsx

Project 2:

Cash Flow

Gears is a five-year-old company that specializes in bike components. The company is having trouble paying for its monthly supplies and would like to perform a cash flow analysis so it can understand its financial position. Cash flow represents the money an investment produces after subtracting cash expenses from income. The statement of cash flows summarizes sources and uses of cash, indicates whether enough cash is available to carry on routine operations, and offers an analysis of all business transactions, reporting where the firm obtained its cash and how it chose to allocate the cash. The cash flow statement shows where money comes from, how the company is going to spend it, and when the company will require additional cash. Gears would like to project a cash flow statement for the next month.

Project Focus

Using the data file AYK2_Data.xlsx complete the cash flow statement for Gears using Excel. Be sure to create formulas so the company can simply input numbers in the future to determine cash flow.

Data File: AYK2_Data.xlsx

Project 3:

Technology Budget

Tally is a start-up Web site development company located in Seattle, Washington. The company currently has seven employees and is looking to hire six new employees in the next month.

Project Focus

You are in charge of purchasing for Tally. Your first task is to purchase computers for the new employees. Your budget is $250,000 to buy the best computer systems with a scanner, three color printers, and business software. Use the Web to research various products and calculate the costs of different systems using Excel. Use a variety of Excel formulas as you analyze costs and compare prices. Use the data file AYK3_Data.xlsx as a template.

Data File: AYK3_Data.xlsx

Project 4:

Tracking Donations

Lazarus Consulting is a large computer consulting company in New York. Pete Lazarus, the CEO and founder, is well known for his philanthropic efforts. Pete knows that most of his employees contribute to nonprofit organizations and wants to reward them for their efforts while encouraging others to contribute to charities. Pete began a program that matches 50 percent of each employee donation. The only stipulations are that the charity must be a nonprofit organization and the company will only match up to $2,000 per year per employee.

Project Focus

Open the data file AYK4_Data.xlsx and determine the following:

- What was the total donation amount per organization?
- What were the average donations per organization?

Data File: AYK4_Data.xlsx

Project 5:

Convert Currency

You have decided to spend the summer traveling abroad with your friends. Your trip is going to take you to France, England, Italy, Switzerland, Germany, Norway, and Ireland. You want to use Excel to convert currencies as you travel around the world.

Project Focus

Locate one of the exchange rate calculators on the Internet (www.xe.com or www.x-rates. com). Find the exchange rates for each of the countries listed above and create formulas in Excel to convert $100, $500, and $1,000. Use the data file AYK5_Data.xlsx as a template.

Data File: AYK5_Data.xls

Project 6:

Cost Comparison

You are thinking about purchasing a new computer since the machine you are using now is four years old, slow, not always reliable, and does not support the latest operating system. Your needs for the new computer are simple: anti-virus software, e-mail, Web browsing, word processing, spreadsheet, database, iTunes, and some light-weight graphical tools. Your concern is what the total cost of ownership will be for the next three years. You have to factor in a few added costs beyond just the initial purchase price for the computer itself, such as: added hardware (this could include a new printer, docking station, or scanner), software (purchase of a new operating system), training (you're thinking about pursuing Web training to get an internship next term), subsequent software upgrades, and maintenance.

Project Focus

- It is useful to think about costs over time—both direct as well as indirect costs. Part of the reason this distinction is important is that a decision should rest not on the nominal sum of the purchase, but rather on the present value of the purchase.
- A dollar today is worth more than a dollar one year from now.
- The relevant discount rate (interest rate) is your marginal cost of capital corresponding to a level of risk equal with the purchase.
- Use the data file AYK6_Data.xlsx as a template.

	A	B	C	D	E	F
1		COST OF NEW COMPUTER				
2	Discount Rate	1	0.9325	0.9109	0.7051	
3		Time 0	Year 1	Year 2	Year 3	Present Value Costs
4	Computer					
5	Software					
6	Additional Hardware					
7	Training					
8	Software upgrades					
9	Maintenance					
10						
11	Total Costs					
12						

Data File: AYK6_Data.xlsx

Project 7:

Time Management

You have just been hired as a business analyst by a new start-up company called Multi-Media. Multi-Media is an interactive agency that constructs phased and affordable Web site marketing, providing its clients with real and measurable solutions that are supported by easy-to-use tools. Since the company is very new to the business arena, it needs help in creating a project management plan for developing its own Web site. The major tasks for the development team have been identified but you need to create the timeline.

Project Focus

1. The task names, durations, and any prerequisites are:
   - Analyze and plan—two weeks. Cannot start anything else until done.
   - Create and organize content—four weeks. Can start to develop "look and feel" before this is done.
   - Develop the "look and feel"—four weeks. Start working on graphics and HTML at the same time.
   - Produce graphics and HTML documents—two weeks. Create working prototype after the first week.
   - Create a working prototype—two weeks. Give to test team when complete.
   - Test, test, test—four weeks.
   - Upload to a Web server and test again—one week.
   - Maintain.
2. Using Microsoft Excel or Microsoft Project, create a Gantt chart using the information provided above.

Project 8:

Maximize Profit

Books, Books, Books is a wholesale distributor of popular books. The business buys overstocked books and sells them for a discount of more than 50 percent to local area bookstores. The owner of the company, BK Kane, would like to determine the best approach to boxing books so he can make the most profit possible. The local bookstores accept all shipments from Books, Books, Books because of BK's incredibly low prices. BK can order as many overstocked books as he requires, and this week's options include:

Title	Weight	Cost	Sale Price
Harry Potter and the Deathly Hallows, J. K. Rowling	5 lb	$9	$17
The Children of Húrin, J. R. R. Tolkien	4 lb	$8	$13
The Time Traveler's Wife, Audrey Niffenegger	3.5 lb	$7	$11
The Dark River, John Twelve Hawks	3 lb	$6	$ 9
The Road, Cormac McCarthy	2.5 lb	$5	$ 7
Slaughterhouse-Five, Kurt Vonnegut	1 lb	$4	$ 5

Project Focus

When packing a single box, BK must adhere to the following:

- 20 books or less.
- Books by three different authors.
- Between four and eight books from each author.
- Weight equal to or less than 50 pounds.

BK has come to you to help him determine which books he should order to maximize his profit based on the above information. Using the data file AYK8_Data.xlsx, determine the optimal book order for a single box of books.

Data File: AYK8_Data.xlsx

Project 9:

Security Analysis

SecureWorks, Inc., is a small computer security contractor that provides computer security analysis, design, and software implementation for the U.S. government and commercial clients. SecureWorks competes for both private and U.S. government computer security contract work by submitting detailed bids outlining the work the company will perform if awarded the contracts. Because all of the work involves computer security, a highly sensitive area, almost all of SecureWorks tasks require access to classified material or company confidential documents. Consequently, all of the security engineers (simply known as "engineers" within the company) have U.S. government clearances of either Secret or Top Secret. Some have even higher clearances for the 2 percent of SecureWorks work that involves so-called "black box" security work. Most of the employees also hold clearances because they must handle classified documents.

Leslie Mamalis is SecureWorks' human resources (HR) manager. She maintains all employee records and is responsible for semiannual review reports, payroll processing, personnel records, recruiting data, employee training, and pension option information. At the heart of an HR system are personnel records. Personnel record maintenance includes activities such as maintaining employee records, tracking cost center data, recording and maintaining pension information, and absence and sick leave record keeping. While most of this information resides in sophisticated database systems, Leslie maintains a basic employee worksheet for quick calculations and ad hoc report generation. Because SecureWorks is a small company, Leslie can take advantage of Excel's excellent list management capabilities to satisfy many of her personnel information management needs.

Project Focus

Leslie has asked you to assist with a number of functions (she has provided you with a copy of her "trusted" personnel data file, AYK9_Data.xlsx):

1. Copy the worksheet Data to a new worksheet called Sort. Sort the employee list in ascending order by department, then by last name, then by first name.

2. Copy the worksheet Data to a new worksheet called Autofilter. Using the Autofilter feature, create a custom filter that will display employees whose birth date is greater than or equal to 1/1/1965 and less than or equal to 12/31/1975.

3. Copy the worksheet Data to a new worksheet called Subtotal. Using the subtotal feature create a sum of the salary for each department.

4. Copy the worksheet Data to a new worksheet called Formatting. Using the salary column, change the font color to red if the cell value is greater than or equal to 55000. You must use the conditional formatting feature to complete this step.

Data File: AYK9_Data.xlsx

Project 10:

Gathering Data

You have just accepted a new job offer from a firm that has offices in San Diego, Los Angeles, and San Francisco. You need to decide which location to move to. Because you have not visited any of these three cities and want to get in a lot of golf time, you determine that the main factor that will affect your decision is weather.

Go to www.weather.com and locate the box in which you can enter the city or ZIP code for which you want information. Enter San Diego, CA, and when the data appears, click the Averages and Records tab. Print this page and repeat this for Los Angeles and San Francisco. You will want to focus on the Monthly Average and Records section on the top of the page.

Project Focus

1. Create a spreadsheet to summarize the information you find.

2. Record the temperature and rainfall in columns, and group the cities into four groups of rows labeled Average High, Average Low, Mean, and Average Precipitation.

3. Fill in the appropriate data for each city and month.

4. Because rain is your greatest concern, use conditional formatting to display the months with an average precipitation below 2.5 inches in blue and apply boldface.

5. You also want to be in the warmest weather possible while in California. Use conditional formatting to display the months with average high temperatures above 65 degrees in green and apply an italic font face.

6. Looking at the average high temperatures above 65 degrees and average precipitation below two inches, to which city do you think you should relocate? Explain your answer.

Project 11:

Scanner System

FunTown is a popular amusement park filled with roller coasters, games, and water features. Boasting 24 roller coasters, 10 of which exceed 200 feet and 70 miles per hour, and five water parks, the park's attendance remains steady throughout the season. Due to the park's popularity, it is not uncommon for entrance lines to exceed one hour on busy days. FunTown would like your help to find a solution to decrease park entrance lines.

Project Focus

FunTown would like to implement a hand-held scanner system that can allow employees to walk around the front gates and accept credit card purchases and print tickets on the spot. The park anticipates an overall increase in sales of 4 percent per year with online ticketing, with an expense of 6 percent of total sales for the scanning equipment. FunTown has created a data file for you to use, AYK11_Data.xlsx, that compares scanning sales and traditional sales. You will need to create the necessary formulas to calculate all the assumptions including:

- Tickets sold at the booth.
- Tickets sold by the scanner.
- Revenues generated by booth sales.
- Revenues generated by scanner sales.
- Scanner ticket expense.
- Revenue with and without scanner sales.
- Three year row totals.

Data File: AYK11_Data.xlsx

Project 12:

Competitive Pricing

Bill Schultz is thinking of starting a store that specializes in handmade cowboy boots. Bill is a longtime rancher in the town of Taos, New Mexico. Bill's reputation for honesty and integrity is well-known around town, and he is positive that his new store will be highly successful.

Project Focus

Before opening his store, Bill is curious about how his profit, revenue, and variable costs will change depending on the amount he charges for his boots. Bill would like you to perform the work required for this analysis and has given you the data file AYK12_Data.xlsx. Here are a few things to consider while you perform your analysis:

- Current competitive prices for custom cowboy boots are between $225 and $275 a pair.
- Variable costs will be either $100 or $150 a pair depending on the types of material Bill chooses to use.
- Fixed costs are $10,000 a month.

Data File: AYK12_Data.xlsx

Project 13:

Adequate Acquisitions

XMark.com is a major Internet company specializing in organic food. XMark.com is thinking of purchasing GoodGrow, another organic food Internet company. GoodGrow has current revenues of $100 million, with expenses of $150 million. Current projections indicate that GoodGrow's revenues are increasing at 35 percent per year and its expenses are increasing by 10 percent per year. XMark.com understands that projections can be erroneous, however; the company must determine the number of years before GoodGrow will return a profit.

Project Focus

You need to help XMark.com determine the number of years required to break even, using annual growth rates in revenue between 20 percent and 60 percent and annual expense growth rates between 10 and 30 percent. You have been provided with a template, AYK13_Data.xlsx, to assist with your analysis.

Data File: AYK13_Data.xlsx

Project 14:

Customer Relations

Schweizer Distribution specializes in distributing fresh produce to local restaurants in the Chicago area. The company currently sells 12 different products through the efforts of three sales representatives to 10 restaurants. The company, like all small businesses, is always interested in finding ways to increase revenues and decrease expenses.

The company's founder, Bob Schweizer, has recently hired you as a new business analyst. You have just graduated from college with a degree in marketing and a specialization in customer relationship management. Bob is eager to hear your thoughts and ideas on how to improve the business and help the company build strong lasting relationships with its customers.

Project Focus

Bob has provided you with last year's sales information in the data file AYK14_Data.xlsx. Help Bob analyze his distribution company by using a PivotTable to determine the following:

1. Who is Bob's best customer by total sales?
2. Who is Bob's worst customer by total sales?
3. Who is Bob's best customer by total profit?
4. Who is Bob's worst customer by total profit?
5. What is Bob's best-selling product by total sales?
6. What is Bob's worst-selling product by total sales?
7. What is Bob's best-selling product by total profit?
8. What is Bob's worst-selling product by total profit?
9. Who is Bob's best sales representative by total profit?
10. Who is Bob's worst sales representative by total profit?
11. What is the best sales representative's best-selling product (by total profit)?
12. Who is the best sales representative's best customer (by total profit)?
13. What is the best sales representative's worst-selling product (by total profit)?
14. Who is the best sales representative's worst customer (by total profit)?

Data File: AYK14_Data.xlsx

Project 15:

Shipping Costs

One of the main products of the Fairway Woods Company is custom-made golf clubs. The clubs are manufactured at three plants (Denver, Colorado; Phoenix, Arizona; and Dallas, Texas) and are then shipped by truck to five distribution warehouses in Sacramento, California; Salt Lake City, Utah; Chicago, Illinois; Albuquerque, New Mexico; and New York City, New York. Since shipping costs are a major expense, management has begun an analysis to determine ways to reduce them. For the upcoming golf season, the output from each manufacturing plant and how much each warehouse will require to satisfy its customers have been estimated.

The CIO from Fairway Woods Company has created a data file for you, AYK15_Data.xlsx, of the shipping costs from each manufacturing plant to each warehouse as a baseline analysis. Some business rules and requirements you should be aware of include:

- The problem presented involves the shipment of goods from three plants to five regional warehouses.
- Goods can be shipped from any plant to any warehouse, but it costs more to ship goods over long distances than over short distances.

Project Focus

1. Your goal is to minimize the costs of shipping goods from production plants to warehouses, thereby meeting the demand from each metropolitan area while not exceeding the supply available from each plant. To complete this project it is recommended that you use the Solver function in Excel to assist with the analysis.

2. Specifically you want to focus on:
   - Minimizing the total shipping costs.
   - Total shipped must be less than or equal to supply at a plant.
   - Total shipped to warehouses must be greater than or equal to the warehouse demand.
   - Number to ship must be greater than or equal to 0.

Data File: AYK15_Data.xlsx

Project 16:

Formatting Grades

Professor Streterstein is a bit absentminded. His instructor's grade book is a mess, and he would like your help cleaning it up and making it easier to use. In Professor Streterstein's course, the maximum possible points a student can earn is 750. The following table displays the grade equivalent to total points for the course.

Total Points	Calculated Grade
675	A
635	A-
600	B
560	B-
535	C
490	C-
450	D
0	F

Project Focus

Help Professor Streterstein rework his grade book. Open the data file AYK16_Data.xlsx and perform the following:

1. Reformat the workbook so it is readable, understandable, and consistent. Replace column labels, format and align the headings, add borders and shading as appropriate.
2. Add a column in the grade book for final grade next to the total points earned column.
3. Use the VLookup Function to automatically assess final grades based on the total points column.
4. Using the If Function, format the workbook so each student's grade shows a pass or fail—P for pass, F for fail—based on the total points.

Data File: AYK16_Data.xlsx

Project 17:

Moving Dilemma

Pony Espresso is a small business that sells specialty coffee drinks at office buildings. Each morning and afternoon, trucks arrive at offices' front entrances, and the office employees purchase various beverages such as Java du Jour and Café de Colombia. The business is profitable. Pony Espresso offices, however, are located north of town, where lease rates are less expensive, and the principal sales area is south of town. This means the trucks must drive across town four times each day.

The cost of transportation to and from the sales area plus the power demands of the trucks' coffee brewing equipment are a significant portion of variable costs. Pony Espresso could reduce the amount of driving and, therefore, the variable costs, if it moved the offices closer to the sales area.

Pony Espresso presently has fixed costs of $10,000 per month. The lease of a new office, closer to the sales area, would cost an additional $2,200 per month. This would increase the fixed costs to $12,200 per month.

Although the lease of new offices would increase the fixed costs, a careful estimate of the potential savings in gasoline and vehicle maintenance indicates that Pony Espresso could reduce the variable costs from $0.60 per unit to $0.35 per unit. Total sales are unlikely to increase as a result of the move, but the savings in variable costs should increase the annual profit.

Project Focus

Consider the information provided to you from the owner in the data file AYK17_Data.xlsx. Especially look at the change in the variability of the profit from month to month. From November through January, when it is much more difficult to lure office workers out into the cold to purchase coffee, Pony Espresso barely breaks even. In fact, in December, the business lost money.

1. Develop the cost analysis on the existing lease information using the monthly sales figures provided to you in the data file.
2. Develop the cost analysis from the new lease information provided above.
3. Calculate the variability that is reflected in the month-to-month standard deviation of earnings for the current cost structure and the projected cost structure.
4. Do not consider any association with downsizing such as overhead—simply focus on the information provided to you.
5. You will need to calculate the EBIT (earnings before interest and taxes).

Data File: AYK17_Data.xlsx

Project 18:

Operational Efficiencies

Hoover Transportation, Inc., is a large distribution company located in Denver, Colorado. The company is currently seeking to gain operational efficiencies in its supply chain by reducing the number of transportation carriers that it is using to outsource. Operational efficiencies for Hoover Transportation, Inc., suggest that reducing the number of carriers from the Denver distribution center to warehouses in the selected states will lead to reduced costs. Brian Hoover, the CEO of Hoover Transportation, requests that the number of carriers transporting products from its Denver distribution center to wholesalers in Arizona, Arkansas, Iowa, Missouri, Montana, Oklahoma, Oregon, and Washington be reduced from the current five carriers to two carriers.

Project Focus

Carrier selection should be based on the assumptions that all environmental factors are equal and historical cost trends will continue. Review the historical data from the past several years to determine your recommendation for the top two carriers that Hoover Transportation should continue to use.

1. Analyze the last 24 months of Hoover's Transportation carrier transactions found in the data file AYK18_Data.xlsx.
2. Create a report detailing your recommendation for the top two carriers with which Hoover Transportation should continue to do business. Be sure to use PivotTables and PivotCharts in your report. A few questions to get you started include:
   - Calculate the average cost per carrier.
   - Calculate the total shipping costs per state.

- Calculate the total shipping weights per state.
- Calculate the average shipping costs per pound.
- Calculate the average cost per carrier.

Data File: AYK18_Data.xlsx

Project 19:

Too Much Information

You have just landed the job of vice president of operations for The Pitt Stop Restaurants, a national chain of full-service, casual-themed restaurants. During your first week on the job, Suzanne Graham, your boss and CEO of the company, has asked you to provide an analysis of how well the company's restaurants are performing. Specifically, she would like to know which units and regions are performing extremely well, which are performing moderately well, and which are underperforming. Her goal is to identify where to spend time and focus efforts to improve the overall health of the company.

Project Focus

Review the data file AYK19_Data.xlsx and determine how best to analyze and interpret the data. Create a formal presentation of your findings. A few things to consider include:

- Should underperforming restaurants be closed or sold?
- Should high-performing restaurants be expanded to accommodate more seats?
- Should the company spend more or less on advertising?
- In which markets should the advertising budget be adjusted?
- How are The Pitt Stop Restaurants performing compared to the competition?
- How are units of like size performing relative to each other?

Data File: AYK19_Data.xlsx

Project 20:

Turnover Rates

Employee turnover rates are at an all-time high at Gizmo's Manufacturing plants. The company is experiencing severe worker retention issues, which are leading to productivity and quality control problems. The majority of the company's workers perform a variety of tasks and are paid by the hour. The company currently tests each potential applicant to ensure they have the skills necessary for the intense mental concentration and dexterity required to fill the positions. Since significant costs are associated with employee turnover, Gizmo Manufacturing wants to find a way to predict which applicants have the characteristics of being a short-term versus a long-term employee.

Project Focus

1. Review the information that Gizmo Manufacturing has collected from two of its different data sources. The first data file, AYK20_Data_A.xlsx, contains information regarding employee wages. The second data file, AYK20_Data_B.xlsx, contains information regarding employee retention.

2. Using Excel analysis functions, determine the employee characteristics that you would recommend Gizmo Manufacturing look for when hiring new personnel. It is highly recommended that you use PivotTables as part of your analysis.

3. Prepare a report based on your findings (which should include several forms of graphical representation) for your recommendations.

Data Files: AYK20_Data_A.xlsx and AYK20_Data_B.xlsx

Project 21:

Vital Information

Martin Resorts, Inc., owns and operates four Spa and Golf resorts in Colorado. The company has five traditional lines of business: (1) golf sales; (2) golf lessons; (3) restaurants; (4) retail and rentals; and (5) hotels. David Logan, director of marketing technology at Martin Resorts, Inc., and Donald Mayer, the lead strategic analyst for Martin Resorts, are soliciting your input for their CRM strategic initiative.

Martin Resorts' IT infrastructure is pieced together with various systems and applications. Currently, the company has a difficult time with CRM because its systems are not integrated. The company cannot determine vital information such as which customers are golfing and staying at the hotel or which customers are staying at the hotel and not golfing.

For example, the three details that the customer Diego Titus (1) stayed four nights at a Martin Resorts' managed hotel, (2) golfed three days, and (3) took an all-day spa treatment the first day are discrete facts housed in separate systems. Martin Resorts hopes that by using data warehousing technology to integrate its data, the next time Diego reserves lodging for another trip, sales associates may ask him if he would like to book a spa treatment as well, and even if he would like the same masseuse that he had on his prior trip.

Martin Resorts is excited about the possibility of taking advantage of customer segmentation and CRM strategies to help increase its business.

Project Focus

The company wants to use CRM and data warehouse technologies to improve service and personalization at each customer touch point. Using a data warehousing tool, important customer information can be accessed from all of its systems either daily, weekly, monthly, or once or twice per year. Analyze the sample data in AYK21_Data.xlsx for the following:

1. Currently, the quality of the data within the above disparate systems is low. Develop a report for David and Donald discussing the importance of high quality information and how low quality information can affect Martin Resorts' business.

2. Review the data that David and Donald are working with from the data warehouse in the data file AYK21_Data.xlsx.

   a. Give examples from the data showing the kind of information Martin Resorts might be able to use to gain a better understanding of its customers. Include the types of data quality issues the company can anticipate and the strategies it can use to help avoid such issues.

   b. Determine who are Martin Resorts' best customers, and provide examples of the types of marketing campaigns the company should offer these valuable customers.

   c. Prepare a report that summarizes the benefits Martin Resorts can receive from using business intelligence to mine the data warehouse. Include a financial analysis of the costs and benefits.

Data File: AYK21_Data.xlsx

Project 22:

Breaking Even

Mountain Cycle specializes in making custom mountain bikes. The company founder, PJ Steffan, is having a hard time making the business profitable. Knowing that you have great business knowledge and solid financial sense, PJ has come to you for advice.

Project Focus

PJ would like you to determine how many bikes Mountain Cycle needs to sell per year to break even. Using Goal Seek in Excel solve using the following:

- Fixed cost equals $65,000.
- Variable cost equals $1,575.
- Bike price equals $2,500.

Project 23:

Profit Scenario

Murry Lutz owns a small shop, Lutz Motors, that sells and services vintage motorcycles. Murry is curious how his profit will be affected by his sales over the next year.

Project Focus

Murry would like your help creating best, worst, and most-likely scenarios for his motorcycle sales over the next year. Using Scenario Manager, help Murry analyze the information in the data file AYK23_Data.xlsx.

Data File: AYK23_Data.xlsx

Project 24:

Electronic Résumés

Résumés are the currency of the recruitment industry. They are the cornerstone of communication between candidates, recruiters, and employers. Technology is automating elements of the recruitment process, but a complete solution requires proper handling of the actual development of all the pieces and parts that comprise not just a résumé, but also an e-résumé. Electronic résumés, or e-résumés, have moved into the mainstream of today's job market at lightning speed. E-résumés have stepped up the efficiency of job placement to such a point that you could get a call from a recruiter just hours after submitting your e-résumé. With this kind of opportunity, you cannot afford to be left in the dark ages of using only a visual résumé.

Project Focus

In the text or HTML editor of your choice, write your e-résumé as though you were really putting it online and inviting prospective employers to see it. We recommend typing in all the text and then later adding the HTML tags (rather than trying to type in the tags as you go).

Use the following checklist to make sure you're covering the basics. You do not need to match it exactly; it just shows what can be done.

- Add structural tags.
- Add paragraphs and headings.
- Find an opportunity to include a list.
- Add inline styles.
- Play with the alignment of elements.
- Add appropriate font selection, font size, and color.

Project 25:

Gathering Feedback

Gathering feedback from Web site's visitors can be a valuable way of assessing a site's success, and it can help build a customer or subscriber database. For example, a business could collect the addresses of people who are interested in receiving product samples, e-mail newsletters, or notifications of special offers.

Project Focus

Adding form elements to a Web page is simple: They are created using a set of HTML form tags that define menus, text fields, buttons, and so on. Form elements are generally used to collect information from a Web page.

In the text or HTML editor of your choice, create a Web form that would collect information for a customer ordering a customized bicycle. Use proper Web design and HTML tools to understand the process and function of form elements. Be sure to pay attention to:

- Form layout and design.
- Visual elements, including labels, alignment, font selection, font size, color.
- Required versus nonrequired fields.
- Drop-down boxes, text fields, and radio buttons.

Project 26:

Daily Invoice

Foothills Animal Hospital is a full-service small animal veterinary hospital located in Morrison, Colorado, specializing in routine medical care, vaccinations, laboratory testing, and surgery. The hospital has experienced tremendous growth over the past six months due to customer referrals. While Foothills Animal Hospital has typically kept its daily service records in a workbook format, it feels the need to expand its reporting capabilities to develop a relational database as a more functional structure.

Foothills Animal Hospital needs help developing a database, specifically:

- Create a customer table—name, address, phone, and date of entrance.
- Create a pet table—pet name, type of animal, breed, gender, color, neutered/spayed, weight, and comments.
- Create a medications table—medication code, name of medication, and cost of medication.
- Create a visit table—details of treatments performed, medications dispensed, and date of the visit.
- Produce a daily invoice report.

Figure AYK.2 displays a sample daily invoice report that the Foothills Animal Hospital accountants have requested. Foothills Animal Hospital organizes its treatments using the codes displayed in Figure AYK.3. The entities and primary keys for the database have been identified in Figure AYK.4.

The following business rules have been identified:

1. A customer can have many pets but must have at least one.
2. A pet must be assigned to one and only one customer.
3. A pet can have one or more treatments per visit but must have at least one.
4. A pet can have one or more medications but need not have any.

Project Focus

Your job is to complete the following tasks:

1. Develop and describe the entity-relationship diagram.
2. Use normalization to assure the correctness of the tables (relations).
3. Create the database using a personal DBMS package (preferably Microsoft Access).
4. Use the data in Figure AYK.3 to populate your tables. Feel free to enter your own personal information.
5. Use the DBMS package to create the basic report in Figure AYK.2.

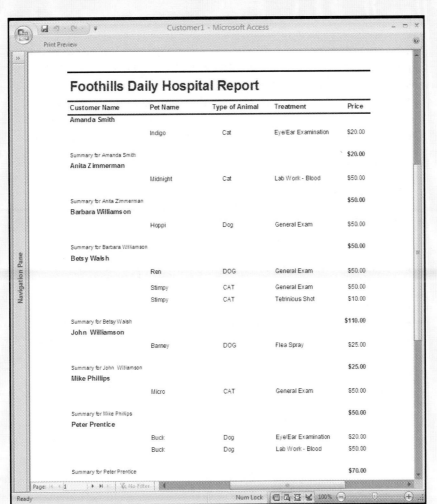

Foothills Daily Hospital Report

Customer Name	Pet Name	Type of Animal	Treatment	Price
Amanda Smith				
	Indigo	Cat	Eye/Ear Examination	$20.00
Summary for Amanda Smith				$20.00
Anita Zimmerman				
	Midnight	Cat	Lab Work - Blood	$50.00
Summary for Anita Zimmerman				$50.00
Barbara Williamson				
	Hoppi	Dog	General Exam	$50.00
Summary for Barbara Williamson				$50.00
Betsy Walsh				
	Ren	DOG	General Exam	$50.00
	Stimpy	CAT	General Exam	$50.00
	Stimpy	CAT	Tetrinious Shot	$10.00
Summary for Betsy Walsh				$110.00
John Williamson				
	Barney	DOG	Flea Spray	$25.00
Summary for John Williamson				$25.00
Mike Phillips				
	Micro	CAT	General Exam	$50.00
Summary for Mike Phillips				$50.00
Peter Prentice				
	Buck	Dog	Eye/Ear Examination	$20.00
	Buck	Dog	Lab Work - Blood	$50.00
Summary for Peter Prentice				$70.00

Treatment Code	Treatment	Price
0100	Tetrinious Shot	$10.00
0201	Rabonius Shot	$20.00
0300	General Exam	$50.00
0303	Eye/Ear Examination	$20.00
0400	Spay/Neuter	$225.00
0405	Reset Dislocation	$165.00
0406	Amputation of Limb	$450.00
0407	Wrap Affected Area	$15.00
0408	Cast Affected Area	$120.00
1000	Lab Work—Blood	$50.00
1003	Lab Work—Misc	$35.00
2003	Flea Spray	$25.00
9999	Other Not Listed	$10.00

Entity	Primary Key
CUSTOMER	Customer Number
PET	Pet Number
VISIT	Visit Number
VISIT DETAIL	Visit Number and Line Number (a composite key)
TREATMENT	Treatment Code
MEDICATION	Medication Code

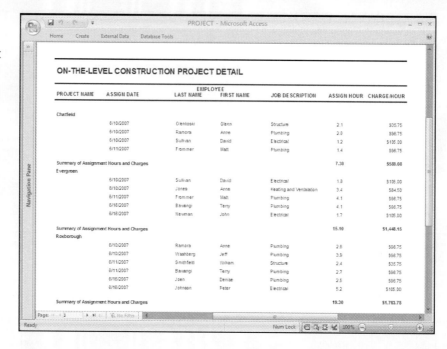

Project 27:

Billing Data

On-The-Level Construction Company is a Denver-based construction company that specializes in subcontracting the development of single-family homes. In business since 1998, On-
The-Level Construction has maintained a talented pool of certified staff and independent
consultants providing the flexibility and combined experience required to meet the needs of
its nearly 300 completed projects in the Denver metropolitan area. The field of operation methods that On-The-Level Construction is responsible for includes structural development, heating and cooling, plumbing, and electricity.

The company charges its clients by billing the hours spent on each contract. The hourly billing rate is dependent on the employee's position according to the field of operations (as noted
above). Figure AYK.5 shows a basic report that On-The-Level Construction foremen would like
to see every week concerning what projects are being assigned, the overall assignment hours,
and the charges for the assignment. On-The-Level Construction organizes its internal structure in four different operations—Structure (500), Plumbing (501), Electrical (502), and Heating
and Ventilation (503). Each of these operational departments can and should have many subcontractors who specialize in that area. Due to the boom in home sales over the last several
years, On-The-Level Construction has decided to implement a relational database model to
track project details according to project name, hours assigned, and charges per hour for
each job description. Originally, On-The-Level Construction decided to let one of its employees handle the construction of the database. However, that employee has not
had the time to completely implement the project. On-The-Level Construction
has asked you to take over and complete the development of the database.

The entities and primary keys for the database have been identified in
Figure AYK.6.

The following business rules have been identified:

1. A job can have many employees assigned but must have at least one.
2. An employee must be assigned to one and only one job number.

Entity	Primary Key
PROJECT	Project Number
EMPLOYEE	Employee Number
JOB	Job Number
ASSIGNMENT	Assignment Number

3. An employee can be assigned to work on one or more projects.

4. A project can be assigned to only one employee but need not be assigned to any employee.

Project Focus

Your job is to complete the following tasks:

1. Develop and describe the entity relationship diagram.

2. Use normalization to assure the correctness of the tables (relations).

3. Create the database using a personal DBMS package (preferably Microsoft Access).

4. Use the DBMS package to create the basic report in Figure AYK.5.

5. You may not be able to develop a report that looks exactly like the one in Figure AYK.5. However, your report should include the same information.

6. Complete personnel information is tracked by another database. For this application, include only the minimum: employee number, last name, and first name.

7. Information concerning all projects, employees, and jobs is not readily available. You should create information for several fictitious projects, employees, and jobs to include in your database.

Project 28:

Inventory Data

An independent retailer of mobile entertainment and wireless phones, iToys.com has built its business on offering the widest selection, expert advice, and outstanding customer service. However, iToys.com does not use a formal, consistent inventory tracking system. Periodically, an iToys.com employee visually checks to see what items are in stock. Although iToys.com does try to keep a certain level of each "top seller" in stock, the lack of a formal inventory tracking system has led to the overstocking of some items and understocking of other items. On occasion, a customer will request a hot item, and it is only then that iToys.com realizes that the item is out of stock. If an item is not available, iToys.com risks losing a customer to a competitor.

Lately, iToys.com has become concerned with its inventory management methods. The owner of iToys.com, Dan Connolly, wants to better manage his inventory. The company receives orders by mail, by telephone, or through its Web site. Regardless of how the orders are received, Dan needs a database to automate the inventory checking and ordering process.

Project Focus

Dan has provided you with a simplified version of the company's current system (an Excel workbook) for recording inventory and orders in an Excel spreadsheet data file AYK28_Data.xlsx.

1. Develop an ERD diagram before you begin to create the database. You will need to use the information provided here as well as the data given in the Excel workbook.

2. Create the database using a personal DBMS package (preferably Microsoft Access) that will track items (i.e., products), orders, order details, categories, suppliers, and shipping methods.

3. In addition to what is mentioned above, the database needs to track the inventory levels for each product, according to a reorder level and lead time.

4. At this time, Dan does not need information stored about the customer; he simply needs you to focus on the inventory structure.

5. Develop a query that will display the products that need to be ordered from their supplier. To complete this, you will want to compare a reorder level with how many units are in stock.

6. Develop several reports that display:

    a. Each product ordered by its supplier. The report should include the product name, quantity on hand, and reorder level.

    b. Each supplier ordered by shipping method.

    c. Each product that requires more than five days lead time. (Hint: You will want to create a query for this first).

    d. Each product ordered by category.

7. Here are some additional business rules to assist you in completing this task:

    a. An order must have at least one product, but can contain more than one product.

    b. A product can have one or more orders, but need not have any orders.

    c. A product must belong to one and only one category, but a category many contain many different products.

    d. A product can only be stocked by one supplier, but a supplier can provide more than one product.

    e. A supplier will use one type of shipping method, but shipping methods can be used by more than one supplier.

Data File: AYK28_Data.xlsx

Project 29:

Call Center

A manufacturing company, Teleworks, has been a market leader in the wireless telephone business for the past 10 years. Other firms have imitated its product with some degree of success, but Teleworks occupies a dominant position in the marketplace because it has a first morer advantage with a quality product.

Recently Teleworks began selling a new, enhanced wireless phone. This new phone does not replace its current product, but offers additional features, greater durability, and better performance for a somewhat higher price. Offering this enhanced phone has established a new revenue stream for the company.

Many sales executives at Teleworks seem to subscribe to the-more-you-have, the-more-you-want theory of managing customer data. That is, they believe they can never accumulate too much information about their customers, and that they can do their jobs more effectively by collecting infinite amounts of customer details. Having a firm grasp on a wide range of customer-focused details—specifically reports summarizing call center information—can be critical in enabling your company to successfully manage a customer relationship management (CRM) solution that creates a positive impact.

To continue to provide excellent customer support, and in anticipation of increased calls due to the release of its new product, Teleworks needs a database that it can use to record, track, and query call center information. Teleworks CIO KED Davisson has hired you to develop this database.

Project Focus

1. Teleworks has provided you with a data file AYK29_Data.xlsx; its current approach for recording cell center information is a spreadsheet file.

2. Develop an ERD diagram before you begin to create the database.

3. Create the database using a personal DBMS package (preferably Microsoft Access) that will allow data analysts to enter call center data according to the type of issue and the customer, assign each call to a consultant, and prioritize the call.

4. Develop a query that will display all issues that are "open."

5. Develop a screen form to browse all issues.

6. Develop several reports that display:

   a. All closed issues.

   b. Each issue in detail ordered by issue ID.

   c. Each issue in detail ordered by consultant.

   d. Each issue in detail ordered by category.

   e. Each issue in detail ordered by status.

7. Here are some additional business rules to assist you in completing this task:

   a. An issue must have at least one customer.

   b. A customer can have more than one issue.

   c. Each issue must be assigned to one consultant.

   d. Each consultant can be assigned to more than one issue.

   e. An issue can only belong to one category.

   f. An issue must be assigned only one status code.

   g. An issue must be assigned a priority code.

8. Priorities are assigned accordingly:

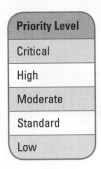

9. Status is recorded as either open or closed.

10. The categories of each issue need to be recorded as:

Data File: AYK29_Data.xlsx

Project 30:

Sales Pipeline

Sales drive any organization. This is true for every for-profit business irrespective of size or industry type. If customers are not buying your goods or services, you run the risk of not having a business. This is when tough decisions have to be made like whether to slash budgets, lay off staff, or seek additional financing.

Unfortunately, you do not wield ultimate power over your customers' buying habits. While you can attempt to influence buying behavior through strategic marketing, smart businesses remain one step ahead by collecting and analyzing historical and current customer information from a range of internal and external sources to forecast future sales. In other words, managing the sales pipeline is an essential ingredient to business success.

You have recently been hired by RealTime Solutions, a new company that collects information to understand, manage, and predict specific sales cycle (including the supply chain and lead times) in the automobile business. Having an accurate forecast of future sales will allow the company to increase or decrease the production cycle as required and manage personnel levels, inventory, and cash flow.

Project Focus

Using a personal DBMS package (preferably Microsoft Access) create a sales pipeline database that will:

1. Track opportunities from employees to customers.
   - Opportunities should have a ranking, category, source of opportunity, open date, closed date, description.
2. Create a form for inputting customer, employee, and opportunity data.
3. Create a few reports that display:
   - All open opportunities, including relevant customer and employee information.
   - Closed opportunities, including relevant customer and employee information.
   - All customers.
4. Create your own data to test the integrity of the relationships. Use approximately 10 records per table.

Project 31:

Second Life—Virtual Networking

Second Life is a whole new society that exists only in cyberspace. What this shared 3-D space offers is wide open—anything is possible. It will grow and evolve and become what the inhabitants make of it. You are about to enter a new world where you can be or do almost anything. If you can imagine it, you can do it in Second Life.

Right now, Second Life is fresh and new and most inhabitants can do the following:

- Explore.
- Meet others with similar (or new) interests, network, make friends.
- Participate in social events.
- Participate in deadly battles in the Outlands.
- Participate in various contests.
- Create things and places others will want to explore.
- Experiment with scripting.
- Create textures and sounds out-of-world, and upload them.
- Collaborate with others to build something big.
- Start businesses that charge for Second Life products or services.

Opening a virtual office, selling and market-testing digital replicas of products, and asking employees to create 3-D online personas or "avatars" are quickly becoming action items at companies seeking to brand themselves as hip, or simply wanting to reach Second Life users, nearly half of whom are female and whose median age is 32.

This has made the online world a hot advertising outlet for brands ranging from Warner Bros. to Adidas to Microsoft. While advertising's traditional media seem to be losing eyeballs, the population of Second Life is growing at 35 percent per month and its economy at 15 percent per month. Or in terms of annual growth rates, the population is growing at 978 percent and the economy at 270 percent.

In Second Life, the products offered by true-life brands can be customized by the people using them—a growing trend in the real-world marketplace. Second Life is an interactive, social-networking zone where companies hope not only to find customers but also to connect remote employees to one another and recruit new hires.

For a company considering jumping into Second Life now, serious homework is needed. Competition among big brands is heating up. It's no longer enough to be the first in an industry to launch a presence in Second Life. Just as Toyota, and now Nissan and General Motors, conducted market research in the digital world before unveiling its plan to sell virtual cars, savvy corporations and their Second Life developers must carefully analyze the competition and differentiate their products.

Project Focus

1. Go to www.secondlife.com, and click on the "Join Now" button (membership is free). Fill out the Second Life registration details, including choosing an Avatar and a Second Life name (alias).

2. Log in with the name and password you selected when you signed up.

3. Point to the Downloads menu and select Second Life Client from the drop-down menu.

4. Download Second Life Setup and save it to your hard drive in a place where you can find it easily, then run Second Life Setup.

5. Follow the instructions on the screen.

6. Double-click the Second Life icon on your desktop. You will see the Second Life sign-on screen.

7. Enter your first and last name, and your password. Click on "Connect." Within seconds, you will be in your Second Life.

8. Project Challenge:
   - Create a business for Second Life that involves concepts from this course, such as supply chain management, decision support, or e-marketing. There are as many opportunities for innovation and profit in Second Life as in the real world. Open a nightclub, sell jewelry, become a land speculator; the choice is yours to make. Thousands of residents are making part or all of their real life income from their Second Life Businesses. By way of example, here are just a few in-world business occupations that Residents founded and currently run, and make part or all of their real life living from.
     - Party and wedding planner.
     - Pet manufacturer.
     - Tattoo artist.
     - Nightclub owner.
     - Fashion designer.
     - Game developer.

Project 32:

Creating a Podcast

Podcasting is a form of audio broadcasting on the Internet. The reason it became linked with the iPod in name was because people download podcasts (audio shows) to listen to on their iPods. However, you don't have to listen to podcasts only on iPods; you can use your computer with some music software such as Windows built-in Media Player or Winamp, or other portable music players (iPod competitors) such as Creative Zen or iRiver. It really does not matter. As long as you have some way to play music on your computer, you will be able to listen to podcasts.

Project Focus

1. Download Audacity from audacity.sourceforge.net. It is open source, cross-platform, free and lets you mix multiple audio files. There are Windows, Mac OS 9 or X, and Linux/Unix versions available. You will also have to download the LAME MP3 encoder, which allows Audacity to export MP3 files. You will see the download link for that on the same page as the Audacity download. Once you download the LAME MP3 encoder, place it in the Audacity program folder (C:\Program Files\Audacity\Plug-Ins\). Then, open a .WAV file in Audacity, and select the menu option "File" then choose "Export As MP3." When you do, you will see this message: At this Point, browse to where you placed the "lame_enc.dll" file (such as C:\Program Files\Audacity\Plug-Ins). Click on the "lame_enc.dll" file. Once finished, you can now effectively use the Export As MP3 menu option to create MP3 files.

2. Open Audacity and check the preferences. Make sure your playback and recording device are set. If you are going to record a stereo signal, set the number of channels to record to 2 (Stereo) on the Audio I/O preferences. When picking a device to record from, make sure you have set up all the connections properly, such as plugging a microphone into the Mic Input, and any other device into the Line In of your sound card.

3. Click on the red "Record" button to begin recording. You can also:
   - Click on the blue "Pause" button to pause the recording. Press it again to continue.
   - Click on the yellow "Stop" button to cease recording. The cursor will return to its previous position, before the recording was started.

4. MP3 is the de facto standard format for podcasts. When saving, use the minimum bit rate that provides good results. Here are some suggested settings:
   - 48–56k Mono—sermons, audio books, talk radio.
   - 64k+ Stereo—music, music and talk combinations.
   - 128k Stereo—good quality music.

5. Create a two to three minute podcast that you can share with your class about a successful entrepreneurial e-business. Here are a few suggestions:
   - SecondLife.com
   - YouTube.com
   - Zillow.com
   - Linkedin.com
   - Digg.com
   - CraigsList.com
   - Karmaloop.com

6. Before you get the ball rolling on creating a podcast, it is important to figure out what will be said (or not said) during the show. What limits are there when it comes to choosing content? In short, there are almost no limits to what can be included in podcasts. Podcasting allows you to create shows, dramatizations, vignettes, commentaries, documentaries, and any other content imaginable. Indeed, podcasting is limited only by individual podcasters' imaginations. However, you need to script out your content before you start to record.

Project 33:

Google Earth—Geographic Information

Google Earth combines the power of Google Search with satellite imagery, maps, terrain, and 3-D buildings to put the world's geographic information at your fingertips. Using Google Earth, you can:

- Fly to your house. Just type in an address, press "Search," and you will zoom right in.
- Search for schools, parks, restaurants, and hotels. Get driving directions.

- Tilt and rotate the view to see 3-D terrain and buildings.
- Save and share your searches and favorites.

Since Google Earth was launched, users have been exploring the world and creating content overlays (otherwise known as KML files) to share their explorations with others. Google Earth is a broadband, 3-D application that not all computers can run. Desktop computers four years and older and notebook computers two years and older might not be able to run Google Earth. Go to earth.google.com/download-earth.html to see specific requirements for each operating system on this page. If your computer has the needed requirements, click on the "Download Google Earth" button. This is a free application.

Once you download and install Google Earth, your computer becomes a window to anywhere on the planet, allowing you to view high-resolution aerial and satellite imagery, elevation terrain, road and street labels, business listings, and more.

Try any of the following:

1. View an image of your home, school, or any place on Earth—click "Fly To." Enter the location in the input box and click the "Search" button. In the search results (Places panel), double-click the location. Google Earth flies you to this location.

2. Go on a tour of the world—in the Places panel, check the Sightseeing folder, and click the "Play Tour" button.

3. Get driving directions from one place to another and fly (follow) the route.

4. View other cool locations and features created by other Google Earth users—in the Layers panel, check Community Showcase. Interesting places and other features appear in the 3-D viewer. Double-click these points of interest to view and explore.

5. View 3-D terrain of a place—this is more fun with hilly or mountainous terrain, such as the Grand Canyon. Go to a location (see number 1 above). When the view shows the location, use the tilt slider to tilt the terrain.

Project Focus

1. Google Earth Enterprise Solutions are also available for on-site deployment of custom Google Earth databases within an enterprise. List a few ways an enterprise could take advantage of this application.

2. Since Google Earth has been released as a free application, numerous people have expressed concerns over the availability of such data for either individual privacy or the possibility of terrorists using the satellite photos. Do you agree or disagree? Explain your position.

Project 34:

Photo Story 3—Show-n-Tell

Microsoft Photo Story 3 for Windows helps create exciting video stories from pictures. For example, you could create a video story that features narrated photographs from a family vacation or a video story that includes pictures and sounds of an athletic race or game.

In a few simple steps, you can import and edit your pictures, add titles, record narration, add background music, and save your story using the optimal quality settings (profile) for the way your story will be played.

Download Photo Story 3 from www.microsoft.com/windowsxp/using/digitalphotography/photostory/default.mspx. Review the requirements section to make sure your computer is able to run this application. Click the "Continue" button in the Validation Required section to begin the short validation process. Once validated, you will be sent to a page with specific instructions for obtaining the download.

When you run Photo Story 3, with the view to making a new project, the first option is to select "Begin a new story." After clicking this option your first task is to "import" pictures. You can import pictures from your computer, a network folder, or a Web site. For each story, you can import up to 300 pictures, which can be files with .bmp, .dib, .eps, .gif, .jhif, .jpe, .jpeg, .jpg, .pcd, .pcx, .png, .psd, .rle, .tga, and .tif file name extensions.

Your pictures appear in the filmstrip at the bottom of the page. If you import more pictures, Microsoft Photo Story 3 adds them at the end of the filmstrip.

By clicking on a series of buttons or options, you can remove black borders, add titles to your picture, add narration and custom motion, and add background music to your story.

Project Focus

1. Develop a 30-second professional commercial. This is a short description of who you are, what job you are looking for, and the skills that make you suited for the job.

2. Building a quality 30-second commercial can be tougher than it sounds. The goal is to be able to contact a stranger and let him or her know who you are, what your skills are, and why you are approaching the person.

3. Create a list of words describing your skills and interests. Begin broadly and then narrow your list to skills related to your current job search.

4. Compile your script and present it to the class.

Project 35:

Sticky Wiki

Wiki (Hawaiian for "quick") is software that allows users to freely create and edit Web page content using any Web browser. The most common Wiki is Wikipedia. Wikis offer a powerful yet flexible collaborative communication tool for developing Web sites. The best part of a wiki is that it grows and evolves by the collaborative community adding content – the owner of the wiki does not have to add all of the content as is typical in a standard Web page.

There are many sites which offer free wiki software such as Socialtext, a group-editable Web site. As one of the first wiki companies, Socialtext wikis are designed for anyone that wants to accelerate team communications, better enable knowledge sharing, foster collaboration, and build online communities. Socialtext also offers WikiWidgets, which make it easy for non-technical business users to create rich, dynamic wiki content. Today, over 3,000 organizations use Socialtext, including Symantec, Nokia, IKEA, Conde Nast, Ziff-Davis, Kodak, University of Southern California, Boston College, and numerous others.

Project Focus

Create your own wiki. Wikis can address a variety of needs from student involvement, fraternities and sororities, group activities, sport team updates, local band highlights, etc. Choose a free wiki software vendor and create a wiki for any of the following:

- Student organization
- Fraternity or sorority
- Academic organization
- Favorite author or book
- Favorite band or musician
- Favorite sports team
- Favorite movie
- Basically, anything you are involved in or excited about and want to create a site to collaborate with other

Wiki Software Sites

- www.socialtext.com – easy-to-use, business-grade wikis proven by Fortune 500 companies
- www.wetpaint.com – a free easy-to-use wiki building site
- www.CentralDesktop.com – Easy-to-use, a wiki for non-techies
- www.xwiki.com – Open source and free hosting with professional services

If you have different wiki software you prefer to use please feel free to use it to create your wiki.

A

acceptable use policy (AUP)   A policy that a user must agree to follow in order to be provided access to a network or to the Internet.

accounting   Analyzes the transactional information of the business so the owners and investors can make sound economic decisions.

accounting and finance ERP component   Manages accounting data and financial processes within the enterprise with functions such as general ledger, accounts payable, accounts receivable, budgeting, and asset management.

accounting department   Provides quantitative information about the finances of the business including recording, measuring, and describing financial information.

adware   Software that generates ads that install themselves on a computer when a person downloads some other program from the Internet.

agile methodology   A form of XP, aims for customer satisfaction through early and continuous delivery of useful software components.

analysis phase   Analyzing end-user business requirements and refining project goals into defined functions and operations of the intended system.

analytical CRM   Supports back-office operations and strategic analysis and includes all systems that do not deal directly with the customers.

analytical information   Encompasses all organizational information, and its primary purpose is to support the performing of managerial analysis tasks.

anti-spam policy   States that e-mail users will not send unsolicited e-mails (or spam).

application architecture   Determines how applications integrate and relate to each other.

application generation component   Includes tools for creating visually appealing and easy-to-use applications.

application programming interface (API)   A set of routines, protocols, and tools for building software applications. A good API makes it easier to develop a program by providing all the building blocks.

application service provider (ASP)   A company that offers an organization access over the Internet to systems and related services that would otherwise have to be located in personal or organizational computers.

application software   Used for specific information processing needs, including payroll, customer relationship management, project management, training, and many others.

arithmetic/logic unit (ALU)   Performs all arithmetic operations (for example, addition and subtraction) and all logic operations (such as sorting and comparing numbers).

artificial intelligence (AI)   Simulates human intelligence such as the ability to reason and learn.

As-Is process model   Represent the current state of the operation that has been mapped, without any specific improvements or changes to existing processes.

asset   Anything owned that has value or earning power.

associates program (affiliate program)   Businesses can generate commissions or royalties from an Internet site.

association detection   Reveals the degree to which variables are related and the nature and frequency of these relationships in the information.

attribute   Characteristics or properties of an entity class.

authentication   A method for confirming users' identities.

authorization   The process of giving someone permission to do or have something.

automatic call distribution   A phone switch routes inbound calls to available agents.

autonomic computing   A self-managing computing model named after, and patterned on, the human body's autonomic nervous system.

availability   Addresses when systems can be accessed by employees, customers, and partners.

B

backdoor program   Viruses that open a way into the network for future attacks.

backup   An exact copy of a system's information.

backward integration   Takes information entered into a given system and sends it automatically to all upstream systems and processes.

balance sheet   Gives an accounting picture of property owned by a company and of claims against the property on a specific date.

balanced scorecard   A management system (not only a measurement system) that enables organizations to clarify their vision and strategy and translate them into action.

banner ad   Small ad on one Web site that advertises the products and services of another business, usually another dot-com business.

benchmark   Baseline values the system seeks to attain.

benchmarking   The process of continuously measuring system results, comparing those results to optimal system performance (benchmark values), and identifying steps and procedures to improve system performance.

binary digit (bit)   The smallest unit of information that a computer can process.

biometric   The identification of a user based on a physical characteristic, such as a fingerprint, iris, face, voice, or handwriting.

black-hat hacker Breaks into other people's computer systems and may just look around or steal and destroy information.

blog Web site in which items are posted on a regular basis and displayed in reverse chronological order.

Bluetooth An omnidirectional wireless technology that provides limited-range voice and data transmission over the unlicensed 2.4-GHz frequency band, allowing connections with a wide variety of fixed and portable devices that normally would have to be cabled together.

bookkeeping The actual recording of the business's transactions, without any analysis of the information.

break-even point The point at which revenues equal costs.

brick-and-mortar business A business that operates in a physical store without an Internet presence.

bullwhip effect Occurs when distorted product demand information passes from one entity to the next throughout the supply chain.

business-critical integrity constraint Enforces business rules vital to an organization's success and often requires more insight and knowledge than relational integrity constraints.

business facing process Invisible to the external customer but essential to the effective management of the business and includes goal setting, day-to-day planning, performance feedback, rewards, and resource allocation.

business intelligence Refers to applications and technologies that are used to gather, provide access to, and analyze data and information to support decision-making efforts.

business process A standardized set of activities that accomplish a specific task, such as processing a customer's order.

business process management (BPM) Integrates all of an organization's business processes to make individual processes more efficient.

business process management tool Used to create an application that is helpful in designing business process models and also helpful in simulating, optimizing, monitoring, and maintaining various processes that occur within an organization.

business process model A graphic description of a process, showing the sequence of process tasks, which is developed for a specific purpose and from a selected viewpoint.

business process modeling (or **mapping**) The activity of creating a detailed flow chart or process map of a work process showing its inputs, tasks, and activities, in a structured sequence.

business process outsourcing The contracting of a specific business task, such as payroll, to a third-party service provider.

business process reengineering (BPR) The analysis and redesign of workflow within and between enterprises.

business requirement The detailed set of business requests that the system must meet in order to be successful.

business-to-business (B2B) Applies to businesses buying from and selling to each other over the Internet.

business-to-business (B2B) marketplace An Internet-based service that brings together many buyers and sellers.

business-to-consumer (B2C) Applies to any business that sells its products or services to consumers over the Internet.

business wiki Collaborative Web pages that allow users to edit documents, share ideas, or monitor the status of a project.

buyer power High when buyers have many choices of whom to buy from and low when their choices are few.

byte Group of eight bits represents one natural language character.

C

cache memory A small unit of ultra-fast memory that is used to store recently accessed or frequently accessed data so that the CPU does not have to retrieve this data from slower memory circuits such as RAM.

call scripting system Accesses organizational databases that track similar issues or questions and automatically generate the details for the CSR who can then relay them to the customer.

campaign management system Guides users through marketing campaigns performing such tasks as campaign definition, planning, scheduling, segmentation, and success analysis.

capacity planning Determines the future IT infrastructure requirements for new equipment and additional network capacity.

capital Represents money whose purpose is to make more money, for example, the money used to buy a rental property or a business.

central processing unit (CPU) (or **microprocessor**) The actual hardware that interprets and executes the program (software) instructions and coordinates how all the other hardware devices work together.

change control board (CCB) Responsible for approving or rejecting all change requests.

change management A set of techniques that aid in evolution, composition, and policy management of the design and implementation of a system.

change management system Includes a collection of procedures to document a change request and define the steps necessary to consider the change based on the expected impact of the change.

chief information officer (CIO) Responsible for (1) overseeing all uses of information technology and (2) ensuring the strategic alignment of IT with business goals and objectives.

chief knowledge officer (CKO) Responsible for collecting, maintaining, and distributing the organization's knowledge.

chief privacy officer (CPO) Responsible for ensuring the ethical and legal use of information within an organization.

chief security officer (CSO) Responsible for ensuring the security of IT systems and developing strategies and IT safeguards against attacks from hackers and viruses.

chief technology officer (CTO) Responsible for ensuring the throughput, speed, accuracy, availability, and reliability of an organization's information technology.

click-and-mortar business A business that operates in a physical store and on the Internet.

clickstream Records information about a customer during a Web surfing session such as what Web sites were visited, how long the visit was, what ads were viewed, and what was purchased.

clickstream data Exact pattern of a consumer's navigation through a site.

click-through A count of the number of people who visit one site and click on an advertisement that takes them to the site of the advertiser.

click-to-talk   Buttons allow customers to click on a button and talk with a CSR via the Internet.

client   Computer that is designed to request information from a server.

client/server network   A model for applications in which the bulk of the back-end processing, such as performing a physical search of a database, takes place on a server, while the front-end processing, which involves communicating with the users, is handled by the clients.

cluster analysis   A technique used to divide an information set into mutually exclusive groups such that the members of each group are as close together as possible to one another and the different groups are as far apart as possible.

coaxial cable   Cable that can carry a wide range of frequencies with low signal loss.

cold site   A separate facility that does not have any computer equipment, but is a place where employees can move after a disaster.

collaboration system   An IT-based set of tools that supports the work of teams by facilitating the sharing and flow of information.

collaborative demand planning   Helps organizations reduce their investment in inventory, while improving customer satisfaction through product availability.

collaborative engineering   Allows an organization to reduce the cost and time required during the design process of a product.

commercial off-the-shelf (COTS)   A software package or solution that is purchased to support one or more business functions and information systems.

communication device   Equipment used to send information and receive it from one location to another.

competitive advantage   A product or service that an organization's customers place a greater value on than similar offerings from a competitor.

complex instruction set computer (CISC) chip   Type of CPU that can recognize as many as 100 or more instructions, enough to carry out most computations directly.

computer   Electronic device operating under the control of instructions stored in its own memory that can accept, manipulate, and store data.

computer-aided software engineering (CASE)   Software suites that automate systems analysis, design, and development.

computer simulation   Complex systems, such as the U.S. economy, can be modeled by means of mathematical equations and different scenarios can be run against the model to determine "what if" analysis.

confidentiality   The assurance that messages and information are available only to those who are authorized to view them.

consolidation   Involves the aggregation of information and features simple roll-ups to complex groupings of interrelated information.

consumer-to-business (C2B)   Applies to any consumer that sells a product or service to a business over the Internet.

consumer-to-consumer (C2C)   Applies to sites primarily offering goods and services to assist consumers interacting with each other over the Internet.

contact center (call center)   Customer service representatives (CSRs) answer customer inquiries and respond to problems through a number of different customer touch points.

contact management CRM system   Maintains customer contact information and identifies prospective customers for future sales.

content filtering   Occurs when organizations use software that filters content to prevent the transmission of unauthorized information.

content management system   Provides tools to manage the creation, storage, editing, and publication of information in a collaborative environment.

content provider   Companies that use the Internet to distribute copyrighted content, including news, music, games, books, movies, and many other types of information.

continuous process improvement model   Attempts to understand and measure the current process, and make performance improvements accordingly.

control unit   Interprets software instructions and literally tells the other hardware devices what to do, based on the software instructions.

cookie   A small file deposited on a hard drive by a Web site containing information about customers and their Web activities.

copyright   The legal protection afforded an expression of an idea, such as a song, video game, and some types of proprietary documents.

core competency   An organization's key strength or business function that it does better than any of its competitors.

core competency strategy   When an organization chooses to focus specifically on what it does best (its core competency) and forms partnerships and alliances with other specialist organizations to handle nonstrategic business processes.

core ERP component   Traditional components included in most ERP systems and they primarily focus on internal operations.

corporation (also called **organization, enterprise,** or **business**)   An artificially created legal entity that exists separate and apart from those individuals who created it and carry on its operations.

counterfeit software   Software that is manufactured to look like the real thing and sold as such.

cracker   A hacker with criminal intent.

critical path   A path from the start to the finish that passes through all the tasks that are critical to completing the project in the shortest amount of time.

critical success factor (CSF)   A factor that is critical to an organization's success.

CRM analysis technologies   Help organizations segment their customers into categories such as best and worst customers.

CRM predicting technologies   Help organizations make predictions regarding customer behavior such as which customers are at risk of leaving.

CRM reporting technologies   Help organizations identify their customers across other applications.

cross-selling   Selling additional products or services to a customer.

cube   The common term for the representation of multidimensional information.

customer facing process   Results in a product or service that is received by an organization's external customer.

customer metric   Assesses the management of customer relationships by the organization.

customer relationship management (CRM)   Involves managing all aspects of a customer's relationship with an organization to increase customer loyalty and retention and an organization's profitability.

cyberterrorist   Seeks to cause harm to people or to destroy critical systems or information and use the Internet as a weapon of mass destruction.

cycle inventory   The average amount of inventory held to satisfy customer demands between inventory deliveries.

D

data   Raw facts that describe the characteristics of an event.

data administration component   Provides tools for managing the overall database environment by providing facilities for backup, recovery, security, and performance.

database   Maintains information about various types of objects (inventory), events (transactions), people (employees), and places (warehouses).

database-based workflow system   Stores documents in a central location and automatically asks the team members to access the document when it is their turn to edit the document.

database management system (DBMS)   Software through which users and application programs interact with a database.

data definition component   Helps create and maintain the data dictionary and the structure of the database.

data dictionary   A file that stores definitions of information types, identifies the primary and foreign keys, and maintains the relationships among the tables.

data-driven Web site   An interactive Web site kept constantly updated and relevant to the needs of its customers through the use of a database.

data flow diagram (DFD)   Illustrates the movement of information between external entities and the processes and data stores within the system.

data manipulation component   Allows users to create, read, update, and delete information in a database.

data mart   Contains a subset of data warehouse information.

data mining   The process of analyzing data to extract information not offered by the raw data alone.

data-mining tool   Uses a variety of techniques to find patterns and relationships in large volumes of information and infer rules from them that predict future behavior and guide decision making.

data model   A formal way to express data relationships to a database management system (DBMS).

data warehouse   A logical collection of information—gathered from many different operational databases—that supports business analysis activities and decision-making tasks.

decision support system (DSS)   Models information to support managers and business professionals during the decision-making process.

demand planning software   Generates demand forecasts using statistical tools and forecasting techniques.

denial-of-service attack (DoS)   Floods a Web site with so many requests for service that it slows down or crashes the site.

dependency   A logical relationship that exists between the project tasks, or between a project task and a milestone.

design phase   Involves describing the desired features and operations of the system including screen layouts, business rules, process diagrams, pseudo code, and other documentation.

development phase   Involves taking all of the detailed design documents from the design phase and transforming them into the actual system.

digital asset management system (DAM)   Though similar to document management, DAM generally works with binary rather than text files, such as multimedia file types.

digital Darwinism   Organizations that cannot adapt to the new demands placed on them for surviving in the information age are doomed to extinction.

digital dashboard   Integrates information from multiple components and tailors the information to individual preferences.

digital divide   When those with access to technology have great advantages over those without access to technology.

digital ink (or electronic ink)   Technology that digitally represents handwriting in its natural form.

digital paper (or electronic paper)   Any paper that is optimized for any type of digital printing.

digital wallet   Both software and information—the software provides security for the transaction and the information includes payment and delivery information (for example, the credit card number and expiration date).

disaster recovery cost curve   Charts (1) the cost to the organization of the unavailability of information and technology and (2) the cost to the organization of recovering from a disaster over time.

disaster recovery plan   A detailed process for recovering information or an IT system in the event of a catastrophic disaster such as a fire or flood.

disruptive technology   A new way of doing things that initially does not meet the needs of existing customers.

distributed denial-of-service attack (DDoS)   Attacks from multiple computers that flood a Web site with so many requests for service that it slows down or crashes.

distribution management software   Coordinates the process of transporting materials from a manufacturer to distribution centers to the final customer.

dividend   A distribution of earnings to shareholders.

document management system (DMS)   Supports the electronic capturing, storage, distribution, archival, and accessing of documents.

drill-down   Enables users to get details, and details of details, of information.

E

e-business   The conducting of business on the Internet, not only buying and selling, but also serving customers and collaborating with business partners.

e-business model An approach to conducting electronic business on the Internet.

e-commerce The buying and selling of goods and services over the Internet.

effectiveness IT metric Measures the impact IT has on business processes and activities including customer satisfaction, conversion rates, and sell-through increases.

efficiency IT metric Measures the performance of the IT system itself including throughput, speed, and availability.

e-government Involves the use of strategies and technologies to transform government(s) by improving the delivery of services and enhancing the quality of interaction between the citizen-consumer within all branches of government.

electronic bill presentment and payment (EBPP) System that sends bills over the Internet and provides an easy-to-use mechanism (such as clicking on a button) to pay the bill.

electronic catalog Presents customers with information about goods and services offered for sale, bid, or auction on the Internet.

electronic check Mechanism for sending a payment from a checking or savings account.

electronic data interchange (EDI) A standard format for exchanging business data.

electronic marketplace (e-marketplace) Interactive business communities providing a central market space where multiple buyers and suppliers can engage in e-business activities.

electronic tagging A technique for identifying and tracking assets and individuals via technologies such as radio frequency identification and smart cards.

elevation of privilege Process by which a user misleads a system into granting unauthorized rights, usually for the purpose of compromising or destroying the system.

e-logistics Manages the transportation and storage of goods.

e-mail privacy policy Details the extent to which e-mail messages may be read by others.

e-mall Consists of a number of e-shops; it serves as a gateway through which a visitor can access other e-shops.

employee monitoring policy States how, when, and where the company monitors its employees.

employee relationship management (ERM) Provides employees with a subset of CRM applications available through a Web browser.

encryption Scrambles information into an alternative form that requires a key or password to decrypt the information.

enterprise application integration (EAI) middleware Represents a new approach to middleware by packaging together commonly used functionality, such as providing prebuilt links to popular enterprise applications, which reduces the time necessary to develop solutions that integrate applications from multiple vendors.

enterprise architect (EA) Person grounded in technology, fluent in business, a patient diplomat, and provides the important bridge between IT and the business.

enterprise architecture Includes the plans for how an organization will build, deploy, use, and share its data, processes, and IT assets.

enterprise resource planning (ERP) Integrates all departments and functions throughout an organization into a single IT system (or integrated set of IT systems) so that employees can make decisions by viewing enterprisewide information on all business operations.

entity In the relational database model, a person, place, thing, transaction, or event about which information is stored.

entity class In the relational database model, a collection of similar entities.

entity-relationship diagram (ERD) A technique for documenting the relationships between entities in a database environment.

entry barrier A product or service feature that customers have come to expect from organizations in a particular industry and must be offered by an entering organization to compete and survive.

environmental scanning The acquisition and analysis of events and trends in the environment external to an organization.

ePolicies Policies and procedures that address the ethical use of computers and Internet usage in the business environment.

e-procurement The B2B purchase and sale of supplies and services over the Internet.

e-shop (e-store or e-tailer) A version of a retail store where customers can shop at any hour of the day without leaving their home or office.

ethernet A physical and data layer technology for LAN networking.

ethical computer use policy Contains general principles to guide computer user behavior.

ethics Principles and standards that guide our behavior toward other people.

executive information system (EIS) A specialized DSS that supports senior level executives within the organization.

expense Refers to the costs incurred in operating and maintaining a business.

expert system Computerized advisory programs that imitate the reasoning processes of experts in solving difficult problems.

explicit knowledge Consists of anything that can be documented, archived, and codified, often with the help of IT.

extended ERP component The extra components that meet the organizational needs not covered by the core components and primarily focus on external operations.

extraction, transformation, and loading (ETL) A process that extracts information from internal and external databases, transforms the information using a common set of enterprise definitions, and loads the information into a data warehouse.

extranet An intranet that is available to strategic allies (such as customers, suppliers, and partners).

extreme programming (XP) methodology Breaks a project into tiny phases, and developers cannot continue on to the next phase until the first phase is complete.

F

failover Backup operational mode in which the function of a computer component (such as a processor, server, network, or database) is assumed by secondary system components when the primary component becomes unavailable through either failure or scheduled down time.

fair use doctrine In certain situations, it is legal to use copyrighted material.

fault tolerance   A computer system designed so that in the event a component fails, a backup component or procedure can immediately take its place with no loss of service.

feasibility study   Determines if the proposed solution is feasible and achievable from a financial, technical, and organizational standpoint.

feature creep   Occurs when developers add extra features that were not part of the initial requirements.

fiber optic (optical fiber)   The technology associated with the transmission of information as light impulses along a glass wire or fiber.

finance   Deals with the strategic financial issues associated with increasing the value of the business while observing applicable laws and social responsibilities.

financial accounting   Involves preparing financial reports that provide information about the business's performance to external parties such as investors, creditors, and tax authorities.

financial cybermediary   Internet-based company that facilitates payments over the Internet.

financial EDI (financial electronic data interchange)   Standard electronic process for B2B market purchase payments.

financial quarter   A three-month period (four quarters per year).

financial statement   Written records of the financial status of the business that allow interested parties to evaluate the profitability and solvency of the business.

firewall   Hardware and/or software that guards a private network by analyzing the information leaving and entering the network.

first-mover advantage   An organization can significantly impact its market share by being first to market with a competitive advantage.

Five Forces model   Helps determine the relative attractiveness of an industry.

flash memory   A special type of rewriteable read-only memory (ROM) that is compact and portable.

for profit corporations   Primarily focus on making money and all profits and losses are shared by the business owners.

forecast   Predictions made on the basis of time-series information.

foreign key   A primary key of one table that appears as an attribute in another table and acts to provide a logical relationship between the two tables.

forward integration   Takes information entered into a given system and sends it automatically to all downstream systems and processes.

fuzzy logic   A mathematical method of handling imprecise or subjective information.

G

Gantt chart   A simple bar chart that depicts project tasks against a calendar.

genetic algorithm   An artificial intelligence system that mimics the evolutionary, survival-of-the-fittest process to generate increasingly better solutions to a problem.

geographic information system (GIS)   Designed to work with information that can be shown on a map.

gigabyte (GB)   Roughly 1 billion bytes.

gigahertz (GHz)   The number of billions of CPU cycles per second.

global inventory management system   Provides the ability to locate, track, and predict the movement of every component or material anywhere upstream or downstream in the supply chain.

global positioning system (GPS)   A device that determines current latitude, longitude, speed, and direction of movement.

goal-seeking analysis   Finds the inputs necessary to achieve a goal such as a desired level of output.

graphical user interface (GUI)   The interface to an information system.

groupware   Software that supports team interaction and dynamics including calendaring, scheduling, and videoconferencing.

GUI screen design   The ability to model the information system screens for an entire system using icons, buttons, menus, and submenus.

H

hacker   People very knowledgeable about computers who use their knowledge to invade other people's computers.

hactivist   Person with philosophical and political reasons for breaking into systems who will often deface Web site as a protest.

hard drive   Secondary storage medium that uses several rigid disks coated with a magnetically sensitive material and housed together with the recording heads in a hermetically sealed mechanism.

hardware   Consists of the physical devices associated with a computer system.

hardware key logger   A hardware device that captures keystrokes on their journey from the keyboard to the motherboard.

help desk   A group of people who respond to internal system user questions.

hierarchical database model   Information is organized into a tree-like structure that allows repeating information using parent/child relationships, in such a way that it cannot have too many relationships.

high availability   Refers to a system or component that is continuously operational for a desirably long length of time.

historical analysis   Historical events are studied to anticipate the outcome of current developments.

hoaxes   Attack computer systems by transmitting a virus hoax, with a real virus attached.

hot site   A separate and fully equipped facility where the company can move immediately after a disaster and resume business.

human resource ERP component   Tracks employee information including payroll, benefits, compensation, and performance assessment, and assures compliance with the legal requirements of multiple jurisdictions and tax authorities.

human resources management (HRM)   Includes the policies, plans, and procedures for the effective management of employees (human resources).

hypertext transfer protocol (HTTP)   The Internet standard that supports the exchange of information on the WWW.

I

identity theft   The forging of someone's identity for the purpose of fraud.

implementation phase   Involves placing the system into production so users can begin to perform actual business operations with the system.

income statement   (also referred to as **earnings report, operating statement,** and **profit-and-loss (P&L) statement**) Reports operating results (revenues minus expenses) for a given time period ending at a specified date.

information   Data converted into a meaningful and useful context.

information accuracy   Extent to which a system generates the correct results when executing the same transaction numerous times.

information architecture   Identifies where and how important information, like customer records, is maintained and secured.

information cleansing or scrubbing   A process that weeds out and fixes or discards inconsistent, incorrect, or incomplete information.

information granularity   Refers to the extent of detail within the information (fine and detailed or "coarse" and abstract information).

information integrity   A measure of the quality of information.

information partnership   Occurs when two or more organizations cooperate by integrating their IT systems, thereby providing customers with the best of what each can offer.

information privacy policy   Contains general principles regarding information privacy.

information reach   Refers to the number of people a business can communicate with, on a global basis.

information richness   Refers to the depth and breadth of information transferred between customers and businesses.

information security   A broad term encompassing the protection of information from accidental or intentional misuse by persons inside or outside an organization.

information security plan   Details how an organization will implement the information security policies.

information security policy   Identifies the rules required to maintain information security.

information technology (IT)   The study, design, development, implementation, support or management of computer-based information systems, particularly software applications and computer hardware.

information technology monitoring   Tracking people's activities by such measures as number of keystrokes, error rate, and number of transactions processed.

infrastructure architecture   Includes the hardware, software, and telecommunications equipment that, when combined, provide the underlying foundation to support the organization's goals.

input device   Equipment used to capture information and commands.

insider   Legitimate users who purposely or accidentally misuse their access to the environment and cause some kind of business-affecting incident.

insourcing (in-house development)   A common approach using the professional expertise within an organization to develop and maintain the organization's information technology systems.

instant messaging (IM or IMing)   A type of communications service that enables someone to create a kind of private chat room with another individual in order to communicate in real-time over the Internet.

integration   Allows separate systems to communicate directly with each other.

integrity constraint   The rules that help ensure the quality of information.

intellectual property   Intangible creative work that is embodied in physical form.

intelligent agent   A special-purpose knowledge-based information system that accomplishes specific tasks on behalf of its users.

intelligent system   Various commercial applications of artificial intelligence.

interactive voice response (IVR)   Directs customers to use touch-tone phones or keywords to navigate or provide information.

interactivity   Measures the visitor interactions with the target ad.

intermediary   Agents, software, or businesses that bring buyers and sellers together that provide a trading infrastructure to enhance e-business.

Internet   A global public network of computer networks that pass information from one to another using common computer protocols.

Internet service provider (ISP)   A company that provides individuals and other companies access to the Internet along with additional related services, such as Web site building.

Internet use policy   Contains general principles to guide the proper use of the Internet.

interoperability   Capability of two or more computer systems to share data and resources, even though they are made by different manufacturers.

intranet   An internalized portion of the Internet, protected from outside access, that allows an organization to provide access to information and application software to only its employees.

intrusion detection software (IDS)   Searches out patterns in information and network traffic to indicate attacks and quickly responds to prevent any harm.

inventory management and control software   Provides control and visibility to the status of individual items maintained in inventory.

IT infrastructure   Includes the hardware, software, and telecommunications equipment that, when combined, provide the underlying foundation to support the organization's goals.

J

joint application development (JAD)   A session where employees meet, sometimes for several days, to define or review the business requirements for the system.

K

key logger, or **key trapper, software**   A program that, when installed on a computer, records every keystroke and mouse click.

key performance indicator (KPI)   Measures that are tied to business drivers.

kiosk   Publicly accessible computer system that has been set up to allow interactive information browsing.

knowledge management (KM)   Involves capturing, classifying, evaluating, retrieving, and sharing information assets in a way that provides context for effective decisions and actions.

knowledge management system (KMS)   Supports the capturing, organization, and dissemination of knowledge (i.e., know-how) throughout an organization.

L

liability   An obligation to make financial payments.

limited liability   Means that the shareholders are not personally liable for the losses incurred by the corporation.

limited liability corporation (LLC)   A hybrid entity that has the legal protections of a corporation and the ability to be taxed (one time) as a partnership.

limited partnership   Much like a general partnership except for one important fundamental difference; the law protects the limited partner from being responsible for all of the partnership's losses.

list generator   Compiles customer information from a variety of sources and segments the information for different marketing campaigns.

local area network (LAN)   Computer network that uses cables or radio signals to link two or more computers within a geographically limited area, generally one building or a group of buildings.

logical view   Focuses on how users logically access information to meet their particular business needs.

logistics   The set of processes that plans for and controls the efficient and effective transportation and storage of supplies from suppliers to customers.

loss   Occurs when businesses sell products or services for less than they cost to produce.

loyalty program   Rewards customers based on the amount of business they do with a particular organization.

M

magnetic medium   Secondary storage medium that uses magnetic techniques to store and retrieve data on disks or tapes coated with magnetically sensitive materials.

magnetic tape   Older secondary storage medium that uses a strip of thin plastic coated with a magnetically sensitive recording medium.

mail bomb   Sends a massive amount of e-mail to a specific person or system resulting in filling up the recipient's disk space, which, in some cases, may be too much for the server to handle and may cause the server to stop functioning.

maintenance   The fixing or enhancing of an information system.

maintenance phase   Involves performing changes, corrections, additions, and upgrades to ensure the system continues to meet the business goals.

maintenance, repair, and operations (MRO) materials (also called **indirect materials**)   Materials necessary for running an organization but that do not relate to the company's primary business activities.

malicious code   Includes a variety of threats such as viruses, worms, and Trojan horses.

management information systems (MIS)   A general name for the business function and academic discipline covering the application of people, technologies, and procedures—collectively called information systems—to solve business problems.

managerial accounting   Involves analyzing business operations for internal decision making and does not have to follow any rules issued by standard-setting bodies such as GAAP.

market basket analysis   Analyzes such items as Web sites and checkout scanner information to detect customers' buying behavior and predict future behavior by identifying affinities among customers' choices of products and services.

marketing   The process associated with promoting the sale of goods or services.

marketing communication   Seeks to build product or service awareness and to educate potential consumers on the product or service.

marketing mix   Includes the variables that marketing managers can control in order to best satisfy customers in the target market.

market maker   Intermediaries that aggregate three services for market participants: (1) a place to trade, (2) rules to govern trading, and (3) an infrastructure to support trading.

market segmentation   The division of a market into similar groups of customers.

market share   Calculated by dividing the firm's sales by the total market sales for the entire industry.

mashup editor   WYSIWYGs (What You See Is What You Get) for mashups that provide a visual interface to build a mashup, often allowing the user to drag and drop data points into a Web application.

mass customization   Ability of an organization to give its customers the opportunity to tailor its products or services to the customers' specifications.

megabyte (MB or **M** or **Meg)**   Roughly 1 million bytes.

megahertz (MHz)   The number of millions of CPU cycles per second.

memory card   Contains high-capacity storage that holds data such as captured images, music, or text files.

memory stick   Provides nonvolatile memory for a range of portable devices including computers, digital cameras, MP3 players, and PDAs.

messaging-based workflow system   Sends work assignments through an e-mail system.

metropolitan area network (MAN)   A computer network that provides connectivity in a geographic area or region larger than that covered by a local area network, but smaller than the area covered by a wide area network.

microwave transmitter   Commonly used to transmit network signals over great distances.

middleware   Different types of software that sit in the middle of and provide connectivity between two or more software applications.

mobile commerce, or **m-commerce**   The ability to purchase goods and services through a wireless Internet-enabled device.

model   A simplified representation or abstraction of reality.

modeling   The activity of drawing a graphical representation of a design.

multisourcing   A combination of professional services, mission-critical support, remote management, and hosting services that are offered to customers in any combination needed.

multitasking   Allows more than one piece of software to be used at a time.

N

nearshore outsourcing   Contracting an outsourcing agreement with a company in a nearby country.

net income   The amount of money remaining after paying taxes.

network   A communications, data exchange, and resource-sharing system created by linking two or more computers and establishing standards, or protocols, so that they can work together.

network database model   A flexible way of representing objects and their relationships.

network operating system (NOS)   The operating system that runs a network, steering information between computers and managing security and users.

network topology   Refers to the geometric arrangement of the actual physical organization of the computers (and other network devices) in a network.

network transmission media   Various types of media used to carry the signal between computers.

neural network (an **artificial neural network**)   A category of AI that attempts to emulate the way the human brain works.

nonrepudiation   A contractual stipulation to ensure that e-business participants do not deny (repudiate) their online actions.

not for profit (or **nonprofit**) **corporation**   Usually exists to accomplish some charitable, humanitarian, or educational purpose, and the profits and losses are not shared by the business owners.

O

offshore outsourcing   Using organizations from developing countries to write code and develop systems.

online ad   Box running across a Web page that is often used to contain advertisements.

online analytical processing (OLAP)   The manipulation of information to create business intelligence in support of strategic decision making.

online broker   Intermediaries between buyers and sellers of goods and services.

online service provider (OSP)   Offers an extensive array of unique services such as its own version of a Web browser.

online training   Runs over the Internet or off a CD-ROM.

online transaction processing (OLTP)   The capturing of transaction and event information using technology to (1) process the information according to defined business rules, (2) store the information, and (3) update existing information to reflect the new information.

onshore outsourcing   The process of engaging another company within the same country for services.

open system   A broad term that describes nonproprietary IT hardware and software made available by the standards and procedures by which their products work, making it easier to integrate them.

operating system software   Controls the application software and manages how the hardware devices work together.

operational CRM   Supports traditional transactional processing for day-to-day front-office operations or systems that deal directly with the customers.

operations management (also called **production management**)   Includes the methods, tasks, and techniques organizations use to produce goods and services.

opportunity management CRM system   Targets sales opportunities by finding new customers or companies for future sales.

opt-in   Indicates that a company will contact only the people who have agreed to receive promotions and marketing material via e-mail.

output device   Equipment used to see, hear, or otherwise accept the results of information processing requests.

outsourcing   An arrangement by which one organization provides a service or services for another organization that chooses not to perform them in-house.

owner's equity   The portion of a company belonging to the owners.

P

packet-switching   Occurs when the sending computer divides a message into a number of efficiently sized units called packets, each of which contains the address of the destination computer.

packet tampering   Altering the contents of packets as they travel over the Internet or altering data on computer disks after penetrating a network.

partner relationship management (PRM)   Focuses on keeping vendors satisfied by managing alliance partner and reseller relationships that provide customers with the optimal sales channel.

partnership   Similar to sole proprietorships, except that this legal structure allows for more than one owner.

partnership agreement   A legal agreement between two or more business partners that outlines core business issues.

peer-to-peer (P2P) network   Any network without a central file server and in which all computers in the network have access to the public files located on all other workstations.

performance   Measures how quickly a system performs a certain process or transaction.

personalization   Occurs when a Web site can know enough about a person's likes and dislikes that it can fashion offers that are more likely to appeal to that person.

PERT (Program Evaluation and Review Technique) chart   A graphical network model that depicts a project's tasks and the relationships between those tasks.

phishing   Technique to gain personal information for the purpose of identity theft, usually by means of fraudulent e-mail.

physical view   The physical storage of information on a storage device such as a hard disk.

pirated software   The unauthorized use, duplication, distribution, or sale of copyrighted software.

planning phase   Involves establishing a high-level plan of the intended project and determining project goals.

podcasting   Distribution of audio or video files, such as radio programs or music videos, over the Internet to play on mobile devices and personal computers.

polymorphic virus and worm   Change their form as they propagate.

pop-under ad   Form of a pop-up ad that users do not see until they close the current Web browser screen.

pop-up ad   Small Web page containing an advertisement that appears on the Web page outside the current Web site loaded in the Web browser.

portal   A Web site that offers a broad array of resources and services, such as e-mail, online discussion groups, search engines, and online shopping malls.

predictive dialing   Automatically dials outbound calls and when someone answers, the call is forwarded to an available agent.

primary key   A field (or group of fields) that uniquely identifies a given entity in a table.

primary storage   Computer's main memory, which consists of the random access memory (RAM), cache memory, and read-only memory (ROM) that is directly accessible to the CPU.

privacy   The right to be left alone when you want to be, to have control over your own personal possessions, and not to be observed without your consent.

private exchange   A B2B marketplace in which a single buyer posts its need and then opens the bidding to any supplier who would care to bid.

process modeling   Involves graphically representing the processes that capture, manipulate, store, and distribute information between a system and its environment.

product life cycle   Includes the four phases a product progresses through during its life cycle including introduction, growth, maturity, and decline.

production and materials management ERP component   Handles the various aspects of production planning and execution such as demand forecasting, production scheduling, job cost accounting, and quality control.

profit   Occurs when businesses sell products or services for more than they cost to produce.

project   A temporary endeavor undertaken to create a unique product or service.

project deliverable   Any measurable, tangible, verifiable outcome, result, or item that is produced to complete a project or part of a project.

project exclusion   Products, services, or processes that are not specifically a part of the project.

project management   The application of knowledge, skills, tools, and techniques to project activities in order to meet or exceed stakeholder needs and expectations from a project.

project management software   Supports the long-term and day-to-day management and execution of the steps in a project.

project manager   An individual who is an expert in project planning and management, defines and develops the project plan, and tracks the plan to ensure all key project milestones are completed on time.

project milestone   Represents key dates when a certain group of activities must be performed.

project objective   Quantifiable criteria that must be met for the project to be considered a success.

project plan   A formal, approved document that manages and controls project execution.

project product   A description of the characteristics the product or service has undertaken.

project risk   An uncertain event or condition that, if it occurs, has a positive or negative effect on a project objective(s).

project scope   Defines the work that must be completed to deliver a product with the specified features and functions.

protocol   A standard that specifies the format of data as well as the rules to be followed during transmission.

prototype   A smaller-scale representation or working model of the user's requirements or a proposed design for an information system.

public key encryption (PKE)   Encryption system that uses two keys: a public key that everyone can have and a private key for only the recipient.

pull technology   Organizations receive or request information.

pure-play (virtual) business   A business that operates on the Internet only without a physical store.

push technology   Organizations send information.

Q

query-by-example (QBE) tool   Allows users to graphically design the answers to specific questions.

R

radio frequency identification (RFID)   Technologies using active or passive tags in the form of chips or smart labels that can store unique identifiers and relay this information to electronic readers.

RadioPaper   A dynamic high-resolution electronic display that combines a paper-like reading experience with the ability to access information anytime, anywhere.

random access memory (RAM)   The computer's primary working memory, in which program instructions and data are stored so that they can be accessed directly by the CPU via the processor's high-speed external data bus.

rapid application development (RAD) (also called rapid prototyping) methodology   Emphasizes extensive user involvement in the rapid and evolutionary construction of working prototypes of a system to accelerate the systems development process.

read-only memory (ROM)   The portion of a computer's primary storage that does not lose its contents when one switches off the power.

real simple syndication (RSS)   Family of Web feed formats used for Web syndication of programs and content.

real-time information   Immediate, up-to-date information.

real-time system Provides real-time information in response to query requests.

recovery The ability to get a system up and running in the event of a system crash or failure and includes restoring the information backup.

reduced instruction set computer (RISC) chip Limits the number of instructions the CPU can execute to increase processing speed.

redundancy The duplication of information or storing the same information in multiple places.

reintermediation Using the Internet to reassemble buyers, sellers, and other partners in a traditional supply chain in new ways.

relational database model A type of database that stores information in the form of logically related two-dimensional tables.

relational integrity constraint The rules that enforce basic and fundamental information-based constraints.

reliability Ensures all systems are functioning correctly and providing accurate information.

report generator Allows users to define formats for reports along with what information they want to see in the report.

requirements definition document Contains the final set of business requirements, prioritized in order of business importance.

response time The time it takes to respond to user interactions such as a mouse click.

revenue Refers to the amount earned resulting from the delivery or manufacture of a product or from the rendering of a service.

reverse auction An auction format in which increasingly lower bids are solicited from organizations willing to supply the desired product or service at an increasingly lower price.

RFID tag Contains a microchip and an antenna, and typically works by transmitting a serial number via radio waves to an electronic reader, which confirms the identity of a person or object bearing the tag.

risk management The process of proactive and ongoing identification, analysis, and response to risk factors.

rivalry among existing competitors High when competition is fierce in a market and low when competition is more complacent.

router An intelligent connecting device that examines each packet of data it receives and then decides which way to send it onward toward its destination.

S

safety inventory Includes extra inventory held in the event demand exceeds supply.

sales The function of selling a good or service that focuses on increasing customer sales, which increases company revenues.

sales force automation (SFA) A system that automatically tracks all of the steps in the sales process.

sales management CRM system Automates each phase of the sales process, helping individual sales representatives coordinate and organize all of their accounts.

scalability Refers to how well a system can adapt to increased demands.

scope creep Occurs when the scope of the project increases.

script kiddies or **script bunnies** Find hacking code on the Internet and click-and-point their way into systems to cause damage or spread viruses.

search engine optimization (SEO) Set of methods aimed at improving the ranking of a Web site in search engine listings.

secondary storage Consists of equipment designed to store large volumes of data for long-term storage.

secure electronic transaction (SET) Transmission security method that ensures transactions are secure and legitimate.

secure socket layer (SSL) (1) Creates a secure and private connection between a client and server computer, (2) encrypts the information, and (3) sends the information over the Internet.

selling chain management Applies technology to the activities in the order life cycle from inquiry to sale.

semantic Web An evolving extension of the World Wide Web in which Web content can be expressed not only in natural language, but also in a format that can be read and used by software agents, thus permitting them to find, share, and integrate information more easily.

sensitivity analysis The study of the impact that changes in one (or more) parts of the model have on other parts of the model.

server Computer that is dedicated to providing information in response to external requests.

service level agreement (SLA) Defines the specific responsibilities of the service provider and sets the customer expectations.

service-oriented architecture (SOA) A collection of services that communicate with each other, for example, passing data from one service to another or coordinating an activity between one or more services.

shareholder Another term for business owners.

shopping bot Software that will search several retailer Web sites and provide a comparison of each retailer's offerings including price and availability.

sign-off The system users' actual signatures indicating they approve all of the business requirements.

slice-and-dice The ability to look at information from different perspectives.

smart card A device that is around the same size as a credit card, containing embedded technologies that can store information and small amounts of software to perform some limited processing.

sniffer A program or device that can monitor data traveling over a network.

social engineering Using one's social skills to trick people into revealing access credentials or other information valuable to the attacker.

social networking analysis (SNA) A process of mapping a group's contacts (whether personal or professional) to identify who knows whom and who works with whom.

software The set of instructions that the hardware executes to carry out specific tasks.

sole proprietorship A business form in which a single person is the sole owner and is personally responsible for all the profits and losses of the business.

solvency Represents the ability of the business to pay its bills and service its debt.

source document Describes the basic transaction data such as its date, purpose, and amount and includes cash receipts, canceled checks, invoices, customer refunds, employee time sheet, etc.

spam Unsolicited e-mail.

spamdexing Uses a variety of deceptive techniques in an attempt to manipulate search engine rankings, whereas legitimate search engine optimization focuses on building better sites and using honest methods of promotion.

spoofing The forging of the return address on an e-mail so that the e-mail message appears to come from someone other than the actual sender.

spyware Software that comes hidden in free downloadable software and tracks online movements, mines the information stored on a computer, or uses a computer's CPU and storage for some task the user knows nothing about.

statement of cash flow Summarizes sources and uses of cash, indicates whether enough cash is available to carry on routine operations, and offers an analysis of all business transactions, reporting where the firm obtained its cash and how it chose to allocate the cash.

statement of owner's equity (also called the **statement of retained earnings** or **equity statement**) Tracks and communicates changes in the shareholder's earnings.

structured collaboration (or **process collaboration**) Involves shared participation in business processes, such as workflow, in which knowledge is hard coded as rules.

structured query language (SQL) A standardized fourth-generation query language found in most DBMSs.

supplier power High when buyers have few choices of whom to buy from and low when their choices are many.

supplier relationship management (SRM) Focuses on keeping suppliers satisfied by evaluating and categorizing suppliers for different projects, which optimizes supplier selection.

supply chain Consists of all parties involved, directly or indirectly, in the procurement of a product or raw material.

supply chain event management (SCEM) Enables an organization to react more quickly to resolve supply chain issues.

supply chain execution (SCE) software Automates the different steps and stages of the supply chain.

supply chain management (SCM) Involves the management of information flows between and among stages in a supply chain to maximize total supply chain effectiveness and profitability.

supply chain planning (SCP) software Uses advanced mathematical algorithms to improve the flow and efficiency of the supply chain while reducing inventory.

supply chain visibility The ability to view all areas up and down the supply chain.

sustaining technology Produces an improved product customers are eager to buy, such as a faster car or larger hard drive.

switching cost The costs that can make customers reluctant to switch to another product or service.

system availability Number of hours a system is available for users.

systems development life cycle (SDLC) The overall process for developing information systems from planning and analysis through implementation and maintenance.

system software Controls how the various technology tools work together along with the application software.

T

tacit knowledge The knowledge contained in people's heads.

telecommunication system Enables the transmission of data over public or private networks.

teleliving Using information devices and the Internet to conduct all aspects of life seamlessly.

telematic Blending computers and wireless telecommunications technologies with the goal of efficiently conveying information over vast networks to improve business operations.

terabyte (TB) Roughly 1 trillion bytes.

test condition The detailed steps the system must perform along with the expected results of each step.

testing phase Involves bringing all the project pieces together into a special testing environment to test for errors, bugs, and interoperability and verify that the system meets all of the business requirements defined in the analysis phase.

threat of new entrants High when it is easy for new competitors to enter a market and low when there are significant entry barriers to entering a market.

threat of substitute products or services High when there are many alternatives to a product or service and low when there are few alternatives from which to choose.

throughput The amount of information that can travel through a system at any point in time.

time-series information Time-stamped information collected at a particular frequency.

To-Be process model Shows the results of applying change improvement opportunities to the current (As-Is) process model.

token Small electronic devices that change user passwords automatically.

transaction Exchange or transfer of goods, services, or funds involving two or more people.

transaction processing system (TPS) The basic business system that serves the operational level (analysts) in an organization.

transaction speed Amount of time a system takes to perform a transaction.

transactional information Encompasses all of the information contained within a single business process or unit of work, and its primary purpose is to support the performing of daily operational tasks.

Transmission Control Protocol/Internet Protocol (TCP/IP) Provides the technical foundation for the public Internet as well as for large numbers of private networks.

transportation planning software Tracks and analyzes the movement of materials and products to ensure the delivery of materials and finished goods at the right time, the right place, and the lowest cost.

trend analysis A trend is examined to identify its nature, causes, speed of development, and potential impacts.

trend monitoring Trends viewed as particularly important in a specific community, industry, or sector are carefully monitored, watched, and reported to key decision makers.

trend projection When numerical data are available, a trend can be plotted to display changes through time and into the future.

Trojan-horse virus Hides inside other software, usually as an attachment or a downloadable file.

twisted-pair wiring A type of cable composed of four (or more) copper wires twisted around each other within a plastic sheath.

U

unstructured collaboration (or **information collaboration**) Includes document exchange, shared whiteboards, discussion forums, and e-mail.

up-selling Increasing the value of a sale.

user documentation Highlights how to use the system.

utility software Provides additional functionality to the operating system.

V

value-added network (VAN) A private network, provided by a third party, for exchanging information through a high-capacity connection.

value chain Views an organization as a series of processes, each of which adds value to the product or service for each customer.

videoconference A set of interactive telecommunication technologies that allow two or more locations to interact via two-way video and audio transmissions simultaneously.

view Allows users to see the contents of a database, make any required changes, perform simple sorting, and query the database to find the location of specific information.

viral marketing Technique that induces Web sites or users to pass on a marketing message to other Web sites or users, creating exponential growth in the message's visibility and effect.

virtual assistant A small program stored on a PC or portable device that monitors e-mails, faxes, messages, and phone calls.

virtualization Protected memory space created by the CPU allowing the computer to create virtual machines.

virtual private network (VPN) A way to use the public telecommunication infrastructure (e.g., Internet) to provide secure access to an organization's network.

virus Software written with malicious intent to cause annoyance or damage.

voice over IP (VoIP) Uses TCP/IP technology to transmit voice calls over long-distance telephone lines.

volatility Refers to RAM's complete loss of stored information if power is interrupted.

W

waterfall methodology A sequential, activity-based process in which each phase in the SDLC is performed sequentially from planning through implementation and maintenance.

Web 2.0 A set of economic, social, and technology trends that collectively form the basis for the next generation of the Internet—a more mature, distinctive medium characterized by user participation, openness, and network effects.

Web-based self-service system Allows customers to use the Web to find answers to their questions or solutions to their problems.

Web conference Blends audio, video, and document-sharing technologies to create virtual meeting rooms where people "gather" at a password-protected Web site.

Web content management system (WCM) Adds an additional layer to document and digital asset management that enables publishing content both to intranets and to public Web sites.

Web log Consists of one line of information for every visitor to a Web site and is usually stored on a Web server.

Web mashup A Web site or Web application that uses content from more than one source to create a completely new service.

Web service Contains a repertoire of Web-based data and procedural resources that use shared protocols and standards permitting different applications to share data and services.

Web traffic Includes a host of benchmarks such as the number of page views, the number of unique visitors, and the average time spent viewing a Web page.

what-if analysis Checks the impact of a change in an assumption on the proposed solution.

white-hat hacker Works at the request of the system owners to find system vulnerabilities and plug the holes.

wide area network (WAN) Computer network that provides data communication services for business in geographically dispersed areas (such as across a country or around the world).

wiki Web-based tools that make it easy for users to add, remove, and change online content.

wireless fidelity (wi-fi) A means of linking computers using infrared or radio signals.

wireless Internet service provider (WISP) An ISP that allows subscribers to connect to a server at designated hotspots or access points using a wireless connection.

wireless media Natural parts of the Earth's environment that can be used as physical paths to carry electrical signals.

wire media Transmission material manufactured so that signals will be confined to a narrow path and will behave predictably.

workflow Defines all the steps or business rules, from beginning to end, required for a business process.

workflow management system Facilitates the automation and management of business processes and controls the movement of work through the business process.

workshop training Set in a classroom-type environment and led by an instructor.

World Wide Web (WWW) A global hypertext system that uses the Internet as its transport mechanism.

worm A type of virus that spreads itself, not only from file to file, but also from computer to computer.

NOTES

Unit One

1. Joshua Ramo, "Jeffrey Bezos," www.time.com/time/poy2000/archive/1999.html, accessed June 8, 2004; "Shop Amazon.com with Your Voice," www.amazon.com/exec/obidos/subst/misc/anywhere/anywhere.html/ref=gw_hp_ls_1_2/ 002-7628940-9665649, accessed June 8, 2004; "Apple Profit Surges 95 Percent on iPod Sales," *Yahoo! News,* news.yahoo.com/s/afp/20060118/bs_afp/ uscompanyearningsit_060118225009, accessed January 18, 2005; "Apple's IPod Success Isn't Sweet Music for Record Company Sales," Bloomberg.com, quote.bloomberg.com/apps/news?pid=nifea&&sid=aHP5Ko1pozM0, accessed November 2, 2005; Peter Burrows, "How Apple Could Mess Up Again," *BusinessWeek* online, yahoo.businessweek.com/technology/content/jan2006/tc20060109_432937.htm, accessed January 9, 2006; www.apple.com/iphone, accessed June 7, 2007; news.com.com/NikeiPod+raises+RFID+privacy+concerns/2100-1029_3-6143606.html, accessed June 7, 2007.

2. Jon Surmacz, "By the Numbers" *CIO Magazine,* www.cio.com, accessed October 2004.

3. IT Centrix, "Optimizing the Business Value of Information Technology", http://www.unisys.com/products/mainframes/insights/insights_compendium, accessed December 10, 2004.

4. *Glossary of Business Terms,* www.powerhomebiz.com/Glossary/glossary-A.htm, accessed December 15, 2003; *Financial Times,* "Mastering Management," www.ft.com/pp/mfm, accessed December 15, 2003; *Glossary of Financial Terms,* www.nytimes.com/library/financial/glossary/bfglosa.htm, accessed December 15, 2003; *Business Dictionary,* www.glossarist.com/glossaries/business/, accessed December 15, 2003; *Glossary of Business Terms,* www.smallbiz.nsw.gov.au/smallbusiness/, accessed December 15, 2003.

5. Ibid.

6. Booze, Allen, Hamilton, *Information Sharing* (New York: HarperCollins, 2006).

7. www.boozallen.com/publications/article/659327, accessed November, 10, 2003.

8. Thomas, Friedman, www.thomaslfriedman.com, accessed September 14, 2005.

9. Michael E. Porter, Competitive Strategy: Techniques for Analyzing Industries and Competitors.

10. Gabriel Kahn and Cris Prystay, "'Charge It' Your Cellphone Tells Your Bank," *The Wall Street Journal,* August 13, 2003.

11. Oracle Customer Study, "Trek Standardizes Worldwide Operations for Boost in Decision-Making Power Business Driver: Standardization for Cost and Process Efficiency," www.oracle.com/customers/snapshots/trek, accessed October 11, 2003; "Trek Standardizes Worldwide Operations on J. D. Edwards," www.jdedwards.com, accessed November 15, 2003.

12. Christopher Koch, "The ABC's of Supply Chain Management," www.cio.com, accessed October 12, 2003; Ben Worthen, "ABC: An Introduction to SCM," www.cio.com/article/40940/ABC_An_Introduction_to_Supply_Chain_Management, accessed May 30, 2007.

13. *CRM Enterprise,* www.cio.com.au/index.php/secid;2, *CIO Magazine,* accessed May 28, 2007; "Customer Success Stories – Charles Schwab," www.siebel.com, accessed November 12, 2003.

14. "Kaiser's Diabetic Initiative," www.businessweek.com, accessed November 15, 2003.

15. "Integrated Solutions—The ABCs of CRM," www.integratedsolutionsmag.com, accessed November 12, 2003.

16. Maureen Weicher, "Business Process Reengineering: Analysis and Recommendation," www.netlib.com, accessed February 12, 2005.

17. Michael Hammer and James Champy, *Reengineering the Corporation* (New York: HarperCollins, 2001).

18. Ibid.

19. Bruce Caldwell, "Missteps, Miscues—Business Reengineering Failures," *InformationWeek,* June 20, 1994, p. 50.

20. Ibid.

21. Ibid.

22. Thomas H. Davenport, "Will Participative Makeovers of Business Processes Succeed Where Reengineering Failed?" *Planning Review,* January 1995, p. 24.

23. Saul Berman, "Strategic Direction: Don't Reengineer Without It; Scanning the Horizon for Turbulence, Planning Review," November 1994, p. 18, ERP White Paper, www.bitpipe.com/rlist/term/ERP.html, accessed July 3, 2007.

24. Exact Software, ERP-II, www.exact.com, accessed April 17, 2007.

25. "Customer Success Stories—Saab," www.siebel.com, accessed November 12, 2005.

26. The Business World According to Peter Drucker, www.peter-drucker.com, accessed May 25, 2007.

27. Ken Blanchard, "Effectiveness vs. Efficiency," *Wachovia Small Business,* www.wachovia.com, accessed October 2003.

28. Barbara Ettorre, "Reengineering Tales from the Front," *Management Review,* January 1995, p. 13.

29. Dave Lindorff, "General Electric and Real Time," www.cioinsight.com/article2/0,3959,686147,00.asp, accessed October 2003.

30. Cisco Press, www.ciscopress.com/index.asp?rl=1, accessed October 2003.

31. United Nations Division for Public Economics and Public Administration, www.un.com, accessed November 10, 2003.

32. Google Analytics, www.google.com/analytics, accessed July 13, 2007.

33. Ibid.

34. Supply Chain Metrics.com, www.supplychainmetric.com/, accessed June 12, 2007.

35. Robert, Kaplan and David Norton, *The BSC: Translating Strategy into Action* (Vintage Books 1998); The Balanced Scorecard Institute, www.balancedscorecard.org/, accessed May 15, 2007.

36. Ibid.

37. Ibid.

38. John Heilmann, "What's Friendster Selling?" *Business 2.0,* March 2004, p. 46.

39. "IT Master of the Senate," *CIO Magazine online,* www.cio.com/archive/050104/tl_govt.html, accessed May 1, 2004.

40. Ibid.

41. "What Concerns CIOs the Most?" www.cio.com, accessed November 17, 2003.

42. *eBay Financial News,* Earnings and Dividend Release, January 15, 2002.

43. "Integrating Information at Children's Hospital," *KMWorld,* www.kmworld.com/Articles/ReadArticle.aspx?ArticleID=10253, accessed June 1, 2005.

44. Michael Schrage, "Build the Business Case," *CIO Magazine* online, www.cio.com, accessed November 17, 2003.

45. "Enron, Who's Accountable?" www.time.com/time/business/article/0,8599,193520,00.html, accessed June 7, 2005.

46. Privacy.org, www.privacy.org/, accessed July 3, 2004.

47. Sharon Gaudin, "Smokers Open the Door for Hackers," www.informationweek.com/news/articleID=9875367, accessed August 23, 2007.

48. Scott Berianato, "Take the Pledge," *CIO Magazine* online, www.cio.com, accessed November 17, 2003.

49. www.hipaa.org, accessed June 14, 2007; "Health Information Management," www.gartner.com, accessed November 16, 2003.

50. Ibid.

51. "2005 CSI/FBI Computer Crime and Security Survey," www.usdoj.gov/criminal/cybercrime/FBI2005.pdf, accessed February 2005.

52. Ibid.

53. www.norcrossgroup.com/casestudies.html, accessed October 2004.

54. Kim Girard, "How Levi's Got Its Jeans into Wal-Mart," *CIO Magazine*, July 15, 2003.

55. "Top 10 Bad Business Decisions," www.business20.com, accessed April 16, 2007.

56. Ibid.

57. "The New Real Minority Report," www.dailygalaxy.com/my_weblog/2007/08/project-hostile.html, accessed June 13, 2003.

58. *Nicomachean Ethics: Aristotle,* with an introduction by Hye-Kyung Kim, translated by F.H. Peters (Oxford, 1893) (Barnes & Noble, 2004).

59. Bittorrent, http://www.bittorrent.com/, accessed June 15, 2004.

Unit Two

1. Daniel Pink, "The Book Stops Here," *Wired,* March 2005, pp.125–39; "Tapping the World's Brainpower with Wiki," *BusinessWeek,* October 11, 2004, p. 132; www.wikipedia.com, accessed November 2005; Robert Hoff, "Something Wiki This Way Comes," *BusinessWeek* online, accessed June 7, 2004; www.wikipedia.org, accessed May, 22, 2007.

2. "Google Reveals High-Profile Users of Data Search Machine," Reuters News Service, August 13, 2003, www.chron.com, accessed September 3, 2003.

3. Mitch Betts, "Unexpected Insights," *ComputerWorld,* April 14, 2003, www.computerworld.com, accessed September 4, 2003.

4. Ibid.

5. "Data Mining: What General Managers Need to Know," *Harvard Management Update,* October 1999.

6. Barbara DePompa Reimers, "Too Much of a Good Thing," *ComputerWorld,* www.computerworld.com, April 14, 2003.

7. Ibid.

8. "MSI Business Solutions Case Study: Westpac Financial Services," www.MSI.com, accessed August 4, 2003.

9. "Why Data Quality," www.trilliumsoft.com, accessed October 3, 2003.

10. Ibid.

11. "Alaska Fish and Game Yields a Bounty of High-Quality Information to Manage Natural Resources," www.oracle.com, accessed September 20, 2003.

12. Webopedia.com, www.webopedia.comTERM/d/database.html, accessed May 15, 2007; Wikipedia, The Free Encyclopedia, en.wikipedia.org/wiki/Wiki, accessed May 22, 2007; Oracle Database, www.oracle.com/database/index.html, accessed May 17, 2007.

13. Ibid.

14. Ibid.

15. Chicago Police Department, gis.chicagopolice.org/, accessed June 23, 2004.

16. "Ford's Vision," donate.pewclimate.org/docUploads/Ford.pdf, accessed June 18, 2003.

17. Webopedia.com, www.webopedia.comTERM/d/database.html, accessed May 15, 2007; Wikipedia, The Free Encyclopedia, en.wikipedia.org/wiki/Wiki, accessed May 22, 2007; Oracle Database, www.oracle.com/database/index.html, accessed May 17, 2007.

18. Ibid; www.sitepoint.com/article/publishing-mysql-data-web, accessed May 16, 2007.

19. Ibid.

20. "Oracle Success Stories," www.oracle.com/successstories/army, accessed May 15, 2003.

21. "Massachusetts Laws About Identity Theft," www.lawlib.state.ma.us/identity.html, accessed June 10, 2007.

22. Kathleen Melymuka, "Premier 100: Turning the Tables at Applebee's," *ComputerWorld,* www.computerworld.com, accessed February 24, 2003.

23. Webopedia.com, www.webopedia.comTERM/d/database.html, accessed May 15, 2007; Wikipedia, The Free Encyclopedia, en.wikipedia.org/wiki/Wiki, accessed May 22, 2007; Oracle Database, www.oracle.com/database/index.html, accessed May 17, 2007; www.sitepoint.com/article/publishing-mysql-data-web, accessed May 16, 2007.

24. Ibid.

25. Ibid.

26. Alice LaPante, "Big Things Come in Smaller Packages," *ComputerWorld,* June 24, 1996, pp. DW/6–7.

27. Julia Kiling, "OLAP Gains Fans among Data-Hungry Firms," *ComputerWorld,* January 8, 2001, p. 54.

28. Nikhil Hutheesing, "Surfing with Sega," *Forbes,* November 4, 2002, p. 58.

29. Tommy Perterson, "Data Cleansing," *ComputerWorld,* www.computerworld.com, accessed February 10, 2003.

30. "Dr Pepper/Seven Up, Inc.," www.cognos.com, accessed September 10, 2003.

31. "Sun Tuz on the Art of War," www.chinapage.com/sunzi-e.html, accessed September 15, 2007.

32. Webopedia.com, www.webopedia.comTERM/d/database.html, accessed May 15, 2007; Oracle Database, www.oracle.com/database/index.html, accessed May 17, 2007; www.sitepoint.com/article/publishing-mysql-data-web, accessed May 16, 2007.

33. Julie Schlosser, "Looking for Intelligence in Ice Cream," Fortune, March 17, 2003; Leslie Goff, "Summertime Heats Up IT at Ben & Jerry's," Computer World, July, 2001; Customer Success Stories, www.cognos.com, accessed January 2005.

34. Meridith Levinson, "Harrah's Knows What You Did Last Night," May 2001; "Harrah's Entertainment Wins TDWI's 2000 DW Award," www.hpcwire.com, accessed October 10, 2003; Gary Loveman, "Diamonds in the Data Mine," *Harvard Business Review,* May 2003, p. 109; "NCR—Harrah's Entertainment, Inc.," www.ncr.com, accessed October 12, 2003; "Cognos and Harrah's Entertainment Win Prestigious Data Warehousing Award," www.cognos.com, accessed October 14, 2003; Kim Nash, "Casinos Hit Jackpot with Customer Data," www.cnn.com, accessed October 14, 2003; Michael S. Malone, "IPO Fever," Wired, March 2004.

35. "Cyber Bomb—Search Tampering," *BusinessWeek,* March 1, 2004; "Google Knows Where You Are," *BusinessWeek,* February 2, 2004 www.google.com, accessed September 13, 2003.

Unit Three

1. Secondlife.com, accessed May, 28, 2007; "Linden Lab to Open Source Second Life Software," Linden Lab (January 8, 2007), accessed May 22, 2007; secondlife.com/community/land-islands.php; Irene Sege; "Leading a double life," *The Boston Globe* 25, October 2006; accessed June, 22, 2007; James Harkin, "Get a (second) life," *Financial Times,* November 2006, accessed June 15, 2007.

2. "1,000 Executives Best Skillset," *The Wall Street Journal,* July 15, 2003.

3. "The Visionary Elite," *Business 2.0,* December 2003, pp. S1–S5.

4. "Boston Coach Aligns Service with Customer Demand in Real Time," www-1.ibm.com/services/us/index.wss, accessed November 4, 2003.

5. "Industry Facts and Statistics," Insurance Information Institute, www.iii.org, accessed December 2005.

6. Neil Raden, "Data, Data Everywhere," DSSResources.com, February 16, 2003.

7. Technology terms, www.techterms.com/, accessed May 3, 2003; Whatis.com, whatis.techtarget.com, accessed May 4, 2003 Webopedia, www.webopedia.com, accessed May 14, 2003.

8. "The Corporate Portal Market 2005," BEA White Paper, www.bea.com, January 2005.

9. "Verizon Executives," newscenter.verizon.com/leadership/shaygan-kheradpir.html, accessed may 17, 2003;

Christopher Koch, "How Verizon Flies by Wire," *CIO Magazine,* November 1, 2004; and "Sleepless in Manhattan," CIO.com, cio.de/news/cio_worldnews/809030/index7.html, accessed May 4, 2005.

10. Beth Bacheldor, "Steady Supply," *InformationWeek,* November 24, 2003, www.informationweek.com, accessed June 6, 2003.

11. Neil McManus, "Robots at Your Service," *Wired,* January 2003, p. O59.

12. "Put Better, Faster Decision-Making in Your Sights," www.teradata.com, accessed July 7, 2003; Neural Network Examples and Definitions, ece-www.colorado.edu/ ~ecen4831/lectures/NNdemo.html, accessed June 24, 2007; S. Begley, "Software au Natural," *Newsweek,* May 8, 2005; McManus, "Robots at Your Service"; Santa Fe Institute, www.dis.anl.gov/abms/, accessed June 24, 2007; Michael A. Arbib, (Ed.) (1995). *The Handbook of Brain Theory and Neural Networks;* L. Biacino and G. Gerla, 2002, "Fuzzy logic, continuity and effectiveness," *Archive for Mathematical Logic.*

13. Ibid.

14. Ibid.

15. Ibid.

16. Ibid.

17. "Smart Tools," *BusinessWeek,* March 24, 2003.

18. S. Begley, "Software au Natural," *Newsweek,* May 8, 2005.

19. "Maytag—Washing Away Maintenance," www.sas.com, accessed October 3, 2003.

20. Ibid.

21. "How Creamy? How Crunchy?" www.sas.com, accessed October 3, 2003.

22. "Forecasting Chocolate," www.sas.com, accessed October 3, 2003.

23. "Darpa Grand Challenge," www.darpa.mil/grandchallenge/, accessed September 1, 2005.

24. John Hagerty, "How Best to Measure Our Supply Chain," www.AMRresearch.com, March 3, 2005.

25. "Finding the Best Buy," www.oracle.com, accessed April 4, 2003.

26. "Smart Tools," *BusinessWeek,* March 24, 2003.

27. Hagerty, "How Best to Measure Our Supply Chain."

28. Andrew Binstock, "Virtual Enterprise Comes of Age," *InformationWeek,* November 6, 2004.

29. "Bullwhips and Beer: Why Supply Chain Management Is So Difficult" forio.com/resources/bullwhips-and-beer/, accessed June 10, 2003.

30. Ibid.

31. Mitch Betts, "Kinks in the Chain," *ComputerWorld,* December 17, 2005.

32. Ibid.

33. Walid Mougayar, "Old Dogs Learn New Tricks," *Business 2.0,* October 2000, www.Business2.com, accessed June 14, 2003.

34. Ibid.

35. "Creating a Value Network," *Wired,* September 2003, p. S13.

36. www.dell.com, accessed September, 15, 2003.

37. Mitch Betts, "Kinks in the Chain," *ComputerWorld,* December 17, 2005.

38. "The e-Biz Surprise," *BusinessWeek,* May 12, 2003, pp. 60–65.

39. Keving Kelleher, "BudNet: 66,207,896 Bottles of Beer on the Wall," *Business 2.0,* February 2004.

40. "1800 flowers.com," *Business 2.0,* February 2004.

41. "The 'New' New York Times," *Business 2.0,* January 2004.

42. "New York Knicks—Success," www.jdedwards.com, accessed January 15, 2004.

43. www.usps.com, accessed June 17, 2004.

44. "Barclays, Giving Voice to Customer-Centricity," crm.insightexec.com, accessed July 15, 2007.

45. www.usps.com, accessed June 17, 2004.

46. "50 People Who Matter Now," money.cnn.com/magazines/business2/peoplewhomatter/, *Business 2.0,* accessed July 16, 2007.

47. "Customer Success—Brother," www.sap.com, accessed January 12, 2004.

48. "Finding Value in the Real-Time Enterprise," *Business 2.0,* November 2003, pp. S1–S5.

49. "Customer Success—PNC Retail Bank," www.siebel.com, accessed May 5, 2003.

50. "Creating a Value Network," *Wired,* September 2003, p. S13; Fred Hapgood, "Smart Decisions," *CIO Magazine,* www.cio.com, August 15, 2001.

51. "Customer First Awards," *Fast Company,* May, 2005.

52. "Customer Success—UPS," www.sap.com, accessed April 5, 2003.

53. Ibid.

54. Exact Software, "ERP-II: Making ERP Deliver on Its Promise to the Enterprise," jobfunctions.bnet.com/whitepaper.aspx?docid=144338, accessed July 25, 2007.

55. Ibid.

56. Ibid.

57. "Del Monte Organic RFID," *Business Week,* March 15, 2007.

58. "ERP Success," www.sap.com, accessed March 15, 2007.

59. "Customer Success—Cisco," www.sap.com, accessed April 5, 2003.

60. "REI Pegs Growth on Effective Multi-channel Strategy," *Internet Retailer,* www.internetretailer.com, accessed February 17, 2005; Alison Overholt, "Smart Strategies: Putting Ideas to Work," *Fast Company,* April 2004, p. 63.

61. "REI Pegs Growth on Effective Multi-channel Strategy," *Internet Retailer,* www.internetretailer.com, accessed February 17, 2005; Alison Overholt, "Smart Strategies: Putting Ideas to Work," *Fast Company,* April 2004, p. 63.

62. Bill Breen, "Living in Dell Time," *Fast Company,* November 2004, p. 86.

63. www.investor.harley-davidson.com, accessed October 10, 2003; Bruce Caldwell, "Harley-Davidson Revs up IT Horsepower," Internetweek.com, December 7, 2000; "Computerworld 100 Best Places to Work in IT 2003," *Computerworld,* June 9, 2003, pp. 36–48; Leroy Zimdars, "Supply Chain Innovation at Harley-Davidson: An Interview with Leroy Zimdars," April 15, 2000; "Customer Trust: Reviving Loyalty in a Challenging Economy," Pivotal Webcast, September 19, 2002; "Harley-Davidson Announces Go-Live: Continues to Expand Use of Manugistics Supplier Relationship Management Solutions," www.manugistics.com, May 7, 2002; Roger Villareal, "Docent Enterprise Increases Technician and Dealer Knowledge and Skills to Maximize Sales Results and Customer Service," www.docent.com, August 13, 2002.

64. "ERP Success," www.sap.com, accessed April 5, 2003.

65. www.netflix.com, accessed May 23, 2007.

66. www.wal-mart.com, accessed May 26, 2007.

67. www.bae.com, accessed May 24, 2007.

68. www.secondlife.com, accessed May 25, 2007.

Unit Four

1. Robert Hof, "Pierre M. Omidyar: The Web for the People," *BusinessWeek,* December 6, 2004; Margaret Kane, "eBay picks up PayPal for 1.5 Billion," *Cnet News,* news.com.com, July 8, 2002; John Blau, "Are eBay and Skype a Good Fit?" *Infoworld,* www.inforworld.com, September 8, 2005; "Better Ask: IRS May Consider eBay Sales as Income," *USA Today,* March 27, 2005.

2. Cisco Press, www.ciscopress.com, accessed March 23, 2005.

3. Adam Lashinsky, "Kodak's Developing Situation," *Fortune,* January 20, 2003, p. 176.

4. www.wired.com, accessed November 15, 2003.

5. Adam Lashinsky, "The Disrupters," *Fortune,* August 11, 2003, pp. 62–65.

6. Clayton Christensen, *The Innovator's Dilemma* (Boston: Harvard Business School, 1997).

7. Internet World Statistics, www.internetworldstats.com, accessed January 2007.

8. "Internet Pioneers," www.ibiblio.org/pioneers/andreesen.html, accessed June 2004.

9. Ibid.

10. Gunjan Bagla, "Bringing IT to Rural India One Village at a Time," *CIO Magazine,* March 1, 2005.

11. Tim O'Reilly, "What Is Web 2.0: Design Patterns and Business Models for the Next Generation of Software," 9/30/2005, www.oreillynet.com/pub/a/oreilly/tim/news/2005/09/30/what-is-web-20.html, accessed June 25, 2007; "Web 2.0 For CIOs," www.cio.com/article/16807, *CIO Magazine,* accessed June 24, 2007.

12. Ibid.

13. Ibid.

14. Ibid.

15. *The Complete Web 2.0 Directory,* www.go2web20.net/, accessed June 24, 2007.

16. "Web 2.0 for CIOs," www.cio.com/article/16807, *CIO Magazine,* accessed June 24, 2007.

17. Jim Rapoza, "First Movers That Flopped," etech.eweek.com/slideshow/index.php?directory=first_movers, accessed June 26, 2007.

18. "A Site Stickier than a Barroom Floor," *Business 2.0,* June 2005, p. 741.

19. ww.emarketer.com, accessed January 2006.

20. www.ebags.com, accessed June 21, 2007.

21. Heather Harreld, "Lemon Aid," *CIO Magazine,* July 1, 2000.

22. Internet World Statistics, www.internetworldstats.com.

23. Anne Zelenka , "The Hype Machine, Best Mashup of Mashup Camp 3," gigaom.com/2007/01/18/the-hype-machine-best-mashup-of-mashup-camp-3/, accessed june 14, 2007.

24. Webmashup.com, www.webmashup.com/ Insert New 25, accessed June 14, 2007.

25. Ibid.

26. "Amazon Finds Profits in Outsourcing," *CIO Magazine,* October 15, 2002, www.cio.com/archive/101502/tl_ec.html, accessed November 14, 2003.

27. "D-FW Defense Contractors Show Mixed Fortunes since September 11," www.bizjournals.com/ dallas/stories/2002/09/09/focus2.htm, accessed June 8, 2004; Steve Konicki,

"Collaboration Is Cornerstone of $19B Defense Contract," www.business2.com/content/ magazine/indepth/ 2000/07/11/17966, accessed June 8, 2004.

28. www.lockheedmartin.com, accessed April 23, 2003.

29. "Knowledge Management Research Center," *CIO Magazine,* www.cio.com/research/knowledge, December 2005; Technology terms, www.techterms.com/, accessed May 3, 2003; Whatis.com, whatis.techtarget.com, accessed May 4, 2003; Webopedia, www.webopedia.com, accessed May 14, 2003.

30. Ibid.

31. Ibid.

32. Thomas Claburn, "Law Professor Predicts Wikipedia's Demise," www.informationweek.com/showArticle.jhtml;jse ssionid=2ZYHJY4LGVHBOQSNDLRSKHSCJUNN2JVN?arti cleID=196601766&queryText=wikipedia, accessed June 8, 2007.

33. Ibid.

34. "Toyota's One-Stop Information Shop," www.istart.co.nz/ index/HM20/PC0/PV21873/EX236/ CS25653, accessed June 8, 2004.

35. "Knowledge Management Research Center," *CIO Magazine,* www.cio.com/research/knowledge, December 2005; Technology terms, www.techterms.com/, accessed May 3, 2003; Whatis.com, whatis.techtarget.com, accessed May 4, 2003; Webopedia, www.webopedia.com, accessed May 14, 2003.

36. Ibid.

37. Megan Santosus, "In The Know," *CIO Magazine,* January 2006.

38. Ibid.

39. "The 21st Century Meeting," February 27, 2007, www.businessweek.com/magazine/content/07_09/b4023059. htm, accessed June 2, 2007.

40. Video Conference, en.wikipedia.org/wiki/Video_conference, accessed June 1, 2007.

41. Ibid.

42. "Toyota's One-Stop Information Shop," www.istart.co.nz/ index/HM20/PC0/PV21873/EX236/ CS25653, accessed June 8, 2004.

43. "The 21st Century Meeting," February 27, 2007, www. businessweek.com/magazine/content/07_09/b4023059.htm, accessed June 2, 2007; Video Conference, en.wikipedia.org/ wiki/Video_conference, accessed June 1, 2007; Technology terms, www.techterms.com/, accessed May 3, 2003; Whatis.com, whatis.techtarget.com, accessed May 4, 2003; Webopedia, www.webopedia.com, accessed May 14, 2003.

44. Ibid.

45. Ibid.

46. Ibid.

47. Ibid.

48. "HP Unveils Halo Collaboration Studio," www.hp.com, December 12, 2005.

49. Chris Murphy, "RIM Settles BlackBerry Suit," *Information Week,* March 6, 2006; "Handheld 2006—2010 Forecast and Analysis," IDC, www.idc.com, accessed March 2006.

50. www.fedex.com, accessed March 13, 2006.

51. Technology terms, www.techterms.com/, accessed May 3, 2003; Whatis.com, whatis.techtarget.com, accessed May 4, 2003; Webopedia, www.webopedia.com, accessed May 14, 2003.

52. Ibid.

53. Ibid.

54. "The I-Tech Virtual keyboard," www.laser-keyboard.com, accessed September 2005.

55. Technology terms, www.techterms.com/, accessed May 3, 2003; Whatis.com, whatis.techtarget.com, accessed May 4, 2003; Webopedia, www.webopedia.com, accessed May 14, 2003.

56. Ibid.

57. Ibid.

58. "Airbus Working with LogicaCMG on Tracking," www.usingrfid.com, accessed August 16, 2004.

59. Technology terms, www.techterms.com/, accessed May 3, 2003; Whatis.com, whatis.techtarget.com, accessed May 4, 2003.

60. "Howard Stern Making Jump to Satellite Radio,

61. Ibid. www.msnbc.msn.com, October 6, 2004.

62. "SiRF Technology and NEC Electronics Partner," www.sirf .com, accessed February 2002.

63. "GM Owners Are Finding an Easy and Convenient Way to Manage Car Care Through E-Mail," www.cnnmoney.com, accessed April 10, 2006.

64. Joe Wilcox, "Sit and Surf," Cnet news, news.com.com, accessed May 2, 2003.

65. Tiffany Kary, "Palm Plugs and Premiers," Cnet news, news. com.com, March 47, 2005.

66. Galen Gruman, "UPS vs. FedEx: Head-to-Head on Wireless," *CIO Magazine,* www.cio.com, accessed June 1, 2004.

67. Laurie Sullivan, "Collaboration Can Better Highway Safety," *Information Week,* August 9, 2004.

68. Beth Bacheldor, "From Scratch: Amazon Keeps Moving," *Information Week,* March 5, 2004; Gary Wolf, "The Great Library of Amazonia," *Wired,* October 23, 2003; "Amazon Company Information," *Forbes,* www.forbes.com, September 2005; Rob Hof, "Amazon's Newest Product: Storage," *BusinessWeek,* March 13, 2006.

69. "10 Tips for Wireless Home Security," compnetworking. about.com/od/wirelesssecurity/tp/wifisecurity.htm, accessed September 15, 2006.

70. "GPS Innovation give Weather Bots a New Ride", www.cio.com/article/108500/GPS, accessed September 15, 2007.

71. Evolution of Wireless Networks, www.cisco.com, accessed September 15, 2007.

72. www.wikipedia.org, accessed September 18, 2007

73. Whitfield Diffie, "Sun's Diffie AT&T Cyber Security Conference," accessed September 2, 2007.

Unit Five

1. Timothy Mullaney and Arlene Weintraub, "The Digital Hospital," *BusinessWeek,* March 28, 2005; Michelle Delio, "How Secure Is Digital Hospital," *Wired,* March 28, 2001.

2. www.businessweek.com, accessed November 1, 2005.

3. "Software Costs," *CIO Magazine,* www.cio.com, accessed December 5, 2003.

4. Ibid.

5. Ibid.

6. "Defective Software Costs," National Institute of Standards and Technology (NIST), June 2002.

7. Ibid.

8. Technology terms, www.techterms.com/, accessed May 3, 2003; Whatis.com, whatis.techtarget.com, accessed May 4, 2003; Webopedia, www.webopedia.com, accessed May 14, 2003.

9. Ibid.

10. "Customer Success Story—PHH," www.informatica.com, accessed December 12, 2003.

11. "Building Events," www.microsoft.com, accessed November 15, 2003.

12. Agile Alliance Manifesto, www.agile.com, accessed November 1, 2003.

13. www.gartner.com, accessed November 3, 2003.

14. "Software Metrics," *CIO Magazine,* www.cio.com, accessed December 2, 2003.

15. "Building Software That Works," www.compaq.com, accessed November 14, 2003.

16. "Software Metrics," *CIO Magazine,* www.cio.com, accessed December 2, 2003.

17. www.agile.com, accessed November 10, 2003.

18. "Customer Success—Horizon," www.businessengine.com, accessed October 15, 2003.

19. "Top Reasons Why IT Projects Fail," *InformationWeek,* www.infoweek.com, accessed November 5, 2003.

20. Ibid.

21. Ibid.

22. Christopher Null, "How Netflix Is Fixing Hollywood," *Business 2.0,* July 2003, pp. 31–33.

23. "Merrill Lynch and Thomson Financial to Develop Wealth Management Workstation," www.advisorpage.com/modules.php?name= News&file=print&sid=666, accessed June 8, 2004.

24. Charles Pelton, "How to Solve the IT Labor Shortage Problem," www.informationweek.com/author/eyeonit15.htm, accessed June 8, 2004.

25. "Future Three Partners with Ideal Technology Solutions, U.S. for Total Automotive Network Exchange (ANX) Capability," www.itsusnow.com/news_future3.htm, accessed June 8, 2004.

26. Technology terms, www.techterms.com/, accessed May 3, 2003; Whatis.com, whatis.techtarget.com, accessed May 4, 2003; Webopedia, www.webopedia.com, accessed May 14, 2003.

27. "Sneaker Net," *CIO Magazine,* www.cio.com/archive/webbusiness/080199_nike.html, accessed June 8, 2004.

28. Art Jahnke, "Kodak Stays in the Digital Picture," www.cnn.com/TECH/computing/9908/06/ kodak.ent.idg/, accessed June 8, 2004.

29. Michael Kanellos, "IDC: PC market on the Comeback Trail," news.com.com/2100-1001-976295. html?part=dtx&tag=ntop, accessed June 8, 2004.

30. Technology terms, www.techterms.com/, accessed May 3, 2003; Whatis.com, whatis.techtarget.com, accessed May 4, 2003; Webopedia, www.webopedia.com, accessed May 14, 2003.

31. Stephanie Overby, "In or Out?" *CIO Magazine,* www.cio.com/archive/081503/sourcing.html, accessed June 8, 2004.

32. Jaikumar Vijayan, "Companies Expected to Boost Offshore Outsourcing," www.computerworld.com/managementtopics/outsourcing/story/0,10801,78583,00.html, accessed June 8, 2004.

33. Geoffrey James, "The Next Delivery? Computer Repair," CNNMoney.com, July 1, 2004.

34. Technology terms, www.techterms.com/, accessed May 3, 2003; Whatis.com, whatis.techtarget.com, accessed May 4, 2003; Webopedia, www.webopedia.com, accessed May 14, 2003.

35. Adam Lashinsky, "The Disrupters," *Fortune,* August 11, 2003, pp. 62–65.

36. www.wired.com, accessed October 15, 2003.

37. "A New View," *Business 2.0,* November 10, 2003, pp. S1–S5.

38. Technology terms, www.techterms.com/, accessed May 3, 2003; Whatis.com, whatis.techtarget.com, accessed May 4, 2003; Webopedia, www.webopedia.com, accessed May 14, 2003.

39. Tom Schultz, "PBS: A Clearer Picture," *Business 2.0,* January 2003.

40. Julia Scheeres, "Three R's: Reading, Writing, and RFID," *Wired,* October 14, 2003; John Blau, "German Researchers Move Forward on Plastic RFID," *Computer World,* January 13, 2005.

41. Kevin Kelleher, "The Wired 40," *Wired,* www.wired.com, accessed March 3, 2004; "The Web Smart 50," *BusinessWeek,* www.businessweek.com, accessed March 3, 2004.

Plug-In B1

1. Julie Schlosser, "Toys 'R'Us Braces for a Holiday Battle," *Money,* December 22, 2003.

2. *Glossary of Business Terms,* www.powerhomebiz.com/Glossary/glossary-A.htm, accessed December 15, 2003; *Financial Times,* "Mastering Management," www.ft.com/pp/mfm, accessed December 15, 2003; *Glossary of Financial Terms,* www.nytimes.com/library/financial/glossary/bfglosa.htm, accessed December 15, 2003; *Business Dictionary,* www.glossarist.com/glossaries/business/, accessed December 15, 2003; *Glossary of Business Terms,* www.smallbiz.nsw.gov.au/smallbusiness/, accessed December 15, 2003.

3. Ibid.

4. Ibid.

5. Alison Overholdt, "The Housewife Who Got Up Off the Couch," *Fast Company,* September 2004, p. 94.

6. *Glossary of Business Terms,* www.powerhomebiz.com/Glossary/glossary-A.htm, accessed December 15, 2003; *Financial Times,* "Mastering Management," www.ft.com/pp/mfm, accessed December 15, 2003; *Glossary of Financial Terms,* www.nytimes.com/library/financial/glossary/bfglosa.htm, accessed December 15, 2003; *Business Dictionary,* www.glossarist.com/glossaries/business/, accessed December 15, 2003; *Glossary of Business Terms,* www.smallbiz.nsw.gov.au/smallbusiness/, accessed December 15, 2003.

7. Ibid.

8. Ibid.

9. Ibid.

10. Ibid.

11. Ibid.

12. Adrian Danescu, "Save $55,000," *CIO Magazine,* December 15, 2004, p. 70.

13. *Glossary of Business Terms,* www.powerhomebiz.com/Glossary/glossary-A.htm, accessed December 15, 2003;

Financial Times, "Mastering Management," www.ft.com/pp/mfm, accessed December 15, 2003; *Glossary of Financial Terms,* www.nytimes.com/library/financial/glossary/bfglosa.htm, accessed December 15, 2003; *Business Dictionary,* www.glossarist.com/glossaries/business/, accessed December 15, 2003; *Glossary of Business Terms,* www.smallbiz.nsw.gov.au/smallbusiness/, accessed December 15, 2003.

14. Ibid.

15. Ibid.

16. "Can the Nordstroms Find the Right Style?" *BusinessWeek,* July 30, 2001.

17. Geoff Keighley, "Will Sony's PSP Become the iPod of Gaming Devices?" *Business 2.0,* May 2004, p. 29.

18. *Glossary of Business Terms,* www.powerhomebiz.com/Glossary/glossary-A.htm, accessed December 15, 2003 *Financial Times,* "Mastering Management," www.ft.com/pp/mfm, accessed December 15, 2003; *Glossary of Financial Terms,* www.nytimes.com/library/financial/glossary/bfglosa.htm, accessed December 15, 2003; *Business Dictionary,* www.glossarist.com/glossaries/business/, accessed December 15, 2003; *Glossary of Business Terms,* www.smallbiz.nsw.gov.au/smallbusiness/, accessed December 15, 2003.

19. Ibid.

20. "From the Bottom Up," *Fast Company,* June 2004, p. 54.

21. Glossary of Business Terms, www.powerhomebiz.com/Glossary/glossary-A.htm, accessed December 15, 2003; *Financial Times,* "Mastering Management," www.ft.com/pp/mfm, accessed December 15, 2003; *Glossary of Financial Terms,* www.nytimes.com/library/financial/glossary/bfglosa.htm, accessed December 15, 2003; *Business Dictionary,* www.glossarist.com/glossaries/business/, accessed December 15, 2003; *Glossary of Business Terms,* www.smallbiz.nsw.gov.au/smallbusiness/, accessed December 15, 2003.

22. Ibid.

23. "Harley-Davidson: Ride Your Heritage," *Fast Company,* August 2004, p. 44. "Ford on Top," *Fast Company,* June 2004, p. 54.

24. Michael Hammer, *Beyond Reengineering: How the Process-Centered Organization Is Changing Our Work and Our Lives* (New York: HarperCollin, 1997).

25. Progressive Insurance, *BusinessWeek,* March 13, 2004.

26. "Toy Wars," www.pbs.org, accessed December 23, 2003.

27. "Innovative Managers," *BusinessWeek,* April 24, 2005.

Plug-In B2

1. "What Is BPR?" searchcio.techtarget.com/sDefinition/0,sid182_gci536451,00.html, accessed October 10, 2005; BPR Online, www.prosci.com/mod1.htm, accessed October 10, 2005; "Business Process Reengineering Six Sigma," www.isixsigma.com/me/bpr/, accessed October 10, 2005; SmartDraw.com, www.smartdraw.com/, accessed October 11, 2005.

2. Ibid.

3. Ibid.

4. Ibid.

5. Michael Hammer, *Beyond Reengineering: How the Process-Centered Organization Is Changing Our Work and Our Lives* (New York: HarperCollin, 1996).

6. Richard Chang, "Process Reengineering in Action: A Practical Guide to Achieving Breakthrough Results (Quality Improvement Series)," 1996; H. James Harrington, *Business Process Improvement Workbook: Documentation, Analysis, Design, and Management of Business Process Improvement* (New York: McGraw-Hill, 1997); Hammer, *Beyond Reengineering;* Michael Hammer and James Champy, "Reengineering the Corporation: A Manifest for Business Revolution," 1993; *Government Business Process Reengineering (BPR) Readiness Assessment Guide,* General Services Administration (GSA), 1996.

7. Ibid.

8. Ibid.

9. Ibid.

10. Ibid.

11. Ibid.

12. H. James Harrington, *Business Process Improvement: The Breakthrough Strategy for Total Quality, Productivity, and Competitiveness* (New York: McGraw-Hill, 1991); Hammer, *Beyond Reengineering.*

13. "What Is BPR?" SmartDraw.com, www.smartdraw.com/, accessed October 11, 2005; BPR Online, www.prosci.com/mod1.htm, accessed October 10, 2005; "Business Process Reengineering Six Sigma," www.isixsigma.com/me/bpr/, accessed October 10, 2005.

14. Ibid.

15. Ibid.

16. Ibid.

17. Bjorn Andersen, *Business Process Improvement Toolbox* (Milwaukee, WI: ASQ Quality Press, 1999).

18. "What Is BPR?" SmartDraw.com, www.smartdraw.com/, accessed October 11, 2005; BPR Online, www.prosci.com/mod1.htm, accessed October 10, 2005; "Business Process Reengineering Six Sigma," www.isixsigma.com/me/bpr/, accessed October 10, 2005

19. Chang, "Process Reengineering in Action"; Harrington, *Business Process Improvement Workbook;* Hammer, *Beyond Reengineering;* Hammer and Champy, "Reengineering the Corporation"; *Government Business Process Reengineering (BPR) Readiness Assessment Guide.*

20. "Customer Success Stories: Adidas," www.global360.com/collateral/Adidas_Case_History.pdf, accessed October 10, 2005.

21. "Savvion Helps 3Com Optimize Product Promotion Processes," www.savvion.com/customers/marketing_promotions.php, accessed October 10, 2005.

Plug-In B3

1. Tom Davenport, "Playing Catch-Up," *CIO Magazine,* May 1, 2001.

2. "Hector Ruiz, Advanced Micro Devices," *BusinessWeek,* January 10, 2005.

3. www.powergridfitness.com, accessed October 2005.

4. Denise Brehm, "Sloan Students Pedal Exercise," www.mit.edu, accessed May 5, 2003.

5. Margaret Locher, "Hands That Speak," *CIO Magazine,* June 1, 2005.

6. www.needapresent.com, accessed October 2005.

7. Aaron Ricadela, "Seismic Shift," *InformationWeek,* March 14, 2005.

8. www.mit.com, accessed October 2005.

9. "The Linux Counter," counter.li.org, accessed October 2005.

10. Meridith Levinson, "Circuit City Rewires," *CIO Magazine,* July 1, 2005.

11. "Electronic Breaking Points," www.pcworld.com, accessed August 2005.

Plug-In B4

1. Christine McGeever, "FBI Database Problem Halts Gun Checks," www.computerworld.com, accessed May 22, 2000.

2. Agile Enterprise, www.agiledata.org/essays/enterpriseArchitecture.html, accessed May 14, 2003; Institute for Enterprise Architecture, www.enterprise-architecture.info/, May 2, 2003; Technology terms, www.techterms.com/, accessed May 3, 2003; Whatis.com, whatis.techtarget.com, accessed May 4, 2003; Webopedia, www.webopedia.com, accessed May 14, 2003.

3. Christopher Koch, "A New Blueprint for the Enterprise," *CIO Magazine,* March 1, 2005.

4. "Distribution of Software Updates of Thousands of Franchise Locations Was Slow and Unpredictable," www.fountain.com, accessed October 10, 2003.

5. Agile Enterprise, www.agiledata.org/essays/enterpriseArchitecture.html, accessed May 14, 2003; Institute for Enterprise Architecture, www.enterprise-architecture.info/, May 2, 2003; Technology terms, www.techterms.com/, accessed May 3, 2003; Whatis.com, whatis.techtarget.com, accessed May 4, 2003; Webopedia, www.webopedia.com, accessed May 14, 2003.

6. "What Every Executive Needs to Know," www.akamai.com, accessed September 10, 2003.

7. Agile Enterprise, www.agiledata.org/essays/enterpriseArchitecture.html, accessed May 14, 2003; Institute for Enterprise Architecture, www.enterprise-architecture.info/, May 2, 2003; Technology terms, www.techterms.com/, accessed May 3, 2003; Whatis.com, whatis.techtarget.com, accessed May 4, 2003; Webopedia, www.webopedia.com, accessed May 14, 2003.

8. www.marshall&swift.com, accessed November 2005.

9. Martin Garvey, "Manage Passwords," *InformationWeek,* May 20, 2005.

10. Ibid.

11. Martin Garvey, "Security Action Plans," *InformationWeek,* May 30, 2005.

12. Agile Enterprise, www.agiledata.org/essays/enterpriseArchitecture.html, accessed May 14, 2003; Institute for Enterprise Architecture, www.enterprise-architecture.info/, May 2, 2003; Technology terms, www.techterms.com/, accessed May 3, 2003; Whatis.com, whatis.techtarget.com, accessed May 4, 2003; Webopedia, www.webopedia.com, accessed May 14, 2003.

13. www.gartner.com, accessed November 2005.

14. www.websidestory.com, accessed November 2005.

15. "Can American Keep Flying?" *CIO Magazine,* www.cio.com, February 15, 2003.

16. Agile Enterprise, www.agiledata.org/essays/enterpriseArchitecture.html, accessed May 14, 2003; Institute for Enterprise Architecture, www.enterprise-architecture.info/, May 2, 2003; Technology terms, www.techterms.com/, accessed May 3, 2003;

Whatis.com, whatis.techtarget.com, accessed May 4, 2003; Webopedia, www.webopedia.com, accessed May 14, 2003.

17. www.abercrombie&fitch.com, accessed November 2005.

18. "Looking at the New," *InformationWeek,* May 2005.

19. Koch, "A New Blueprint for the Enterprise."

20. Agile Enterprise, www.agiledata.org/essays/enterpriseArchitecture.html, accessed May 14, 2003; Institute for Enterprise Architecture, www.enterprise-architecture.info/, May 2, 2003; Technology terms, www.techterms.com/, accessed May 3, 2003; Whatis.com, whatis.techtarget.com, accessed May 4, 2003; Webopedia, www.webopedia.com, accessed May 14, 2003.

21. Ibid.

22. Ibid.

23. John Fontana, "Lydian Revs up with Web Services," *Network World,* March 10, 2004.

24. www.websidestory.com, accessed November 2005.

25. Ibid.

26. Tim Wilson, "Server Consolidation Delivers," *InformationWeek,* May 30, 2005.

27. Erick Schonfeld, "Linux Takes Flight," *Business 2.0,* January 2003, pp. 103–5;
Otis Port, "Will the Feud Choke the Life Out of Linux?" *BusinessWeek,* July 7, 2003, p. 81.

Plug-In B5

1. Technology terms, www.techterms.com/, accessed May 3, 2003; Networking.com, www.networking.com, accessed May 15, 2003; Whatis.com, whatis.techtarget.com, accessed May 4, 2003; Webopedia, www.webopedia.com, accessed May 14, 2003.

2. Ibid.

3. Eva Chen, "Shop Talk," *CIO Magazine,* October 15, 2004.

4. Technology terms, www.techterms.com/, accessed May 3, 2003; Networking.com, www.networking.com, accessed May 15, 2003; Whatis.com, whatis.techtarget.com, accessed May 4, 2003; Webopedia, www.webopedia.com, accessed May 14, 2003.

5. Ibid.

6. Ibid.

7. Ibid.

8. Ibid.

9. Ibid.

10. www.perrio.com, accessed November 2005.

11. Technology terms, www.techterms.com/, accessed May 3, 2003; Networking.com, www.networking.com, accessed May 15, 2003; Whatis.com, whatis.techtarget.com, accessed May 4, 2003; Webopedia, www.webopedia.com, accessed May 14, 2003.

12. Ibid.

13. Ibid.

14. Ibid.

15. Ibid.

16. Ibid.

17. "Overcoming Software Development Problems," www.samspublishing.com, October 7, 2002, accessed November 16, 2003.

18. "The Security Revolution," *CIO Magazine,* www.cio.com, accessed June 6, 2003.

Plug-In B6

1. "2002 CSI/FBI Computer Crime and Security Survey," www.gocsi.com, accessed November 23, 2003.
2. www.ey.com, accessed November 25, 2003.
3. "The Security Revolution," *CIO Magazine,* www.cio.com, accessed June 6, 2003.
4. Ibid.
5. "Losses from Identity Theft to Total $221 Billion Worldwide," *CIO Magazine,* www.cio.com, May, 2005.
6. "Sony Fights Intrusion with 'Crystal Ball,'" *CIO Magazine,* www.cio.com, accessed August 9, 2003.
7. Mark Leon, "Keys to the Kingdom," www.computerworld.com, April 14, 2003, accessed August 8, 2003.
8. "Spam Losses to Grow to $198 Billion," *CIO Magazine,* www.cio.com, accessed August 9, 2003.
9. "Teen Arrested in Internet 'Blaster' Attack," www.cnn.com, August 29, 2003.
10. Scott Berinato and Sarah Scalet, "The ABCs of Information Security," *CIO Magazine,* www.cio.com, accessed July 7, 2003.
11. "Hacker Hunters," *BusinessWeek,* May 30, 2005.

Plug-In B7

1. Scott Berinato, "Take the Pledge—The CIO's Code of Ethical Data Management," *CIO Magazine,* July 1, 2002, www.cio.com, accessed March 7, 2004.
2. Ibid.
3. "FedLaw Computers and Information Technology," www.thecre.com/fedlaw/legal8.htm, accessed March 21, 2004.
4. "Information Security Policy World," www.information-security-policies-and-standards.com/, accessed March 23, 2004; Computer Security Policy, www.computer-security-policies.com/, accessed March 24, 2007: Technology terms, www.techterms.com/, accessed May 3, 2003; Whatis.com, whatis.techtarget.com, accessed May 4, 2003; Webopedia, www.webopedia.com, accessed May 14, 2003.
5. Ibid.
6. Ibid.
7. Ibid.
8. Ibid.
9. Alice Dragon, "Be a Spam Slayer," *CIO Magazine,* November 1, 2003, www.cio.com, accessed March 9, 2004.
10. Information Security Policy World, www.information-security-policies-and-standards.com/, accessed March 23, 2004; "Computer Security Policy," www.computer-security-policies.com/, accessed March 24, 2007; Technology terms, www.techterms.com/, accessed May 3, 2003; Whatis.com, whatis.techtarget.com, accessed May 4, 2003; Webopedia, www.webopedia.com, accessed May 14, 2003.
11. Ibid.
12. Paul Roberts, "Report: Spam Costs $874 per Employee per Year," www.computerworld.com, July 2, 2003, accessed March 9, 2004.
13. "Information Security Policy World," www.information-security-policies-and-standards.com/, accessed March 23, 2004: Computer Security Policy, www.computer-security-policies.com/, accessed March 24, 2007; Technology terms, www.techterms.com/, accessed May 3, 2003; Whatis.com, whatis.techtarget.com, accessed May 4, 2003; Webopedia, www.webopedia.com, accessed May 14, 2003.

14. AMA Research, "Workplace Monitoring and Surveillance," www.amanet.org, April 2003, accessed March 1, 2004.
15. www.vault.com, accessed January 2006.
16. AMA Research, "Workplace Monitoring and Surveillance." www.amanet.org, April 2003, accessed March 1, 2004.
17. "Information Security Policy World," www.information-security-policies-and-standards.com/, accessed March 23, 2004; Computer Security Policy, www.computer-security-policies.com/, accessed March 24, 2007; Technology terms, www.techterms.com/, accessed May 3, 2003; Whatis.com, whatis.techtarget.com, accessed May 4, 2003; Webopedia, www.webopedia.com, accessed May 14, 2003.
18. "Sarbanes-Oxley Act," www.workingvalues.com, accessed March 3, 2004.
19. AnchorDeskStaff, "How to Spy on Your Employees and Why You May Not Want To," www.reviews-zdnet.com, August 21, 2003, accessed March 5, 2004.

Plug-In B8

1. Frank Quinn, "The Payoff Potential in Supply Chain Management," www.ascet.com, accessed June 15, 2003.
2. Supply Chain Council, www.supply-chain.org/cs/root/home, accessed June 22, 2003; Logistics and Supply Chain, logistics.about.com, accessed June 2, 2003; Technology terms, www.techterms.com/, accessed May 3, 2003; Whatis.com, whatis.techtarget.com, accessed May 4, 2003; Webopedia, www.webopedia.com, accessed May 14, 2003.
3. Ibid.
4. Ibid.
5. Ibid.
6. Ibid.
7. Walid Mougayar, "Old Dogs Learn New Tricks," *Business 2.0,* October 2000, www.Business2.com, accessed June 14, 2003.
8. Supply Chain Council, www.supply-chain.org/cs/root/home, accessed June 22, 2003; Logistics and Supply Chain, logistics.about.com, accessed June 2, 2003; Technology terms, www.techterms.com/, accessed May 3, 2003; Whatis.com, whatis.techtarget.com, accessed May 4, 2003; Webopedia, www.webopedia.com, accessed May 14, 2003.
9. Ibid.
10. Ibid.
11. Ibid.
12. Ibid.
13. Ibid.
14. Ibid.
15. Ibid.
16. Quinn, "The Payoff Potential"; William Copacino, "How to Become a Supply Chain Master," *Supply Chain Management Review,* September 1, 2001, www.manufacturing.net, accessed June 12, 2003.
17. Bob Evans, "Business Technology: Sweet Home," *InformationWeek,* February 7, 2005.
18. Navi Radjou, "Manufacturing Sector IT Spending Profile for 2004," www.forrester.com, September 12, 2003, accessed March 15, 2004.
19. Jennifer Bresnahan, "The Incredible Journey," *CIO Enterprise,* August 15, 1998, www.cio.com, accessed March 12, 2004;

20. Justin Fox, "A Meditation on Risk," *Fortune,* October 3, 2005.
21. Parija Bhatnagar, "Wal-Mart Closes 123 Stores from Storm," www.cnnmoney.com, accessed August 2005.

Plug-In B9

1. "Barclays, Giving Voice to Customer-Centricity," crm. insightexec.com, accessed July 15, 2003.
2. California State Automobile Association Case Study, www.epiphany.com/customers/detail_csaa.html, accessed July 4, 2003.
3. www.salesforce.com, accessed June 2005.
4. "Vail Resorts Implements FrontRange HEAT," *CRM Today,* October 16, 2003, www.crm2day.com/news/crm/ EpyykllFyAqEUbqOhW.php, accessed December 2, 2003.
5. "3M Accelerates Revenue Growth Using Siebel eBusiness Applications," www.siebel.com, July 30, 2002, accessed July 10, 2003.
6. Ibid.
7. "Avnet Brings IM to Corporate America with Lotus Instant Messaging," websphereadvisor.com/doc/12196, accessed July 11, 2003.
8. www.nicesystems.com, accessed June 2005.
9. www.FedEx.com, accessed July 13, 2003.
10. "Documedics," www.siebel.com, accessed July 10, 2003.
11. Bob Evans, "Business Technology: Sweet Home," *InformationWeek,* February 7, 2005.
12. Customer Success—UPS," www.sap.com, accessed April 5, 2003.
13. "Sears: Redefining Business", *BusinessWeek,* www.businessweek.com, accessed April 15, 2003.
14. "Supply Chain Planet," June 2003, newsweaver.co.uk/ supplychainplanet/e_article000153342.cfm, accessed July 12, 2003.
15. "Customer Success," www.costco.com, accessed June 2005.
16. "Customer Success," www.rackspace.com, accessed June 2005.
17. "Partnering in the Fight Against Cancer," www.siebel.com, accessed July 16, 2003.
18. "The Expanding Territory of Outsourcing," www.outsourcing. com, accessed August 15, 2003.

Plug-In B10

1. "Customer Success Story—Turner Industries," www. jdedwards.com, accessed October 15, 2003.
2. "Harley-Davidson on the Path to Success," www.peoplesoft. com/media/success, accessed October 12, 2003.
3. "Customer Success Story—Grupo Farmanova Intermed," www.jdedwards.com, accessed October 15, 2003.
4. "Customer Success Stories," www.jdedwards.com, accessed October 15, 2003.
5. Ibid.
6. Michael Doane, "A Blueprint for ERP Implementation Readiness," www.metagroup.com, accessed October 17, 2003.
7. Ibid.
8. "Customer Success Story—PepsiAmerica," www.peoplesoft. com, accessed October 22, 2003.
9. Thomas Wailgum, "Big Mess on Campus," *CIO Magazine,* May 1, 2005.

Plug-In B11

1. ColdStone Creamery Talk, www.creamerytalk.com/press/ in_the_news_2005.html, accessed September 23, 2004.
2. "Info on 3.9M Citigroup," *Money,* June 6, 2005.
3. Amy Johnson, "A New Supply Chain Forged," *ComputerWorld,* September 30, 2002.
4. "Pratt & Whitney," *BusinessWeek,* June 2004.
5. "Let's Remake a Deal," *Business 2.0,* March 2004.
6. Laura Rohde, "British Airways Takes Off with Cisco," *Network World,* May 11, 2005.
7. www.t-mobile.com, accessed June 2005.
8. www.idc.com, accessed June 2005.
9. Rachel Metz, "Changing at the Push of a Button," *Wired,* September 27, 2004.
10. www.hotel-gatti.com, accessed June 2003.
11. Frank Quinn, "The Payoff Potential in Supply Chain Management," www.ascet.com, accessed June 15, 2003.
12. www.oecd.org, accessed June 2005.
13. www.vanguard.com, accessed June 2005.
14. "Watch Your Spending," *BusinessWeek,* May 23, 2004.
15. Jack Welch, "What's Right About Wal-Mart', *CIO Magazine,* www.cio.com, accessed May 2005.
16. www.yankeegroup.com, accessed May 2005.
17. www.ingenio.com, accessed July 2005.
18. Joshua Ramo, "Jeffrey Bezos," www.time.com/time/poy2000/ archive/1999.html, accessed June 8, 2004.
19. "Manage Your Mailing Experience Electronically, All in One Place," United States Postal Service, www.usps.com, accessed July 2005.
20. Penelope Patsuris, "Marketing Messages Made to Order," *Forbes,* August 2003.

Plug-In B12

1. "The Art of Foresight," *The Futurist,* May–June 2004, pp. 31–35.
2. Marvin Cetron and Owen Davies, "50 Trends Shaping the Future," *2003 World Future Society Special Report,* April 2004.
3. William Halal, "The Top 10 Emerging Technologies," *The Futurist Special Report,* July 2004.
4. Penelope Patsuris, "Marketing Messages Made to Order," *Forbes,* August 2003.
5. Stacy Crowley, "IBM, HP, MS Discuss Autonomic Computing Strategies," *Infoworld,* May 19, 2004.
6. Denise Dubie, "Tivoli Users Discuss Automation," *Network World,* April 14, 2003.
7. "Progressive Receives Applied Systems' 2003 Interface Best Practices Award," www.worksite.net/091203tech.htm, accessed June 18, 2004.

Plug-In B13

1. "IBM/Lotus Domino Server Hosting Service," www. macro.com.hk/solution_Outsourcing.htm, accessed June 8, 2004.
2. www.forrester.com/find?SortType=Date&No=350&N=32, accessed June 8, 2004.
3. Deni Connor, "IT Outlook Declines Due to Outsourcing, Offshoring," www.nwfusion.com/careers/2004/0531manside. html, accessed June 8, 2004.

4. "BP: WebLearn," www.accenture.com/xd/xd.asp?it=enweb
&xd=industries%5Cresources%5Cenergy%5Ccase%5Cener_
bpweblearn.xml, accessed June 8, 2004.

5. Todd Datz, "Outsourcing World Tour," *CIO Magazine,* July 15,
2004, pp. 42–48.

6. "Call Center and CRM Statistics," www.cconvergence.com/
shared/printableArticle. jhtml?articleID=7617915, accessed
June 8, 2004.

7. Stan Gibson, "Global Services Plays Pivotal Role,"
www.eweek.com/article2/0,1759,808984,00.asp, accessed
June 8, 2004.

8. "Coors Brewing Company," www.eds.com/case_studies/
case_coors.shtml, accessed June 8, 2004.

Plug-In B14

1. "Python Project Failure," www.systemsdev.com, accessed
November 14, 2003.

2. Gary McGraw, "Making Essential Software Work," *Software
Quality Management,* April 2003, www.sqmmagazine.com,
accessed November 14, 2003.

3. www.standishgroup.com, accessed November 14, 2003.

4. "Overcoming Software Development Problems,"
www.samspublishing.com, October 7, 2002, accessed
November 16, 2003; "Baggage Handling System Errors,"
www.flavors.com, accessed November 16, 2003.

5. www.microsoft.com, accessed November 16, 2003.

Plug-In B15

1. www.calpine.com, accessed December 14, 2003.

2. "The Project Manager in the IT Industry," www.si2.com,
accessed December 15, 2003.

3. www.standishgroup.com, accessed December 12, 2003.

4. www.snapon.com, accessed December 13, 2003.

5. www.change-management.org, accessed December 12, 2003.

6. www.altria.com, accessed December 15, 2003.

7. "Supply and Demand Chain," www.isourceonline.com,
accessed December 14, 2003.

8. www.microsoft.com, accessed December 13, 2003.

9. "Staying on Track at the Toronto Transit Commission,"
www.primavera.com, accessed December 16, 2003.

10. "Taking On Change," *CIO Magazine,* June 2005.

P 1.1A, page 3, ©McGraw-Hill Companies/Jill Braaten, photographer.

P 1.1B, page 3, The McGraw-Hill Companies, Inc./Lars A. Niki, photographer.

P 1.1C, page 3, The McGraw-Hill Companies, Inc./Christopher Kerrigan, photographer.

Figure 1.1, page 8, Paige Baltzan.

Figure 1.2, page 9, www.cio.com, accessed August 2005.

Figure 2.3a, page 21, Photo courtesy of Hyundai Motor America.

Figure 2.3b, page 21, Photo courtesy of Audi.

Figure 2.3c, page 21, Copyright © 2004 Kia Motors America, Inc. All Rights Reserved.

Figure 2.5, page 22, Porter, Michael E., Competitive Strategy: Techniques for Analyzing Industries and Competitors, The Free Press, 1998.

Figure 3.4, page 30, Caldwell, Bruce, "Missteps, Miscues—Business Reengineering Failures," *Information Week*, June 20, 1994, p. 50.

Figure 3.10, page 33, ERP White Paper, www.bitpipe.com/rlist/term/ERP.html, accessed July 3, 2007.

Figure 4.6, page 41, Google Analytics, www.google.com/analytics, accessed July 13, 2007.

Figure 4.7, page 41, Google Analytics, www.google.com/analytics, accessed July 13, 2007.

Figure 4.8, Supply Chain Metrics.com, www.supplychainmetric.com/, accessed June 12, 2007.

Figure 4.9, Kaplan, Robert, Norton, David, "The BSC: Translating Strategy into Action" (Vintage Books: 1998) The Balanced Scorecard Institute, www.balancedscorecard.org/, accessed May 15, 2007.

Figure 5.5, page 50, Scott Berimano, Take the Pledge, www.cio.com, accessed November 17, 2003.

Figure 5.6, page 51, Computer Security Institute.

P 1.2A, page 55, © Louise Gubb/The Image Works.

P 1.2B, page 55, © Amy Etra/ Photo Edit.

P 1.2C, page 55, © James Leynse/ Corbis.

Page 57 (left): The McGraw-Hill Companies, Inc. / John Flournoy, photographer.

Page 57 (middle): Steven Brahms / Bloomberg News/ Landov.

Page 57 (right): PRNewsFoto / Bank of America / AP / Wide World Photos.

P 2.1A, page 69, Digital Vision / Getty Images.

P 2.1B, page 69, BananaStock/PictureQuest.

P 2.1C, page 69, Jason Reed/Getty Images.

Figure 7.4, page 87, Webopedia.com, www.webopedia.comTERM/d/database.html, accessed May 15, 2007; Wikipedia, The Free Encyclopedia, en.wikipedia.org/wiki/Wiki, accessed May 22, 2007; Oracle Database, www.oracle.com/database/index.html, accessed May 17, 2007; www.sitepoint.com/article/publishing-mysql-data-web, accessed May 16, 2007.

P 2.2A, page 102, PhotoLink / Photodisc / Getty Images.

P 2.2B, page 102, Jack Star/PhotoLink/Getty Images.

P 2.2C, page 102, Oleg Svyatoslavsky/Life File/Getty Images.

P2.3, page 104, Photo courtesy of Cray, Inc.

Page 113 (all): Courtesy of Linden Labs.

P9.1, page 125, Alexander Heimann/AFP/Getty.

P9.2, page 125, AP/Wide World Photos.

P9.3, page 125, © Jeff Greenberg/Photo Edit.

P9.4, page 130, Photo courtesy of NCR Corporation.

Figure 12.13, page 155, Exact Software, "ERP-II: Making ERP Deliver On Its Promise to the Enterprise", jobfunctions.bnet.com/whitepaper.aspx?docid=144338, accessed July 25, 2007.

Figure 12.14, page 155, Exact Software, "ERP-II: Making ERP Deliver On Its Promise to the Enterprise", jobfunctions.bnet.com/whitepaper.aspx?docid=144338, accessed July 25, 2007.

P 3.2A, page 163, C. Sherburne/PhotoLink/Getty Images.

P 3.2B, page 163, Digital Vision / Getty Images.

P 3.2C, page 163, Ryan McVay/Getty Images.

P3.2D, page 165, AP/Wide World Photos.

P3.2E, page 165, Scott Olson/Getty Images.

P3.2F, page 165, PRNewsFoto/Harley-Davidson/AP/Wide World Photos.

P 4.1A, page 175, Don Farrall/Getty Images.

P 4.1B, page 175, PhotoLink/Getty Images.

P 4.1C, page 175, Jason Reed / Ryan McVay/Getty Images.

Figure 13.1, page 180, http://www.internetworldstats.com/stats.htm, accessed January 15, 2005.

Figure 13.8, page 184, Tim O'Reilly, "What Is Web 2.0: Design Patterns and Business Models for the Next Generation of Software", 9/30/2005.

Figure 13.9, page 185, Tim O'Reilly, "What Is Web 2.0: Design Patterns and Business Models for the Next Generation of Software", 9/30/2005.

Figure 14.9, page 194, Ecommerce Taxation, www.icsc.org/, accessed June 8, 2004.

Figure 15.10, page 210: Cartesia / PhotoDisc Imaging / Getty Images.

Figure 15.11, page 211: © Tom Grill / Corbis.

P 4.2A, page 224, Creatas/PunchStock.

P 4.2B, page 224, Dynamic Graphics / JupiterImages.

P 4.2C, page 224, PhotoLink/Getty Images.

P 4.2D, page 225, © Macduff Everton/Corbis.

P 4.2E, page 225, AP/Wide World Photos.

P 4.2F, page 225, © Jack Kurtz/The Image Works.

P 5.1A, page 237, Dynamic Graphics / JupiterImages.

P 5.1B, page 237, © Image100/PunchStock.

P 5.1C, page 237. Dynamic Graphics / JupiterImages.

Figure 17.5, page 249, *Information Week.*

Figure 18.1, page 253, Common Outsourcing, www.cio.com, accessed June 15, 2004.

Figure 19.1, page 259, www.expedia.com, www.apple.com, www.dell.com, www.lendingtree.com, www.amazon.com, www.ebay.com, accessed October 13, 2004.

Figure 19.3, page 260, 2005 SCOnline.com, accessed January 2005.

P 5.2A, page 266, © Digital Vision/PunchStock.

P 5.2B, page 266, Royalty-Free/CORBIS.

P 5.2C, page 266, Ryan McVay/Getty Images.

P 5.2D, page 267, Mario Tama/Getty Images.

P 5.2E, page 267, Justin Sullivan/Getty Images.

P 5.2F, page 267, Dan Krauss/Getty Images.

Figure B2.6, page 303, Michael Hammer. *Beyond Reengineering, How the Process-Centered Organization Is Changing Our Work and Our Lives, New York:* HarperCollins, Publisher, 1996.

P B3.1A, page 319, Royalty-Free/CORBIS.

P B3.1B, page 319, Stockbyte/Punchstock Images.

P B3.2, page 320, SimpleTech Inc.

P B3.3A, page 320, Getty Images.

P B3.3B, page 320, Daisuke Morita/Getty Images.

P B3.4A, page 320, © Stockbyte/PunchStock.

P B3.4B, page 320, © Stockbyte/PunchStock.

P B3.5A, page 320, Courtesy of Panasonic

P B3.5B, page 320, Courtesy of Dell Inc.

P B3.6A, page 320, Getty Images.

P B3.6B, page 320, Royalty-Free/CORBIS.

Figure B3.3, page 321, "Chip Wars," *PC World,* August 2005.

Figure B3.11, page 328, Ricadela, Aaron, "Seismic Shift," Information Week, March 14, 2005.

Figure B4.1, page 338, *Business Week,* January 10, 2005.

Figure B4.3, page 341, *Information Week,* August 9, 2004.

Figure B5.5, page 357, www.pcmagazine.com, accessed October 10, 2005.

Figure B5.12, page 361, www.cio.com, accessed October 20, 2005.

Figure B6.3, page 373, www.ey.com, accessed November 25, 2003.

Figure B6.4, page 374, "The Security Revolution," www.cio.com, accessed June 6, 2003.

Figure B6.6, page 376, "Spam Losses to Grow to $198 Billion," www.cio.com, accessed August 9, 2003.

Figure B7.10, page 392, Paul Roberts, "Report Span Costs $874 per Employee per Year," www.computerworld.com, July 2, 2003, accessed March 9, 2004.

Figure B7.11, page 393, AMA Research, "Workplace Monitoring and Surveillance," www.amanet.org, April 2003, accessed March 1, 2004.

Figure B10.1, page 433, "ERP Knowledge Base, " www.cio.com, accessed June 2005.

Figure B11.9, page 456, www.w3.org, W3C Security resources, accessed June 2005.

Figure B12.2, page 470, "50 Trends Shaping the Future," *2003 World Future Society Special Report,* April 2004.

Figure B12.3, page 470, Ibid.

Figure B12.4, page 471, Ibid.

Figure B13.3, page 485, Datz, Todd, "Outsourcing World Tour," *CIO Magazine,* July 15, 2004, pp. 42–48.

Figure B15.6, page 523, "The Change Management Guide for Managers and Supervisors," www.changemeanagement.org, accessed December 12, 2003.

Figure B15.11, page 526, "Successful Project Management Strategies," CIO, www.cio.com, accessed December 12, 2003.

BUSINESS DRIVEN TECHNOLOGY CASES

Business Driven Technology offers over 60 cases on current companies ranging from Apple to Wikipedia. Unit opening cases have questions spread throughout the Unit to help students analyze the case according to material. Each chapter has a smaller case that focuses on specific chapter content. Unit closing cases are in-depth cases covering all Unit material. Each business plug-in has two cases which explore the plug-in topics further. Cases include:

- 3Com Optimizes Product Promotion Processes
- Amazon.com—Not Your Average Bookstore
- Apple—Merging Technology, Business, and Entertainment
- Autonomic Railways
- Banks, Banking on Network Security
- Battle of the Toys—FAO Schwarz is Back
- Business 2.0 – Bad Business Decisions
- BudNet
- Calling All Canadians
- Campus ERP
- Change at Toyota
- Changing Circuits at Circuit City
- *Chicago Tribune's* Server Consolidation a Success
- Consolidating Touchpoints for Saab
- Creating a Clearer Picture for Public Broadcasting Service (PBS)
- Defense Advanced Research Projects Agency (DARPA) Grand Challenge
- Dell's Famous Supply Chain
- Disaster at Denver International Airport
- Dreamworks Animation Collaboration
- eBay—The Ultimate Business
- eBiz
- Electronic Breaking Points
- Executive Dilemmas in the Information Age
- Failing to Innovate
- Fear the Penguin
- Fighting Cancer with Information
- Fishing for Quality
- Gearing Up at REI
- Hacker Hunters
- Harrah's—Gambling Big on Technology
- How Do You Value Friendster?
- How Levi's Jeans Got into Wal-Mart

- Improving Highway Safety Through Collaboration
- Innovative Business Managers
- Invading Your Privacy
- It Takes a Village to Write an Encyclopedia
- Katrina Shakes Supply Chains
- Keeper of the Keys
- Listerine's Journey
- Made-to-Order Businesses
- Mail with PostalOne
- Masters of Innovation, Technology, and Strategic Vision
- Mining the Data Warehouse
- Mobil Travel Guide
- Outsourcing Brew
- PepsiAmericas' Enterprises
- Reducing Ambiguity in Business Requirements
- Revving Up Sales at Harley-Davidson
- RFID—Future Tracking
- Sarbanes-Oxley: Where Information Technology, Finance, and Ethics Meet
- Say "Charge It" with Your Cell Phone
- Searching for Revenue—Google
- Second Life: Succeeding in Virtual Times
- Staying on Track—Toronto Transit
- Streamlining Processes at Adidas
- The Digital Hospital
- The Ritz-Carlton—Specializing in Customers
- Thinking like the Enemy
- Thomas Friedman's The World is Flat
- Transforming the Entertainment Industry—Netflix
- UPS in the Computer Repair Business
- UPS versus FedEx: Head-to-Head on Wireless
- Watching Where You Step—Prada
- Wireless Progression